Contemporary British Politics & Government

Fourth Edition

Phil Cocker &
Alistair Jones

ISBN 1-903-499-83-6
978-1-903499-83-2

Printed and bound in the United Kingdom by 4edge Ltd, 7a Eldon Way Industrial
Estate, Hockley, Essex, SS5 4AD.

Profit Through Change contact details
Email: info@profitthroughchange.com

CONTENTS //

CENTRAL GOVERNMENT INSTITUTIONS

PARTICIPATION IN BRITISH POLITICS

GOVERNMENT BEYOND THE CENTRE

Policy Issues

Conclusion

List of Tables and Figures

Acknowledgements

Writing this book has taken a very long time. It was started just after the 2010 General Election, and has taken the best part of four years to write. During this time, politics in the UK changed significantly, making the writing of this book even more difficult. I can safely say, however, that it has been a labour of love.

There are many people that I must thank for their help and support during this time. At the top of the list is my wife, Claire, whose support, encouragement and enthusiasm has been never ending. A number of current and former colleagues at De Montfort University must also be thanked for their comments on draft chapters, their advice and support.

In no particular order, I would like to thank David Wilson, Alasdair Blair, Alison Statham, Colin Copus, Rob Baggott, Clive Gray, Melvin Wingfield, Tor Clark, Chris Goldsmith, Kathryn Jones, Sheree Peaple, Neil Parpworth, Fred Mear and Yulia Rodionova. I would also like to thank all of my students who read the chapters and passed on their comments as well.

From the publishers, the Cambridge Media Group, I would like to thank Ken Sewell for the e-mails asking about progress.

Finally, and by no means lastly, I would like to thank all of my pets for providing a range of distractions, and reminding me that their welfare and entertainment is always a priority. Thanks, therefore, go to Max, Sasha and Toby (all of whom sadly died while this book was being written), and to Tiny, Miss Kitty Fantastic and to all of our chickens.

I hope that you get as much enjoyment out of reading this book as I have in writing it. As ever, any errors and mistakes within the book are mine.

Alistair Jones

CHAPTER 1 // INTRODUCTION

Contents

Introduction

There is an argument that the study of British Politics is in decline; that it is being surpassed by much more sexy subjects such as globalisation or international relations, or regional studies – be it Europe, the Americas or South East Asia. With the move to £9000 university tuition fees in England, students are going to want more 'bang' for their buck. Students in Scotland or Wales are more likely to want to study Scottish and Welsh politics respectively. There is a suggestion that stand-alone courses in British Politics are dead in the water. To what sort of career would the study of British Politics lead? A politician – be it an MP, a councillor or some other elected position? What about the teaching of politics and other related subjects to the next generation? The paths to get to the elected posts do not require a politics degree; in most cases, they require party membership, loyalty, and an ability to toe the party line. The idea of questioning your instructions should not register.

For those considering teaching, reflect on what other teaching is, or has to be, done by current staff members who teach politics. Is politics their dominant discipline or is it some other academic subject? This is by no means meant to put you off such a career – in fact, I would encourage such a career. Rather, it is to make you aware of the size of the politics discipline.

Despite this gloomy outlook, there is a need for the study of British Politics. Rather than it being the entire degree, it might need to be part of a bigger package – be it in Politics or Government. It is also part of the study of Citizenship – and a key component at that. Yet the study of British Politics should go much further. Somebody studying business, for example, ought to have an awareness of the fundamentals of British Politics. Such knowledge may give a greater awareness of the role and function of the public sector, or sources of start-up funds for new businesses. The list goes on.

So the study of British Politics is very important. This book attempts to encapsulate much of what is taught in a Politics syllabus. It also includes other areas of politics, which students of British Politics might not consider important. To those studying law, history, business and citizenship – to name but four subjects – this book draws in aspects of your subjects and links them to the politics of the United Kingdom.

What is Politics?

An introductory Politics 101 lecture is likely to start off with this seemingly simple question: what is politics? There is no simple answer to such a question. For example, it could be argued that politics pervades every single subject: fashion, the moon, the food you eat (or choose not to eat) – all of these topics can have elements of politics within them. Sometimes the politics is overt; other times it is far less obvious. All of the books, newspapers or magazines that you read will have a political aspect. There are arguments that, for example, politics should be kept out of sport. There is no chance of this happening. Sport is a hugely political subject. During the Cold War, for example, East and West competed against each other at every Olympic Games (unless there was a boycott – which, on each occasion, was political). There is politics in business, nursing, journalism, accountancy and any other subject that you care to study at school, college or university. Even something like mathematics can be political. You are told that parallel lines do not intersect. On an atlas, take a map of the world and examine the lines of longitude – those that travel north-south. They are parallel, and do not intersect. Take that map, and make it into a globe. The lines of longitude intersect at the poles; thus parallel lines intersect. Does this mean that your mathematics teachers have been lying to you? Here, there is a conflict: two answers that are contradictory but both are correct.

Politics is to do with conflict and conflict resolution. While people tend to associate conflict with violence, it can also be associated with far more mundane matters such as a dispute over by how much the government is planning to cut public spending. Conflict, and its resolution, is everywhere. It is an inherent part of politics, as is demonstrated in the title of Harold Lasswell's text: *Politics: Who Gets What, When, How*. There is conflict over the distribution of scarce resources. Political parties fight elections in an attempt to gain power to be able to allocate these resources. The election campaign is the battlefield – the scene of the conflict. Opinion polls give progress reports on how the war is progressing. The conflict is resolved after polling day, when the votes are counted, the seats allocated and a government formed – even a coalition government. This resolution is but a temporary lull, as campaigning starts for the next election.

As the conflict is resolved, a form of control emerges, which becomes a source of more conflict. In George Orwell's *Animal Farm*, the animals rebelled against control by the farmer. Once the conflict was over, with the farmer driven away, a new form of control emerged – that of the pigs over the rest of the animals. From Orwell's perspective, the pigs became more and more like the former rulers, the human farmers. There was nothing the rest of the animals could do. At least in a democracy, voters (in theory) can pass judgement over the control exerted by the government, at the ballot box. Looking at the 2010 General Election, nobody voted for a coalition government but there were few objections. Compare that to the first free elections in Egypt in 2012, where many people objected to the winner – Mohamed Morsi of the Muslim Brotherhood. A year after his election, Morsi was ousted in a coup, and the Muslim Brotherhood declared a terrorist organisation. Conflict leading to control, leading to more conflict: an endless circle.

Overview of the book

Criticisms are often made of text books that they do not cover subjects adequately. Such a criticism may be valid, but the idea of a text book is to whet the appetite; to give a taste of the subject. From this taste, the specialist books and journal articles should then be accessed to further knowledge and understanding. Each chapter contains some guided reading and internet sites for points of further reference.

There is no expectation that anyone will read this book from cover to cover. Students may wish to cherry-pick from particular chapters in preparation for assignments or exams. Each chapter can be treated in isolation, although there are clear links between many of them: the Prime Minister and the cabinet; the House of Commons and the House of Lords. Each of these have links to others, such as the various chapters on devolution, local government or the European Union. At times, these links may not be obvious, such as quangos and ethnicity or gender – until you examine ethnic minority or female representation on these bodies.

British politics is at an interesting point in time. The 2010 General Election resulted in a coalition government – the first since the Second World War. A referendum has been held on changing the voting system, and was roundly defeated. Elected Police and Crime Commissioners have been introduced, but, noting the phenomenally poor turnout, very few people seemed to notice. The Scots are demanding a vote on independence and by September 2014, the United Kingdom as we understand it today may no longer exist. There are demands for Britain to withdraw from the European Union: this is most clearly seen with the rise of the UK Independence Party. The elections to the European Parliament in May 2014 may see a UKIP victory, but will this lead to UKIP success at the 2015 general election? One of the rather sad aspects of British politics is most commentators look no further than the next general election. This may be understandable when there is a coalition government, but it was the same after all previous elections. With all of this as the current backdrop, the study of British politics is exciting.

This book is divided into six sections. The first sets the context for 'where we are today'. There is coverage of the political, social and economic development of the United Kingdom in the post-war era. There is also coverage of the UK constitution and the idea of a bill of rights. All of this section underpins the changes that have taken place in the UK.

The second section focuses on central government. This is considered to be the bread-and-butter of British Politics. There is an obvious fixation on this area: it is a fundamental part of most British Politics syllabuses, covering Parliament, the Executive and the judiciary. Accountability aspects are also covered through chapters on regulation and redress. Kerr & Kettell (2006, p. 6) bemoan that the study of British politics "has suffered from the deficiencies of the so-called 'Westminster model' and its central concern with examining the narrow mechanics of British central government". Such a criticism is valid. The problem is those who write the syllabus – particularly at 'A'-level – appear to have such a fixation. In a very simple case of market economics, the text book writers will respond to market demand. Around a third of this book focuses on central government institutions.

Section three examines different forms of participation in British Politics. There is the obvious voting behaviour, political parties, pressure groups and electoral systems. The concepts of participation and citizenship are also covered, as well as the most recent form of participation: the media.

The fourth section goes beyond the centre, to examine other forms of government at the local, regional and European levels. Grant (2012, p. 33) has questioned these types of chapters: "there is a tendency in British politics text books to think that the European Union (EU) can be satisfactorily dealt with in a distinct chapter rather than reflecting the way in which it is integrated on a daily basis in many aspects of British policy-making". While acknowledging the importance of this point, it is imperative to reiterate that these chapters gave an introduction to the subject. There is no need for a British politics text book to provide an indepth examination of the pros and cons of, for example, comitology. That would go far beyond the remit of such a text, but is likely to be covered in more specialist EU textbooks instead.

The fifth section covers policy issues: those of equality and the environment. Foster *et al* (2013) raise the concern that a solitary chapter on, for example, gender is little more than tokenism. The suggestion here is such topics are being sidelined or trivialised. It can only be argued that such chapters do not, under any circumstance, try to sideline such mainstream subjects. Again, one chapter is used to highlight the subject, but – in this case, gender issues – arise in other chapters as well.

The final section pulls together the disparate strands of the book. The way in which the governing of the UK is conducted has changed significantly over the last two or three decades. This chapter sets out the way forward in the study of the subject. It examines how the governing of the UK has changed over the past few decades.

This textbook will not provide all of the answers, nor all of the questions to ask. It will provide information, with comment and analysis. Alternative or supplementary sources of information are cited at the end of each chapter, and there is also a comprehensive bibliography at the end of the book. There are also questions for you to consider at the end of each chapter. The answers may not be provided in the chapter. Rather, the questions are there for you to focus your thoughts in a particular direction, and to appraise the information in each chapter.

Selected Bibliography

Gamble, Andrew. (2003). *Between Europe and America: The future of British Politics*: Palgrave.

Hay, Colin. (2007). *Why We Hate Politics:* Polity Press.

Hay, Colin. (2009). "Disenchanted with democracy, pissed off with politics", *British Politics* vol. 4-1, pp. 92-99.

Kerr, Peter & Kettell, Simon. (2006). "In Defence of British Politics: The Past, Present and Future of the Discipline", *British Politics* vol. 1-1, pp. 3-25.

Stoker, Gerry. (2006). *Why Politics Matters:* Macmillan.

Websites

www.bbc.co.uk/news/politics/
This is one of many media outlets which have an excellent coverage of politics. You could also look to ITN, Sky News or any of the broadsheet newspapers

www.politics.co.uk/
This is a wide ranging website covering a range of topical issues

www.ukpolitics.org.uk/
This is an excellent website as a starting point for topical political issues

Questions
1. What is politics?
2. Can there ever be an ideal form of political control?
3. Why does the Western model of democracy seem to fail elsewhere?

CHAPTER 2 // POST-WAR DEVELOPMENT OF BRITAIN: POLITICAL CHANGE

Contents
- **Introduction**
- **The Post-War Consensus**
- **Consensus broken**
- **A new consensus?**
- **Conclusion**

Introduction

The Britain of the early 21st Century is unrecognisable from one hundred years ago. At that time, the Great War – the war to end all wars – had broken out. Since then, the franchise has been extended to women, the world experienced an economic depression before fighting another war, and atomic weapons were used for the first time to end that war.

Much could be written about how Britain has changed throughout the twentieth century. This chapter (the first of three) will focus on how Britain has changed politically in the period since the end of the Second World War in 1945. It will also look at how attitudes to politics have changed. The subsequent two chapters will examine the social and the economic changes over that same time period. Thereafter, there is a chapter on Britain's place in the world, and how that has changed.

It is difficult to separate what is 'political', 'social' and 'economic'. In fact, there is likely to be some overlap between the chapters – not to mention links to other chapters in the book. The idea of the post-war consensus, for example, was a political consensus about the economy and the welfare state. Thus it could be seen as a political, economic and social consensus. The idea, therefore, is to get people to think about the types of change that have taken place. From this, it will be possible to set the scene for the rest of the book – painting a broad picture of how Britain has changed over the past seventy years to then be able to appreciate the finer detail of how Britain functions today.

The Post-War Consensus

The idea of the post-war consensus was that a broad agreement was necessary between the politicians of the major political parties – Conservative and Labour – as to how the country should be run. In effect, there would be a combination of Keynesian demand-led economics (which will be examined in chapter four), with an emphasis on achieving full employment in a mixed economy (a mixture of public and private ownership). Added to this was a commitment to the provision and maintenance of a welfare state.

Having this consensus did not mean there was total agreement on how things should be done. For example, in a mixed economy, what should be the degree of mix? How much public or private sector involvement should there be? These were the political battlegrounds at general elections.

There was also a broad consensus as to how the country should be managed. Parliamentary sovereignty was unquestioned. Even though there was a commitment from the Labour Party to abolish the House of Lords, there was no political will to see such a reform through. In fact, the Labour Government had to use the 1911 Parliament Act to force through the 1949 Parliament Act. The former enabled the House of Lords to delay legislation for up to two years; the latter reduced the delay to a year. In effect, there was a high degree of resistance to change. There was an old adage about the constitution: 'if it ain't broke, don't fix it'. Arguably, this applied to the running of the country as well.

On a simple left-right continuum, the vast majority of British politicians were either centre-left or centre-right. Figure 2.1 presents a simple perspective as to where the vast majority of politicians were located during the era of consensus. There were individual politicians, such as Enoch Powell and Tony Benn, who were more to the extreme end of their own party's ideological position.

Figure 2.1 Left-Right Continuum

During the 1970s this consensus started to come under pressure. Economic problems arose to which the politicians appeared to have no answer. Added to this, confidence in the political structures began to wane, with demands, for example, for devolution (and even independence) in Scotland. Hence the consensus began to fracture. By the 1980s, it had clearly broken.

Consensus broken
The politician who is credited with breaking the post-war consensus is Margaret Thatcher. This, however, is not wholly accurate. The consensus was already breaking during the Labour Government of 1974-79, under Harold Wilson and James Callaghan. It must be noted this was not voluntary. Due to economic pressures, the government was forced to go to the International Monetary Fund (IMF) for a loan. One of the conditions of the loan was, in effect, to replace the Keynesian model of running the country. It was Anthony Crosland who warned local government in 1975, "the party is over" with regard to spending plans. He

was not promising cuts; merely a cessation of spending increases. Thatcher, on the other hand, adopted the neo-liberal strategy of rolling back the frontiers of the state far more enthusiastically. This approach is examined in much greater detail in chapter 8.

In this way, the political consensus on how to run the state was broken in the early 1980s. One of the consequences was the way in which British politics became even more polarised. The neo-liberal strategy adopted by the Thatcher Governments saw the Conservative Party moving away from the centre-right position that had been adopted during the post-war period. It was gradually replaced by a more right wing position i.e. moving further from the centre-ground of British politics. At the same time, the Labour Party moved to the left, arguing for a greater role for the state in running the economy and society. This opened up the centre ground of British politics. One consequence of this was a split in the Labour Party. Many of those members who saw the party as deserting its centre-left position, joined the new Social Democratic Party (SDP). The SDP formed an alliance with the Liberals, in the hope of taking over the centre ground of British politics.

It must be noted the Conservatives under Thatcher wanted to reduce the role of government, but not necessarily central government. Tiers of local government were abolished in 1986 (see chapter 25), and parts of central government were streamlined. The police, armed forces and the judiciary did not suffer in the same way. A small state was what Thatcher desired, but also a strong state.

The 1983 General Election saw the Labour Party suffer its worst defeat in the post-war era. In response to this electoral disaster, the Labour Party started a gradual move back to the centre ground. In doing this, it started to alienate the more left wing support within the party. One of the aims of the move to the right was to re-engage with many Social Democrats who had left the party in the early 1980s.

Throughout the 1980s and into the early 1990s, there was no longer a consensus on how to run the country. The Conservative Party, in power from 1979 to 1997, was able to set the agenda on how the country should be run. Labour's original response was to oppose the minimalist state agenda most vigorously. Yet this seemed to fail. Consequently, the Labour Party moved dramatically towards the centre ground – in effect taking over some centre-right positions that had been held by the pre-Thatcher Conservative Party – in the hope of gaining electoral credibility and, ultimately, the opportunity to gain office.

A new consensus?

What was seen to develop from the mid-1990s was an apparent new political consensus between the Conservatives and Labour. It was built on the neo-liberal foundations of the Thatcher Governments. The Labour version of events came under the broad label of the Third Way – the idea being that the party was neither left nor right. In effect, the Labour Party under Tony Blair appeared to cherry pick a range of policies it felt would be successful. These were chosen to display a caring side, which the Conservatives appeared not to have, but also an awareness of the prevalent global neo-liberal economic agenda.

There are two moments, prior to Labour gaining power in 1997, where it became evident the Labour Party under Blair was moving to the right of its social democratic base. The first of these was the so-called battle over Clause 4 of the Labour Party constitution. This clause committed the Labour Party to the policy of nationalisation, although it must be noted not even the Attlee Government had pursued this policy with any great vigour. The clause was replaced. The two versions can be seen in Table 2.1.

Table 2.1 New and Old Clause 4 of the Labour Party constitution

Old Clause 4	New Clause 4
To secure for all the workers by hand or by brain the full fruits of their industry and the most equitable distribution thereof that may be possible upon the basis of the common ownership of the means of production, distribution and exchange, and the best obtainable system of popular administration and control of each industry of service.	The Labour Party is a democratic socialist party. It believes that by the strength of our common endeavour we achieve more than we achieve alone, so as to create for each of us the means to realise our true potential and for all of us a community in which power, wealth and opportunity are in the hands of the many, not the few.

Another marker that highlighted the extent to which the Labour Party had changed was in an interview that Tony Blair gave to the *Financial Times*. Blair compared the new Labour Party with that of the Democrats in the United States. "People don't even question for a single moment that the Democrats are a pro-business party. They should not be asking the question about New Labour" (*Financial Times* 16 January 1997). Rather than being the party that represented the workers and working class interests, Blair wanted businesses to trust Labour, arguably in a similar vein to that of business and the Conservatives.

With regard to the so-called 'new' Labour, Gamble (2003) has made some interesting observations – and these highlight just how far to the right Labour moved under Tony Blair's leadership. "If Labour was new, this meant that it was no longer a socialist party, no longer a social democratic party, no longer even a party of Labour. It had turned its back on the working class, on the poor, on the trade unions and on its active membership, and was looking for new allies and new voters" (Gamble, 2003, p. 192). In effect, Labour was looking to disaffected

Conservatives (and other disaffected centre or centre-right voters) in an attempt to broaden its support base, but at the expense of its traditional support – which appeared to be taken for granted. This strategy, to give Blair credit, was successful, with three consecutive election victories – the first Labour leader to do so. The question remains, in the post-Blair/Brown era, at what cost to the party?

Thus there was a new consensus that appeared to form. Both of the major parties were happy to adopt the neo-liberal platform that had been established by the Thatcher and Major Governments. The frontiers of the state had been rolled back, and that was not going to be reversed.

Constitutional reforms introduced by the 'New' Labour Government, such as devolution, were not going to be reversed either. Under 'New' Labour, the universality of the welfare state, and specifically the benefit programme, was also reversed. Gordon Brown, as Chancellor of the Exchequer, talked of "targeted universalism". In effect, the emphasis was placed upon the individual. This is clearly a neo-liberal provision with regard to the role of the state – or, more accurately, the minimal role of the state. The need for a benefit had to be proven before it could be received. The current Coalition Government has not reversed such a position. Instead, they tightened up the process even further.

Even the deficit reduction plans of all of the major parties were not too dissimilar. They all agreed that cuts were necessary. The disagreement was over the speed and the depth of the cuts. Such a debate was carried out in the 1950s and the 1960s over the mixed economy of the UK. The questions were about the degree of mix.

In 2013, there appears to be a consensus between all three major parties over the role of the state in political, economic and social matters. There are specific policy disagreements, even between the coalition partners. Nick Clegg, for example, wants a largely elected upper chamber. The Conservative Party, on the other hand, is far from enthusiastic in supporting such a policy. Consequently, there has been a stalemate on any major reforms. There is, however, agreement that a second chamber is necessary.

Where a consensus is not so apparent, is over the issue of Europe. There is broad agreement among many politicians in the major political parties that Britain should remain a member of the European Union. It must be noted, however, that there are growing numbers who are dissatisfied about British membership – especially in light of the ongoing Euro-zone crisis. David Cameron saw a significant number of his own MPs fail to toe the party line in a parliamentary vote on a referendum on continued British membership of the EU. The apparent rise in popularity for the UK Independence Party (UKIP) has resulted in a more euro-sceptical stance from David Cameron and the Conservative Party. Cameron plans to renegotiate the terms of entry and to put them to the country in an 'In-Out' referendum in 2017. Some of his backbenchers would like such a referendum to be held much sooner, regardless of renegotiating the terms of entry!

It must be noted the issue of Europe is not one that sits nicely on party lines. It straddles all parties; i.e. all of the major parties have members who see themselves as 'pro-Europeans', and others who see themselves as 'anti-Europeans'. The Liberal Democrats have presented themselves as the only consistently pro-European party. Yet even they now have anti-European members. Overall, 'apathetic acceptance of membership' may be the best way to describe Britain's relationship with the EU – at least among mainstream politicians, but could that really be called a consensus?

Conclusion

When talking of a political consensus in British politics, it is important to note this does not mean there is total agreement on all policies. The consensus is at the strategic level. There will be specific policy differences. As was noted at the time of the post-war consensus, there was agreement about Keynesian economics, a welfare state, a mixed economy and the aim of achieving full employment. There were, for example, clear policy divisions over the level of mix in a mixed economy – how much public ownership and how much private? Regardless of this, there was a perceived consensus.

That consensus was shattered, but now appears to have been replaced by a new consensus. There are still policy divisions between the major parties, but there appears to be a broad agreement over how the economy should be run and how government should be structured. The composition of the House of Lords, or the introduction of elected mayors, are policy debates, but there is no talk of abolishing the House of Lords or local government.

A final point to note is all of this could still change. A consensus takes time to bed down. A surprise outcome at the next general election could throw this apparent consensus out of the window. A week, after all, is a long time in politics. Things can, and do, change. External factors may influence thinking e.g. fighting in the Middle East, the price of oil, the on-going Euro-crisis, a resurrection of pro-democracy campaigning in China. Anything like this will impact upon British politics and has the potential to shake up a consensus.

Selected Bibliography

Butler, David & Stokes, Donald. (1976). *Political Change in Britain:* Macmillan, 2nd edition.

Gamble, Andrew. (2003). *Between Europe and America: The Future of British Politics:* Palgrave.

McCormick, John. (2012). *Contemporary Britain:* Palgrave, 3rd edition.

Mycock, Andrew. (2010). "British Citizenship and the Legacy of Empires", *Parliamentary Affairs* vol. 63-2, pp. 339-355.

Panitch, Leo. (1977). "Profits and Politics: Labour and the Crisis of British Capitalism", *Politics & Society* vol. 7-4, pp. 477-507.

Websites

www.bbc.co.uk/history/british/modern/thatcherism_01.shtml
The BBC history pages give a balanced insight into the political development of Britain post-Second World War

www.britannia.com/history/nar20hist5.html
This website gives a fascinating overview of British history for the Americans. Note how the words Britain and England appear interchangeable.

www.history.org.uk/resources/student_resource_4701,4708_110.html
The Historical Association's podcasts are a useful supplement

Questions

1. Is a new political consensus developing in the UK in the early twenty-first century?
2. "The social democratic, welfare state model was no more than a flawed experiment." Discuss.
3. "The post-war consensus was little more than an excuse by politicians not to introduce any radical policies." Discuss.

CHAPTER 3 // POST-WAR DEVELOPMENT OF BRITAIN: SOCIAL CHANGE

Contents
- **Introduction**
- **The British Political Culture – does it even exist?**
- **Changing class cleavages**
- **The Changing Family**
- **Religion in Britain**
- **Is Britain a multi-cultural society?**
- **Conclusion**

Introduction

Society is continually changing and evolving. Advancements in, for example technology, have a huge impact upon people's lives. At the beginning of the twentieth century, socialisation – how people learn about society, and their role within it – was largely conducted through the family unit. By the late 1970s, there was a strong argument that television had a significant impact upon socialisation, and was possibly becoming the primary source of information. Today, the most significant factor in socialisation appears to be the internet – with many people living their lives on Facebook or other social networking sites, blogging about every miniscule activity in their lives.

British society as it exists in the early part of the twenty first century is significantly different to that in the immediate post-war period. There was rationing of food, with, for example, bread being rationed until the 1950s. This is seen as a basic staple of life, that is taken for granted. Today, people get upset if their local supermarket is not stocking particular food products when they want them. Thus strawberries are eaten all year round, rather than in June.

The composition of society has also changed significantly. This is not just through immigration, although there is a clear impact here, but also through who goes to work, where and when they work, etc. The concept of 'flexi-time' was not in the vocabulary until the late twentieth century. Traditionally, people worked 9-5, Monday to Friday. The weekend was a time of rest, with Sundays set aside for religious observances.

Attitudes have changed as well. Britain has been perceived as a tolerant society – throughout history, refugees have fled Europe, or other parts of the world, for Britain, where it was felt their lives could be lived more safely. Today, this is even more the case. Britain, collectively, is more tolerant of people of different ethnic or religious backgrounds, as well as a person's sexuality, than many other countries. It is possibly only queue-jumping that is not tolerated.

The British Political Culture – does it even exist?

Before examining the question of whether a British political culture exists, it is important to examine the concept 'political culture'. In broad terms, political culture is to do with what people think about politics, government, etc. It is also an acknowledgement that what people think, and how they act, may not be the same.

Political culture is developed through socialisation. There are a number of different stages, known as patterns of orientation. These show how a political culture may develop. The first stage is about **cognition** – knowledge of your country, the politics of the country, the political system as a whole, etc. This is the most basic level of political culture. In some countries, there may be people who are unaware as to the country in which they live, or the politics of the country.

Once cognition has developed, the second pattern evolves naturally. This is the **affection** stage. Feelings develop for your country or the political system. It is important to note that these feelings do not have to be positive.

The final stage here is **evaluative**. The affection could lead to very negative evaluations of a political culture. A person could despise the political regime within their country, or feel that they are being forced to belong to a particular nationality rather than some other self-perceived nationality. The alternative – a very positive evaluation – is also most feasible.

A political culture may be influenced by many factors. These include:

1. the political system – e.g. how 'open' or 'closed' is the system. Compare, for example, the totalitarian regime of North Korea with that of the United States.
2. input factors – these include such things as the divisions within society, as well as the political parties, their leaders, etc. These are the factors that have inputs into the political system.
3. output factors – this is to do with the expectations that people may have from the political system. What are the policies of the regime? What are the expectations that these policies are going to be implemented?
4. individual – this is the role of socialisation. How are people socialised? What are the factors that influence their perceptions?

Finally, when examining political culture, there are different types of political culture. There are three broad categories:

1. Parochial – this is where the population look up to a leader to guide them in what to do, or even how to think. Such a typology is said to exist in 'traditional' societies, where groups look to tribal leaders for guidance.
2. Subject – this is where the state imposes its will on the population, who, in

turn, accept these instructions unquestioningly. The former Soviet Union was seen to have such a political culture.

3. Participant – this is seen as the ideal type, whereby people are involved in politics and society. They are able to interact with the organs of the state, with the possibility of influencing said organs.

Having examined the concept of political culture, there than arises the question as to whether or not there exists a 'British' political culture. Noting that the concept 'political culture' is a contested one, the evidence would suggest a lack of a British political culture. There are, however, cases both for and against the idea of a British political culture.

Almond & Verba (1963); *The Civic Culture* is seen as the classic text on the idea of political culture. They conducted a series of surveys about the attitudes people held towards their political system. The interviews were conducted in West Germany, Italy, Mexico, the United States and the United Kingdom. The British, according to this study, were seen as a deferential people, who held the monarchy and other institutions of state in high regard, and who felt they could influence the government if they so chose. The British were seen to have a high degree of trust in the institutions of state, including politicians, the police, etc. There was also much pride in the national identity of 'being British'.

Fifty years on, levels of trust in the state have diminished, while deference is near to non-existent. Pride in national identity has also been brought into question, especially with the rise in, for example, Scottish nationalism. Many Scots see themselves as Scottish rather than British. Similarly, many in Wales see themselves as Welsh rather than British (McCormick, 2012). Much of this changed with the 2012 Olympic Games, where there was a very visible – if short term – surge in the levels of British patriotism.

Respect for the monarchy has also fluctuated since the writings of Almond & Verba. In 1977, at the time of the Silver Jubilee, there were street parties across many parts of the country to commemorate the celebrations. By the time of the Golden Jubilee, such celebrations were few and far between. There was talk of the monarchy – or, more broadly, the Royal Family – being aloof, distant and unengaged with the country. Much of this had been in response to the mixed messages that came from Buckingham Palace over the death of the Princess of Wales a few years earlier. Ten years later, with the Diamond Jubilee, there were celebrations across the country to mark the sixtieth year of the monarch's reign. This was nothing when compared to the excitement of the Royal Wedding between Prince William and Kate Middleton. Their marriage and then the birth of their first child highlighted the fascination many people still have with the Royal Family. There may not be the same respect for the monarchy as in the early 1960s, but those arguing for the abolition of the monarchy are still a distinct and very small minority.

It is difficult to ascertain whether or not there is a British political culture. There is little conformity over attitudes towards the political institutions of the country. The levels of trust and deference seen in the time of Almond & Verba have largely disappeared, seemingly being replaced by public apathy. Some of this is a clear result of the actions of many politicians e.g. MPs expenses. Yet it may also be a response to the lack of speed in changing policies, especially when compared to the near instant responses people get when voting contestants out of the X-Factor or Strictly Come Dancing. Conversely, national pride is still strong, although the issue may be more about identifying in which nationality there is such pride.

Changing class cleavages

As will be seen in the chapter on voting behaviour (Chapter 21), class has always been a significant factor in voting behaviour. Pulzer (1967, p. 98) noted that class was "the basis of British party politics; all else is embellishment and detail".

In broad terms, Britain was divided into two classes: the working class and the middle class. Linked to employment, the working class are the manual workers; those in the middle class are in non-manual employment. There is also a so-called 'upper class' – the gentry or aristocracy. They comprise a very small percentage of the population, but in relation to the rest are largely inconsequential. It must be noted, however, there is a newer perception of an upper class, and this is linked to wealth. Not all members of the aristocracy are wealthy. Instead, there is a new super-wealthy elite in the UK, with incomes in the millions of pounds. Again, they comprise a miniscule percentage of the population, and, in relation to changing class cleavages, are not of great consequence. There are different ways of classifying class that have been developed. These are also examined in chapter 21.

What has changed over the post-war period is the size of each class – although some of this may be linked to self-perception of class. In sum, the size of the working class has shrunk. In the 1950s and 1960s, the working class comprised approximately two thirds of the population. This dropped to below 50% at the beginning of the twenty-first century, and is now at around one third of the population. Conversely, a survey in 2007 found that over half of the population saw themselves as working class. Noting that, conventionally, the working class comprises those in manual employment, Bryson & Forth (2010) found that 37% of employees were in manual employment in 2005. This has led to suggestions of a growth in 'inverse' snobbery, where people take pride in claiming working class origins.

The shrinking of the working class can be related to the contraction of manufacturing and heavy industry in the UK. This will be examined in chapter 4, where the changes in the structure of the British economy in the post-war period are evaluated. The decline and disappearance of some heavy industries in the 1980s is in line with the decline of the British working class.

As the working class has shrunk, those in non-manual work (i.e. the middle class) have increased in number. The middle class comprised approximately a third of the population in the 1950s and 1960s. It now appears those in middle class occupations comprise over half of the population.

With this growth in middle class occupations, there is an associated suggestion that 'we are all better off'. This is anything but the case, as Hutton (1995) presented in his description of Britain as a 30:30:40 society. Hutton argued that British society had fractured under the Thatcher years. Around 30% of the population, he claimed, were marginalized. These were the unemployed, or those (today, at least) who are on the minimum wage and are dependent upon benefits to survive. A further 30% were what he termed "insecure". They may be better off financially, but there is a high degree of job insecurity. The remaining 40% were privileged. These are the people with full-time, permanent jobs, who are comfortably off. Hutton may have hoped that an incoming Labour government might do something to address these imbalances. This did not happen. Disparities in wealth and income increased under Labour, more so than they had done under Thatcher or Major. Social immobility is extremely high in the UK, in fact, higher than in the USA (Sloam, 2012). When drawing on the idea of a 30:30:40 society, this appears unlikely to change.

The Changing Family
Society may have changed quite significantly in the second half of the twentieth century, but aspects within this have changed as well. Family structures have changed. There are fewer people getting married, but divorce levels have increased. There is not just co-habitation, but also civil partnerships (both gay and heterosexual). The conventional nuclear family appears far from the norm. With potentially both adults in work, the traditional family has changed significantly over the past sixty to seventy years.

The family used to be the main source of socialization, which fed into the political culture of a country. Whatever needed to be learned was done so at the dinner table. This was surpassed by the media: firstly, television, and now the internet. The family's role in socialization has diminished significantly.

The family unit has changed. Divorce rates were very low in the 1950s – less than 30 000 per year in the UK (Allen & Crow, 2001). Divorce laws were relaxed in 1969 (Divorce Reform Act), and since then rates of divorce have increased. There was speculation in the mid-1990s that about 40% of all first-time marriages would end in divorce (Allen & Crow, 2001). Divorce rates peaked in 1991 and have gradually declined (with the occasional upsurge). By 2007, divorce rates were closer to that of the 1970s.

Marriage rates have also fluctuated. They were declining during the 1990s before picking up in the early years of the 21st century, and then declining further. In 2007, for example, there were just over 235 000 marriages in England

and Wales, of which around 146 000 were first time marriages (Marriage, Divorce and Adoption Statistics, England and Wales (Series FM2), No. 35, 2007). It is also interesting to note that almost two thirds of the marriages in 2007 were civil marriages, as opposed to religious marriages. Added to this in over 80% of marriages in 2007, both partners gave an identical address prior to marriage. This suggests the vast majority of those getting married co-habit first. Even in the early 1980s, around 30% of couples were cohabiting prior to marriage. In the early 1960s, the figure was closer to 3% (Beaujouan & Ní Bhrolcháin, 2011).

With the increase in divorce rates post-1969, and many cohabiting couples separating, there has been an increase in single parent families. In the mid-1970s, around 10% of all births were to single mothers. This had increased to over a third of all births by the mid-1990s. In 2011, there were approximately 2 million single parents with dependent children. This number has been increasing steadily. Of these, women accounted for over 90% of all lone parents.

Another factor to note is that of teenage pregnancy. The UK has some of the highest rates of teenage pregnancy in Western Europe, and this figure increased regularly throughout the 1980s and 1990s. Much media coverage was given to the topic. In 2010, UK teenage pregnancy rates dropped by 7% compared to 2009 figures. The 2010 figures are the lowest rates of teenage pregnancy since 1969. Figures covering the early part of the 21st century show that of all mothers giving birth, 5.6% were teenage mothers.

Another area that has seen significant change in the post-war period is the number of working mothers. The stereotypical perception of women (and this will be examined in much greater detail in chapter 32) was that upon getting married, a woman would stop working and run the household, raise the family, etc. Such a perception, assuming it was ever wholly accurate, is no longer valid. Bear in mind even in the 1980s, some women were sacked because they were pregnant.

The number of women in the workplace is similar to that of men. This, however, masks a number of issues: the type of work done; the hours worked (part-time or full-time employment); wages for comparable jobs with those done by men; and, the existence of the glass ceiling (see chapter 32). Over 70% of women work in paid employment. At the end of the working day many of them return home to complete the domestic chores as well.

Finally, the UK has an ageing population. In 1951, about 10% of the population were aged over 65. By the turn of the century, it was over 15%. Most people are living longer, and this is causing a burden on the state through the provision of welfare and health care, as well as the paying of the state pension. Consequently, the retirement age – i.e. the age at which you can draw your state pension – has been increased, and is likely to be increased again in the future.

Religion in Britain

An interesting aspect of British society that is often overlooked is the role of religion. Religion plays a prominent, if declining, role in our society – and most people do not even notice. Take, for example, the legislative process. Within the House of Lords sit 26 bishops, all of whom represent the Church of England. Thus, the Church of England is guaranteed input into the legislative process, as it is the **Established Church**. Whether this remains the case in the future is unclear. The Wakeham Commission into the reform of the House of Lords planned to broaden out religious representation, but those reforms have not proceeded (see chapter 10). Nick Clegg's proposals to reform the House of Lords planned a reduction in the number of bishops, but did not guarantee representation for any other religious groups. Again, these reforms have not been implemented.

Religious practice has been in decline since the 1960s. Many people may identify with a particular religion, but do not necessarily attend any religious observances. It is interesting to note that Christmas is celebrated across the UK – as a time of giving and receiving presents. There are apocryphal stories of people complaining that religion gets in the way of Christmas.

In the 2001 census, 170 different religions were listed. This included "Jedi". There was an internet campaign at the time of the census to get "Jedi" or "Jedi Knight" recognised as an official religion. The story was that if enough people claimed to practice such a religion, it would be recognised as such. This was, however, an urban myth. It did not stop almost 400 000 people claiming to practice "Jedi" (more than who claimed to be Sikh, Jewish or Buddhist).

The data of the major religions practised in the UK, as cited in Table 3.1, is significantly different to actual religious practice. In 1999, a third of people claimed to visit a place of religious observance at least once a year (Social Trends, 2000), but around half of the population claimed to belong to the Church of England.

Table 3.1 Religious Practice in the UK (2001 census)

Religion	% Population
Christian	71.6
Muslim	2.7
Hindu	1.0
Sikh	0.6
Jewish	0.5
Buddhist	0.3
None (including Jedi)	15.5

Thus, although Christianity is by far the dominant religion in the UK, it covers a diverse range of interpretations. The Anglican/Church of England faith dominates, but there is also Catholicism, Church of Scotland, Church in Wales, Baptist, Methodist, etc. Added to this, many people may identify with a religion, but may not practice it on a regular basis.

Is Britain a multi-cultural society?

The subject of ethnicity is covered in Chapter 33. This section here is to highlight just how much Britain has changed in the post-war period. It is often pointed out, for example, that around 8% of the population belong to ethnic minorities in Britain. This is not wholly accurate – these are the non-white ethnic minorities. With the enlargement of the European Union in 2004 and 2007, many people from Eastern Europe came to the UK to work. Some have settled. White non-British comprise around 5% of the UK population. Not only does this include people from the EU, but also Australia, New Zealand, Canada and the United States. Collectively, they comprise a higher percentage of the population than any other ethnic minority.

Britain has an ethnically diverse society. There are different cultures, different religious practices co-existing in a high degree of harmony. This is significantly different to the early post-war period.

The *Empire Windrush* docked in June 1948 in London. This is seen as the start of mass immigration as we understand it today. Most of the passengers on the *Windrush* came from the Caribbean to the UK looking for work, or with the promise of jobs upon their arrival. During the 1950s and 1960s, many people came to the UK from the disparate parts of the Commonwealth, looking for work. It was only in the 1970s that restrictions were placed on immigration into the UK. In 1972, around 80 000 African Asians were expelled from Uganda. They arrived in the UK with little more than the baggage they could carry, and settled in cities such as Leicester.

Leicester, as an example, claims to be a multi-ethnic, multi-faith and multi-cultural city. It celebrates its diversity. Over half of the city's population is not of English origin. Around half of primary school children in Leicester do not have English as a first language. Celebrations such as Diwali (the Hindu Festival of Light) are as prominent as Christmas festivities within the city. Leicester claims to have the largest Diwali celebrations outside of India. The diversity of the city is both highlighted and enjoyed.

Conclusion

UK society has changed significantly in the seventy years since the end of the war. Immigration has been one of the catalysts of change, but by no means is it the sole reason for change. Technology has changed the way in which society operates. It is almost impossible for many young people today to imagine life without a mobile phone or the internet. These types of change have enabled society to develop – and some would argue such change is not necessarily for the best. Being so attached to technology has meant that some people may not have learned the basic skills of human interaction, except via technology.

Where technology has been a benefit can be seen in the advances in healthcare. People tend to live longer as a result of the advances in healthcare, in conjunction with a better diet. A consequence of this is people draw their state pensions for many more years than originally anticipated when the state pension scheme was first established. Thus the cost to the state increases. One response has been to raise the retirement age. Yet by making people work for longer means there are fewer jobs available for younger people, and, consequently, there are increases in unemployment of the young. In 2013, the figure for unemployed 18-24 year olds stood at about a million! Another lost generation of unemployed people will have a significant impact upon how our society develops over the next ten or twenty years.

Selected Bibliography

Almond, Gabriel & Verba, Sydney. (1963). *The Civic Culture*: Princeton University Press.

Furlong, Andy & Cartmel, Fred. (2012). "Social Change and Political Engagement Among Young People: Generation and the 2009/2010 British Election Survey", *Parliamentary Affairs* vol. 65-1, pp. 13-28.

McCormick, John. (2012). *Contemporary Britain*: Palgrave, 3rd edition.

Parliamentary Affairs vol. 63-2. (2010). A special edition on Britishness.

Uberoi, Varun & Modood, Tariq. (2013). "Inclusive Britishness: A Multiculturalist Advance", *Political Studies* vol. 61-1, pp. 23-41.

Weakliem, David & Adams, Julia. (2011). "What Do We Mean by 'Class Politics'?", *Politics & Society* vol. 39-4, pp. 475-495.

Websites

www.bbc.co.uk/history/british/modern/
The BBC pages give a fascinating overview of how Britain has changed in the post-war era.

www.nationalarchives.gov.uk/
The National Archives have a huge store of data. Census data, among many other things, can be accessed from here.

www.ons.gov.uk/ons/index.html
The Office of National Statistics web pages provide much data. For example, Marriage, Divorce and Adoption Statistics, England and Wales (Series FM2), No. 35, (2007) is available at www.ons.gov.uk/ons/publications/re-reference-tables. html?edition=tcm%3A77-39669

Questions
1. What are the main features of the British political culture in the 21st century?
2. To what extent has Britain become a secular society?
3. "Deference is still prominent in Britain today. It's just that people are now deferential to money and celebrity." Discuss.

CHAPTER 4 // THE CHANGING BRITISH ECONOMY

Contents
- **Introduction**
- **Keynesianism**
- **The neo-liberal response**
- **"We don't make things any more!" – the decline of manufacturing**
- **A service economy?**
- **Conclusion**

Introduction

One of the major criticisms of the British economy in recent times has been that Britain "doesn't make things anymore". Along with such a criticism comes a harking back to the times when Britain was a manufacturing giant; a global leader in manufacturing. What has been seen, especially in the post-Second World War period, has been a managed decline. As Pollard (1984, p. 14) noted, in this period "virtually all our economic policies and all the major economic and political controversies surrounding them (with a very few exceptions) have not been about how to improve the growth performance of the British economy, but how to slide down gracefully and elegantly rather than in ungainly and demoralising lurches". This is a rather pessimistic description of Britain's economic position. It is reinforced with phrases such as "industrial disease", or periods of "stagflation".

Yet, is this description of the British economy wholly accurate? Britain was the first country to industrialise – and that came with some economic cost. Other countries were able to copy and improve upon British industrial developments, at far less cost. There is no doubt Britain is no longer the world's economic superpower; but bear in mind Britain had already slipped to fourth in the rankings of GDP per head of population by the early 20th century (behind Australia, the USA and New Zealand). Throw in two world wars, which crippled the British economy, and it may be something of a surprise Britain is still ranked so highly compared to other economies around the world.

In a range of sectors, such as finance, pharmaceuticals and armaments, British firms are among the world leaders. Maybe, therefore, one of the problems is the British do not like to boast about their economic successes – it is seen as being very brash, boastful and "American". If anything goes wrong with the economy, there is likely to be a collective wailing and gnashing of teeth. With regard to the economy, we appear to belong to the "glass half empty" brigade, rather than the "glass half full".

This is not to say there have not been any economic disasters in the post-war period. This chapter was written during an alleged double-dip recession! Rather, as can be seen in the rest of this chapter, there have been peaks and troughs, as there have been in every other economy around the world.

The Keynesianism Economy

As was noted in chapter 2, there was broad general agreement as to how the British economy should be run in the post-war period; i.e. there was a consensus. Both the Conservatives and Labour were committed to a mixed economy, the utilisation of Keynesian demand-led economics, and an aim of achieving full employment. Alongside this was the welfare state. The idea was the state could meet your welfare needs, 'from the cradle to the grave', if an individual so chose. The choice of seeking private sector alternatives was not stopped.

In the immediate aftermath of the Second World War, the first ever majority Labour Government decided to use the state to rebuild the economy. The way in which this was to be achieved was by taking over the 'commanding heights of the economy'. In effect, this meant nationalising key industries (as can be seen in Table 4.1). While a major policy platform (and a commitment in the Labour Party constitution), the nationalisation programme covered approximately 15% of the British economy. There was no wholesale nationalisation. On top of this, there was also very generous compensation for the former-owners of the industries that were nationalised.

Table 4.1 Industries nationalised by the Labour Government 1945-1950

The Bank of England (1946)
Civil Aviation (1946)
Cable & Wireless (1946)
Coal (1946)
Road and Rail Transport (1946)
Electricity (1947)
Land Development Rights (1947)
Gas (1948)
Iron and Steel (1949)

The Keynesian approach to running the economy was relatively straightforward. Keynes had looked at the disaster of the Great Depression, where the government had failed to intercede to help people find work. Added to this, successive governments had appeared more concerned about balancing the budget and eliminating a budget deficit, rather than focusing upon the welfare of the people. The argument at that time was the market was the most efficient method for allocating resources, and the state should not intervene. Such an approach appeared to fail.

Keynes turned all of this on its head. A market economy could not utilise all available productive resources, therefore the state had to intervene. The government should manage demand, and should stimulate demand primarily through fiscal policy (tax and spend) and monetary policy (interest rates). To stimulate demand, a government could, for example, increase public spending, reduce taxes or cut interest rates. If demand got too high, it could be dampened down, again using fiscal and monetary policy – by cutting spending, increasing taxes or increasing interest rates.

In effect, Keynes argued a government should spend its way out of an economic downturn or recession. A balanced budget was not the most important factor in running the economy. Rather, it should be full employment. If people were in work, even in the public sector, they would be contributing to the growth of the economy. People out of work could be a burden on the economy. In economic bad times, a government should overspend on public projects e.g. roads, schools, hospitals, railways, etc. These would be an investment for the future. Such overspending would be recouped over the longer term.

Figure 4.1 The Stop-Go Cycle

Subsequent governments of both political persuasions followed this approach. There was some tweaking to the nationalisation programme, with a Conservative Government denationalising iron and steel, and road haulage, in 1953. Added to this, consultative bodies were established to enable trades unions and business leaders to have some input into the development of economic policy. Harold Macmillan introduced the National Economic Development Council (NEDC, but known as Neddy) in 1961. Achieving full employment meant working with the unions and business leaders.

The Keynesian approach to running the economy can be seen as a Stop-Go Cycle (as demonstrated in Figure 4.1). All economic approaches utilise such a cycle, highlighting the very close relationship between economic success and electoral success. Demand is stimulated to grow the economy. The problem is such stimulation may not help the economy. There is a time lag of several months between the stimulus being introduced and the national economy responding. People, with extra money to spend, are not going to wait to 'buy British'. Hence, the shortfall in supply is met by increased imports. This could lead, in a worst-case scenario, to a run on the currency. Consequently, demand needs to be dampened down. Yet, it is normally the state of the economy that enables a government to win an election. It is very rare for a government to retain power during an economic downturn. Thus, governments of all political persuasions attempt to stimulate the economy, in an attempt to make the economic picture look good and thus gain re-election.

Figure 4.2 The Phillips Curve

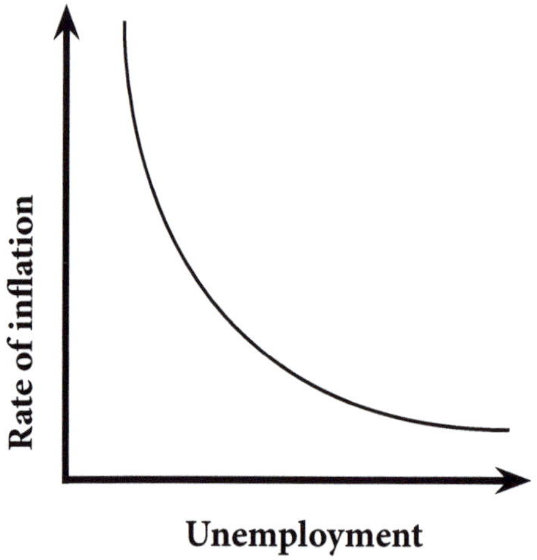

Rate of inflation

Unemployment

The Keynesian approach to running the economy dominated in the post-war period, but was seen to 'fail' in the 1970s. In an attempt to stimulate the economy, governments spent more. This caused inflation to increase – which was an acknowledged by-product of increased government spending. The idea is to achieve a balance between levels of unemployment and inflation, as demonstrated by the Phillips Curve (see Figure 4.2), although the target was still full employment. The optimum level, utilising the Phillips Curve, is an unemployment rate of around 2.5%. Yet in the 1970s, unemployment remained high, and Britain entered a period of "stagflation" – high inflation, stagnant economic growth and high unemployment. It must be noted unemployment hit one million in 1972, for the first time since the Great Depression. In a period where the objective was full employment, this was seen as an unacceptably high rate of unemployment. The Keynesian approach appeared to have no answers to what was described as the "British economic disease".

The problems with the British economy can be seen quite clearly in Tables 4.2 – 4.4. Unemployment kept on rising, as did inflation. Economic growth, on the other hand, was nowhere near as strong.

Table 4.2 Unemployment in the UK, 1950-1979

Time Period	Rate of Unemployment
1950s	1.6%
1960s	1.9%
1970s	3.2%
1970-74	2.4%
1975-79	4.0%

Table 4.3 Inflation in the UK, 1950-1979

Time Period	Rate of Inflation
1950s	3.0%
1960s	4.5%
1970s	12.5%
1970-74	9.0%
1975-79	15.0%

Table 4.4 UK economic growth, 1950-1979

Time period	Average economic growth
1950s	2.5%
1960s	3.3%
1970s	2.3%
1950-73	3.0%
1974-79	1.4%

(Developed from Johnson (1991)

The Keynesian approach appeared to have no answers as to why the British economy was seen to be failing. Thus, alternative strategies were needed, and the one that dominated was the neo-liberal approach.

The neo-liberal response

The neo-liberal role of the state is explained in chapter 8. The focus in this section is the neo-liberal approach to the running of the economy – although there is a clear overlap between the two. With the apparent failure of the Keynesian approach to running the economy, the Conservative Party under Margaret Thatcher took on wholeheartedly the neo-liberal approach.

What this entailed was a reduction in public spending (as a proportion of GDP) and a reduction in the public part of the mixed economy. Added to this was an emphasis upon monetary policy, rather than fiscal policy, to control and manipulate the economy. Finally, contact with outside bodies – most notably the trades unions, but also many business organisations – was reduced significantly. If Keynes saw a demand-led economy, the Thatcherite approach was clearly supply-side economics.

In sum, there was a reduced role for the state. Thatcher described it as 'rolling back the frontiers of the state'. The emphasis was very much upon the market, rather than the state, leading the economy. It is interesting to note, however, there was no actual plan for how to reduce the role of the state. Rather, as will be seen later in this chapter, there were a number of policies that were developed in a piecemeal fashion, which collectively reduced the role of the state in the economy.

The ease with which this was done was aided by the imagery of the so-called 'Winter of Discontent' of 1978-79. As Hay (2010, pp. 446-447) has noted, it was a "tale of how the country was 'held to ransom', of how 'the dead were left unburied' and of how the 'bins were left unemptied' during a 'Winter of Discontent' in which 'Britain was under siege' from 'militant trade unionists' and their extremist leaders". This imagery, which was far from accurate, enabled Thatcher and her government to reduce the role of the state, and to attack trade union power and influence. With regard to trade union power and influence, most commentators accept, in retrospect, it had grown to undesirable levels by the 1970s. If anything, this was the symbolic end of the period of consensus.

Under a Keynesian approach, the emphasis was upon achieving full employment. This was abandoned in the early 1980s. Instead, the emphasis was on fighting inflation, with the aim being to squeeze inflation out of the economic system. Thus, unemployment was allowed to rise. Thatcher's governments did little to intercede in fighting unemployment. The argument was the market would set the levels of unemployment. If unemployment rose, wages would fall as business cut their cloth to meet their needs. Lower wages would mean the opportunity to employ more staff and, thus, employment levels would rise again (soon to be followed by rises in wages).

Table 4.5 Inflation in the UK 1980-2009

Time Period	Rate of Inflation
1980-89	7.0%
1990-99	3.3%
2000-09	1.9 %
1980-97	5.7%
1997-2009	1.8%

In the 1980s, unemployment levels averaged at 9.6%, peaking in 1986 at 11.8% of the workforce. In effect this meant almost one in every eight people was unemployed. Compare this to the levels in Table 4.2, where people were concerned that unemployment levels had reached one million. Under Thatcher, they passed three million. In the 1990s, unemployment levels dropped to an average of 8.0% – still significantly higher than the pre-Thatcher years.

Table 4.6 Unemployment in the UK, 1980-2009

Time Period	Rate of unemployment
1980-89	9.6%
1990-99	8.0%
2000-09	5.4%

This neo-liberal approach places an emphasis upon the role of the individual rather than society. In fact, Thatcher was to comment 'there was no such thing as society'. Individuals were to be encouraged to become more entrepreneurial, and less dependent on the state. Incentives were introduced to encourage such practices. The most obvious of these were reductions in the rate of income tax. In Geoffrey Howe's first budget as Chancellor of the Exchequer in 1979, the top rate of income tax was reduced from 83% to 60%, while the basic rate was reduced from 33% to 30%. Further reductions were made in 1988, when the top rate was reduced to 40%, and the basic rate to 25%. Howe did increase the rate of VAT, from 8% to 15%. As with all indirect taxes, this hurt the least well off in society, who pay a larger share of their total income in such taxes.

One of the key objectives of the Thatcher Government was to reduce the role of the state in the economy. This was carried out via a range of different policies, including privatisation of nationalised industries (see Table 4.7), the placing out to tender of public sector services, and a reduction in regulations in some sectors. Retrospectively, this is sometimes presented as a coherent package of policies. The reality was that it was significantly different. The first Thatcher Government (1979-1983) had no plans for mass privatisation. Rather there were strategies to discipline the nationalised industries, to make them more efficient.

Table 4.7 The Main Privatisations by the Thatcher Governments*

Amersham International
British Aerospace
British Airports Authority (BAA)
British Airways
British Gas
British Petroleum (BP)
British Steel
British Sugar Corporation
British Telecom
Britoil
Cable & Wireless
Electricity
Jaguar
Rolls Royce
Rover
Water

* There have been no dates placed against the industries that were privatised. The reason for this is that many industries were privatised in phases e.g. BP in 1979, 1983, 1987, 1988 and 1989.

Along with privatisation, there was a range of other policies that reduced the role of the state in both the economy and in the provision of services. These included Compulsory Competitive Tendering (CCT), where local authorities were required to put some of their services (e.g. refuse collection) out to tender. The idea was to try and get a cheaper, more efficient service. Particular local authority services, such as public transport, were opened up to competition from the private sector. Council tenants were given the right to buy their own houses. There was also the alternative of changing from a public sector landlord to one from the private sector. In effect, public services that were not in the market sector were opened up to competition.

In having a reduced role for the state in running the economy, the importance of fiscal policy was seen to decline. Instead, far greater emphasis was placed on control of the money supply – monetary policy – to influence the economy. The theory was that by controlling and manipulating interest rates, inflation could be brought under control and then squeezed out of the system. The reality was significantly different – the major problem being the different definitions of 'money supply', as can be seen in Table 4.8.

Table 4.8 Different explanations of 'Money Supply'

M0	All cash in circulation. It is sometimes known as 'narrow money' because it is the most narrow definition of the money supply
M1	This includes everything under M0 plus assets that may be quickly converted into cash
M2	This includes everything under M1 plus all time-related deposits, saving deposits and non-institutional money market funds
M3	This includes M2 plus all large time deposits, institutional money market funds, short-term repurchase agreements, along with other larger liquid assets
M4	This includes everything under M3 plus all other deposits

From the mid-1980s onwards, governments of all political persuasions have utilised both monetary and fiscal policy to influence the economy. Policies of privatisation continued under the Major and Blair Governments, as well as the Coalition Government. The idea of the minimal role for the state has been retained as well.

Under the Blair Government, the idea of "the Third Way" was introduced. This approach was described as "neither Left nor Right". The argument was there was no longer a need for the ideologically-charged arguments over how the economy and the state should be run. If a particular policy worked, regardless of who first thought of it, then it should be implemented. This approach led some commentators to describe the Third Way as warmed up neo-liberalism, or Thatcherism with a smile. In effect, the argument went that the Third Way simply tried to make neo-liberalism 'nicer'. This is discussed in greater detail in chapter 23.

Table 4.9 Economic Growth in the UK, 1980-2009

Time Period	Average economic growth
1980-89	2.2%
1990-99	2.2%
2000-09	2.0%

In many respects, the neo-liberal response to the apparent failure of Keynesianism became the new consensus. This came under threat during the financial crisis of 2008, where the markets – and in particular the finance and mortgage sector – failed. Across the world, banks had to be bailed out. This has raised questions over whether or not the neo-liberal approach has reduced the power of the government to influence the economy too far. Such debates could be seen in the French Presidential and Assembly elections in 2012, as well as both assembly elections in Greece in 2012. The austerity approach to resolving the financial crisis, as espoused by the neo-liberal mainstream, has been brought into question.

In 2008 and 2009, the British economy contracted (by about 4.5% in 2009). By the end of 2013, the UK economy had still not reached the position it had been in prior to the crash. In some quarters, it is suggested the austerity measures introduced by the Coalition Government have failed to stimulate economic growth, and alternative strategies need to be developed.

"We don't make anything anymore!" – the decline of manufacturing
One of the major concerns expressed about the state of the British economy has been the decline in the importance of manufacturing. There has been a belief that for an economy to be successfully, it must 'make' things. Yet, what has been seen in Britain during the post-war era has been the gradual decline of the manufacturing base of the economy.

In 1958, manufacturing comprised over one third of the total UK economy. This had dropped to around 28% by 1979, and to 22% by 1989. It had dropped even further – to below a fifth of the economy – by the turn of the century, and to an eighth (12.5%) by 2007. Yet, as Davies (2011) has noted, while the numbers employed in manufacturing have decreased, and the percentage contribution to GDP has also decreased, there is still some good news. In 1987, manufacturing contributed almost £90 billion to the UK economy. By 1997, this had increased to almost £105 billion to the UK economy. Ten years later, that had increased to £109 billion. This demonstrates there is still a vibrant, if rather small, manufacturing base to the British economy.

No longer do British industries mass produce goods – the textiles, clothing, vehicles, etc that were produced in the 1950s and 1960s. Many of these industries have relocated overseas, where costs are lower. Even some of the more successful modern British manufacturers, such as Dyson vacuum cleaners, have relocated overseas (in Dyson's case, to Malaysia). Some, however, have stayed in the UK. Companies such as McLaren, or BAE Systems, have remained in the UK. Their manufacturing is at the high end of the economic scale. Mass production of clothing, for example, has a very low return on investment. A super car, retailing for hundreds of thousands of pounds, on the other hand, has a very high return. It is this top end of the market to which the remaining British manufacturers are aiming. What this means is massive investment in research and design.

One of the problems with the British economy – and more broadly with the Anglo-American model – is research and design does not always feature very highly. Concern is far more about shareholder returns in the short term. It is this short-termism that has had a massive negative impact on the British economy. The more successful businesses are those which develop a longer term strategy, rather than focussing simply upon the returns for the next financial quarter.

A service economy?

As manufacturing has declined within the structure of the UK economy, it is the service industries that have grown. This is not simply about retail. The service sector covers a much broader range of areas. Wholesale and retail, as of 2007, comprised a slightly smaller share of the UK economy (11.4%) than manufacturing (12.5%). Services include window cleaning, as well as retail and wholesale, not to forget finance as well (Davis, 2011). According to the OECD (2011), the UK has run a trade surplus in services every year since 1966, peaking with a surplus of $US101.4 billion in 2008. Only the United States surpasses the UK in such a surplus, but in per capita terms, the UK is the world leader by far, as can be seen in Table 4.10 – although the list is by no means exhaustive.

Table 4.10 UK service exports (2008)

Service	Value (US$ billion)	World Ranking in per capita terms
Communications	9	1st
Insurance	15	1st
Financial services	69	1st
Computer and information services	13	1st
Other business services	82	1st
Total services	286	1st
Total, excluding finance	217	1st

Developed from Davis (2011)

Concern has often been expressed that jobs in the service sector are insecure, part-time, minimum-waged, etc. Examining the services listed in Table 4.10 should demonstrate otherwise. In sectors such as retail, telemarketing, catering, hotels, many jobs do fit such a description. It is these jobs that can be lost most easily in an economic downturn. Other parts of the service sector, especially those in the public sector (e.g. education, health, police), tended to see greater job security but not necessarily better pay than their private sector counterparts.

In the economic climate in 2013, even these jobs were under threat. It is clear the British economy is very reliant on the service sector, and some may argue too reliant.

Conclusion

The British economy has evolved significantly during the post-war period. There have been significant ideological shifts with regard to how the economy should be run. The Keynesian approach of demand-led economics, with the state playing an active role in the economy and in society, dominated the British political landscape from the 1940s to the 1970s. With its apparent failure, the neo-liberal approach of supply-side economics, with a minimal role for the state came to the fore. A consensus seemed to develop on this approach until the banking crisis of 2008. For now, at least, the neo-liberal approach dominates the British economy. The question is for how much longer?

Added to this, the make-up of the British economy has evolved, with far less dependence upon manufacturing and a far greater role for services. Mass production of goods has been sent overseas, where costs are far lower. Instead, the high end of manufacturing has remained in the UK, building on the knowledge economy – the developments in technology that spearhead change. At the same time, the service economy has grown in both size and breadth, and has become an integral part of the global economy. Britain is the world leader in the export of services.

Yet all of this is rather fragile. An economic downturn could see less investment in research and design, with fewer people being able to afford to go to university. Fewer graduates, in turn, means greater dependence upon overseas graduates, or businesses relocating overseas to tap those specific graduate markets. Consequently, the knowledge economy shrinks, the service sector shrinks, and the British economy suffers more. An economic upturn would see the opposite happen. The question is then about what, if anything, should the government do to stimulate that more positive outcome?

Selected Bibliography

Davis, Evan. (2011). *Made in Britain:* Little, Brown.

Grant, Wyn. (2002). *Economic Policy in Britain:* Palgrave.

Hay, Colin. (2010). "Chronicles of a Death Foretold: the Winter of Discontent and Construction of the Crisis of British Keynesianism", *Parliamentary Affairs* vol. 63-3, pp. 446-470.

Johnson, Christopher. (1991). *The Economy under Mrs Thatcher 1979-1990:* Penguin.

McCormick, John. (2012). *Contemporary Britain:* Palgrave, 3rd edition.

Minford, Patrick. (1988). "Mrs Thatcher's Economic Reform Programme" in Sidelsky, Robert (ed.). *Thatcherism:* Chatto & Windus, pp. 93-106.

Pollard, Sidney. (1984). *The Wasting of the British Economy*: Croom Helm, 2nd edition.

Websites

www.bankofengland.co.uk/publications/Documents/quarterlybulletin/threecenturiesofdata.xls
This Bank of England publication provides three centuries of data about the state of the British economy.

www.bbc.co.uk/news/special_reports/uk_economy/
This BBC web page has links to a number of very useful reports on the state of the British economy

www.economist.com
The Economist *runs a number of features and articles on Britain and the state of the British economy*

Questions
1. To what extent, if at all, does it matter if the British economy does not 'make' things anymore?
2. "The idea of the state playing a significant role in running the economy was little more than a failed experiment. The neo-liberal approach is the economic norm." Discuss.
3. Running the economy successfully requires balancing the fiscal and monetary pressures. Such a balancing act is nigh on imposible to achieve. Comment.

CHAPTER 5 // BRITAIN'S POSITION IN THE WORLD

Contents
- **Introduction**
- **The Three Concentric Circles**
- **Empire and Commonwealth**
- **The United States**
- **Europe**
- **Britain and the rest of the World**
- **Conclusion**

Introduction

At the beginning of the twentieth century, Britain was still seen as the dominant power in the world. The British Empire, which reached its peak in size in 1923, was the largest of all the colonial powers. Compared to other colonial powers, Britain was very good at managing its empire. Yet, if need be, gunboat diplomacy was a viable option. If the natives in any of the colonies got restless, military intervention was the response.

In the aftermath of the Second World War, Britain was still one of the 'Great Powers' of the world. Britain was represented at the conferences at Yalta and Potsdam, where the post-war political (and ideological) lines were drawn up. Churchill sat alongside Stalin and Roosevelt as an equal at Yalta. At the Potsdam summit, Attlee may not have been seen as an equal to either Stalin or Truman, but nobody questioned Britain's right to be at the top table. That Britain should be a Permanent Member of the newly created United Nation's Security Council was taken as read.

During the latter half of the 20th century, and into the 21st century, things have changed significantly. Having fought two world wars, Britain was economically exhausted. Since the end of the Second World War, there has been a gradual decline in Britain's position in global affairs. As Hearl (1995, p. 17) notes, "[f]rom having been a world power with global interests and responsibilities, Britain has steadily and unquestionably become less and less significant an actor on the world stage".

A major turning point in Britain's global decline was the Suez crisis of 1956. The Egyptian Government, under the leadership of Nasser, had nationalised the Suez Canal – ostensibly to fund the building of a new dam on the River Nile at Aswan. The British response, in collusion with the French and the Israelis, was to invade; the canal was deemed to be the property of an Anglo-

French company. The backlash from the rest of the world, but most notably the Americans, was such that the British withdrew – leaving the French to clean up the mess. It was this event that signalled the end of any aspirations of British global influence via gunboat diplomacy.

Despite this decline, Britain is still a significant actor on the world stage – just less so than before. Many countries – most notably within the Commonwealth – look to Britain for leadership. Britain remains a Permanent Member of the UN Security Council. This collection of small islands off the northwest coast of Europe punches well above its weight. It is merely in relation to the historic position that Britain is seen as being a declining influence in world affairs.

The Three Concentric Circles

It was Winston Churchill who spoke of seeing the Western world as three concentric circles. This was at the onset of the Cold War, with the fear of a Soviet invasion of Western Europe, if not of the entire world. Churchill's three circles comprised of the English-speaking world (but, specifically, the United States), the British Empire/Commonwealth and Europe. As can be seen in Figure 5.1, where these three circles intersected was Britain. Britain had a 'special relationship' with the United States; Britain was head of the Empire; and, of those participating in the Second World War, Britain was the only West European state to be undefeated. Thus, Britain was the lynchpin of the free world in the fight against communism.

These concentric circles are a useful starting point from which to examine Britain's position in the world today. Obviously, with the end of the Cold War, the influence is no longer about leading the fight against communism. Consequently, it is not just these three concentric circles that need to be examined. Britain has a relationship with the rest of the world, or, more accurately, a series of relationships with different parts of the world.

Empire and Commonwealth

At its height, the British Empire covered around a third of the globe. Many explorers and pioneers in the 19th century dreamt of world maps being painted pink. There was an aura of invincibility within the British Empire, with Britain at the helm. Such a perception started to disintegrate during the Second World War, with the fall of Singapore to the Japanese. Australian troops returned home with a threat of a Japanese invasion. Britain no longer had that aura.

Figure 5.1 Churchill's three concentric circles

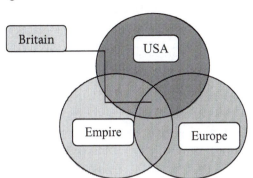

After the war, in countries such as Singapore, the British returned. There was a perception among the British that life would carry on as it had done prior to the war. Local populations held strongly divergent views. Demands for independence grew. The so-called "jewel" in the crown of the Empire, India, gained independence in 1947 (as did Pakistan, as a result of the partition of India). Many other countries in the Empire followed suit.

In 1960, Harold Macmillan made a speech in Cape Town, where he spoke of the "winds of change" blowing through Africa. This heralded a significant change in Britain's colonial policies in that continent, with many colonies gaining independence – the first had been Ghana (formerly known as the Gold Coast) in 1957.

Today, there is the Commonwealth – a collection of 55 states, of which Britain is but one. The Queen, is Head of State not just in Britain, but also in 16 other Commonwealth countries. Some of them, such as Australia and Jamaica, would like to see that arrangement changed. In a number of Commonwealth countries, there is a growing feeling the British monarchy has very little to do with the day-to-day life of their citizens, and that they should choose their own Head of State.

It is interesting to note when the law on primogeniture was changed to enable the eldest child of a future monarch (William), rather than the eldest son, to succeed to the throne, it was not just Britain that had to legislate. The other 16 Commonwealth countries that had the Queen as Head of State had to pass similar legislation. There was no way whatsoever the British could impose their will on those countries.

A final point to note about the Commonwealth is some countries, which have no historical ties with Britain, want to join the organisation. The newest member, Rwanda, is a former German and former Belgian colony, with French as the national language, although English became the language of education in 2008. Rwanda had no historical links to Britain, but still wanted to join the Commonwealth.

The United States

There is a perception in Britain that a 'special relationship' exists between the UK and the United States. Although, as Dumbrell (2009, p. 65) notes, "if indeed it does exist, is spoken of largely in British accents. Its most common invocations – shared values, shared history, shared language – arguably reflect sentiment and wishful thinking as much as the real world of material interests".

The origins of the 'special relationship' date back to the aftermath of the Second World War, where Britain and the USA were seen to be defending the so-called 'free world' from the Soviet Union. It was the USA, with Britain as a junior partner, that established the International Monetary Fund (IMF), the World Bank, and the General Agreement on Tariffs and Trade (GATT). In defending the West from Soviet invasion, it was the USA that established the North Atlantic Treaty Organisation (NATO), with Britain again as a junior partner. The formation of NATO was, arguably, a way of preventing the USA from returning to a policy of isolationism (as had happened after the First World War).

It becomes obvious very quickly this so-called 'special relationship' is, at best, asymmetrical. The US is the dominant partner. Political cartoonists best exemplified this relationship during the war in Iraq, where Tony Blair was portrayed as George W. Bush's poodle.

This so-called 'special relationship' has not always been a cosy affair. There have been times where Anglo-American relations have been strained. Examples include the refusal of the Wilson Government to send troops to Vietnam in the mid-1960s, or the US invasion of the Commonwealth country of Grenada in 1983. Even the build-up to the invasion of Iraq in 2003 saw US-UK relations become rather fragile. On top of this, allegations of the NSA tapping the telephones of European leaders – although they were adamant not that of Prime Minister David Cameron – has also strained the relationship.

As noted above in the quote from Dumbrell (2009), the 'special relationship' tends to be seen as such by the British. The US, on the other hand, has a series of 'special relationships' with other prominent countries around the world e.g. Japan and Germany. For example, in 1989 President Bush when visiting Europe "talked of a 'partnership' between America and Germany" (Coker, 1991, p. 411). Unsurprisingly, this went down very badly in Britain.

It must be noted, however, Presidents Clinton, George W. Bush and Obama each spoke of the special relationship the US had with Britain. There was some resonance here with President Reagan doing the same in the latter days of his presidency with Margaret Thatcher. In each of these cases, there has been a suggestion the importance of the relationship was used to bolster the position of the British Prime Minister rather than because there actually was a 'special relationship'. George W. Bush, in particular, developed a very close relationship with Tony Blair. Arguably, this was detrimental to the standing of Tony Blair within the UK.

Question marks have been raised as to whether or not the 'special relationship' still exists. Wallace (2005, p. 64), for example, stated, "the 'special relationship' is dead". He points out many other states "have special relations with Washington: Israel, Australia, Mexico, Italy, Poland, even Saudi Arabia. We are not as special as successive prime ministers... have wanted to believe" (p. 65). This is a major concern. Whenever a British Prime Minister goes to the United States, or a US President visits the UK, the concept of the 'special relationship' is invoked by the participants, and is played up in the British media. It is presented in the UK as if there is only one such relationship, and this is clearly not true. It is a resonance from history, and one to which Britain appears desperate to cling.

Europe

The European circle was always considered to be the least important of the three concentric circles. Since Britain joined the then-EEC in 1973, the reality is this circle has become the most important of the three. Some of this may be linked to the declining importance of the other two circles. Britain's relationship with the European Union is examined in Chapter 31, but there are some issues that need to be examined in the context of Britain's position in the world.

In December 1962, Dean Acheson, a former-US Secretary of State under President Truman, made a speech at West Point. In it, he said that Britain had lost an empire but not found a role. Today, whether Britons like it or not, that new role is Europe. Shlaim (1975, p. 856) noted:

> The challenge consists of maximising the political benefits of the European option by pooling resources and equipping the EEC with the instruments which would make its economic weight felt in world affairs. There is no other way in which Britain's long, painful and protracted quest for a world role can be brought to a satisfactory conclusion.

None of the European powers had the wherewithal to compete with the US or the Soviet Union on their own. There was a need for those countries to work together. Today, the situation is no different, except some of the rivals are different.

Britain's role within Europe has changed. The importance of having won the war has diminished in the new world order. Britain is not leading Europe, but is – or, rather, has the potential to be – one of the leaders of Europe. The problem is successive British leaders appear not to have wanted the role. This is exacerbated by the attitudes of a largely euro-phobic domestic media. Consequently, even when British Prime Ministers such as John Major and Tony Blair have announced their desire to place Britain at the heart of Europe, domestic pressures have compelled them to back away from such desires. At times, Dean Acheson's description of Britain resonates still.

Britain and the rest of the world

In the immediate aftermath of the Second World War, Britain was perceived as one of the Great Powers. As has been noted throughout this chapter, there has been a decline in Britain's position. This decline appears pronounced, but must be taken in conjunction with the position of Britain as the pre-eminent world power in the late 19th century.

In 1968, Britain announced the withdrawal of its military presence from "East of Suez". While this directly affected the "Empire" of the three concentric circles, the reality was it demonstrated the extent to which Britain was withdrawing from a global role. The big military bases in Aden and Singapore were closed. A British military presence was withdrawn from many countries, including Sharjah, Bahrain, Malaysia and Brunei. Britain withdrew from the Indian Ocean, South East Asia and the Far East, and from much of the Middle East. "Withdrawal was more of a realisation of the fact that Britain had no genuine 'role' to play east of Suez in the 1960s and beyond" (McCourt, 2009, p. 469).

As Britain, and arguably the rest of Europe, has declined, other countries have risen. Economically, the BRIC countries (Brazil, Russia, India and China) are growing rapidly, and are likely to pass Britain (if they have not already done so) in the next few years in terms of the size of their economy. Yet this is only one aspect of having influence in global affairs. Political and military power is also very important. Britain carries these as, for example, a nuclear-armed power. In fact, Britain is "one of only five recognised to do so under the Nuclear Non-Proliferation Treaty" (Morris, 2011, p. 332). Thus, the decline in global power may not be quite as pronounced, as many believe.

Added to this, Britain plays a significant humanitarian role in global politics. For example, Britain is one of the world's largest contributors to international aid, being surpassed only by the United States (Morris 2011).

Britain retains a significant influence upon the world – and in ways that do not always appear obvious. The use of English as the language of business may be a result of American influences, but very few people would claim to speak "American". The Westminster model of government has been retained by many former colonies, and derivatives have been replicated around the world. British sports teams – one of the most notable being Manchester United – are instantly recognizable. Television programmes such as 'Coronation Street' and 'East Enders' have global audiences, as does the FA Cup final. The BBC is considered to be one of the most trusted news agencies in the world. All of this links back to Britain; a form of soft power in global affairs.

Conclusion

Britain's position in the world has changed markedly over the past hundred years. Even in the post-war era, Britain's role has changed significantly. To some who glory in the memories of Empire, Britain joining the EEC was the nadir of

Britain's global role. Yet, the reality is the world has changed. No longer do British Governments send in gunboats to protect the Empire (although the Falklands War in 1982 suggested otherwise). If nothing else, the cost of maintaining such a prominent global role is far beyond Britain's capabilities. Instead, Britain's role is one as a partner, sharing responsibilities.

The fortieth anniversary of Britain joining the EEC was held on 1 January 2013. This should have been a cause for celebration. It is the one remaining circle of Churchill's three concentric circles that retains a prominent role in British politics. That role still does not get the acknowledgement it deserves. Dean Acheson said Britain had lost an Empire but not found a role. The reality is the role is waiting but no politicians appear willing to take it up.

Selected Bibliography

Barder, Brian. (2001). "Britain: Still Looking for that Role?", *Political Quarterly* vol. 72-3, pp. 366-374.

Dumbrell, John. (2009). "The US-UK Special Relationship: Taking the 21st-Century Temperature", *British Journal of Politics and International Relations* vol. 11-1, pp. 64-78.

Gamble, Andrew. (2003). *Between Europe and America: The Future of British Politics*: Palgrave.

Morris, Justin. (2011). "How Great is Britain? Power, Responsibility and Britain's Future Global Role", *British Journal of Politics and International Relations* vol. 13-3, pp. 326-347.

Niblett, Robin. (2007). "Choosing between America and Europe: a new context for British foreign policy", *International Affairs* vol. 83-4, pp. 627-641.

Shlaim, Avi. (1975). "Britain's Quest for a World Role", *International Relations* vol. 5-1, pp. 838-856.

Questions
1. What is Britain's role in the world in the 21st century?
2. *"Between Europe and America: should Britain have to choose?"* Discuss.
3. "Britain is still a global player. Few other countries wish to take on such a responsibility." Comment.

CHAPTER 6 // THE CHANGING CONSTITUTION OF BRITAIN

Contents
- **Introduction**
- **The Traditional Westminster/Whitehall model of the Constitution**
- **Changes to the Constitution**
- **Conclusion**

This particular chapter should be studied in conjunction with the chapter on the Bill of Rights. Students often confuse these two concepts, hence their separation. Therefore the broad idea of a constitution will be introduced, with an evaluation of certain aspects of constitutions, before moving on to issues around human rights in the subsequent chapter.

In the UK we do not have a written constitution – rather it is partially written and uncodified. There is a demand to change this situation (see Bogdanor *et al* (2007)). Yet the demand for a written constitution cannot be understood fully without appreciating how the constitution and the political system upon which it is based have been undergoing both subtle and radical modifications.

From the student's point of view the constitution is a subject that will well reward attention, not simply for examination purposes, but as a key towards an understanding of the nature of British politics. In many respects, awareness of the importance of the constitution provides an ideal backdrop for the entire book.

Introduction
A constitution allocates formal power within a state. It outlines what powers may be wielded by which institutions. In simple terms, a constitution is a set of rules: the rules of the political game. This tells us what a constitution 'is', but not really what a constitution 'does'. It allocates power to various institutions, as well as setting parameters by which those wielding the power may be held to account for their actions. Thus, a constitution could prescribe specific powers to state institutions, as well as placing limits on how such powers may be wielded.

The Magna Carta may be seen as the starting point for the British constitution as we understand it today. As a result of the Magna Carta, the monarch could no longer raise taxes without the formal approval of the rest of parliament. Some powers were, in effect, transferred from the monarch to some members of the aristocracy. Yet, as well as this, the basis of Britain's constitutional government owes a great deal to the events of the Glorious Revolution of 1688 and the Bill of Rights that followed in 1689. More power passed from the monarch to Parliament – as the protector of the rights of citizens. In retrospect, this also created the conditions for transferring power from Parliament to the Executive. It is this development, more than anything else, which has created the concern and movement towards limiting the power of government by subjecting it to the law of a written constitution.

The argument is that despite the virtue of flexibility the constitution is, in the phrase of Lord Hailsham, "wearing out" and is nothing short of a shambles. Hence the movement advanced to short-circuit the process of deterioration in one fell swoop by incorporating the European Convention of Human Rights (ECHR) as the basis of a written constitution which will at least curb the overwhelming power of the Executive. This has been realised to some extent via the implementation of the Human Rights Act (1998). It has caused a number of changes to the way in which politics operates in the UK.

What has become more noticeable with the piecemeal changes to the British constitution introduced by the Blair Government is the extent to which British political institutions and procedures appear to be divorced from constitutional theory. It could be argued there is almost a crisis at the heart of the political system. With devolution for Scotland, Wales and Northern Ireland, and the prospect of greater integration with the European Union (EU), the situation can only get worse. Yet many politicians and commentators refuse to recognise much of the traditional language of constitutional comment has lost its relevance and vitality.

The Traditional Westminster/Whitehall model of the Constitution

The view of the British constitution that dominated analysis of the political system throughout the twentieth century had been based on the classical, liberal interpretations of Walter Bagehot and A.V. Dicey in particular. In the early years of the 21st century, little appears to have changed. These interpretations are covered under the following broad headings:

1. *Uncodified (rather than "unwritten")*
2. *Unitary Nature*
3. *Parliamentary Sovereignty*
4. *Partial Separation of Powers*
5. *The Rule of Law*
6. *Conventions*

1. Uncodified (rather than "unwritten")

A common error, expressed even by some politicians and academics, is to describe the British constitution as "unwritten". At best, it could be described as "partially written". All forms of statute law, judicial interpretations, royal prerogatives and even authoritative works like those of Blackstone and Dicey are included as part of the constitution (see Bogdanor *et al*, 2007). Thus a huge section of the constitution is in fact "written". The British constitution is actually *uncodified*.

Compare this to the US constitution: a single document which comprises all the legal rights and liberties of the citizen which is revered by all. Instead, in the case of the UK, by tradition and precedent there is a reliance on a mixture of statute law (Acts of Parliament), common law, conventions and authoritative works, with an Act of Parliament overriding all other forms of law (see Table 6.1).

Table 6.1 The British Constitution: Sources and Constituents

COMPONENT OF THE CONSTITUTION	EXPLANATION	EXAMPLES
Statute Law	Acts of Parliament which override other constitutional sources	Act of Union 1707 Parliament Act 1949 European Communities Act 1972
Common Law	Judicial decisions which establish legal precedents	Freedom of speech, association, movement, etc. Royal Prerogative
Conventions	Rules, customs and practices which are considered binding (normally applicable to Parliament)	Collective responsibility of the Cabinet Prime Minister is a member of the Commons Government should resign if it loses a vote of no confidence
European Union Law	This takes precedence over national law (where the two conflict)	Treaty on European Union (1992)
Law and Custom of Parliament	Guidelines as to how Parliament may operate	Impartiality of the Speaker
Works of Authority	Books and writings which are considered as expert guidance on the constitution	A. V. Dicey (1885); *An Introduction to the Study of the Law of the Constitution* Erskine May (1844); *Treatise on the Law, Privileges, Proceedings, and Usage of Parliament*

To complicate matters further, there is also no definitive authority on the British constitution. Commentators such as Bagehot and Dicey have had their interpretations of the constitution included into the constitution (the works of authority). This, in a way, highlights the flexibility of the British constitution: that it can be re-interpreted as times change. A further example of this evolving constitution is through membership of the European Union: EU law takes precedence over national law should the two conflict.

2. Unitary Nature

The term "unitary" refers not just to the concept of a *United Kingdom* (England, Scotland, Wales and Northern Ireland) but also to the principle that there is only one source of legality: Parliament. There has been a rejection of federalism - of having more than one source of legality. Although there is a devolved Parliament in Scotland, and devolved Assemblies in Wales, Northern Ireland and London, constitutional theory stipulates that all political and legal power emanates from Parliament. When other bodies such as local government, or even the devolved institutions, exercise forms of power and rule it is only with the permission of Parliament. On top of this, Parliament may at any time revoke that permission. That is why in any contest between local authorities like Liverpool or Lambeth and the central government, the latter is almost certain to be the winner in both the financial and legal senses. Central government can restructure, or even abolish local government, and did so in the 1980s and 1990s. The same can apply to devolved government: the Northern Ireland Assembly has been suspended on four occasions as of 2013; and central government also abolished the unelected English Regional Assemblies in 2010 (see Chapter 30).

While the unitary nature of the constitution has been much applauded as giving cohesion to disparate forces and institutions, it is now seen by many commentators as reinforcing too heavily the over-centralisation of the country. Devolution may have gone some way to dissipating this concern in Scotland, Wales and Northern Ireland. However, a consequence of this has been to increase the sense of remoteness from government being experienced in the outer regions of England.

3. Parliamentary Sovereignty

As previously stated, one of the cardinal components of the constitution is the supremacy of Parliament over all other forms of institutional power. More realistically, this could be described as parliamentary government under a constitutional monarchy. Since Parliament derived its legitimacy and strength from the consent of the governed and was accountable to the voters, it was considered that adequate checks and balances existed to prevent the emergence of a dangerous and autocratic executive. Thus a written constitution would be pointless, and ideas such as judicial review of legislation were deemed to be unnecessary – especially as it could mean unelected judges could strike down legislation agreed by the elected representatives of the people.

It should be remembered, however, the constitution always favoured a strong executive, so that the notion of a "golden age" of the legislature controlling governments in the 19th century, if not a myth, was always rather fanciful. As the debate on the desirability of a Bill of Rights showed, there is serious concern the strength of the executive has become so great as to be positively dangerous by distorting the original notion of parliamentary sovereignty.

4. Partial Separation of Powers

This is a theoretical position which has practical implications but has tended to be neglected in any consideration of the constitution. When examined in conjunction with the distortion to the notion of parliamentary sovereignty, a huge concern is further highlighted. The English philosopher, Locke, but even more so the French philosopher, Montesquieu, maintained that to attain pure democracy in a nation state the three branches of government (the Legislative, the Executive and the Judiciary) should be separated completely and a system of checks and balances devised, as a prescription to prevent a tyranny developing. The United States adopted Montesquieu's ideas almost wholesale so that in their system the presidency, Congress and Supreme Court are fully separated and an elaborate web of checks and balances erected to prevent the emergence of any one arm of the government becoming too strong.

In Britain, however, such a total separation was never really contemplated. The entire British system has gradually evolved. The Executive and the Legislative are both contained within Parliament and the Lord Chancellor, who is a member of the Executive, is involved in the appointment of judges. When Jack Straw was the Secretary of State for Justice, he was also effectively the Lord Chancellor (the chief of the judiciary), as well as being in the Cabinet (Executive) and the MP for Blackburn (member of the legislature). Thus he represented all three branches of government. He was also appointed to his cabinet post by the prime minister, highlighting yet again the dominance of the executive (if not specifically the prime minister). The establishment of the UK Supreme Court (see chapter 15) has diluted this concentration of power. Unlike the Supreme Court of the United States, the British judiciary has no constitutional right to reject or override the legislation of Parliament as long as the due legal processes have been observed.

The Prime Minister and most of the Cabinet are also ordinary MPs so the distinction between the government and the legislative is much more blurred in Britain than in the US. The experience of some US presidents such as Bill Clinton and George W. Bush in having legislation and appointees rejected is unthinkable in the British context. It is purely a matter of opinion as to which system yields a purer form of "democracy".

5. *The Rule of law*
This concept, usually attributed to A.V. Dicey, refers to procedural substantive rights, e.g. an independent judiciary, but there has never been agreement as to the meaning of the phrase "the rule of law". According to Dicey, there were certain accepted unwritten principles that transcended any law passed by a particular parliament, e.g. the prolongation of a parliament's life beyond the statutory five years even if such an amendment was legitimised by an Act of Parliament. The trouble with Dicey's concept couched in almost mystical terms is it has no legal validity and most commentators tend to give little credence to it. Other versions of the "rule of law" – such as an independent judiciary, the application of the law to all citizens irrespective of their station in life and the need to obey the law in a democratic country – are generally accepted.

6. *Conventions*
These can be regarded as maxims and practices that regulate the conduct of the Crown, of ministers, of politicians and civil servants. They are strictly non-legal rules but have acquired through tradition and practice almost the force of law – to the extent that flouting them is regarded as a highly serious matter. The use of conventions fits in well with the notion of flexibility that so permeates the British Constitution. Hence, many of the most noted of political institutions and practices are based on convention and usage; their universal acceptance obviates any need to convert them into rigid legal rules. An example would be the notion of 'the rule of law'.

Yet there appears to be a contradiction here. While the use of conventions suggests flexibility, their status in almost having the force of law is such that they are rather inflexible. Amongst the most famous of the conventions are: cabinet government; collective (cabinet) responsibility; that the Prime Minister should come from the House of Commons (Lord Salisbury was the last PM to come from the Lords in 1899, although Alec Douglas Home resigned his peerage and fought a by-election to enter the Commons to become PM in 1963); and the relationship between civil servants and ministers. The system based on conventions generally works very well since their force is recognised and any serious breach of them would almost certainly result in having to enact a law to enforce them.

The above traditional model continues to be included in many textbooks on British politics and whilst there is still validity in much of the description, it is becoming increasingly clear that events and developments are fast altering the picture. The whole model is based on assumptions of parliamentary sovereignty in the 19th century. There is no consideration of a mass electorate or the monolithic political parties that exist today. Added to this, little attention is paid to pressure groups, public opinion or the influence of a mass media. Yet even in the 1960s little attention was paid to constitutional innovation on the grounds that for all its limitations the British constitutional/political system by and large answered the nation's needs.

Changes to the Constitution

When the Labour Party was returned to power in 1997, constitutional reform was high on the agenda. The Liberal Democrats supported what was termed the "big bang" approach – a single act to radically overhaul the constitution. However, Labour adopted a piecemeal approach, identifying particular sections of the constitution in need of reform and updating or modernising them. This process, though far slower than desired by many, has had a profound effect upon the constitution. What is interesting to note is the constitutional reforms are an on-going process. As Prime Minister, Tony Blair felt all of the constitutional changes were carried out during the first term of office. The reality was there were a series of knock-on effects that continue far beyond his time as prime minister.

A master stroke of constitutional reform came at the end of the second term of the Blair Government, with the Constitutional Reform Act (2005) – although the government had been criticised in 2003, when the changes were first announced, for a lack of consultation about the proposals. This was an attempt to develop a separation of powers in the UK – to remove the judiciary from the legislature and the executive. Thus judicial independence was enshrined in law for the first time in over 900 years.

In effect, the Constitutional Reform Act (2005) removed the judicial role from the post of the Lord Chancellor. There was, in fact, an attempt to abolish the post altogether, but this was reversed. The judicial powers of the Lord Chancellor were transferred to the Lord Chief Justice, under a new title: President of the Courts of England and Wales. This new post is responsible for the training, guiding and deployment of judges in England and Wales. The Lord Chancellor also lost the post of Speaker in the House of Lords (see chapter 15). That chamber now appoints its own Speaker – in 2013, this post was held by Baroness D'Souza.

On top of this, the appellate role of the House of Lords was abolished by the Constitutional Reform Act. No longer is the House of Lords the highest court of appeal in the land. This power has been transferred to the new Supreme Court, which started sitting in 2010. The Supreme Court has its own budget, staffing, building, etc. The title "Supreme Court" is actually misleading as it will not have the powers of other supreme courts such as in the USA, or countries in the Commonwealth such as Australia. The UK Supreme Court, for example, will not be able to strike down unconstitutional laws.

The removal of the Law Lords from the House of Lords raised some eyebrows. While this attempt at separation of powers garnered support, the Law Lords had played a valuable role in the House of Lords. Of greatest note was their participation in select committees – especially on the European Union. The removal of the Law Lords deprives the House of their expertise.

The final part to note about this separation of judicial powers from the legislature and executive was to do with the appointment of judges. The Constitutional Reform Act established a Judicial Appointments Commission, removing this power of appointment from the Secretary of State for Justice. The sole criterion for judicial appointments is by merit.

The Constitutional Reform Act (2005) also established a new government department: the Department for Constitutional Affairs. The functions of the Lord Chancellor (excluding those cited above) were transferred to this department.

Below is a brief examination of some of the other key areas of constitutional reform. A number of them are examined in greater detail in subsequent chapters. This section should whet the appetite for more, while focusing upon some of the constitutional issues. One omission is human rights, although it and the related constitutional issues are covered in chapter seven. The areas to be examined are:

1. *Devolution*
2. *House of Lords*
3. *Electoral Reform*
4. *Freedom of Information*
5. *European Union*
6. *Guardians of the constitution.*

1. Devolution
At first sight this does not appear to be too radical a reform. While Maer *et al* (2004, p. 254) have suggested the UK is no longer a unitary state, and that devolution cannot be rolled back, constitutionally this is not the case. Parliament remains supreme, any devolved powers can be returned to the centre. There are also lists of issues beyond the remit of the devolved bodies – known as the reserved powers.

Yet devolution may also be perceived as a weakening of central government or even as a weak form of central government. Maer *et al* (2004) are right to suggest the UK is no longer a highly centralised state. The powers devolved to the Scottish Parliament and to the Welsh Assembly are unlikely to be returned. Northern Ireland contains such a complex number of issues that such a categoric statement cannot be made. The Northern Ireland Legislative Assembly has already had its powers both removed and returned on four occasions. Yet, the longer that the legislative assembly operates in Northern Ireland, the less likely it appears that powers will be returned to London.

There were also plans to introduce directly elected regional assemblies into the regions of England. One region, the North East, held a referendum on this issue and it was resoundingly defeated.

There is, however, the idea that devolution is fundamentally changing the constitutional landscape of the UK. Hazell (2006), for example, has suggested that devolution in the UK has led to the formation of a quasi-federal system. It could be a stepping stone to overhauling the House of Lords into a directly-elected chamber on a regional basis – possibly similar to that in the USA (Senate) or Germany (Bundesrat).

Tam Dalyell argued that devolution would lead to the break-up of the United Kingdom. It would be the "thin end of the wedge" leading to an independent Scotland. Many Scottish Nationalist Party (SNP) supporters hope he is right and with a referendum on independence in September 2014, there is an opportunity for Dalyell's fears to be realised. Support for devolution, however, does not necessarily mean support for independence. In fact many devolutionists would not describe themselves as nationalists. They wish for some powers to be devolved from the centre but the centre must also carry out many functions as well.

A significant aspect within the devolution debate applies specifically to Scotland – the right to raise or lower taxation rates by up to 3 pence in the pound. This power, over and above that of the Treasury is significant. It presents the appearance of real power for the Scottish Parliament – although as of 2013, it has not been used.

The talk of devolution as being something radical and new must also be tempered. Devolution existed in many forms even in the 19th century. The Scottish Office was set up in 1885, with the Welsh Office in 1964 and the Northern Ireland office in 1972. On top of this, the Scottish education system is different to that of England and Wales. Scottish and Irish banks issue their own bank notes, including £1 notes in Scotland. Welsh is taught as a first language in many schools, and is used on the Welsh television channel, SC4, and Welsh radio. Finally, there are the great many sporting teams in Scotland, Wales and Northern Ireland – each represented with flag, national anthem, and competitors at the Commonwealth Games, in football and rugby tournaments, as well as many other sports. These are closer to symbols of independent states than devolved components of a "greater" body.

2. House of Lords

Reform of this chamber, if not outright abolition, has always been high on the Labour Party's agenda. Yet, whenever in office, Labour has avoided this issue. Although moves were made in the late 1960s to abolish the House of Lords, these were rather half-hearted and were easily defeated. The Blair Government appeared to be the exception. Rather than outright abolition or replacement with an elected second chamber, the process has been gradualist. In 1999, the right of hereditary peers to sit and vote in the chamber was removed. Not all hereditary peers were excluded. A select few, 92 in fact, were permitted to stay as working members of the second chamber. This was step one of the process. Step two was to decide on the next part of the process. For this, the Royal Commission on Reform of the House of Lords was set up.

This commission comprised twelve members and was chaired by Lord Wakeham. Its terms of reference were made very clear. The House of Commons was to remain the pre-eminent chamber. Thereafter, the commission could examine the role and function of the second chamber, and the method(s) of composition.

From a constitutional perspective, the Wakeham Report changed very little. This report is examined in much greater detail in chapter 10. In brief, it proposed a second chamber of around 550 members, a small number of whom (between 20% and 35%) would be elected for a single 15-year term. The remainder would be effectively appointed for life. The powers of the second chamber would effectively remain unchanged. A slightly more radical step was to alter the religious representation. The Church of England would still dominate, but other Christian denominations would also be represented, along with non-Christian faiths.

In 2007, the House of Commons voted on the percentage of members of the House of Lords who should be elected. They voted in favour of 100% elected, and 80% elected. The House of Lords, on the other hand, voted for 100% appointed. Consequently, reform of the membership of the House of Lords remains in limbo.

Surprisingly, there were plans to reform the House of Lords from the Coalition Government – or at least from the Liberal Democrats. Party leader, Nick Clegg, wanted at least 80% of the House to become wholly elected. Such plans were blocked by the Conservatives in 2012.

One change that has taken effect is the separation of judicial powers from the House of Lords, as noted earlier in this chapter. The Law Lords have been removed from the House of Lords and are now the UK Supreme Court. The post of Lord Chancellor was also separated from the House of Lords in that the post-holder was no longer Speaker of the House of Lords – and in fact did not even have to be a member of that House. Jack Straw, MP for Blackburn, became the first Lord Chancellor under the new system.

3. Electoral Reform

There were many debates throughout the 20th century on this issue. It was not always widespread, sometimes only in academic circles. The Blair Government pulled it on to the political agenda. Elections to the devolved bodies in Scotland, Wales and Northern Ireland were carried out under different forms of Proportional Representation (PR). A different form of PR was used for the 1999 elections to the European Parliament. From 2007, Scottish local government elections utilised the Single Transferable Vote (STV), as is the case in Northern

Ireland's local elections. This only really leaves central government as yet untouched by any form of PR.

Prior to the 1997 General Election a pact was made between Labour and the Liberal Democrats on electoral reform. Labour pledged a referendum on the issue in return for support on other issues, in particular to do with the Constitution. An Independent Commission on the Voting System was set up to investigate electoral reform, and reported back in 1998. It was chaired by Lord Jenkins, and is covered in chapter 20.

The remit of the Jenkins Commission was to recommend the best alternative system, or combination of systems, to that currently in use for parliamentary elections. Key areas of focus were:

- Proportionality
- Stable government
- Voter choice
- Preserving some form of MP-constituency link

The Jenkins Report advocated a system called AV Plus, or AV "Top Up". It is a hybrid of two electoral systems – the Alternative Vote (AV) as used in Australia, with the "top up" to ensure some degree of proportionality similar to the Mixed Member-Proportional (MMP) systems as used in New Zealand and Germany. The plan was to have a referendum on the electoral system, with voters having a straight choice between Simple Plurality and AV Plus. After reporting back in October 1998, there was very little movement towards the proposed referendum. In fact, the Jenkins Report was quietly pushed to one side.

The Coalition Government instituted a referendum on electoral reform, asking voters to choose between the Alternative Vote and Simple Plurality. This was part of the coalition agreement from 2010. The referendum was held in 2011, and led to a resounding defeat for change.

4. Freedom of Information

The underpinning of the entire system of British central government has been secrecy, or at least this has been the traditional portrayal. There are, for example, Official Secrets Acts. Many of the proceedings of government are carried out behind closed doors. Rhodri Morgan, former leader of the Welsh Assembly, took a radical step in April 2000 by promising the publication of cabinet minutes six weeks after each meeting. By UK standards, this was a giant leap forward in the concept of "open government". Yet it is argued that what is really needed is a Freedom of Information Act.

Labour published a white paper in 1997 on a proposed Freedom of Information Act. It was a wide ranging paper focusing upon a citizen's "right to know". The legislation was delayed, but eventually passed in 2000, and came into effect in January 2005. Included in the legislation were the following themes:

- To provide a right of access to information held by over 100 000 public authorities
- To create exemptions from the duty to disclose information
- To establish arrangements for enforcement and appeal

The idea was to make not just government but the whole public sector more transparent and more accountable to the public.

Yet many critics argue the Freedom of Information Act does not go far enough. Too much discretionary power is left in the hands of the Secretary of State for Justice in deciding which information can and which cannot be released. The former Chairman of the Committee of Standards of Public Life, Lord Neill, complained of formidable obstacles being created to prevent disclosure of secret meetings between government ministers, civil servants and lobbyists, as well as sensitive policy discussions, for example scientific advice on BSE. In sum, the legislation appeared to be written to strengthen the secrecy within British Government.

5. European Union

Membership of the EU (or the European Economic Community [EEC] as it was known when Britain joined in 1973) has probably had the greatest impact upon the constitution. By becoming a member, Britain for the first time in its history accepted the rulings of a supranational body and hence surrendered the rights of Parliament to be the supreme law making institution if any of its laws conflict with those of the EU. It has been suggested the body Britain joined in 1973 bears little resemblance to the current organisation.

The Single European Act of 1986, the Treaty on European Union (also known as the Maastricht Treaty) of 1992, the Amsterdam Treaty of 1997 and the EU Reform Treaty of 2008 have eroded features of the British constitution, in particular with regard to sovereignty. Despite this, Britain remains a sovereign state for the simple reason it has the right to withdraw from the EU. This may not be a practical option from an economic perspective as the UK economy is so closely tied to that of the EU, but it still remains an option – and one which organisations such as the UK Independence Party (UKIP) would like to see realised.

6. Guardians of the constitution

One of the interesting aspects of much of the constitutional change is the extent to which there are different bodies to protect the UK constitution from abuse. The list is quite extensive, as can be seen in Table 6.2. Some of the bodies are well known to the public, others far less so. Unfortunately, many of them could be abolished by the Government at any time.

Table 6.2 Guardians of the British Constitution

Judiciary/UK Supreme Court
Joint Committee on Human Rights
Constitutional Affairs select committee
Ombudsman
Comptroller and Auditor General
Commission on Standards in Public Life
Commission for Public Appointments
Civil Service Commissioner
Electoral Commission
Lords Appointments Commission
Judicial Appointments Commission
Information Commissioner

Source: developed from Hazell (2006)

Many of the bodies listed in Table 6.2 were created by the Blair-led Labour Government. The Ombudsman, on the other hand, was created in the 1960s, while the post of Comptroller and Auditor General dates back to the 1860s.

Conclusion

The British constitution can best be described as continuously evolving. Until the election of the Blair Government in 1997, much of this process was almost unnoticeable. Since then, however, great strides appear to have been taken in reforming the constitution. There has been some devolution for Scotland, Wales and Northern Ireland; the introduction of forms of PR for elections to these devolved bodies, for the European Parliamentary elections, and for Scottish local government elections; tentative and gradual reform of the House of Lords; separation of the judiciary from the executive and legislature; and the opening up of the public sector through the Freedom of Information Act.

Yet it must be questioned as to the extent of this constitutional reform. While there is the appearance of opening up government and dispersing power from the centre, all of these processes are being controlled by the executive. As will be seen in subsequent chapters, central government is the key. The devolving of powers is decided by the executive – which powers are devolved and which are reserved. Electoral reform is now off the political agenda, especially with the defeat of the AV option in the referendum in 2011. Reform of the House of Lords has proceeded in a rather haphazard manner. Finally, the Freedom of Information legislation has delivered far less than expected. Each of these is a consequence of central interference. Yet constitutional issues are not deemed newsworthy. They appear dull, mundane and boring. The economic situation – especially in terms of austerity – is deemed much more important. Consequently, the UK constitution is tweaked as and when those in power deem it necessary. Our evolving, flexible constitution can remain in the shadows.

Selected bibliography

Bagehot, Walter. (1963). *The English Constitution:* Fontana.

Bogdanor, Vernon. (2011). *The Coalition and the Constitution*: Hart Publishing.

Bogdanor, Vernon; Khaitan, Tarunabh & Vogenauer, Stefan. (2007). "Should Britain Have a Written Constitution?", *Political Quarterly* vol. 78-4, pp. 499-517.

Hazell, Robert. (2006). "The Continuing Dynamism of Constitutional Reform", *Parliamentary Affairs* vol. 60-1, pp. 3-25.

Jowell, Jeffrey & Oliver, Dawn (eds.). (2000). *The Changing Constitution:* Oxford University Press, 4th edition.

Maer, Lucinda; Hazell, Robert; King, Simon; Russell, Meg; Trench, Alan & Sandford, Mark. (2004). "The Constitution: Dragging the Constitution out of the Shadows", *Parliamentary Affairs* vol. 57-2, pp. 253-268.

Parpworth, Neil. (2013). "The Succession to the Crown Act 2013: Modernising the Monarchy", *Modern Law Review* vol. 76-6, pp. 1070-1093.

Websites

ico.org.uk/for_organisations/freedom_of_information/guide
This site provides information on the Freedom of Information Act from the Information Commissioner's Office

www.justice.gov.uk/information-access-rights/foi-guidance-for-practitionershtm
Guidance on how to access Freedom of Information material from the Ministry of Justice

www.ucl.ac.uk/constitution-unit/
The Constitution Unit at University College London. This site gives a comprehensive overview of many constitutional issues and changes

new.wales.gov.uk/about/cabinet/cabinetmeetings/?lang=en
Follow the links to access the minutes of the Welsh Assembly cabinet meetings

Questions
1. What are the advantages and disadvantages of a written constitution for Britain?
2. The constitution is "wearing out". How is this description of the British Constitution justified at this time?
3. What organisations are likely to have the most profound influence upon the British Constitution in the early part of the 21st century?

CHAPTER SEVEN // A BILL OF RIGHTS

Contents
- **Introduction**
- **Human Rights Act 1998**
- **Advantages**
- **Disadvantages**
- **Conclusion**

Introduction

No modern consideration of the British constitution could be complete without reference to the demands for a Bill of Rights. These come from many disparate quarters, encompassing a wide range of the political and academic spectrum. Within the academic spectrum, there is a whole debate over whether rights are 'universal' – in that the same set of rights ought to be applied to everyone – or whether rights are 'particular' – in that there will be different interpretations of human rights in different countries. There is no agreement as to which interpretation is more accurate.

Within the United Kingdom, the traditional merits of an uncodified constitution (flexibility, the sovereignty of a parliament answerable to the electorate, of ministers accountable to Parliament, of the use of conventions where appropriate rather than rigid statute law) have come to be regarded, in some quarters, as insufficient to protect basic human liberties. This again highlights the confusion between a constitution and a Bill of Rights. As stated in the previous chapter, a constitution is to do with the rules of the political game – if you like, how politics operates. A Bill of Rights, on the other hand, is to do with individual rights, duties, obligations and the relationship of the citizen to the state. It can almost be seen as a code of political conduct (Hiebert, 2005). Ultimately, such legislation can protect the individual from inappropriate state actions – and note the State (the roles and functions of which are examined in chapter 8) includes the legislature, the executive and the judiciary. The legislation may be enshrined within a constitution, but not necessarily so. A Bill of Rights – or more accurately, an Act of Rights should it become law in the UK – could easily be free standing. With an uncodified constitution in Britain, this may well become the case. Currently, what exists within the UK is the Human Rights Act (1998).

A number of eminent authorities like Lord Hailsham, Michael Zander and movements such as Charter 88, have claimed that a single, all embracing document incorporating the liberties and rights of citizens should form a key part of the constitution. Instead there is a reliance on a combination of statutes (made by a strong executive which appears largely unrestrained by a weak legislature – even in the times of a coalition government), common law, judicial precedents and administrative rules which go to make up the law in Britain. One major concession has been the incorporation of the European Convention of Human Rights (ECHR) into legislation as the Human Rights Act. This, however, is still not seen as going far enough in protecting peoples' rights. The legislation may be repealed by a future government (as, constitutionally, no Parliament may bind its successors). It may also be suspended – as was the case after the 11 September 2001 terrorist attacks in the USA. All of this is examined in greater detail later in the chapter.

It must also be acknowledged such a movement is by no means universally welcomed. Besides the understandable reservations of some major political figures, particularly in the Conservative Party, who fear the diminution of their executive powers while in office, a number of constitutional arguments have been advanced against such a radical departure from the traditional constitutional structures.

On top of this, parts of the British media have run sensationalist stories on how some people have abused the Human Rights Act, while at the same time harking back to some halcyon days when everyone knew their place. In parts of the tabloid media, the Human Rights Act has been described as a "rogues' charter", where criminals use the legislation to protect their own rights at the expense of the victims of crime.

Prior to the election of the Labour Government in 1997, Britain was a party to all major United Nations human rights treaties as well as important European instruments including the ECHR. These treaties were not actually incorporated into the constitution. Rather, successive British Governments highlighted the merits of the flexible nature of the British constitution and how it could adapt and evolve to protect individual liberties and promote justice and fairness.

As part of its proposed package of constitutional reforms the Labour Party included in its 1997 manifesto the commitment to incorporate the ECHR into British law. This manifesto commitment was realised with the Human Rights Act 1998. Although not a full Bill of Rights, the Human Rights Act goes some way towards clarifying the rights of an individual. In some respects, the Human Rights Act 1998 may better protect the rights of individuals than a conventional Bill of Rights. This has not stopped David Cameron from arguing the case to repeal the Human Rights Act, and to replace it with a more flexible British Bill of Rights.

Human Rights Act 1998

The first thing to note about the Human Rights Act (HRA) is that it is significantly different, not just from the US Bill of Rights, but almost every other equivalent document. In almost every case, a Bill of Rights is focused upon events **after** legislation has been passed. Under the HRA there is a requirement for all public authorities to consider their actions and the compatibility of said actions with the HRA. Under the HRA, according to Hiebert (2006, p.3), rights will not just be protected by the courts but "by establishing opportunities and obligations for political rights review by ministers, parliamentarians, and public authorities that are distinct from, and prior to, judicial review." Thus, for ministers, there is a requirement for them to report to parliament (in both Houses), **prior to the second reading of the legislation**, on the compatibility of the proposed legislation with the HRA.

Note here the judiciary, which is part of the State, is seen as being a neutral and impartial player. There appears to be no comprehension of the judiciary as a source of human rights abuse (see Hiebert (2005) for an excellent overview of this argument).

The HRA came into force in October 2000. The reason for the delay between passing the legislation and its enforcement was to allow government time to train their staff as to how the legislation had to be incorporated into their work. In January 1999, a Human Rights Task Force was set up by the Home Office to increase awareness among young people of their rights and responsibilities. At the same time, it entered it a dialogue with other branches of government and non-governmental organisations on ways in which the legislation could be properly implemented.

As can be seen in Tables 7.1 and 7.2, a wide range of areas are included in the legislation. Many of the articles and protocols appear to be part of the accepted norm as to what are an individual's rights. Yet without their codification into a single document, many of these rights could be forfeited without an individual necessarily even knowing that such forfeiture had happened.

Table 7.1 The Rights and Freedoms included in the Human Rights Act 1998

Article	Title
2	Right to Life
3	Prohibition of Torture
4	Prohibition of Slavery and Forced Labour
5	Right to Liberty and Security
6	Right to a Fair Trial
7	No Punishment Without Law
8	Right to Respect for Private and Family Life
9	Freedom of Thought Conscience and Religion
10	Freedom of Expression
11	Freedom of Assembly and Association
12	Right to Marry
14	Prohibition of Discrimination
16	Restrictions on Political Activity of Aliens
17	Prohibition of Abuse of Rights
18	Limitation on Use of Restrictions on Rights

Table 7.2 Protocols within the Human Rights Act 1998

Protocol	Article	Title
First Protocol	1	Protection of Property
	2	Right to Education
	3	Right to Free Elections
Sixth Protocol	1	Abolition of Death Penalty
	2	Death Penalty in Time of War

There are several things to note about the Human Rights Act 1998. Firstly, it is not an entrenched piece of legislation. This means any government can amend or repeal the Act through another Act of Parliament. In other words, the Act is not protected from the whims of a new government. Secondly, as can be seen in Tables 7.1 and 7.2, there are a number of omissions from the Act. Articles 1, 13 and 15 from the ECHR are missing, as are a number of Protocols. These omissions were extensively debated in both the House of Commons and the House of Lords during the progress of the legislation.

Article 1 placed an obligation on a contracting state to secure the convention rights to everyone within the jurisdiction of that state. It was argued this already happened under the rule of law in Britain. This same line was used when justifying the exclusion of Article 13, which focussed on effective domestic remedies for claims of breach of the convention. Article 15 permits a state to derogate from certain articles in the convention in times of war or other public emergency threatening the life of the state. This was also omitted from the HRA.

Advantages

There are a number of advantages for the citizen with the introduction of the HRA. Some of these will be outlined briefly.

1. A curb on potential abuse of executive power

This restraint on the executive is seen as a fundamental part of any Bill of Rights. The idea appears to be the individual needs to be protected from the State. Therefore, all legislation that passes through the British Parliament must now be compatible with the HRA. This applies not only to all present and future legislation, but also to legislation pre-dating the HRA as well. As noted earlier, Government ministers are already expected to make some sort of statement to Parliament outlining the compatibility of their legislative proposals with the HRA. Yet the implementation of this Act on past legislation will probably be exceedingly difficult to implement. Although the Act will not prevent the abuse of power by an executive with a huge majority in the Commons, it will at least go some way towards protecting the rights of the citizen. Curbing the powers of the executive is more closely linked to the constitution than to the HRA *per se*.

The formation of a select committee on Human Rights has also helped to monitor the Executive. The Joint Committee on Human Rights (JCHR) has 12 members, six from each House. Unlike other select committees, this committee does not have an in-built government majority, although in 2013 there were seven Coalition Government members. The key role of the JCHR is scrutiny of bills for compatibility with the HRA, as well as scrutiny of the ministerial statements to Parliament (prior to the Second Reading, as noted earlier) on compatibility.

2. Protect Parliamentary sovereignty

With the HRA, there is a clear idea to keep Parliamentary sovereignty. What can be seen is an attempt to balance the idea of judicial review with Parliamentary sovereignty (see Hiebert, 2006). This is something of a conflict of opposites. Judicial review and Parliamentary sovereignty do not appear compatible. The idea in the HRA is to blend 'best practice' from each perspective. The idea of ministers making statements on the compatibility of proposed legislation with the HRA – in other words, taking legal advice and making it public prior to Parliament passing the legislation – is a case in point.

3. Redress of citizen's grievances

This issue, in many respects, is the primary focus of the HRA. Individual rights are outlined very clearly but what happens if these rights are abused? Prior to this legislation, redress of grievances had been a relatively unimportant feature of government. Various channels already existed for individuals to voice their complaints – MPs, the Ombudsman, the courts (see chapter 17). The Major Government introduced the Citizen's Charter in 1991, which focused on the quality of public service delivery and avenues of redress where standards were not met. While many mocked the Citizen's Charter, it was a major step forward in compelling service deliverers to examine the type of service delivered and the methods of redress when services were not up to an acceptable standard.

The interesting point in the redress of citizen's grievances is the way in which there is a subtle shift in emphasis with the introduction of the HRA. English law (as opposed to Scottish law, which has significant differences) has traditionally been based upon 'freedoms'. The idea has been the individual is free to do whatever he or she likes, as long as it is within the bounds of the law. The individual is free to do anything, but exceptions are then stated. Under the ECHR, it is the opposite way around. The practice is to specify a fundamental right and elaborate upon what it means to the individual. In other words, to stipulate very clearly what are the rights of the individual. This then links to the next point.

4. Raising awareness of Human Rights

One of the hopes linked to the introduction of this legislation was that it would raise the levels of awareness of an individual's rights – in fact it was one of the goals of the HRA to build a 'rights culture'. It will be highly educative in influencing public opinion, in enlightening citizens on the principles of human rights and, more broadly, democracy. There is even some anticipation the HRA may become a central part of the British constitution, similar to the situation in the United States. It is often asserted that US citizens are much more aware than their British counter-parts of their constitutional and basic rights because they learn and absorb the clauses of their Declaration of Rights.

5. Role of judges

Prior to the introduction of the HRA, one of the main objections to such legislation had always been that it would transfer power from an elected parliament to an unelected body, the judiciary. Such a position is not strictly accurate. The courts themselves will have to operate in a manner consistent with the Convention of Human Rights. To meet this requirement, extensive training programmes have been set up to provide knowledge and awareness of the implications and potential effect of the HRA.

Yet, as Hiebert (2005, p. 236) has pointed out, "an effective bill of rights requires more than judicial review", and the HRA is no different. The courts are not able to strike down legislation which is incompatible with the HRA. They are required to interpret legislation, working on the assumption that it is compatible with the HRA (see Juss (2006) and Kavanagh (2006) for more detailed coverage).

Disadvantages

There are also a number of disadvantages to having a HRA. Some critics are totally opposed to such legislation, while others argue that it does not go far enough in protecting the rights of the individual.

1. Loss of constitutional flexibility

Britain is losing the traditional advantages of relying on custom, convention and judicial precedent. Consequently, Britain has become subject to the straitjacket of a rigid set of principles and regulations. It would be much more difficult to alter and mould the constitution or the HRA as needs arise or older ones become obsolete. Even with the HRA being unentrenched, change would be difficult – although David Cameron has talked of abolishing the HRA and replacing it with a British Bill of Rights. Even with such a move, the loss of constitutional flexibility is likely to remain. The US experience is often cited as an example of the rigidities that can hamper the ability to adapt to change, for example, on the gun laws. The right to bear arms embedded in a constitution created in the 18th century has become so sacrosanct that besides the opposition of pressure groups like the American Rifle Association, ordinary Americans are loath to abandon a fundamental tenet of the founding fathers of the constitution. Despite several massacres of school children in school grounds, change still appears unlikely. After all, as the gun lobby claims, the argument goes it is people who fire the guns; guns cannot fire themselves.

2. No guarantee of liberties

The experience of a number of countries as diverse as the former-USSR, apartheid-South Africa, and even the USA with their written constitutions/Bills of Rights ensuring freedoms and rights illustrates that pious or allegedly cynical statements of intention do not in themselves guarantee those freedoms and rights. The former-USSR claimed to have the most democratic constitution in the world with its right to freedom of speech, universal suffrage for those aged over 18 years, equality of opportunity, etc. Despite these claims, what existed in the former-USSR did not exactly gel with western liberal perspectives. During the Second World War, US citizens of Japanese origin were interned in a flagrant breach of their constitutional rights. The US army's treatment of its Black troops was little better. In effect, a piece of parchment in itself as a proof of civic liberties and human rights is worthless unless there are also present democratic institutions and processes of accountability to the electorate that are seen to work effectively.

On top of this, the British government reserves the right to suspend the HRA in particular circumstances. While Home Secretary, David Blunkett suspended the HRA after the attack on the World Trade Centre in 2001. Part of the defence of his actions was that the innocent have nothing to fear. The reality is in Britain we are seeing the departure from over 300 years of constitutional and legal practice. It appears the elements of democracy and accountability that had been so firmly established within Britain are now to be ignored at the convenience of the government.

Ewing (2004) has noted the extent to which human rights have been restricted in the UK, despite the existence of the HRA. This includes the Criminal Justice Act (2003), where individuals may be denied access to a lawyer for the first 48 hours in which they are held in custody. The idea of freedom of association has been brought into question, with there being many organisations that are banned, i.e. it is illegal to be a member of such organisations, or to give support to them. There are over 40 such organisations e.g. ETA (Basque separatists), the PKK (a Kurdish guerilla organisation operating in Turkey and Iraq), Hamas, and Al-Qaeda. In many cases, the bans have been imposed utilising secondary rather than primary legislation! Hence the title of Ewing's article: "The Futility of the Human Rights Act".

3. Erosion of parliamentary sovereignty

The adoption of the ECHR through the Human Rights Act 1998 will fundamentally erode the most important feature of the British political system

– parliamentary sovereignty. Parliament has developed over more than eight centuries. This will be checked because instead of depending upon a body elected by the people and responsible to them for guaranteeing freedoms and rights, citizens will have to place a greater reliance on a document of abstract principles interpreted by unelected judges.

This may go even further, with what is called "a process of juridification – the replacing of politics with the formality of law and legal decisions" (Davis, 2010, p. 91). Such a process may enable the government to avoid blame over failed policies, especially in areas such as counter-terrorism. Davis (2010) gives examples of such blame avoidance, with the Home Office claiming "its decisions to alter the counter-terrorism regime as mandated by judicial interference" (p. 94).

Despite the protestations of Charter 88, there can be little doubt the concept of parliamentary sovereignty may be eroded. It has always been the case that parliament and judges created law where new cases demanded it. The HRA is a set of principles couched in abstract terms, which is already taking precedence over parliamentary law. Legislation must be framed in accordance with notions of 'liberties' and 'rights' instead of considering such legislation on its merits.

4. Role of judges

This is the real sticking point for most opponents of a Bill of Rights and even for those unenthused about the HRA. Basically, the judiciary will have a prominent role in the interpretation and implementation of the provisions of the HRA, although it could be argued this has always been the case – the role of case-law in the constitution being such an example. It is a matter of opinion as to the fitness of judges throughout Britain to assume such a crucial part in the British constitutional process. The track record of the judiciary is such as to raise serious misgivings of judges as being the great defenders of liberties and rights.

Under the HRA, the judiciary can issue a declaration of incompatibility if there is a belief legislation or actions are not compatible with the HRA legislation. Seventeen were issued in the first five years (Klug & Starmer, 2005, p. 721). The problem is Parliament has the final say. Thus, a government with a large majority (or even a small majority) in Parliament could decide to ignore the judicial declaration of incompatibility.

Added to this is the potential for the politicisation of the judiciary. Concern has been raised with regard to the potential shift of power away from the elected representatives (Parliament) to unelected appointees (the judges). As in the USA there would be the great temptation of governments to ensure 'suitable' candidates were chosen for the judiciary. There will be mechanisms to lessen this possibility but the taint of political opportunism will probably still remain. Currently in the UK, as was noted in the previous chapter, there is an independent appointments board (the Judicial Appointments Commission) which selects judges. Yet there could still be politicisation with regard to the appointments to the Judicial Appointments Commission.

5. *The Act is not extensive enough*

While the previous comments have been directed at possible problems with the HRA, there is also the perspective of the legislation not being extensive enough. It has been suggested, with some justification, the HRA is not a sufficient replacement for a Bill of Rights. Not only can the government suspend the legislation, but there are a number of gaps in the legislation as well. For example, many campaigners have argued the courts should have been given the power to strike down legislation contrary to the ECHR/Human Rights Act. A further weakness is the state can ignore the legislation if it so wishes, in areas such as privacy. In Article 8 – Right to Respect for Private and Family Life – paragraph 2 states:

There shall be no interference by a public authority with the exercise of this right except such as in accordance with the law and is necessary in a democratic society in the interests of national security, public safety or the economic well-being of the country, for the prevention of disorder or crime, for the protection of health or morals, or for the protection of the rights or freedoms of others.

There is a similar problem in paragraph 2 of Article 9 – Freedom of Thought, Conscience and Religion:

Freedom to manifest one's religion or beliefs shall be subject only to such limitations as are prescribed by law and are necessary in a democratic society in the interests of public safety, for the protection of public order, health or morals, or for the protection of the rights and freedoms of others

The interpretation of what is necessary is to be carried out by the courts. As stated above, their track record does not inspire confidence.

Finally, it was also felt the original ECHR was out of date. It had been written in the late 1940s, being ratified in Britain in 1951. There has been little done to update it. Such a position suggests rights are 'particular' rather than 'universal'.

The Coalition Government has a major problem with the HRA. The Conservatives committed themselves, in the 2010 election manifesto, to repealing the HRA and replacing it with a British Bill of Rights – which is something that would be opposed most fundamentally by the Scottish Nationalist Government in Edinburgh. The Liberal Democrats had been rather scathing of this idea throughout the election campaign. They want a much stronger piece of legislation, not the abolition of the HRA. As of 2013, no move had been made to repeal the legislation – and it appears unlikely to happen prior to the 2015 general election. Some Conservative cabinet ministers, such as Dominic Grieve (Attorney General), have stated that they are broadly comfortable with the HRA. Amendments may need to be made to the legislation but a repealing of the legislation would be unnecessary.

Conclusion

There is a huge amount of literature on the subject of a Bill of Rights incorporated in a written constitution for Britain. Some of this literature is in the realms of speculation and conjecture, drawing ideas from other countries, in particular the United States of America. The Human Rights Act 1998 has changed this situation dramatically. Supporters look to protect their rights and freedoms as enshrined in the legislation. Antagonists, on the other hand, hark back to the days where parliamentary sovereignty underpinned the entire constitution, where conventions, customs and precedent gave Britain the flexibility to protect its citizens. Both perspectives contribute to a potentially lively debate; each having valid points to make, and each having flaws they do not want made public. From a constitutional perspective at least, we continue to live in interesting times.

Selected bibliography

Erdos, David. (2010). "Smoke but No Fire? The Politics of a 'British' Bill of Rights", *Political Quarterly* vol. 81-2, pp. 188-197.

Ewing, K. D. (2004). "The Futility of the Human Rights Act", *Public Law* pp. 829-852.

Hiebert, Janet. (2006). 'Parliament and the Human Rights Act: Can the JCHR help facilitate a culture of rights?', *International Journal of Constitutional Law* vol. 4-1, pp. 1-38.

Juss, Satvinder Singh. (2006). "Constitutionalising Rights Without a Constitution: The British Experience under Article 6 of the Human Rights Act 1998", *Statute Law Review* vol. 27-1, pp. 29-60.

Kavanagh, Aileen. (2006). "The Role of Parliamentary Intention in Adjudication under the Human Rights Act 1998", *Oxford Journal of Legal Studies* vol. 26-1, pp. 179-206.

Zander, Michael. (1997). *A Bill of Rights?*: Sweet and Maxwell

Websites

www.bihr.org
The British Institute of Human Rights home page

www.direct.gov.uk/en/Governmentcitizensandrights/index.htm
An explanation of the various rights people hold in the workplace

www.justice.gov.uk/human-rights
The Ministry of Justice information on human rights

www.opsi.gov.uk/acts/acts1998/ukpga_19980042_en_1
The Human Rights Act 1998

www.parliament.uk/business/committees/committees-a-z/joint-select/human-rights-committee/
The Joint Committee on Human Rights home page

Questions

1. To what extent, if at all, are individual rights protected by the Human Rights Act 1998?
2. The Human Rights Act has been described as a "rogues' charter". Why has this been the case? To what extent is it an accurate assessment?
3. The HRA needs to be replaced by a proper British Bill of Rights. What might constitute such a bill? How would it differ from the current HRA?

CHAPTER 8 // THE BRITISH STATE

Contents
- **Introduction**
- **What is a State?**
- **Public Sector – Private Sector**
- **Government and the State**
- **Theories of the State**
- **The British State**
- **Conclusion**

Introduction

The concept 'state' is utilised frequently within the framework of British politics. There is the welfare state, the regulatory state, the hollowed out state, not to forget the Head of State (which, in the UK, is the monarch, while the prime minister is merely the Head of Government). Added to this, Margaret Thatcher, when she was prime minister, spoke of 'rolling back the frontiers of the state'. This highlights how the role of the state can be a major underpinning of ideology. After all, within any ideology, there will be a perception of what role the state should play.

This chapter will explore the concept 'state' to set the scene for subsequent chapters in this section on central government institutions. It will, however, also form a basis for other sections, such as Section 4 – Government Beyond the Centre, as well as specific chapters such as that on regulation. Some theoretical approaches to the role of the state will also be examined briefly. That section should be read in conjunction with chapter two. Finally in this chapter, there is a summary of the components of the British State.

What is a State?

There are a range of different approaches to addressing this question. Most people would tend to think of a country. The United Kingdom of Great Britain and Northern Ireland is a state, as is the United States of America, the Federal Republic of Germany, and the People's Republic of China. Firstly, therefore, a state can be a territorial unit.

A different perspective focuses upon the institutions within a country. Thus in the UK, people might think of Parliament, the judiciary, local government and the police force as being part of the state. Within each country, similar institutions exist. These are seen as being part of the state.

The state may also be seen as an instrument of force and coercion. Rather than leaving individuals to get on with their lives, the state intercedes in almost all aspects of people's lives – telling them what to do, and punishing them if there is a lack of conformity (see George Orwell's *Animal Farm* for a fascinating take on this approach). The state may therefore be seen as an oppressive body, imposing itself on people and curtailing their rights and freedoms.

There are many other answers to the question 'what is a state?'. The above ideas give a flavour as to how such a question could be answered. Andrew Heywood (2007, p. 91) has identified five key features of a state.

1. A state is *sovereign*. This means the state is the body which has the right to make, and to enforce, laws. No other organisations may challenge this position of the state.
2. The state's institutions are *'public'*. This point is examined in greater detail later in the chapter. In effect, the state makes and enforces decisions for the benefit of all members of society.
3. The state is an exercise in *legitimation*. All decisions taken by the state are normally accepted as binding on all members of society. The state is the only body which has the right to wield such power.
4. The state is an instrument of *domination*. This is linked to enforcement. The state needs to have the capacity to ensure all members of society obey the laws. Those that do not are punished, but are also seen to be punished (as a warning to all members of society).
5. The state is a *territorial* association. The powers of the state may only be wielded legitimately within the geographical borders of the state. These borders are normally recognized by other states.

All states share these key features. They overlap with the different perspectives of the state that were described earlier in the chapter. Some states are described as 'failing' because they are unable to meet all of the above features. Countries such as Somalia and Yemen are deemed to be failing states. Their sovereignty may be questioned, as well as their legitimacy and domination. Even their geographical borders may be brought into question.

Later in this chapter, the focus will move to the features of the British state. This will build on the features cited above.

Public Sector – Private Sector

State institutions are public institutions, working for the benefit of all members of society. This is significantly different to private organisations, which focus on the interests of the owners and shareholders. It is easier to examine this issue in greater detail by focusing on the terms 'public sector' and 'private sector'.

The public sector is a system of organisations concerned with achieving State purposes. This includes, for example, government departments, nationalised industries, and the NHS. Such bodies will be involved primarily in the implementation of government and state policies. These organisations are run for the benefit of **all** members of society (whether or not all members of society choose to use such organisations and their services).

The private sector is a collective term for organisations which are neither state-owned nor operating specifically to achieve state goals. This includes businesses such as British Telecom, or, on a much smaller scale, a corner shop. Private sector organisations are profit driven. Their *raison d'être* is profit maximisation. This ensures financial gain for their owners or shareholders.

Basically the private sector will not provide some essential services as they are most unlikely to generate a profit e.g. libraries. Thus, such service provision is left to the public sector. Similarly, there are some services the private sector could provide – such as street lighting – but has no adequate way in which to get users to pay for such a service. This is, therefore, left to the public sector, which compels most users to pay through general taxation. For a discussion of the pros and cons of having a public sector, see P. Cocker & A. Jones (2005); *Essential Topics in Modern British Politics and Government* chapter 16.

Conventionally, distinguishing between the public and private sectors was relatively straight forward. A solitary question was needed: who benefits from the organisation? The answer to this question would reveal whether the organisation was in the public or private sector. More recently, the answer to this question has become somewhat less clear. This point will be developed later in the chapter.

Government and the State

The concepts 'state' and 'government' are often used interchangeably. This is an error. If anything, the government is part of the state. To use a mathematical analogy, the government is a subset of the state. The state is far more extensive (specific detail as to what comprises the British state is given later in this chapter). It is also permanent; whereas governments are temporary. For example, the Blair Government was replaced by the Brown Government, which was, in turn, replaced by the Cameron-Clegg coalition Government. Throughout all of this time, the state of the United Kingdom of Great Britain and Northern Ireland remained. The policies of these governments had different priorities, and this had some impact upon the functioning of the state.

While the state is permanent, it also represents the permanent interests of society. Thus, there is in the UK a welfare system, or a military. Government is partisan – it is biased. Therefore the extent of spending on said welfare state or military is likely to vary between different governments. They have different political priorities. This can be seen more clearly when various theoretical approaches to the state are examined.

Theories of the State

The different ideological approaches to the role of the state have a huge impact upon the role of the public and private sectors. Not all ideological approaches are covered here. For greater detail see P. Dunleavy and B. O'Leary (1987); *Theories of the State*, C. Hay *et al* (eds.); (2006) *The State: Theories and Issues*, or J. Dryzek & P. Dunleavy (2009); *Theories of the Democratic State*.

The different approaches to be covered here are:
1. Liberal State
2. Marxist State
3. New Right
4. Environmental State

Supporters of each approach will argue the merits of their ideas, and will be disparaging of others. Yet no single approach is necessarily the 'best' way for a state to be run. This is where the partisanship of governments comes into play.

1. Liberal State

The liberal model of the state places great emphasis upon the role of the individual. States are merely "caretakers of the rule of law and the rights of citizens to life, liberty and property" (Sørensen, 2004, p. 17). It is the individual who is important. Sørensen uses the term "caretaker" – although Dunleavy & O'Leary (1987, p. 6) argue that liberals believe "the state should be an 'umpire', a 'referee', a regulator and an arbiter... of conflicting interests in society."

Either way, the state has a minimal role to play. From this perspective, it is important to note the state "is derived from the people, the individuals. Without them the state would have no power and no legitimacy"(Sørensen, 2004, p. 182). The emphasis is, thus, upon the role of the individual.

There is, it must be noted, a role for the state. King & Kendall (2004, p. 195) argue, from the liberal perspective, it is to equip citizens (or subjects) with the wherewithall to govern themselves. This links in with Sørensen's approach. From a liberal perspective, there is a fear that state or government involvement in almost any activities is likely to do more harm than good. The state is needed, but only in a minimal sense.

2. Marxist State

A Marxist approach to the role of the state would see the interests of the ruling class as the most important. The ruling class dominates the organisation and the function of the state (McAuley, 2003). The state is used to reinforce the existing social order i.e. everything is done in the interests of the ruling class. How this is carried out is a point of debate.

Hay (2006, pp. 60-62) notes there are a range of different perspectives within the Marxist approach to the role of the state – and there is a distinct lack of agreement between these sub-groups. One approach focuses on the state as an "instrument of the ruling classes". This is the dominant Marxist position, whereby the ruling classes use the state to maintain their dominant position.

A slightly different perspective sees the state as being a repressive tool of the ruling classes. Rather than maintaining their position, the state is used by the ruling classes to crush the workers – the emphasis is very much upon the repression of the proletariat. Lenin, for example, saw the state as a coercive apparatus. His argument was the only way to change things was through violent revolution – to meet force with force!

A third perspective sees the state as an ideal collective capitalist. From this perspective, 'capital' is not seen as self-reproducing, nor can it create the environment for its own reproduction. Thus, the state intervenes to create those conditions which are conducive to the reproduction of capital.

> Capitalist production and exchange are inherently "anarchistic". Individuals, each in pursuit of his or her private interests, cannot possibly take "the common interest" – even of the capitalist class – into account in their actions. Thus, the capitalist State has also to function as a vehicle through which the class interests of the capitalists are expressed in all fields of production, circulation and exchange.
>
> State intervention is necessary... because a system based on individual self-interest and competition cannot otherwise express a collective class interest.
>
> (Harvey, 1976, p. 84)

The state is not, in itself, capitalist, and the idea of collective capitalism appears illogical – as capitalism depends upon competition for the movement of capital. There is bound to be competition and struggle within the elite or capitalist class (Tsolakis, 2010). But, this is presented as an 'ideal' type – a theoretical concept. The organs of the state are used to intercede on behalf of the long-term interests of capital.

All these Marxist approaches (and this list is not exhaustive) fall in line with the definitions and roles of the state cited earlier in this chapter. It is where the emphasis is placed that differences can be seen. For example, is the state primarily a coercive or dominant body, or is it sovereign? Developing Lenin's perspective, once the violent revolution is over, a state is still required to see the transition from a capitalist society to a socialist society.

3. New Right

Prior to examining the approach of the New Right to the role of the state, a warning must be given. Some people use the phrases "New Right", "radical right", "neo-liberalism" and "neo-conservatism" interchangeably. It is wrong to do so. While there may be broad brush similarities between these different ideological approaches, there are many subtle differences.

Followers of the New Right sees a limited role for the state; any interventions by the state should be "specific, fine-tuned, remedial and authoritative" (King & Kendall, 2004, p. 123). There is, however, a clear hostility towards the state. This is broadly in line with the liberal approach to the state.

Much of the New Right literature bears similarities with Public Choice Theory (also known as Rational Choice Theory). Public Choice theorists see the state as being phenomenally inefficient. Those who work for the state are budget maximisers – because there is no concern over profits and losses, the only thing left is budget maximisation. Public Choice Theory provided the New Right "with a particular language in which the failings of the state could be dissected and a set of policy recommendations to deal with them" (Hindmoor, 2006, p. 97).

There is also an assumption within Public Choice Theory that every individual is a "rational self-interested utility-maximizer" (Hindmoor, 2006, p. 81). In other words, everybody does whatever they like to further their own self-interest. As rational individuals, we will each explore all of the options available to us, and then choose that which will give us most satisfaction (utility). The state does not do this. The state does not provide choice. Rather, the state provides a 'one size fits all' approach. Without competition and choice, there is only inefficiency.

Much of the thinking behind the New Right, and its application to the UK, was examined in chapters 2 and 4. It can also be seen in Chapter 13 (civil service) and Chapter 16 (The Regulatory State).

4. Environmental State

In some respects, the idea of an environmental state is a bit of an oxymoron. As Paterson et al (2006, p. 138) note: "since states are irredeemably oriented around protecting the interests of those within their own territory, they will never be able to pursue environmental co-operation to the extent necessary to avoid ecological collapse". There is a fight for scarce resources – between states, businesses, people, etc. – around the world. This is prioritised over ecological sustainability. With this in mind, Dryzek & Dunleavy (2009, p. 244) see an environmental theory of the state as a critique of how the modern state "is a product of an industrialist era in which economic growth and technological change were unquestioned goods".

Such a perspective suggests 'Green' theorists are likely to reject the state. This is not necessarily the case. For example, Paterson et al (2006, pp. 146-152) highlight the idea of "Greening the state". To the forefront in all of this is the risk society (see chapter 16 for risk and regulation). Greening the state looks at how states can respond to the environmental and ecological concerns of the day. For some, the underpinning is to transform the economy "in an ecological direction" (p. 147). This is seen as a weak form of ecological modernisation. A far stronger form involves "the development of deliberative decision-making procedures, the decentralization of decision-making combined with a range of participative processes" (p.148). Such an approach goes far beyond what might be perceived as an environmental perspective. Different approaches to 'green' politics are examined in chapter 34.

The British State

> As late as 1870, most Britons assumed that the only tasks that should be entrusted to the central and local authorities were the defence of the realm, the maintenance of public order, the prevention of destitution, a modicum of workplace and sanitary regulation, and the provision of basic amenities such as street lighting. (Harling, 2001, p. 2)

The above quote highlights the liberal approach to the state, which was prominent at that time. The perception as to the role of the British state has changed significantly since 1870. Yet, as can be seen from the ideological perspectives from earlier in this chapter, there are people who believe what the state was providing in 1870 was still too much – and what is being provided today is excessive!

The current British state includes the Monarchy, Parliament, the police and other emergency services, all of the government departments, the devolved governments, local government, the judiciary, quangos, nationalised industries, etc. The list is extensive. Yet, as noted in the introduction, Margaret Thatcher spoke of 'rolling back the state'. Thus there was privatisation – which took the nationalised industries out of state control. There were policies at the local government level, such as Compulsory Competitive Tendering (CCT), which forced local authorities to put some of their services out to private tender. Ideologically, all of this can be linked to the New Right – the idea of reducing the size of the state. Arguably, the state was far smaller in the 1990s than it had been thirty years earlier.

A line of thought was developed in the 1990s that the British state was 'hollowing out'. In effect, central government was fragmenting. Consequently, it was losing its grip on the rest of the state. Powers were being ceded to the European Union (which is both a supra-national and an intergovernmental organisation – see chapter 31). Added to this, there were local government reforms which saw local authorities being stripped of some powers. Across all of the public sector, there were massive reforms which saw "power flow sideways and downwards from the central state to a myriad of subsidiary bodies, both within and without the formal boundaries of the state" (Holloway, 2000, p. 168). The extent of these changes is such the central state apparatus appears to no longer control or direct policy making and policy implementation.

In retrospect, this 'hollowing out' thesis overstated the extent to which the role of the central state had been reduced. There was, clearly, a reduction in what the state did. It was the way in which policies were directed that changed.

Similarly, the attempts to roll back the frontiers of the state did not lead to a massive reduction of the role of the state. Rather, there was a transformation in what the state does (Flinders, 2006, p. 224). The state is no longer a provider of all services. Instead, it may regulate the private (or voluntary) sector provision of these services. The state still has to ensure that the services are provided – and to a specified minimum standard, with penalties for failure. The state is still present. Part of its role has changed. This can be seen in Table 8.1.

Table 8.1 Public and Private Provision and Financing of Services

		Provision of Services	
		Public	Private
Financing of Services	Public	State education Old-age benefits NHS	Scholarships Vouchers Insurance programmes
	Private	User fees Trust hospitals Road tariffs	Fee for service Insurance Private doctors Private education

Source: Nisar (2007) p. 149

The state also works in partnership with other sectors in the provision of services. This has been most prominent in the UK through things such as the Private Finance Initiative (PFI) and Public-Private Partnerships (PPPs). Nisar (2007, p. 147) presents three broad arguments about the benefits of PPPs to the state:

1. there is a benefit to the Treasury of enabling public sector projects to be undertaken without swelling the government debt or triggering the need for tax rises
2. they provide a competitive and cost-attractive alternative to traditional public sector projects
3. they bring in proven project management expertise

Much of this has transformed the role of the British state. The language of the 1980s and 1990s spoke of the state being an 'enabler' rather than a 'provider' of services. Today, the emphasis is more upon 'partnership'.

Yet many questions have been raised as to the benefits to the state of these partnerships. Flinders (2005, p. 216) has argued that "PPP represents a Faustian bargain in that forms of PPP may deliver efficiency gains and service improvements in some policy areas but these benefits may involve substantial political and democratic costs". In other words, are the short-term benefits of PPP being highlighted, with the long-term costs being ignored? Faust sold his soul to the devil in return for unlimited knowledge. When Faust died, after a life of pleasure, he was damned for eternity! Was the short-term pleasure worth eternal damnation?

Flinders (2005, pp. 224-234) highlights five themes around PPP. Similarities may be noted with the benefits cited by Nisar (above). Yet Nisar's positive outlook is not shared.

1. **Efficiency** – the idea is PPPs increase efficiency. Evidence of this is mixed. Success stories include road building. Failures include some hospitals and schools.

2. **Risk** – the idea behind PPP is the risk is transferred from the public sector to the private sector. This is debatable. With PFI, it is even more so. As Weihe (2008, p. 157) points out – with regard to PFI – "risk sharing is absent". Many services, such as the London Underground, are heavily subsidised. Others, such as the National Air Traffic Services, have seen the government intervene and subsidise them because the projects were in danger of failing. Some projects are too important to be allowed to fail, thus the contractors are bailed out.

3. **Complexity** – there are now so many non-state service providers involved in service provision that the whole system has become phenomenally complex. This has led to a high degree of public confusion. Quangos have had to be established (such as the Better Regulation Delivery Office) to report to the government on how well all the PPPs are operating. There has also been a lot of difficulty in getting long-term contracts changed e.g. trying to introduce healthy school meals.

4. **Accountability** – issues of complexity have had a huge impact upon accountability. Not only this, but when PPPs fail, or need bailing out, who is accountable for the failure, and to whom? How are the service providers in a PPP held to account? It is not uniform across different policy sectors.

5. **Governance and the future of state projects** – the more PPPs are used, the less direct control there is for central government. "PPPs challenge central tenets of the British welfare state: a commitment to universal and equal public service, the public service ethos and an implicit rejection of profit-making in certain core public services" (Flinders, 2005, p. 234). The problem is if the state cannot fund the projects, but there is demand for the service, alternative providers must be found. The question then becomes: which services should be prioritised for public service provision?

Conclusion

There is an argument the state is disappearing; it is being replaced by the market. This is not the case. The state is not disappearing. Instead, its role is changing.

There is a process which is moving away from government (not just in the UK, but around the world) to governance. This perspective will be examined in chapter 35. The idea is the state (or, more specifically, the government) works with a range of organisations to deliver the services to the public. Within this, there should be choice – including both public and private sector alternatives.

Yet there are certain core functions the vast majority of Britons believe ought to be funded and run by the state. This includes the judiciary, policing, the military, education, social services, the emergency services and the NHS. For the NHS, as with education, there is a line of argument that the state should not be the sole provider. There should be alternatives – be they from the private or voluntary sector. It is important to note, however, that the teachers, doctors, nurses, etc. who work in the private and voluntary alternatives are likely to have been trained by state-funded institutions!

Selected bibliography

Cocker, Phil & Jones, Alistair. (2005). *Essential Topics in Modern British Politics and Government:* Liverpool Academic Press, 2nd edition, chapter 16.

Dryzek, John & Dunleavy, Patrick. (2009). *Theories of the Democratic State:* Palgrave.

Dunleavy, Patrick & O'Leary, Brendan. (1987). *Theories of the State: The Politics of Liberal Democracy:* Macmillan.

Flinders, Matthew. (2005). "The Politics of Public-Private Partnerships", *British Journal of Politics and International Relations* vol. 7-2, pp. 215-239.

Hay, Colin; Lister, Michael & Marsh, David (eds.). (2006). *The State: Theories and Issues:* Palgrave.

McAuley, James. (2003). *An Introduction to Politics, State and Society:* Sage.

Sørensen, Georg. (2004). *The Transformation of the State: Beyond the Myth of Retreat:* Palgrave.

Websites

www.royal.gov.uk/RoyalEventsandCeremonies/StateVisits/InwardStatevisits.aspx
State visits highlight the role of the Monarch as Head of State for the UK

www.theguardian.com/commentisfree/2013/nov/15/cambridge-university-british-state-questions
This is an interesting article from The Guardian *about the British state and spying*

Questions
1. What is the ideal role of the state?
2. How might a 'green' state function?
3. "The state is first and foremost about repression. It stipulates what can and cannot be done, and compels everyone to obey its orders. Anything else is window dressing." Discuss.

CHAPTER 9 // THE HOUSE OF COMMONS

Contents
- **Introduction**
- **Functions of the House of Commons**
- **Scrutiny of the Executive**
- **Reform of the Commons**
- **Conclusion**

The role and work of the House of Commons is a vast subject and a potentially daunting one for many students. Some students wish to focus on procedural rules and the conduct of business in the Commons. Yet these aspects must not obscure other important features of the chamber's role as a supportive and influencing mechanism of Executive power, as well as one of restraint on the use (and potential abuse) of Executive power.

Introduction

Formally, Parliament consists of three component parts, which are collectively termed the legislature: the House of Commons; the House of Lords; and, the Crown (monarchy). Of these, the Commons is now so dominant in relation to the other two parts it has become practically synonymous with Parliament itself. Arguably, this underplays the role and influence of the House of Lords (which is covered in the next chapter).

The development of the power of the Commons became more evident in the late 19th century with the emergence of two monolithic parties, the Conservatives and the Liberals. Such a growing dominance of what was to be termed "party politics" soon ensured Commons business was directed towards retaining the government in power through its own party support. On top of this, the 1911 and 1949 Parliament Acts reduced the powers of the House of Lords, leaving the Commons as the dominant House with the focus more and more upon the parties and their attempts to gain and stay in Office. Consequently, throughout the latter half of the 20th century and into the 21st, the supremacy of the Commons over the rest of Parliament has been taken as read. The focus has moved to the role of the Commons and its relationship with the Executive. If there was ever a "golden age" of the Commons in the mid-19th century where it could dominate the government of the day – and this is viewed more as myth than fact – it is now clearly not the case.

In turn, the Commons has become subordinate to the needs and desires of the government of the day, depending upon the size of the government's majority – the larger the majority, the more sub-ordinate the Commons. Thus, with a coalition government, there is an expectation of seeing a more lively and far from sub-ordinate Commons. The Commons has an opportunity to reassert itself. This aspect will be discussed later.

Initially, the functions of the Commons will be outlined and analysed. Following this, ways in which the Commons can scrutinise the Executive will be examined, along with their effectiveness. Finally in this chapter, the issue of reform of the Commons will be raised. Some reforms have already taken place, others, possibly viewed as necessary, are awaited.

Functions of the House of Commons

At the outset it is important to distinguish between the functions performed by individual MPs and those performed by the House of Commons acting collectively. It is quite difficult to describe the latter as an entity because it comprises a number of disparate parts – the Government, the governing party, the Opposition front bench, the opposition party, as well as the other so-called minor parties. With a coalition government, it gets even more complicated, with two governing parties forming the Government. Added to this, there are the various factions within each party, each of which may be vying to dominate their own party – and, again, this is made even more complicated with a coalition government as different factions within one coalition partner may work with (or against) factions in the other partner.

Before examining the various functions of the House of Commons, it is worth emphasising certain points. The most important of these is the influence of the party. It is a fact of life in the Commons that the role of the party dominates. It is through party support and organisation that a team of leading figures can occupy ministerial posts, that backbenchers are strengthened in their support for their party's programme, and that the shape and content of the party battle eventually percolates down to the public. Thus the role of the party appears paramount.

A consequence of this influence is the decline of the Commons as a brake on the ever-increasing power of the Executive buttressed by party support. Throughout the 20th century there were complaints about the lack of power and influence in the Commons. Of these, possibly the most damning was Lord Hailsham's charge of "elective dictatorship" – a clear comment on the powerlessness of the Commons to check the 'dictatorship' of modern executives. Concern about such a dictatorship was raised during the 2001 General Election campaign. Added to this, in the 2005 election campaign the Conservative Party utilised the slogan "Vote Blair, Get Brown". Although the Conservatives were pointing out Gordon Brown was likely to take over as prime minister during the subsequent Parliament, the emphasis upon the party leader (and potential prime minister) highlights the centralisation of power in one political post, thus reinforcing Hailsham's claim of an "elective dictatorship". There was no constitutional requirement for Gordon Brown to call a general election in order to gain a personal mandate as prime minister (in the same way as John Major and James Callaghan did not call immediate general elections when they both became Prime Minister). A counterbalance to such criticism, however, is the relationship between the Legislative and the Executive arms of government have become more intertwined. In terms of modern government, it is unlikely the Commons can aspire to a governing role. Depending upon the size of a government's majority, it may not even have a controlling role.

All of this is considered in keeping with the nature of Britain's uncodified constitution. The flexibility and adaptability are qualities that can be applied to the function of the Commons as it evolved, in the same way in which they have been applied to the constitution. Despite the changes, both politicians and students still insist on emphasising the formal functions as if they were real. For example, liberal thinkers may prefer to stress the classic virtues of the sovereignty of Parliament and its functions in controlling the Executive. An alternative focus places the emphasis upon the legislative functions. Neither approach is strictly accurate. Instead, there are a number of functions that are generally accepted. There are, of course, disagreements on their significance.

1. *Representation*
2. *Legislation*
3. *Recruitment*
4. *Scrutiny and influence of the Executive*
5. *Miscellaneous*

1. Representation
Walter Bagehot chose the electoral function as the main task of the House of Commons, acting as an electoral college selecting the nation's leaders. This was in a time prior to the development of strong political parties. Today it is the general election that decides the party composition in the Commons, and thus *indirectly* chooses the government. The exception is in the case of a 'hung' parliament, where no single party has an overall majority in the Commons. This happened in February 1974 (which led to a minority government, and a second election in October 1974) and in 2010 (which led to a coalition government).

The concept of representation is still the foundation of the other roles of the Commons. It imparts the essential element of *legitimacy* to its deliberations. In a democracy the principle of representation underpins the right of the representatives to act on behalf of the voters and endorse or reject the legislation of the government.

It would appear therefore the representative, the MP, is there to represent the voters of a specific geographical constituency. Yet the question of representation can go much further. An MP does represent a constituency, but he/she will also represent a political party (except in the case of Independent MPs), as well as other pressures. These pressures could include an MPs (former) occupation, sponsor (who may have assisted in the funding of the constituency election campaign), or interest groups. Which of these take priority in the event of conflict of interests? To present a hypothetical example: an MPs constituents overwhelmingly oppose a road building development in the constituency. The MPs party is in favour of the development, as are the MPs sponsors – an organisation involved with road haulage. On top of this, the MP will be lobbied by a number of disparate pressure groups – in favour and opposed to the development. Which way should the MP go? If the MP supports the development, the constituents may not give their support at the next election, leading to possible electoral defeat for the MP. Yet if the MP opposes the development, the party may deselect the MP or the sponsors may withhold future financial support. Representation is not as clear cut as many imagine. Each of these roles is combined into the person of the MP.

The 650 constituencies, each with their own MP, fulfil the principle that all areas of the UK are represented in the Commons (Sinn Fein MPs have experienced difficulties here as they refuse to swear an oath of allegiance to the monarch and cannot therefore sit in the House). This geographical concept has assumed paramount importance in the sense that the individual MP representing his/her constituency is supposed to cater for all electors in that constituency, including those who did not vote for him/her. Dealing with constituents concerns and problems is a large part of an MPs work. In addition, the MP is expected to put the constituency 'on the map' by, for example, being zealous in improving employment opportunities, improving health and education, etc.

There is a small, little noticed caveat here. For Ministers of State, as well as cabinet members, it is very difficult to 'represent' their constituencies in the House. By convention, such ministers do not get the opportunity to ask questions or to raise constituents concerns in the House. And, as one Minister of State has pointed out, some of his constituents asked him: "What the hell do you actually do to represent us in Parliament?"

In passing it should be noted the principle of representation does not necessarily endorse the idea that MPs have to correspond to a social microcosm of the nation. The vast majority of MPs are white, middle class, middle aged males, as can be seen in Table 9.1. Almost a fifth of MPs are female, yet women make up over 50% of the population. The number of ethnic minority MPs has risen to over 2% of all MPs, compared with about 5% of the population. In both cases, there is still huge under-representation but these numbers are considered an improvement on pre-1997 Parliaments.

Table 9.1 Social breakdown of MPs

Election Year	Number of Female MPs	Number of Ethnic Minority MPs	Number of MPs aged between 40 and 59 years	Average Age of MPs
1997	121/659	9	481	48.8
2001	118/659	12	483	49.8
2005	125/646	15	440	50.6
2010	143/650	27	397	50.0

A final comment on representation is with regard to representing the party. The vast majority of MPs are elected under a party label. The exceptions include Martin Bell (MP for Tatton 1997-2001) and Richard Taylor (MP for Wyre Forest 2001-2010). MPs are all expected to 'toe their party line' on virtually every issue. This includes voting and speaking in the Chamber, as well as promoting and defending the party position in all external engagements. Not upsetting the party increases the chances of promotion. There are MPs, often labelled 'the awkward squad', who realise they have little chance of promotion within their party. Consequently, they sometimes act as if they have *carte blanche* with regard to what they say and do.

This 'toeing the party line' does not always stand true. There have been exceptions – such as voting on the war in Iraq or the campaign for an immediate referendum on continued EU membership – where large numbers of MPs refused to follow their party line. In such cases, there is very little the party leadership can do. A solitary MP, or even a small group of MPs, may be isolated from the rest of the party. When the numbers are vast, it is impossible for the party leadership to discipline their members.

2. Legislation

In constitutional theory, Parliament is the legislature – the law-making body – as epitomised in the concept of parliamentary sovereignty. This perspective is best demonstrated when examining the legislative process as shown in Table 9.2. Both Houses of Parliament have three readings of each piece of legislation. Legislation may be introduced in either House, but must go through both before going to Royal Assent. The three readings within the House of Lords are not shown in Table 9.2, as the House of Lords is quite restricted in what it can do.

Table 9.2 The Legislative Process

House of Commons	First Reading	Introduce the bill
	Second Reading	Debate and vote on thinking behind the bill
	Public Bill Committee	Cross-party committee which works through the detail of the legislation
	Report Stage	Report of the Public Bill Committee
	Third Reading	Debate and vote on the text of the legislation
House of Lords	Accept legislation	Goes straight to Royal Assent
	Finance legislation	No opportunity to change the legislation. Straight to Royal Assent
	Amend legislation	Amendments may be proposed. They go to the Commons Public Bill Committee. If accepted, straight to Royal Assent. If not the legislation is delayed for up to one year before going for Royal Assent
Monarchy	Royal Assent	

There is one other caveat to Table 9.2. A Government may force legislation through the House of Lords using the 1949 Parliament Act. This only applies, however, if the bill originated in the House of Commons. If a bill starts in the House of Lords, and there is disagreement between the two chambers, the 1949 Parliament Act may not be utilised.

Although we can see legislation progressing through Parliament, the idea Parliament makes the laws is largely a myth. Political reality demonstrates legislation is made by the Executive with Parliament there to criticise and possibly influence it, but largely to *legitimise* the legislation by voting for it. Parliament rarely initiates legislation or even makes policy – the exception being Private Member's Bills, which are discussed below.

The stages in the passage of a bill are little more than an elaborate process for sanctioning or legitimating government legislation. On top of this, much of the legislation is 'whipped'. This means, depending upon the importance of the legislation, MPs are almost compelled into voting for their party's position on any legislation, highlighting yet again the importance of party. There is a one-line whip, where attendance is 'requested'; a two-line whip where attendance is 'expected'; and, a three-line whip, where attendance is regarded as 'essential'. An alternative is the non-whipped legislation, known as a 'free' vote, where MPs vote according to their conscience. This is used for contentious non-partisan legislation, for example the re-introduction of the death penalty.

The legislative timetable works around annual sessions. In effect, this means if legislation is not passed by the end of session, it falls. Thus, towards the end of each session, there is great pressure to force legislation through (Korris, 2011), or for the Opposition to attempt to gain as many concessions as possible. This is no longer necessary, as there is now the opportunity to make provision for legislation to be carried over from one session to the next. Around half of all carry-over motions are uncontested (Korris, 2011, p. 571). Yet this provision is rarely used, leaving the parties to battle things out at the end of each session.

Where Parliament can initiate legislation – through Private Member's Bills – the fact is the government decides the time and procedure of these bills. If hostile, or even merely unenthusiastic, towards the bill, the government can 'kill' them off, for example in 2012-13 to repeal the European Communities Act, 1972. The vast proportion of Private Members' legislation never reaches the statute book. This is not to say Private Member's Bills are futile. Almost every year sees Private Member's Bills being enacted. The last year in which no Private Member's Bills became law was in 2004-5. Prior to that, it was 2000-1. In both cases, these were short Parliamentary sessions where a general election was called. The time before was 1974 – when there were two general elections in the year.

It is often perceived, when looking at whipped legislation, the role of MPs within the House of Commons is little more than cannon – or more accurately, lobby – fodder for their respective parties. This, though, was inevitable in a representative democracy based on a parliamentary model which is dominated by party factions. Power will shift to the Government with the Parliament having little more than a supportive, if sometimes critical, role. Other countries have similar experiences, most notably New Zealand.

There are commentators and MPs who, while not wishing to usurp the legislative role of government, do desire a Commons strengthened by organisation and procedures to be much more influential on the quality and nature of the legislation. We will look at some of these later in this chapter.

In addition, it should be pointed out that powerful bodies outside Parliament such as pressure groups or the International Monetary Fund (IMF), exercise their own form of legitimisation on the Commons and government, who may depend upon those sources for advice and co-operation. The European dimension is another potent source of legitimisation. There are many observers who now believe this extra-Parliamentary form of legitimisation is far more significant than that conferred by voters through the House of Commons.

3. Recruitment

Most ministers are also members of the House of Commons. There are some that sit in the Lords. MPs who wish to climb this greasy pole to power first have to work their way through a number of other positions. Their performance in the Chamber – voting and speaking – needs to be exemplary from a party perspective. Thereafter, there is the possibility of sitting on a select committee, or even becoming a Parliamentary Private Secretary, which is an unpaid post as a ministers' helper. From there an MP could move up to a junior ministerial post, then a non-cabinet minister of state and finally into the cabinet.

4. Scrutiny and influence of the Executive

This section will be dealt with in greater detail later in this chapter. It is important to note here this is now considered the most critical role of the Commons, involving scrutinising, amending and possibly rejecting legislative proposals from the Executive, as well as harrying them in the Chamber in debates and through questioning ministers. The ultimate sanction for the Commons is to defeat government policy or legislation. A vote of 'no confidence' on a government or a rejection of a major piece of legislation, constitutionally at least, should lead to the resignation of the government and thus a general election. This, however, only happened on three occasions in the 20th century – 1924, 1929, and 1979. In each case, it was a minority Labour Administration. Much more common since the 1970s have been defeats of minor legislative measures. When this occurs, it is normally a consequence of the government losing the support of its backbenchers. Throughout the 1980s and 1990s, and again during the latter days of the Blair Government, this seemed to happen much more frequently, suggesting MPs were becoming far more rebellious. This has continued under the Coalition Government.

5. Miscellaneous

On top of all the formal parts of MPs work, there are a number of other areas that may or may not take up much time. There are various meetings with pressure groups, constituency party activists or the media; correspondence must be dealt with; speaking engagements; and possibly even holding down another job, for example as a journalist.

This all highlights the problem of identifying the work of an MP. Tony Wright wrote an article entitled "What are MPs for?" He noted that as an MP, "I found a job without any job description at all, no means of knowing what I should be doing, and with no means of assessing how well I was doing it" (Wright, 2010, p. 299). With such a degree of flexibility, it is hardly surprising to see so many MPs taking up so many other miscellaneous roles.

Scrutiny of the Executive

As stated above, scrutiny of the Executive is now probably the key role for the Commons. The pressures on scrutiny continue to grow, but the resources to do so have not. The role of scrutiny goes far beyond looking at legislation, and is not always carried out through voting in the House. It may be the most newsworthy – especially if it leads to the defeat of the government – but there are a range of other options.

1. *Question Time*
2. *Debates/Speaking in the House*
3. *Select Committees*
4. *Public Bill Committees*
5. *Opposition*

Each of these will be evaluated, highlighting their respective strengths and weaknesses. This section then leads on to the question of reform for the House of Commons.

1. Question Time

This is a distinctive feature of British constitutional procedures. Ministers and the Prime Minister must face the legislature and be held to account for policies and actions. Prime Minister's Question Time is perceived as the highlight of each Parliamentary week. Prior to 1997, the PM would face oral questions from the House on Tuesdays and Thursdays from 3:15-3:30pm. Tony Blair unilaterally changed the format to Wednesdays from 3:00-3:30pm. For this he was heavily criticised, with suggestions he was trying to avoid the House and thus his accountability to it. The session was later pushed back to 12noon on a Wednesday, enabling reports from Prime Minister's Question Time to be seen and heard on the lunch time news.

The PM is obliged to answer questions on a variety of topics from MPs and especially the Leader of the Opposition who has two opportunities to ask a series of questions. The whole process is broadcast live on television and radio and highlights the apparent strengths and weaknesses of this form of scrutiny.

On the surface, Question Time portrays a packed House with MPs grilling the PM – British democracy at work. The purpose is for opposition MPs to attempt to embarrass the government, to elicit information and to boost the morale of their party. Yet there is also a much harsher, more cynical interpretation. The PM, or for that matter any government minister at their own question time, while obligated to provide a response to each question, does not actually have to answer the question. A long-winded response can enable the PM to avoid answering tricky questions. On top of this, half of the questions are asked by government backbenchers. Many of these questions are a sycophantic waste of time, in particular when government MPs ask 'planted' questions designed to enhance the reputation of the government.

In judging the value of Question Time the wider context should always be kept in mind. Despite time wasting, tedious point scoring and quite often general unruliness in the Chamber, it should be noted Question Time is the one occasion where the Executive has to face MPs in a direct confrontation and account for its policies and actions. Ministerial careers can be made or broken at the Dispatch Box. There is clearly a need for an improvement to the procedures, or at least the elimination of the abuses.

2. Debates/Speaking in the House

Apart from participating in the debates on legislation in the House, there are also other opportunities for MPs to raise their own issues or concerns.

Adjournment Debates are a way in which influence and scrutiny of the Executive may be carried out. These normally occur at the end of normal business, and enable MPs to pursue a subject unsatisfactorily dealt with at Question Time, or to raise particular issues, grievances or matters of concern to their constituents (see Table 9.3). MPs gain the right to speak by 'winning' a ballot held every fortnight, but on one day each week the Speaker chooses the subject for debate from a list submitted by MPs. The government will have a ministerial representative, usually a junior minister, to respond to the speech of the backbencher concerned. It is also open to an MP to move the immediate adjournment of the House to 'discuss a specific and important matter that should have urgent consideration'. It is up to the Speaker to allow the debate, or not.

Table 9.3 Adjournment Debate Subjects

Date	MP	Subject
18/01/13	Sir Tony Baldry	Planning Guidance
21/01/13	John Mann	East Midlands Ambulance Service
22/01/13	Daniel Kawczynski	UK Trade and Investment
23/01/13	Hazel Blears	Access to Postgraduate study
24/01/13	Sir Alan Beith	Freedom of Information
25/01/13	Liam Byrne	High Speed 2

Attendance at Adjournment Debates is often woefully thin and their impact on government policy negligible but they do act as a safety valve for many MPs who have failed to gain satisfaction from ministers through other means. A wide range of topics will be covered (as can be seen in Table 9.3), and a good performance from an MP may go some way towards enhancing his/her reputation, possibly even resulting in promotion. In the end, adjournment debates are another device by which backbenchers may confront the Executive and influence the timetable of the House.

Adjournment Debates are held both on the floor of the House and at Westminster Hall. This has enabled more MPs to raise issues of concern. With only half an hour set aside for such debates, there may be a feeling they are rather pointless.

Emergency Debates can be requested by MPs but it is up to the Speaker to grant them. The normal business of the House is suspended for such debates to occur. These debates can cover a wide range of issues, and as their name suggests are supposed to be debated at the earliest opportunity. Opposition MPs in particular constantly request such debates as a means of embarrassing the government but the Speaker rejects more requests than are granted. Between 1979 and 1997 only 13 Emergency Debates took place. Only three took place between 1997 and 2010, and there have been four between 2010 and 2013 – on phone hacking, the European Union, the Health and Social Care bill, and the Royal Charter on press conduct.

Early Day Motions (EDMs) are motions given by MPs that are not generally expected to be debated. An EDM draws attention to a particular issue. MPs who put forward such motions also try to persuade colleagues to support the motion by adding their signatures to it. These motions often attract publicity and can be used to gauge levels of opinion with regard to a given issue.

3. *Select Committees*

This form of scrutiny takes place outside the chamber of the House of Commons. These committees can interrogate ministers, civil servants and even members of the public, and can call for any papers or documents. They are often viewed as being far more effective than questioning ministers on the floor of the House.

Select committees usually comprise between eleven and fourteen backbench MPs, with an in-built government majority. The chairs of the committees are shared across the parties (see Table 9.4). They are all prominent backbench MPs, with the exception of the chair of the Modernisation Committee, which is held by the Leader of the House of Commons (a cabinet member). The chairpersons of the select committees normally stay in post for two terms of Parliament. Half of the committees 'shadow' a specific government department. Consequently they are often known as Departmental Select Committees. Their specific remit is to examine the expenditure, administration and policies of their respective departments (as is detailed in Table 9.5). There are also other "cross-cutting" committees, which look at issues that cut across departmental lines, as can be seen in Table 9.4.

Table 9.4 Select Committees and their Chairs (February 2014)

Type of Select Committee	Title of Select Committee (Number of Members)	Chair of Select Committee
Departmental	Business, Innovation and Skills (11)	Adrian Bailey (Lab)
	Communities and Local Government (11)	Clive Betts (Lab)
	Culture, Media and Sport (11)	John Whittingdale (Con)
	Defence (12)	James Arbuthnott (Con)
	Education (11)	Graham Stuart (Con)
	Energy and Climate Change (11)	Tim Yeo (Con)
	Environment, Food and Rural Affairs (11)	Anne McIntosh (Con)
	Foreign Affairs (11)	Sir Richard Ottaway (Con)
	Health (11)	Stephen Dorrell (Con)
	Home Affairs (11)	Keith Vaz (Lab)
	International Development (11)	Malcolm Bruce (Lib Dem)
	Justice (12)	Sir Alan Beith (Lib Dem)
	Northern Ireland Affairs (14)	Laurence Robertson (Con)
	Scottish Affairs (10)	Ian Davidson (Lab)
	Transport (11)	Louise Ellman (Lab)
	Treasury (13)	Andrew Tyrie (Con)
	Welsh Affairs (12)	David T. C. Davies (Con)
	Work and Pensions (11)	Dame Anne Begg (Lab)
Scrutiny	European (16)	William Cash (Con)
	Political and Constitutional Reform (11)	Graham Allen (Lab)
	Statutory Instruments (7)	David Tredinnick (Con)

Joint (Membership is from both Houses)	Human Rights (12) Security (12) Statutory Instruments (12)	Dr Hywel Francis (Lab) John Randall (Con) George Mudie (Lab)
Domestic (Management of the House)	Administration (16) Backbench Business (8) Finance and Services (11) Members Expenses (8) Procedure (12)	Sir Alan Haselhurst (Con) Natasha Engel (Lab) John Thurso (Lib Dem) Adam Afriyie (Con) Charles Walker (Con)
External Matters	Environmental Audit (16) Public Accounts (14) Public Administration (11)	Joan Walley (Lab) Margaret Hodge (Lab) Bernard Jenkin (Con)
Others	Backbench Business (8) Liaison (Heads of most Select Committees) (33) Privileges (10) Regulatory Reform (14) Science and Technology (11) Selection (9) Standards (10)	Natascha Engel (Lab) Sir Alan Beith (Lib Dem) Kevin Barron (Lab) James Duddridge (Con) Andrew Miller (Lab) Geoffrey Clifton-Brown (Con) Kevin Barron (Lab)

One of the strengths of the select committee system is they can call for any person or papers. This enables the members to be more fully informed than possibly otherwise. When grilling ministers or civil servants, the members of the committees are able to repeat the questions until they get a satisfactory answer. Compare this with Question Time in the Commons where ministers can avoid answering difficult embarrassing questions.

Select committees may carry out detailed investigations on particular issues or concerns related to their department. Their core tasks are detailed in Table 9.5 – most of which applies to the Departmental Select Committees (as listed in Table 9.4). These were agreed by the Liaison Select Committee in 2002. At the conclusion of an investigation, the select committee will draw up a report which is published. Most of these reports will include recommendations for government action, some of which will be acted upon. There is no way in which select committees can compel the government to act upon their recommendations.

Table 9.5 Core Tasks for Select Committees

OBJECTIVE A: To examine and comment on the policy of the Department

Task 1 To examine policy proposals from the UK Government and the European Commission in Green Papers, White Papers, draft Guidance etc, and to inquire further where the Committee considers it appropriate.

Task 2 To identify and examine areas of emerging policy, or where existing policy is deficient, and make proposals.

Task 3 To conduct scrutiny of any published draft bill within the Committee's responsibilities.

Task 4 To examine specific output from the department expressed in documents or other decisions.

OBJECTIVE B: To examine the expenditure of the Department

Task 5 To examine the expenditure plans and out-turn of the department, its agencies and principal NDPBs.

OBJECTIVE C: To examine the administration of the Department

Task 6 To examine the department's Public Service Agreements, the associated targets and the statistical measurements employed, and report if appropriate.

Task 7 To monitor the work of the department's Executive Agencies, NDPBs, regulators and other associated public bodies.

Task 8 To scrutinise major appointments made by the department.

Task 9 To examine the implementation of legislation and major policy initiatives.

OBJECTIVE D: To assist the House in debate and decision

Task 10 To produce reports which are suitable for debate in the House, including Westminster Hall, or debating committees.

Developed from www.parliament.uk/commons/lib/research/notes/snpc-03161.pdf

An obvious weakness of the select committee system is the in-built government majority. While the chairs of most select committees are elected by the House of Commons, appointments to these committees is not so open. The party whips can be very influential. Consequently there may be "tame" membership on some committees, with members not willing to rock the boat of government too much. There is also the suggestion select committees are taking the focus of scrutiny and influence of the Executive away from the floor of the House, and thus undermining the role of MPs in the Commons.

4. Public Bill Committees

Public Bill Committees are sometimes known as General Committees. Prior to the 2006/2007 Parliamentary session, they were known as Standing Committees. As pointed out in Table 9.2, Public Bill Committees are cross-party committees which work on the specific details of legislation after the Second Reading in the Commons. Each public bill committee is named after the relevant bill e.g. the Counter-Terrorism Bill Committee. Public Bill Committees usually comprise between 16 and 50 members, and, as with select committees, there is an in-built government majority. Since the reforms of 2006/2007, public bill committees, like select committees, can take written and oral evidence from the public. The idea is to enable the committee to make a more fully informed evaluation of the proposed legislation.

The theory is in a cross-party atmosphere, public bill committees can examine legislation in detail and amend and improve it where appropriate, away from the party pressures that exist within the House itself. Under the old Standing Committee system, however, with party whips and ministers and shadow ministers keeping an eye on proceedings, such an ideal was undermined. If the government really wished, they could railroad any legislation through the committee stage. In such a case, without any amendments, there would be no report stage in the legislative process. As a result of the 2006/2007 reforms, "the scrutiny that these committees now provide can not only be described as informed and engaging, but also as effective" (Levy, 2010, p. 534). There remains, however, an in-built government majority, and the presence of the party whips.

5. The role of the Opposition

The concept of an official Opposition is peculiar to Westminster-style systems in the sense the largest losing party at a general election is given that title and a number of concessions, which may be denied to smaller parties, in order to make the Government more accountable, for example:

> *i.* 29 Opposition days when the Opposition has the sole right to choose the subject of debate.
>
> *ii.* The Opposition Leader is given priority over other backbenchers and Opposition frontbenchers, to speak in debates, to ask two sets of questions at Question Time, to be consulted on certain bi-partisan matters, etc.

Like other critical devices, the effectiveness of the Opposition's function is seriously blunted because of the numerical supremacy of the governing party, the Government's control of the civil service and its extensive power of patronage – even when there is a coalition government. It has always been a matter of contention whether an Opposition should always oppose on the grounds it represents citizens who did not vote for the Government, or act 'responsibly' and as an alternative government when it does agree with Government policy. What was particularly interesting is during the Blair Government years, on three occasions legislation was passed where many Labour MPs voted against the proposals, but the Opposition voted in favour and thus enabled the legislation to be passed e.g. the vote in 2007 to update the Trident missile system saw 90 Labour MPs vote against a three-line party whip, but the legislation cleared the Commons due to the support from David Cameron and the Conservative Party.

Reform of the Commons

What can be clearly seen in this chapter is an elected House dominated by political parties and by the Government. Reform of this chamber is desperately needed. Over the latter part of the 20th century and into the 21st, some reforms were carried out. The Blair and Brown Governments continued in this piecemeal format. David Cameron and Nick Clegg promised a radical overhaul of Parliament, but have not delivered. Cameron wanted to overhaul the Commons, including reducing the number of MPs to 600. Clegg wanted to overhaul the House of Lords. Yet the coalition partners failed to support each others proposals and the reforms stalled. The rest of this chapter is going to examine some of the reforms and highlight others that may be desirable.

1. Standards in Public Life

The Committee on Standards in Public Life was set up in October 1994 under the Chairmanship of Lord Nolan (and has been chaired by Lord Bew since January 2013). As the title of the committee suggests, it was set up to examine concerns about standards of conduct in public office (not just MPs). The Prime Minister at the time, John Major, had been concerned about the misconduct and unethical behaviour of a number of politicians. This was encompassed under the broad label of "sleaze". There were allegations of MPs taking vast sums of money for asking questions in Parliament. Most prominent among these was the then-MP for Tatton, Neil Hamilton.

As a consequence of these investigations, the House of Commons came up with a new set of rules on the behaviour of its members:

- Paid advocacy should not be allowed. In other words, MPs should not be paid for speaking on behalf of an interest, asking questions on behalf of an interest, or arranging or participating in meetings with ministers on behalf of an interest.
- A post entitled Parliamentary Commissioner for Standards (held by Kathryn Hudson since January 2013) was created, with the appointment on a fixed five year term. The post holder could advise MPs on their conduct, investigate complaints, and keep the Register of Members' Interests up to date.
- A new select committee was established – the Committee on Standards and Privileges (which has since been separated into two committees, see Table

9.4) – with a number of functions, including overseeing the work of the Parliamentary Commissioner for Standards.

The effectiveness of this committee was brought into question over the MP's expenses scandal. While much of the scandal was actually beyond the remit of the Committee of Standards in Public Life, a clear code of conduct for MPs has had to be established. This applies to all MPs in all facets of their public lives – their private lives are exempt. The general principles, as described by the Committee of Standards in Public Life, form the basis for much of the code (see www.publications.parliament.uk/pa/cm200809/cmcode/735/73502.htm#a1 for the full text of MPs code of conduct).

2. Hours of Sitting

This aspect of reform of the House of Commons has caused much discussion both within and outside the House. The real issue is over when the House should rise. Traditionally, there has been the possibility of all-night sittings in the Commons and this has been a feature with contentious legislation. In a move to make the hours of sitting more 'family friendly', a decision was taken in July 2000 to stop proceedings at 10:30pm. The hours of sitting have been changed since then as well. As of October 2012, the Commons sits as follows:

Monday 2:30pm – 10:00pm
Tuesday 11:30am – 7:00pm
Wednesday 11:30am – 7:00pm
Thursday 9:30am – 5:00pm
Friday 9:30am – 2:30pm

Since 30 November 1999, however, the Commons has also convened in Westminster Hall. These sittings are a little more restricted and are for specific functions – such as adjournment debates. Currently, the House sits in Westminster Hall on Mondays (4:30-7:30pm), Tuesdays and Wednesdays (9:30-11:30am and 2:30-5:00pm) and Thursdays (1:30-4:40pm).

3. Office support

Office support for MPs has always been contentious. For the year from April 2013 MPs were paid £66 396. There is a further Staffing Allowance which can cover secretarial support, general office expenses, employment of research assistants, etc. All of this must be documented. Office space itself is also at a premium, with many MPs no longer having offices in the Parliament buildings – although those in Portcullis House are far more luxurious.

There has been abuse of the staffing allowances for MPs. Over the past few years it has come to light that many MPs have paid their spouses or their children for providing office support. In one case, Derek Conway paid his sons as office staff while they were studying at university. One son was studying in Newcastle while apparently working in London. The consequence of the Conway case was for all MPs to declare if their spouses were employed in any capacity, and the remuneration.

This, it later transpired, was merely the tip of the iceberg of abuse of the expenses system. Many MPs, quite often legally, claimed whatever expenses they could. One MP claimed for the cleaning of his moat, while others claimed the employment of cleaners, the refurbishment of their homes, etc. As a result, many MPs had to repay their expenses, while some MPs were charged and found guilty of fraud. Consequently, the public perception of MPs diminished even further

5. Procedures

There has already been some tinkering with the procedures in the Commons, most notably the changes in Prime Ministers Question Time. This superficial change was imposed without debate. Yet this tinkering has done very little to make features of parliamentary scrutiny more effective. A radical overhaul is needed to ensure that this role is carried out thoroughly.

During the Blair years, it sometimes appeared as if ministers could not be bothered with Parliament. Attendance by Blair was the worst for a sitting PM. Added to this, former Speaker of the House, Betty Boothroyd, complained of ministers making statements on the Today Programme on Radio 4, announcing government policy to the media prior to announcing it to Parliament. She condemned such action as it undermined the role of Parliament.

One procedural change that could be introduced is the automatic timetabling of legislation. Currently, very little of the legislation that passes through Parliament has a fixed timetable slot. An obvious example of automatic timetabling of legislation is the budget. This could be broadened out to include much more legislation. Critics of such an idea point to the way in which adequate scrutiny of any legislation could be reduced as a consequence of automatic timetabling of legislation. The suggestion is it could lead to greater Executive dominance within both the legislative process and within the running of Parliament in general.

Other procedural changes, such as electronic voting, appear not to be feasible. The Scottish Parliament uses such a system. For Westminster, the problem is that it is impossible to sit all 650 MPs in the chamber – and this is prior to giving the MPs the facilities with which to utilise electronic voting. As a result, the conventional way of moving through the 'Aye' or 'No' lobbies persists.

Where steps have been taken is over e-petitioning. The Select Committee on Procedures has published a report on e-petitioning. While the 10 Downing Street website has such a facility, the Procedure Committee has suggested Parliament is the more appropriate place for such petitioning, and there should be an obligation for Parliament to respond, if not to debate such issues.

6. Electoral Reform

The issue of electoral reform will be discussed in chapter 20. It is important to note here the issue is not new in debates on reforming the Commons. In fact, the issue was discussed in great depth in the early 20th century, in particular during the inter-war period. In more recent times, the Jenkins Committee had the potential to highlight this issue but did not really succeed. The current coalition government held a referendum on changing the electoral system to the Alternative Vote in May 2011. This was defeated comprehensively.

7. European Union

The EU has an ever-growing role in British politics. This will be discussed in chapter 31, but there are a few key points worth noting here on the relationship between Parliament and the EU. As already mentioned earlier, if there is legislative conflict, EU law takes precedence over national law. All EU legislation is supposed to be scrutinised by Parliament prior to going on to the Statute Books. As there is quite often a backlog of legislation, however, the so-called scrutiny has been known to take place after the law has been imposed. The Select Committee on Europe has an important role here in reporting on the legal and political importance of each EU document (see Jones, 2007a). In 1995 this committee highlighted the problem of proposed laws emanating from Europe having to be considered without there being a formal text of the laws available for scrutiny.

8. Fixed Term Parliaments

This proposal was part of the reform package introduced by the coalition government. Rather than permitting the government to choose when a general election will be held, the time should be fixed. Thus the next general election is set for 7 May 2015. Fixed term parliaments can prevent the government building up the economy prior to calling an election, or calling snap elections. The down side of this idea is the government may simply attempt to build their economic policies around the electoral cycle.

Conclusion

Despite the immense wealth of material there is no general consensus amongst practising politicians, academics, or journalists as to how effectively Parliament, and particularly the House of Commons, fulfils its tasks. In fact, there is no consensus as to which tasks should take priority. Different degrees of emphasis are placed on the various functions, such as representation, legislation, constituency work, redress of grievances, and scrutiny. If any, it is probably scrutiny of the Executive that dominates. Yet, in the event of a governing party with a healthy working majority, in conjunction with strict party discipline, the Executive is clearly in a position to be able to dominate Parliament. The majority party sustains its government while the minority parties do whatever they can to oppose the government's policies, dent its majority, and even try to bring down the government.

During the Major Government, particularly 1992-1997, there were many calls for a return to strong executive government. It was suggested in many quarters, especially in the media, that Major was a weak prime minister and that he should be replaced with a stronger individual. In other words, come back Margaret Thatcher, all is forgiven. No one ever asks if Thatcher could have survived as prime minister for five years with a Parliamentary majority that started at 21 and shrank to nothing.

Conversely, during the Blair years 1997-2007, there were loud cries from the very same sections of society that the Executive was too dominant, that the prime minister was interfering too much, that there was a 'presidential' prime minister, and that power should be returned to Parliament. A strong Executive has clearly become an embedded element in modern British Parliamentary democracy, but there is also the suggestion that it must not be too strong. It is up to Parliament to rein in the Executive.

Selected bibliography

Cairney, Paul. (2007). "The Professionalisation of MPs: Refining the 'Politics-Facilitating' Explanation", *Parliamentary Affairs* vol. 60-2, pp.212-233.

Flinders, Matthew. (2007). "Analysing Reform: The House of Commons, 2001-5", *Political Studies* vol. 55-1, pp. 174-200.

Judge, David. (2004). "Whatever Happened to Parliamentary Democracy in the United Kingdom?", *Parliamentary Affairs* vol. 57-3, pp. 682-701.

Kelso, Alexandra. (2007a). "The House of Commons Modernisation Committee: Who Needs It?", *British Journal of Politics and International Relations* vol. 9-1, pp. 138-157.

Russell, Meg. (2011). "'Never Allow a Crisis Go To Waste': The Wright Committee Reforms to Strengthen the House of Commons", *Parliamentary Affairs* vol. 64-4, pp. 612-633.

Whitaker, Richard. (2006). "Backbench Influence on Government Legislation? A Flexing of Parliamentary Muscles at Westminster", *Parliamentary Affairs* vol. 59-2, pp. 350-359.

Wright, Tony. (2010). "What are MPs for?", *Political Quarterly* vol. 81-3, pp. 298-308.

Websites

epetitions.direct.gov.uk/
E-petitions are run by the government rather than Parliament. This is the website for current petitions.

www.parliament.uk
The starting point for any investigation into Parliament. From here you can go to the House of Commons, select committees, or any other part of Parliament.

www.parliament.uk/site-information/glossary/select-committees/
This site details the core tasks of select committees.

www.publications.parliament.uk/pa/cm200708/cmselect/cmproced/136/136.pdf
Report of the House of Commons Procedure Committee; e-petitions 19 March 2008.

Questions

1. "Parliament's role is to legitimise the government of the day rather than to legislate." Discuss.
2. What is the function of Question Time in the House of Commons? How successful is it?
3. "MPs are little more than lobby-fodder. They toe their party line unquestioningly." Evaluate the accuracy of such a claim.
4. What are the most effective forms of scrutiny performed by the House of Commons? Why are they so effective?

CHAPTER 10 // THE HOUSE OF LORDS

Contents

Introduction

Until recently, the composition of this House was a mixture of hereditary peers, bishops, life peers and law lords. None of these groups were elected but they had the constitutional right to amend and delay government legislation. They could also introduce bills and, in a particular constitutional crisis, veto the attempt of a government to extend its parliamentary life. They appeared to be no line of accountability for any of their actions. Unsurprisingly, there was a lengthy list of critics who wanted to restructure or even abolish this chamber. Yet the House of Lords continues. It is only in recent times there has been significant attempts at restructuring. The future of the House of Lords has been assured; the question is in what form?

Before examining the House of Lords in greater detail, a point needs to be made about the structure of Parliament. The UK has a bicameral parliament. This means it has two chambers. New Zealand, on the other hand, has a unicameral parliament i.e. only one chamber. Questions have been raised over the extent to which the UK has a fully bicameral structure. The reason for this, as will be seen in this chapter, is the weakness of the House of Lords. Consequently, the UK Parliament is sometimes cited as an example of *weak bicameralism*. Parkinson (2007) has suggested as the House of Lords is so subordinate to the Commons, Britain does not have a truly bicameral Parliament but rather a split unicameral Parliament.

This then raises a rather interesting question, as Russell (2001) asks: "What are Second Chambers for?" There can be seen to be four key roles:

i.   Representation
ii.   Scrutiny of the Executive
iii. Checks and Balances
iv.   Performing different parliamentary duties

With regard to representation, a second chamber will represent different interests to those in the first chamber. This is regardless as to whether or not the second chamber is elected. The Scrutiny of the Executive role is about the second chamber being less under the control of the Executive than the first chamber and can bring different perspectives to legislative proposals. Even where a second chamber has limited powers, it is possible to raise issues and concerns. This links in with the third point of Checks and Balances. It is possible for the second chamber to re-evaluate legislative proposals, and possibly even delay them.

The final point is one that is often neglected. The second chamber enables the work of Parliament to be shared across both chambers. This is not just about ministerial appointments, but also quite probably the scrutiny of legislation, the introduction of legislation, and holding other bodies (such as the European Union) to account for their actions. Across all four roles, issues may arise as to the effectiveness of the second chamber. Regardless, all second chambers perform these roles.

Background and Development

The origins and development of the House of Lords can be traced to the Norman era when it was the practice of the monarch to consult collectively with the nobility. By the 16th century a separate institution had developed whose membership was confined to those with a hereditary peerage.

When the franchise was extended by the 1832 Reform Act (known as the Great Reform Act), the House of Commons acquired a greater constitutional validity than the House of Lords. The latter was not prepared to surrender power easily; throughout the 19th century the Lords asserted itself by periodically rejecting bills coming from the Commons, e.g. in 1872 on the Secret Ballot and Home Rule for Ireland in 1886. The Lords' justification was such measures had not been put to the people in previous elections and hence the Government did not have a mandate for implementing them.

The tension between the two Houses reached a climax in 1909 when Lloyd George's 'Peoples' Budget' was rejected by the Lords. A grave constitutional crisis was averted when the Lords reluctantly gave way after two general elections in 1910 returned the Liberals to power, pledged to force through Lloyd George's measures. It was the threat to flood the Lords with sufficient new peers to give the Liberals a majority in the upper chamber which ensured the final victory of the Commons. The result was the 1911 Parliament Act. The House of Lords power to delay bills from the Commons was limited to two years and their right to delay finance bills to one month (in reality there is automatic passage of a money bill through the Lords). In 1949 the delaying power was reduced from two years to one year, under the Parliament Act (1949) – although this was passed using the 1911 legislation.

In 1958, the **Life Peerages Act** was introduced. This meant that:
1. The Crown was given the power to appoint peers, including women, for life. There was no limit set on numbers.
2. Peers were to be paid an attendance allowance.

3. Every peer must declare at the beginning of a session whether he/she intended to take up his/her seat in the House. This precaution was taken to lessen the power of the 'backwoodsmen' (peers who only attend to defeat a particular bill from the Commons).

The significance of the Life Peerages Act was quite profound for the composition and political future of the Lords. A large number of former Labour MPs and Labour appointees entered the House. This went some way towards redressing the imbalance that existed at that time between Conservative and Labour peers.

A number of eminent people from various sectors of the community – the professions, the City, education, the arts, and trade unions – were admitted to the House. Many of these were people who would not normally have concerned themselves with political life but were given the opportunity to participate in the legislative process.

The 1963 **Peerages Act** was the result of the campaign by Anthony Wedgwood-Benn (Tony Benn) to renounce his inherited title of Lord Stansgate. The Act allows peers to surrender their titles but not to disqualify their heirs from succeeding to the peerage. Since the Act was passed, the most notable peers to give up their titles have been Lord Hailsham and Lord Home, both of whom did so to enter the contest for the premiership after the resignation of Harold Macmillan. Lord Home became Prime Minister as Sir Alec Douglas-Home and Lord Hailsham reverted to his original name, Quentin Hogg. Both men later re-entered the House of Lords as life peers. The point of the Peerages Act was to prevent the destruction of the political careers of ambitious politicians like Tony Benn and to allow existing peers to enter the political arena in a way not possible from the Lords.

During the Thatcher years, the House of Lords enjoyed something of a revival. With the Thatcher government enjoying huge majorities in the Commons after the 1983 and 1987 elections, it was the House of Lords that actually tried to stand up to the "elective dictatorship" in the Commons. It was under Thatcher that there was the first use of the 1949 Parliament Act to force legislation through the House of Lords (War Crimes Bill). Throughout the 1980s, there were well over a hundred defeats inflicted on the government. These included government attempts to charge local authorities for school transport, and to include council houses especially built for the elderly as part of the sale of these houses. This belligerent mood of the Lords against the Thatcher government mellowed to some extent when Major replaced Thatcher in 1990.

Despite having problems with the House of Lords, neither Thatcher nor Major sought its reform. The Blair Government, on the other hand, sought to reform the House of Lords, but not its abolition. Legislation included the **House of Lords Act (1999)**, which removed hereditary peers from the Lords, leaving an appointed House with a residue of 92 hereditary peers as an interim measure.

The Wakeham Commission was set up to examine the future of the chamber, the findings of which are examined later in this chapter.

Reform of the House of Lords

In the 1997 Labour manifesto there was a clear commitment to reform the House of Lords. Previous Labour manifestos had called for the abolition of the Lords. The idea of reform suggested a far more gradual approach, without necessarily including outright abolition. This is indeed what has happened.

In February 1999 a **Royal Commission on the Reform of the House of Lords** was established, chaired by Lord Wakeham. The Commission had twelve members and very clear terms of reference. The House of Commons was to remain the pre-eminent chamber. The role and function of the second chamber was to be examined, along with possible methods of composition. The Commission was given nine months to issue a consultation paper, hold public meetings around the country, read written submissions, question selected witnesses, and then write the report. This report, entitled "A House for the Future", was published in January 2000.

The Wakeham Commission described its proposals as "radical evolution" but was largely condemned in the press with headlines such as "The empty chamber" (Polly Toynbee) and "No more than a House of corrupted legitimacy" (Hugo Young). The key points of the report are listed in Table 10.1.

Table 10.1 Proposals from the Wakeham Report

• Second Chamber to contain around 550 members
• An Independent Commission to select most members
• Some members (either 65, 87 or 195) to be elected on a regional basis
• Composition of chamber to be regularly adjusted to reflect voting patterns
• Targets to reflect the UK's population by gender, ethnicity and religious denomination
• Link between Honours list and membership of the Chamber to be dropped
• Powers of the Chamber to be no less than those currently wielded by the Lords

What made the issue more complicated was the proposals were presented as the first step in an ongoing reform process. This has left the House in a transitory state, as the reform process has since stalled.

Unsurprisingly, the Wakeham Commission's proposals came under much criticism. The number of elected members was castigated in some quarters as being far too small. This was exacerbated with members being elected or appointed for a single 15-year term. The time span may actually leave many members as being unrepresentative of their region. Added to this, the length of term may make it very difficult to change the composition of the chamber to reflect voting patterns. It will also be difficult for the chamber to be representative of the political balance of the country while keeping the total number of members at 550. Current life peers were allowed to remain in office, even though they already exceeded the total number recommended in the chamber. Further, the issue of the number of elected peers appeared as a stumbling block, with some critics demanding a wholly elected chamber. This is examined further later in the chapter.

Targets to reflect the UK's population by gender, ethnicity and religious denomination have also been heavily criticised. The religious representation was denounced by the National Secular Society who pointed out the religious representation was being increased in the Wakeham recommendations while the population as a whole appeared to be abandoning religion. It is important to note, however, that religious diversification in the new chamber is a great step forward in attempting to achieve a more balanced representation of the population. The concern is really over which faiths gain representation of the 26 seats available for the Christian denominations, and the 5 seats available for non-Christian faiths.

A key recommendation of the Wakeham report was the statutory duty to ensure at least 30% of members in the new chamber be women and at least 30% men. Organisations such as Fawcett had previously argued this should be a statutory duty. Although women comprise a majority of the population, and 30% is still therefore hugely under-representative, it appeared to be a step in the right direction in attempting to make this chamber more representative of society with respect to gender. How this will gel with regard to the elected element of the House remains unclear.

Another important part of the Wakeham Report was the proposal to set up an independent commission to select most of the non-elected members. The **House of Lords Appointments Commission** was established in May 2000. All nominations to the House of Lords – partisan and non-partisan – are vetted by the Commission. One of the major concerns for the Commission has been the nominations for appointment which are linked to party funding. The Commission's rule of thumb appears to be that giving money to a political party, either in the form of a donation or a loan, is insufficient on its own to warrant a peerage. With that type of issue swirling around, the Commission has also to ensure that targets for representation by gender and ethnicity are achieved, and some balance in representation by religious denomination.

Membership of the Appointments Commission is unelected. Three members are partisan appointments – one from each of the three major parties. The remaining five positions, including the chairperson of the Commission (in 2013 this was Lord Ajay Kakkar), are made after an open recruitment competition, with all of these appointments being vetted by the Commissioner for Public Appointments (see chapter 14). The Commission is formally independent of the government, although a government department – the Cabinet Office, sponsors it. Staff for the Commission are civil servants, most of whom also come from the Cabinet Office.

Membership of the House of Lords

Trying to get agreement on the membership of the House of Lords has proved to be hugely problematic. Although the Wakeham Commission proposed three alternatives with regard to the proportion of elected members, little progress has been made.

In February 2003, the House of Commons voted on seven alternatives (a wholly appointed chamber, 20% elected, 40%, 50%, 60%, 80% and a wholly elected chamber), as well as on abolishing the House of Lords. Tony Blair's preferred option was wholly appointed, while the Conservative Party supported 80% elected. Each alternative was defeated in the Commons. This left the status quo in place – a largely appointed chamber – and Tony Blair kicked the issue into the long grass.

The issue of membership was revisited in March 2007. On this occasion, the House of Commons voted for both a wholly elected chamber and 80% elected. Blair's position had moved to support of a 50% elected chamber, while the new Conservative Party leader, David Cameron, voted against a wholly elected chamber. The House of Lords, unsurprisingly, voted for a wholly appointed chamber – all of the other alternatives were defeated. Yet again, this left the membership of the House of Lords unchanged.

Nick Clegg, as Deputy Prime Minister, tried to revisit the idea of making the House of Lords wholly elected. According to the Bishop of Leicester, Clegg appeared "driven" to make the chamber democratically accountable. In August 2012, Clegg dropped the plans, even though it had been written into the Coalition Agreement, blaming both the Conservatives and Labour over political opportunism. At the same time, he declared plans to revisit making the House of Lords wholly elected after the 2015 general election.

There are two ways of examining the current membership of the House of Lords – by party strength and by type of peerage (as can be seen in Tables 10.2 and 10.3). Prior to the Blair Government coming to power in 1997, the Conservative Party had dominated the House of Lords. By 2005, there were more Labour peers than Conservative peers, but nowhere near a majority, and the position has since changed. Included under 'Other' is the Lord Speaker of the House, Baroness D'Souza. Her predecessor, Baroness Hayman, was the first Speaker of the House who had not held the post of Lord Chancellor. Under the Constitutional Reform Act (2005), the role of the Speaker was removed from the post of Lord Chancellor.

Table 10.2 Membership of the House of Lords by Party (February 2013)

Conservative	220
Labour	220
Liberal Democrat	99
Crossbench	180
Bishop	26
Non-affiliated	19
Other	15
Peers on leave of absence/excluded	56
Total	835

Source: www.parliament.uk/mps-lords-and-offices/lords/composition-of-the-lords/

Table 10.3 Membership of the House of Lords by Type (February 2013)

Archbishops and Bishops	26
Life peers	666
Peers under the House of Lords Act (1999)	87
Peers on leave of absence/excluded	56
Total	835

Source: www.parliament.uk/mps-lords-and-offices/lords/composition-of-the-lords/

What is not clear in either table is where the People's Peers (or more accurately, the Non-Party Political Peers) sit. They sit as Crossbenchers. The idea of People's Peers was to enable members of the public to put their names forward to sit in the House of Lords. This, it was felt, might bring the House of Lords closer to the public. All such appointments need to be approved by the House of Lords Appointments Commission. When the People's Peers were first introduced, the first round of appointments was castigated for being more like 'the great and the good' rather than being average members of the public. Unattributed comments suggesting hairdressers and mechanics knew nothing about how to pass laws and should not therefore be eligible for membership as People's Peers, did nothing to enhance their reputation. Up to February 2013, 63 People's Peers have been nominated.

Many of these appointments still smack of the great and the good. Very few of the appointments would be considered as being in touch with everyday life for the average person in the UK. The possible exceptions here may be Nicola Chapman (who works with disabled and disadvantaged people), Kamlesh Patel (who is a government adviser on mental health, drugs and ethnicity) and Tanni Grey-Thompson (former-paralympic athlete, and patron of numerous charities).

Functions

The terms of reference for the Wakeham Commission were very clear. The House of Commons was to remain the pre-eminent chamber. Arguably, everything else could be reformed. As part of the radical evolution, the Wakeham Commission decided the powers of the new chamber were to remain largely unchanged. Thus, in the legislative process, as outlined in the previous chapter in Table 9.2, the powers of the reformed chamber remain the same. The actual functions of the House are detailed below.

1. Delaying Power

The power to delay Commons legislation for one year is easily the most controversial function the Lords can perform. The justification for such a function is that it will be used only for highly contentious pieces of legislation and hence used sparingly. In this sense the delaying power gets enmeshed with the doctrine of the mandate. If a bill is not part of a government's election manifesto, is highly controversial, has a tiny majority approved in the Commons and arouses public ire, then it is contended that the Lords should have the constitutional right to send back the bill for further consideration by the Commons. It is further argued the absence of a codified constitution, the presence of a strong Executive, and tightly whipped parties need a check other than that provided by the Opposition in the Commons.

Problems arose over the changes in the electoral system for the 1999 elections to the European Parliament. The Blair Government forced the adoption of a party list system through the Commons. This system was to be 'closed' which meant voters could only vote for a particular political party within their multi-member constituency. The Lords argued the lists should be 'open', which would allow for voters to cast their ballot for a specific individual candidate if they so wished. On seven occasions the Lords refused to accept the will of the Commons, and on the same number of occasions the Commons refused to accept the amendment proposed by the Lords. The then-Prime Minister, Tony Blair, argued the unelected Lords were attempting to usurp the powers of the democratically elected House of Commons. Members in the House of Lords argued voters had the right to be able to cast their ballot for a specific candidate rather than a party list, imposed by unelected party members upon a constituency. Not being able to do so was an affront to voters and broke away from the convention underpinning all electoral systems used in Britain – that voters elected a candidate to represent them. While this may seem a little hypocritical coming from an unelected chamber, there was much popular support for the Lords on this issue, although ultimately, the House of Lords was forced to back down.

Since the removal of most of the hereditary peers, critics expected the transitional chamber to be little more than a puppet of the Blair Government. Surprisingly, the chamber asserted itself. It has defeated the government on over

500 separate pieces of legislation since the removal of most of the hereditary peers, up to February 2014. In the 2002-03 Parliamentary session, the House of Lords defeated government legislation on 88 separate occasions. What has happened is the rump of the Lords has reasserted its status as a revising chamber, which will be explained below.

Where there is agreement for the House of Lords not to have a delaying power is over any legislative proposals that were in a governing party's election manifesto. Under the Salisbury Convention, if it was in the party manifesto, the Lords will not delay the legislation. This approach caused a problem after the 2005 General Election when the Labour Government passed legislation to ban hunting with dogs. This had not been in the 2005 election manifesto, but had been in the previous election manifestos. The House of Lords argued the Salisbury Convention did not apply, but the government resolved the problem by using the 1949 Parliament Act.

2. Revising Legislation

All bills must be passed by both Houses before they can become law. In the case of finance the Lords rarely debate – let alone alter – such legislation. For the other three quarters of bills, members of the Lords undertake a welter of revision. The House of Lords presents thousands of proposed legislative amendments each year, some of which are government-sponsored. If importance is measured by the amount of effort expended then it can safely be stated the revising function comes into this category, and the Wakeham reforms may well have enhanced this function still further.

The thorough, painstaking examination and revision of bills emanating from the Commons has undoubtedly relieved that House of much of its legislative burden. Amendments to bills can be moved either by the government ministers in the Lords or by other members of the Chamber. These government amendments may result from the flaws in the drafting of bills or because there was insufficient time to introduce the amendments when the bill was in the Commons. All members of the Lords have the right to introduce their own amendments but if the government or the Commons refuses to accept them they are generally withdrawn. The above example of the changes to the electoral system for European Parliamentary elections is very much the exception rather than the rule.

Without the constant close scrutiny the House of Lords devotes to the examination and revision of bills, the strain on the Commons under the present procedure would become intolerable. By relieving MPs from the arduous task of detailed scrutiny, the House of Lords allows the elected chamber to concentrate more on the political principles of legislation. In many ways the upper house is more fitted to the task of close examination since it has more time at its disposal, contains many members with experience of this kind of work, and the party battle is not so fierce, so a more 'objective' judgement can be brought to bear on legislative matters. With the removal of most of the hereditary peers, it is argued the partially reformed upper house is more legitimate than its predecessor, and is arguably more objective – especially with no party having an overall majority.

3.   Initiating Legislation

The Commons acquired almost by constitutional convention the right to introduce all important legislation. Non-controversial proposals, however, and those of a moral nature can be introduced by either House. The Lords can certainly introduce public bills but these tend to be of a technical nature, for example, on weights and measures, investment trusts, or land compensation. On private bills, the Lords share an equal burden with the Commons and in delegated legislation it has an equal power with the Commons.

It is in the sphere of legislation on moral themes particularly that the chamber has revealed its usefulness. Subjects like abortion, divorce and homosexuality have all been introduced in the Lords and more recently animal rights and environmental concerns have occupied the attention of the peers. This is not to suggest that the Lords support all matters in these areas – as the opposition to Section 28 (on whether or not homosexuality should be included as part of sex education) demonstrated – but rather that legislation can be developed in these areas in what is considered a less partisan atmosphere.

4.   Discussion – Deliberation

Part of the function of Parliament is to question, to debate and to hold the government to account. On most Wednesdays when the House is sitting, the Lords debates motions put forward by the opposition, cross-bench and government party backbench peers. In the ensuing debates, covering a vast array of subjects, the façade at least of governmental accountability is maintained. Since party discipline is quite lax and members are still not accountable to voters, speakers can debate freely and in a leisurely manner.

It is difficult to assess the value of these debates, even after the reforms initiated by the Wakeham Commission. Peers themselves are divided on their worth, although there is far greater enthusiasm – and some peers would argue legitimacy – in trying to hold the government to account. A great deal is made of the quality and degree of expertise displayed in the debates. At the same time it also has to be admitted that a great many speeches are boring and ill-informed; in any case it is dubious whether most speeches make much of an impact on the electorate despite the innovative mediums of television and now the internet. Some of the greatest fans of these debates are viewers of cable television in the United States, often demonstrating far greater interest than the British public.

Yet the Lords are attempting to reach out to the public, with the **Lords Digital Chamber**. The aim is to encourage interaction between members of the House of Lords and the public, via a range of social media tools. The Lords Digital Chamber was launched in 2014.

Future

The future role of the House of Lords is still unclear. Currently the overwhelming majority of members are appointed – although most of the 92 hereditary peers can at least claim to have been elected, even if it was by fellow members of their party groups in the Lords. All of the major political parties have come round to the idea of reforming the House, with some suggestions for a regionally based form of representation, similar to that of Germany. One thing is clear: the future of the House is guaranteed. Unlike in New Zealand, where an unelected Upper House was voted out of existence in 1950 with nothing to replace it, the House of Lords will remain. As things currently stand, a reformed House is going to be very similar to its predecessor. With similar powers, and even if elected, the House may end up being subservient to the government of the day. The positive aspects in attempting to gain representation for women, ethnic minorities and broadening the religious base are laudable, yet may be viewed as tokenism. They may also clash with any future electoral accountability.

Conclusion

What is most obvious about the House of Lords is both how little and how much it has changed as a consequence of the Wakeham Report. The radical evolution proposed by the Wakeham Commission has left all the old power structures in place. Effectively, the House of Lords is going to remain an unelected House in the short term. In the future, there may be the introduction of a nominal number of elected members. As to how many, and how and when they will be elected, has not yet been decided. Instead, there is currently an appointed chamber. Although the current chamber has stood up to the Government on a number of issues, they can still do no more than the unreformed predecessor could do. Issues and concerns may be highlighted but if the government of the day wish for legislation to be passed, it can indeed be forced through. The Wakeham proposals, although presented as being spectacular, radical, and a host of other adjectives, in reality changed very little.

Selected bibliography

Kelso, Alexandra. (2006). "Reforming the House of Lords: Navigating Representation, Democracy and Legitimacy at Westminster", *Parliamentary Affairs* vol. 59-4, pp. 563-581.

Parkinson, John. (2007). "The House of Lords: A Deliberative Democratic Defence", *Political Quarterly* vol. 78-3, pp. 374-381.

Russell, Meg. (2001). "What are Second Chambers for?", *Parliamentary Affairs* vol. 54-3, pp. 442-458.

Shell, Donald. (1992). *The House of Lords*: Harvester Wheatsheaf, 2nd edition.
Shell, Donald. (2004). "The Future of the Second Chamber", *Parliamentary Affairs* vol. 57-4, pp. 852-866.
Whitaker, Richard. (2005). "Ascendant Assemblies in Britain? Rebellions, Reforms and Inter-Cameral Conflict", *Parliamentary Affairs* vol. 59-1, pp. 173-180.

Websites
www.legislation.gov.uk/ukpga/1999/34/contents
The House of Lords Act, 1999

www.lordsappointments.gov.uk/
Home page of the House of Lords Appointments Commission

www.parliament.uk/business/lords/
The starting point for any investigation into the House of Lords

Questions

- "An undemocratic appendage to the Constitution." Is this still a justifiable comment on the House of Lords?
- What reforms could be imposed on the House of Lords? What would be their consequences?
- Why may a second chamber, in whatever form, be an essential part of government in the 21st century?
- What is the case for a wholly elected second chamber? What powers should such a chamber wield?

CHAPTER 11 // CABINET

Contents

The role of the Cabinet is a central issue in any study of British government and politics. Along with the Office of the Prime Minister, the Civil Service and the Departments of State, it forms the **Executive**. Students should pay particular attention to the changing developments in Cabinet structure and its significance, relative to the other arms of the Executive, the Legislature, and the political scene generally. A favourite topic of examiners is the alleged decline of Cabinet government and the rise of the Presidential Prime Minister. A coalition government, of course, throws that hypothesis on its head.

Introduction

Bagehot (1867) described the Cabinet as "a combining committee – a hyphen which joins, a buckle which fastens the legislative part of the State to the executive part of the State". This picturesque description gets to the heart of the nature of Cabinet government. The Cabinet is indeed a committee based on the convention of collective responsibility, exercising both executive and legislative functions (through its preparation of the legislative programme). The emphasis placed here by Bagehot has been reinforced by countless writers, highlighting the importance of the Cabinet in the constitutional and political institutions and climate of Britain.

Like so many British political institutions, the Cabinet has its origins in the medieval past where it acted as an advisory body to the monarch. As the authority of the monarch declined to be replaced by that of Parliament, ministers had to switch their allegiance to Parliament, and then, more specifically, to the House of Commons. In order to formulate their policies more effectively, secrecy (or at least confidentiality) became crucial; hence was born the doctrine of collective responsibility. The integral ties between the Cabinet and Parliament as a whole became conditional on the ever increasing element of party politics, not just in the 19th century but especially so in the 20th century. The majority party supplied the ministers for the cabinet with a vested interest in ensuring government policies were implemented effectively. Control of Parliament, therefore, became almost essential. Without this control, Cabinet policies and major decisions could be defeated in the Commons, necessitating the resignation of ministers and/or the dissolution of Parliament. Effective party discipline ensured this was a very rare occurrence. Hence instead of a true separation of powers between the Executive and the Legislative there developed a fusion of these powers. The Cabinet evolved into a co-ordinating centre. Through its committees and 'inner' groupings Cabinets arrived at decisions and with party majority support saw to it that these were legitimised by parliamentary approval.

One quick word of warning: the terms 'government' and 'Cabinet' are often used interchangeably, and inaccurately so. The term 'government' refers to *all* the ministers and their aides down to parliamentary private secretaries, altogether numbering over 100. The term 'Cabinet' technically refers to those politicians invited by the Prime Minister to give collective advice to the monarch. In modern terms, this generally refers to the specific heads of departments, and is applied to the 20 or so ministers chosen by the prime minister to take up such posts (although not all Cabinet Ministers are Heads of Departments e.g. the Chief Secretary to the Treasury). There is no constitutional restriction on the number but through pragmatism and experience a membership of around 20 has proved most suitable for manageable government.

The Functions of Cabinet

In modern government you would expect to be able to obtain an idea as to what the Cabinet actually does. However, it is not quite so easy. The major problem is everything is shrouded in secrecy. Open government is still a theory rather than an actuality. On the positive side, there are some obvious functions that can be examined. These functions, and the general role of the Cabinet have evolved in a pragmatic fashion, moulding themselves to meet changing constitutional and political demands, for example the role of the territorial (Scottish, Welsh and Northern Ireland) offices have altered post-devolution. Yet other bodies such as 'inner Cabinets', Cabinet committees, and special advisory groups have, at times, usurped parts of Cabinet business. It is therefore by no means certain what are the precise functions or roles of the Cabinet.

According to James (1992, pp. 4-10), there are some underlying principles of the British cabinet system. These are: collegiality; the importance of Parliament; ministerial responsibility; and, collective responsibility. The latter two will be explained later in this chapter.

The idea of collegiality is relatively simple. It is the idea of all of the cabinet members working together. Across all parts of government in the UK, we see groups of people working together – at local council level, as well as at the devolved level. Central government is no different. Collegiality sees decision-making being taken by more than one person. Thus, a range of ideas may be drawn into the decision-making process, rather than one person moving unilaterally.

An obvious drawback is that collegiality may slow down the decision-making process. Within a collegial system, it is still possible for an individual, or two or three individuals, to dominate. Thus, the prime minister is likely to play a major role, as are the other 'big beasts' of the cabinet. Collegiality is also the basis of collective responsibility.

Parliament is also important within a cabinet system. The cabinet may propose laws, but these still have to be ratified by Parliament. This process is dominated by the annual Parliamentary sessions. Thus, there is pressure on the cabinet members to get their legislative proposals prepared accurately. Ministers are also accountable to Parliament, and must explain their actions – or the actions of their department – to Parliament. In fact, Parliament can make or break a ministerial career! This is one aspect of ministerial responsibility.

With the cabinet system evolving, the shroud of secrecy, and Parliamentary pressures, it is not always easy to see what the cabinet actually does. There are, however, a number of functions that can be discerned:

1. The Determination of Policy
2. Co-ordination of Government Policy and Administration
3. Parliamentary Business
4. Political Leadership of the Party

1. The Determination of Policy
In 1918 the Haldane Committee in its 'Report on the Machinery of Government' stated clearly 'the final determination of policy to be submitted to Parliament' rests with the Cabinet. The accuracy of such a statement has been called into question, particularly with regard to the role of the Cabinet. The sheer volume of government business alone makes the determination of policy by the full Cabinet a virtual impossibility. The work of the department occupies most of a minister's time, to the extent that he or she may have little time to consider the overall strategy of Cabinet policy or even important itemised business. Consequently, extra-Cabinet bodies such as Cabinet committees and advisory groups have become significant in formulating policy with the Cabinet acting as either a rubber stamp for decisions arrived at elsewhere, or, more positively, as the final arbiter in differences not already settled. In either respect, the role of the Cabinet appears to have been somewhat marginalised.

Nevertheless it would be foolish to dismiss the status of the Cabinet in the field of policy making to that of a cypher. While the Cabinet may not necessarily decide the actual policies, it is the arena where most important decisions are taken.

The Cabinet meets weekly on a Thursday to consider a whole range of items, including both Parliamentary business for the forthcoming week and foreign and Commonwealth matters. The prime minister chairs the meeting, and sums up the mood of the meeting (voting never takes place), which is then transferred to the minutes and becomes the final Cabinet decision. Quite clearly, the role of the prime minister is very important within the Cabinet. The role of the prime minister is examined in chapter 12.

2. Co-ordination of Government Policy and Administration

Since the Cabinet is supposed to be the engine room of government policy making, the co-ordination of policy and administration would seem to be vital. Bagehot (in his analogy of 'the hyphen which joins, the buckle that fastens') certainly thought so. In fact Bagehot raised co-ordination to the highest function the Cabinet should exercise. He may, however, have overstated the case. Individual departments tend to work as autonomous units rather than working collectively. In fact, there is at times the perception that individual departments are competing with each other rather than working collectively to enact the government's legislative programme.

Such a situation is made worse by the way in which Cabinet members perceive their roles. The position of being a *representative* of a department comes ahead of being a member of a collective decision making body, at least in the eyes of many ministers and civil servants. Added to this, emphasis was placed upon the internal aspects of a minister's work – the managing and administering of the department. This led Headey (1974) to conclude Britain had departmental rather than Cabinet government.

But it would be absurd to conclude that co-ordination is entirely missing from the work of the Cabinet – the Blair Government, for example, emphasised 'joined up' government; and with a coalition government, co-ordination between the two partners is essential. The task of co-ordination is taken partially by the Prime Minister's Office and the Cabinet Office, but also by non-departmental ministers like the Lord President of the Council (Leader of the House) and the Chancellor of the Duchy of Lancaster. It is also carried out in conjunction with other non-Cabinet ministers, senior civil servants, policy advisors and military chiefs, depending upon what issue is being addressed.

The tasks of co-ordination are being performed more often by the Cabinet Committees chaired by the Prime Minister and senior Cabinet members, with the Cabinet acting as a final court of appeal or as a rubber stamp. Acting in parallel with the Cabinet Committees are the Official Committees composed of senior officials. Constant informal consultations take place between these officials and the departmental ministers. The Cabinet Office, by servicing the Cabinet and its committees, also assists in the work of co-ordination.

The Treasury is regarded as the most 'important' of the various government departments. It co-ordinates public spending and through its annual spending reviews and dealings with individual spending ministries provides at least some oversight of the government machine.

Yet there is general agreement despite the assistance of the above mechanisms, the vital task of co-ordination is not achieved in an efficient and coherent manner. This is usually explained by the weight of 'overload' – too much material to digest and the inordinate time devoted to departmental work by individual ministers. For evidence of this you only need to examine ministerial memoirs by Tony Benn, Barbara Castle, Alan Clarke and Richard Crossman.

Remedies have been suggested to this problem, such as smaller or 'inner' cabinets, or the amalgamation of departments. Yet they do not appear to have more than minimal success. Other suggested remedies, like a prime ministers department, tend to be opposed on constitutional and practical grounds. With a dominant prime minister in the mould of Margaret Thatcher or Tony Blair, a prime ministers department may move power further away from the Cabinet. With a coalition government, there would probably be concern from the junior partner about being side lined by the creation of a prime ministers department.

3. Parliamentary Business

The other functions of the Cabinet might appear more mundane but serve to emphasise the controlling influence this body exercises over both parliamentary and party political business. The parliamentary timetable is planned in Cabinet, usually a week or so in advance and announced by the Leader of the House in the Commons. Time allocated to debates, whether to use the guillotine or other closure devices are determined not necessarily by the whole Cabinet but with Cabinet approval. Such prosaic procedures have political overtones in maximising the weight of government impact and minimising the influence of the opposition parties.

4. Political Leadership of the Party

It should always be kept in mind the modern Cabinet is essentially a party-political body designed to achieve the smooth running of the administrative machine and ensuring electoral success. Hence its policies are often shaped with a narrow party interest in view, within the broader sweep of a national policy. Such a leadership role is not so easily performed within a coalition government, where concessions may have to be made to the coalition partner. One of the interesting points that came up at the 2011 Conservative Party annual conference was the demand for David Cameron to show greater leadership within the coalition – there was a perception in some quarters of the Conservative Party that too many concessions had been made to the Liberal Democrats.

The Size of the Cabinet

A preoccupation with the size of the Cabinet is simply an indication of the desire to extract maximum efficiency from this ruling body. As the workload of government business increased dramatically in the 20th century, it was natural the size and composition of the Cabinet would become a concern. In the 19th century a rather leisurely approach was taken towards Cabinet business, mirroring the lack of government involvement in economic and social matters. Thus a Cabinet of between 10 and 12 ministers was considered perfectly adequate. Even the Haldane Report (1918) recommended not more than 12 members to keep a sharp cutting edge to policymaking and administration. With the growth of state activity, particularly after the Second World War, the Cabinet size expanded to over 20 members.

What we see is the prime minister involved in a balancing act between the needs of policymaking and representativeness. The Cabinet has to include the ministers of the important departments and one or two non-departmental ministers (ministers without portfolio) for specific tasks. The latter can be used by a prime minister to include in the Cabinet an inexperienced minister or a close ally (e.g. the inclusion of Peter Mandelson by Tony Blair after his first Cabinet reshuffle, or of Oliver Letwin by David Cameron). At the same time it is essential to contain the numbers to manageable proportions to facilitate the processes of decision-making and discussion.

Thus, in an attempt to make things more manageable, a prime minister may revert to any one of a number of strategies to keep Cabinet numbers down. Some prime ministers have amalgamated departments into 'super ministries'. An alternative is to create 'inner' cabinets to direct broad policy and to focus upon strategic policy. The hope in such a situation might be to achieve better co-ordination of policy making. Thatcher never formalised her 'inner' Cabinet. She worked with a few trusted ministers. These ministers changed over time and sometimes with regard to the issue as well. Finally, there is always the option of looking beyond the Cabinet, using task forces. Ted Heath used this option, drawing in the senior civil service to policy initiatives. Tony Blair looked further afield, to people from outside government. He also preferred to utilise what was termed 'sofa government', where he would have a one-to-one chat with a specific minister rather than discussing something with the full cabinet.

Within the coalition government, a balance of the distribution of portfolios was needed between the coalition partners. It is much more difficult to get things done away from the cabinet, without informing the junior coalition partner. David Cameron has his trusted ministers, as does Nick Clegg. Even by late 2013, the Cameron-Clegg relationship seemed strong enough to keep the front benches of both parties reasonably happy.

The assessment to be made after the experimentation of post-war prime ministers is separating policy from administration is a task fraught with difficulties, bordering on the impossible. Adopting a system of inner Cabinets concentrating on policy has certainly not solved the problem. Looking to outsiders appears to be faring little better. The political dimension, in which ministers excluded from the charmed circle resent the 'demotion' is a factor too often overlooked by prime ministers. This was most noticeable with the need to form a coalition government after the 2010 General Election. The Conservatives had to cede some posts to the Liberal Democrats, which displeased a number of senior Conservative MPs who had expected to receive a cabinet post.

The Composition of the Cabinet

The decision as to who should be in the Cabinet is determined not only by its size but also by a number of other considerations: the changing demands of economic, social and political factors; the needs of a particular governing party, or of coalition partners; the judgement of prime ministers on the competence and loyalty of individual ministers; and the necessity to balance the competing forces within the party or across a coalition.

It might be superfluous to state all Cabinet members must come from Parliament but it is worth remembering in Britain, the Executive and the Legislature are not clearly separated as in the USA. Prime ministers, therefore, can only choose from those elected as MPs or members of the House of Lords. It is highly unusual for a newly elected MP to be catapulted into the Cabinet. The Wilson Government of 1964-70 created a by-election to enable Frank Cousins (a trade union leader) to become an MP and immediately a Cabinet member as Minister of Technology. This appointment was not overly successful. The other route for prime ministers to install a person they want in the Cabinet who is not an MP is to create a Life Peerage for that person. In 1997 Tony Blair elevated Derry Irvine to the Lords (Lord Irvine of Lairg) in order to include him in the Cabinet as the Lord Chancellor.

1. Changing Demands of Government

The composition of the Cabinet has of necessity to reflect the changes in economic, social, political and international demands. It is educative to compare the posts of Cabinet rank in the 1940s and 1950s with those of the first coalition government of the 21st century (as can be seen in Table 11.1). The India and Commonwealth Offices have long since disappeared. The Housing and Local Government post (which was formed in 1951) was subsumed into the Department of the Environment, which then became part of the Department of Environment, Transport and the Regions. It has now resurfaced as the Department of Communities and Local Government. The Department of Health and Social Security has been both merged and separated. The latter has evolved into part of the Department of Work and Pensions. As the workload of the Treasury has increased, the Chancellor of the Exchequer's 'assistant' – the Chief Secretary to the Treasury – has been elevated to Cabinet rank. It is worth noting John Major occupied both Treasury positions prior to becoming Prime Minister.

Table 11.1 Cabinet posts under the Attlee and Cameron Governments

Attlee Government (1945)	Cameron Coalition Government (2013)
Prime Minister (Clement Attlee)	Prime Minister (David Cameron)
Lord Chancellor (Lord Jowitt)	Deputy Prime Minister and Lord President of the Council (Nick Clegg*)
Lord President (Herbert Morrison)	Chancellor of the Exchequer (George Osborne)
Lord Privy Seal (Arthur Greenwood)	Secretary of State for Foreign and Commonwealth Affairs (William Hague)
Chancellor of the Exchequer (Hugh Dalton)	Lord Chancellor and Secretary of State for Justice (Chris Grayling)
Minister of Economic Affairs (Sir Stafford Cripps)	Secretary of State for the Home Department (Theresa May)
Foreign Secretary (Ernest Bevin)	Secretary of State for Business, Innovation and Skills (Vince Cable*)
Home Secretary (Chuter Ede)	Secretary of State for Energy and Climate Change (Edward Davey*)
First Lord of the Admiralty (A. V. Alexander)	Secretary of State for Education (Michael Gove)
Minister of Agriculture and Fisheries (Tom Williams)	Secretary of State for Communities and Local Government (Eric Pickles)
Secretary of State for Air (Lord Stansgate)	Secretary of State for Transport (Patrick McLoughlin)
Colonial Secretary (George Hall)	Secretary of State for Scotland (Alistair Carmichael*)
Secretary of State for the Dominions (Lord Addison)	Culture, Media and Sport Secretary (Maria Miller)
Minister of Defence (Clement Attlee)	Secretary of State for International Development (Justine Greening)
Minister of Education (Ellen Wilkinson)	Work and Pensions Secretary (Iain Duncan Smith)
Minister of Fuel and Power (Emanuel Shinwell)	Environment, Food and Rural Affairs Secretary (Owen Paterson)
Minister of Health (Aneurin Bevan)	Leader of the House of Lords and Chancellor of the Duchy of Lancaster (Lord Hill of Oareford)
Secretary of State for India and Burma (Lord Pethwick-Lawrence)	Secretary of State for Health (Jeremy Hunt)
Minister of Labour and National Service (George Isaacs)	Secretary of State for Wales (David Jones)
Secretary of State for Scotland (J. Westwood)	Secretary of State for Northern Ireland (Theresa Villiers)
President of the Board of Trade (Sir Stafford Cripps)	Secretary of State for Defence (Philip Hammond)
Secretary of State for War (J. J. Lawson)	Chief Secretary to the Treasury (Danny Alexander*)
	Minister without Portfolio and Conservative Party Chair (Grant Shapps)
	Minister for the Cabinet Office (Francis Maude)
	Minister without Portfolio (Kenneth Clarke)
	Leader of the House and Lord Privy Seal (Andrew Lansley)
	Minister for Government Policy (Oliver Letwin)
	Chief Whip (Conservative) – Sir George Young

* Liberal Democrat

Sources: K. Morgan (1984) Labour in Power 1945-1951 Oxford University Press; www.parliament.uk/mps-lords-and-offices/government-and-opposition1/her-majestys-government/; www.gov.uk/government.ministers

2) Personality: Competence in political and administrative spheres

Politics is often as much about personality and competence as it is about institutions, principles and policies. The composition of a Cabinet proves no exception to the rule. Although in theory every party MP of the House of Commons is eligible to enter the Cabinet, in practice the choice is limited to a narrow band of MPs. Some by sheer experience and standing almost choose themselves, except when they have incurred the wrath of the Prime Minister. Thus Tony Blair had to include Gordon Brown and Robin Cook in his Cabinet, but was able to remove Jack Cunningham and to push Mo Mowlam to a less important post and eventually out of the Cabinet. Robin Cook was effectively demoted after the 2001 General Election from Foreign Secretary to Leader of the Commons, allegedly over his overt enthusiasm for the Euro. Others are earmarked for Cabinet status – even though inexperienced – because of special qualities discerned by the Prime Minister. Michael Gove, within the coalition government, would be such an example.

Generally, however, it is the trait of administrative skill, the ability to manage a department, absorb and present a brief at least competently for which prime ministers look, but indications of loyalty are also considered to be of great importance. All prime ministers view this latter quality very highly indeed. The phrase 'One of Us' became a common expression under Thatcher, indicating loyalty to Thatcherite beliefs. 'Tony's cronies' was the rather derogatory version applied to Blair.

3) A Balance of the Main Forces in the Party

This topic is to some extent dealt with in the next chapter on the Prime Minister. Here it is sufficient to emphasise large political parties in the UK are 'umbrella' or 'broad church' groups. Each encompasses a number of different and competing strands, all dedicated to their concepts of Conservatism, Liberalism or Labourism. A Cabinet, as both an Executive Committee and representative of the party, is supposed to reflect at least a semblance of a compendium of right, centre and left wing factions of the party. Blair needed to keep both 'old' and 'new' Labour represented in his Cabinet. Thus John Prescott and Margaret Beckett remained in place during the first term of Office. It was noticeable that the majority of Cabinet members belonged to the New Labour wing of the party. Over time, most of the remnants of 'old' Labour were weeded out.

Within a coalition government, as well as the balancing within a party of government, there is also the balancing between coalition partners. In other countries, most notably Italy, failure to keep coalition partners happy has resulted in the disintegration of governments. The failure to build coalitions – as in the case of Belgium – has seen political stagnation and a lack of political leadership. As of 2013, such a problem had not arisen within the coalition government.

Collective Responsibility

The notion of the collective responsibility of the Cabinet was an almost inevitable development of Cabinet government within the context of exclusive party government. In order to maintain the vital element of unity it was natural that *all* members of the Cabinet were expected to speak with one voice.

The doctrine of collective responsibility is quite clear. All members of the government (all ministers, not just the Cabinet) must agree *publicly* with government policy and action, even if they have *private* doubts. If they cannot do this, they must resign. Surprisingly, the 'Ministerial Code' which lays down guidelines for Cabinet ministers (see www.cabinetoffice.gov.uk/sites/default/files/resources/ministerial-code-may-2010.pdf for specific details) does not state this explicitly. It does state ministers should ensure their statements are consistent with collective Government policy, and ministers will only stay in post while they have the confidence of the prime minister. Resignation is more implicit than explicitly stated.

The purpose of collective responsibility is quite clear; to ensure government authority is maintained and party (or coalition) unity preserved. Of course this is not necessarily an aim in itself but it is done to present to the electorate the image of a strong government and united party in order to win the next general election. It is almost certainly this consideration rather than constitutional concerns that keeps the doctrine alive at a time when it is incurring a great deal of criticism. An obvious underpinning of this doctrine is *secrecy*, which characterises not just Cabinet decisions but many government dealings as well. Yet leaks and coded messages undermine the entire doctrine.

The application of collective responsibility is, however, by no means as watertight as perhaps prime ministers would wish. In fact it was Harold Wilson who made the clearest breach of the principle in 1975 when he suspended it over the referendum on continued EEC membership. The Cabinet was notoriously divided on the issue of whether Britain should remain in the EEC. Thus, by allowing Cabinet members to express their own opinions on the issue, Wilson felt he might be able to solve the 'problem' of Cabinet disunity. Immediately after the referendum, collective responsibility was re-imposed on the issue.

In general, it appears the principle of collective responsibility is being eroded. It is not just through the suspension of the convention as done by Wilson, but by veiled disagreements between ministers, 'leaks' to the press, publication of memoirs and diaries by former ministers. Although the latter are supposed to be 'cleared' by the Cabinet Office, they still reveal the amount of dissent in Cabinet.

These instances and many others serve to illustrate how difficult it is in practice to adhere rigidly to the doctrine of collective responsibility. This is not surprising for the following reasons:

1. The increase in government size to about 100 members makes it so much harder to preserve unity and secrecy.

2. It is sometimes by no means clear exactly what Cabinet policy is since the whole process of policy making is diffused through the Cabinet system with its numerous committees and sub-committees, as well as the use of external groups.

3. With the preference of prime ministers for inner Cabinets or groups there is a tendency to commit the whole Cabinet to a policy not yet examined thoroughly or even discussed.

The above remarks might well suggest the doctrine of collective responsibility is outmoded or at least impossible to implement rigidly or even consistently. It is alleged that leaks to lobby correspondents have become so commonplace as to make a nonsense of the doctrine.

There have been calls for the total abandonment of the doctrine. Tony Benn was to the forefront here, arguing MPs should elect the Cabinet, which would enable Cabinet members to express their own ideas. It has also been suggested the electorate has become much more sophisticated and will not necessarily punish the government or opposition for allowing ministers and shadow ministers to disagree publicly.

Within a coalition government, the doctrine of collective responsibility may appear problematic. For the coalition government, this problem was circumvented with the coalition agreement. The document specified where both coalition partners would work in tandem, and both would accept collective responsibility e.g. reducing the deficit. It also specified opt outs e.g. the Conservatives, while acceding to a referendum on electoral reform, were under no obligation to campaign for a 'yes' vote. Thus, the convention of ministerial responsibility is actually reinforced, in some respects, by the coalition agreement. Where a problem remains could be over the response to any unforeseen event. It remains to be seen how the coalition will respond to an issue that divides both partners.

The truth is governments find the doctrine very useful for maintaining party discipline – even within a coalition. Leaks can be tolerated as long as they are not too damaging and do not become too frequent. After all it would be extremely difficult for a government to maintain cohesion without retaining collective responsibility.

Individual or Ministerial Responsibility
Basically there are three parts to the doctrine of individual responsibility. In legal terms it refers to the minister being responsible to Parliament for a particular aspect of government action so the monarch may be absolved from responsibility. Specifically, each minister is responsible for:
1) their own personal conduct
2) the conduct and policies of their department
3) the conduct of their civil servants within the department.

There have been numerous examples of ministers resigning over their own personal conduct. Within the Blair Government there was Peter Mandelson and Ron Davies. The coalition government received the resignation of David Laws within days of the coalition being formed. The most infamous of all such resignations was John Profumo, who resigned from the Macmillan Government in 1963 over misleading the House of Commons about an extra-marital relationship with Christine Keeler. This was the first modern day public scandal, and was epitomised in the film *Scandal*.

While there is an extensive list of ministers who have resigned over personal indiscretions, the list of non-resignations is also very long. Robin Cook decided to choose his mistress over his wife but remained Foreign Secretary. Jack Straw stayed in the Home Office despite his son's entrapment in the sale of cannabis. Steven Norris remained a junior Transport Minister in the Major Government despite the revelation of numerous mistresses. Liam Fox retained the support of David Cameron despite errors of judgement in relation to a close personal friend and Department of Defence matters (although Fox eventually resigned). There are clear inconsistencies in who remains and who resigns. Much of it is down to the personal standing of a minister and their relationship with the prime minister. Sometimes it becomes impossible for a PM to save a colleague. Tony Blair 'lost' Peter Mandelson twice in two years.

Resignations over failed policies or departmental conduct are much rarer. Lord Carrington and his two deputies, Humphrey Aitkins and Richard Luce, resigned from the Foreign Office over the Argentine invasion of the Falkland Islands in the early 1980s. Norman Lamont resigned as Chancellor over Britain being ejected from the European Exchange Rate Mechanism in 1992. More often than not, ministers will attempt to brazen things out in the hope of either the issue blowing over, or the prime minister invoking collective responsibility.

Resignation over the actions of the civil servants is called *vicarious* responsibility. Such resignations have been virtually non-existent in the times of modern government. It may have been feasible in the 19th century for a minister to resign over the action of his civil servants. In those days, a minister probably knew the name of every civil servant who worked for him. This is simply not the case any longer with over half a million civil servants spread across the country and around 100 ministers. Some authors have considered the resignation of Sir Thomas Dugdale over the Crichel Down affair in 1954 to be the only post-war example of vicarious responsibility. This was to do with the compulsory acquisition of a piece of land in 1940 and its resale. For many years it was portrayed as Dugdale being misinformed by his civil servants over the entire case. Yet when the official documents were released 30 years later, there was evidence of Dugdale's involvement throughout the entire affair. The pressures on Dugdale to resign should see this example included as a failed policy, or even a personal indiscretion. With regard to vicarious responsibility, a minister may be responsible as head of the department but is he/she really to blame?

In sum, with regard to individual responsibility there is a clear pattern. It has nothing to do with the type of indiscretion committed, nor the extent of the failed policy. It is to do with the minister's relationship with the prime minister. If the minister is viewed as dispensable, it is most likely he/she will resign. Otherwise, the prime minister may give public support to their beleaguered colleague, or collective responsibility may be invoked.

Cabinet Structure

The Cabinet as the supreme Executive Committee has a clearly defined structure to enable it to perform its duties in the most efficient manner. The component parts of the structure are meant to dovetail into each other for maximum effectiveness but like most machines performance does not always match expectations. The main components are:

1. *The Cabinet Office*
2. *The Cabinet Committees*

1. The Cabinet Office

It is surprising to learn, considering the volume of Cabinet business, it was not until 1916 that a permanent Secretariat was established by Lloyd George to handle and co-ordinate the conduct of the First World War. Basically it was regarded as the 'Civil Service' of the Cabinet situated at the heart of the government machine. Until 2012, the Secretary of the Cabinet headed the Cabinet Office, coupling the post with the Head of the Home Civil Service. It was then split, with Sir Jeremy Heywood as Cabinet Secretary, Sir Bob Kerslake as Head of the Home Civil Service, and Ian Watmore as Permanent Secretary at the Cabinet Office. The overarching role of the Cabinet Office can be summarised as the work of co-ordination and the smooth running of government.

In 2013, the Minister for the Cabinet Office was Francis Maude (who attended cabinet meetings), and was assisted by Grant Shapps. Maude's post was responsible areas such as co-ordinating and presenting government policies. Shapps was responsible for the 'political' side of the Cabinet Office, including the link between government and the Conservative Party. Added to this, Nick Clegg and Oliver Letwin both appeared to play key roles within the Cabinet Office. Clegg was responsible for political and constitutional reform; Letwin provided policy advice for the Prime Minister.

The Cabinet Office has long outgrown its original function of simply being an instrument for recording decisions and circulating information. To some extent the Cabinet Office as a whole has become an instrument for aiding the prime minister, although it could never be described as being a 'Prime Minister's

Department' as its functions are still, constitutionally at least, linked in with the Cabinet rather than the Prime Minister (the PM being 'first among equals' within the Cabinet). Having said this, it was not stated so clearly on the Cabinet Office's web pages in 2013: "We support the Prime Minister and the Deputy Prime Minister, and ensure the effective running of government. We are also the corporate headquarters for government, in partnership with HM Treasury, and we take the lead in certain critical policy areas" (www.cabinetoffice.gov.uk/content/about-cabinet-office). From this, it could be argued the Cabinet Office has clearly become an instrument for aiding the prime minister and deputy prime minister, rather than the cabinet.

2. Cabinet Committees

The proliferation of cabinet committees is ample evidence of the huge increase in the work of the Cabinet and the 'overload' of government; hence the necessity to improve co-ordination. In theory the committees were bound by secrecy – in fact, their existence was not even confirmed until the 1980s. The chairs of committees were revealed by John Major. Tony Blair revealed the full membership of each Committee. Examples are given in Table 11.2.

With the formation of the coalition government, many aspects had to be agreed formally by both partners. This included the role and membership of cabinet committees. There was a document from the Cabinet Office in September 2010, which stated very clearly the role of the cabinet and cabinet committees:

> Cabinet and Cabinet Committees are groups of Ministers that can take collective decisions that are binding across Government. The Cabinet is the supreme decision-making body in government, dealing with the big issues of the day and the Government's overall strategy. Cabinet Committees reduce the burden on Cabinet by enabling collective decisions to be taken by a smaller group of Ministers. The composition and terms of reference of Coalition Cabinet Committees are a matter for the Prime Minister, in consultation with the Deputy Prime Minister.

> **Source: www.gov.uk/government/uploads/system/uploads/attachment_data/file/60639/cabinet-committees-system.pdf**

This document listed 12 cabinet committees and three cabinet sub-committees, including their membership and terms of reference.

Table 11.2 Examples of the Composition of Cabinet Committees (October 2011)

Economic Affairs	European Affairs
Chancellor of the Exchequer (Chair)	Foreign Secretary (Chair)
Business, Innovation & Skills Secretary	Energy & Climate Change Secretary
Foreign Secretary	Chancellor of the Exchequer
Defence Secretary	Home Secretary
Work & Pensions Secretary	Defence Secretary
Energy & Climate Change Secretary	Business, Innovation & Skills Secretary
Communities & Local Government Secretary	Communities & Local Government Secretary
Transport Secretary	International Development Secretary
Chief Secretary to the Treasury	Chief Secretary to the Treasury
Minister of State – Cabinet Office	Minister of State – Cabinet Office
Minister of State – Universities & Skills	Chief Whip
Minister of State – Communities & Local Government	Minister of State – Europe
	Minister of State – FCO
	Deputy Chief Whip

Source: www.gov.uk/government/uploads/system/uploads/attachment_data/file/60639/cabinet-committees-system.pdf

There are different types of Cabinet Committees:

Standing Committees. These are permanent during the prime minister's tenure of office and reflect the range and requirements of that particular government. Each committee connects departments associated with common policies (e.g. Economic Affairs is listed in Table 11.2).

Ad hoc. These committees are set up to examine specific issues or concerns as they arise. Examples from the past include committees being set up in response to the inner city riots of 1981, and the miners' strike of 1984-85. During the Blair years, and under the Coalition Government, the use of such committees has virtually ceased. There is an expectation the appropriate department(s) will deal with these issues and report back to full cabinet.

Official Committees. These consist solely of civil servants and run in parallel to the Standing Committees.

The number of Cabinet Committees declined during the Thatcher years, and again during the Blair years. The first post-war Labour Government under Clement Attlee had over 450 such committees. Thatcher reduced the number to 135. Under Blair, the number stood between 20 and 30. By 2009, under

Gordon Brown, this had dropped to 11 standing and six ad hoc committees (plus sub-committees). In the first two years of the David Cameron-led Coalition Government, the number stood at around a dozen, plus sub-committees.

The decline in the number of Cabinet Committees has not seen a concurrent resurgence in the use of the full Cabinet. If anything, it has further reduced the importance of the Cabinet. Blair, in particular, used bilateral meetings with specific ministers rather than using the traditional collegial methods. Many of the complaints about Cabinet Committees being used to bypass the full Cabinet now seem inconsequential. The Cabinet Committees themselves appear to be less important.

Conclusion

During the Thatcher years there was a great emphasis among commentators and politicians on the breakdown of Cabinet government. During the Major years, however, this argument was, to some extent at least, reversed. Under Blair, the arguments on the demise of the Cabinet resurfaced, only to disappear with the formation of a coalition government.

What is definitely clear is over time there has been a growth in the prestige and presidential style of some prime ministers. Added to this, there has been the 'overload' of ministers with departmental work, the emergence of extra-Cabinet bodies like advisory groups, 'kitchen' or inner Cabinets, task forces, etc. all leading to the claim Cabinet has been undermined as a fully-functioning Executive body. The problem really stems from the origins of the Cabinet. What currently exists is a body not too dissimilar to that which existed in the 19th century. It has not really evolved to take on the needs of the 21st century.

Not all critics would present such a doom and gloom summary of the Cabinet, but there is no doubt the body is under considerable strain. This may be the reason why the Blair government in particular took to almost avoiding the use of the Cabinet except when it was really necessary. At the same time, an emphasis was placed on 'joined up' government, with a Cabinet minister heading a department which co-ordinated government. This role, very clearly now within the Cabinet Office, has been strengthened by the Coalition Government. It is interesting to speculate about the extent to which this would have happened had there not been a coalition government. Regardless, at least until the 2015 general election, the cabinet will remain a key body the prime minister cannot take for granted.

Selected bibliography

Barberis, Peter. (2000). "Prime Minister and Cabinet" in Pyper, Robert & Robins, Lynton (eds.), *United Kingdom Governance*: Macmillan, pp. 14-38.
Berlinski, Samuel; Dewan, Torun & Dowding, Keith. (2007). "The Length of Ministerial Tenure in the United Kingdom, 1945-1997", *British Journal of Political Science* vol. 37-2, pp. 245-262.

Flinders, Matthew. (2002). "Shifting the Balance? Parliament, the Executive and the British Constitution", *Political Studies* vol. 50-1, pp. 23-42.

Headey, Bruce. (1974). *British Cabinet Ministers*: Allen and Unwin.

Richards, David. (2011). "Changing Patterns of Executive Governance" in Heffernan, Richard; Cowley, Philip & Hay, Colin (eds.), *Developments in British Politics 9*: Palgrave, pp. 29-50.

Thomas, Graham. (1998). *Prime Minister and Cabinet Today*: Manchester University Press.

Websites

www.cabinet-office.gov.uk/
This is the general link to the Cabinet Office, from where you can access all sources of government information.

www.gov.uk/government/uploads/system/uploads/attachment_data/file/60639/cabinet-committees-system.pdf
This document outlines the cabinet committee system (September 2010) and lists all of the cabinet committees and their membership, for the coalition government

www.number10.gov.uk/news/her-majestys-government/
This will give you a complete list of all Cabinet and ministerial posts

Questions

1. "The main function of the Cabinet is to determine policy and keep the government in power." Discuss.
2. Evaluate the usefulness of the conventions collective and individual responsibility.
3. Justify the view that the Cabinet is now a superfluous part of British government.
4. How may the Cabinet be made to run more effectively and more efficiently?

CHAPTER 12 // PRIME MINISTER

Contents

- **Introduction**
- **The Sources and Strengths of the Prime Minister's Power**
- **Constraints on a Prime Minister's Power**
- **The Case against the Concept of Prime Ministerial Government**
- **The Case for the Existence of Prime Ministerial Government**
- **Conclusion**

The extent and limitations of a prime minister's power is one of the perennial examination subjects. Students should have no particular difficulty in assessing the respective arguments advanced as to whether prime ministerial government has superseded Cabinet government, or even whether or not there has ever been a 'presidential' prime minister. The formation of a coalition government after the 2010 General Election has, however, muddied some of these waters, especially with regard to the dominance of the prime minister.

Introduction

The dramatic, unexpected demise of Margaret Thatcher in November 1990 revived the controversy over the limits of prime ministerial power, just as it appeared the advocates of the 'prime ministerial' government thesis were in the ascendancy. When Tony Blair was Prime Minister, these advocates resurfaced, only to disappear again with the demise of Blair's premiership. Much of their argumentation can be sourced from Richard Crossman. In his introduction to the 1963 version of Walter Bagehot's *The English Constitution*, Crossman insisted cabinet government had given way to prime ministerial government. The idea of Prime Minister being *primus inter pares* (first among equals) was antiquated; an inadequate description of a modern prime minister's authority. While there was some support for Crossman, the majority of political scientists believed such a stance to be an over-exaggeration. The idea a prime minister could be 'presidentialist' or an 'elected monarch' was considered totally inappropriate since there were sufficient checks and balances within the political system to curb even the most dominant of prime ministers.

The controversy was given an extra impetus by the authority Margaret Thatcher wielded over the cabinet, parliament and Conservative Party (particularly after the 1983 General Election), and the style with which she embellished the office. Her fall from power added another twist to the debate, especially as her successor, John Major, adopted a far more collegial approach. Tony Blair gave the debate yet another twist, as his approach appeared far closer to that of Thatcher than Major. The coalition government, on the other hand, has a high degree of collegiality – far higher, it seems, than ever experienced during the Major years. While collegiality might be necessary in a coalition, it is the degree of apparent collegiality that is quite surprising.

None of this is a new debate. In the mid-nineteenth century, Bagehot professed in the natural development of party politics the Prime Minister would eventually come to dominate the cabinet. Whenever there is an assertive or dominant prime minister – Lloyd George, Thatcher or Blair – the arguments resurface. Consequently, the debate has become a little tiresome. Simply listing the powers of a prime minister and their limitations does not help it. What is too often missing is the significance of personality and the social, economic, political and policy contexts in which particular prime ministers operated and currently operate. There is too strong a reliance on the institutional sources of power and the checks on these powers, which is then linked to the problems of having an uncodified constitution.

The office of a prime minister does not lend itself easily to a 'job description'. It is an adjustable, flexible constitutional position, far more flexible than the presidency of the USA. Comparisons between the two posts do not actually help matters. The terms 'president' and 'presidential government' can only in the most superficial way be applied to the British system of a prime minister and cabinet. Heffernan (2003a, p. 349), for example has argued that the notion of presidentialism "may illuminate, but it also confuses". The problem has become the emphasis placed upon the post (and the potential post-holders) by the media. In fact, the post of the Prime Minister is whatever the holder chooses to make of it. This may be the most appropriate description of the post. The powers available to one prime minister are also available to all others; it is how they are wielded that matters. This can be linked to the size of parliamentary majority or events that happen while in office. Such factors may enhance or reduce the potential for a prime minister to use these powers. The full list of 20th century prime ministers can be seen in table 12.1.

Since the topic is of significance in understanding the British political system there can be no shirking a consideration of the power of a modern prime minister. Despite the restrictions levelled above at the 'list' method of drawing up 'powers' and 'limitations', it is still the conventional device designed to reach some meaningful conclusions and lends itself to examination answers for students. It should be stressed as many relevant examples should be introduced not merely to illustrate generalised statements but to demonstrate how much personality and circumstance figure in any worthwhile assessment of the power of a British prime minister.

Table 12.1 Prime Ministers of the 20th and 21st centuries

Prime Minister	Party	Took office
The Marquess of Salisbury	Unionist (Conservative)	25 June 1895
Arthur James Balfour	Unionist (Conservative)	12 July 1902
Sir Henry Campbell-Bannerman	Liberal	5 December 1906
Herbert Henry Asquith	Liberal (1)	8 April 1908
David Lloyd George	Liberal (2)	7 December 1916
Andrew Bonar Law	Unionist (Conservative)	23 October 1922
Stanley Baldwin	Unionist (Conservative)	22 May 1923
J. Ramsay MacDonald	Labour	22 January 1924
Stanley Baldwin	Conservative	4 November 1924
J. Ramsay MacDonald	Labour	5 June 1929
J. Ramsay MacDonald	National Labour (3)	24 August 1931
Stanley Baldwin	Conservative (3)	7 June 1935
Neville Chamberlain	Conservative (3)	28 May 1937
Winston S. Churchill	Conservative (4)	10 May 1940
Clement Attlee	Labour	26 July 1945
Sir Winston S. Churchill	Conservative	26 October 1951
Sir Anthony Eden	Conservative	6 April 1955
Harold Macmillan	Conservative	10 January 1957
Sir Alec Douglas-Home	Conservative	19 October 1963
Harold Wilson	Labour	16 October 1964
Edward Heath	Conservative	19 June 1970
Harold Wilson	Labour	4 March 1974
James Callaghan	Labour	5 April 1976
Margaret Thatcher	Conservative	4 May 1979
John Major	Conservative	28 November 1990
Anthony Blair	Labour	1 May 1997
Gordon Brown	Labour	27 June 2007
David Cameron	Conservative (5)	11 May 2010

Notes:

(1) Coalition government from May 1915

(2) Coalition government

(3) National government

(4) Coalition government from May 1940 until 1945; national government from May 1945 until July 1945

(5) Coalition government

The Sources and Strengths of the Prime Minister's Power
For convenience of study these can be summarised under five main headings:

1. *Control of the Cabinet*
2. *Prime Minister and Parliament*
3. *Prime Minister and Party*
4. *Prime Minister and Administration*
5. *Powers of Patronage, Media Attention, etc.*

1. Control of the Cabinet
The phrase 'primus inter pares' suggests the Prime Minister is but one, the most influential one certainly, amongst his/her cabinet colleagues and equals. It is debatable as to the accuracy of such a statement. To be little more than 'first among equals' suggests a very weak prime minister. The development of the office of prime minister, along with the power of patronage and media attention, has reinforced the controls over the cabinet existing since the 19th century. Even a so-called weak prime minister such as John Major was able to manipulate his cabinet. He was far more than first among equals.

a) The Powers of Appointment and Dismissal
The Prime Minister has the right to appoint, promote, demote, transfer and dismiss any Cabinet member. A quick footnote here is this may depend upon political considerations as to how these rights may be utilised. How this is applied within a coalition government is not necessarily clear. In the coalition, is it the Prime Minister who sacks a Liberal Democrat cabinet member, or the Deputy Prime Minister, or both?

There have been some dramatic examples of how a Prime Minister can elevate Ministers of State, backbench MPs or even outsiders to Cabinet rank. Harold Wilson promoted Frank Cousins, the Transport and General Workers Union (TGWU) General Secretary, straight into the Cabinet as Minister of Technology in 1964. Cousins did not become an MP until after his by-election victory at Nuneaton in January 1965, which in effect legitimised his position. James Callaghan promoted David Owen to Foreign Secretary in 1977 even though Owen's previous experience was only as Minister of State (i.e. outside the Cabinet). Margaret Thatcher more than any other Prime Minister shaped her Cabinet to produce a loyal team by a constant succession of hiring and firings. Those not of a Thatcherite line, such as Gilmour and St. John Stevas were replaced gradually by the likes of Brittan, Lawson and Major. These newcomers were seen as sympathetic to Thatcher's policies. Since they owed their promotion to her, and not because of their standing in the party, they would presumably remain loyal. When one of her most loyal supporters, Geoffrey Howe, refused to toe the Thatcher line on Europe, he was demoted from Foreign Secretary and replaced by the relatively inexperienced John Major.

Tony Blair's position was not too dissimilar to that of Margaret Thatcher. Many MPs who desired promotion owed their position to Blair. All cabinet promotions, demotions and reshuffles were always measured against the TB-GB scale – whether there were more or fewer Blair supporters promoted than Brown supporters.

The resignation and re-appointment of Peter Mandelson to the Blair Cabinet also demonstrates the power of appointment that can be wielded. Ten months after resigning over a loan scandal in December 1998, Mandelson was rehabilitated and promoted to the Northern Ireland Office. Yet in January 2001, Mandelson was again forced to resign because of further alleged personal indiscretions. Mandelson was reinstated under the Brown Premiership to an even more prominent position within the cabinet.

Within the coalition government, the prominence of both party leaders is important, in their respective roles of Prime Minister and Deputy Prime Minister. While there is no equivalent of the TB-GBs, Liberal Democrat promotions have seen the rise of the Cleggites e.g. Danny Alexander replacing David Laws. Within the Conservative Party, the resignation of Liam Fox saw the promotion of Justine Greening – who is clearly part of the Cameron-Osborne axis within the party. This caused some rumblings of discontent from the Euro-sceptic right of the Conservative party – but no more than this.

b) The Summoning of Cabinet Meetings and Setting of the Cabinet Agenda

Although these powers might appear routine they do give the Prime Minister the initiative in the exercise of Cabinet business. Tony Benn gave a shrewd account of how thoroughly a prime minister can exercise personal control of the conduct of government business including Cabinet discussion and the decision on the circulation of Cabinet papers. Martin Burch has supported these statements by pointing out that as a result of the sheer volume of government transactions the prime minister wields ultimate authority through by-passing the cabinet and relying on Cabinet Committees, inner Cabinets, the Prime Minister's Office and informal groupings. To this list can be added task forces, focus groups and political advisers.

Prime Ministers can use their position as chair of the Cabinet to prevent issues from being raised in Cabinet. In the late 1960s, Wilson went to extraordinary lengths to keep devaluation off the Cabinet agenda. Two decades later, Thatcher rode roughshod over anyone who wished to raise issues or questions that she did not want to discuss; examples include: blocking Geoffrey Howe from asking a question on the issue of the sovereignty of the Falklands; and, allegedly removing an item from the Cabinet agenda at the time of the Westland Affair. This was to do with the takeover of the Westland Helicopter Company. Michael Heseltine, who resigned over the affair, suggested the item was left off the agenda to enable an American-Italian offer (which supposedly had the tacit support of Thatcher) to succeed.

Blair took a step sideways by actually downplaying the importance of the cabinet. It became little more than a forum for informal discussion, without a fixed agenda. The order of items to be discussed tended to be set at the meeting. In fact the meetings themselves often lasted less than an hour. This may have strengthened Blair's position. He was able to bypass the full cabinet more easily by underplaying its usefulness, or, alternatively, reporting *fait accomplis* decisions back to the cabinet. Contentious issues were normally resolved between the PM and the individual ministers concerned – which was also very much a Thatcher tactic. Blair would also make decisions and then announce them to the cabinet. Examples of such actions include the announcement of a pay freeze for ministers, and the go-ahead for the Millennium Dome.

In sum, it has generally come to be accepted as a customary practice the Prime Minister controls the Cabinet and timing of Cabinet meetings. This has changed somewhat under the coalition government. Cabinet has become reinvigorated, with the Prime Minister not able to dominate to the same extent – unless there has been agreement reached between the coalition partners prior to the meeting of the full cabinet.

c) Appointment of Chairpersons of Cabinet Committees
The subject of Cabinet Committees often looms large, particularly with reference to executive power and dominance. There was a perception the Prime Minister had come to rely on these committees. This, in turn, was partly instrumental in undermining the authority of Cabinet government. The Prime Minister would ensure those senior Cabinet colleagues most sympathetic to his/her policies would chair many of these committees (unless the PM appointed him/herself as chair). The role of these Cabinet Committees has diminished somewhat under both the Brown and the coalition government. While they still exist, as noted in the previous chapter, they are far fewer in number. The Coalition Agreement stipulates very clear rules on the chair and deputy chair of any such committees – neither party may hold both posts within a given committee. Consequently, one of the prime ministerial powers of appointment has been diminished quite significantly.

d) Determination of the Composition and Size of the Cabinet
Through the lessons of experience and practicality modern Cabinets comprise 20-24 members, although constitutionally there is nothing to prevent a prime minister from reducing or increasing the numbers. The coalition cabinet contains 23 members, with a number of other ministers attending some cabinet meetings (without actually being full cabinet members).

In the past there have been vague suggestions of increasing the size of the cabinet so all major areas of government policy and administration are covered. This would present a cabinet of around 40 members. Such ideas have been ignored as it is difficult enough to conduct Cabinet business with the present size. It is most likely that the majority of prime ministers would actually prefer to work with a smaller Cabinet but the demands of policy and administration militate against this. Within the limits of size, however, there is scope for the prime minister to alter and shape the personnel and the departmental structure (see Table 11.1 in the previous chapter).

Over the years the departments of state and ex-portfolio posts have altered to reflect changing needs and prime ministerial preferences. It is a reflection of the importance attached to the economy that in addition to the Chancellorship of the Exchequer another Treasury post – the Chief Secretary of the Treasury – also occupies a Cabinet seat. The growing significance given to ecology and the environment persuaded Edward Heath to create a new department – that of the Environment; incorporating housing, local government and transport. The last named (Transport) had previously been a separate Cabinet post, and was later reinstated as such. Under the 1997-2001 Blair Government, there was another merger with the creation of the Department of the Environment, Transport and the Regions. John Prescott headed this huge department. It was restructured again after the 2001 election to Transport, Local Government and the Regions, with Prescott making way for Stephen Byers. Education and Employment were separate departments until they were merged by John Major. Blair maintained this merger until after the 2001 election, when the department was renamed Education and Skills. The coalition government reverted back to the Department for Education. Other changes under Blair and Brown saw the creation of a Department for Business, Enterprise and Regulatory Reform, and a Department for Innovation, Universities and Skills. The coalition government drew these departments together with the creation of the Department for Business, Innovation and Skills.

The constant change in the personnel of Cabinets does not necessarily make much difference to its size or composition of posts but it does help to demonstrate the power a prime minister can wield within the Cabinet itself. Margaret Thatcher holds the record for the number of dismissals from her Cabinet – although this may be attributed to her longevity in office. The resurrection of ministerial careers can be almost at the whim of the prime minister. Tony Blair, for example, returned Peter Mandelson (after his first resignation) to the Cabinet at the earliest opportunity. David Cameron made it clear he did not want to have endless reshuffles. He had only one complete cabinet reshuffle during his first term of office – at the mid-point of the term. The occasional ministerial resignation saw the odd minister climb the greasy pole of cabinet promotions.

e) Existence of 'Inner Cabinets'
It would be misleading to judge the extent of prime ministerial power simply through the channels of the Cabinet and Cabinet committees. Most prime

ministers in the twentieth century relied heavily on a group of advisors both in and out of the Cabinet. The existence of these 'inner cabinets' (sometimes called 'kitchen cabinets') has often been denied or at least acknowledged only on an informal basis. It is in times of crisis the secrecy is discarded and the 'Inner Cabinet' placed on a more formal basis e.g. the Falklands and Gulf Wars or the coal miners strike of 1984-85. On matters of national security the prime minister assumes full responsibility and shares information with only a handful of chosen senior ministers. Security matters of this calibre never go before the full Cabinet. It is by working through such small groups of 'loyalists' that prime ministers have an enhanced opportunity of extending their power base. Cabinet business is controlled more easily by restricting it to those few members who are fully trusted or who are regarded as vital to a particular strategy.

The assessment of a prime minister's power in relation to his/her Cabinet in the end depends not just upon the formal arrangements described above but also on the standing a particular prime minister enjoys with his/her colleagues. There have been domineering PMs before Thatcher and Blair, like David Lloyd George and Winston Churchill. Interestingly, though, both of these were in war-time, when special circumstances apply. Thatcher's dominance over her Cabinet appeared almost absolute and shakeable – to the extent the Crossman thesis of the demise of Cabinet government was resurrected. Her fall from power, at the hands of her Cabinet, shows how foolish it is to rely on a single theory for an explanation of prime ministerial power. Supporters of this theory gathered again, talking of Prime Ministerial Government under Blair. Again, they were brought up short with his demise.

2) Prime Minister and Parliament

It may be stating the obvious, but it is still highly pertinent to point out no prime minister can maintain power without a majority in the House of Commons. Such a majority is never taken for granted. The performance of the prime minister at the dispatch box at Question Time and in important debates is regarded as highly important, even when there is a large majority as under the Conservative Government of 1987-92 or the Labour Government of 1997-2001. When the majority is wafer thin or non-existent, as experienced by the Conservative Government of 1992-97, performances must be nothing less than brilliant. With a coalition government, even more of a balancing act becomes necessary. This was most obvious for David Cameron over the issue of Europe in late 2011, when there was a debate and a vote on whether to have a referendum on continued membership of the European Union.

Party morale, regardless of the size of the majority, constantly needs boosting and now that millions of voters can watch the Prime Minister and the Leader of the Opposition facing each other at lunchtime every Wednesday, the performance of both protagonists takes on an added electoral significance. It is generally agreed that Thatcher 'defeated' Neil Kinnock in their duels. The contests between Major and each of Kinnock, Smith and Blair were far more even. William Hague, on the other hand, tended to come out ahead against Tony Blair on many occasions. Blair's performances beyond the Dispatch Box tended to more than make up for these 'defeats'. Cameron regularly defeated the rather dour Gordon Brown, but it was a far more even contest between Ed Miliband and David Cameron. Regardless, Parliamentary skill is an important ingredient in helping a prime minister to exert authority over his/her party and, through the party, Parliament.

3) Prime Minister and Party

If viewed logically, all prime ministers' powers emanate from command of the party. Without this support a prime minister's position becomes untenable as Neville Chamberlain (1940) and Margaret Thatcher (1990) found to their cost. Eden (1957) and to a lesser extent Macmillan (1963) might well have been deposed if convenient illnesses had not intervened. The Blair-Brown years were significant here. Within the Labour Party, there was a clear divide between the supporters of the then-Prime Minister and his Chancellor. Brown commanded such support from within the party as to be able to stand up to Blair with near impunity.

A prime minister is constantly engaged in ensuring party loyalty mainly through the power of patronage. We have already seen how Cabinet positions can be allocated according to prime ministerial choice. Added to this, through the use of the party whips, carrots are offered to backbench MPs and junior ministers to retain loyalty (such as peerages and knighthoods). Regardless of ability, some MPs will remain on the backbenches if they are regarded as sceptical or disloyal. Again, the vote in 2011 on whether to have a referendum on continued EU membership is significant. Backbench Conservative MPs were warned not to vote against the government position i.e. they must vote against the motion. Some of these euro-sceptic MPs were potentially about to lose their seats (as there were proposals to reduce the number of MPs from 650 to 600 – although this proposed legislation later fell). It is alleged some of these MPs were warned they would receive no party support in finding a new seat if they failed to toe the government line!

Ultimately there is the weapon of parliamentary dissolution to bring a recalcitrant party to heel. The fear of MPs losing their seats at an ensuing general election is supposed to act as a deterrent against a party dethroning its leader. While there is no *evidence* that any prime minister has ever considered using such a drastic weapon, there are many *reports* that John Major threatened such action over the Maastricht debate. What a party has to consider is whether replacing a prime minister will win or lose the next general election.

John Major once took the radical action of resigning as party leader, while still retaining the post of Prime Minister. The aim of this action was to force any internal opposition in the Conservative Party into the open. John Redwood stood against Major and was soundly defeated. This action strengthened Major's position over what was clearly a divided Conservative Party.

A prime minister's authority over the party is very much a two-way process. The party realises its fortunes are tied to the ability of the leader, while the prime minister by controlling appointments and using powers of patronage seeks to maintain authority over the party. The two-way process is much more obvious within a coalition government. With the Prime Minister's party having to make some concessions to the junior coalition partner, this often causes some rancour within the party – be it over policy or appointments.

4) Prime Minister and Administration

A prime minister's authority is far more wide-ranging than just the control of the Cabinet, Parliament and Party. It embraces all aspects of government business and appointments. The First Lord of the Treasury is the official title bestowed on a prime minister, indicating command of the civil service machine. Prime ministers in the past were theoretically entitled to appoint senior civil service positions, yet Thatcher was the first to supposedly 'interfere' in the appointments process. There is now supposed to be open competition for many senior posts, although the Civil Service Commission and the Senior Appointments Selection Committee may set out the required procedures.

The prime minister is supported by the Prime Minister's Office, which is part of the Cabinet Office. In 2001, it was restructured into three directorates:

Policy and Government – focuses on medium- and long-term policy analysis
Communications and Strategy – is, in effect, a press office. Under some prime ministers (most notably Thatcher and Blair) the person in charge of press relations (Bernard Ingham and Alastair Campbell, respectively) were seen as being phenomenally influential in getting the PM's version of events publicised.

Government and Political Relations – handles party-political matters.

The important thing to note here is this is not a Prime Minister's Department. There has been much talk about whether or not the Prime Minister's Office (or even the Cabinet Office) should become a proper department for the prime minister. Sir Richard Wilson (Cabinet Secretary during part of Tony Blair's premiership) was adamant there was "no need for a formal Prime Minister's Department" (Hennessy, 2000b, p. 491).

5) Powers of Patronage, Media Attention, etc.

Amongst the various writers on the position of the prime minister, it was Tony Benn who placed the greatest emphasis on patronage as a source of power and authority rather than on the institutional or constitutional sources. This is indeed a very important point. A modern prime minister does indeed possess very wide discretionary powers on a whole range of appointments that often have little to do with the business of government *per se*. It is difficult to trace exactly how a prime minister came to acquire some of these powers. They appear simply to have grown with the constant extension of government authority. These powers range from the appointment of bishops (in conjunction with the monarch, who acts upon the PM's advice) to the chairs of the BBC and ITC, from the creation of peers to quango appointments and the recommending of persons for honours (such as baronetcies, knighthoods, OBEs, MBEs).

This patronage comes 'with the job'. Yet some prime ministers have used it unscrupulously, as Lloyd George did in selling honours. Margaret Thatcher used this patronage to ensure those sympathetic to her ideology were rewarded or placed in important positions to facilitate her policies. Tony Blair appeared little different, with allegations of cronyism appearing in the first term of office. 'Tony's cronies' was a label used to describe the appointed peers remaining in the partially reformed House of Lords, as well as anyone else who had links to the Labour Party and who was appointed to any post.

Television and 24 hour-a-day news enables a prime minister to receive an inordinate amount of attention which helps not just to project his/her image before the public gaze but enhances the status of the Office itself. This, though, is a double-edged sword – especially if the publicity starts to generate hostility as could be seen in the fuel protests of September 2000, or the protests about university tuition fees in 2011, or those about spending cuts. Yet a prime minister must always try to utilise the publicity to best advantage. Thus Blair brought attention to the numerous problems being caused and exacerbated by the fuel protests, rather than trying to deal with them. Similarly, Cameron threw his support behind the judges who came down hard on protesters who had broken the law.

From the above assessment it can be seen on paper and often in reality a British prime minister does appear to possess quite formidable sources of power and authority. An understandable follow-on from this is to suggest a prime minister might be 'quasi-presidential', or cabinet government is now virtually extinct and is being replaced by prime ministerial government. When Margaret Thatcher assumed such commanding authority for eleven years it was tempting to subscribe to the Crossman thesis; but Thatcher was eventually removed by her cabinet. Tony Blair had comparisons being drawn between himself and Thatcher prior to completing his first term in office. He was also undone by cabinet colleagues. Commentators appear to forget Britain's strong parliamentary democratic tradition, based on a cabinet system of government, is not so easily subverted by a Lloyd George, Churchill, Thatcher or Blair. This is clearly the case when examining the coalition government.

Constraints on a Prime Minister's Power

The fall of Margaret Thatcher should be an object lesson to those who believe in untrammelled prime ministerial power. Prior to her demise there were some commentators who were sceptical as to whether Cabinet government had given way to prime ministerial government. This perspective of questioning prime ministerial dominance was again undermined by the Blair premiership. Yet there are constraints upon the powers of a prime minister that need to be borne in mind.

1) Prime Minister and Cabinet

The prime minister's position is still supposed to be 'primus inter pares'. This assumes the cabinet is a collection of equals headed by a prime minister whose authority is only slightly stronger than his/her colleagues. Added to this, unlike Chief Executives in many other systems (e.g. USA), the British Prime Minister is not the Head of State, hence the 'primus inter pares' position.

According to this doctrine the Cabinet collectively possesses greater legal authority than the prime minister heading it. Since Cabinet government is only a convention, it requires more than a mere statement of the doctrine to prove it has greater authority than the prime minister. In reality it can exert its control through a number of practical devices.

a) The Formation of Cabinet

Theoretically there is no legal constraint on a prime minister choosing any member of his/her party in the Commons or Lords as a Cabinet minister. As is common in political tradition, practice can diverge sharply from theory. After all, there are really only a small number of party members who can qualify for membership of the Cabinet. Some senior colleagues can hardly be omitted without them attracting sympathetic support on the backbenches. Ted Heath took a calculated risk when dismissing Enoch Powell from his Shadow Cabinet in the late 1960s. In 1979, Margaret Thatcher was almost compelled to keep most of the senior colleagues inherited from her predecessor, but she gradually removed them once her position was established. When John Major replaced Thatcher, he was forced to include Michael Heseltine and Douglas Hurd (the two candidates he defeated in the leadership election) in his first cabinet. Tony Blair had little option but to include Gordon Brown, Margaret Beckett, Robin Cook and John Prescott in his first Cabinet. Within the coalition government, Chris Huhne was always going to be one of the Liberal Democrat cabinet members, as was Vince Cable. David Cameron took a calculated risk with the resignation of Liam Fox not to appoint a new standard bearer for the euro-sceptic right of the Conservative Party.

In an ideal situation, from a prime minister's perspective at least, any prime minister would dearly love to select those who share his/her views and are at the same time reasonably competent. Thatcher came closest to this ideal among modern prime ministers as the slogan 'one of us' became one of the criteria for entry into her Cabinet. Yet these close supporters cannot necessarily gain immediate access to the Cabinet. Tony Blair could not promote Peter Mandelson straight into the Cabinet. Instead, Mandelson was given an influential junior ministerial post. David Cameron gave Oliver Letwin a junior ministerial post in the Cabinet Office, but Letwin's role is to provide policy advice to the Prime Minister.

The composition of a Cabinet has always proved a difficult task for a prime minister because, apart from balancing the different wings of the party, he/she has to blend experience with youthfulness. This is made even more difficult with a coalition government, as the wings of each coalition partner need to be appeased.

b) The Question of Dismissal

There is no constitutional restraint on the right of prime ministers to dismiss any of their colleagues or even a whole batch of them as in the infamous case of 'The Night of the Long Knives' in 1962 when Harold Macmillan sacked seven Cabinet members, including his Chancellor of the Exchequer, Selwyn Lloyd. Dismissal is a matter of calculation on the part of the prime minister - although in Macmillan's case it turned out to be a miscalculation. Senior ministers can be dismissed without damaging a prime minister's authority, but only if they do not have a strong following in the party. Thus Thatcher could dismiss John Biffen, but not Nigel Lawson or Geoffrey Howe (although both eventually resigned) because of the possibility of repercussions among the backbenches. Similarly, John Major could never dismiss Michael Portillo or any other of the so-called 'Cabinet Bastards', and Tony Blair could not dismiss Gordon Brown.

Dismissal can be seen as a form of restraint on a prime minister. It is a weapon that needs careful handling, with a full realisation of its consequences. Thatcher used this weapon more often than any other prime minister. Major and Blair both clearly learned from its potentially disastrous overuse.

c) Control of the Agenda

Michael Heseltine complained it was the refusal of Margaret Thatcher to table the European offer for the Westland Helicopter Company on the Cabinet agenda and tampering with the minutes that precipitated his resignation and the ensuing Westland crisis. This accusation was, unsurprisingly, strongly denied by Thatcher. Regardless, this is a very rare example of the Cabinet agenda figuring crucially in a crisis.

Theoretically, the prime minister has the right to determine the agenda of Cabinet meetings. In the realm of practical politics it is hardly likely a prime minister can postpone indefinitely the inclusion of a subject other Cabinet members wish to discuss. What was interesting with the Blair Government was Cabinet meetings often did not even have an agenda. This placed Blair in a very dominant position; he could influence what his Cabinet colleagues discussed. The coalition government could not even consider such an approach.

d) Control of the Cabinet

The 'Spitting Image' programme gave viewers a jaundiced picture of the docility, even craven cowardice, of Margaret Thatcher's Cabinet. There are some allegations this picture was actually very close to the truth. Thatcher always made it known that 'as Prime Minister, I could not waste time with any internal arguments' but also denied she always won the arguments in Cabinet. A similar example was presented about Tony Blair when he decided Cabinet members would not take a pay increase in the late 1990s. No member of the Cabinet questioned the decision until he had left the room, whereupon, it is alleged, there was uproar.

There is no record of any prime minister getting his/her way with every proposed measure; it is a matter of judgement as to how far a Cabinet can really control a prime minister considering the adroit way in which the latter can sidestep or bypass the Cabinet by working through Cabinet committees or through informal meetings of trusted allies. In the last resort, though, as in the case of Margaret Thatcher, the attitude of the Cabinet can be largely instrumental in deciding the fate of a prime minister.

2) Prime Minister and Parliament

Unlike the President of the USA who is elected directly by popular vote through an electoral college and constitutionally operating outside Congress, the British Prime Minister is elected not as a prime minister but as an ordinary MP who happens to be head of his/her party. Since 1902, all prime ministers have come from the House of Commons and hence command of Parliament is essential to their survival. A successful vote of 'No Confidence' in the Commons either leads to the resignation of the Prime Minister or, more likely, the dissolution of Parliament and the calling of a general election. In 1940, Neville Chamberlain resigned despite winning a vote of 'no confidence' because of the large numbers who voted against him. James Callaghan lost a vote of 'no confidence' in 1979 and called a general election, which he lost. Successful votes of 'No Confidence' are very rare but they are threats no prime minister can take lightly.

More customarily prime ministers' performances at the dispatch box can be taken as one of the barometers of their hold and command of their party and Parliament. In crucial debates, and week by week at Question Time, parliamentary performances by the prime minister impose their own discipline. Margaret Thatcher was able to dominate both in the late 1980s. John Major, at times, proved to be surprisingly adept. Tony Blair dominated his party even though he did not always 'win' at Prime Minister's Question Time. Gordon Brown, on the other hand, was not able to dominate his party in the way many people expected. Added to this, his performances at the dispatch box were not exactly scintillating. There were pressures from within the party for him to stand down.

Indirectly, therefore, Parliament does impose restraints upon a prime minister because poor performance in the Commons can induce discontent in the party and, combined with other factors, might lead to his/her downfall. Many Tories feared John Major would look weak when compared to Margaret Thatcher but he demonstrated some Parliamentary skills not even Thatcher could match – especially in brinkmanship. Tony Blair was a more than capable performer in the Chamber but was not a natural debater, sometimes struggling with spontaneity. Gordon Brown was somewhat dour and lacking in spontaneity. Cameron, on the other hand, appears more capable in the House, but has a far more difficult balancing act to play than any of his post-war predecessors.

3) Prime Minister and Party

It cannot be emphasised enough that a British prime minister's position rests wholly on the support of his/her party. As long as the party retains electoral popularity the prime minister will almost certainly continue to enjoy the support of the party. Even total domination over the party for eleven years cannot save a prime minister who looks likely to lose a subsequent general election. The fall of Thatcher will always be an object lesson on the degree of ruthlessness displayed by a party (particularly the Conservatives) when it senses electoral disaster if the existing leader is retained. Yet in the latter days of the Major Government, the prime minister was not replaced, possibly because the party was too divided, and possibly because there was no viable alternative to John Major.

Tony Blair appeared to enjoy unrivalled dominance over his party. The huge majority in the Commons in 1997 meant he could get his legislative programme through the House with relative ease. In the year 2000, for example, commentators were talking not about who would win the 2001 General Election but rather by how many seats Blair would win. Arguably Thatcher enjoyed a similar experience prior to the 1987 election, but only three and a half years later, she was removed. Blair survived somewhat longer, but there were clear divisions within the Labour Party throughout his time in office.

In many ways it may well be said a prime minister's most difficult task is to command the party rather than Parliament and the country, although the three are inextricably linked. Attempting to reconcile the many policy objectives a party pursues, and keeping important influential colleagues reasonably happy, while at the same time having to give the impression of strong leadership, requires outstanding abilities from a prime minister. Thatcher, for much of her time in office, was able to do so, with her emphasis upon 'conviction politics'.

Overall, Major struggled but was able to remain almost unchallenged in office until electoral defeat. Tony Blair, with a clearly compliant party, appeared to succeed. Yet questions remain as to the extent of this 'compliance' without the support of Gordon Brown.

4) Prime Minister and the Media

The office of prime minister grew immensely in stature during the twentieth century. It is not just the 'glamour' of the post that is important. Particular attention has to be paid to personality, actions and general demeanour as presented in the media but especially on television. Even the most trivial of events can be highlighted, whether it was John Major eating at a 'Happy Eater' restaurant or Tony Blair wearing short-sleeved shirts or his sweating profusely at the Labour Party Conference in 2000, or the first Cameron-Clegg press conference in the gardens of 10 Downing Street. Modern prime ministers have to accustom themselves to living in a goldfish bowl – as do their families. Prime ministers are constantly on television whether in the broadcasts of the House of Commons proceedings, being interviewed and photographed, or taking part in more mundane activities like attending church fêtes. Their private lives are dissected. The Blair family were pursued wherever they went on holiday, and ended up giving photo opportunities in a manner not unlike the Royal family. For the Camerons, it was similar, especially with the birth of their daughter, Florence, in 2010. The birth occurred while the family were on holiday in Cornwall, and the media were there to report the entire event.

Prime ministerial leadership style and substance is a constant fixation for the media. The polling organisations – including MORI, NOP and Gallup – highlight the standing of the prime minister not only against his/her rival in the leader of the opposition, but also in relation to the party, or with regard to particular qualities – toughness, integrity, and competence.

There is a price to be paid for this intense media exposure. Whilst prime ministers attract more attention than the other party leaders, any major slip they make can cost them and their parties the next general election. Popularity alone is not sufficient to win or lose an election. In 1970, Harold Wilson was far more popular than Ted Heath, but still lost the election; similarly, James Callaghan over Margaret Thatcher in 1979. Quite clearly prime ministers have to rely on far more than just their personal reputations to win elections.

5) Conclusion

The idea that the office of the prime minister is 'what the holder makes of it' may not be constitutionally correct but it does emphasise the *personal element* so often neglected. The debate on the nature of prime ministerial power appears to ebb and flow according to who holds the office and their relationship with their Cabinets and party.

The Case against the Concept of Prime Ministerial Government

The essence of the case against prime ministerial government is based on a number of factors which can constrain a prime minister. These can be summarised under three headings: political; administrative; and, personal constraints.

Politically, as head of the party any prime minister has to heed the wishes of the party and the competing factions within it, particularly within the Cabinet. Senior colleagues' ambitions have to be appreciated and the dangers of rivals' challenges overcome. It took Thatcher until her third term of office (1987-90) before she had the Cabinet she wanted – and it eventually unseated her. Tony Blair clearly shared power with Gordon Brown. Brown withdrew from the leadership contest after the death of John Smith. This prevented a civil war breaking out in the party but in office Brown had a position and status unachieved by any previous Chancellor of the Exchequer or even Deputy Prime Minister. A number of authors (including Hargrove, 2001; Heffernan, 2005b) have pointed out institutional factors make it near to impossible for a prime minister to become a president.

Administratively, the prime minister has a number of constraints forced upon him/her. A resignation by a key member of the Cabinet can question the extent of control over the Cabinet agenda (e.g. Heseltine in 1986). External factors always impinge upon what should be discussed in the Cabinet. Within the Cabinet itself there is bound to be argument between a group of powerful ministers each with their own axe to grind. This is even more the case in a coalition government, as can be seen by the relationship between George Osborne and Vince Cable.

Even the notion that prime ministers always get their own way in Cabinet flies in the face of known opinion. Thatcher was defeated on numerous issues, including subsidies to nationalised industries, the extent of public expenditure, and joining the European Exchange Rate Mechanism (ERM). It is also most likely the Falklands' Task Force would never have sailed in 1982 without Cabinet approval. Blair never got to have a referendum on Britain joining the Euro; he was blocked by Brown. As for a coalition cabinet; it is very unlikely the prime minister will get his/her own way on everything.

Personally, the very nature of a prime minister's position is a limiting factor. No single person could possibly oversee the enormous amount of work emanating from the various government departments. If anything, a prime minister may actually be in a weak position compared to fellow Cabinet members. The Prime Minister's Office is relatively small (currently around 200 members) when compared to over half a million civil servants working for the various departments. Even if a prime minister wished to intervene in a particular issue or concern, he/she may actually lack the full policy information needed to do so effectively.

The dominant personality of particular prime ministers sometimes gives the illusion this domination is constant and unquestioned; whereas it is much more evident at certain periods, for instance after a general election. Thatcher appeared to dominate and thus her fall came as something of a shock. Yet the reality was she had been losing control over the previous two years, especially on the issues of Europe and the Poll Tax. Major had the exact opposite problem. He appeared never to be in control after winning the 1992 election. This, combined with his 'grey' image and his emphasis upon collegiality, meant he never had a chance to visibly wield the same authority as Thatcher. Blair, on the other hand, asserted his authority from day one. Jokes about Blair being a control freak and jokes about 'Tony's cronies' added to the image of his dominance.

The Case for the Existence of Prime Ministerial Government

Despite the above sceptical observations concerning the limitations on prime ministerial authority, there still remains a powerful body of thought which believes there is an inexorable drift towards prime ministerial government. Arguably, this drift has ceased with the coalition government, but it is more than likely it will resurface again. Even with as collegially-oriented a prime minister as John Major, the arguments were Cabinet government was doomed. With Tony Blair as prime minister, such arguments gained momentum.

One of the most prominent advocates of prime ministerial government was Tony Benn. In 1985 he published an article entitled "The Case for a Constitutional Premiership" (in the journal *Parliamentary Affairs*). While this article did acknowledge a prime minister could be removed through constitutional and party mechanisms, the main thrust of the argument was the increasing centralisation of power would make such action extremely unlikely. Added to this, with the increasing powers of patronage and greater emphasis upon personal rule, the prime minister has become the central focus of our parliamentary democracy.

In addition, Cabinet business is controlled completely by the prime minister through his/her setting of the agenda, on the circulation of Cabinet papers, on the establishment of Cabinet committees and who should chair them, all unbeknown to Parliament and the public. The most powerful weapon of all is the calling of a general election. A prime minister has the right to determine when a general election shall be held (within the constitutional five year span). With this weapon a prime minister can manipulate his/her Cabinet and party, and the economy of the country. Yet David Cameron yielded this power with the introduction of a fixed-term parliament. This may have been more to do with making sure the coalition stayed in power for the full term rather than wishing to lose such a potent weapon. It may, after all, only be yielded temporarily.

In some respects, the debate has moved on from Benn's article. There are suggestions we now have some form of presidential-styled politics. This argument arose during the Thatcher years, disappeared while Major was Prime Minister, and reappeared under Blair. 'Has Prime Minister Major been

Replaced by President Blair?' asked Thomas (2000). With the media emphasis now so much upon the prime minister, it may well be there is a development of presidential-styled politics within a Parliamentary framework – and even within a coalition government. The role and importance of the Cabinet has clearly been reduced. The emphasis moved to Cabinet committees, and has since moved again to focus groups, and bilateral meetings. These can all be engineered by the Prime Minister.

There is a collorary. A prime minister can only dominate if the Cabinet lets him/her do so. To dominate, a prime minister needs a range of power resources, including a strong reputation, an association with political success, a high standing within his/her political party, and public popularity (Heffernan, 2003a). A dominant prime minister may be able to intercede on many issues, but that does not make them presidential. "Too often the presidential thesis treats intervention as control" (Bevir & Rhodes, 2006, p. 682). Prime Minister Attlee "always insisted that the Prime Minister was not and should not be a presidential figure" (Theakston, 2005, p. 18).

Conclusion

The position of the Prime Minister is what the holder makes of it. The powers any single prime minister can wield are the same as any other prime minister. Some of the constraints are clearly different. A prime minister with a large majority in the House of Commons is less constrained by the party than a prime minister with a wafer thin majority, or one in a coalition. Yet, both Thatcher and Blair were removed as Prime Minister despite sizeable majorities in the Commons. There is, therefore, a clear need for a prime minister to stay in touch with his/ her Cabinet colleagues and, perhaps more importantly, with the backbench MPs. Ultimately, a prime minister depends upon them for the retention of the post.

Selected bibliography

Bevir, Mark & Rhodes, R. A. W. (2006). "Prime Ministers, Presidentialism and Westminster Smokescreens", *Political Studies* vol. 54-4, pp. 671-690.

Denver, David & Garnett, Mark, (2012). "The Popularity of British Prime Ministers", *British Journal of Politics and International Relations* vol. 14-1, pp. 57-73.

Hargrove, Erwin. (2001). "The presidency and the prime ministership as institutions: an American perspective", *British Journal of Politics and International Relations* vol. 3-1, pp. 49-70.

Heffernan, Richard. (2005a). "Exploring (and Explaining) the British Prime Minister", *British Journal of Politics and International Relations* vol.7-3, pp. 605-620.

Heffernan, Richard. (2005b). "Why the Prime Minister cannot be a President: Comparing Institutional Imperatives in Britain and America", *Parliamentary Affairs* vol. 58-1, pp. 53-70

Hennessy, Peter. (2000b). *The Prime Minister: The Office and its Holders since 1945*: Allen Lane

Theakston, Kevin & Gill, Mark. (2006). "Rating 20th-Century British Prime Ministers", *British Journal of Politics and International Relations* vol.8-2, pp. 193-21.

Websites
www.cabinet-office.gov.uk/
Home page of the Cabinet office

www.number-10.gov.uk/
The home page of 10 Downing Street

Questions
1. Comment on the view that prime ministerial government has arrived in Britain.
2. How is the role of a prime minister in a coalition government any different to that of a prime minister of a single party in power?
3. "President Blair". Is this an exaggerated assessment of the powers that Tony Blair wielded?

CHAPTER 13 // CIVIL SERVICE

Contents
- **Introduction**
- **The Whitehall Model**
- **The Managerial Revolution?**
- **Ministers and Civil Servants**
- **The civil service code of conduct**
- **Special Advisers**
- **Politicisation?**
- **Conclusion**

Introduction

An appreciation of the role of the Senior Civil Service in its relationship with the government is a necessity for all students wishing to understand the nature of the British political and administrative system. This is important not just for those students studying Politics and Government, but also Public Policy and Public Administration. It is the intention of this chapter to examine the development of the Civil Service, particularly the so-called managerial revolution that has been implemented; to analyse the nature of the relationship between the top civil servants and their political masters, the ministers; to examine the charges of social elitism and excessive secrecy levelled at the Service; and to consider whether politicisation is occurring and whether such a process could be good for the Civil Service and for government *per se*.

The generally agreed definition of a 'civil servant' is one adapted from the Tomlin Commission (1931): 'a person employed by the Crown, other than holders of political or judicial posts, to carry out the work of the Government in a civil capacity and who is paid completely and directly with money voted by Parliament'. This definition covers around 450 000 employees divided into administrative, executive and clerical levels (the latter are confusingly known as Administrative Officers and Administrative Assistants), with scientists, technologists, lawyers, accountants, medical officers, psychologists, the tax inspectorate and Customs and Excise officers also included. Within the definition are also the staff who work for the Executive Agencies. The definition excludes ministers and MPs, members of the armed forces, employees of Parliament, local government and National Health Service (NHS) staff, employees of public corporations (such as the BBC), and members of quasi-governmental bodies (quangos).

Further adaptations have been made to the Tomlin Commission definition. It was broadened out to include holders "of certain other offices in respect of whose tenure of office special provision has been made". This includes special advisers and other staff.

A further change came about as a result of the Constitutional Reform and Governance Act (2010). One consequence of this legislation was "civil servants are no longer constitutionally servants of the Crown but of the state" (Van Dorpe & Horton, 2011, p. 245).

Generally when talking about the 'Civil Service', it is the senior civil service – the 'mandarins' – who are the subject of conversation. These are the policy advisers; those who generally assist with the co-ordination and improvement of the machinery of government; those who head the civil servants within a department. The actual grading structure of the civil service changed significantly in the 1990s. The current grading structure is listed below:

1. Senior Civil Service (SCS)
2. Level 6
3. Level 7
4. Senior Executive Officer
5. Higher Executive Officer
6. Executive Officer
7. Administrative Officer
8. Administrative Assistant

The SCS comprises approximately 5 000 staff. Formerly, they were graded from Level 5 up to Level 1. These are the Permanent Secretaries, the directors and deputy directors, who tender advice to ministers and who manage the machinery of government. Most attention is therefore focused upon this tier, especially the Permanent Secretaries – the administrative heads of department.

The Whitehall Model

The Whitehall Model is a label given to the role of civil servants, which includes their relationship with government ministers. Arguably, this dates back to the Northcote-Trevelyan Report (1854), which laid the foundations of the British Civil Service. It introduced a number of principles that have come to typify and indeed constitutionally to represent the nature of the Service. Although these principles have come under some pressure, they are still of great importance today:

1. *Neutrality/Impartiality*
2. *Permanence*
3. *Anonymity*
4. *Generalist tradition*

1) Neutrality/Impartiality

Although civil servants are there to assist the government of the day to achieve its aims, they remain servants of the state and are not therefore supposed to indulge in any *open* support or denigration of government policies. If a government is defeated in a general election, the Civil Service must transfer its allegiance to the incoming government. If this means reversing previous measures which it had helped to draft, so be it.

In the event of a change in government, this may appear to cause a huge upheaval. It is not necessarily the case. The mandarins will know the policy plans of both major parties at the time of a general election. Thus they prepare contingency plans for each outcome (i.e. a Labour victory or a Conservative victory). Prior to the 2010 General Election, for the first time ever, the civil service prepared for a 'hung' parliament and a possible coalition government.

The impartiality of the Civil Service is regarded as a crucial principle that needs to be preserved as a constitutional desirability. There have, however, been allegations made of attempts at politicising the Civil Service. This concern will be examined later in the chapter.

2) Permanence

Senior British Civil Servants, unlike their counterparts in for example the USA, are in permanent tenure since they are not employed by the Government, but by the Crown or state. This ensures a career Civil Service with officials acquiring experience over many years, not afraid of a change of government. As a consequence, however, a particular ethos and culture has developed which has been criticised for its rather blinkered outlook. In an attempt to reverse this attitude, there have been many attempts to reform the civil service. For example, outsiders have been employed in the upper echelons of the civil service, particularly in the Government's Executive Agencies, on fixed-term, renewable contracts. This will be discussed further later in the chapter.

3) Anonymity

In order to reinforce the doctrine of neutrality, civil servants are expected to remain silent in public on any political or contentious issue connected with government business. Civil servants are not elected and must leave their ministers to deal with the political implications of policy and action. The doctrine of ministerial responsibility (see chapter 11) should be involved in any instance where a glaring error involves a civil servant.

This is the theory. The reality is significantly different as the cloak of anonymity is being lifted more and more frequently to expose civil servants not just to the public gaze but to comment and blame. The most prominent example in recent times was Dr David Kelly, a civil servant (or, more specifically, a scientist) in the Ministry of Defence. Kelly had alleged a dossier on Iraqi weapons of mass destruction had been "transformed" in such a way as to make some of the claims sound scarier than reality – the Iraqis could deploy these weapons within 45 minutes. Kelly leaked these concerns to a BBC journalist, Andrew Gilligan, who ran with the story. Upon finding out the source of the leak, the government-of-the-day let it be known Kelly was the source of the leak (and his claims to be unfounded). Sadly, with all of the pressure brought to bear on Kelly, he committed suicide. What makes matters worse is his allegations were true.

Ministers still defend their civil servants in Parliament and public but it is becoming increasingly difficult to preserve their anonymity, as they appear on radio and television broadcasts of Select Committee investigations. How far, however, the principle of anonymity can remain compatible with the doctrine of ministerial responsibility is a matter of concern to both civil servants and constitutional commentators, especially where it is often the ministers themselves who breach the doctrine.

4) Generalist tradition

This tradition has its origins not in the Northcote-Trevelyan Report, but in the reforms introduced in the 1920s and 1930s by Warren Fisher and Edward Bridges, both of whom held the most senior civil service posts (Rhodes, 2001, p. 148). Civil servants should not be 'specialists' in a particular subject area. Rather, the idea of the 'gifted amateur' should apply. A civil servant should be able to turn their hand to anything, regardless as to the department in which he or she is located. An ideal administrator was a gifted layperson who could move from job to job within the Civil Service, who could turn their hands to any task, irrespective of the subject matter, and use their knowledge and experience of the machinery of Government to aid such problem solving. Much of this generalist approach is still visible today among the upper echelons of the civil service.

The Managerial Revolution?

In the 1970s and 1980s, a concept called **New Public Management (NPM)** came to the fore. Supporters of NPM argued management needed to be introduced into the civil service, if not the entire public sector. This was to become known as the managerial revolution. Yet the demands for greater or better management in the civil service go back much further.

In 1968, the **Fulton Report** was published. It made a number of serious criticisms of the Civil Service. Fulton argued the structure of the civil service was out of date; it had been functioning virtually unchanged for over one hundred years. Included in this was an attack on the philosophy of the 'gifted amateur', as well as the lack of training for recruits who joined the civil service.

Fulton felt there was not enough contact between the Civil Service and the rest of the community and thus an insufficient awareness of how the world outside Whitehall worked. To break down this excessive 'hothouse' atmosphere and to introduce innovations, Fulton felt more 'outsiders' from business, commerce and the professions were needed.

Fulton recommended a number of 'improvements'. Most of them were implemented but without really changing the philosophy and practices of the Civil Service. A Civil Service Department was established for staffing matters and recruitment, and a Civil Service College for training in management and other skills was also established. The structure of the Civil Service was reformed; not by introducing a single grading structure as envisaged by Fulton, but by creating a series of new classes. More specialists were recruited and promoted in an attempt to introduce greater professionalism. The principle of 'accountable management' was to be applied to the work of all departments. Where it was feasible, individual civil servants were to have job specifications and be held responsible for carrying out allotted tasks or accounting for output and costs.

Despite all of this, very little had actually changed within the civil service when Margaret Thatcher came to power in 1979, It was the Thatcher Government that introduced the most radical changes to the Civil Service since Northcote-Trevelyan – bringing in NPM. A process of change was started that was built upon by all subsequent governments.

NPM needs to be seen as part of an ideological attack on the role of the state and the public sector (see chapters 2 and 8). The underpinning belief was private sector techniques were far more effective and efficient than those in the public sector. They were, in effect, imposed on all parts of the public sector, including the civil service. "The basic idea of NPM is to make public sector organizations – and the people working in them! – much more 'business-like' and 'market-oriented', that is, performance-, cost-, efficiency- and audit-oriented" (Diefenbach, 2009, p.893).

The Reduction in the Number of Civil Servants
On the grounds of 'less government' and perceived waste in administration, Thatcher vowed to drastically reduce the number of officials. From a total of approximately 750 000 they were cut down to under 600 000 by the Thatcher Government. This process has continued, and the number of civil servants in 2012 stood at about 450 000 (although this was an increase on the previous year).

The Next Steps Report
This was a report written by Sir Robin Ibbs (originally from ICI), the full title of which was: *Improving Management in Government: The Next Steps*. It was published in February 1988. The underpinning of this document was to break the monolithic civil service machine down into a number of smaller units or agencies. Yet, although this idea was not radically new (Fulton had suggested some 'hiving off' of particular aspects of civil service work into agencies) it was heralded as the greatest shake-up of the civil service since Northcote-Trevelyan.

The advantages the agencies offer is they can carry out daily management without much interference from ministers. They can also provide the government with a degree of flexibility lacking in the more rigid departmental structure.

The Ibbs Report (or the Next Steps Report) took the idea of agencies further than any other supporter of agencies had ever suggested. The Civil Service was to be left with a core of approximately 20 000 officials who would form the heart of the Whitehall machine. The remainder would be employed by these agencies, focusing upon service delivery.

Agencies were to be used to develop the other strands of the Ibbs Report. For example, Ibbs pointed out there was insufficient focus on the delivery of government services – 95% of civil servants worked in this area. Each agency would be able to focus specifically on their service. Ibbs also suggested there was too much emphasis upon spending and not enough on getting results. In conjunction, long term planning was squeezed out by short term political pressures. Agencies could address both of these issues as well. Table 13.1 highlights the vast array of executive agencies that now exist in the UK.

There were many fears about the agencies, some of which have been realised. In some quarters it was suggested the creation of agencies was a stepping stone to privatisation. While such ideas were dismissed at the time, a small number of agencies have been privatised, for example the trading functions of Her Majesty's Stationery Office (HMSO) have become The Stationery Office Limited.

There was also a concern about the lines of accountability. While ministers were to remain accountable and responsible for policy, the Chief Executives of the agencies were to be responsible for their day-to-day running. The problem is: where does policy making end and day-to-day running commence? Each affects the other, to the extent there is no clear cut division. This has been demonstrated on a number of occasions, one of the more recent of which was between the Home Secretary, Theresa May and the then-head of the UK Border Agency, Brodie Clark. In 2011, Clark resigned from the Border Agency after being blamed by the Home Secretary for relaxing some border controls. The issue was the extent to which this had gone on. The Home Office had approved some changes but appeared to object to Clark's interpretation of the extent to which those changes applied.

Table 13.1 Executive Agencies (September 2013)

Animal Health and Veterinary Laboratories Agency	National Museums Liverpool
Arts Council England	National Offender Management Service
British Film Institute	National Portrait Gallery
British Library	Natural History Museum
British Museum	Office of the Public Guardian
Centre for Environment, Fisheries and Aquaculture Science	Olympic Delivery Authority
Companies House	Olympic Lottery Distributor
Defence Science and Technology Laboratory	Ordnance Survey
Defence Support Group	Planning Inspectorate
Driver and Vehicle Licensing Agency	Public Health England
Driving Standards Agency	Public Lending Right
Education Funding Agency	Queen Elizabeth II Conference Centre
English Heritage	Royal Armouries Museum
Equality and Human Rights Commission	Royal Museums Greenwich
Gambling Commission	Rural Payments Agency
Geffrye Museum	Science Museum Group
Government Procurement Service	Service Children's Education
Heritage Lottery Fund	Service Personnel and Veterans Agency
Highways Agency	Sir John Soane's Museum
HM Courts and Tribunals Service	Skills Funding Agency
HM Passport Office	Sport England
HM Prison Service	Sports Grounds Safety Authority
Horniman Public Museum and Public Park Trust	Standards and Testing Agency
Imperial War Museum	The Food and Environment Research Agency
Intellectual Property Office	The Insolvency Service
Land Registry	The National Archives
Legal Aid Agency	UK Anti-Doping
Maritime and Coastguard Agency	UK Debt Management Office
Medicines and Healthcare Products Regulatory Agency	UK Hydrographic Office
Met Office	UK Space Agency
National College for Teaching and Leadership	UK Sport
National Fraud Office	Vehicle and Operator Services Agency
National Gallery	Vehicle Certification Agency
National Heritage Memorial Fund	Veterinary Medicines Directorate
National Lottery Commission	Victoria and Albert Museum
National Measurement Office	VisitBritain
	Wallace Collection

Developed from www.gov.uk/government/organisations

Modernising Government

Over the years, the language of NPM has changed significantly. While, in its early incarnations, the language was about cutting spending, privatisation, better management, and the primacy of the market, the emphasis changed in the Major and Blair years. It became more about modernising government. This saw a continuing reform agenda, but one 'sold' to the public as being for their benefit rather than being ideologically-driven.

This modernisation agenda attempted to change the priorities of the civil service, as well as the public sector as a whole. An emphasis was placed on the needs of the service users ahead of the service providers, as well as on the use of technology to enhance the quality of service delivery. In many respects, from the Citizen's Charter, through Best Value and the modernisation agenda, the emphasis was upon building on the Ibbs reforms, but with a 'human face'.

NPM has altered significantly how the civil service operates. There is a far greater emphasis upon performance, as well as on budgets and cost-cutting. The belief is this has led to a far more effective and efficient civil service, one in touch with the world beyond Whitehall. Despite this, the reform agenda continues today, with even greater demands for cuts and efficiency savings. The creation of agencies, as well as the privatisation of some of them, has seen the monolithic civil service machine broken up.

Conversely, the more things change, the more they stay the same. There are still, for example, many generalists in the upper echelons of the civil service – although they are diminished in number. The permanence of the civil service has been reduced, with only a quarter of civil servants seeing it as a career (Greer & Jarman, 2010). Yet the use of special advisers (see later in this chapter) has highlighted the need for a strong and stable core for any government. The Whitehall model may be altered, but it has not fundamentally changed.

Ministers and Civil Servants

The relationship between Ministers and Civil Servants is a complex one. Viewers of the television series *Yes, Minister* saw an overbearing civil service (represented by Sir Humphrey Appleby) manipulating the inexperienced minister (Jim Hacker), out-thinking him, out-manoeuvring him all of the time. While the series may have overplayed the powers of the Civil Service, it should not be dismissed lightly.

The formal or constitutional relationship between ministers and civil servants is quite straight forward. Ministers make policy, and are accountable to Parliament for those policies. The civil service advises ministers on policy, and is involved in the implementation of the policies. The civil servants are, ultimately, accountable to the minister.

This follows very clearly from the Whitehall model, where civil servants are non-political or neutral. They obey 'their' minister. If there is a change in government, or a change in minister, the civil servants will follow the instructions of the new post-holder. Ministers come and ministers go; the civil service is a constant.

There is an argument, however, that says the formal or constitutional position oversimplifies reality. Can it really be a minister can 'control' their civil servants? Is it possible for a newly-appointed minister to be able to direct the policy-making within a new department? When making policy, it is the civil service that advises the minister. As a new minister does not get to see the papers of his or her predecessor, how can a newly-appointed minister know the worth of the advice being proffered? Under the Whitehall model, it could be argued the civil service holds a near-monopoly on the advice being given to ministers. If a lobbyist or a pressure group wishes to gain access to the minister, they must first get past the minister's gatekeepers: the civil servants.

Thus what was portrayed in *Yes, Minister* highlighted the extent to which a minister can be dominated by the civil service. The tenure of the civil service – and especially the senior civil service – leaves a minister at a distinct disadvantage. One avenue out of this is the use of special advisers, which is examined later in this chapter.

This idea of conflict and confrontation between a minister and the civil service is but one perspective. If a minister can be dominated by his or her departmental civil servants, then it is likely this same minister will be dominated in the same way within cabinet. The UK governmental system is based on government by department. There is almost a silo mentality here, with the different departments competing for scarce resources – and especially so in times of austerity. The last thing the civil servants in a given department would want is a weak minister. Thus there needs to be a balance of perspective. There are, in effect, two fights: the first is the political versus the administrative wings; the second is the inter-departmental conflict. In the case of the latter, the civil service would want a strong minister, capable of fighting the departmental corner. Consequently, the relationship between ministers and civil servants is likely to be far more fluid.

The civil service code of conduct

There is a specific code of conduct for civil servants. It details the standards of behaviour to be expected; the core values of the civil service as a whole; and is, in effect, part of the terms and conditions of employment for every civil servant. This is all part of the Civil Service Management Code, which was established in the Constitutional Reform and Governance Act (2010).

There is an argument that the Constitutional Reform and Governance Act (2010) started a more overt politicisation of the civil service. The introduction to the Civil Service Management Code states: "the Minister for the Civil Service has the power to make regulations and give instructions for the management of the Civil Service, *including the power to prescribe the conditions of service* of civil servants" (Civil Service Management Code, 2011, p. 4, emphasis added).

A code of conduct for civil servants was first published in 1996. It detailed clearly the requirements for the behaviour of all civil servants. This code of conduct, which has been retained in the 2010 legislation, highlights key aspects of any civil servants behaviour:

- *integrity*
- *honesty*
- *objectivity*
- *impartiality*

Similar codes have been established for civil servants working for the Scottish Executive, the Welsh Assembly Government and the Northern Ireland Civil Service. All of this collectively reinforces many of the standards first outlined at the time of the Northcote-Trevelyan Report.

Special Advisers

The use of special advisers to aid ministers became prominent during the Blair years – although these advisers had been used for many decades before. The difference under the Blair premiership was their proliferation.

Among other things, they were used as an alternative source of policy advice to that of the civil service. In particular during the Blair years, there was a degree of mistrust of the civil service. It had served the Thatcher and Major Governments for 18 years; consequently, there was some uneasiness as to whether or not the civil service would follow the instructions of the new government. Would, for example, the advice given to the new Labour ministers be objective, given these same civil servants had been advising a Conservative Government for so long. This lack of trust caused a number of problems between the political and administrative arms of government.

Some special advisers became very prominent: Alastair Campbell, Ed Balls, Jo Moore, to name but three. Jo Moore came to prominence while working for Stephen Byers at the Department of Transport, Local Government and Regions. There were rumours of a rather abrasive relationship with the civil servants in that department. It all came to a head on 11 September 2001 (the day passenger planes were flown into the twin towers of the World Trade Centre in New York) when an e-mail was leaked. The e-mail sent by Moore to the department's press office said it was a good day to bury bad news. Moore was eventually forced to resign in early 2002.

Such actions highlighted both the conflict between special advisers and the civil service, and the need to introduce a code of conduct for special advisers. The most recent version of this code of conduct was published in June 2010.

This document describes special advisers as "temporary civil servants", who are there "to serve the Government as a whole, and not just their appointing Minister". Special advisers are not bound by the need for objectivity in their advice. Integrity and honesty are still expected. The code of conduct for special advisers highlights how their role straddles the party-political and the governmental needs of ministers. Special advisers are, however, bound by the civil service code of conduct as well.

Politicisation?

Two questions need to be raised briefly in this section. Firstly is the civil service becoming politicised? and, secondly, should it be? A key underpinning of the British civil service has been its political neutrality, enabling the bureaucracy to serve the government of the day – and the government being able to trust civil servants to implement their policies properly. This is a key part of the constitutional relationship. Under the early years of the Blair Government, this trust was lacking. Interestingly, with the coalition government, this constitutional relationship appears to be operating well.

Despite the importance of this constitutional relationship, there have been many suggestions the civil service is becoming politicised. In the 1960s, with a Labour Government in power, there were accusations the civil service was 'conservative' (note the small 'c') in that it was opposed to any change and in particular any radical change. Allegations were made of a conspiratorial civil service blocking the implementation of a socialist agenda. Interestingly enough, such allegations about a conspiratorial and reactionary civil service were also raised during the Thatcher years!

It has been since the 1980s that accusations of politicisation have emerged more strongly than ever. Margaret Thatcher, with her 'Is he one of us?' request, made clear she wished to be more involved in senior civil service appointments. This led to grave concern the upper echelons of the civil service were being 'Thatcherised' if not politicised.

The Blair Government, possibly even more than the Thatcher Government, was also involved in the politicisation of the civil service. While there was greater use of outsiders rather than using the civil service (in such things as special advisers and task forces), there were also some controversial civil servant appointments. One of the most prominent of these was Ed Balls, who was an adviser to Gordon Brown before being appointed as a civil servant to the position of economic adviser to the Chancellor of the Exchequer. Since then, Balls has become an elected politician, a cabinet member, and a prominent shadow cabinet member.

While there has been both overt and covert politicisation of the civil service, it begs the question of *should* the civil service be politicised? There is no easy answer to this question. Neutrality has been a key feature of the civil service but it is clearly being undermined. The introduction of formal politicisation would cause a massive upheaval in the civil service. If a line similar to that of the USA was used, then after every election, or more precisely after every change of government, the upper echelons of the civil service would probably be replaced. Clearly this does not happen in Britain at the moment. With greater use of political advisers by the Blair Government, and their apparent mistrust of a civil service moulded by 18 years of Conservative rule, we saw possibly the *indirect* politicisation of the civil service. This has continued, although not quite to the same extent, under the coalition government. The closest advisers to the ministers may no longer be their Permanent Secretaries but rather their political advisers. Thus the civil service is possibly now one step removed from advising ministers. These political advisers have much more in common with the senior appointments within the US bureaucracy than with the British civil service. The extent to which this is a good thing for the civil service, or for government, is still unclear. Some of the powers of these unelected personnel may be reduced but with reduced involvement in the policy making process, it may not be so easy to implement the spirit of the law as well as the letter of the law.

Conclusion

The civil service in the 21st century is very different to that envisaged in the Northcote-Trevelyan Report, although many key features still remain. The formal constitutional position of a permanent, neutral and anonymous civil service is still evident – although all three aspects have come under significant pressure. Changes to the civil service have been taking place since the 1980s, with greater emphasis upon management, upon budgets, and an apparent ideological underpinning of "the market knows best". There does not appear to be any plan to let up on this process either. The emphasis appears to be continuous modernisation.

Selected bibliography

Chapman, Richard & O'Toole, Barry. (2010). "Leadership in the British Civil Service: An Interpretation", *Public Policy and Administration* vol. 25-2, pp. 123-136.
Greer, Scott & Jarman, Holly. (2010). "What Whitehall? Definitions, Demographics and the Changing Home Civil Service", *Public Policy and Administration* vol. 25-3, pp. 251-270.
Hood, Christopher & Dixon, Ruth. (2012). "A Model of Cost-cutting in Government? The Great Management Revolution in UK Central Government Reconsidered", *Public Administration* vol. 91-1, pp. 114-134.
Page, Edward. (2010). "Has the Whitehall Model survived?", *International Review of Administrative Sciences* vol. 76-3, pp. 407-423.
Rhodes, R.A.W. & Wanna, John. (2009). "Bringing the Politics Back In: Public Value in Westminster Parliamentary Government", *Public Administration* vol. 87-2, pp. 161-183.

Van Dorpe, Karolien & Horton, Sylvia. (2011). "The Public Service Bargain in the United Kingdom: The Whitehall Model in Decline?", *Public Policy and Administration* vol. 26-2, pp. 233-252.

Websites

www.cabinet-office.gov.uk/ is the home page of the Cabinet Office. *From here you can access many parts of the civil service.*

www.civilservice.gov.uk/ *The homepage of the UK civil service*

www.civilservice.gov.uk/about/resources/civil-service-management-code *Where the Civil Service Management Code can be accessed*

www.gov.uk/government/organisations/cabinet-office/series/special-advisers-conduct-and-guidance *Where the rules of conduct of special advisers are detailed*

Questions

1. How accurate is it to describe the functions of the Civil Service as being politically neutral?
2. Assess the view that in Britain senior civil servants have too much influence on policy.
3. "The use of special advisers means there is less need to politicise the civil service." Comment.

CHAPTER 14 // QUANGOS

Contents

Introduction

Quangos, or Quasi-Autonomous Non-Governmental Organisations, have become an integral part of British Government. They are used extensively by central government in areas such as service delivery. They are also used at the sub-national level of government – both regional and local levels. Yet the term Quango is not officially recognised in Whitehall circles. They come under a list of other labels, such as ALBs (Arm's Length Bodies), EGOs (Extra-Government Organisations) or NDPBs (Non-Departmental Public Bodies). Added to this, it is often unclear as to the functions of specific quangos. They are unelected, appointed bodies, and they add to the levels of secrecy that pervade British Government. The world of the quango is indeed a murky one. Within this murkiness, quangos have developed a rather poor reputation – which may not always be justified. This chapter will attempt to unravel some of the key aspects of quangos, starting off with definitional issues before moving on to their functions, advantages and disadvantages.

Definition

Although quangos have been around since the Second World War, if not earlier, the first major official investigation into their existence in Britain, which was carried out by Sir Leon Pliatzky, was only published in 1980 (*Report on Non-Departmental Bodies* Cmnd. 7797). It found 489 executive non-governmental bodies with regulatory functions and over 1500 advisory and other bodies. Pliatzky, however, adopted a very narrow definition, using the term Non-Departmental Public Body (NDPB). This excluded the nationalised industries, public corporations (such as the BBC) and any local government quangos. Thus Pliatzky was able to conclude he could only find 2167 such bodies. His definitional approach has been maintained by the government ever since. According to Pliatzky, quangos, or rather, NDPBs "have a role in the processes of government in the United Kingdom but which are not Government Departments or part of a Government Department." (Cmnd. 7797, 1980, p. 1).

The Pliatzky Report then proceeded to give a list of other types of bodies which have been described as quangos, but are excluded from this narrow definition.

This has been maintained ever since, and includes:

- NHS bodies, including local Trusts
- Nationalised Industries, Public Corporations, and Non-Ministerial Government Departments (such as the Regulatory Agencies of the privatised utilities e.g. Ofgem)
- Local Public Spending Bodies e.g. further and higher education bodies, Grant-Maintained Schools, Training and Enterprise Councils, Local Enterprise Companies, Registered Social Landlords (formerly the Directory of Housing Associations)

By 2009, the Cabinet Office identified 766 NDPBs (down from 827 in 2007). Again, all of the bodies listed above were excluded. The inclusion of such bodies as part of the quango count is clearly important. Weir & Hall came up with the label EGOs (Extra-Government Organisations). They define EGOs as "executive bodies of a semi-autonomous nature which effectively act as agencies for central government and carry out government policies" (Weir & Hall, 1994, p. 8).

Flinders (1999a, p. 4) gives an even broader definition of a quango. "Any body that spends public money to fulfil a public task but with some degree of independence from elected representatives." Flinders acknowledges this is a very loose, catch-all definition. Under this definition, Next Steps Agencies (see Chapter 13) would be included. Weir & Hall argue these agencies should not be included in the quango count. This shows very clearly even the so-called experts cannot agree on what should be included under this concept.

Regardless of which definition is used, there have been a number of allegations made against quangos: they are non-elected, secretive, and unaccountable. What is interesting is Opposition MPs complain about these bodies, claiming Government Ministers make political appointments to these bodies. Thatcher complained about 'jobs for the boys' in the late 1970s, with the then-Labour Government appointing trade unionists to all sorts of posts. When Thatcher became Prime Minister, the number of NDPBs was reduced. At the same time, both the number of EGOs, and their powers, was increased.

In the build-up to the 1997 General Election, Labour promised a bonfire of the quangos. Upon obtaining office, the matches were not even lit. Similarly, the Conservative-Liberal Democrat coalition pledged to reduce the number of quangos, but with only marginal success – although there is a clear plan to abolish some quangos, and to merge others. As with all governments, the current incumbents found quangos can actually prove to be useful organisations. Within days of taking office, George Osborne (Chancellor of the Exchequer) established the Office of Budget Responsibility. This is a quango. Gash and Rutter (2011, p. 95) highlight what they call the quango conundrum: "hated as a class, but individually seen as valuable devices for improving effectiveness and increasing public confidence in government".

Functions of Quangos

While there have been many attacks on quangos, with accusations of unaccountability, unrepresentativeness, and being undemocratic, what is often omitted is a basic list of what quangos actually do. Quangos perform a role of 'government-at-arm's length' – they carry out a specific task on behalf of the government. Such tasks may be of a controversial nature where it is argued basic party politics ought to be excluded; thus a quango may be the most appropriate body (e.g. the **Commission for Racial Equality**).

The Commission for Racial Equality (CRE) was set up in 1976 to fight racial discrimination and promote racial equality. It came under the auspices of the Home Office. Such a body is supposed to act with the support of all political parties, but without attaching itself to any one in particular. Bodies such as the CRE are established in the hope of creating a more conducive atmosphere to enable intelligent discussion to take place. The CRE has since been merged with the Disability Rights Commission and the Equal Opportunities Commission (both of which were also quangos), to form a new super-quango – the **Equality and Human Rights Commission**.

The role of quangos may include providing advice for government ministers. Research may be carried out by a quango for a particular government department. Coming from a quango, the advice is more likely to be impartial, as opposed to containing in-built government, or even party-political, biases. Quangos may also be able to provide specialist advice or information beyond the ability of a particular government department. This wide range of advisory quangos includes the Low Pay Commission and the Marine Management Organisation.

Some quangos are involved in service delivery. These bodies cover a wide range of functions across the entire remit of government, and can be national or local in nature. The Higher Education Funding Council (HEFC) deals with the myriad of problems in funding higher education in England. A school that has either opted out of Local Authority control or become an Academy is technically a quango that provides education for the pupils. Health Trusts are also quangos delivering a number of services. A tier of government may previously have carried out the range of services provided by any quango. The various bodies have, however, been given the opportunity to run their own affairs. This is co-ordinated by a Board of Governors (or some other such body) that comprises the quango members.

With regard to the functions of quangos, they are clearly wide-ranging. These functions may be advisory or executive in nature. Quangos are able to deliver services of a potentially contentious nature outside of the party political atmosphere of government. These bodies can be of a national or local nature. They have become a key element for governments of all persuasions in areas such as service delivery and provision of advice.

The former-Labour Government identified different types of NDPB, based on the Pliatzky model. These were:

- *executive bodies*
- *advisory committees*
- *tribunals*
- *prison boards of visitors*

Each of these types of NDPB has specific functions. As noted by Greenwood, Pyper & Wilson (2002), the executive bodies have a range of potential functions. These could be administrative, regulatory, executive or even commercial. These functions are carried out on behalf of the government. Examples of such executive NDPBs include the Arts Council and the Equality and Human Rights Commission.

Advisory committees tend to provide some sort of 'expert' advice. This advice could be for ministers, officials, or even the public. An example of such an advisory committee would be the Low Pay Commission.

Tribunals, such as the Employment Tribunal, have a role to play in specialised legal areas, while the prison boards of visitors are bodies that oversee the prison system. Each government department has quangos operating under its auspices. The extent and type is detailed in Table 14.1.

Disadvantages of Quangos

There have been numerous criticisms of quangos. In fact most texts on the subject are of a highly critical nature. Although the functions outlined above are clearly important, and are probably best carried out by quangos, the criticisms need to be taken on board. The list of disadvantages of quangos is by no means exhaustive. The key areas are:

1. *Unrepresentative*
2. *Undemocratic*
3. *Unaccountable*
4. *Patronage State*

1. Unrepresentative

Quangos are generally considered to be unrepresentative of society. Flinders *et al* (2011) ask the question: are they "pale, male and stale?" The vast majority of appointments to quangos appear to be party-political, or from the world of business. The various sections of society are not always represented - gender, ethnicity, class or religion. It is the idea of the white, middle class male who is considered to be a 'safe pair of hands' that is applied, just as in the selection of MPs. Consequently there is no counterbalance to the very narrow range of experience (business and politics) of quangocrats. Denton (2006) questions this lack of representativeness by highlighting an interesting conflict: diversity versus appointment on merit. It is a case of trying to find the best people for the job, and there should also be a balance between skills and background.

Table 14.1 Number of NDPBs (March 2009)

DEPARTMENT	Executive NDPBs	Advisory NDPBs	Tribunal NDPBs	Other NDPBs	TOTAL
Cabinet Office	2	9	0	0	11
Business, Enterprise & Regulatory Reform	17	11	3	0	31
Children, Schools & Families	9	4	0	0	13
Communities & Local Government	11	5	2	0	18
Culture, Media & Sport	34	10	1	0	45
Environment, Food & Rural Affairs	28	37	3	0	68
Innovation, Universities & Skills	20	2	1	0	23
International Development	1	0	0	0	1
Transport	6	3	1	0	10
Work and Pensions	8	5	2	0	15
Energy & Climate Change	4	6	0	0	10
Health	11	31	0	0	42
Foreign & Commonwealth Office	4	2	1	0	7
Home Office	6	7	4	0	17
Defence	5	23	0	1	29
Justice	14	218	0	146	378

Source: adapted from *Public Bodies* 2009.

Accusations of unrepresentativeness in quango appointments were levelled at the Thatcher and Major Governments, yet the Blair Government was similarly tainted. A positive aspect drawn from the unrepresentative nature of quangos is we are now able to find out who sits on which quango. At this stage, it could simply mean we can strengthen the accusations of unrepresentativeness with actual examples. The Bank of England, for example, has a Governor, three Deputy Governors and ten Non-Executive Directors. Of these thirteen members, many have a business background. The exceptions, as of 2013, are Charles Bean (a Deputy Governor, with a civil service and academic background), Sir Jon Cunliffe (civil servant), Nils Blythe (journalism background), and Paul Fisher (academic background). All bar one of the appointments (Joanna Place) are male, and none are from ethnic minorities. The Chief Operating Officer and the Adviser to the Governor are both female as well.

Steps have been taken to address the accusations of unrepresentativeness by various Governments. The **Commissioner for Public Appointments** (CPA) was set up in 1995. This came about from investigations by the Committee on Standards in Public Life. It was hoped an independent body to appoint quango members would increase public confidence in the system. The current post-holder is Sir David Normington, who took up the position in 2011. The Office for the Commissioner for Public Appointments home page on the internet outlines the role of the Commissioner:

> The Commissioner for Public Appointments regulates the processes by which Ministers (including Welsh Assembly Government Ministers) make appointments to the boards of national and regional public bodies. He also currently regulates appointments processes in relation to some bodies in Northern Ireland.
> **(source: publicappointmentscommissioner.independent.gov.uk/ whatwedo/commissionersrole/index.html)**

Added to this, the Blair Government made commitments to increase the participation of under-represented groups in public life. Aims included getting an equal gender balance in representation, and representation of ethnic minorities in line with their overall population size. Increased participation by disabled people was also an aim.

By 1999, women held 33% of quango posts, while ethnic minorities held fewer than 5% (www.cabinet-office.gov.uk/central/2000/OpenPA/foreword.htm). By 2009, the figure for women holding public appointments had remained almost static (32.6%). Ethnic minority representation had risen to 6.9%, while disabled people held 3.5% of public appointments (*Public Bodies 2009*). Individual quangos may have very good levels of representation by gender, ethnicity and disability. Others, such as the Bank of England, do not.

2. Undemocratic

Quangos are accused of being undemocratic for the simple reason members are appointed rather than elected. A key feature of any democratic system is open and free elections. In the USA, for example, almost all public posts are open to election. In Britain, quangos are definitely public posts but their membership is appointed. This also raises accountability issues, which are examined below.

On top of this, quangos may also undermine other elected bodies. This is particularly evident when touching upon local government. For example, councils and councillors can be held responsible for schools under Local Authority control. They must explain and defend their actions. An inability to do so may result in defeat at the next elections. Opted out schools and the new Academies do not experience this form of democratic control.

The phrase used to describe this problem of quangos being undemocratic is a **democratic deficit**. There is quite simply a lack of direct democratic control over quangos. Arguably there is indirect democratic control via central government. In such a situation, the parent government department may be held to account for the actions of a quango. Yet it is difficult, if not impossible, to hold central government to account for a localised problem. It may not even be appropriate to hold a government minister to account for the actions of a group of appointed people – even if the minister appointed them. The remit of a quango is clearly stated. If a minister is to be held to account for the actions of a quango, then possibly the ministers' department ought to be carrying out the work of the quango rather than providing the quango with some degree of autonomy (a degree of freedom to provide the service as they see fit).

In the past, the high levels of secrecy surrounding quangos made all of this worse. Under previous governments, even the membership of quangos was concealed. Secrecy is a feature of British politics, but at least there is the opportunity for the public to voice their opinions via elections. No such opportunity exists over quangos.

Instead, the CPA monitors quango membership and also investigates complaints about quangos and departmental practices. While openness (or **transparency** to use the official jargon) is encouraged, this democratic accountability is indirect rather than direct. It is still very difficult to hold quango members to account for their actions.

This issue of transparency can cause politicians a problem, as noted by Bertelli (2008). The more transparent an organisation, the more information there will be in the public domain. This then leads to pressure groups lobbying ministers or MPs when the group's interests are not being met by a specific quango.

3. Unaccountable

Through the previous two points it ought to be apparent there is a problem of accountability with quangos. Many structures exist to hold the various tiers of government to account; yet quangos appear to be excluded from them. For example, while all quangos are obliged to produce an annual report, there may be no obligation to hold any public meetings. The Ombudsman (who investigates maladministration – see chapter 17) can inspect around three quarters of all executive quangos. Around half are not even subject to a public audit (although almost all quangos produce annual accounts). Things have now changed with the National Audit Office involved in auditing the majority of executive NDPBs. Advisory quangos are more opaque when it comes to scrutiny and accountability. Consequently, there are increased opportunities for corrupt practices to occur.

This apparent lack of accountability has been recognised by both the former Labour Government and by the Coalition Government. Labour found a lack of procedures by which quangos could be held to account, and attempted to open up the quango system to greater public scrutiny. As has already been stated, information about membership is now in the public domain. The powers of the CPA were broadened in 1998 to include a greater number of quangos and individual appointments. A Code of Practice was established for all ministerial appointments to public bodies. The CPA monitors this process.

The Coalition Government have compiled a list of quangos to be abolished and another list of those to be merged (for example, the Competition Commission and the Office of Fair Trading are to be merged in 2014). There is a third list of those to be retained. What is not always clear with the bodies to be abolished is who will provide the services? All of the Regional Development Agencies were abolished, with their powers given to either central or local government. Which of these represents regional interests at Brussels? Many bodies such as the Committee on Medical Effects of Air Pollutants are being abolished, but their role is to be taken over by a committee of experts – another quango!

Although there is this apparent lack of accountability, it is possibly not quite as clear-cut as to say there is, or there is not, any accountability. Rather, it may be more pertinent to look at levels or forms of accountability. As a consequence of media scrutiny, many quangos have raised their levels of publicity through holding public meetings, publishing minutes of meetings, publishing annual reports, and even publishing business plans. Under the Freedom of Information Act (2000), every public authority must produce a publication scheme. This means all Advisory Bodies should make information available to the public, as part of their activities e.g. an annual report.

As of June 2010, the Coalition Government published all members of NDPBs who earned more than £150 000 in their post. At that time, there were 345 post holders included in this list. Among the highest earners were David Higgins, Chief Executive of the Olympic Delivery Authority (who earned between £390 000 and £394 999, with a stake holder pension) and Tony Fountain, Chief Executive of the Nuclear Decommissioning Authority (who earned between £365 000 and £369 999, excluding £70 810 allowance in lieu of pension and excluding £91

000 assistance with relocation costs which will reduce to zero over three years) (source: www.cabinetoffice.gov.uk/resource-library/non-departmental-public-bodies-high-earners-data-release).

Simply because there are no elections to these bodies, it does not mean they are not accountable. Yet, regardless of these steps – which appear more to do with openness than accountability – there is still a feeling that quangos are unaccountable. In affairs of quangos, as in politics as a whole, if something is unelected, the presumption is that it is unaccountable.

Where the issue of unaccountability is often driven home is over finance. In 1996, it was estimated NDPBs collectively spent over £21 billion. The official government figure for 1999/2000 was £24 billion (*Public Bodies 2000*, p. v). Of this, £18.5 billion was funded directly by the government. Note this applies only to the Government's narrow definition of quangos. Estimations for the amount spent by EGOs in the mid-1990s came to around £50 billion (Flinders, 1999). By 2008/2009, spending on Executive NDPBs had risen to £46.5 billion, of which about £38.4 billion was funded directly by the government (*Public Bodies 2009*, p. 6). In March 2011, it was announced spending by NDPBs would be reduced by £11 billion per year by 2014/15.

4. Patronage State

This label has been used to describe public appointments and quango appointments in particular. In the 1970s Labour was accused of stacking quangos with their supporters. The same applied to the Thatcher and Major Governments, and also to the Blair Government. It is important to note the Blair Government moved to advertising quango posts. This patronage state, however, was best epitomised by Lady Denton, a junior minister at the Department of Trade and Industry under the Major Government. With regard to quango appointments, she was reported as saying: "I can't remember knowingly appointing a Labour supporter" (*Independent on Sunday*, 23 March 1993).

To ensure quangos operate in the way the government wishes, it is best to make sure trusted and loyal supporters staff such bodies. Thus it is clearly a case of who you know rather than what you know. This is not unusual in politics. In the case of quangos, however, it could be as many as 10 000 appointments or renewal of appointments each year. The power of patronage in the quango state is very extensive.

The Committee on Standards in Public Life investigated this concern, and came up with the CPA. The hope was to rebuild public confidence in quango appointments by ensuring they were made under strict rules and guidance from an independent body. It was essential the CPA was independent of the government as part of the confidence rebuilding process. The CPA regulates the processes by which appointments are made to certain public bodies. There is a comprehensive list of bodies whose appointments are regulated by the CPA.

These include Executive and Advisory NDPBs. A full list can be accessed on the CPA web pages.

Advantages of Quangos
To some extent this section overlaps with the functions of quangos. The actual roles of quangos – in the functions they provide – are an obvious advantage. Despite some repetition, it is important to highlight the advantages of quangos.

1. Advice
2. Depoliticisation
3. Improving Service Delivery
4. Addressing Democratic Deficit

1. Advice
The primary function of many quangos is to provide expert impartial advice to the government. This could be on very sensitive issues such as BSE or GM crops. Added to this, some quangos can provide a rapid response to matters of concern. The Committee on Standards in Public Life was set up to investigate sleaze in public life, and to define acceptable standards of conduct for those who work in this area. The CPA, as proposed by the Committee on Standards in Public Life, monitors quango membership. This is to assist in ensuring the impartiality of the advice given by quangos

2. Depoliticisation
This is an important aspect in the role of quangos. As already stated, there are some aspects of government better addressed beyond the party-political sphere. Political considerations often need to be dropped in the hope of achieving a sensible outcome to a problem or concern. Issues as diverse as race relations, health and safety, and higher education funding are likely to benefit from their depoliticisation. Much of this was covered under the functions of quangos, earlier in this chapter.

This is closely linked to the idea of arm's length government. Quangos are government appointed (following guidelines set down by the CPA), but quangos are then distanced from the government. There is supposed to be no government interference in the operation of quangos, which clearly assists in their depoliticisation. Again, it is the CPA that ensures that this depoliticisation is maintained.

3. Improving Service Delivery
Governments perceive quangos to be an essential part of the service delivery sector. Being at arm's length from government enables a quango to concentrate specifically upon their task at hand (in the same way as agencies function in the

civil service, as was explained in the previous chapter). Single purpose bodies are able to specialise and develop new and hopefully more efficient practices, in the way local authorities or other multi-purpose service providers cannot. There are no party political constraints upon quangos, unlike that which can encumber both local and central government. The service delivery is left to the quango, but the politicians retain overall policy formulation and development. The quango is able to give the expert advice governments need to develop and improve policy. Thus both benefit from their mutual co-existence.

4. Addressing Democratic Deficit

There is a very important line of argument that quangos aid and improve democracy. At first, this does not seem apparent. Quangos are unelected, which is equated with being undemocratic. Although unelected, quangos can still improve democracy. At one level, democracy is improved via openness and accountability. Quangos are ultimately accountable to their parent department and thus to the minister, who is, in turn, responsible to Parliament and to the public. Through openness, information about quango activity – both positive and negative – gets into the public domain.

Secondly, and more importantly, the public are empowered as consumers of public services. It does not really matter who provides the service as long as it is responsive to the demands of the user. If you are dissatisfied with the quality of service being delivered then you change service provider. You can lobby your council to improve a given service, but councils have a reputation for being rather distant from the public. There are similar problems with all services being provided by the local council. If they are inadequate, your only options appear to be either lobby the council for change, vote the council out at the next election, or move house. The former option is very difficult. Generally in local government elections, the turnout averages around 40%, which highlights the levels of disinterest in local politics. It may actually be the case the voting public is dissatisfied with local government processes, and does not believe anything can be done about the various problems via the ballot box. Democracy through the ballot box does not always appear to work.

Thus quangos empower the people. They are considered to be far more responsive to public demands, because the public, as consumers of a service, demand the best possible service and will change service provider if it is not the case. Ultimately democracy is also improved as accountability is increased. Quangos, as service providers, must operate in the best interests of the consumers because the consumers, if dissatisfied, have the opportunity to change service provider. This may not, however, be the case if the quangos are monopoly providers. If there is no alternative in service provision, then the same problems may arise as with the former council provision. Fragmenting the service provision, while increasing the options available to the consumer, may actually cause a multiplication of problems (e.g. potentially different forms of accountability).

Conclusion

Quangos are both a problem and an essential part of the British system of government. They are problematic as they are unelected, not easily held to account for their actions, unrepresentative, and secretive. Some of these problems have been addressed – such as secrecy and the lack of representativeness – but there is still a lack of public confidence in these bodies. Paramount here is the lack of direct accountability. Ministers remain accountable to Parliament, and ultimately to the public, for the actions of quangos. The quangocrats themselves appear unaccountable.

Yet, at the same time, quangos are needed. In the case of contentious issues, the use of quangos can depoliticise sensitive issues. While in the past the government of the day might simply have filled these quangos full of their supporters, the Commissioner for Public Appointments provides guidelines and monitors quango membership and the actions of quangos. Independent bodies set up by the government, such as the Equality and Human Rights Commission, instil far greater confidence than a party-political body ever could.

Quangos (or ALBs or EGOs or NDPBs or whatever term is used) will remain a feature of British Government. Concerns around secrecy and representativeness continue to be addressed. The hope is the issue of accountability can be approached and possibly even resolved. When in Opposition, a political party may sound off about the problems of unelected government; when in Office there is a sudden realisation quangos are necessary. Quangos work for the Government - but they need to be made to work for the public as well.

Selected bibliography

Bertelli, Anthony. (2008). "Credible Governance? Transparency, Political Control, the Personal Vote and British Quangos", *Political Studies* vol. 56-4, pp. 807-829.

Denton, Matthew. (2006). "The Impact of the Committee on Standards in Public Life on Delegated Governance: The Commissioner for Public Appointments", *Parliamentary Affairs* vol. 59-3, pp. 491-508.

Flinders, Matthew & Smith, Martin. (eds.). *Quangos, Accountability and Reform: The Politics of Quasi-Government*: Macmillan.

Flinders, Matthew & Skelcher, Chris. (2012). "Shrinking the quango state: five challenges in reforming quangos", *Public Money & Management* vol. 32-5, pp. 327-334.

Gash, Tom & Rutter, Jill. (2011). "Reports and Surveys: The Quango Conundrum", *Political Quarterly* vol. 82-1, pp. 95-101.

Van Thiel, Sandra. (2001). *Quangos: Trends, Causes and Consequences:* Ashgate.

Websites

publicappointmentscommissioner.independent.gov.uk/index.html
This is the homepage of the Office of the Commissioner for Public Appointments

www.cabinetoffice.gov.uk/resource-library/non-departmental-public-bodies-high-earners-data-release
Cabinet Office web page which links to the posts and salaries of all NDPB members earning over £150 000

www.cabinetoffice.gov.uk/search/apachesolr_search/quangos
This is the Government's homepage for information on quangos

www.direct.gov.uk/en/Dl1/Directories/A-ZOfCentralGovernment/index.htm
This web site provides all of the information about NDPBs, including their web addresses

Questions
1. What is a quango?
2. To what extent may quangos be viewed as an aid to democracy?
3. How may quangos be held to account? In what ways can their levels of accountability be increased?

CHAPTER 15 // THE JUDICIAL SYSTEM

Contents

Introduction

The judicial system is a fundamental part of the structure of any state. When examining the UK judicial system, this cannot be done in isolation. Thus, this chapter needs to be read in conjunction with a number of others: those on the constitution, the bill of rights, the state, the House of Lords, and redress. There can be significant overlap between each of these chapters. In this chapter, there will be some coverage of the implications of the Human Rights Act. That is covered in greater detail in the chapter on a bill of rights. Similarly, although judicial review would clearly come under this chapter, it is also included under the chapter on redress.

To complicate matters in the UK, there is no single legal system. There are in fact three: Scotland and Northern Ireland each have their own separate legal systems. The focus of this chapter will be, for the most part, on the legal system of England and Wales. A further caveat here is Wales has gained more devolved powers and there are those who would argue Wales ought now to become a separate legal jurisdiction.

There will also be a brief examination of the role and function of the Police and Crime Commissioners. Although not part of the judiciary, they play an important role in the interplay between the police and the judiciary.

What is the judiciary?

When describing judges, a stereotypical image is presented by Foster (2006, p. 40). "A common image of a judge is that of an ill-tempered, somewhat crusty old gentleman whose role is akin to that in a sporting contest." In effect, a judge is often portrayed like a referee, giving the prosecution and defence in a trial a fair opportunity to present their respective cases, before summing up and advising the jury. Foster adds this perception is not wholly accurate.

The judiciary needs to be impartial. If this cannot be done in a given case, then a judge ought to recuse him or herself i.e. withdraw from the case to enable it to be allocated to another judge. According to Foster (2006), this impartiality should cover three aspects:

1. Disinterest – a judge should have no personal interest whatsoever in any cases before him or her. This could be financial or even familial interests.
2. Open-mindedness – or impartiality. A judge should weigh up the arguments and the evidence from both sides in a dispassionate manner.
3. Objectivity – the chief concern for a judge should be in weighing up the facts before them, in conjunction with the demands of the law. Nothing else should impact upon the decision.

One of the problems when examining the UK judicial system is the complexity of the structures. A first problem is the distinction between the civil and the criminal courts (see Table 15.1). Then, within each of these, there are different tiers of courts, as well as the different courts of appeal (see Table 15.2).

Table 15.1 Definitions of Civil Courts and Criminal Courts

Civil Courts
These courts deal with non-criminal law. The county courts and, on occasions, the magistrates court deal with such matters. These can be disputes between individuals, or between individuals and organisations. They consider private controversies, rather than dealing with the public collectively. Guilt – or, more accurately, liability – is decided on the balance of probability, rather than beyond reasonable doubt, and compensation may be awarded to the victim. The emphasis in the civil courts is upon conflict resolution rather than punishment.

Criminal Courts
These courts deal with people who break the law. If found guilty, there is some form of punishment. All criminal cases start in a magistrates court, although the more serious offences will be sent to the Crown Court.

Table 15.2 The Court Structures in England and Wales

County Courts
Magistrates Courts
The Crown Court
The High Court
Court of Appeal
The UK Supreme Court
(The Court of Justice of the European Union)
(The European Court of Human Rights)

In Scotland, there is a **Justice of the Peace Court**, which deals with less serious matters. There is a **Sheriffs Court**, which is sub-divided into civil and criminal jurisdictions. Above all of this are the **Supreme Courts**, which are also divided into civil and criminal jurisdictions – the **Court of Session** and the **High Court of Justiciary** respectively. The UK Supreme Court is the highest court of appeal.

In Northern Ireland, there are county courts and magistrates courts which deal with civil matters. There is also the **Court of Judicature**, which comprises the Crown Court, the High Court and the Court of Appeal. Each of these follow their English and Welsh equivalents. As with the rest of the UK, the UK Supreme Court is the highest court of appeal.

It is interesting to note the Court of Justice of the European Union and the European Court of Human Rights (ECtHR) are included as part of the court structures of the UK. The Court of Justice, as noted in chapter 31, may only intercede in matters relating to EU law – and it must be asked to intercede. The Court of Justice is a reactive body, not a pro-active one.

The ECtHR has nothing to do with the EU. It deals with allegations made against signatory states to the European Convention on Human Rights (ECHR) – which is, in effect, the Human Rights Act in the UK (see chapter 7). There are 47 signatory states to the Convention. The ECtHR deals with any allegations concerning the civil and political rights detailed in the Convention.

One of the most powerful positions within the judiciary was the Lord Chancellor. The Lord Chancellor was, as noted by Bradney (1999), a judge, a cabinet member and the speaker of the House of Lords. It was a very powerful political and judicial post. Bradney (1999) argued the judicial role had four clear parts:

i.   Judge – the Lord Chancellor could sit with the 'Law Lords'. Added to this, the Lord Chancellor was President of the Chancery Division of the High Court.

ii. Judicial appointments – the Lord Chancellor was involved in appointing High Court judges, circuit judges, recorders and stipendary magistrates. The Lord Chancellor appointed district judges, lay magistrates and tribunal chairs.

iii. Judicial discipline – the Lord Chancellor had the power to dismiss some judges for misbehaviour or incapacity.

iv. Politician – the Lord Chancellor held a post in cabinet and was also the Speaker in the House of Lords.

In 2003, the government announced in a press release the abolition of the office of Lord Chancellor. The role in judicial appointments was to be passed on to a Judicial Appointments Commission (for England and Wales) – see later in this chapter. The establishment of a new Supreme Court was announced at the same time, which would remove judicial business from the House of Lords.

There was such an outcry the reforms to the post of Lord Chancellor were not implemented as first planned. The post has remained and is currently held by the Secretary of State for Justice. The powers of the Lord Chancellor have been limited (see Prince (2005); Bevir (2008)). The role of the Speaker in the House of Lords is no longer held by the Lord Chancellor. Peers have elected their own Speaker since 2006.

The Appointment of Judges

Just as there are different legal structures in the different parts of the UK, so there are different methods of appointment. In the past, senior judicial appointments were made by the Crown, on the advice of the Lord Chancellor and the Prime Minister. Since April 2006, judicial appointments in England and Wales have been made by the **Judicial Appointments Commission**. Although this body does not select the appointments to the UK Supreme Court, it does recommend to the Lord Chancellor the appointment of:

- *the Lord Chief Justice*
- *Heads of Division*
- *Lord Justices of Appeal*
- *judges of the High Court*

There are fifteen commissioners, twelve of whom are recruited and appointed through open competition. The other three are judicial members, selected by the Judges' Council. The important factor in these appointments is the professional ability of the judge.

In Scotland, there is a **Judicial Appointments Board**, which has been in existence since 2002. There are ten members on this body; five from a legal background, and five who are lay people. This body provides a short list of candidates for the First Minister of Scotland for the following posts:

- *Judges in the Court of Session*
- *Sheriffs-Principal*
- *Sheriffs*
- *Part-time Sheriffs*

The First Minister, after consulting with the Lord President, will make a recommendation to the Monarch.

As of June 2005, appointments in Northern Ireland have been made by the **Northern Ireland Judicial Appointments Commission**. They make recommendations up to, and including, the post of High Court judge. The thirteen members of the Commission are drawn from the judiciary, legal and other professional backgrounds. The five 'lay' members are appointed through open competition. The Lord Chief Justice of Northern Ireland, who is also the chair of the Commission, appoints five judicial members. Both legal members are appointed by the Bar Council of Northern Ireland and the Law Society of Northern Ireland.

Accusations have been made against the judiciary of being out of touch with the lives of the everyday person in the street and unrepresentative of society. This was highlighted in 2005, when Mrs Justice Linda Dobbs was appointed to the High Court. She was the first non-white appointment to such a post. As of 2013, there was one female Judge of the Supreme Court (Dame Brenda Hale). Of the 108 High Court judges (there is a fixed number of appointments), seventeen were female. In the Court of Appeal, seven of the 38 judges were female. Around a quarter of district court judges were female, while women comprised a majority of magistrates (52%). Ethnic minority representation within the judiciary "ranges from two to four per cent", and just under eight per cent of all magistrates (www. judiciary.gov.uk/about-the-judiciary/judges-magistrates-and-tribunal-judges/ judges-career-paths/diversity-gender-age-ethnicity). On current rates of growth in the representation of women in the judiciary, it will take around half a century for parity to be reached. Ethnic minority representation, in relation to population size, may well be achieved sooner.

The UK Supreme Court

On 1 October 2009, the UK Supreme Court came into being. Prior to this time, the role had been performed by the 'Law Lords' in the House of Lords. There had been much criticism of the 'Law Lords' in the latter part of the twentieth century. As members of the House of Lords they were involved in the making and passing of laws, as well as the application of these laws. There was a perception of a possibility of a conflict of interest.

The twelve 'Law Lords', when they sat in the House of Lords, were known as the **Appellate Committee**. A panel of the Law Lords would sit as the final court of appeal in the UK. With the establishment of the Supreme Court, the 'Law Lords' became the **Justices of the Supreme Court**. They moved from the House of Lords to a new purpose-built building (which was formerly the Middlesex Guildhall), located on Parliament Square.

The establishment of the Supreme Court, in a separate building to the legislature, gave a visible appearance of the separation of powers. This physical separation strengthens the perception of the independence of the judiciary from the legislature and the executive. Interestingly, as noted by Kavanagh (2011), no new powers were given to the Supreme Court that had not previously been held by the 'Law Lords'. The one caveat here is with regard to devolved issues in Scotland and Northern Ireland. Previously, such appeals had gone to the Judicial

Committee of the Privy Council. Now there is a degree of judicial uniformity across the UK with regard to the appeals process.

Oliver (2004) raises a concern about the perception of the role of the Supreme Court. She argues "[t]he title 'Supreme Court' is misleading since the court will not enjoy the power which the American Supreme Court or Supreme Courts in Australia, Canada and many other Commonwealth countries have to set aside a provision of a statute that is 'unconstitutional'" (Oliver, 2004, p. 758).

This is an important point. Under the British constitution, Parliament is the supreme decision maker. Only Parliament can make or unmake laws. Only Parliament can initiate legislation – even if it is to give that power of initiation to another body, such as the European Union. No Parliament can bind its successors. In theory, therefore, a future government could repeal the Constitutional Reform Act (2005) which established the Supreme Court. The Judges of the Supreme Court could be returned to the House of Lords and reinstated as the 'Law Lords'.

There is, however, a small caveat here. This links to the ECHR, and the Human Rights Act (1998). Under the HRA, it is unlawful for any public authority to act in a way which is incompatible with the legislation. While Parliament is excluded from this particular definition of a public authority, all secondary legislation that goes through Parliament must be compatible with the ECHR. It is the duty of all courts in the UK, including the Supreme Court, to monitor this compatibility. Judges may not strike down any legislation; in fact, they cannot initiate any concerns. They can only respond if an individual or an organisation goes to the courts to argue a particular piece of legislation is unlawful. If the courts decide legislation is not compatible with the ECHR, they must issue a **declaration of incompatibility**. Such a declaration is a measure of last resort. There is no obligation for the government to amend or repeal the legislation, the declaration highlights to the legislators a clear concern.

Woodhouse (2001, p. 234) noted if judges make a declaration of incompatibility, they "will in effect be initiating legislation, a role technically confined to politicians". This may be to overstate the case. The Human Rights Act places a requirement on legislators to ensure compatibility. This judicial role is more akin to a form of judicial review; in this case, through the monitoring and regulating of legislative proposals as they pass through Parliament.

Judicial review is covered in chapter 17. It is worthwhile to reiterate, in brief, an overview of the concept. Judicial review is the right to challenge government decisions, although there are particular procedures and time scales that must be followed. It is about procedural flaws rather than the merits or demerits of a case, where a public authority, for example, may have acted beyond their powers. The coalition government reviewed access to judicial review. According to David Cameron, as reported by the BBC (19 November 2012), this is because so many of the cases are deemed to be "time wasting" (www.bbc.co.uk/news/uk-politics-20389297). Thus there are plans to reduce the time scales and to increase the costs. In other words, making access to judicial review even more difficult.

Returning to the Supreme Court of the UK, it is the final court of appeal for civil and criminal cases. It is a reactive body, and may only intercede in a case if a relevant order has been made in a lower court.

Police and Crime Commissioners

Although not part of the judiciary, the role of Police and Crime Commissioners (PCC) have an impact on the judiciary. In 2011, the Police Reform and Social Responsibility Act was passed. This allowed for the election of PCCs in 41 out of the 43 police forces in England and Wales (excluding London and the City of London). The idea behind the establishment of these bodies was to try to make the police more accountable to the public. One of the roles of a PCC was to make sure the police were delivering an effective and efficient service to the public. Interestingly, judges could not stand for the position of PCC; there could easily be a conflict of interests.

It is the setting of priorities for the police that will impact upon the judiciary. Targeting particular crimes could lead to an increased workload in the magistrates and Crown Courts. Focusing on particular aspects of crime prevention – and if successful – could lead to reduced pressures on the judicial system. The PCCs, in conjunction with senior policing staff, will set these priorities for each police authority.

The elections were held on 15 November 2012, and had a turnout of 17% – one polling station in Newport, Gwent, saw a turnout of zero: not a single vote was cast in that polling station. The plans for increased accountability to the public have yet to be tested. The only consolation with regard to electoral turnout is the next PCC elections (assuming the elected PCCs are not disbanded) will be held at the same time as local elections. This should see an increased turnout.

Conclusion

To describe the British judicial system, or, more accurately, systems, as complicated is something of an understatement. In many respects, it is a labyrinthine organisation, in which the average person can easily get lost. That is why organisations such as the **Public Law Project** have been established – to enable the least secure in society to have access to the system of public law.

Over time, the operations of court proceedings have become a little less formalised. In some cases, in particular where children are involved, the lawyers may remove their wigs in the hope of making the experience less frightening or intimidating. Questions have been raised as to whether or not children should even have to appear in court. There are around 40 000 criminal cases every year where children and young adults have to give evidence. Their treatment, in particular under cross-examination, has raised grave concerns.

The problem is, as has been noted in this chapter, the judicial system of the UK is unrepresentative of society. As with many politicians, many of those working within the judiciary have little or no knowledge or experience about the lives of the most vulnerable in society. Should this matter for a judiciary, when the importance of their job lies with the application of the law equally and fairly across all parts of society? Such a question has no 'right' or 'wrong' answer. A judge has to be disinterested, open-minded and impartial. Arguably, fairness comes alongside all three terms. Everyone is supposed to be equal under the law. One role of the judiciary is to make sure it remains the case.

Selected bibliography

Bevir, Mark. (2008). "The Westminster Model, Governance and Judicial Reform", *Parliamentary Affairs* vol. 61-4, pp. 559-577.

Drewry, Gavin; Blom-Cooper, Louis & Blake, Charles. (2007). *The Court of Appeal*: Hart Publishing.

Foster, Steven. (2006). *The Judiciary, Civil Liberties and Human Rights*: Edinburgh University Press.

Lee, James. (ed.). (2011). *From House of Lords to Supreme Court: Judges, Jurists and the Process of Judging*: Hart Publishing.

Mallesson, Kate. (2009). "Diversity in the Judiciary: The Case For Positive Action", *Journal of Law and Society* vol. 36-3, pp. 376-402.

Patterson QC, Frances (General Editor). (2011). *Judicial Review: Law and Practice*: Jordans.

Phillips of Worth Matravers, Lord. (2012). "The Birth and First Steps of the UK Supreme Court", *Cambridge Journal of International and Comparative Law* vol. 1-2, pp. 9-12.

Websites

jac.judiciary.gov.uk/
Judicial Appointments Commission homepage

scotland-judiciary.org.uk/
The homepage of the Judiciary of Scotland

www.judiciary.gov.uk/
A resource where you can find out much more about judges, magistrates and tribunals, as well as many other aspects of the UK judiciary

www.nijac.gov.uk/index.htm
The homepage of the Northern Ireland Judicial Appointments Commission

www.publiclawproject.org.uk/
A charity which aims to improve access to public law remedies for the least well off in society

www.supremecourt.gov.uk/
The home page of the UK Supreme Court

Questions
1. Examine the case for giving the UK Supreme Court the powers to strike down legislation. What might be the consequences of such a move?
2. How can the judiciary be better representative of society?

CHAPTER 16 // THE REGULATORY STATE

Contents

Introduction

When examining the concept 'regulation', and the idea of a regulatory state, there are numerous misconceptions. Some of this is to do with a misunderstanding of the concept regulation. Working from an apparently opposite direction, people confuse deregulation with privatisation, de-nationalisation, or liberalisation. While these terms do have a strong relationship with regulation, they are not necessarily polar opposites. Regulation, therefore, is not necessarily about the government running things.

It is important to be aware of a number of factors with regard to regulation. Firstly, there are different forms of regulation. The government is normally perceived to be the regulator. As will become apparent, this is not necessarily the case. Secondly, it is important to consider the objectives of introducing regulation – i.e. why put the regulations in place? Thirdly, there is the issue of accountability. How are those being regulated held to account? Just as important is the accountability of the regulators. To whom are they accountable, and how are they held to account? These issues will be addressed in this chapter.

What is regulation?

The idea of regulation is often misunderstood to be the State running particular aspects of the economy. This is not strictly accurate. According to May (2007, p.8), traditional regulation is about the government or government agencies enforcing rules, with penalties for non-compliance. A more comprehensive definition is provided by Black. She states regulation is about

> sustained and focused attempts to change the behavior [*sic*] of others in order to address a collective problem or attain an identified end or ends, usually through a combination of rules or norms and some means for their implementation and enforcement, which can be legal or non-legal. (Black, 2008, p. 139)

The National Audit Office (NAO) has a different perspective. "The purpose of regulation is to protect the public and the environment and provide a level playing field for business" (NAO, 2008, p. 6). To highlight the extent of regulation in the UK, in 2007 it cost UK businesses around £20 billion to comply with regulations in that year!

Regulation can be about monitoring service provision. The aim would be to make sure services are delivered effectively and efficiently. Regulation can also be used to improve service delivery – be these economic or social services. Yet there is no uniformity of regulation across different sectors. The way in which society has changed over the last two or three decades, along with technological developments, has seen not only new forms of regulation but also new bodies to be regulated. For example, a new regulatory body was created with the introduction of the National Lottery.

According to Prosser (2000, p. 231), there are two key reasons for regulation:
 – to prevent profit maximisation of natural monopolies from distorting the efficient distribution of goods
 – to resolve externalities – where the unregulated price of a product does not reflect its true cost to society e.g. pollution

Regardless as to what bodies are conducting the regulation, both of the above reasons should underpin all aspects of regulation, be it economic or social regulation.

There are many different forms of regulation. May (2007) highlights different forms of regulatory regimes. Firstly, there are the traditional ideas of *prescriptive regulation*. This involves telling particular bodies, or even individuals, what to do. This can be a very 'hands-on' approach to regulation. Such an approach is still perceived as the mainstream form of regulation, with the government telling bodies what to do – the other regulatory regimes are alternatives. Thus, secondly, there is *system-based regulation*. Utilising such an approach enables regulatory bodies to monitor systems of production. The emphasis is very much upon having a management plan – the idea of knowing how things are supposed to operate – rather than actually measuring what has been achieved. Thirdly, there is *performance-based regulation*. Such an approach focuses upon the results to be achieved, rather than the way in which the results are achieved. For such an approach to work, the targets of the regulated bodies need to be detailed to be able to measure the extent to which they have been achieved. These different regulatory regimes will be re-visited when we focus on regulation and accountability later in this chapter. Implicit in the next section of this chapter is the idea of prescriptive regulation.

Regulation Pre- and Post-Privatisation
Prior to the privatisations of the 1980s, the idea of regulation was not prominent. Instead, there was nationalisation and subsidisation, alongside economic

regulation. In effect, the government was involved in micro-management of the economy. There were penalties for non-compliance (see Thompson, 1990, chapter 6). There was no external supervision of the nationalised industries. The head of a nationalised industry was accountable to the Secretary of State of the parent department, who, in turn, was accountable to Parliament. The heads of the nationalised industries were also held to account through the select committee on nationalised industries – a body which was established in 1956. There was no external audit. One of the interesting results of privatisation was the greater degree of openness within the newly-privatised industries compared to when they had been nationalised.

With the privatisation of the Thatcher years, the forms of intervention changed. It must be noted that in 1979, there were no major plans for privatisation – the Conservatives "more or less stumbled into large-scale privatization" (Moran, 2003, p. 100). The ideologically-driven privatisation agenda was presented as the deregulation of the economy. In effect, state-owned enterprises were sold (privatisation), and markets were opened up to competition (i.e. they were liberalised). The government became far less involved in running the economy. It was left much more to the private sector. Yet all of this had to be monitored – or regulated. As Rhodes (1997, p. 91) states, the government "substituted regulation for ownership". Majone (1998, p. 199) points out

> regulatory agencies were set up in the 1980s and early 1990s, partly because it was realised that in many cases privatization would only mean the replacement of public by private monopolies unless the newly privatised companies were subjected to public regulation of profits, prices, and entry and service conditions.

Thompson (1990, p. 135) takes this further, describing it as "the paradoxical emergence of extensive *re*regulation of economic activity in a period supposedly typified by drastic *de*regulation". In fact, as Moran (2003, p. 70) notes: "[s]ome of the main arguments for deregulation... are in effect arguments for more self-regulation". There was deregulation, but this does not mean there was no regulation. Rather there was likely to be "less restrictive or rigid regulation" (Majone, 1997, p. 143). Majone concurs with Thompson in many respects, pointing out there was a combination of deregulation *and* reregulation. Moran (2003, p. 70) has pointed out "some of the main arguments for deregulation... are, in effect, arguments for more self-regulation." Self-regulation is examined later in this chapter.

One of the aims of the privatisation agenda was to stimulate economic activity through opening up markets, and encouraging competition. The neo-liberal argument was the state as a monopoly owner was unable to stimulate entrepreneurship. It was cumbersome, reactionary, and, basically, very bad for capitalism. By increasing competition, liberalising markets, and reducing the role of the state, businesses would have far greater opportunities to maximise their profits – without government interference.

Yet, a role was retained for the state, via regulation. Regulation could be used to moderate the excesses of liberalisation by deterring some competition. This could be done by raising the barriers of entry into a given market. Conversely, regulation could also be used to stimulate new economic activity through opening up new markets and increasing competition. This has led Humphreys & Simpson to describe the regulatory state as being "Janus-faced" (2008, p. 853). The idea of regulation could be used to appease opponents of privatisation, demonstrating how the excesses of capitalism could be thwarted. At the same time, regulation could be used to show supporters of the privatisation agenda how market liberalisation could be extended even further.

Self-Regulation

One of the big arguments is over who should carry out regulation. On the one hand, there is regulation by the State. This is "statutory or 'command and control' regulation in which the state, by a variety of means, specifies the regulations and monitors and enforces the conduct of the regulated organizations" (Bartle & Vass, 2007, p. 888). State regulation is often seen as the traditional way in which regulation is carried out.

Self-regulation is often perceived to be a more effective approach to regulation than state regulation. There is the expertise and efficiency within the sector under regulation that is lacking when there is state regulation. Added to this, self-regulation is often seen as being less burdensome than state regulation – there is far less 'red tape'. Alongside the term self-regulation, descriptors such as 'flexible' are utilised. Forms of self-regulation are presented as being informal and responsive. State regulation, on the other hand, is presented as rigid and unresponsive. Self-regulation is often presented as non-state regulation, and possibly even the opposite of state regulation. Quite simply, self-regulation

> involves the regulation of the conduct of individual organizations, or groups of organizations, by themselves. Regulatory rules are self-specified, conduct is self-monitored and the rules are self-enforced.
> (Bartle & Vass, 2007, p. 888)

Thus, self-regulation would appear to be organisations monitoring themselves, without government or state interference. This is, however, inaccurate.

Even where there is self-regulation, there is likely to be a degree of state involvement. It is very rare indeed for there to be total detachment from the state. The reality is there are varying degrees of state involvement in self-regulation. On the one hand, there may be a highly legalised structure, which may have involved government legislation. The government may even designate a specific group as the regulatory body, or merely approve the rules under which a self-regulating body may operate (Black, 2001). At the other end of the scale, there may be voluntary self-regulation with little or no state involvement. Bartle & Vass (2007, p. 895) give the example of complementary health practitioners. Their self-regulation has no legal basis and is totally voluntary, and appears to work. Yet, the Department of Health monitors these practices in case there is ever a need for legislation to be introduced.

Despite this potential state involvement in self-regulation, there is still a degree of public scepticism about self-regulation. How can somebody from a specific economic sector monitor his or her colleagues in an impartial manner? Such a concern became public when Sir James Crosby (of HBOS) was appointed Deputy Head of the Financial Services Authority (FSA). How could a person from the banking sector regulate the banking sector effectively and efficiently? Added to this, *quis custodiet ipsos custodies*? – who shall guard the guards?

Regulation and Accountability

One of the major concerns with regard to regulation surrounds the issue of accountability. There are, in fact, a number of issues here, which come under two sections. The first is the way in which the regulatory bodies are able to hold those organisations under their regulation to account for their actions. The second is the way in which the regulatory bodies are held to account for their actions. Such an issue came to the fore with the alleged failings of the FSA with regard to the partial collapse of the British banking system (with the associated need for the government to bail out many of Britain's banks).

Yet, a brief explanation of the concept 'accountability' is also needed in the context of regulation. Accountability encompasses "the formal duties of public bodies to account for their actions to ministers, Parliament, and to courts" (Scott, 2000, p. 40). While this is a rather narrow definition, it can be supplemented by three simple questions:

1. Who is accountable?
2. To whom are they accountable?
3. For what are they accountable?

Whenever the issue of accountability is being considered, these questions ought to be borne in mind.

Earlier in this chapter, the approach of May (2007) to regulatory regimes was introduced. He has taken this further to highlight **how** each form of regulatory regime can be held to account. There are four levels of accountability: legal, bureaucratic, professional and political. Each of these is applied to each regulatory regime, as can be seen in Table 16.1.

Legal accountability is all about the transparency with which the rules and regulations are established. The focus is upon their suitability and their fairness. There may be issues with regard to who makes the rules and regulations. For example, there is always the possibility of regulatory capture (where the regulatory bodies may be very strongly influenced by those being regulated and to the detriment of the public). Under the prescriptive regime, it is most likely to be the state which makes the rules.

Bureaucratic accountability is about the answerability of the regulators with regard to how the provisions are implemented. How and when should rules be enforced rigorously? Should there be any degree of leeway in the application of the rules? These are the types of issues that arise under this form of accountability.

Professional accountability is more likely (but not exclusively) to be seen under the system-based and performance-based regimes. Prescriptive regimes tend to focus more on accountability through bureaucratic controls. For the system-based and performance-based regimes, this professional accountability is the self-regulation that is so desired. The 'professionals' have to demonstrate their ability to keep their colleagues under regulatory control. Failure to do so in one professional sector may have repercussions in others.

Political accountability is seen more as a response to failure within the regulatory regimes. As May (2007, p. 14) notes, political attention arises only when there is regulatory failure or a scandal. For the system-based and performance-based regimes, it may be the time where the state has to intercede with more prescriptive regulation.

Table 16.1 summarises how regulatory bodies may be held to account. There remains still the question as to how the regulators are held to account.

> The privatisation of public utilities has transferred public sector monopolies into private sector monopolies. Accountability through Parliament has been replaced with a number of regulators who are supposed to supervise the behaviour of the new monopolies, yet these regulators themselves are not directly accountable to Parliament. (Mullard, 1995, p. 4)

This begs the questions not only how, as stated above, the regulators are held to account, but also to whom?

The powers of many regulatory bodies are established through statute. In effect, it is the government who decides what powers they wield. Accountability is carried out through greater transparency. Ofgem (the Office of the Gas and Electricity Markets), for example, promotes competition in the gas and electricity markets, protects consumers in these markets, as well as a range of other things.

Table 16.1 Regulatory Regimes and Accountability

Accountability levels	Regulatory Regime		
	Prescriptive Regulation	System-based Regulation	Performance-based Regulation
Legal	Transparency in setting the rules and regulations	Transparency in establishing the features of the system	Transparency in establishing goals
Bureaucratic	Monitoring of organisations to ensure adherence to rules	Monitoring of organisations to ensure the effectiveness and efficiency of the management structures	Monitoring of organisations to ensure adherence to performance goals
Professional	Regulatory inspectors used to enforce the rules and regulations	System design decisions by the regulated entities	Adherence to performance goals by the regulated entities
Political	Tends to occur when there are complaints about the regulatory process	Tends to occur when there are multiple system breakdowns	Triggered by undesired outcomes

Developed from May (2007) p. 13

Ofgem is governed by an Authority, consisting of non-executive and executive members and a non-executive chair. Non-executive members bring experience and expertise from a range of areas including industry, social policy, environmental work, finance and Europe. (Ofgem web page, 2010)

They are held to account through publishing the minutes of the Authority's meetings, and holding public meetings. There are also very clear complaints procedures. Added to this, Ofgem is monitored by the Energy Ombudsman (see chapter 17 for more on the role of the ombudsman).

While not uniform across all sectors of regulation, the Ofgem example presents the ways in which regulators are held to account. Yet the whole issue of accountability is ever-changing. This can be seen best through the concept of 'Better Regulation'.

Better Regulation

According to the Comptroller and Auditor General (2001, p. 1), it is government policy "that regulation, where it is needed, should have a light touch with the right balance struck between under-regulating (so failing to protect the public) and over-regulating (so creating excessive bureaucracy)." This quote highlights the balancing act needed to ensure good regulation. Consequently, regulatory procedures are evaluated frequently to make certain the right balance is achieved.

The original idea behind better regulation was about making it more efficient and more transparent. Radaelli & Meuwese (2009) suggest this can be done in a number of different ways, or even in a combination of different ways. Better regulation could be a new version of deregulation i.e. reducing the amount of regulation. It could be about "risk-tolerant regulation" (Radaelli & Meuwese, 2009, p. 640), which prioritises regulatory activity through risk assessments. With such an approach, resources are targeted at risks which pose the greatest threat to the ability of the regulator to achieve its objectives (Black, 2007). Finally, better regulation could be about open governance, where the focus should be upon the quality of regulation, not the quantity.

In 1997, when the Blair Government came to power, the emphasis appeared to be upon better forms of regulation rather than the apparent deregulation of the Thatcher and Major years. A number of bodies were established to monitor regulation:

- Better Regulation Unit (which later became the Regulatory Impact Unit)
- Better Regulation Task Force (which later became the Better Regulation Commission)
- Panel for Regulatory Accountability
- Better Regulation Executive

The Better Regulation Unit, and its successor, conducted Regulatory Impact Assessments (RIAs). RIAs are carried out by the government whenever new regulation is to be introduced. They should examine the potential risks, as well as the expected benefits of the proposed regulations, and the costs for the different bodies involved. The RIA should be signed off by the appropriate minister, and submitted to Parliament alongside the legislation which introduces the regulation (Comptroller and Auditor General, 2001).

The Better Regulation Task Force (BRTF) was established to advise the government on the effectiveness of regulation. Its successor organisation worked in conjunction with the Better Regulation Executive in doing this. Their key points of focus for regulation and its enforcement were:

- that it was **proportionate**
- that there was **accountability**
- that there was **consistency**
- that there was **transparency**
- that it was **targeted**

All of this can be seen to be part of what has been called 'responsive regulation'. The idea being that the regulation can respond to a range of different, and potentially changing, factors. The approach utilised by the UK Government has been **risk-based**. Risk-based regulation refers to "a targeting of inspection and enforcement resources that is based on an assessment of the risks that a regulated person or firm poses to the regulators objectives" (Baldwin & Black, 2008, p. 66. See also Moran, 2003, pp. 26-31). This type of approach was highlighted in the Hampton Report (2005) as being the most appropriate for all regulatory agencies in the UK.

The Hampton Report (2005) aimed to make regulation more effective. This report highlighted the complexity of the UK's regulatory structures, and their need for streamlining. For example, according to the Hampton Report (2005, p. 11), in 2003/4 regulatory inspection and enforcement was divided between

- 63 national regulators
- 203 trading standards offices
- 408 environment health offices

The latter two were located across 468 local authorities. Between them, they employed over 41 000 people, utilising a budget of around £4 billion.

Hampton wanted regulation across the UK to be streamlined. He wanted inspections and enforcement to be carried out more effectively and more efficiently. For Hampton, the underpinning of all regulation was to be, as noted above, through risk assessment, or risk-based regulation.

The question then arises as to how such risk-based regulation can be enforced? There are a number of tools available to the regulators.

What can be seen in Table 16.2 (overleaf) is the potential for escalation with the enforcement tools that are available for regulatory bodies. Just as importantly, although far more difficult to implement, is de-escalation. Much of the enforcement of regulations may depend upon simple things, such as clear communication between those who are being regulated and the regulators.

Table 16.2 Regulatory Enforcement Tools

Pre-enforcement tools	Warnings, notices, etc.
Investigations	These are used in an attempt to prompt compliance
Continuation of Business Operations	Licence amendments, disqualification, removal of assets, etc.
Finance	Fines, monetary penalties, etc.
Restorative tools	Re-mediation orders, restorative conferences, etc.
Undertaking and Compliance Management	Compliance audits, voluntary or enforceable undertakings
Performance Disclosure	League tables, naming-and-shaming, etc.

Developed from Baldwin & Black (2008), p. 83

The whole idea of sanctions – in fact, responsive regulation as a whole – has been presented as a pyramid strategy (Ayres & Braithwaite, 1992). Thus Table 16.2 may be presented as a pyramid strategy can be seen in Figure 16.1. The sanctions at the base of the pyramid are broadest. As you progress up the pyramid, the sanctions become far more draconian. This works on the line of the worse the offence, the greater the sanction.

With this pyramid approach, in theory, some emphasis is placed upon the opportunities for escalation and de-escalation (although the latter is much harder to implement). For any regulator, escalation of sanctions is one potential strategy. Yet, through simple things, such as better communication, an opportunity for a de-escalation of sanctions may present itself.

Figure 16.1 Pyramid of Sanctions

Developed from Ayres & Braithwaite (1992) and Baldwin & Black (2008).

Conclusion

Regulation is often presented as the state interfering in the free market. In many respects, such a perspective is wholly inaccurate. "It is one of the many paradoxes of the success of capitalism that it owes its very survival to regulatory and state intervention and yet it continues to rail at it as an unjustified burden and interference in the sacred freedom of the market" (Clarke, 2000, p. 26). Regulation is seen as undesirable, as a cost on business, and a restraint on free trade. Opponents of regulation argue only the free market can drive out bad practice.

Yet regulation is not necessarily about the state interfering in the free market. Where there is such 'interference', there is normally a clearly stipulated objective e.g. to prevent the abuse of a dominant market position; to protect the most vulnerable in society from the worst excesses of capitalism; or to protect people from market failure. As has been seen in this chapter, governments do not have a monopoly on regulation. Self-regulation has normally been perceived as the best way forward, at least for the economy. Most governments would prefer to utilise a 'hands-off' approach to regulation, leaving organisations to regulate themselves. The *quid pro quo* for this freedom is the sanctions available to the government if self-regulation fails.

Regulation is not necessarily about control. Rather, it can be about guiding or directing according to the rules or norms under which organisations operate.

There should be uniformity of regulation within a given sector e.g. finance, but not necessarily across sectors e.g. should the finance sector and the National Lottery be regulated in a similar manner? Ultimately, as long as the regulation is implemented effectively and efficiently, it does not matter who carries out the regulatory activities.

Selected bibliography

Baldwin, Robert & Black, Julia. (2008). "Really Responsive Regulation", *The Modern Law Review* vol. 71-1, pp. 59-94.

Bartle, Ian & Vass, Peter. (2007). "Self-Regulation within the Regulatory State", *Public Administration* vol. 85-4, pp. 885-905.

Black, Julia. (2007). "Tensions in the Regulatory State", *Public Law* vol. 51-1, pp. 58-73.

May, Peter. (2007). "Regulatory regimes and accountability", *Regulation & Governance* vol. 1-1, pp. 8-26.

Nielsen, Vibeke & Parker, Christine. (2009). "Testing responsive regulation in regulatory enforcement", *Regulation & Governance* vol. 3-4, pp. 376-399.

Ogus, Anthony. (1995). "Rethinking Self-Regulation", *Oxford Journal of Legal Studies* vol. 15-1, pp. 97-108.

Radaelli, Claudio & Meuwese, Anne. (2009). "Better Regulation in Europe: Between Public Management and Regulatory Reform", *Public Administration* vol. 87-3, pp. 639-654.

Websites

www.ukwebstart.com/listwatchdogs.html
This website provides a link to a number of UK regulatory bodies

www.ofgem.gov.uk/About%20us/Pages/AboutUsPage.aspx
This is the Ofgem website which explains their powers and accountability

Questions
1. "Self-regulation enables businesses to do what they like. It is non-regulation." Discuss.
2. In what ways can regulation be carried out more effectively and more efficiently?
3. "Regulation is little more than state interference in the market economy." Discuss.

CHAPTER 17 // REDRESS IN BRITISH POLITICS

Contents
- **Introduction**
- **Accountability and Answerability**
- **Ministerial Accountability**
- **Ombudsman**
- **Judicial Review**
- **Tribunals**
- **European Convention on Human Rights**
- **Audit and Inspection**
- **Conclusion**

Introduction

The issue of redress in the public sector appears in many places. Some of it – such as holding ministers to account for their actions – is covered in greater detail elsewhere in this book (although it is also covered – briefly – in this chapter). Yet the whole system of public sector accountability and redress is something of which most students (not to mention members of the public) are distinctly unaware. This, in itself, causes a degree of confusion. Stories appear in the media highlighting problems with the public sector (e.g. people unable to get treatment on the NHS) with an implicit idea the public sector is not accountable but for the media. Such stories tend to be inaccurate with regard to the accountability of those employed in the public sector. The reality is there are numerous forms of redress available. It is their accessibility that may be more problematic, not to mention the length of time some investigations may take. There appears to be a belief if a story can be reported in the media, there is a greater likelihood of immediate redress.

In 1988, Seneviratne & Cracknell highlighted the extent of complaints procedures in local government at that time. Not only did this include electoral accountability, but also other forms of "legal and political control" over local government activities. These included "applications for judicial review under Order 53 of the Supreme Court Act 1981, liability under contract and tort, various statutory rights of appeal, and... fiduciary control exercised by the local government auditor." (Seneviratne & Cracknell, 1988, p. 181). This list was by no means exhaustive in 1988 – and it is even more extensive today.

Accountability and Answerability

One of the first things to consider with regard to redress is a definition of key concepts. The idea is public sector workers should be both accountable and answerable to the public for their actions. Pyper (1994) raises some key questions about all of this:

- Accountable for what?
- Accountable to whom?
- How are people held to account?
- What is the difference between accountability and answerability?

Accountable for what?
Public sector workers are accountable for 'what they do' and for 'how they conduct themselves'. There are numerous tiers of workers within the public sector, each with their own responsibilities. Some senior civil servants, for example, may be held to account for the policy advice they provide to their ministers. Others, at a lower rank, may be held to account for the way in which they interact with members of the public.

Accountable to whom?
The public sector is hierarchical. This means those working at one level in their organisation will be accountable to someone in a higher tier. Senior civil servants are accountable to their minister, and the minister is accountable to parliament, and thus to the public. As will become apparent in this chapter, there are also other bodies which audit and inspect the actions of public bodies as well.

How are people held to account?
As Pyper (1994, p. 7) notes, this is closely related to the question of *accountability to whom*. There are audits and inspections which monitor the ways in which public services are delivered. There are autonomous bodies which may be requested to investigate the actions of public sector bodies. Ultimately, the government is held to account via the ballot box.

What is the difference between accountability and answerability?
This is a tricky question. Put simply, *answerability* can be seen as being little more than a commitment to provide an answer, whereas *accountability* suggests some form of redress should there have been proven errors. When pursuing redress, there is normally a demand for accountability. A minister may answer to Parliament for the actions of civil servants within his/her government department. Should that minister be held to account for said actions – especially noting the accepted form of redress is a ministerial resignation?

Ministerial Accountability
While ministerial responsibility was covered in some detail in chapters 11 and

12, it is useful to reiterate the key points. Ministerial responsibility (also known as individual responsibility) covers three aspects:
1. a minister is responsible for his or her own personal conduct;
2. a minister is responsible for the policies that come from his or her department;
3. a minister is responsible for the conduct of the civil servants within his or her department.

In each of these areas, if there are faults or omissions, there is an expectation the minister will resign. A ministerial resignation is seen as the key form of accountability among government ministers. Ministers are accountable to parliament, and must explain their actions to parliament. The convention is if a minister fails in his or her duties, then resignation is seen to be the only option.

There is also **collective responsibility**. This is where **all** government ministers support the policies of the government. Failure to give such support will see the prime minister sack a minister. More likely, the minister will tender his or her resignation prior to being sacked. The enforcement of collective responsibility is in the hands of the prime minister.

One caveat here, with regard to the Conservative-Liberal Democrat coalition, is the enforcement of collective responsibility over the Liberal Democrat ministers. While the convention of collective responsibility states it is the prime minister, it is more likely the deputy prime minister (and leader of the Liberal Democrats) will be the person to wield the sword should any Liberal Democrat ministers fail to toe the coalition government line.

Ombudsman

The office of ombudsman was introduced into the UK in 1967. The Ombudsman (officially known as the **Parliamentary Commissioner for Administration**, or PCA) was established to investigate *maladministration*. Surprisingly, within the legislation, the concept maladministration was not explained! The minister involved in establishing the Ombudsman, Richard Crossman, suggested maladministration included "bias, neglect, inattention, delay, incompetence, ineptitude, perversity, turpitude, arbitrariness, and so on" (House of Commons debates, 18 October 1966). This was later broadened to include decisions that were thoroughly bad in quality or clearly wrong.

There is an important point to note about the ombudsman. Complaints are only about the implementation of policies. Whether the policy is good or bad, right or wrong, is immaterial. Maladministration is solely about policy implementation.

When the original ombudsman was established, there was a fear it might supplant the role of MPs (see chapter 9 for the role of MPs). Traditionally, constituents were expected to go to their MP if they had any complaints. Some MPs expressed the fear the creation of the ombudsman would undermine this role. Consequently, an MP filter was established for the Parliamentary

Commissioner for Administration (but not any other ombudsman system). A complainant should go to his or her MP, who may, in turn, take the grievance to the ombudsman on behalf of the constituent.

Since the establishment of the PCA in 1967, many other ombudsman systems have been established. There is one for local government and one for the NHS (although this is actually the same body as the Parliamentary Commissioner for Administration, but without the MP filter). Ombudsman systems have also been established in the private sector. In 1981, for example, the Insurance Ombudsman Bureau was established. In 2007, the Financial Ombudsman Service was established through the merger of seven ombudsman bodies, including the Insurance Ombudsman Bureau.

There are significant differences between public sector and private sector ombudsman systems. While they all investigate the poor implementation of policies, how this is done – and how it is reported – is different. The Local Government Ombudsman, for example, publishes an annual register of complaints for each council (see Table 17.1), as well as the investigations that have been carried through, and their outcomes. This is available to all members of the public. Private sector ombudsman systems, on the other hand, argue the need to maintain confidentiality within the private sector (see Gilad 2008).

Table 17.1 Local Government Ombudsman Report to Leicester City Council for the year ending 31 March 2010 – Local Government Advice Team

	Formal or informal premature complaints	Advice given	Forwarded to investigative team (resubmitted prematures)	Forwarded to investigative team (new)	Total
Adult care services	1	3	0	4	8
Children & family services	4	0	5	1	10
Education	0	6	0	8	14
Housing	12	4	2	18	36
Benefits	6	1	0	4	11
Public finance	1	2	0	7	10
Planning & building control	0	2	1	4	7
Transport & highways	2	1	1	8	12
Other	7	9	3	10	29
Total	33	28	12	64	137

Developed from Local Government Ombudsman (2010); "The Local Government Ombudsman's Annual Review: Leicester City Council for the year ending 31 March 2010" Appendix 2.

Today, the role of the ombudsman has changed. A former ombudsman highlighted the need to focus upon good administration rather than maladministration (Abraham (2008); Abraham (2009)). With this in mind, her office published the *Principles of Good Administration* (Parliamentary and Health Service Ombudsman, 2009b). There are six key principles:

– Getting it right
– Being customer focussed
– Being open and accountable
– Acting fairly and proportionately
– Putting things right
– Seeking continuous improvement

There are also *Principles of Good Complaint Handling* (Parliamentary and Health Service Ombudsman, 2009c), and *Principles for Remedy* (Parliamentary and Health Service Ombudsman, 2009a). All of this is about setting the standards for effective service delivery, and – should there be complaints about such services – dealing with the complaints in an appropriate manner. The British and Irish Ombudsman Association have developed their *Principles and guide to good governance* (2009). This promotes similar ideas, but for application across both public and private sector ombudsman systems. As of 2012, the ombudsman was Dame Julie Mellor.

Judicial Review

This is another way in which administrative decisions may be challenged. It is conducted through the High Court. O'Donnell (1994, p. 106) notes judicial review "is primarily concerned with the provision of remedies against administrative authorities and bodies on the traditional grounds of *ultra vires* and/or a breach of natural justice". The concept *ultra vires* is explained in Table 17.2. Patterson (2011), in a similar vein, points out judicial review can be on the grounds of illegality (*ultra vires*), irrationality (or unreasonableness) or procedural impropriety (fairness).

Table 17.2 What is *ultra vires*?

The term *ultra vires* is used to describe a way in which a public body acts beyond its powers. It could be because a public body has exercised powers it does not have the right to wield. Alternatively, it could be because a public body has acted in a way which is incompatible with decisions taken by a higher authority, such as the European Union. A third way in which the concept *ultra vires* can be utilised is when a public body fails to exercise powers through a prescribed procedure (normally laid out by statute).

Judicial Review is a right to challenge government decisions. It can be carried out through either private law or public law.

The private law approach involves taking legal action against a government body, in the same way as against an individual. It could involve taking out an injunction against the government body. An injunction is "a coercive order requiring a defendant to cease a particular course of behaviour" (Loveland, 2003, p. 491).

The public law approach appears to be a little more complicated. It contains

> the three so-called 'prerogative remedies' of certiorari, prohibition and mandamus. Certiorari was a device to quash (or invalidate) unlawful decisions; prohibition had the same effect as the injunction; and mandamus was intended to force a government body to exercise its legal powers when it was refusing to do so. (Loveland, 2003, p. 492)

All of these proceedings, under public law, will be heard by a single judge in the Administrative Courts. In England and Wales, there are Administrative Courts in Birmingham, Cardiff, Leeds, London and Manchester. In Scotland, proceedings are conducted through the Court of Session, while in Northern Ireland it is through the High Court of Justice. In both Scotland and Northern Ireland, if any case is linked to powers reserved by Westminster (see Section 4 of this book – Government Beyond the Centre), it must be referred to the Upper Tribunal of the Tribunal Service, based in London.

To seek redress through judicial review can be difficult. There are strict procedures to which complainants must adhere. For example, the complainant must seek permission to commence proceedings – and this must be done within three months after the grounds for the complaint arose. There is also an obligation to have exhausted all other alternatives of dispute resolution prior to utilising judicial review (Law Commission, 2008). It is interesting to note around 60% of judicial review cases are resolved prior to a formal claim being submitted. Around a third are settled or withdrawn after a case has been issued; leaving less than 10% going to a final hearing.

As with the ombudsman system, judicial review is a reactive rather than a pro-active system. Whereas the ombudsman system has tried to be more pro-active – through the *Principles of Good Administration* – it is more difficult for the legal system to operate in such a manner. However, the introduction of the Human Rights Act (HRA) enabled a degree of proactivity.

Tribunals

These are part of the judicial system, but need to be acknowledged in their own right – even though they were merged with the courts in 2011. As O'Donnell (1994, p. 97) points out, tribunals "are independent adjudicatory bodies usually established by statute to deal with disputes in a particular area of law". Tribunals are normally seen as being less formal than the courts, as well as being more accessible to the public.

A Council on Tribunals was established in 1958. It was replaced by a quango (see chapter 15), the **Administrative Justice and Tribunals Council (AJTC)**, in 2007. This legislation, more broadly, aimed at addressing "concerns regarding the importance of providing proportionate and accessible redress to those citizens who experience injustice at the hands of the public sector" (Kirkham *et al*, 2009, p. 600). The AJTC was abolished in 2011.

There are many tribunals in existence. There are the First-tier Tribunals, which are made up of seven chambers, within each of which are more specific jurisdictions

- The General Regulatory Chamber
- Health, Education and Social Care Chamber
- Immigration and Asylum Chamber
- The Property Chamber
- Social Entitlement Chamber
- Tax Chamber
- War Pensions and Armed Forces Compensation Chamber

There is also an Upper Tribunal, which comprises four chambers, one of which deals with appeals from decisions (on points of law) taken by the First-tier Tribunals:

- The Administrative Appeals Chamber
- The Immigration and Asylum Chamber
- The Lands Chamber
- The Tax and Chancery Chamber

There is a clear set of values to which the tribunals must adhere – they look remarkably similar to those of the ombudsman.

- openness and transparency
- fairness and proportionality
- impartiality and independence
- equality of access to justice

European Convention on Human Rights (ECHR)

The Human Rights Act (HRA) was covered in chapter seven. Thus this section on the ECHR will be brief, as the HRA was built upon the ECHR.

Britain ratified the ECHR in 1951, but it was not incorporated into British law until the Human Rights Act was passed in 1998, and it did not come into effect until 2000. This meant that, since 2000, all British laws have had to be interpreted in a way that was compatible with the ECHR. This has given another tier of redress for people who feel the public sector has, in some way, infringed upon their rights. The processes – be they judicial review, tribunal, or the ombudsman – are still the same. The ECHR has merely given greater clarity to people's rights. Anyone wishing to make a claim using the ECHR must do so within one year of the date when the act or omission took place.

The ECHR appears to be a very popular form of redress. The downside of this has been a backlog of cases: by 2009, the backlog stood at around 90 000 cases.

This does not mean there are even more opportunities for people to make financial claims against the public sector (as the HRA is sometimes portrayed in the British media). Rather, "damages are awarded only exceptionally rather than as a rule" (Law Commission, 2008, p. 50).

Audit and Inspection

This is a way in which both public and private bodies may be held to account for their actions. Some of this is covered under Regulation in chapter 16. As a form of redress, however, it needs to be covered here.

Clarke (2009, p. 201) noted audit "has historically meant the practice of scrutinising financial control processes and financial decision-making". Today, the idea of an audit goes much further. The financial aspects are still important, but an audit could also involve, for example, an assessment of service performance.

The way in which auditing has changed can be seen in the roles of the **National Audit Office** and the **Audit Commission** (which the coalition government has been proposing to close since gaining office, but was still operating in 2013). Both bodies were involved in assessing the efficiency and evaluating the effectiveness of public sector bodies. According to Flynn (2007, p. 169), the Audit Commission has become "more like a management consultancy, with powers to impose management methods on local authorities as well as assessing and reporting on performance."

The National Audit Office (NAO) was established in 1983, under the control of the **Comptroller and Auditor General**. Civil servants must account for their actions, especially over government spending, to the Comptroller and Auditor General, who is, in turn, accountable to the appropriate select committee. The Comptroller and Auditor General can conduct 'value-for-money audits', but may not investigate the allocation of contracts (Woodhouse, 1997). It must be noted the Comptroller and Auditor General is an officer of the House of Commons, and is appointed by the Monarch.

The aim of the NAO is to promote economy, effectiveness and efficiency across (and within) government departments, alongside routine audits of public sector bodies. It is **not** involved in auditing local government spending, or the spending of the devolved bodies across the UK. Local government spending is audited by the Audit Commission, while there are separate bodies for the devolved bodies: Audit Scotland, the Wales Audit Office and the Northern Ireland Audit Office. When the Audit Commission is abolished, Parliament will legislate on the bodies to pick up the Audit Commission's functions.

The Audit Commission "is an independent watchdog driving economy, efficiency and effectiveness in local public services to deliver better outcomes for everyone" (www.audit-commission.gov.uk/Pages/default.aspx). Not only does it cover local authorities, but also health, housing, community safety, and the fire and rescue services. Annual reports are compiled on how money is spent in all of these bodies. In 2008-2009, the Audit Commission covered public spending of over £45 billion. Again, as with other auditors, it is not just about spending money. In the health sector, for example, the Audit Commission carries out local evaluations, investigates into fraud, collates and monitors the 'Payment by Results' data (which includes establishing national benchmarks), as well as focusing upon examples of good practice which could be utilised elsewhere. If the coalition government's plans to abolish the Audit Commission finally go ahead, many of its functions may be transferred to the NAO.

In the UK, there has been a long tradition of inspectorates, often linked to regulation. Since 2009, within the public sector, there have been four umbrella inspectorates:
– children's services, education and skills
– adult and social care and health
– justice and community safety
– local services

The inspectorate under the banner of children's services, education and skills is Ofsted, which is short for the Office for Standards in Education, Children's Services and Skills. Ofsted inspect a wide range of bodies, as can be seen in Table 17.3. The aim of Ofsted is to achieve educational excellence through regulation and inspection, as well as focusing upon the care and education of children and young people. All of the inspections carried out by Ofsted are available to the public. These can be accessed through the Ofsted web pages.

Table 17.3 Organisations inspected by Ofsted in England (2013)

– childminders
– early years and child care
– adoption and fostering services and agencies
– residential schools, family centres and homes for children
– all state maintained schools some independent schools
– pupil referral units
– the Children and Family Courts Advisory Service (Cafcass)
– the quality of services and outcomes for children and young people in each local authority
– further education and 14 to 19 provision
– Initial Teacher Training
– publicly funded adult skills and employment based training
– learning in prisons, the secure estate and probation
– maintained schools and academies

Developed from Ofsted web pages at www.ofsted.gov.uk/about-us/who-we-are-and-what-we-do/services-we-inspect-or-regulate

There are also other independent inspectorates, such as HM Inspectorate of Constabulary (HMIC) and the Independent Chief Inspector of the Border Agency. HMIC inspects the policing of the UK, to make sure that it is carried out in the public interest. The UK Borders Act (2007) established the statutory framework for the Chief Inspector of the Border Agency, which came into being in 2008. The post holder assesses the effectiveness and the efficiency of the Border Agency, including the Agency's overall performance, the treatment of claimants, and the handling of complaints.

Added to this, there is a profusion of other inspectorates, some of which also perform a regulatory role. These include:

The **Planning Inspectorate**, which was established in 1909. It examines planning proposals, as well as a host of other planning related tasks including listed building consent appeals.

The **Royal Pharmaceutical Society of Great Britain**, which was founded in 1841, is not only the professional body for pharmacists, but it is also an inspectorate. It ensures that the Society fulfils its statutory duties, and that all members of the Society do so, under the Poisons Act (1972), through inspecting the premises of all registered pharmacists.

It is through these inspectorates public welfare can be protected. Added to this, if there are any grievances, these inspectorates have significant powers to punish offenders.

Conclusion

There are many alternatives for people who wish to complain about public sector bodies. As noted at the beginning of this chapter, people appear unaware of the alternatives that exist. One of the problems is in selecting the most appropriate alternative to get a grievance addressed. Sometimes it is down to good (or bad) fortune: "it is largely a matter of 'pot luck' whether a citizen with a grievance about public administration ends up in front of a court with a judicial review claim or an Ombudsman with a complaint" (Abraham, 2008, p. 374).

In our more litigious society, some people are looking for ways to complain in an attempt to make financial gain. What is interesting about many of the forms of grievance procedure covered in this chapter is financial compensation is not a priority. It is about addressing the complaints to ensure they are not repeated. Where there is financial compensation, vast sums of money are not being proffered.

Selected bibliography

Abraham, Ann. (2009). "Good Administration: Why We Need It More Than Ever", *Political Quarterly* vol. 80-1, pp. 25-32.
Abraham, Ann. (2008). "The Ombudsman and Individual Rights", *Parliamentary Affairs* vol. 61-2, pp. 370-379.

Brewer, Brian. (2007). "Citizen or consumer? Complaints handling in the public sector", *International Review of Administrative Sciences* vol. 73-4, pp. 549-556.

Kirkham, Richard; Thompson, Brian & Buck, Trevor. (2009). "Putting the Ombudsman into Constitutional Context", *Parliamentary Affairs* vol. 62-4, pp. 600-617.

Law Commission. (2008). "Administrative Redress: Public Bodies and the Citizen", Consultation Paper No. 187.

Patterson QC, Frances (General Editor). (2011). *Judicial Review: Law and Practice*: Jordans.

Websites

www.audit-commission.gov.uk
The home page of the Audit Commission.

www.justice.gov.uk/about/hmcts
The home page of HM Courts and the Tribunals Service.

www.nao.org.uk/
The home page of the National Audit Office

www.ofsted.gov.uk/
Home page of Ofsted

Questions
1. What are the most effective forms of redress? What makes them so effective?
2. "The MP filter for the Parliamentary Commissioner for Administration means that many cases never get that far. The MP filter should be removed." Discuss.
3. What is 'maladministration'?

CHAPTER 18 // PARTICIPATION

Contents
- **Introduction**
- **Political Parties and Pressure Groups**
- **New Forms of Participation**
- **The Big Society**
- **Conclusion**

Introduction

This chapter needs to be read in conjunction with the next chapter, on Citizenship. Added to this, there is clear reference to the possibility of participation via political parties and pressure groups. Thus, reference will need to be made to subsequent chapters on those specific areas.

Over the last decade or so, there appears to have been a crisis in participation. People, and especially the young, are not joining political parties, are not bothering to vote, and, generally, seem disengaged in, or apathetic about, politics. Such a perception, while not inaccurate, masks a simple concern: what is meant by the concept 'participation'? Is participation merely about voting? At the most basic level, for those eligible to vote, the answer is 'Yes'. Yet this ignores a myriad of other forms of participation, or opportunities to participate. Many people may feel disengaged with mainstream politics in the Westminster village and do not, therefore, vote, but work actively through volunteering in community centres, or attending park user group meetings, or becoming community governors in a local school. These are all forms of participation. The option of 'not voting' could be seen as a deliberate choice, especially if a voter has no confidence in any of the candidates: an active decision to withdraw participation. A simple response here is for this hypothetical non-voter to at least go and spoil their ballot paper; thus meeting the 'mainstream' criteria of participating, while refusing to express a positive choice. Compelling participation, through compulsion, undermines the ideas behind participation: most notably, that of volunteering.

Crouch (2001, p. 150) highlights the problem of participation. The disillusioned may ask how do you participate?

> By voting in elections for a choice between parties which increasingly differ more in their presentation than their substance? By joining a party which will be seen by its leaders as either a flock of sycophantic cheerleaders or an irritating nuisance, to be rendered dispensable as soon as the flow of corporate campaign funding allows? By sending messages to party websites managed by lower-level employees of spin doctors? Or by becoming a corporate lobbyist, waiting for the revolving door to come round, and hoping to hang on to my principles as I hurtle through it?

Such a quote presents a rather gloomy outlook on participation, highlighting the negative aspects, and many of the problems, in attempting to participate. The reality may not be quite so bad.

Political Parties and Pressure Groups
After voting, the most conventional forms of participation include joining a political party or a pressure group. Originally, political parties were the most significant form of participation in the 20th century, but they were gradually replaced by pressure groups.

Political Parties
In the immediate post-war period, when Britain was effectively a two party political system, the most effective form of participation was seen to be through political parties. Thus, people joined a party, or lobbied or campaigned on behalf of the party. The mass memberships of the two major parties – Conservative and Labour – were very influential.

In the early part of the twentieth century, political parties moved from being elite-based cadre parties (which were dominated by political elites) to being mass membership parties. As Sartori (2005, p. 13) pointed out, "a mass party must have masses of people behind it". Such parties tended to be equated with working class or proletarian parties. There is a debate as to whether or not there could be mass middle class parties. Sartori is of the opinion there could be such a party; others are less convinced. Regardless of this debate, the two major political parties in the UK – Conservative and Labour – had significant mass memberships.

During the 1960s, these mass parties started to move to become 'catch-all' parties. The parties started to move away from their mass base of support, and to target floating voters; developing policies to appeal to the 'undecided' voter rather than targeting the wishes of their core support. More recently, they have evolved into electoral professional parties (Heffernan, 2003) or modern day cartel parties (Blyth & Katz, 2005). In these parties, ideology plays a much-reduced role; competence is the key to electoral success (Heffernan, 2003, p. 138). Even the space for competing 'catch-all' parties has been reduced. As Lees-Marshment (2008) points out, parties focus on satisfying voters' demands. In such a model, political parties act more like a business, with voters treated more like consumers. This was epitomised by New Labour, which, in the build up to the 1997 General Election, "was united in the desire to change all aspects of its behaviour in order to win" (Lees-Marshment, 2008, p. 181). In doing so, Labour alienated its traditional supporters. As a result of this desire to win office, it could be argued Labour "lost all its ideology and beliefs and stands for nothing" (Lees-Marshment, 2008, p. 181).

This professionalisation of political parties, especially in the development from mass membership parties, has seen a reduction in the opportunities to influence policy. With such a reduction, along with the downplaying of ideology or political ideas, sees far less participation by members – in fact, membership of such parties diminishes. These new electoral machines appear far less interested in the wishes of their grass-roots members, and far more concerned about avoiding risks. Consequently, as an avenue of participation, membership of a political party is no longer perceived as a viable option to the average citizen.

Pressure Groups

Pressure group action, as it is understood today, originated in the 1960s. Political parties appeared to be less in touch with the issues or concerns of many parts of society. Consequently, pressure groups started to develop in an attempt to influence government – be it local or national – to change a particular policy or to address a particular interest. This *interest articulation* was seen to be very important – and has remained so.

Often, people join a pressure group because of a particular issue, more often than not at a local level. These activists are labelled NIMBYs – Not In My Back Yard. Such a label is often used in a derogatory manner: NIMBYs are self-interested, and are watching out for their own welfare rather than that of society or the nation. Such denigration is neither wholly fair, nor wholly accurate. It is fair to acknowledge the 'personal' concerns such campaigners express. Yet they are attempting to participate in the local (or national) policy formulation and implementation process. The comments by Lees-Marshment (2008) about voters and political parties apply just as much to pressure group campaigners. There is a desire – self-interested though it may be – to participate; to satisfy their own demands. Pressure groups are about a single issue or concern affecting members of the organisation. NIMBYism is no different.

While local pressure groups come and go, in relation to the issues and concerns of the day, national and international pressure groups remain. These bodies, such as Green Peace, Friends of the Earth, the Campaign for Nuclear Disarmament (CND), have strong memberships, who are willing to participate. Yet, with the professionalisation of lobbying by these organisations, some people are no longer drawn to such groups. They see them as tied in to 'the system', no longer activists but professional lobbyists. With such professionalism, the link to the membership is lost, in just the same way as political parties appear to have lost touch with their core membership. Thus people, and especially younger people, look for alternative forms of participation.

Direct Action

This is a form of pressure group activity that tends not to be supported by the professional lobbyists. Rather than campaigning to persuade elected representatives to address a particular interest or concern, direct action uses other means. This could be through violence and illegality, or simply through protests (see chapter 22). The idea is to be 'doing' something, rather than working through a (party) political filter.

Direct action is something of a double-edged sword. When students protested about the imposition of the new system of tuition fees, by organising a march through central London, some of those protests turned into riots. Later that evening, through a streak of misfortune, the Prince of Wales and his wife got caught up in the trouble. The late evening news and the headlines of the following day were all about the threat to the Royals, and the violence of some of the protestors, rather than about the reason for the protests. Such problems with direct action are not new. Anti-capitalism protests have got out of hand on more than one occasion, when the lunatic fringe or the hard-line protestors hijack such protests and demonstrations.

New Forms of Participation

From the mid-1990s, new forms of participation have developed. Governments, intent on encouraging new forms of participation, engineered some of these. It must be noted some of the government-led forms of participation look more akin to consultation. The Labour Government under Tony Blair exhibited "a deep commitment to processes of consultation, participation and 'listening' to citizens in the widest sense" (Clarke, 2005, p. 450). The emphasis was on the active citizen, but questions were raised with regard to the extent of citizens being empowered. Added to this, technological developments enabled new forms of participation to develop. The internet, in particular, has been a major force in such developments.

Citizens' Juries

These were used extensively by the Labour Government of Tony Blair, but also at the level of local government. In effect, a citizens' jury was putting a policy on trial (Pratchett, 1999). It was a form of consultation (which, it could be argued, was different to participation).

These juries comprised a group of randomly chosen citizens, who would gather and discuss a particular issue or policy. Information was provided for the participants to make the deliberations far better informed. On top of this, witnesses could be called to provide further evidence. Although there appears to be a legal underpinning, these juries worked more like select committees. A moderator, who had been trained for such a role, facilitated all of this. The citizens' juries would produce a recommendation, or series of recommendations, although there was no obligation for the government to adhere to them.

Citizens' juries were seen as a form of deliberative democracy. It offered increased chances for citizen participation (Smith & Wales, 2000). The problem was usually very few people were invited to participate. These juries took up a lot of time at both evenings and weekends.

Table 18.1 Deliberative Democracy

Deliberative democracy concerns itself with the process through which political decisions are made. The idea is to encourage political dialogue, aimed at developing mutual understanding. Politics is often seen as being confrontational. Look, for example, at the layout and the processes of the House of Commons: Her Majesty's Loyal Government and Her Majesty's Loyal Opposition. Rather than imposing ideas on to people, deliberative democracy is aimed at conflict resolution. This is done through argument and debate. It does not mean that both sides have to agree.

Focus Groups

Like citizens' juries, focus groups are consultative bodies established to discuss a particular topic. Focus groups are very clearly modelled on the private sector; a group is established to comment on or evaluate a particular product. Again, it was the Labour Party who started using such a technique prior to the 1997 General Election.

A focus group could comprise between half-a-dozen and a dozen people. They would be selected to meet specific criteria. These criteria could be linked to age, ethnicity, gender, educational qualifications, or users of public transport. Those selected would also receive a small remuneration for their time.

As with citizens' juries, a question must be raised as to whether or not these groups can be seen as a form of participation. In that a small number of people are chosen to provide their opinions on a particular topic, there is a form of participation. That the participants are carefully selected to meet specific criteria suggests the link to participation is a little tenuous.

New Media

It is in the area of the new media – most notably through the internet – that opportunities for participation have arisen, and have been taken. In many respects, this is a move away from the more traditional forms of participation, such as voting, campaigning for a party or lobbying an elected representative – which has been described as citizen-oriented action (Norris, 2003). The use of new technology has seen a rise in "cause-oriented repertoires" (Norris, 2003). This can be about a specific issue – similar to pressure group activity – but could be more about consumer politics, petitioning, as well as protests and demonstrations. Norris (2003) notes how young people, in particular, are more engaged politically via the new media, but not in the conventional forms of political activity.

Successive governments have looked to tap into the new media, and attempted to encourage participation by the population via such media. Thus there is the opportunity to start an e-petition on the 10 Downing Street web pages. There is a commitment: any petition which receives over one hundred thousand signatures will be debated in the House of Commons. There have been e-petitions on a range of issues, including: to reconsider the West Coast rail franchise; to protect police pensions; to save children's cardiac surgery at the EMCHC [East Midlands Congenital Heart Centre] at the Glenfield Hospital, Leicester; and, a referendum on the European Union. E-petitions that have received over one hundred thousand signatures include: the demand for full disclosure of all Government documents relating to the 1989 Hillsborough disaster; and, a demand for cheaper petrol and diesel.

Yet the new media goes so much further. Many people, in effect, live their lives via social media such as Twitter and Facebook. This new media is also used to highlight issues. Dissatisfaction with a retailer may get highlighted on social media pages. Accidents or other incidents may get broadcast on YouTube. Such stories or videos may go viral, compelling some form of response from the retailer. This is a new form of participation with which politicians and business leaders have to deal – but it is always a reactive response. Arguably, it is impossible to be proactive here, but such participation does compel a response.

One of the reasons why this new media is so popular is often to do with the immediacy of the response. Just as in television programmes such as The X Factor or Strictly Come Dancing, a vote (or multiple votes) gets a near immediate response. A competitor is eliminated by the following week. Broadcasts on YouTube can evoke a near-similar response. Compare this with the mainstream political response, which requires debates in the Houses of Parliament or in the local council chamber, multiple votes, and a vague attempt to address the issue either weeks or, more likely, months later. There are many justifications for the apparent slowness of the response, including considering the consequences of introducing some legislation. Such considerations are deemed irrelevant when voting a contestant from a game show.

The Big Society

Prior to becoming prime minister, David Cameron introduced his idea of the Big Society. This was his plan to fix 'Broken Britain', not by heavy-handed state intervention (as the Blair and Brown Governments were accused of doing) but by getting society to sort itself out. Critics were quick to suggest Cameron's vision of the Big Society was little more than an excuse to further roll back the frontiers of the state, reinforcing the neo-liberal ideals of the Thatcher years (see chapter 8).

The ideas behind the Big Society are not new. Both the Blair and the Major Governments had similar ideas that were introduced. As Davies & Pill (2012, p. 193) have noted: "From the Major premiership onwards, successive administrations have increasingly invested in the potential of civic renewal for reinvigorating self-help, volunteering and political participation and for taking ownership of public assets and running public services". If anything, the difference with the Big Society is the scale by which public services would no longer be run by the state.

The ideal was for community groups to run parks, post offices, libraries, local transport services and so forth (Kisby, 2010). The active citizen would become even more of a philanthropist; a culture of volunteering would be instilled in everyone. The Big Society, however, is not just about individual participation; it is also about empowering communities. On the Cabinet Office website, there is a claim:

> We will introduce new powers to help communities save local facilities and services threatened with closure, and give communities the right to bid to take over local state-run services.
> **www.cabinetoffice.gov.uk/sites/default/files/resources/building-big-society_0.pdf**

This is a most laudable idea. If communities want to keep their services, they should do something about it, rather than looking to the state. Yet what must be asked is **why** are these local services under threat? Is it due to lack of use, or lack of funds?

Shortly after the 2010 General Election, four areas were declared the vanguard of the Big Society: Liverpool, Eden Valley (Cumbria), Windsor & Maidenhead, and the London borough of Sutton. The aim was to reduce the role of the state in these areas, and to encourage communities, in conjunction with businesses, voluntary organisations, and community groups, to take over some provision of services, to streamline the amount of planning regulations, and, ultimately, remove bureaucratic barriers to participation. In February 2011, Liverpool withdrew from the vanguard because of the public spending cuts being imposed on all parts of the public sector.

One of the problems facing the Big Society is funding. In healthy economic times, funding would be available to support these voluntary groups take over the running of public services. As Davies & Pill (2012, p. 193) have highlighted: "unless it is backed by substantive public investment, the 'big society' risks being little more than 'laissez-faire' by another name, with disastrous consequences". If, for example, these organisations are unable to continue running the services – for whatever reason – who would take over the provision? The suggestion in the Big Society is **not** the state. The quote from the Cabinet Office (above) highlights how communities can take over local facilities, but is light on information about finance. Apart from the establishment of a Big Society bank, there is little information about funding the provision of services. Instead, there is talk of increased charitable donations.

Kisby (2010, p. 491) highlights the core issue surrounding the idea of the Big Society.

> The 'big society' idea seems to be one of two things. At best, it is essentially empty, nothing more than an encouragement to citizens to do 'good deeds' in the community; nothing particularly objectionable but equally lacking in substance and destined to have a minimal impact on public policy. At worst it is dangerous, a genuine belief that charities and volunteers, rather than the state, can and should provide numerous, core public services.

It could be argued that Kisby is overstating the problem: presenting a 'worst-case' scenario. Even his positive perspective is somewhat dismissive of the Big Society. The idea of participating in, for example, your local community is not to be dismissed. It would probably work best through complementing state provision of services, rather than replacing them. For example, volunteers may join in on a litter pick to tidy up a local park – something that is easily co-ordinated by the local council. Those same volunteers are unlikely to want to maintain the park and its facilities. That is a task suited to the local council. A private provider of such a park – who needs to make a profit on the running of the facility – is far less likely to get the local community involved in a litter pick, when the users have to pay directly for the service (rather than paying for the service via taxation).

The idea voluntary organisations may provide schooling is not unusual. There have always been private (and voluntary) providers of education, complementing state provision. What is odd is, under the system of free schools, they may be exempt from the national curriculum and do not need to have fully qualified schoolteachers taking the classes. Some groups, for example, are looking to former members of the military to run their classes, to instil some discipline in the pupils. While that may be seen as a worthy ideal, how is this going to contribute to pupil attainment? The government blocked a proposal for a 'military' free school in Oldham, but the group involved (the Pheonix Academy) are looking elsewhere to establish their school. One of the criticisms from the Department for Education, in an otherwise 'strong bid', was a lack of trained teachers!

Conclusion

The idea of participation is not new. Successive governments have re-branded the concept, in an attempt to instil greater desire to participate – be it citizenship under the Blair Government, or the Big Society under Cameron. What needs to be asked is why are governments encouraging participation? What forms of participation would they like people to do? At the most basic level, voting is seen as a form of participation. All politicians would like to see increased turnouts, especially as that can give them a clearer mandate from the people.

When people go out to protest about government policy, or to go on strike in response to government policy e.g. public sector workers over pensions, governments tend to complain about such actions. Yet these are valid forms of participation – a form of lobbying or pressure group activity. It is interesting to note the selectivity of politicians with regard to what is considered 'acceptable' participation, and what is not.

Modern technology has opened up a whole new range of opportunities to participate, and this is being picked up by the younger generations. Young people are often castigated for not participating i.e. not voting. Yet these people are far from disengaged from politics – they are merely uninterested in the stuffy formal politics of Westminster or the town hall. They adopt a far more consumerist approach to participation i.e. what is of interest to them. With such participation comes a feeling of being able to get things done. Whether or not things change is open to question. Yet it is the feeling of doing so that sees higher levels of participation.

Selected bibliography

Davies, Jonathan & Pill, Madeleine. (2012). "Empowerment or abandonment? Prospects for neighbourhood revitalization under the big society", *Public Money & Management* vol. 32-2, pp. 193-200.

Farthing, Rys. (2010). "The politics of youthful antipolitics: representing the 'issue' of youth participation in politics", *Journal of Youth Studies* vol. 13-2, pp. 181-195.

Furlong, Andy & Cartmel, Fred. (2012). "Social Change and Political Engagement Among Young People: Generation and the 2009/2010 British Election Survey", *Parliamentary Affairs* vol. 65-1, pp. 13-28.

Henn, Matt & Foard, Nick. (2012). "Young People, Political Participation and Trust in Britain", *Parliamentary Affairs* vol. 65-1, pp. 47-67.

Kisby, Ben. (2010). "The Big Society: Power to the People?", *Political Quarterly* vol. 81-4, pp. 484-491.

Lees-Marshment, Jennifer. (2008). *Political marketing and British political parties*: Manchester University Press, 2nd edition.

Websites

www.cabinetoffice.gov.uk/news/building-big-society
An outline of the government's programme of policies in support of the Big Society.

www.hks.harvard.edu/fs/pnorris/Acrobat/COE%20Young%20People%20 and%20Political%20Activism.pdf
This is a report by Pippa Norris entitled "Young People & Political Activism: From the Politics of Loyalties to the Politics of Choice" for the Council of Europe Symposium: "Young people and democratic institutions: from disillusionment to participation", Strasbourg, 27-28 November, 2003.

www.number10.gov.uk/take-part/public-engagement/petitions/
10 Downing Street e-petition page

Questions
1. What are the most effective forms of participation? What makes them so effective?
2. "Participation requires incentives and compulsion. Without incentives and compulsion, there will be no participation." Discuss.
3. The Big Society is not about participation but about rolling back the frontiers of the State. Comment.

CHAPTER 19 // CITIZENSHIP

Contents
- **Introduction**
- **What is Citizenship?**
- **Theories of Citizenship**
- **Citizenship and Nationality**
- **Citizenship and Gender**
- **Can Citizenship be taught?**
- **Conclusion**

The previous chapter examined issues surrounding the concept of participation. In many respects, this chapter builds upon the idea of participating. There is a belief that an *active citizen* is somebody who is willing to participate – be it through voting, writing a letter to an elected representative, joining a pressure group, etc. Yet citizenship encompasses far more than just participating.

Introduction
A problem with citizenship is it is a contested concept. As will become apparent through this chapter, there are a number of different understandings of the concept – and these are sometimes contradictory. King & Waldron (1988, pp. 431-432) highlight one interpretation: "when we say 'X is a citizen of the United Kingdom', what we mean is that he or she is a fully-fledged *member* of this community, entitled to live here and make a life here". While this is a useful starting point, it raises some interesting questions. The most prominent of these – and this is clearly linked to the idea of citizenship – is: what does being "entitled to live here" include? Responses to this question could include a list of rights that are generally seen as being bestowed upon people who live in the United Kingdom. Less acknowledged is there are many duties and obligations that come along with these rights. There are many television programmes, for example, where characters claim they have, or they know their rights. The duties and obligations appear to fall by the wayside.

What is Citizenship?
The idea of citizenship can be traced back to Ancient Greece, where the citizens of Athens were involved in running the city. These "citizens" were male, over 30 years of age, born in the city, and were free (i.e. not a slave). This totalled about an eighth of the population of the city. Women, slaves, foreigners and minors were not seen as citizens.

There is broad agreement the modern understanding of citizenship can be attributed to the work of T. H. Marshall; *Citizenship and Social Class* (1950). Since that time, there have been many criticisms of Marshall's work, including the lack of focus on gender and ethnicity, and the emphasis upon class. Yet, despite such criticisms, modern understandings of citizenship are built upon Marshall's ideas.

Marshall saw three strands to citizenship: civic, political and social. He argued these strands were interwoven. In the past, they had been separated, but during the twentieth century they knitted back together.

The **civil** strand of citizenship was about equality before the law. Marshall stated it was "composed of the rights necessary for individual freedom – liberty of the person, freedom of speech, thought and faith, the right to own property and to conclude valid contracts, and the right to justice" (1963, p. 74). These civil, or legal, rights started to become prominent during the eighteenth century.

The **political** strand has many of its origins in the nineteenth century, especially with legislation such as the Great Reform Act of 1832. According to Marshall, this strand was about "the right to participate in the exercise of political power, as a member of a body invested with political authority or as an elector of the members of such a body" (1963, p. 74). Some of this political citizenship did not occur until the twentieth century e.g. votes for women. Marshall acknowledged there was overlap in the timescales of each strand and they were not tied down to a particular century. Rather, it was during a specific century the awareness and the creation of such rights and duties within a particular strand commenced.

The **social** strand is placed in the twentieth century. Often it is related to the welfare state. For Marshall, it was about "the whole range from the right to a modicum of economic welfare and security to the right to share to the full in the social heritage and to live the life of a civilized being according to the standards prevailing in the society" (1963, p. 74).

While this was a useful exercise in examining how modern citizenship has developed, Marshall felt it was important for the three strands not to be kept separate. As Lister (2005, p. 473) argues, there is a need to focus on "the unified nature of citizenship and the need to consider civil, political and social rights in relation to, not isolation from, each other". Lister points out the relationship between these component parts may not be harmonious, but should not be a justification for separating each section of rights. Legal rights impact upon political rights, which impact upon social rights, and so forth.

With this base of knowledge about citizenship, there is still a need to define the concept. As noted earlier, it is a contested subject. Below is a range of definitions of citizenship:

> Citizenship is a set of norms, values and practices designed to solve collective action problems which involve the recognition by individuals that they have rights and obligations to each other if they wish to solve such problems.
> (Pattie, Seyd & Whiteley, 2004, p. 22)

Citizenship: membership, determined by factors such as place of birth, parentage or naturalisation, of a political community (generally a nation-state), in virtue of which one has legally defined rights and duties, significant identity and (on some counts) moral responsibility to participate in public affairs.
(Dower, 2003, p. xi)

Citizenship is linked with obtaining the nationality of the country of residence and sharing full and equal rights with the 'original' citizens.
(van den Anker, 2002, p. 165)

...the term 'citizenship' is a very broad concept and it encompasses questions of identity, ethnicity, gender, participation, attitudes and values as well as perceptions of rights and obligations.
(Pattie, Seyd & Whiteley, 2004, p. 129)

[Citizenship] can be reduced to the dialectical relationship between state, the protection it offers to its citizens as rights, and the duties to the state that those citizens are expected to offer in return.
(Lambert & Machon, 2001, p. 4)

Citizenship is a status bestowed on those who are full members of a community. All who possess the status are equal with respect to the rights and duties with which the status is endowed. There is no universal principle that determines what these rights and duties shall be...
(Marshall, 1963, p. 87)

Prominent in each definition is the idea of both rights and duties (or obligations). Marshall (1963, p. 17) noted "[i]f citizenship is invoked in the defence of rights, the corresponding duties of citizenship cannot be ignored". There is also an emphasis placed upon the state, and interactions between the citizen and the state. Quite often, in definitions of citizenship, there is a muddying of the waters with nationality. This will be examined later in the chapter.

When looking at citizenship, Dobson (2003) suggests thinking of four contrasts:
1. rights and obligations
2. territorial and non-territorial concepts of citizenship
3. public and private arenas as possible sites of citizenship activity
4. virtue- and non-virtue-based ideas of citizenship

Each contrast will be explained briefly. Prior to this, it is important to note they should not be seen in isolation of each other. As with Marshall's strands of citizenship, there is overlap.

1. rights and obligations are the fundamental part of citizenship. As has been noted frequently throughout this chapter, there are both rights and obligations for citizens. There are the obvious rights, such as freedom of speech or freedom of religious practice. The obligations or duties include obeying the law and paying taxes.
2. territorial and non-territorial concepts of citizenship can be related to nationality. A territorial link can be seen through a geographical attachment – a specific country or region. Yet a non-territorial link could be seen in the idea of global citizenship.
3. the public and private arenas as possible sites of citizenship activity raises some interesting issues. Conventionally, citizenship is seen as being in the public sphere. The private sphere (e.g. within the home) is seen as belonging to the private individual. Yet what happens in the public sphere will influence the private. Much of this is linked to gender issues, which will be examined later in the chapter.
4. virtue- and non-virtue-based ideas of citizenship may straddle ideological perceptions of the role of the state. Dobson (2003, p. 57) notes "conceptions of citizenship that do not subscribe to public reasonableness, for example, are very unlikely to get a purchase in liberal or social democratic societies". Within illiberal societies, it may be different. This still leaves the issue of which virtues should be included or excluded in our liberal or social democratic society.

Dobson's contrasts highlight just how difficult it can be to pin down the concept of citizenship. There are many filters influencing an individual's understanding of not just the concept 'citizenship', but also with regard to how to be a 'good' or an 'active' citizen.

Theories of Citizenship

There are many different ways of examining citizenship. Later in this chapter, perspectives on gender and nationality will be raised. Prior to this it will be useful to assess two different sets of approaches to citizenship:
1. liberal versus civic republican
2. choice theories versus structural theories

The 'liberal' and 'civic republican' strands of citizenship dominate the academic landscape. The liberal side places far greater emphasis upon rights, while the civic republican side stresses duties and obligations. This is not an exclusive division, merely the dominant divide. It is also not to say the liberal approach ignores duties, nor the civic republican approach the idea of rights. Rather, it is where the emphasis is placed. It is interesting to note the ideological underpinning of the Blair Government – the Third Way – included the importance of citizen's rights and responsibilities. As Giddens (1998, p.66) stated: "no rights without responsibilities". This appears to be like a contractual obligation, although how it would be enforced is not always clear. Not paying taxes could lead to a fine or even incarceration. Not voting registers no penalty at all (although there is an obligation to be on the electoral register). By complying with these responsibilities, a citizen gets to enjoy the same rights as everyone else.

The 'choice' and 'structural' theories are explained by Pattie *et al* (2004). Under each label, there are subsets.

Choice theories

These theories place the emphasis very much upon the actions of the individual i.e. his or her choice to do, or not to do, something.

Cognitive engagement theory – participation depends upon the extent to which a citizen has access to information. If there is no access to information, there is most unlikely to be any action. Thereafter, assuming there is such access to information, there is then the question as to whether the citizen has the desire, or the capability, to use said information to make choices.

General incentives theory – this is straight-forward rational choice theory. A citizen needs an incentive to participate. If there is no incentive or perceived benefit to doing something, then it is most unlikely that a citizen will participate. The incentive to vote, for example, is to see your favoured candidate get elected, or your favoured party to win the election and implement its manifesto programme. If there is little chance of your favoured party or candidate winning, what incentive is there to participate? A feel-good factor, or a sense of fulfilling a social obligation, is unlikely to be an adequate incentive.

Structural theories

The citizen is a product of social forces. He or she is moulded by everything around them. It is not about the choices that are made. The available choices are a result of social forces.

Civic volunteerism model – most simply put, this is about volunteering. Citizens who have the time, money or skills to be able to volunteer will do so.

Equity-fairness theory – various groups in society are in competition with each other. A citizen will compare him or herself with his or her peers. If the comparison is not favourable, the citizen will compete with his or her peers to improve his or her status.

Social capital model – this is more about collective action. If citizens trust each other, they will work together to solve common problems. The consequence is everyone benefits as a result. This model can be seen in the Third Way, as well as the Big Society.

Citizenship and Nationality

Many authors note the concepts of "citizenship" and "nationality" get merged, or used in an apparently interchangeable manner. This is somewhat unfortunate, as the concept of citizenship can mean far more than nationality. The concept "nationality" is explained in chapter 26 on devolution.

In the definitions presented earlier in this chapter, both van den Anker (2002) and Dower (2003) highlighted the link between citizenship and nationality. It is interesting to note van den Anker suggests the duties of citizenship requires some integration for immigrants, and there should be active participation in society for the 'traditional' citizens (2002, p. 165). There appears to be a distinction here between who is or is not a citizen – and it is linked to nationality. Durose *et al* (2009, p. 2) have also noted a similar distinction. Like children, "new immigrants are understood as almost, but not quite, full citizens". Heater (2004, p. 144) goes much further:

> In its main basic sense, citizenship still involves living in and being committed to a nation-state, with the rights and duties prevailing in that form of polity. But, in addition, it is expected that the citizen should participate in some manner in the generally accepted culture of the community. All should be able to communicate in the country's main language or use one of its main languages. All should be tolerant of the different religions, social habits and political beliefs that make up today's variegated countries – that is, modes of social identity outside citizenship.

In this context, while nationality is clearly the base for citizenship, there is a clear distinction between the two concepts. For example, as Heater later notes (pp. 144-145), it is possible to have multiple social identities and multiple political citizenships. One of the authors of this book, for example, is Welsh by birth, resident in England, holds a British/EU passport, and is also a citizen of New Zealand.

What makes things more complicated with regard to nationality and citizenship in the UK can be linked to Britain's colonial past. Lester (2008, p. 389) attributes "a lack of coherent concept of British citizenship" to that past. In 1948, the passing of the British Nationality Act meant a Commonwealth citizen had the status of a British subject – the concepts of citizen and subject were apparently interchangeable terms. Until 1962, Commonwealth citizens "were entitled freely to travel to this country [the UK] and to settle here. Once here, they enjoyed equal rights with United Kingdom citizens and could acquire United Kingdom citizenship automatically by registering after a period of residence" (Lester, 2008, p. 390). Added to this, citizens of the Republic of Ireland were also treated as if they were British subjects – and much of that still applies today!

The Treaty on European Union (also known as the Maastricht Treaty) introduced the idea of EU citizenship. On the one hand, the idea was "to foster trust among citizens of the Union" (Follesdal, 2002, p. 73). On the other hand, it was also seen "as a purely decorative and symbolic institution" (Kostakopoulou, 2008, p. 286). The treaty further enshrined the idea of the free movement of people across all EU states (with some caveats). To make this easier, the idea of EU passports and EU citizenship was introduced. This appears to be an attempt to create a clear break between the idea of nationality and citizenship, while fostering the idea of all residents in all member states having the similar rights as citizens. Yet, as Dobson (2003, p. 35) notes, "we find it hard to entertain the idea now that citizenship can have meaning outside the nation-state".

Despite this rather pessimistic outlook, there are a number of authors who are looking to the idea of global citizenship e.g. Dower & Williams (eds.); *Global Citizenship: A Critical Reader* (2002). Such a text looks at breaking – or at least loosening – the nationality-citizenship link.

Citizenship and Gender

A concern not often noted with regard to citizenship is its relationship with gender. Jones (1990, p. 785) notes that "[w]hom we recognize as citizens depends upon what qualifies as the behavior [*sic*] of citizens" – see also Durose *et al* (2009), as noted earlier in this chapter on immigrants. Lowndes (2000, p. 535), more precisely, argues "women's maternal and care-giving roles have traditionally been seen as *barriers* to full citizenship". This is linked to the public-private divide mentioned earlier in this chapter.

Citizenship is seen as being in the public sphere, where good citizens help in their community, or do good deeds; acting unselfishly for the benefit of others. The private sphere – for example, within one's home – is seen as being beyond the remit of the good citizen. This is very much gender-related. The man is seen as the head of the household – in times gone by, he effectively 'owned' his wife. She was in charge of the domestic duties, but was seen as subservient to the head of the household. What went on behind those closed doors, stayed there – and was of nobody else's concern.

The reality is much of what goes on in the public sphere impacts upon the private, and vice versa. As Lister (2003, p. 30) notes, "actions in both public and private spheres can interact to enhance the capacity to act as a citizen. Thus, involvement in collective action can strengthen the ability to resist oppressive practices such as domestic violence in the private sphere; conversely such resistance can lead to and inform more public collective citizen action".

Jones (1990) highlights how many women in Western democracies do not have the same rights as men – more specifically, they have fewer rights than men – under the banner of citizenship. More broadly, the concept of citizenship, she argues, needs to be challenged:

the conceptualisation of citizenship in these systems [western democracies] – the characteristics, qualities, attributes, behavior [sic], and identity of those who are regarded as full members of the political community – is derived from a set of values, experiences, modes of discourse, rituals, and practices that both explicitly and implicitly privileges men and the "masculine" and excludes women and the "female". (1990, p. 781)

Some of this can be seen in classical approaches to citizenship, where courage, leadership and self-sacrifice were seen as the virtues of a good citizen. These are very much seen as "masculine" perspectives, and they are still there within modern ideas of citizenship. Ideas such as nurturing, caring or compassion are not really seen within citizenship – they may be taught in the classroom, but they are far less evident in practical citizenship. If they were to be included, it would alter not only the ways in which citizens are defined, but also the study of citizenship (Jones, 1990, p. 789-790).

Even the language used to describe citizenship is distinctively different. The "masculine" perspective focuses upon duty to the body politic, and the activities and characteristics of citizenship. On the other hand, the "feminine" perspective is more about friendship, community and family. These are significantly different perspectives, both of which need to be understood to gain a more rounded understanding of citizenship.

Can Citizenship be taught?

The impact of Marshall's three parts or strands of citizenship could be seen very clearly in the development of the academic syllabus. The original structure to the A/S level syllabus saw three papers: law; politics; and, sociology (see Jones (2007b) for a critique of this syllabus and its successor). Yet there appears to be an assumption citizenship can be taught. It is included in the national syllabus, and there is a citizenship test for immigrants who wish to take up British citizenship (see Table 19.1).

The problem is about how citizenship is assessed. Taking an exam – be it GCSE, A/S, A2 or the test to gain British citizenship – it is merely testing knowledge. The citizenship questions, as shown in Table 19.1 demonstrate this 'knowledge' aspect very clearly. Do you have knowledge about Parliament, local government, society and the legal system? Can you relate that knowledge back to a series of specific questions? This is fine for an academic subject, but the 'doing' is not so apparent.

Table 19.1 A sample range of questions from the Official Practice Citizenship Test

---

Is the statement below TRUE or FALSE?

'In the 1980s, the largest immigrant groups were from the West Indies, Ireland, India and Pakistan.'

Is the following statement TRUE or FALSE?

'Ulster Scots is a dialect which is spoken in Northern Ireland.'

In which year did married women get the right to divorce their husband?

1837; 1857; 1875; 1882

Which of the following TWO types of people get their prescriptions free of charge?

People aged 60 or over

People aged 18 or under

Pregnant women or those with a baby under 12 months old

People on the minimum wage

Is the statement below TRUE or FALSE?

'You can attend a hospital without a GP's letter only in the case of an emergency.'

Source: www.ukcitizenshiptest.co.uk/

One way around this is to encourage active citizen portfolios, where students keep a record of all the citizenship activity they have carried out. The compilation of such a portfolio encourages students to think about the activities they are doing, and to evaluate their actions. The stumbling block, again, is how this is measured. What is to stop a student from compiling a fabricated portfolio and to use that to answer their exam questions? How can there be consistency of assessment across all schools and colleges in the UK with regard to these portfolios? How much support will each individual school or college give to each pupil? The logistics are simply not feasible.

Citizenship *per se* cannot be taught. Instead, the teaching of citizenship should enable students to participate fully, if that is what each student wishes to do. The political, legal and social strands, as taken from Marshall, are a useful starting point. The problem is there is so much more that could be included. The issues surrounding gender and citizenship highlight the extent to which citizenship is an all-encompassing subject, and what is taught today does little more than scratch the surface.

A final point to note about the teaching of citizenship to would-be citizens of the UK is there is no such requirement for UK nationals to sit such a test. Sample questions are included in Table 19.1 – the website will take you to them all. The reality is those passing the citizenship test (needing a grade of at least 75%) are likely to be far better informed citizens than many UK nationals, and, consequently, far more able to engage with society and the state.

Conclusion

The idea of an *active* citizen, who is informed on a range of issues, knows their way around legal, political and social issues, and knows how to interact with the political system is an ideal type. It is one to which the teaching of citizenship aspires. Informed, participating citizens not only can keep the government to account, but they can also protect those same institutions and structures that are an essential part of modern democracy. Feminist critics would argue, and rightly so, this is a very "masculine" perspective on citizenship. The caring, sharing and nurturing parts – the "feminine" parts – of our lives and communities must also be included. This may actually mean a radical overhaul of the concept citizenship – but that would be no bad thing if the end result were a far more inclusive approach to citizenship.

Bibliography

Crick, Bernard (ed.). (2001). *Citizens: Towards a Citizenship Culture*: Blackwell
Dower, Nigel. (2003). *An Introduction to Global Citizenship:* Edinburgh University Press.
Jones, Alistair. (2007b). "Teaching Citizenship?", *Teaching Public Administration* vol. 27-2, pp. 1-14.
Jones, Kathleen. (1990). "Citizenship in a Woman-friendly Polity", *Signs: Journal of Women in Culture and Society* vol. 15-4, pp. 781-812.
Kisby, Ben. (2007). "New Labour and Citizenship Education", *Parliamentary Affairs* vol. 60-1, pp. 84-101.
Lister, Ruth. (2003). *Citizenship: Feminist Perspectives*: Palgrave 2nd edition.
Pattie, Charles; Seyd, Patrick & Whiteley, Paul. (2004). *Citizenship in Britain: Values, Participation and Democracy*: Cambridge University Press.

Websites

www.citizenshipfoundation.org.uk/
The Citizenship Foundation is an organisation that encourages young people to take a more active part in society

www.gov.uk/browse/citizenship/citizenship
This site gives the government's explanations of British citizenship

www.ukcitizenshiptest.co.uk/
This site will give you access to the Official Practice Citizenship Test.

Questions
1. What makes a good citizen?
2. "Everyone in the UK ought to sit and pass a Citizenship test in order to exert their political and social rights." Discuss.
3. Can citizenship be taught?

CHAPTER 20 // ELECTORAL SYSTEMS

Contents

- **Introduction**
- **Main features of Simple Plurality**
- **Arguments for retaining Simple Plurality**
- **Arguments against Simple Plurality**
- **The Multi-Dimensional Approach to Electoral Systems**
- **Alternative Electoral Systems**
- **Conclusion**

Introduction

This topic is a favourite one with examiners. The public has become aware of the discrepancies of the present Simple Plurality system and some of the alternatives available. Different electoral systems are used in elections to the European Parliament, Scottish Parliament, Welsh Assembly, Northern Ireland Assembly, and some parts of local government across the United Kingdom. Added to this, there was the Jenkins Report on electoral reform which investigated replacing Simple Plurality in parliamentary elections. At the 2010 general election, and within the coalition negotiations, the replacement of Simple Plurality with some alternative form of electoral system featured prominently.

The mechanics of these and other electoral systems should be studied but it is the principles which need to be noted. Students often fall into the trap of merely describing how alternative electoral systems function instead of analysing the justification for these systems. Another mistake made by students and politicians alike is to assume when talking about electoral reform, we mean replacing Simple Plurality with some form of Proportional Representation (PR). The reality is there are many non-proportional systems used around the world, some of which may be more appropriate for Britain than many of the forms of PR. A final danger when comparing electoral systems is in the comparing of results. Many people attempt to demonstrate how clever they are by working out the election results if a different system had been used. This is impossible. The systems may have different district magnitudes (number of MPs in a constituency), or different types of ballot (vote for one person, two or more people, or ranking of preferences), as well as different formulae for translating the votes into seats. Each of these has a huge impact upon the result. Anyone transposing election results across electoral systems ignores at least the first two of these variables which results in them making rather empty 'what if...' types of statement.

This chapter will outline the features of Simple Plurality before evaluating its strengths and weaknesses. Thereafter, the chapter will focus on alternative electoral systems that could be employed in Britain.

Main features of Simple Plurality

It is often suggested electoral systems arise in a country because of a range of factors. These may include things such as tradition, or a system has proved its worth, the electorate accepts it, or it produces clear choices or results. If this is the case, why do countries look at reforming their electoral systems? The British Parliamentary electoral system of Simple Plurality is considered a product of factors peculiar to Britain, especially so when compared to systems used in continental Europe. It is not always relevant to compare or imitate the customs of other countries when adopting electoral systems or other institutions but there is also a danger of being completely insular by refusing to consider their merits. There is sometimes a sense of smugness in the British regard for their own practices and institutions.

This smugness extends to the name of the electoral system. Many electoral commentators describe the UK Parliamentary electoral system as 'First-Past-the-Post'. This is, at best, a partially accurate statement. All electoral systems are, technically, first-past-the-post (see *Politics Pal 2010* for a greater discussion of this point). The UK electoral system for Parliamentary elections is Simple Plurality.

If there is ever to be electoral reform, the same criteria concerning general elections will apply. These are: they confer legitimacy on the chosen government for a set period; and, the government is itself a product of choices exercised by the electorate between competing political parties. In addition, general elections afford the opportunity to voters to remove one party and install another, thus preserving the principle of accountability in that governments only derive authority from the consent of voters.

1. The Franchise

The right to vote in elections in Britain is given to all British citizens and those of the Republic of Ireland aged over 18 years at the time of the election. There has been discussion about lowering the voting age to 16, but no legislation has been proposed to do so – although the voting age has been lowered to 16 for the Scottish referendum on independence. Certain groups are not permitted to vote, including: royalty, peers, bankrupts, convicted felons, the mentally impaired, those convicted of serious criminal offences or illegal and corrupt practices at elections in the preceding five years, and those not on the electoral register.

The responsibility for voting rests entirely on the elector by ensuring his/her name appears on the electoral register, which is renewed annually. It is illegal for people not to be registered when they turn 18 years of age.

2. Constituencies

A general election is about constituents electing their MPs. At the same time, an election is about voting in a government from one of the major competing parties. These two features are often blurred. For example, many Labour voters in 1997 claimed to be voting for Tony Blair even though they did not live in Sedgefield – the constituency in which Tony Blair was a candidate. To win an election, a party must currently gain a majority of votes in (as of the 2010 election) 326 out of the 650 constituencies.

The boundaries between the constituencies are redrawn every 8 – 12 years by the Boundary Commissioners to accord with the constantly shifting population. This exercise, which was last carried out in 2005, presents peculiar difficulties because the Commissioners have to reconcile an even spread of electors between seats (the 'quota') with the demands of geography. It is clearly desirable for each constituency to contain the same number of electors but in areas of sparse population, e.g. Orkney and Shetland, and parts of the Highlands of Scotland, the geographical size would be too large to justify this average amount of population. At the same time there are problems of natural boundaries e.g. the Isle of Wight. The electoral population of the Isle of Wight is 103 480, while the quota for each constituency is 69 932. The Isle of Wight does not have the population to justify being divided into two constituencies. It will thus remain the largest single constituency.

The Conservative-Liberal Democrat coalition government proposed reducing the number of MPs to 600 and to attempt to standardise the size of the constituencies – at least with regard to population. This raised potential problems for a number of the constituencies in the North of Scotland, which were already quite vast in size. Such a move would have made them even bigger and far more difficult for an MP to get around. The plans were shelved because of disagreements over Parliamentary reform between the coalition partners.

3. Candidates

Any British citizen or citizen of the Republic of Ireland over the age of 21 is eligible to stand as a parliamentary candidate as long as he/she is not disqualified for the same reasons that would disqualify him/her as an elector. In addition clergymen of the Anglican and Roman Catholic Churches, judges, civil servants, members of the armed forces and the police are not entitled to stand as candidates for Parliament.

Those candidates who are eligible to stand must have the support of ten other electors when submitting their names in writing by nomination day. A deposit of £500 is required. This is lost if the candidate fails to win 5% of total votes cast in the constituency.

The selection of candidates remains very largely in the hands of local constituency party organisations. The vast majority of all MPs are elected as party representatives. There are some exceptions. In the 1997 General Election, Martin Bell won in Tatton as an Independent candidate. There were particular circumstances surrounding his election, most notably the allegations of sleaze and corruption against the Conservative incumbent, Neil Hamilton, while Labour and the Liberal Democrats decided not to field candidates but instead gave tacit support to Martin Bell. In the 2001 General Election, Richard Taylor won in Wyre Forest. He was an Independent candidate who stood on the platform of trying to keep the Kidderminster Hospital Accident and Emergency unit open. The Liberal Democrats refused to stand against Taylor, who won most convincingly. Taylor was re-elected in 2005, but lost in 2010. For the main part, however, candidates tend to be party representatives.

The Central Office of the Conservative Party retains a list of approved candidates which the local Conservative associations are expected to consult before making their choice. The Central Office reserves the right of veto on any candidate. There is no need to be a member of the Conservative Party to stand as a candidate. Neil Hamilton, for example, had not joined the Tatton Conservative Association, despite being the local MP until 1997.

The Labour Party has a slightly more complicated procedure. Two lists are kept; list A contains the names of candidates sponsored by trade unions affiliated to the Labour Party; list B the names of other prospective candidates. The local party has the right to choose individuals from outside these lists but the National Executive Committee (NEC) can veto the choice – in fact they can veto any choice.

The main influence on candidate selection is undoubtedly the needs of the political party. The personal standing of the individual counts for very little now. It has been calculated that a 'good' candidate is worth about 500 votes to his/her party but of course there are exceptions. Enoch Powell had enormous prestige in his constituency of Wolverhampton South West in the 1960s and 1970s. More recently, there have been Julian Critchley (Aldershot), Tam Dalyell (Linlithgow), Dennis Skinner (Bolsover), Douglas Carswell (Clacton), Keith Vaz (Leicester East) and Bernie Grant (Tottenham).

4. The Campaign

Election campaigns are conducted on a national basis with local influences still potentially significant but not really explaining the result. The Tatton result in 1997 and Wyre Forest in 2001 and 2005 were down to local concerns rather than national campaigning, due to reasons noted earlier in this chapter. The importance of the local campaign should not be discounted because it helps to revive the morale of constituency parties, enabling party workers to contribute to canvassing and other mundane duties like delivering literature. The extent to which such actions change opinions is often viewed as being minimal at best, but a lack of it could be costly, suggesting either a lack of interest in the constituency or arrogance on behalf of the party or candidate. Specific targeting of constituencies, as carried out by the Liberal Democrats and Labour in the

1997 and 2001 general elections, and the Conservatives in 2010, has on occasions borne results.

The importance of the campaign, even at national level conducted through a powerful medium like television, should not be exaggerated but nor should it be discounted. The 1992 general election campaign certainly had a bearing on the final result. The image built up by the parties in the pre-election period is probably more decisive although, of course, events during the campaign may be influential. Both the 1997 and 2001 results were easily predictable prior to the commencement of the official campaign. The role of the Referendum Party (in 1997) in attempting to split the Conservative vote was also highly influential. The UK Independence Party tried a similar tactic in 2001, but had only a negligible influence. There have been far fewer major election rallies during more recent campaigns than in previous ones – possibly a case of lessons learned from the Sheffield rally in the 1992 campaign where Neil Kinnock was introduced as the next Prime Minister of Britain.

A significant change to the campaign was introduced in the 2010 General Election – the leadership debate. There were three debates on set topics. Gordon Brown, David Cameron and Nick Clegg had the opportunity to present their party's case to the people. Rather than seeing this as such an opportunity, all three party leaders were very cautious in their approach. It was generally felt, prior to the debates, Nick Clegg had the most to gain – and this proved to be the case. Gordon Brown appeared rather wooden (as Lord Kinnock noted on the Andrew Marr Show, "Gordon Brown has a radio face"). Of the three candidates, it was David Cameron who failed to live up to expectations in the debates – although no serious gaffes were made in the debates by any of the leaders.

The main target of the campaign is the 'floating voters'. These are the people who are undecided as to which party or candidate should receive their vote. It is in this area election campaigns can prove decisive. In particular, in the event of an election that is too close to call, these floating voters in marginal constituencies will decide the outcome of the election. This was evident in the 2010 election result.

Any reservations about the influence of the election campaign are not to deride its significance in other areas. Without a campaign, issues and differences between the parties may be blurred and almost certainly the turnout at the election decreased. A long campaign, however, may have the same effect, as can be seen in the turnout for the 1997 general election. The morale and enthusiasm of party workers is boosted by the campaign; party leaders are forced to face the public and hence one of the central principles of a democratic government, accountability, is sustained. The 2001 campaign was four weeks in length but appeared to have little impact upon the public. The turnout was the lowest since 1918, highlighting both apathy and disillusionment with mainstream politics in Britain.

Table 20.1 Election turnouts 1945-2010

Date	Percentage
1945	73.3
1950	84.0
1951	82.5
1955	76.8
1959	78.7
1964	77.1
1966	75.8
1970	72.0
1974 (Feb.)	78.1
1974 (Oct.)	72.8
1979	76.0
1983	72.7
1987	75.3
1992	77.7
1997	71.2
2001	59.4
2005	61.2
2010	65.1

Arguments for retaining Simple Plurality

It should be appreciated, although the following arguments are usually presented in an objective, theoretical manner by the protagonists, there is a great deal of vested interest in the points made. For example it obviously suits the two major parties to preserve the present plurality system as they benefit from it (although the 2010 election result demonstrates otherwise). A system which emphasises competition between potential governments develops a simple adversarial system. This is most clearly seen through the Simple Plurality electoral system. The smaller parties, on the other hand, favour some form of proportional representation. Use of some form of proportional representation tends to lead to more parties gaining representation, with the emphasis being upon a parliament representative of society, rather than competition between competing potential governments. This can be seen in the elections to the Scottish Parliament and the Welsh Assembly. Yet all of this may be a little too cynical a view as there are cogent reasons advanced on both sides which deserve serious attention.

1. Empirical Evidence – Stability

One of the salient and desirable features of any electoral system should be a degree of stability of government. On the whole the present system has given Britain's political system stability based on clear majorities so the programme of government, as set out in a manifesto, can be implemented. The necessity of coalition government during two world wars was discarded in peacetime. The 2010 election result saw the formation of the first coalition government since 1945, although a minority government was elected in February 1974, and there have also been periods of minority government in both the late-1970s and the mid-1990s. The British people, in fact, understand and welcome the present electoral system because, for all its drawbacks, it does provide effective government. This is preferred to a purely mathematical form of representation. The alternatives to Simple Plurality are seen as complex, and this complexity leads to confusion (Kelly, 2008, p. 261).

2. Strong Government Based on Clear Policies

Even though governments today can be termed 'largest organised minorities' because no party has won over 50% of the vote since 1935 (and that was technically a national coalition party), voters are aware under the present electoral system they are electing a government with a defined programme. The doctrine of the mandate based upon the manifesto of the governing party is rightly regarded with suspicion but at least it is a rough yardstick by which the Government's performance can be measured at the next election. The formation of a coalition – as happened in 2010 – saw both coalition partners dropping some of their key manifesto commitments, although there is a document which details the coalition agreement. The coalition could, however, claim to be a strong government, representing over 59% of the votes cast in the election

3. MP – Constituency Relationship

One of the main features of the present electoral system is the close relationship between MPs and their constituents, including those who did not vote for the winning candidate. This aspect of Britain's electoral system should not be tampered with lightly. The MP besides being a representative is also a source of information and a redresser of grievances. Alternative electoral systems, especially those of a proportional nature, will almost certainly affect these roles adversely. With regard to the elections to the European Parliament, it was the House of Lords that attempted to protect this important relationship in the face of extreme pressure from the Blair Government. Any debate over changing the UK Parliamentary electoral system will see a major focus on this point. Hence, the proposal of the Alternative Vote to replace Simple Plurality, as it retained such a link.

4. Adversarial Politics Perpetuated?

One of the charges against the Simple Plurality system is it encourages the practice of adversarial politics and the resulting dire effects. This is a clear feature of the British political system, with Her Majesty's Loyal Government and

Her Majesty's Loyal Opposition. Despite questioning the usefulness of such a setup, there is also a clear counter argument which highlights the benefits of adversarial politics. The various political parties offer clear policy proposals, while the victorious party can be held to account for their policies. It could even be said adversarial politics simply reflects the volatile mood of the electorate who prefer clearly articulated alternative policies rather than a compromising fudging amalgam of them.

The actual evidence of this adversarial system, focusing upon only two parties can be seen in the election results detailed in Table 20.2. The number of seats gained by the two major parties far outstrips the number won by all of the other parties put together, even when one of the major parties has been well and truly beaten e.g. 1983, 1997 and 2001. When looking at the percentages of votes cast (Table 20.3) the two party system of adversarial politics is displayed. Arguably, in 1983, there was some threat to the system. The support for the Liberal-SDP Alliance, however, could not be maintained as the Labour vote started to return to its natural party.

Table 20.2 British Election Results by constituencies gained 1945-2010

Election	Conservative	Labour	Liberal*	Others**	Total
1945	213	393	12	22	640
1950	298	315	9	3	625
1951	321	295	6	3	625
1955	344	277	6	3	630
1959	365	258	6	1	630
1964	304	317	9	0	630
1966	253	363	12	2	630
1970	330	287	6	7	630
1974 (Feb.)	297	301	14	23	635
1974 (Oct.)	277	319	13	26	635
1979	339	269	11	16	635
1983	397	209	23	21	650
1987	375	229	22	24	650
1992	336	271	20	24	651
1997	165	419	46	29	659
2001	166	413	52	28	659
2005	198	356	62	30	646
2010	307	258	57	28	650

* In 1983 and 1987 Liberal figures cover the results for the SDP/Liberal Alliance. The figures since 1992 are for the Liberal Democrats.
** Northern Irish MPs are counted as 'Others' from 1974.

Table 20.3 British Election Results 1945-2010 by percentage of votes cast

Election	Conservative	Labour	Liberal*	Others**
1945	39.8	47.8	9.0	3.4
1950	43.5	46.1	9.1	0.7
1951	48.0	48.8	2.5	0.7
1955	49.7	46.4	2.7	1.2
1959	49.4	43.8	5.9	0.9
1964	43.4	44.1	11.2	1.3
1966	41.9	47.9	8.5	1.7
1970	46.4	43.0	7.5	3.1
1974 (Feb.)	37.9	37.1	19.3	5.7
1974 (Oct.)	35.8	39.2	18.3	6.7
1979	43.9	36.9	13.8	5.4
1983	42.4	27.6	25.4	4.6
1987	42.3	30.8	22.6	4.3
1992	41.9	34.4	17.8	5.9
1997	30.7	43.2	16.8	9.3
2001	31.7	40.7	18.3	9.3
2005	32.3	35.3	22.1	10.3
2010	36.1	29.0	23.0	11.9

* In 1983 and 1987 Liberal figures cover the results for the SDP/Liberal Alliance. The figures since 1992 are for the Liberal Democrats.
** Northern Ireland votes are counted as 'Others' from 1974

Conclusion

The strength of the case for retaining the present system of elections is it places 'effectiveness', 'stability', and 'strong government' above a concept of 'fairer' representation. Electoral systems should reflect the particular strengths of the country in question. What might be construed as suitable for continental countries with different historical and political traditions is not necessarily going to fit into the British political system and vice versa.

Arguments against Simple Plurality

1. Stability?

This is often more apparent than real. Although Margaret Thatcher's election victories in 1979, 1983 and 1987 were substantial in numbers of seats, the actual proportion of votes cast in her favour were less than those obtained by Ted Heath in his much narrower victory in 1970. Similar comparisons can be made with the Blair victories in 1997, 2001 and 2005, and those of the Wilson-led Labour Party in the 1960s.

In three cases since 1945 fresh elections were needed within 18 months – 1951, 1966, 1974. Question marks were raised about the life of the Conservative-Liberal Democrat coalition, with some pundits predicting a further election within 12 months! As voters become more aware of the vagaries of the present system and the Liberal Democrats establish themselves as a clear third force in Britain, stability will be much more difficult to justify as a merit of the present system. Added to this, the major parties cannot really claim to be truly national parties, with none of them have elected MPs in Northern Ireland. Added to this, the Conservatives were wiped out in parliamentary seats in both Scotland and Wales in 1997, although they regained one seat in Scotland in 2001. Even by 2010, they had only one seat in Scotland, and eight in Wales.

There is also the continuing rise in support for the nationalist parties in Scotland and Wales. In Parliamentary elections, Plaid Cymru and the Scottish Nationalists are prominent players. In Scottish Parliamentary and Welsh Assembly elections, both parties have been elected to government – the SNP as a minority and as a majority government, Plaid Cymru as a coalition partner with Labour. In both countries, the nationalist parties are seen as the major opposition party to Labour.

2. Fairness?

This may not be the most significant of criteria in assessing the merits of an electoral system. Allegations are made that Simple Plurality throws up manifestly 'unfair' and 'absurd' results. Thus, suggestions are made the whole democratic structure should be examined in order to preserve the essential element of democracy. In 1983, for example, the Liberal-SDP Alliance obtained over a quarter of all votes cast but won only 23 seats. In the same election, Labour obtained around 28% of the votes cast and won 209 seats.

From the other side of the coin, no single party has won an absolute majority of votes across the country since 1935. In 1959, the Conservative Party came very close by winning 49.7% of the votes cast. Compare this with the October 1974 result where Labour won the election with fewer than 40% of the vote, or 2010, where the Conservatives were the largest party (but short of an overall majority) winning 36% of the votes cast. It is also possible to win the most votes in an election without actually winning the election. This has happened on two occasions in the post-war period: 1951 and February 1974.

Yet, the question must be asked: what is meant by a 'fair' election? Blau (2004) has investigated this issue. He highlights five common specifications on the concept fairness which are detailed in Table 20.4. Blau raises the pertinent question: "*Should* we use fairness to evaluate electoral systems?"(2004, p. 175).

Table 20.4 The concept 'fairness'

Equality	Citizens and parties to be treated equally
Populist	Voters choose governments, not party leaders
Winner-takes-all	The winner should take the electoral 'spoils'
Majority	The majority of voters or the majority party 'deserve' to win
Plurality	The largest group of voters 'deserve' to win

Developed from Blau (2004) pp. 167-168, 177.

Of these different approaches to the concept 'fairness', the most common are the first three cited in Table 20.4. It must be noted, however, all of the above are clearly contradictory. When examining the 'Plurality' interpretation of 'fairness', for example, is the focus on an individual constituency, across the entire country, or both? Which approach to 'fairness' should be utilised? As Blau (2004, p. 173) notes: "fairness in translating votes to seats may lead to unfairness in translating seats to power". To state that "election results are manifestly unfair" requires the concept of 'fairness' to be explained. Otherwise, such a statement is rather meaningless.

3. Discrimination against smaller parties
In the elections in the 1980s, the Liberal-SDP Alliance came second in over 300 constituencies, but won very few seats. The Liberal Democrats in the 1990s suffered similar problems. It is really only with the formation of a coalition government in 2010 aspects of such discrimination became a little less obvious.

This highlights one of the apparent injustices of the present system. Minority parties have to struggle to get to a threshold of around 30%, after which they may win seats in greater numbers. Such concerns were demonstrated in New Zealand as well as Britain. In New Zealand, one minor party, Social Credit, gained around 25% of the votes cast in the late 1970s and early 1980s but won only two seats out of 92. One party, the New Zealand Party, won over 12% of the vote but failed to gain a single seat in 1984.

4. Artificially large majorities
The present system, partly through the concentrated support for the two larger parties, creates an abnormal number (around 70%) of 'safe' seats. These are seats that require a greater than 10% swing against the incumbent for the seat to be lost. This means the elections are decided in the remaining constituencies – the 'marginal' seats. A mere swing of 1% from one major party

to the other can result in a dozen marginal seats changing hands. The whole electoral system and the pattern of voting can be distorted. The majorities in both the 'safe' and 'marginal' seats may well not be a valid reflection of public opinion. Concentrated regional support for Labour and the Conservatives is creating a divided Britain in electoral terms. There have been occasions where Wales has had no Conservative MPs, and, similarly, the Scots. Prior to the 1997 election, the South and South East of England (outside London) was true blue Conservative. The Liberal Democrats and Labour both ate into these regions in 1997 and 2001, with the Conservatives fighting back again in 2010. There is also traditionally an urban-rural divide – which appears to have been reinforced after the 2010 election. In effect, within a crude two-party system, the Conservatives are the party of rural and possibly suburban England, while Labour represents the inner cities. Surprisingly, the major opposition party (at least in England) is the Liberal Democrats. They fight the Conservatives in rural England, and Labour in the inner cities. This divergence of voting patterns cannot be healthy for British democracy reliant as it is upon a unitary state which claims to represent all of Britain.

5. Adversarial Politics – Perpetuation of the two-party system
The present system lauds stability but since it encourages adversarial politics with incoming governments committed to reversing their predecessors' politics, it can actually create instability and discontinuity. Labour fears about this were such in the 1997 election campaign they pledged to stick to the Conservative Government's spending plans for the following two years.

The public has become conditioned to pledging massive support for the two major parties (although this has dropped from 96.8% in 1951 to 65.1% in 2010) and been discouraged from voting for the smaller parties. Such discouragement tends to come not from a rejection of policies but because there is a perception it would be a wasted vote because the party stands no chance of winning. Hence, it could be argued votes are cast not for the party that people support but rather for one they dislike the least.

6. Discrimination against women and ethnic minorities
It cannot be proven Simple Plurality discriminates against females and ethnic minorities. Since the system has promoted the two-party dominance, there is a distinct tendency for these parties to play 'safe' and choose middle-aged, male, white candidates. This situation may be changing. In 1997, over 120 female MPs were elected. This was to do, in part, with the women-only shortlists the Labour Party introduced, although it was successfully challenged. There were nine MPs from ethnic minorities elected in 1997. After the 2001 election, there were 118 female MPs and 12 representing ethnic minorities. By 2010 the numbers were 143 female MPs and 27 ethnic minority MPs. When examining

other countries, there are similar concerns. The choice of electoral system does not guarantee improved representation for women or ethnic minorities. Rather, the focus has to be upon the candidate selection processes adopted by the political parties. This may be where the problem of discrimination really lies.

The Multi-Dimensional Approach to Electoral Systems

What is most noticeable when there is discussion on electoral reform is the focus on the electoral formula: if you like, how the votes are translated into seats. There is also talk as to whether Britain should adopt PR as if it is a single electoral system, when it is actually a label covering many different systems. There is very little debate about the other important features of elections, most noticeably the district magnitude, which is the number of MPs to be elected in a constituency, or the type of ballot, which is how many votes we have and how they can be cast.

What can be seen in Table 20.5 is an overview of how electoral systems could be evaluated and even adopted if there was demand for reform. The focus is upon the district magnitude and the type of ballot, with the formulae being less important, and the labels largely inconsequential. While many people simply focus on the strengths and weaknesses of various systems (or more accurately, the formulae), this approach tries to draw in other important factors. In effect, when using this table, you should focus upon either the number of MPs for each constituency, and/or the type of ballot. Having done this, you can then look to the formulae that could be used when adopting that specific district magnitude or type of ballot. After that, the classification is largely unimportant.

By using this approach, there is also the hope much of the heat can be taken out of the debate surrounding electoral reform. Many writers focus upon the strengths and weaknesses of proportional representation, which immediately eliminates a large number of electoral systems. The ignorance here is in equating electoral reform with adopting some form of PR. Those opposed to electoral reform highlight many deficiencies of forms of PR in an attempt to prevent debate moving on. Consequently supporters of electoral reform are presented as being in favour of PR, and thus in favour of weak coalition governments, with deals done in back rooms and the voters being unable to hold the government to account. Yet electoral reform could be as simple as changing the number of MPs to be elected in a constituency. Many local government elections in Britain see contests in multi-member wards.

The list of electoral formulae cited in Table 20.5 is not exhaustive. Rather than working through all of them, it is far easier and more appropriate for essay and exam preparation to work through the more important systems; although there is a brief overview of each system in the Appendix.

Table 20.5 The Multi-Dimensional Approach to Electoral Systems

Classification	District Magnitude	Type of Ballot	Formula
Plurality	Single member Multi-member	Single vote Multiple vote (votes = seats)	• Simple Plurality • Block Vote
Majoritarian	Single member	Single vote Rank preferences Multiple vote (votes = candidates) Multiple vote (votes < candidates)	• Second Ballot • Condorcet • Borda • Alternative Vote • Supplementary Vote • Approval Voting • Exhaustive Voting
Semi-proportional	Multi-member	Single vote Rank preferences Multiple vote (votes < seats)	• Single Non-Transferable Vote • Cumulative Vote • Limited Vote
Proportional	Multi-member	Rank preferences List (national or regional) • Closed (single vote) • Open (single vote) • Flexible (rank preferences) • Panachage (rank preferences)	• Single Transferable Vote • d'Hondt • Imperiali • Saint Laguë • Niemeyer • Hagenbach-Bischoff • Hare
Hybrid	Single member (with unelected top up) Single and multi-member (with elected top up)	Single vote Rank Preferences Two votes • One constituency (single vote) • One list (single vote or rank preferences)	• Additional Member System • AV Plus • Mixed Member-Proportional

Alternative Electoral Systems

This chapter has already examined one electoral system – Simple Plurality. Here we are going to examine other systems that could be – and in all but one case are – used in Britain. They are:

1. *Alternative Vote (AV)*
2. *Single Transferable Vote (STV)*
3. *Party Lists*
4. *Mixed Member-Proportional (MMP)*
5. *Block Vote*
6. *Supplementary Vote*

The proportionality, or lack thereof, in any of these systems is immaterial. The reality is district magnitude has a far greater impact upon the proportionality of election results than the formula. This section is simply going to present some material on each of these systems, highlighting some of the strengths and weaknesses.

1. Alternative Vote (AV)

This electoral system is used in Australia, and was proposed for a referendum in 2011 to replace Simple Plurality in UK Parliamentary elections. It is broadly similar to Simple Plurality in that single member constituencies are used. The first difference is voters should rank the candidates in order of preference (although if a voter wishes to put a mark against just one candidate, that vote will still be counted).

To gain election, the leading candidate needs an absolute majority of votes i.e. over 50%. Should no candidate receive over 50% of the votes, the last placed candidate is eliminated, and the votes for that candidate are redistributed to the next-placed candidate on each ballot paper. This process continues until a candidate wins over 50% of the votes cast. It is demonstrated in Table 20.6.

An interesting point to note is the candidate who won the most first preference votes in Table 20.6 failed to win the election outright. Ferguson won 43% of the first preference votes. It was only after the final round of exclusions that Campbell passed Ferguson. This shows the importance of each redistribution of votes and, from the voter's perspective, the importance of ranking preferences.

A derivative of AV was proposed by the Jenkins Report in 1999, known as **AV Plus** or **AV Top UP**. Between 80% and 85% of MPs would be elected using AV. The remainder would be a regionally-based top up. There would be 80 regions around the UK, with each region having one or two top up MPs. This would be used to ensure some degree of proportionality. The number of votes for each party in each region would be counted up and divided by the number of constituencies won by that party in that region, plus one.

votes cast for a party in a region

----

seats won by the party in that region + 1

The party with the highest number after this mathematical equation gains the first top up seat. If need be, the mathematics is then recalculated for that party, and the process repeated for the allocation of the other top up seat in that region. Rather than having a separate list for these 'top up' MPs, the Jenkins Report recommended these seats be given to the best placed losing candidates.

After a fanfare of publicity with the publication of the report, very little happened. The report was effectively kicked into the long grass. Most electoral experts were scathing of the Jenkins Report, as it was not considered to be a proportional electoral system, and it allowed defeated candidates to gain election to Parliament without any obvious signs of accountability to the public.

Table 20.6 Australian House of Representatives, constituency of Bass, Tasmania (2007)
Votes cast 63 835. To gain election, a candidate needs 31 918 votes

Count	Wiener (Indep't)	Watts (Citizens Electoral Council)	Campbell (Labor)	Millen (Green)	De Haan (Family First)	Bennett (Liberty and Democracy)	Ferguson (Liberal)
1st	1 123	219	23 764	9 745	930	285	27 769
2nd	95	Excluded	45	32	23	9	15
total	1 218		23 809	9 777	953	294	27 784
3rd	41		60	44	76	Excluded	73
total	1 259		23 869	9 821	1 029		27 857
4th	185		241	168	Excluded		435
total	1 444		24 110	9 989			28 292
5th	Excluded		669	497			278
total			24 779	10 486			28 570
6th			7 774	Excluded			2 712
total			32 553				31 282
			Elected				

2. Single Transferable Vote (STV)
This system uses multi-member constituencies, with voters ranking their preferences. Each party can put forward as many or as few candidates as they wish. The Liberal Democrats advocate this system. It is used in Scottish local elections, and in Northern Ireland for local, European Parliamentary and Northern Ireland Assembly elections.

For voters, this is a straightforward electoral system. As with AV, candidates have to be ranked in order of preference. It is more complicated for the returning officers who have to translate the votes into representation. This is done by a mathematical formula called the **Droop Quota**.

$$\frac{\text{Total Number of Votes Cast in a Constituency}}{\text{Number of Seats in the Constituency} + 1} + 1$$

Thus in a 4 seat constituency which sees 125 000 votes cast, the Droop Quota would be:

$$\frac{125\ 000 \text{ votes cast}}{4 \text{ seats} + 1} + 1 = 25\ 001$$

Candidates who achieve this quota are automatically elected; any votes cast in excess of this quota are redistributed to the other candidates in order of preference. At the same time the candidate with the lowest number of votes is eliminated, and these votes are redistributed according to their next preference (similar to AV). The process is continued until all the seats in the constituency are filled. An example of how the process works is demonstrated in Table 20.7, which includes both redistributions and eliminations.

Table 20.7 East Neuk and Landward ward, Fife Council election 2007
Votes cast 5 455, Seats 3, Droop Quota 1 364

Candidate (Party)	First Preference Votes	Reallocation (Riches surplus)	Reallocation (Scott-Hayward surplus)	Reallocation (Russell votes)	Reallocation (Wight votes)
D. MacGregor (Liberal Democrat)	816	1 041.30825 (+225.30825)	1 087.65015 (+46.34190)	1 247.82269 (+160.17254)	1 794.08222 (+546.25953)
E. Riches (Liberal Democrat)	1 696 (Elected)	1 364 (-332)	1 364	1 364	1 364
R. Russell (Labour)	387	407.16225 (+20.16225)	414.935173 (+7.77348)	0 (-414.935173)	0
M. Scott-Hayward (Conservative)	1 515	1 515 (Elected)	1 364 (-151)	1 364	1 364
M. Wight (Scottish Nationalist)	1 041 -	1 069.18800 (+28.18800)	1 086.62850 (+17.44050)	1 149.04894 (+62.42044)	0 (-1 149.04894)
Non-transferable		58.34150 (+58.34150)	137.78562 (+79.44412)	330.12837 (+192.34275)	932.91788 (+602.78941)

Riches (Liberal Democrat), Scott-Hayward (Conservative) and MacGregor (Liberal Democrat) gained election.

It is interesting to note the vote splitting of the Liberal Democrat voters in the example in Table 20.7. Quite a number of voters who cast their first preference for Riches did not cast their second choice for the other Liberal Democrat candidate (MacGregor). Added to this is the failure of the SNP candidate (Wight) to gain election despite having over 200 more first preference votes than the eventual third placed candidate.

The forecast is, if STV were adopted, voters would be more likely to select candidates from the broad spectrum of parties. The obvious consequence is smaller parties would have a better chance of getting their candidates elected. This may lead to a better representation of parties across the country.

Also, as surplus votes are redistributed there would be fewer wasted votes. Patterns of negative voting, where voters choose the candidate most likely to defeat their most disliked candidate rather than their favourite, would be largely eliminated from first preference (or even higher preference) voting.

There are, however, a number of objections to STV. It is considered more complicated than the present system, ranking preferences rather than making a single categoric choice, and the implementation of the Droop Quota to work out who has been elected (although this does not involve voters directly). There is also no guarantee voting behaviour would fall into the pattern forecast. The method is based very heavily on the assumption voters will record all of their preferences – and the number of non-transferable votes in Table 20.7 is quite marked.

The system allows voters to choose a single candidate if they so wish, or to select only a few preferences. Tactical voting is prevalent under any electoral system. Yet why should redistributed votes with second, third or even ninth or tenth preferences have the same value as first preference votes? Added to this, the links between an MP and his/her constituency might be damaged with new huge constituencies and voters having a choice as to which MP they might wish to approach.

3. Party Lists
The label 'Party List' covers a multitude of areas. Firstly, lists can be national (as in Israel) or regional (as used in mainland Britain in the elections to the European Parliament since 1999). Secondly, lists can be closed (where you vote for a party, with no choice of individual candidate), open (where you can vote for a party list or a specific individual on one list), flexible (where you can rearrange the names on one list), or panachage (where, in effect, you can vote for as many individuals on any party list up to the number of candidates to be elected in that constituency, including voting for your favourite candidate twice). Thirdly, there is the formula to translate the votes into representation. There are a number of different formulae, including: d'Hondt, Hagenbach-Bischoff, Imperiali, Hare-Niemeyer and Saint-Laguë.

Added to this is the complication of thresholds. This is where a minimum percentage of votes is required before a party can gain representation. In theory, this was introduced to prevent radical or extremist parties gaining representation, and to prevent a splintering of the party system with too many parties gaining representation with the subsequent inability to form a cohesive coalition government.

Tables 20.8a and 20.8b show how the votes can be translated into seats on a regional basis (using the d'Hondt divisor system). It highlights very clearly that the system, at a constituency level, may not be truly proportional. The greater the district magnitude (the number of representatives being elected in a given constituency) the more proportional the result.

The strengths of this system are you get a Parliament more reflective of society in its makeup. There tends to be better representation of women and ethnic minorities, and smaller parties also tend to gain representation. This is, however, often more dependent upon larger multi-member constituencies. As can be seen in Table 20.8b, the Greens would need the constituency to elect 11 candidates before they would win their first one.

There are, however, far more critics of this type of electoral system. The likelihood of coalition government is probably at the top of the list, although many supporters of electoral reform would argue coalition government might be a benefit rather than a problem. There could also be the tyranny of the minority, with small or extremist parties holding the balance of power or holding Parliament to ransom. Critics will cite Italy as an example of this instability which may be a consequence of adopting a party list electoral system.

4. Mixed Member-Proportional (MMP)

There are many versions of this system in use around the world. Germany, New Zealand, Japan, Scotland and Wales all use forms of MMP. Sometimes, this system is known as the Additional Member System (AMS). Under MMP, voters cast two ballots. The first is for a constituency representative. This is done using Simple Plurality. The second ballot is for a party list – this could be a regional list (as used in Scotland, Wales and Germany), or a national list (as used in New Zealand). There are other constraints on the lists, as noted earlier in this chapter.

An obvious strength of the MMP system is the split vote. Voters elect a constituency representative with their first vote. The second vote can be described as choosing the party the voter would most like to see form the government. This is often enhanced if parties make clear as to with whom they would be likely to form a coalition government. According to Sartori (1994, p. 19), "the second vote is the crucial one." It influences the overall result far more than the constituency vote.

Table 20.8a European Parliament Election result (UK) East Midlands constituency, 2009
Five MEPs to be elected

Party	Number of votes	Percentage of votes	Number of seats
Conservative	370 275	30.2	2
Labour	206 945	16.9	1
UK Independence	201 984	16.4	1
Liberal Democrat	151 428	12.3	1
British National	106 319	8.7	0
Green	83 939	6.8	0
English Democrats	28 498	2.3	0
UK First	20 561	1.7	0
Christian	17 907	1.5	0
Socialist Labour	13 590	1.1	0
No 2 EU	11 375	0.9	0
Libertas	7 882	0.6	0
Jury Team	7 362	0.6	0

Table 20.8b European Parliament Election result (UK) East Midlands constituency, 2009
Five MEPs to be elected

Party	Conservative	Labour	UKIP	Lib Dem	BNP	Green
Votes (%)	370 275 (30.2)	206 945 (16.9)	201 984 (16.4)	151 428 (12.3)	106 319 (8.7)	83 939 (6.8)
/1	**370 275**	**206 945**	**201 984**	**151 428**	106 319	83 939
/2	**185 137.5**	103 472.5	100 992	75 714	53 159.5	41 969.5
/3	123 425	68 981.667	67 328	50 476	35 439.667	27 979.667
/4	92 568.75	51 736.25	50 496	37 857	26 579.75	20 984.75
/5	74 055	41 389	40 396.8	30 285.6	21 263.8	16 787.8

Two Conservatives, and one Labour, UKIP and Liberal Democrat candidates were elected.

There are serious criticisms of this system. As with the list systems, it is possible for a small party to be able to hold the balance of power. Such a party could play a disproportionate role in deciding government policy. This was best demonstrated in New Zealand after their first elections under MMP in 1996 where the New Zealand First Party, who were the third largest party after the election, and who could form a government with either of the two largest parties, held separate coalition negotiations with the two larger parties at the same time. After the coalition formation, the New Zealand First Party wielded power far above its electoral support both in the cabinet and in Parliament.

Alternatively, if a coalition cannot be formed, a minority government is likely to be established. This happened in Scotland in 2007, as can be seen in Table 20.9.

Table 20.9 Scottish Parliamentary election 2007

Party	Constituency Seats	List Seats	Percentage List Vote	Total Seats
Conservative	4	13	13.9	17
Green	0	2	4.0	2
Labour	37	9	29.2	46
Liberal Democrat	11	5	11.3	16
Scottish Nationalist	21	26	31.0	47
Other	0	1	10.6	1

There is also no getting away from the fact two classes of MPs exist: constituency MPs and List MPs. Many of the latter may even be failed candidates in the constituencies.

The importance of the list seats over the constituency seats is most obvious in Table 20.9. Labour won over half of the constituency seats, but came second in the total votes cast. Both the SNP and the Conservatives won more list seats than Labour.

5. Block Vote

This system is used in many local government elections in England and Wales. There are multi-member constituencies (or more accurately, wards) with voters able to cast as many votes as there are seats available in the ward. In a 2-member ward, voters can cast up to two votes; in a 3-member ward, up to three votes. Voters do not have to use all of their votes, it is entirely up to them how many, or how few, will be cast. After the count, the candidate with the most votes is elected, as is the candidate with the second largest total of votes, and in a 3-member ward the third placed candidate would also be elected. In effect this system is a multi-member constituency version of Simple Plurality.

One of the advantages of this system is it gives greater voter choice. As with many electoral systems using multi-member constituencies, there is intra-party competition as well as competition between the parties. If they so wish, voters can split their votes for candidates of different parties. An example of this is listed in Table 20.10 with a two seat ward.

Table 20.10 Aylestone ward, Leicester City Council election, 2011
Two candidates to be elected

Candidate	Party	Vote
Nigel Porter	Liberal Democrat	1 141
Adam Clarke	Labour	1 124
Anthony Lee	Liberal Democrat	920
Jon Humberstone	Conservative	838
Peter Bedford	Conservative	750
Mohammed Thalukdar	Labour	613
Alison Bannatyne	UKIP	253
Thomas O'Connell	Green	191
Alan Stocker	Green	188
Margaret Green	UKIP	174

One Liberal Democrats and one Labour candidate were elected. Votes were clearly split in this particular ward between the major parties.

A drawback to this system is it may actually reinforce support for parties rather than candidates. This is what is normally expected – hence the name 'Block' Vote. Voters may decide to back all of the candidates from their favourite party rather than examining the specific qualities of individual candidates. Table 20.11 highlights such a possibility, although it is important to note we are looking solely as to the results and not why people voted as they did. The table shows the consistency of party voting in a three seat ward. A possible knock on effect is to increase a party's representation on a council.

6. Supplementary Vote
The Supplementary Vote is used for the elections for London Mayor and other elected mayors in England. It is very similar to the Alternative Vote – the one exception being voters may express only two preferences. To gain election on first preferences – as with AV – a candidate needs to win over 50% of the votes. If this does not happen, all candidates except for the top two are eliminated and their votes are redistributed according to their second choice. Any second preferences for eliminated candidates are ignored. Table 20.12 provides an example. The numbers in italics show the total number of second preferences for each candidate. This includes, for example those voters who placed Boris Johnson first and Ken Livingston second, or vice versa. It also shows how many second preference votes were wasted on lower placed candidates. Over 20% of voters did not cast a second preference. Many voters also voted for the same candidate with each ballot.

Table 20.11 Humberstone and Hamilton ward, Leicester City Council election, 2011
Three councillors to be elected

Candidate	Party	Votes
Barbara Potter	Labour	2 306
Rita Patel	Labour	2 263
Gurinder Singh Sandhu	Labour	2 231
John Mugglestone	Conservative	1 718
Jas Sethi	Conservative	1 460
Stephen Thompson	Conservative	1 460
David Haslett	English Democrats	442
Gita Patel	Independent	274

Three Labour councillors were elected in this ward.

Table 20.12 London Mayoral election, 2012

Candidate	Party	First Preference Votes (%)	Second Preference Votes (%)	Final Total
Boris Johnson	Conservative	971 931 (44.0)	82 880 *253 709 (14.4)*	1 054 811
Ken Livingston	Labour	889 918 (40.3)	102 355 *335 398 (19.0)*	992 273
Jenny Jones	Green	98 913 (4.5)	*363 193 (20.6)*	
Brian Paddick	Liberal Democrat	91 774 (4.2)	*363 692 (20.6)*	
Siobhan Benita	Independent	83 914 (3.8)	*212 412 (12.0)*	
Lawrence Webb	UK Independence	43 274 (2.0)	*161 252 (9.1)*	
Carlos Cortiglia	British National	28 751 (1.3)	*73 353 (4.2)*	
Boris Johnson is elected as mayor.				

Conclusion

The issue of the electoral system which was previously considered rather an academic one has moved on. There is much greater public interest, although with the qualification this is dependent upon media involvement. There is still a great deal of uncertainty in many quarters, with people confusing electoral reform with adopting some form of proportional representation. Added to this is the single-minded focus upon the type of electoral system to be adopted, while ignoring issues such as district magnitude and the type of ballot. This is best exemplified with the referendum on electoral reform held in 2011. No consultation was carried through. The Alternative Vote was proposed, and Prime Minister David Cameron announced he would campaign against reforming the electoral system.

What is interesting is the multiplicity of electoral system in use in the UK – as of 2013, there were five different systems in use. There may be some concern over the complexity of the different systems (as argued by Kelly, 2008), yet they are all very easily explained. For voters, it could be a single choice, multiple choices or ranking preferences. With regard to counting the votes and translating them into seats, the various systems can be explained very easily. Electoral reform is not as scary as many critics would like people to believe.

Selected bibliography

Blau, Adrian. (2004). "Fairness and Electoral Reform", *British Journal of Politics and International Relations* vol. 6-2, pp. 165-181.

Bowler, Shaun & Farrell, David. (2006). "We Know Which One We Prefer but We Don't Really Know Why: The Curious Case of Mixed Member Electoral Systems", *British Journal of Politics and International Relations* vol. 8-3, pp. 445-460.

Dunleavy, Patrick & Margetts, Helen. (2005). "The Impact of UK Electoral Systems", *Parliamentary Affairs* vol. 58-4, pp. 854-870.

Farrell, David. (2011). *Electoral Systems: A Comparative Introduction*: Palgrave, 2nd edition.

Kelly, Richard. (2008). "It's Only Made Things Worse: A Critique of Electoral Reform in Britain", *Political Quarterly* vol. 79-2, pp. 260-268.

Lundberg, Thomas. (2007). "Electoral System Reviews in New Zealand, Britain and Canada: A Critical Comparison", *Government and Opposition* vol. 42-4, pp. 471-490.

Taylor, Andrew. (2007). "The Strategic Impact of the Electoral System and the Definition of 'Good' Governance", *British Politics* vol. 2-1, pp. 20-44.

Websites

libraries.ucsd.edu/locations/sshl/data-gov-info-gis/ssds/guides/lij/
This is the Arend Lijphart Elections Archive at the University of California, San Diego. It contains election results from all over the world up to 2003.

www.citizen.org.uk
Institute for Citizenship homepage, including ways of encouraging participation.

www.electionguide.org
This is the home page of the Consortium for Elections and Political Process Strengthening, which works with the International Foundation for Electoral Systems. From here it is possible to access information about past and future elections from around the world

www.gov.uk/voting-in-the-uk
This is a UK Government site on elections and voting

www.ifes.org
International Foundation for Electoral Systems home page

Questions
1. The virtues of Simple Plurality have been questioned in recent years. Why is this so?
2. Assess the likely benefits and penalties that would follow the adoption of some form of PR in Britain. Are the benefits and penalties similar under different proportional systems?
3. The Jenkins Commission was used to divert attention away from electoral reform in Britain. Why might this be the case?

CHAPTER 21 // VOTING BEHAVIOUR

Contents
- **Introduction**
- **The Current Interpretations**
- **Alternative classifications of class**
- **Alternative factors in explaining voting behaviour**
- **Issue-based Voting**
- **Conclusion**

This topic is often a major component of examination papers. Therefore students need to devote particular attention to a very complex subject. It is vital that up-to-date material is studied since there is a great deal of controversy on the voting habits and trends of the British electorate. This was especially so after profound general election results, which may have seen huge swings, such as in 1979 and 1997. The 2010 General Election is also significant in that the Conservatives failed to gain an outright victory.

Introduction

The analysis of electoral behaviour has been subject to fundamental changes in recent years so even a seminal work like Butler and Stokes' *Political Change in Britain* (1969, 1974) has either undergone a process of serious revision or has had some of its basic conclusions refuted altogether. With class being considered the most important factor in voting behaviour, the overriding question has become the extent to which it is still the main determinant of voting behaviour.

Up until the 1970s two successive models were used to explain voting behaviour. The Classical/Liberal model emphasised the citizens as responsible voters making rational choices based on the national good and giving governments a mandate to carry out policies. These voters would also be fully informed of the consequences of their actions. Arguably a key text here would be Anthony Downs *An Economic Theory of Democracy* (1957). This highly idealised concept gradually gave way to a social deterministic model where such characteristics as ethnicity and religion, but especially class, were stressed as true indicators of voting intentions. Socialisation – cultural background, family, and workplace – reinforced the self-interest of classes to the extent parties could chart or even predict where their support lay with a relatively high degree of accuracy. Any alteration from this settled pattern, regardless of how small, fascinated analysts. Hence there are numerous studies on working class Tories and middle class Labour supporters.

Butler and Stokes synthesised and advanced the disparate explanations from this social deterministic model. They took their cue from a study at Michigan

University entitled *The American Voter*. Long term factors, particularly parental attitudes within a class context were emphasised. Lesser factors such as gender, age, ethnicity, and religion helped to build up a model of voters influenced by a long process of political socialisation giving a remarkable degree of voting stability with elections decided by small turnovers between elections.

It was, however, always recognised specific issues like the performance of the economy, or law and order could have a direct influence on the outcome at the polls. Hence there was always a small element of volatility. The floating voter was waiting to be captured. A number of studies examined this aspect without removing the emphasis upon class-based politics. Peter Pulzer (1967, p. 98) famously summed up the position: "Class is the basis of British party politics; all else is embellishment and detail". After 1970, this perspective was to come under intense scrutiny.

The Current Interpretations

The model offered by Butler and Stokes emphasised party identification, long-term factors, stable voting, and a low priority for issue-based politics. All of these elements were conditioned by class-based voting. Yet from the mid-1970s this was to be seriously questioned.

The decline of class conditioning politics was seen as the catalyst to explain a whole new set of variables to explain voting behaviour in the 1970s and 1980s.

1. The Major Changes in Party Identification and Support

a) The breakdown in support for the two major parties
In 1951 the Conservatives and Labour captured almost 97% of the total votes cast. In 1970, it was a shade under 90%. This period, 1950-1970, has been described as the period of partisan alignment, with two great blocs of solid party support. Only once since then have the Conservatives and Labour collectively captured over 80% of the vote – in 1979 with 80.9%. Since 1970, the label of partisan dealignment has been used to describe the decrease in support for the two major parties. In 2010, the Conservatives and Labour won 65.1% of the votes cast. If this was to be broadened out to examine the share of the total potential electorate, the drop is even more telling. Almost 80% of the potential electorate voted either Conservative or Labour in 1951. It was down to 64% in 1970. Since then, it has only once been over 60% (in 1979 with 61.5%) and was at 43% in 2001. Part of the reason for the low polling in the 2001 election can be attributed to the low turnout – which dropped beneath 60% for the first time ever. Even when turnout rose above 60% in subsequent elections, the collective support for the two major parties decreased further in 2005, and increased only marginally in 2010 (but still remained below the 2001 figure). The full extent of the changes can be seen in Table 21.1.

Table 21.1 Electoral support for Conservative and Labour Parties (1950-2010)

Date of General Election	Con % of vote	Lab % of vote	Other parties % of vote	Con % of electorate	Lab % of electorate	Other parties % of electorate
1950	43.5	46.1	10.4	36.5	38.7	8.7
1951	48.0	48.8	3.2	39.6	40.3	2.6
1955	49.7	46.4	3.9	38.2	35.6	3.0
1959	49.4	43.8	6.8	38.9	34.5	5.4
1964	43.4	44.1	12.5	33.5	34.0	9.6
1966	41.9	47.9	10.2	31.8	36.3	7.7
1970	46.4	43.0	10.6	33.4	31.0	7.6
1974 (F)	37.8	37.1	25.1	29.5	29.0	19.6
1974 (O)	35.8	39.2	25.0	26.1	28.5	18.2
1979	43.9	37.0	19.1	33.4	28.1	14.5
1983	42.4	27.6	30.0	30.8	20.1	21.8
1987	42.3	30.8	26.9	31.9	23.2	20.3
1992	41.9	34.4	23.7	32.6	26.7	18.4
1997	30.7	43.2	26.1	21.9	30.8	18.9
2001	31.7	40.7	27.6	18.8	24.2	16.4
2005	32.3	35.3	32.4	19.7	21.6	19.8
2010	36.1	29.0	34.9	23.5	18.9	22.7

b) The increasing support for minor parties

An obvious corollary to a decline in support for the two major parties has been a clear increase in support for the minor parties. The Liberals and the nationalist parties in Scotland and Wales were the beneficiaries in the 1970s, the Alliance in the 1980s, and the Liberal Democrats and the nationalist parties again in the 1990s. In the 2010 General Election, the votes cast not for either of the two major parties reached an all-time high, with over a third of the votes cast **not** going to the Conservatives or Labour.

The increase in support for the minor parties can probably be explained by both positive and negative factors. There has been much disillusionment with both major parties in conjunction with clear policy platforms from the Liberal Democrats (and their predecessors the SDP/Liberal Alliance and the Liberals) and from the Scottish Nationalist Party and Plaid Cymru (the Welsh nationalists). The latter two were both supplemented by a growth of nationalist feelings. In some elections, and particularly in 1997, there was an increase in tactical voting. In many Southern English constituencies during the 1997 campaign, Labour and the Liberal Democrats gave tacit encouragement to their supporters to vote for the party most likely to defeat the Conservative incumbent.

Such tactical voting continued in the subsequent elections, although without necessarily seeing the same degree of success as in 1997. In Scotland and Wales, with the introduction of political devolution, there has been a suggestion the importance of the Westminster elections are now seen as less significant than the elections to the devolved bodies. Consequently, support for the nationalist parties at general elections has diminished.

2. The Volatility of Voters

The 1970s and 1980s revealed an increasing volatility in voters' intentions as shown not simply by the general elections but also in local government elections, European Parliamentary elections, and especially in by-elections where huge swings have occurred. This also applied to the 2010 General Election.

Volatility is where a voter does not cast his or her ballot for the same party in consecutive general elections – and this is before examining elections at local, regional or European levels. Thus, in one general election, a voter may vote Labour. In the subsequent general election, that voter may cast a ballot for the Green Party, and in the next general election for the Liberal Democrats.

It needs to be noted with a proliferation of parties, the range of choice for voters increases. At the same time, the simple left-right dichotomy decreases. Then, as Evans (2000, p. 407) notes, there is "a fuller representation of the voters' spectrum of choice at the ballot box".

The problem is there is no such thing as a 'typical' floating voter. Some generalisations can be made such as: a decline in partisanship and hence weak party loyalty; the incidence of first time voters; so-called 'rational' voters who make up their minds at the last minute having weighed up very carefully how to cast their ballot; and, protest votes where voters register their dissatisfaction with the mainstream parties by voting for a candidate who has little chance in winning. This use of protest votes has been very influential and is becoming an increasing fact of electoral life.

There was an expectation in the 2005 General Election of a large protest vote over the war in Iraq. The war "was expected to motivate turnout" (Dermody *et al*, 2010, p. 422). Such an improved turnout failed to materialise. The volatility may, therefore, be present through non-voting.

3. Class Dealignment

This is a term used to describe the weakening of the association between occupational class and the normal voting behaviour of this class. Class is still considered to be the single best predictor or indicator of voting intentions. In the 1950s and 1960s **class alignment** was clearly apparent. Approximately two thirds of the manual working class supported Labour, while around four fifths of the non-manual class supported the Conservatives. Since then, class dealignment has occurred. It is now suggested **class dealignment** is so strong class can no longer be regarded as the only serious indicator of voting intentions. There is, however, generally broad agreement among commentators that class is still a major component of voting behaviour.

The British Market Research Society divides class up into six different categories. This classification has been used since the early 20th century. There are other ways of defining class and some of these will be examined later in the chapter.

- A - Upper Middle
- B - Middle
- C1 - Lower Middle
- C2 - Skilled Manual
- D - Semi-skilled and Unskilled workers
- E - State dependents

Classes A, B and C1 are the middle class. Classes C2, D and E are the working class. Social class C was split into C1 and C2 in 1971. It is expected that AB, C1 will mostly voting Conservative and C2, DE Labour. Class dealignment questions the strength of this association.

In 1983 for the first time fewer than half of the voters cast a ballot for their 'natural' class party. This confirmed a trend that appeared to be developing in the 1970s. Throughout the 1980s there was a remarkable growth of Conservative voting amongst manual workers. At the same time there was a decline in non-manual Conservative voting but not to the same degree as the fall in 'natural' Labour support.

The class dealignment explanation, however, focuses on the shrinking working class Labour vote rather than on the desertion of the non-manual class from the Conservatives. The main reason is this feature is regarded as more remarkable and helps to account for the decline in Labour fortunes throughout the 1980s. In 1997, however, there seemed to be a reversal of fortunes as traditional Labour voters returned to the fold. At the same time, many traditional Conservative voters transferred their allegiances to Labour or the Liberal Democrats. The 1997 election was perceived as being an exceptional one. Yet the results of the 2001 election appeared to reinforce them. The gap between Labour and Conservative middle class supporters (AB, C1) was diminished. With the middle classes now comprising almost half of the voting population, these were lost voters the Conservatives needed to win back to gain office. At the same time, it is interesting to note there has been a drift in working class support (C2, DE) towards the Conservatives. Labour still has around half of the working class support but as the party has modernised under Blair, the traditional support base appeared a little reluctant to follow. In the 2005 and 2010 General Elections, there appeared to be a move back to more traditional class-based voting, with middle class voters appearing to return to the Conservative fold – although nowhere near to the extent of elections prior to 1997. Details of class-based voting are presented in Tables 21.2 through to 21.6.

Table 21.2 Vote by social class 1992 General Election (%)

	ABC1	C2	DE
Labour	22	40	49
Conservative	54	39	31
Liberal Democrat	21	17	16

Table 21.3 Vote by social class 1997 General Election (%)

	ABC1	C2	DE
Labour	34	50	59
Conservative	39	27	21
Liberal Democrat	20	16	13

Table 21.4 Vote by social class 2001 General Election (%)

	ABC1	C2	DE
Labour	34	49	55
Conservative	38	29	24
Liberal Democrat	22	15	13

Table 21.5 Vote by social class 2005 General Election (%)

	ABC1	C2	DE
Labour	30	40	48
Conservative	37	33	25
Liberal Democrat	26	19	18

Table 21.6 Vote by social class 2010 General Election (%)

	ABC1	C2	DE
Labour	27	29	40
Conservative	39	37	31
Liberal Democrat	26	22	17

What emerged in the 1980s and persisted into the early 1990s was the fragmentation of the working class and the development of what was labelled the 'new' working class. Many of these people would normally have been considered to be C2s, and they became the target voters for the major parties. The idea of a 'new' working class could be attributed to the growing prosperity that appeared in Britain, with people being given the opportunity to buy their own council houses, or take regular overseas holidays. This prosperity saw peoples' self-perception of class change. In conjunction with the decline of manufacturing across the UK, this brought into question the classification of class.

Alternative classifications of class
There has been much debate over the extent to which the traditional class labels are still appropriate. The concept of class is an essentially contested concept (Evans, 2000). The middle class (AB, C1) and the working class (C2, DE) as defined by the British Market Research Society (BMRS) have been considered inaccurate and out of date. Alternative classifications have been presented but none have succeeded in replacing that of the BMRS.

1. Heath, Jowell and Curtice thesis
The book *How Britain Votes* by Heath, Jowell and Curtice (1985) offered what appeared to be a clear alternative to the BMRS. Not only did they question the

categorisation of the classes but also much of the 'baggage' that came with it, including the idea of a decline in class-based voting. Heath, Jowell and Curtice argued class dealignment ignored fundamental changes in the relative size of social classes. Britain had become a predominantly white-collar (middle class) society and therefore the fall in Labour support in the 1980s could be attributed to a shrinkage in the size of the working class.

On top of this, Heath, Jowell and Curtice raised the question as to whether Labour's decline in working class support in the 1980s was a consequence of long term decay in the basic class structure. They argued not, pointing to a number of short term factors that swung many working class voters behind the Conservatives. These included issues of race, gender, housing, levels of education, and the private/public sector divide.

Instead of the conventional analysis or classification, Heath, Jowell and Curtice offered a more formally class-based set of categories. Each adult would be classified according to his or her own employment. The main categories were:

- *Salariat* – (managers, supervisors, professionals)
- *Routine non-manual* – (clerks, sales workers, secretaries)
- *Petit bourgeoisie* – (farmers, small proprietors, self-employed manual workers)
- *Foreman, technicians* – (blue collar supervisory class)
- *Working class* – (manual workers in industry and agriculture. Regardless of skill levels, what distinguishes this 'class' status is they are subject to detailed supervision)

Generally, the Heath, Jowell and Curtice analysis attempted to demonstrate there had been no significant class dealignment since the 1960s. Class seemed to matter less as a result of conventional polling techniques along with the inaccurate correlation between a decreasing Labour vote and a decrease in working class support for Labour.

The line of argument adopted by Heath, Jowell and Curtice was not greatly favoured by academic opinion. There were suggestions, despite these arguments, of a clear decline in working class support for Labour. The appearance of the 'new' working class arguably highlighted an unmistakable fragmentation of the class structure in Britain.

2. Economic and Social Research Council classification

In December 1997 the Economic and Social Research Council (ESRC) presented an alternative classification of class. As with other classifications, this was also based upon occupation. *The Guardian* (15 December 1997) summarised the classifications as follows:

1. Doctors, lawyers, scientists, and employers, administrators and managers in "large" organisations, i.e., those with 25 or more staff;
2. Nurses, legal executives, laboratory technicians, other "associate professionals", employers, administrators and managers in smaller organisations, supervisors of intermediate staff;
3. Secretaries, sales reps, nursery nurses, computer operators and other intermediate occupations in administrative, clerical, sales and service work;
4. Driving instructors, builders, carpenters and other self-employed non-professionals;
5. Telephone fitters, plumbers and other supervisors and crafts and related works;
6. Lorry drivers, assembly line workers, traffic wardens and workers in routine occupations in manufacturing and services;
7. "All types of labourers, waiters and waitresses and cleaners" and other workers in elementary occupations in manufacturing and services;
8. The underclass of those who have never worked and the long-term unemployed or sick.

The final class is a major step forward. It acknowledges the existence of an underclass. All other classifications have ignored the long term sick and unemployed. Whether this classification can actually be used to help explain voting behaviour will remain to be seen.

It is obvious class still appears to be an important factor in explaining voting behaviour. Unlike in the period of alignment, where class was considered the sole explanation of voting behaviour, class has clearly decreased in importance. Many other factors can be used to explain voting behaviour, and some of these are detailed below. As the Centre for Research into Elections and Social Trends (CREST) has pointed out, class still persists as a key influence in voting behaviour.

Alternative factors in explaining voting behaviour

Class is an important factor in voting behaviour. There are, however, other factors that can explain some features of voting behaviour. These have been described as "[n]ew post-industrial social cleavages" (Evans, 2000, p. 405). Arguably, some of these may be linked to class. As a consequence, they may provide a fuller explanation of how people vote. Issue-based voting, and other related matters, will be examined later in the chapter.

1. *age*
2. *gender*
3. *race/ethnicity*
4. *region/locale*
5. *housing*

Before examining these alternative factors in voting, there are two very important points that need to be noted. Firstly, some of these variables may be linked to class, for example, housing. Such variables need acknowledgement, but their relationship with class is also of importance. Secondly, each of these variables cannot be used in isolation. While they are examined individually, they may actually work in tandem. For example, the combination of age and gender may influence voting.

1. Age

There are two theories with regard to age and voting behaviour. There is the **life cycle** theory and the theory of **political generations**. The life cycle theory suggests that as people get older, they get more 'conservative' in their outlook. By this it is suggested older people look more for security and stability in their lives. The need to pay off mortgages, pay for children to attend university, retirement and pensions are of far greater importance than trying to change the world. Radical politics tends to be associated with the Labour Party. Yet all of this may be confused with the class variable.

The political generations theory looks to defining events in each generation that will mould how they behave. Key events are of great importance e.g. the formation of the Labour Party in 1906, the first majority Labour Government in 1945, Margaret Thatcher's period in office (1979-90), and the Blair-Brown Governments (1997-2010). The first time voters in 2010 would only have knowledge of a Labour Government. There would be no memory of the monumental expectations of the 1997 landslide. They are the Blair Generation – a consequence, possibly, of those voters known as 'Thatcher's children'. It will be interesting to see how their priorities, as voters, lie at the subsequent general elections.

There has, however, been grave concern over young people not voting. There appears to be a huge degree of disengagement of young voters. Dermody *et al* (2010) found almost two thirds of 18-24 year olds did not vote in the 2001 and 2005 General Elections. This does not mean these young people are not participating in politics – they are simply not voting. What is unclear is whether such disengagement will continue into later life, as well as the extent to which such disengagement is passed on to subsequent generations.

2. Gender

Pulzer suggested, in 1967, women are more inclined to vote Conservative than men. The gist of the argument was men, and in particular those in the working class, went out to work, and possibly experienced industrial conflict, whilst women stayed at home and looked after the family. The party which considers itself to best represent family values is the Conservative Party. Such a statement masks a number of other issues linked quite possibly to class, age, and even religion. Since the 1990s, there has been no clear link between gender and voting behaviour.

3. Race/ethnicity

The impact of race or ethnicity on voting behaviour is becoming more powerful. The fact remains, however, about 5% of the total voting population is black or Asian, and the total influence on the outcome of an election is relatively weak. This is not the case in particular constituencies such as Bradford West, Leicester East, or Southall, where the ethnic vote carries considerable weight. Studies on ethnic minority voting patterns confirm the Labour Party tends to benefit from the ethnic vote. There is an important footnote to add here. It may well be the ethnic vote can no longer be classified as a collective group. There was evidence in elections since the early 1990s of sizeable numbers of Asian voters moving towards the Conservative Party. Again, class as an intervening variable is important here, as sections of the Asian population are clearly becoming more affluent and are often in non-manual employment.

4. Region/locale

This label covers a number of geographical cleavages that are becoming much more prominent in the 21st century. There is the urban/rural divide. This states urban, or more specifically inner city voters are more likely to vote Labour, while rural voters and those living in the suburbs are more likely to vote Conservative. There are obviously close links with class in such an explanation. In both the 1997 and 2001 General Elections, the Conservatives failed to win a single inner city constituency.

Another geographical 'cleavage' is the North/South divide. The North traditionally votes Labour, the South votes Conservative. This is best exemplified in the 1983 and 1987 election results, with the South of England, outside Greater London, being a swathe of blue. After the 1997 general election, there were no Conservative MPs in Scotland or Wales. Only one Conservative MP was returned in Scotland in 2001, and that number has remained the same in the subsequent two elections. The south west of England was controlled largely by the Liberal Democrats. If anything, with the heavy defeat of the Conservatives in 1997, they were left with a rump based for the main part in the south of England. The Liberal Democrats had the audacity to claim to be the official national opposition party to the Blair Government as they had MPs throughout mainland Britain. Such a claim could also be made in 2001, despite the single Conservative success in Scotland.

The regional vote has special emphasis in Scotland, Wales and Northern Ireland. In Scotland and Wales there are the nationalist parties (Scottish Nationalist Party and Plaid Cymru). Each wins a sizeable proportion of the vote in their region. In Scotland, the SNP have formed a majority government in the Scottish Parliament in 2011, while in Wales Plaid Cymru were in a coalition administration in the Welsh Assembly with Labour from 2007 to 2011. In Northern Ireland, there are significantly different cleavages, most notably religion and nationalism. So complex is the Northern Ireland situation it has been very rare in recent times for mainland parties to actually contest any of these constituencies.

5. Housing

During the period of alignment, it was generally felt housing tenure was closely linked to class. Housing tenure, in particular since the 1980s, appears to be an important factor in voting. Owner occupiers are far more likely to vote Conservative while council tenants are more likely to vote Labour, and this is regardless of their class. With this sort of information, the Conservative Government's zeal in selling off council housing in the 1980s is even easier to explain.

On housing it might even be said the rapid growth of private sector housing, and especially the sale of council houses, has made this factor a better forecaster of voting intentions than occupational class. Private housing ownership encapsulates the themes of economic self-interest, party policies and community pressures. Thus the sale of council houses was a winning policy for the Conservatives in the 1980s. Labour now subscribes to this policy; the clear partisan divide is diminishing. Those dependent upon state provision of housing may still be more likely to vote Labour. Home-owners or mortgage holders may not be quite so likely to vote Conservative.

Issue-based Voting

Before examining the idea of issue-based voting, there are some important factors that need to be explained. There are some issues about which everyone is in agreement. Nobody is likely to campaign for an increase in crime, or for economic collapse. These are known as **valence** issues, where there is broad agreement about the issue, but disagreement over which party may be best in delivering their promises on such issues. This should be contrasted with **position** issues. These are the issues where people take a position e.g. pro- or anti-fox hunting; pro- or anti-university tuition fees. Thus, when considering issue-based voting, such a classification – valence and position issues – needs to be noted.

1. Issues

During a period of dealignment, issue-based voting may come to the fore. Voters change their opinions on what are regarded as the important issues. In the past, such issues as nationalisation, trade union immunities and the extension of the welfare state appeared attractive to the electorate. These issues were clearly associated with the Labour Party. In the 1980s, the issues that were more prominent included cutting taxes, privatisation, and defence. Quite clearly these issues were associated with the Conservatives. All of these are position issues.

One issue that does not fit comfortably in either party is Europe. Since the mid-1980s, all major parties have claimed to be pro-European, in that the UK should remain a member of the EU. This would, therefore, appear to be a valence issue. Yet all of the parties are divided internally on this issue. There are members of all major political parties who would like the UK to leave the EU.

There are also other issues which do not sit comfortably with either of the major parties, yet there have been attempts to include aspects of them within manifestos. The most obvious example is the environment. Again, this appears to be a valence issue – which party would campaign on polluting the environment? Concerns over conservation, the use of fossil fuels, the safety of nuclear energy, as well as general environmental concerns at local, national or even global levels have forced this issue on to the political agenda. This 'Green' lobby has forced both major parties into changing some of their attitudes. What must be questioned is the level of commitment to the issue of the environment. Are the Conservatives and Labour actually trying to do something to improve the environment or are they simply trying not to lose votes to the Green Party or other more environmentally-sound parties?

A final point on issue-based voting is when an issue dominates an election. In February 1974 it was 'Who governs?'. Some people argue the issue which dominated the 1997 election was 'kicking out the Tories', while in 2010 it was getting rid of Brown. Yet the reality is it tends to be an exceptional election where a single issue dominates. Bland general comments on the state of the economy cover a multitude of issues such as employment, inflation, balance of trade, economic growth, taxation and so forth. Bill Clinton reminded himself: "It's the economy, stupid". Yet the economy, like so many other issues, is a valence issue. It therefore may get reduced to **perceptions** as to who can run the economy best. Perhaps that is why the Conservatives won in 1992, but why Labour won in 1997. The 2010 results suggests the Conservatives failed to demonstrate their economic aptitude.

2. Party leader

As elections in Britain have become more presidentialist in style, there has been more and more focus on the role of the party leader. There has been greater focus on the party leaders – especially the likes of Thatcher and Blair. In 2010, there were the first ever leaders debates – three debates between the three major party leaders during the election campaign. Opinion may be divided as to the importance of party leaders, but these debates almost placed the leaders ahead of any of the issues they were debating. Former-Labour Party leader, Neil Kinnock was unconvinced Gordon Brown would benefit from the debates. On The Andrew Marr Show, Kinnock said Brown had "a radio face".

The party leader is a valence issue. Every voter wants the country to have the best possible prime minister. Thus there is an evaluation of the party leaders. This could be over their competence in handling current issues (in the case of the incumbent), or their potential performance in handling future problems, as well as the ability to deliver on their electoral promises. As Clarke (2009, p. 638) notes:

> [t]he strength of leader effects on electoral choice in Britain should not surprise. Leaders are, and long have been, pre-eminent players on the political stage, and their activities and utterances regularly receive enormous media attention. In a very real sense, the party leaders are the human face of their parties, and they are the focal points of their parties' national campaigns in general elections.

3. Campaign

The election campaign itself can be of great importance, particularly if there is dealignment. Part of the campaign focuses upon the party leaders, and their role was explained above, and summarised succinctly by Clarke (2009). Specific issues can also be highlighted during a campaign in the hope of swinging the undecided voters behind the party.

There may be specific turning points in a campaign. These could be gaffes, such as Gordon Brown's "bigot-gate" in 2010, or particular events or issues, such as Tony Blair being harangued by an angry voter outside a hospital in Birmingham in the 2001 election over a lack of beds in the hospital.

Quite clearly a part of the election campaign, but also extending far beyond, is the role of the media – press coverage and television presentation. It is still a matter of contention as to how much the attitudes and presentation of newspapers and journals really influence voters' intentions. In 1992, *The Sun* famously claimed "It was the Sun wot won it". Such claims actually have little support. It is suggested people purchase newspapers which support their party preferences rather than being converted by them. This, of course, is a generalisation and in the past the Labour Party has complained the vast majority of newspapers support the Conservative Party. There was near silence from the Labour Party when *The Sun* announced it was backing Blair before the 1997 election. Prior to the 2010 General Election, *The Sun* reverted to supporting the Conservatives.

The impact of television is certainly more powerful but again there is disagreement as to the degree of influence on the final outcome of an election. The broadcast media are obligated to be impartial. Yet it is the televisual presentations by the parties, in their party political broadcasts and their election broadcasts, that may have some influence. Added to this, of course, was the party leaders debates in the 2010 campaign – all broadcast live!

For the political parties, the focus is very much upon the swinging voters and the undecided voters; these are the targets. In a close election, they *may* actually decide the outcome. Thus the parties will do whatever they can to persuade these voters to back them. The campaign is simply the last chance.

4. *Tactical voting*

A final aspect in trying to explain voting behaviour is tactical voting. During a period of alignment, this would be largely inconsequential. Yet in the 1980s and 1990s (and especially in 1997), tactical voting came to the fore. In this situation, voters do not cast their ballot for the candidate they would most like to win, but rather for the candidate who is most likely to beat the one they want to lose. In 1997, in a number of constituencies, Liberal Democrats voted Labour, and in others Labour voters cast their ballot for the Liberal Democratic candidate, leading in both cases to the defeat of Conservative candidates. Kettering was won by Labour, while Sutton and Cheam was won by the Liberal Democrats – both as a consequence of tactical voting. Both were retained in 2001. Yet it needs to be noted how isolated are such examples. Tactical voting – if it was ever so overtly encouraged – is often perceived as 'not the done thing'. The perception is voters should cast their ballot for whom they want to win, not for a candidate with the best chance of defeating the candidate they want to lose.

Conclusion

Voting behaviour is very straight forward. Those voters who cast their ballots do so in whatever way they like. It is the explanations as to **why** they voted the way they did that are complicated. No single factor alone can adequately explain voting behaviour. Class is clearly a significant factor, even in the early 21st century. Yet in a period of dealignment, its level of importance may decrease. Other explanators may not be any stronger. Rather we need to look to a range of factors, some of which may be inter-related, in our attempts to explain voting behaviour. Added to this are the valence and position issues that may have an impact upon voting behaviour.

Explanations have changed over time. Pulzer's perspective of class as the basis of British party politics no longer holds true - partly because we can no longer be sure as to who belongs to which class. Other factors have risen in importance. Each election will be different, as will the explanation of each result.

Selected bibliography

Butler, David & Stokes, Donald. (1974). *Political Change in Britain: The Evolution of Electoral Choice:* Macmillan, 2nd edition.

Clarke, Harold; Sanders, David; Stewart, Marianne & Whiteley, Paul. (2009). "The American voter's British cousin", *Electoral Studies* vol. 28-4, pp. 632-641.
Clough, Emily. (2007). "Strategic Voting Under Conditions of Uncertainty: A Re-Evaluation of Duverger's Law", *British Journal of Political Science* vol. 37-2, pp. 313-332.
Denver, David. (2007). *Elections and Voters in Britain*: Palgrave, 2nd edition.
Dermody, Janine; Hanmer-Lloyd, Stuart & Scullion, Richard. (2010). "Young people and voting behaviour: alienated youth and (or) an interested and critical citizenry?", *European Journal of Marketing* vol. 44-3/4, pp. 421-435.
Sanders, David; Clarke, Harold; Stewart, Marianne & Whiteley, Paul. (2011). "Downs, Stokes and the Dynamics of Electoral Choice", *British Journal of Political Science* vol. 41-2, pp. 287-314.

Websites
www.crest.ox.ac.uk/
This will take you to the CREST homepage

www.gallup.com/home.aspx
This is the Gallup opinion pollsters homepage. Mori and ICM are alternatives

www.runnymedetrust.org/projects-and-publications/projects/community-cohesion/voting-behaviour.html
The Runnymede Trust focus on, among other things, issues surrounding ethnicity and voting behaviour

Questions
1. How far does the analysis of voting behaviour confirm the view class is the dominant element?
2. To what extent are we seeing a realignment in British voting behaviour?
3. Evaluate the extent to which election outcomes hang upon the floating voter.

CHAPTER 22 // PRESSURE GROUPS

Contents
- **Introduction**
- **Definition**
- **Development of Pressure Groups**
- **Typology of Pressure Groups**
- **Methods of Operating**
- **Direct Action**
- **Assessment of Pressure Groups**
- **Conclusion**

Introduction

Pressure groups are an integral part of the British political process. Yet when talking about ideas such as democracy or participation (as discussed in chapter 18), the emphasis seems to be on electoral participation, and specifically elections to Parliament. Pressure group activity appears sometimes to be an extra, almost as an afterthought to the Parliamentary processes. It is interesting to note constitutional writers in the 1950s and 1960s ignored such group interests – presumably because they did not fit into the formal structures of government. Admittedly, the explosion in the number of pressure groups in the UK did not occur until the mid-1960s.

To omit the examination of such bodies is no longer tenable in a modern democratic society. The idea of elected representatives being able to look after all of their constituents' needs and concerns is no longer seen as accurate (if it ever was). Hence the growth of pressure groups was an almost inevitable attempt to develop a more open and democratic system. While political parties may satisfy a number of aspirations (see chapter 23), they cannot hope to fulfil the wishes of all citizens. The development of pressure groups has been a partial answer to this problem.

The political system is open to all individuals to exercise their right to influence the ideas and actions of MPs and ministers, preferably by methods that are not illegal. Groups tend to be much more effective in this area than individuals. Experience has taught people group interests, whether through trade unions, environmental movements or animal welfare organisations, have a better chance of achieving their aims than individuals pursuing identical aims separately. In other words, 'collective action' is more effective than individual effort. Pressure groups, it seems, have developed to complement the representation function of MPs rather than to replace them.

Definition

One of the major problems when attempting to define 'pressure group' is it is a contested concept. The idea of a pressure group means different things to different people. There is also the concept 'interest group'. There may be differences between the two concepts, but that may be linked to definitional issues. What some people may call a 'pressure group', others may call an 'interest group'. In practice, these terms can be used interchangeably; as to the average person they probably mean the same thing.

With there being no agreement between experts as to what comprises a pressure group, any text examining pressure groups will present one or more definitions of the term. These definitions will not be the same. There tend to be common themes underpinning these definitions and it is from this point any attempt at a definition ought to start. These are:

1. A pressure group tends **to seek influence**, either of a direct or indirect nature. This may be over a particular government policy such as a road building scheme at local government level, university lecturers pay at a national government level, or standards of cleanliness of beaches at the European Union level. The seeking of influence, however, could be over public opinion, by trying to raise public concern to gain added support for the cause.

2. Most groups have **a narrow range of concerns**; indeed some focus on single issues. Such a concern can be very specific such as the Ramblers' Associations and the right to roam. Alternatively, the issue or concern can also be very widespread. Greenpeace is concerned with environmental issues. These extend far beyond British shores, and range from opposition to the testing of nuclear weapons to saving the Brazilian rain forests. Trade unions are concerned with the well being of their members. This can range from health and safety issues in the workplace through to pay demands and fighting redundancies. It is also worth noting, increasingly groups are working collectively. There were coalitions of interests opposed to the war in Iraq. Similarly, there were coalitions of interests in the fight to protect public sector pensions in 2011.

3. Pressure groups **do not seek to govern**. This means while pressure groups may seek influence, normally they have no desire to form a government – at any level. Traditionally it was argued pressure groups do not fight elections because they do not wish to form part of the government. More and more, pressure group campaigners can be seen standing for Office, particularly in by-elections. While they probably have little chance of winning, they do gain publicity at a local level about their cause. Thus they are able to inform the public more easily. Victory in such a by-election would add great strength to the position of the campaigners.

   Some groups, however, have enjoyed electoral success as part of their campaign. In the 2001 General Election, in the constituency of Wyre Forest, an independent candidate (Dr. Richard Taylor) stood on the issue of the reduction of emergency and health care facilities at Kidderminster Hospital.

He gained election, defeating the Labour junior Health minister in the process and gained much publicity for the cause. Taylor was re-elected in 2005, but lost narrowly in the 2010 General Election. What was less well reported was in 2001 the pressure group (Kidderminster Health and Hospital Concern) was already the largest party on the Wyre Forest district council, and they took control of the council in 2002. Although control was lost, they have remained a prominent group. Added to this, the group has also won council representation on the Worcestershire and Shropshire County Councils, as well as on town and village councils such as Stourport Town Council.

So, in sum, a pressure group is an organisation of people with a specific interest or concern. They may attempt to influence either government (at any level) or the public with regard to that interest or concern. Pressure groups do not normally wish to form part of the government, they may simply wish access to and influence over the decision makers. These themes are evident in the following definitions:

"A pressure group is an organisation which seeks to influence the details of a comparatively small range of public policies and which is not a faction of a recognised political party." (Baggott, 1988, p.26)

Interest group "refers to individuals, organizations or institutions that are associated in a body that aims at influencing public policy." (Eisner, 2008, p. 5)

Development of Pressure Groups

Pressure groups have a long and distinguished history. They have been transformed from something perceived to be akin to mob activity into a form of acceptable participation by citizens. For example in the 19th century Parliament was influenced by powerful interests in the East and West Indies, in land, railways, shipping, Anti-Slavery organisations, Abolition Societies, and most notable because of its organisational methods, the Anti-Corn Law League. The Chartists campaigned for, among other things, an extension of voting rights and a secret ballot. In the 20th century we have seen the achievements of campaigns to promote Clean Air and the Suffragette movement.

It is in the post-1945 era the greatest and most spectacular advances have been made in the development of pressure groups. Currently, the Directory of British Associations (which was established in 1965) lists over 7000 organisations, from CAMRA (the Campaign for Real Ale) to the CBI (Confederation of British Industry), from the Simplified Spelling Society to the TUC (Trades Union Congress).

The explanation for this growth is not difficult to seek. The changing social and economic conditions of post-war Britain contain many of the answers. As the state intervened more and more in such areas as social welfare, industry, planning, education, and so on, it was inevitably drawn into deeper contact with citizens whose expectations had been aroused and who were not satisfied with the solutions offered by, or neglected by, the political parties. The expansion of educational opportunities gave a stimulus to a rising middle class concerned with social and economic issues – to which could later be added environmental issues. These middle classes had the ability to articulate their demands and organise group activity. At the same time, the improvements in living standards generated a consumer-oriented society. Consequently groups developed in each of these areas and many others. The Consumers' Association was set up in 1957 to protect the consumer; the Campaign for Nuclear Disarmament (CND) was formed in 1959. Other groups who formed in the 1960s included the Child Poverty Action Group (CPAG), Shelter, Age Concern and the National Viewers and Listeners Association (now known as Mediawatch – UK).

Not only did these and other groups appreciate the benefits and power of the media, and especially television, but they were professional enough to exploit it. To do so adequately they needed effective organisation and leadership. Hence, over the years, figures such as Mary Whitehouse, Frank Field, Jonathon Porritt and Des Wilson became influential and well-known in pressure groups politics, appearing regularly in the media on their particular issue (broadcasting standards on the BBC, CPAG, the environment, and Shelter respectively). More recently, there has been Peter Tatchell (LBGT rights), Naomi Klein (anti-globalisation) and Shami Chakrabati (Liberty).

Yet it was not just in the media or in the public eye such groups developed. As the activity of the state extended, the civil service found these outside bodies could provide advice and expertise lacking within itself. Pressure groups were given greater opportunities to come into contact with, and to influence, government departments and policy making.

In many respects this situation was a natural extension of the British political system. The unitary nature of the constitution meant the groups could direct their energies towards the centralised machinery of government instead of having to spread their effort across a number of tiers of government. Throughout the 1950s and 1960s, central government was the focus for the most publicised of pressure group activities.

The close relationship between the policy makers and the pressure groups has been encapsulated in the concept of *corporatism*. This can be loosely defined as co-operation between politicians and organisations outside Parliament and Whitehall to formulate policies and activities. It became so important the co-operation of leading pressure groups became almost indispensable to government policy and activity. There was, however, a price to pay for such access to government. In return for being able to influence government policy so closely, the groups had to make sure their members openly supported the policy proposals, possibly assisting in their implementation, and not making too heavy demands on the government. It was very much a case of *quid pro quo*, which loosely translates as 'you scratch my back, I'll scratch yours'.

Margaret Thatcher reversed this trend, promising to roll back the frontiers of the State (see Chapter 8). She detested corporatism and consensus. Many pressure groups (but not all of them) were simply refused access to the decision making process. Others retained links with the civil service even where ministerial relations deteriorated. The relationship sometimes depended upon the minister concerned rather than the Prime Minister (e.g. Kenneth Clarke alienated many groups). Pressure groups were compelled to look elsewhere in their attempts to exert influence. Local government became a target, the European Community (EC) – as it was then known – became another.

When John Major replaced Thatcher as Prime Minister, the access to central government opened up to some extent, although some groups were still not welcome. This process of opening up developed further under Blair and Brown. Under the coalition government, pressure group access to decision makers was variable. Due to pressure politics, the proposed reforms of the NHS were re-opened for broader consultation with a range of bodies across the health sector.

In the post-Thatcher years, not all groups were given access to the decision making process. The system has merely become easier to enter – and the use of new technologies has made it even easier. There is greater opportunity of access to central government. Unsurprisingly, the links pressure groups have developed with other tiers of government have not been dropped. Multiple lines of access to the various tiers of government may actually strengthen a group's position, despite the unitary nature of British politics.

Typology of Pressure Groups

What becomes obvious when examining the development of pressure groups is the vast number of these organisations; they cover almost every aspect of our daily lives, and they each have their own specific aims and objectives. In fact, in almost every area of pressure group activity, where one group is formed, another will form in response to it. A good example is on the issue of abortion, where there are the Pro-Life (anti-abortion) campaigners, and the Pro-Choice (pro-abortion) campaigners.

In an attempt to make the examination of pressure group activity somewhat easier, a number of authors have attempted to categorise the various types of pressure group. Yet, as with the definition of the concept, there is no agreement as to the best classification of these groups. In fact, the typology adopted may depend upon what aspects of pressure group activity the author may wish to highlight.

A major classification of pressure groups focuses upon a basic divide between what are termed 'interest' groups and 'promotional' groups, with each of these having sub-groups. Under this particular classification, 'interest' groups exist to protect the interests of the members. This can be done through attempting to influence government, be it Parliament or the Executive, or employers, or the public. They may have sanctions to impose if their demands are not met (e.g. strikes). It could be to do with rates of pay, health and safety at work, or other such issues. These groups are sometimes called sectional groups. There is a clear divide under this broad label between the groups representing the world of capital (business owners) and those the world of labour (the workers).

Both sub-sets, but particularly 'capital', tend to be well organised and often have expertise to offer the government. Consequently these groups may have direct or indirect access to the decision makers. Included under the general label of 'interest' group would be trade unions, the BMA (British Medical Association), the CBI (Confederation of British Industry) and the Institute of Directors.

'Promotional' groups, on the other hand, promote a particular cause, issue or concern. Often they may be called 'Cause' groups, and sometimes even 'Protest' groups. They may lobby government or the public. Their particular objective is to get the law changed, or often to prevent it from being changed. Such groups include Greenpeace, Friends of the Earth, the RSPCA, and Animal Aid. Promotional groups are very heavily dependent upon the volume and quality of public support. Such support could be membership, financial contributions, or even time. Some of these groups – or, more accurately, their cause – are short-lived. Such protests are "often initiated quickly and finished fast. It is a burst of colour or activity that meets the space/time /entertainment demands of the news media" (Libby, 2006, p. 911).

A problem arises with the classification of groups such as CPAG, the RAC, and Shelter. These groups could be labelled as 'promotional' as they promote a particular cause or concern. It could just as easily be argued they are sectional groups as they are concerned with advancing the interests of a particular section of society. Such quibbling often leads to confusion and is probably best resolved by arguing some groups may actually be listed under both 'interest' and 'promotional' labels.

Wyn Grant (1989) developed a different classification, focusing upon the strategies for pressure groups. There is a clear distinction between 'insider' groups and 'outsider' groups. These refer to the potential access to decision makers, and within each there are sub-groups. The government consults insider groups; outsider groups are far less likely to be consulted, or may not want to be even associated with the government. Table 22.1 outlines the various groupings.

Table 22.1 The Insider/Outsider dichotomy

INSIDER GROUPS	HIGH PROFILE INSIDERS	LOW PROFILE INSIDERS	PRISONER GROUPS
	They are prepared to reinforce contact with government by use of the media	They focus entirely on behind the scenes contact	They are unable to break away from the government position
OUTSIDER GROUPS	POTENTIAL INSIDERS	OUTSIDE GROUPS BY NECESSITY	IDEOLOGICAL OUTSIDERS
	These groups seek insider status	They may wish to become insiders but lack the political skill to succeed	The objectives of these groups are at odds with social and political norms and cannot be achieved within the normal political system

Source: Grant, Wyn. (1989). *Pressure Group Politics and Democracy in Britain*

What is important to note in Table 22.1 is the positions of the groups are fluid – they can change. For many years, trade unions were viewed as high profile insiders. Yet during the Thatcher years they were shunned, becoming outsiders and not even potential insiders. Under Major and Blair, their position changed again, to the extent they were possibly potential insiders. With the coalition government, trade unions were again shunned. Arguably, much depends upon the issue at stake as to the extent of trade union involvement. Such issues as rates of pay and health and safety in the workplace are likely to see a greater level of union involvement.

To become an 'insider' organisation, a pressure group must demonstrate they possess some special attribute or knowledge the government cannot do without. This could be information, authority in a specific field, or the possession of a powerful sanction that could be wielded if they do not get their own way. Yet once this 'insider' status has been achieved, the group must accept certain constraints such as confidentiality, the willingness to compromise, and the avoidance of threats. Some of these may appear incompatible with the attributes of the group, but this is to do with the nature of 'insider' politics. It is very much a case of give and take.

An insider group, in effect, needs the following characteristics:
– to be recognised as the legitimate spokesperson for a particular concern
– to be able to engage in dialogue on this concern
– to agree to abide by the rules of the game (even if the outcome is not what was hoped)

Outsiders, and even potential insiders, are not subject to the last of these points – although potential insider groups may abide by the 'rules' as a sign of good faith (and in the hope of becoming an insider group).

Insider groups are more likely to be successful than outsider groups in achieving their aims and objectives. This does not mean insider groups are guaranteed to get what they want. It may be easy to measure the access insider groups have to decision makers, but not their input into the decision making process. The input might as easily be negligible as being great. Similarly, it does not mean all outsider groups are doomed to failure. For example, campaigns of direct action appear to becoming more effective in achieving their aims. This is especially as a result of technology e.g. social network campaigns and mobile phone video footage. The latter may be downloaded on to the internet and viewed globally within minutes. "The growth in direct action is driven also by growing dissatisfaction with more conventional forms of politics because of their failure to bring quick results" (Grant, 2004, p. 412).

Grant (2004) has acknowledged the insider/outsider dichotomy is diminishing in usefulness. Within the collective label of insider groups, there appears to be a growing distinction between core insiders (such as the CBI) and peripheral insiders. Conversely, the outsider label may be diminishing. In 2000, the Government issued a *Code of Practice on Consultation* (a third version of which was published in 2008). This gave very clear guidelines on how pressure groups could lobby government more effectively. It was replaced by a simple document entitled "Consultation Principles" by the coalition government – although it was noted on the last page of the document that it did not have legal force. As a result, the classification 'Outside Groups by Necessity' may well be defunct.

Table 22.2 Consultation Criteria

Consultation Principles
Subjects of consultation
Timing of consultation
Making information useful and accessible
Transparency and feedback
Practical considerations

Developed from www.gov.uk/government/publications/consultation-principles-guidance

Methods of Operating

Experience has taught pressure groups there are a number of avenues open to them to achieve their objectives. The methods and activities used will to a large extent be dependent upon the strength and financial standing of the groups. The most powerful and influential could use any of a range of methods available, whilst smaller groups may have to confine themselves to a much more limited set of activities.

1. *Violence and illegality*
2. *Denial of function*
3. *Publicity seeking techniques*
4. *Political parties*
5. *Parliament*
6. *Ministers and Civil Servants*

1. Violence and illegality

Not all pressure groups obey the laws of the land. Terrorism and hijacking are forms of pressure group activity. The IRA bombing campaigns raised awareness of problems in Northern Ireland. Had it not been for the campaign conducted by the IRA, would the Legislative Assembly of Northern Ireland be in place today? The Animal Liberation Front (ALF) breaks the law frequently as part of their campaign against, among other things, testing products on animals. Many groups using violence and illegality may not even recognise the right of the government of the day to legislate on their behalf. Many states around the world have been founded on the back of terrorism and/or a war of liberation, including the United States of America. One person's terrorist is another's freedom fighter.

2. Denial of function

This mode of operation is only available to specific groups. Denial of function includes actions such as strikes, working to rule, and lockouts. It is where a particular group refuses to carry out its duties, or to conduct them in a limited capacity, for whatever reason. A strike or a work to rule may be called over an inadequate pay increase proposal. There could be a go-slow, or a refusal to work overtime. On the other hand, a multi-national company may decide to relocate or lock the workers out as part of the dispute (as happened in Dundee at the Timex factory in 2005). Forms of action under this label are restricted to operations in the economic sphere of life.

3. Publicity seeking techniques

Such techniques are used to make the public aware of the issue or concern of the pressure group. Actions include demonstrations, marches, advertisements, and boycotts. Students organised protest marches in London against tuition fees; the Royal College of Nursing organised outdoor 'sleepovers' to protest at the high cost and poor accommodation for student nurses; there was a boycott of South African produce by the anti-apartheid movement in the 1960s-1980s.

Publicity seeking techniques can be a double-edged weapon. If a protest march becomes disruptive or turns into a riot, the original reason for the march is lost in the news reports. Examples here include the Poll Tax demonstration in London, which turned into a riot in 1990; the anti-capitalism march in 2000 that also turned violent and destructive; and the student protests over the new £9000 tuition fees in 2010. In each of these cases, news reports focused upon the violence and illegality rather than the reason for the protest.

Publicity seeking techniques often see groups trying to get celebrity support for their cause. For example, Joanna Lumley was very prominent in campaigning for the rights of the Ghurkhas. While Lumley had a clear association with this cause, the relationship between celebrity and cause is not always so apparent. As Lester (2006, p. 918) notes, "well-knowness is now a legitimate criterion for participation in political debate".

4. Political parties
While most groups tend to avoid getting involved in party-political debates, it is sometimes useful for a group to be associated with a political party. Thus the Campaign for Nuclear Disarmament (CND) actively courted Labour Party support. The hope was, should a Labour Government get into power, CND would be in a position to directly influence defence policy and achieve their aim of unilateral nuclear disarmament. In the 1980s, the Labour Party adopted unilateral nuclear disarmament as one of their policies.

Trade unions have also been closely linked to the Labour Party. It is important to note the trade unions were involved in the formation of the Labour Party. When Tony Blair became party leader, the close links between the two disappeared. Even under the leadership of Ed Miliband, the relationship between the Labour Party and the trade unions was nowhere near as close as it was in the 1960s and 1970s. The relationship was also put under strain by the Blair Government's courting of big business – traditional Conservative Party supporters. Blair argued, like the Democrat Party in the USA, Labour could be the party of business. Such a stance horrified many traditional Labour Party supporters, as well as most rank-and-file union members.

5. Parliament
It is important to note most MPs automatically represent particular interests by virtue of their profession (prior to becoming an MP). Thus there are teachers, lawyers, accountants, business people, and trade unionists in Parliament, who are able to articulate concerns related to their profession.

Outside organisations could pay MPs to act as Parliamentary advisers. In the past there have been many allegations of MPs 'being bought' or being 'under undue influence' from outside organisations. Much of this was brought to light in the 'Cash for Questions' scandals during the Major Government, and the sleaze allegations most notably against Neil Hamilton (former MP for Tatton) prior to the 1997 General Election.

The Committee on Standards in Public Life clamped down on these aspects of MPs work. Despite this additional regulation, allegations of sleaze continued under the Blair and Brown Governments leading to demands for ministerial resignations.

6. Ministers and Civil Servants

This is the nub of the 'insider' access to decision making. It takes place away from public view. In fact, it is often very difficult to know which groups have been consulted, or even who approached whom. As Baggott (2000) points out, these meetings could take place in a very informal atmosphere over lunch, or at a venue such as the Carlton Club. Added to this, former ministers and civil servants (who know the paths to power and influence) are able to use their personal networks to gain access to the decision making process.

Increasingly this process is becoming more open, as shown with the publication of the *Code of Practice on Consultation* and the Consultation Criteria. Attempts have been made to encourage groups to access the government. Also, after any consultation, a list of all groups who participated is published.

Direct Action

Within the list of Methods of Operating, the first three items could easily come under the broad heading of direct action. In fact, in Wyn Grant's Insider/Outsider dichotomy, much of the 'outsider' activity could come under the label of direct action.

Yet direct action receives a lot of bad press. There is a perception direct action is violent – the perpetrators are a bunch of thugs or anarchists who wish to destroy everything. While this perception is not always inaccurate, much of it is down to media reporting of events. McLeod & Detenber (1999, p. 3) note "news stories about protests tend to focus on the protestors' appearances rather than their issues, emphasize their violent actions rather than their social criticism, pit them against the police rather than their chosen targets, and downplay their effectiveness." Much of this misrepresents so much about direct action.

Under the insider/outsider dichotomy, any group moving towards any form of direct action was deemed to be failing. The perception was the groups that shouted the loudest were achieving the least. This was never wholly accurate, and with direct action, such a claim may be challenged even further.

Doherty *et al* (2003, p. 670) argue direct action "is intended to directly change perceived political, social or environmental injustices. Such an approach rejects mediation via political elites or the media". Some groups may utilise methods of violence, but many others are non-violent. It depends upon the type of group as well as their aims and objectives. For example, some forms of direct action involve the establishment of community projects. These could be the establishment of community vegetable gardens, which will provide the neighbourhood with a healthy source of food in a direct challenge to the produce from multi-national supermarkets. With this sort of example, the ideas of success and failure for pressure groups may need to be re-evaluated. Conventional pressure groups might perceive success as obtaining a change in policy. Direct action groups, depending upon the issue, may see success as increasing community participation and creating a healthier community.

Assessment of Pressure Groups
There is no consensus among commentators as to the merits and demerits of pressure groups in the British political system. Just as there is debate over definitions and typologies, so there is debate over the advantages and disadvantages of pressure group politics, and whether or not they enhance democracy.

1. The Benefits of Pressure Groups

a) Participation
Pressure groups provide the means for ordinary citizens to realise their aims and have a voice in public affairs in addition to or as a substitute for joining a political party. Party membership is in decline; pressure groups act as an outlet for those disillusioned with party politics.

Pressure groups enable more frequent participation as well. Through pressure group activity some degree of continuity of representation between elections is maintained. Without it, the only opportunity to exercise influence may be when voting. A general election may occur every four or five years. Local government elections and those for the devolved bodies in Scotland, Northern Ireland and Wales occur every four years. There is actually very little opportunity to influence policy by voting. Between times, participating in pressure group politics may plug that gap.

Through direct action, opportunities to influence policy making have increased. With 24-hour media coverage, publicity for campaigns can be achieved – although for some direct action groups, media publicity may be shunned. Direct action is more likely to get media coverage than "conventional public relations activities" (Gavin, 2010, p. 462). Added to this, with the internet and other forms of new media, publicity is achieved very easily indeed. In fact, direct action groups that distrust conventional media outlets are more likely to utilise these alternative forms of media. This may encourage greater public participation as well.

b) Single Issue Campaigns
By pursuing isolated campaigns pressure groups enable the ordinary citizen to understand the political system more clearly, and give the individual a sense of real commitment. In recent times, the Snowdrop Campaign best exemplified this. In March 1996 a gunman killed 16 school children and their teacher in Dunblane. After this tragedy, a campaign was launched to ban the private ownership of handguns. A high profile campaign was carried out which gained support from the bereaved parents as well as from the general public. This campaign was successful, with a handgun ban being introduced, despite the best efforts of the gun lobby.

c) Protecting minorities
Both political parties and the more powerful pressure groups too often overlook minority interests. Only through banding together can individuals with so-called minority interests hope to have their views represented and articulated. Thus, for example, the elderly can look to Age Concern, the homeless to Shelter, mental health sufferers to MIND.

d) Legitimising function
The strict constitutional interpretation is MPs being the elected representatives of constituents are the channels through which complaints can be expressed. A strong case could be made that the legitimising function of Parliament is incomplete if pressure groups and their leaders are locked out of the consultation process. It makes sense to consult with those who are to be most closely affected by government action. For example, in a road-widening scheme, the local residents ought to be consulted. Yet it is pressure groups who are more successful than political parties in drawing people into the policy making process and bringing to prominence such disparate issues as capital punishment, abortion, fox hunting and health and safety concerns.

e) Critics of Government (i.e. scrutiny and accountability)
Through their zeal, enthusiasm and commitment, pressure groups often serve as acute critics of government. Unlike many MPs they are highly motivated and well-informed (at least with regard to their specific issue). British democracy is not so perfect governments cannot endure checks beyond those offered by opposing MPs. Pressure groups, even if not directly criticising government policy, can at least offer detailed information. Although we are noting criticism of government here, it is also important to note pressure groups may actually praise government action. The Snowdrop Campaign, for example, commended the government on its prompt action to ban handguns.

f) Justification

A theoretical justification can be made for the desirability of pressure group activity. Fundamental freedoms, many of which are supposedly protected under the Human Rights Act (1998) such as speech, religion and association, can be furthered by pressure group action. While the law is supposed to protect the people, it is often pressure group action that makes people aware of the law and their own individual rights. Governments become aware of the strong feelings generated by campaigns and ignore them at their peril. The Blair Government, for example, saw the extent of support both for and against fox hunting. A government needs to balance these demands in what is a zero-sum game – there can be only one winner. The question then becomes: what happens afterwards? Just because legislation has been passed, it does not mean the lobbying stops. Pro-hunting campaign groups have pursued their cause vigorously, despite the legislation banning hunting with hounds.

2. Criticisms of Pressure Groups

a) Undermining Parliamentary democracy

Pressure groups are often perceived as distorting or subverting the democratic process. The traditional view of the role of MPs is as the arbiters of the national interest, rather than outside groups that distract people from the bigger picture. Added to this, of course, MPs are accountable to the public at election time, whereas pressure groups appear to be accountable to no one except possibly their specific membership. By drawing in such groups into the policy making process, the role of the MP is undermined. Policy making appears to be conducted by ministers and civil servants, along with the leaders of 'insider' groups, away from Parliament. This may leave the national representative body as little more than a legitimising husk.

b) Power of strong pressure groups

Pressure groups are intrinsically self-interested and in the contest with governments it is the big battalions who have all of the advantages in the matters of strength, propaganda, wealth and publicity. It follows, the stronger the group is in terms of riches, contacts and size, the greater the chance it has of achieving its aims of influencing the government. Business-related groups tend to be over-represented mainly because of their wealth and ability to organise. The CBI, for example, claims to be the top business lobbying organisation in the country, with ministers, MPs, civil servants, and many other key personnel as contacts. The weaker consumer group interests, like those dealing with children, the elderly, the disabled, and charitable bodies, because of their relative poverty and weak organisation, lose out in these competing stakes. Even within a particular sector, these divisions are clear. Compare the power and influence of the big breweries with those who are after better quality of product, such as CAMRA.

c) Sectional, self-interest tendencies

Pressure groups are accused of being more selfishly concerned with their own sectional interests, often at the expense of the public, than with the national good. The scope for sabotage may be exploited. An obvious example was the fuel protest in 2000. Lorry drivers and farmers forced the country to a halt by blockading fuel depots and preventing fuel being delivered. Their concern was the high taxation duty paid on fuel, and they demanded French, or at least continental, fuel prices. The lorry drivers ignored the higher levels of direct taxation paid by their continental counterparts, or the motorway taxes, and a host of other duties that drive continental costs up. Similarly, the farmers failed to point out 'red' diesel, which may only be used on farms, had 3.13 pence duty on it compared to the 48.82 pence duty paid for normal diesel in 1999. Regardless, as a result of the narrow mindedness of the protesters, along with the frenzy whipped up by the media, Britain almost ground to a halt. Emergency services could not function properly; in rural areas children could not get to school, all for the demand for cheap fuel.

What was also interesting in this example is the way in which the 'insider' groups were marginalized. For example, farmers groups, such as the National Farmers Union (NFU), appeared out of touch with their grassroots membership. Prior to the fuel protests, there had been a degree of dissatisfaction with the NFU, and this resulted in the formation of more radical groups who felt they could better represent farmers' interests utilising more direct methods.

d) Secrecy

One of the major accusations levelled against the conduct of British governments and administrations is the obsession with secrecy. The most powerful pressure groups (Grant's 'insiders') collude with civil servants to perpetuate this situation. Most pressure groups do not operate in full public view except when they want publicity to combat their opponents' views. There is a mitigating circumstance of sorts. Civil servants make it clear they will have no dealings with groups unless secrecy is preserved. Thus the public is unaware of how influential a group's views are when decisions are taken. It is possible to find out who has been consulted, but not who was successful in achieving their aims. If it is felt excessive secrecy undermines the democratic processes, then pressure groups are to blame for helping perpetuate such a system.

Conclusion

Whatever view one takes of the desirability or otherwise of pressure groups there is no denying a modern democracy has to come to terms with them.

Pressure groups can exercise a powerful check on government policy and be instrumental in distorting decision making. Within our modern democracy the most powerful of pressure groups may appear **undemocratic** when compared to MPs and ministers being held accountable to Parliament (note that to some extent Parliament may be controlled or manipulated by the Executive). They cannot be held to account for their actions, unless their operations break the law. A counter argument may be with the proliferation of groups, if there is one group in favour of something, another will form to oppose them and thus a balance of sorts is achieved.

In a democracy so heavily geared towards a Parliamentary representative system, with all of its imperfections, it was inevitable people would bond together in groups to further particular objectives. It was also inevitable the more powerful groups would exert an undue influence on government. It is difficult to see what can sensibly be done to curb such activity. Actions which are closer to corruption are being weeded out by the Committee on Public Standards. Yet it is not really desirable to completely disparage pressure group activity, despite its obvious flaws.

In the modern era of a need for instant gratification, pressure groups appear to give the opportunity for everyone to participate and to achieve their goals. Yet, as Grant (2005, pp. 372-373) points out: "there is a risk that organisations may consider that getting their issue on the political agenda is enough whereas as in fact it is only the start of the battle." This applies very much to groups involved in direct action, or, more generally, to Grant's 'outsider groups'.

Yet direct action is not necessarily the most appropriate form of pressure group activity. "There is mileage in diligent lobbying, careful research, discriminating collaboration, public relations professionalism and the cultivation of the conventional media" (Gavin, 2010, p. 471). The problem is such activity is not sensationalist, and is not likely to gain media headlines. On the other hand, it may be more likely through such activity a pressure group is able to achieve its aims.

Selected bibliography

Baggott, Rob. (2000). *Pressure Groups and the Policy Process:* Sheffield Hallam University Press.

Barker, Rodney. (2011). "Big Societies, Little Platoons and the Problems with Pluralism", *Political Quarterly* vol. 82-1, pp. 50-55.

Cottle, Simon. (2008). "Reporting demonstrations: the changing media politics of dissent", *Media, Culture and Society* vol. 30-6, pp. 853-872.

Doherty, Brian; Plows, Alexandra & Wall, Derek. (2003). "'The Preferred Way of Doing Things': The British Direct Action Movement", *Parliamentary Affairs* vol. 56-4, pp. 669-686.

Lester, Libby. (2006). "Lost in the wilderness? Celebrity, protest and the news", *Journalism Studies* vol. 7-6, pp. 907-921.

Parliamentary Affairs vol. 51-3 special edition on "Protest Politics: Cause Groups and Campaigns", edited with Grant Jordan.

Toke, David. (2010). "Foxhunting and the Conservatives", *Political Quarterly* vol. 81-2, pp. 205-212.

Websites

www.europarl.europa.eu/oeil/popups/ficheprocedure.do?lang=en&reference=2007/2115%28INI%29
This site highlights how the European Parliament and EU deal with lobbying. Clear rules and guidelines were established.

www.politicsdirect.co.uk/portal/pressure-groups
Here is an extensive list of UK pressure groups

www.uknetguide.co.uk/News_and_Weather/Organisations/Pressure_Groups.html
This site gives a an interesting list of the top pressure groups in the UK, and links to their respective web pages

Questions

1. Evaluate the extent to which pressure group activity may distort the democratic process.
2. 'The louder a pressure group shouts, the less likely it is to be achieving its goals'. Discuss this perspective.
3. Lobbying the Government is only one of a range of options open to pressure groups. Examine some alternatives. Which are the most effective?

CHAPTER 23 // POLITICAL PARTIES

Contents

Introduction

Political parties are so much an essential part of the contemporary world it is sometimes difficult to remember how relatively modern a concept they are in the sense we understand them. Their origins are in the 18th century, although they have evolved quite considerably since that time. The ultimate aim of a political party – at a national level – is to form the government and run the country. To achieve such an aim, political parties fight elections and attempt to persuade people to vote for them. If a party is successful in achieving enough representation to form a government, they may claim to have a mandate from the people to govern as they see fit.

Thus political parties should be distinguished from pressure groups. As was shown in chapter 22, pressure groups want to influence the government of the day to carry out specific measures relating to their areas of interest. Political parties, on the other hand, wish not only to originate these measures but also to have a programme covering the whole range of policies. Unlike pressure groups, political parties offer policies in their manifestos to voters in order to be elected to government. It could be argued some of the very poorly supported parties, such as the Socialist Labour Party, are little more than pressure groups since they have no chance of forming a government.

It is worth noting an interesting constitutional point about political parties. Although they very clearly exist, and are accepted by the electorate, their constitutional role has never been legally recognised by statute; nor does the House of Commons and electoral law *officially* acknowledge their existence. Indeed it was not until 1970 party labels were recorded on ballot papers. This reluctance to accept the legal existence of political parties reflects a stubborn belief in an electoral system that considers MPs as being elected as individuals rather than as party representatives. This explains the justification in party defectors not resigning their seats (e.g. Quentin Davis quitting the Conservatives for Labour in 2007, or Bob Spink leaving the Conservatives for UKIP in 2008).

Functions of Political Parties

From the introduction, it could be assumed political parties are an inevitable development and even desirable agents in facilitating the democratic process. There has always been a body of opinion questioning such a perspective. It could be argued, for example, political parties undermine choice. Power is centralised within party leaderships, and these leaderships can dominate the selection of candidates put up for election. Voters get to choose between the chosen candidates of the party leaderships.

Another criticism – although one that is waning – is social divisions are perpetuated by the conflicting ideologies of the Conservative and Labour parties. This line of argument highlights the electoral system aiding and abetting the two major parties in preventing minor parties from participating in the governmental process. Winning elections can become the be-all and end-all for the major parties to the extent any form of 'rebellion' or 'extremism' within these parties is suppressed.

The above criticisms usually receive short shrift within the ethos of a modern democracy such as Britain. This has been most notable in the post-2010 General Election period where there has been a coalition government. Regardless, there is a general agreement for all their deficiencies, political parties do perform a number of important functions:

1. Forming a Government and Opposition – Policy Proposals

Political parties may be viewed as aggregates of a range of interests. They are 'umbrella' or 'catch-all' organisations offering the public a list of policy proposals known as a manifesto. The party that wins a general election is supposed to implement this manifesto. Hence, in Britain we have government by party, even in coalitions.

Having attained power the governing party or parties supply the ministers to administer the various departments of state. This is considered to be more easily achievable by one party controlling the levers of power. A coherent system tends to be more easily constructed through the shared interests of the party than through a collection of individuals with their disparate views or even through sharing power with another party in a coalition. Whether the country receives 'better' government is another matter.

To ensure party government does not become oppressive or unchecked, political parties are also supposed to provide effective opposition. In Britain, this means the party with the second largest number of seats becomes the official opposition, an alternate government in waiting. Only through political parties can an organised opposition be mounted. The effectiveness of such opposition, however, can be questioned. When governments have exceedingly large majorities (such as the Conservatives in 1983 [144] and 1987 [101], and Labour in 1997 [177] and 2001 [165]), the opposition may appear ineffectual. There may be more effective opposition from within the governing party's own ranks than from elsewhere.

2. Participation

Individual citizens find it is often extremely difficult to participate in the political process, to articulate their desires, and to hold governments to account for their actions (or lack thereof). Political parties enable greater opportunities for such aims to be realised, through the organisation and sharing of common interests they offer. The degree of participation can be at any level. It can range from the very low (licking envelopes, delivering leaflets, canvassing), rising to a higher degree of political activity (attending party conferences), and up to the highest level (standing for election and possibly becoming a councillor, an MP, an MEP, or a member of the Government).

It has generally been assumed the motivation for commitment to one party or another, however weak it is, comprises some degree of ideological belief in the doctrines and policies for which the party stands. Cynics may contend the more unscrupulous members simply view advancement in one party as more likely for them than joining its opponents. While such individuals may be a tiny minority in any party, high profile defectors such as Shaun Woodward (Labour MP for St. Helens South, formerly Conservative MP for Witney) add credence to the cynical perspective. This, in turn, leads to a higher degree of disillusionment with party politics.

What is of great concern to party leaderships is the rapid decrease in party membership. This is reflected not only in the decline in numbers who 'identify' with either of the major parties but even in voting for any party. Turnout has been particularly low in all elections in the 21st century. It appears many members of the public are seeking alternative avenues of political participation – particularly through pressure groups. This could detract from one of the key roles of a political party – being an effective channel for political participation. Yet pressure groups appear to be far more popular vehicles for participation – with their 'single issue' focus rather than the morass of issues and concerns included in a political party's remit. Pressure groups *appear* to achieve their goals whereas this is not necessarily the case for political parties (although the reality may actually be the reverse). Thus political parties may be superceded by pressure groups as effective vehicles of participation (see chapter 18 on Participation).

3. Political Recruitment

Generally there is little chance of independent candidates becoming MPs let alone attaining high office. There have been more independent MPs elected in recent elections than ever before, although never more than two in any one election. The most prominent include Martin Bell, who stood in Tatton (in 1997) amid allegations of sleaze directed against the sitting MP (Neil Hamilton). Both Labour and the Liberal Democrats decided against putting up a candidate. In 2001, Richard Taylor stood in Wyre Forest against the junior Health Minister, David Lock, on the issue of the closure of Kidderminster Hospital Accident and Emergency Section. The Liberal Democrats refused to contest the seat. Not only was Taylor elected in 2001; he was re-elected in 2005!

For the most part it is through the party system that candidates for political office are offered the opportunity to enter Parliament, regional or local government. It is also possible to gain positions of stature within a political party as well (e.g. the National Executive Council (NEC) of the Labour Party which is the policy making centre of the party).

4. Representation and Choice

In a complex modern industrial democracy, political parties have the great advantage of offering the electorate a list of itemised policies the party promises to implement if voted into office. In an ideal state where citizens are politically mature, where considered examination of individuals' policies can be evaluated, political parties may be deemed unnecessary. But in an imperfect world where electoral systems are viewed as being 'unfair', where there is a strong streak of apathy, parties have at least the merit of representing an aggregate of interests and presenting policies in a clear and systematic manner. In this vein, political parties may be perceived as democratic educators, eliciting and organising opinions with the possibility of delivering the measures they promise at the next election. Issues considered important to the public can be channelled through the parties. In the 19th century, issues such as free trade and the electoral franchise dominated the party programmes. In the early 20th century, social welfare was the prominent concern that divided the major parties.

The major division between the political parties in the 20th century has been class; although this distinction gradually blurred. The label used to describe this phenomenon was 'dealignment'. The consensus politics of the period 1950-1970 appeared to offer voters much less of a stark choice between the two major parties. Thatcherism broke this consensus by offering the public a much more radical programme. Labour, in response, moved more to the left. By the time of the 1992 election, a new consensus was beginning to appear. This was more marked in all subsequent general elections, where the two major parties broadly agreed on the general sweep of policies, with the possible exception of Europe.

In any event political parties are still the most important agency of representation. Party labels identify candidates and their political beliefs. Voters supposedly understand in making their decisions they are helping to elect a government and not simply an MP.

5. Channels of Communication

In keeping with the purpose of party existence and organisation, political parties are imperfect channels of communication but they still provide the linkages between the leadership, party activists and supporters. It is the political parties which act as sounding boards for governments so they can respond to the developing demands of the public.

Parties have been accused of bureaucratic insensibility in their response to public opinion, often being more concerned with achieving or retaining power. There is also the problem of the converse to this, with parties jumping on any populist bandwagon in an attempt to gain support.

6. Accountability

One of the essentials of the democratic process is the accountability of the government of the day to the electorate through the instrument of a general election. It is much easier for such accountability to be realised if one party can be held responsible for its actions as the government of the day rather than for a collection of independent individuals being blamed. This is a major criticism levelled against the idea of coalition government – which party should be 'blamed' for any problems. In local elections in the years after the 2010 General Election, the Liberal Democrats appeared to be 'blamed' for all of the ills of the coalition government, losing hundreds and hundreds of councillors.

Parties can also mask accountability. If specific individuals within a party raise contentious issues or are 'problematic' within the party, they can be removed even if they have popular local support (e.g. Liz Davies in Leeds North East prior to the 1997 election). Parties may attempt to protect individuals when allegations are made (e.g. Jeffrey Archer or Keith Vaz). It is virtually impossible to hold an entire political party to account for the actions of one individual, unless that individual is the party leader or holds high office within the party.

Development of the Party System in Britain

Britain is normally portrayed as having a two-party system. To most of the electorate in England, this two-party system appears to be the natural order. Yet it is only since 1945 that a two-party system has become pre-dominant. In Scotland and Wales, this situation has been tested already with the rise of the nationalist parties, first in the 1970s and again in the post-devolution era. It is now under pressure in England with the resurgence of the Liberal Democrats, especially as coalition partners at Westminster. When drawing in local government, it becomes apparent there may no longer be a uniform portrayal of the party system in England. Northern Ireland is far more complicated, with multi-party politics and no mainland British party being fully engaged in the domestic politics of the province.

The birth and development of the modern British party system could be seen in the middle of the nineteenth century. This was the time of the Second Reform Act (1867), which extended the franchise. Consequently, the parties of the day – the Whigs and the Tories – were forced to develop into more coherent organisations in order to gain and maintain electoral support. These parties evolved into the Liberals and the Conservatives.

At the beginning of the twentieth century, the Labour Party was formed. There were other parties at that time, including an Irish Home Rule Party.

The inter-war period was a time of multi-party politics. The Conservatives, the Liberals and Labour each formed single party governments – although in the case of Labour, these were minority governments. All three parties were also involved in the formation of coalitions. The 1920s saw the demise of the Liberal Party as a dominant force in British politics. This process was accelerated after the formation of the first minority Labour Government in 1923, and the subsequent general election in October 1924, when the Liberals were almost annihilated as a political force.

The period 1945-1970 has been described as the time where the two-party system became the norm in Britain. Each election was presented as a straight fight between Labour and the Conservatives. Class and party identification accounted for the strength of support for the two major parties. Between them these two parties won about 90% of the votes cast at general elections, and around 98% of the seats. In the 1951 election, the Liberal Party was almost facing extinction, winning 6 seats (five of which were not contested by the Conservatives) and a mere 2.5% of the popular vote.

The post-1970 period has seen the gradual break down of the two-party system in Britain. While elections are still portrayed as a straight choice between Labour and the Conservatives, the minor parties have become far more prominent. In both of the 1974 general elections, the nationalist parties, particularly in Scotland but also in Wales, made significant inroads into the two-party domination of votes. At the same time, the Liberals also experienced a surge in support. The number of seats gained, however, failed to match the rise in support.

During the 1980s, the nationalist challenge receded in both Scotland and Wales. The formation of the Social Democratic Party (SDP) and its relationship with the Liberals led to the formation of the Alliance. This new force in British politics appeared set to challenge the status quo in the early 1980s but the expectations were not met. The Alliance gained over a quarter of all votes cast in the 1983 general election but a mere 23 seats in Parliament. The 1987 election produced a similar result, although slightly down in both votes and seats. In 1989 the SDP and the Liberals merged to form the Liberal Democrats.

The 1990s saw a resurgence in support for the nationalist parties and the Liberal Democrats, and this has continued into the 21st century. As with previous challenges to the two-party system, the seats being won in Parliament bore little relationship to the votes cast for these parties.

There is however, an important factor that needs noting. This challenge to the two-party system is no longer focussed upon Westminster. Where different electoral systems have been used (for non-Westminster elections) many minor parties have gained representation and single party government has not been formed – and this has also been the case in some local government elections under Simple Plurality. Added to this challenge, of course, is the 2010 General Election result.

Single party government has always been portrayed (inaccurately so) as the norm for Britain. Between 1977 and 1979 there was a minority Labour government kept in power by a pact with the Liberal Party, along with support from the Scottish Nationalist Party. The Lib-Lab Pact heavily dented the assumption of single party majority government as the norm for British politics. This was not a formal coalition but rather an agreement of support in Parliament.

The Conservatives under John Major also experienced minority government. During the Maastricht Treaty debates, the Major Government was dependent upon the support of the Ulster Unionists. This was a consequence of the party whip being withdrawn from eight Conservative MPs (with a ninth joining them) over Britain signing the Maastricht Treaty.

Yet despite the optimism over increased minor party support, Britain is still portrayed as a two-party system. Arguably, during the Thatcher years, Britain could easily have been portrayed as a country with continuous one-party government (with no alternation between parties). Looking at the size of the Labour majorities after the 1997 and 2001 elections, the same arguments could be presented. Yet, in 2010, a coalition government was formed.

Reasons for the Domination of the Two Party System

Britain stands out among European democracies as being so closely associated with a two-party system. As can be seen in Table 23.1, during the post-war period there has been irregular alternation in power between the two major parties. There are several possible reasons as to why this is the case, some of which are outlined overleaf.

Table 23.1 Two Party Government 1945-2010

Election	Party returned to Office	Size of overall majority
1945	Labour	146
1950	Labour	5
1951	Conservative	17
1955	Conservative	58
1959	Conservative	100
1964	Labour	4
1966	Labour	96
1970	Conservative	30
1974 (Feb.)	Labour	-33
1974 (Oct.)	Labour	3
1979	Conservative	43
1983	Conservative	144
1987	Conservative	101
1992	Conservative	21
1997	Labour	177
2001	Labour	165
2005	Labour	66
2010	Conservative-Liberal Democrat coalition	78*

* The Conservatives could have formed a minority government, with an overall majority of -19

1. Historical Tradition

In the 18th century, politics polarised around two groups known as Whigs and Tories. Each group sought the support of the Monarch, had particular attitudes towards the Church and the State, and had other particular interests. This set the pattern for the adversarial politics we see today. It solidified in the 19th and early 20th centuries around the party organisations of the Liberals and the Conservatives, with each trying to develop distinctive policies to appeal to the mass electorate. The regular alternations in power between these two parties also strengthened the belief in the merits of the two-party system. As the position of the Liberals waned, Labour effectively replaced them as one of the two major parties. During this period of adjustment there was multi-party politics, but it was an interim period as Labour replaced the Liberals.

2. Electoral System

The evolution of the electoral system based on simple majority, constituency-based representation should be seen in conjunction with the development of the two-party system. In fact, it might well be said the so-called 'first-past-the-post' system was made to measure for the domination of two-party politics. This system disadvantages smaller parties who are often used as a repository for protest votes rather than being perceived as a potential government. Thus the Liberal Democrats, through many of their different guises, have received between 15 and 25% of the national vote but not a similar percentage of seats. Conversely, smaller parties, with concentrated support, such as the Scottish Nationalist Party, tend to fare rather better.

To counteract this problem, the Liberal Democrats have attempted to use the electoral system to their advantage by targeting particular constituencies. By focusing their resources, a concentration of support has been achieved and subsequently greater elected representation.

3. Responsible, Strong Government

It is claimed the two-party system is much more conducive to fulfilling one of the cardinal features of British government, i.e. ministers are responsible to Parliament and hence to the electorate for their actions and policies. Only through clear majority government can such responsible government be discharged unequivocally. Voters know for what a government stands and can support or oppose it. Thus issues tend to resolve themselves into clear alternatives between two choices, rather than being clouded by a range of minor party perspectives. Responsible government allows the existence of an official opposition standing by as an alternative government. It boils down to a simple choice within British politics – yes or no.

4. Class Basis

According to Pulzer (1967), class was the basis of British party politics. Everything else "was little more than embellishment and detail". Despite all the changes in the class structure, and the decline in class-based voting and partisanship, class is still a powerful factor in explaining voting behaviour. The two major parties are still perceived as class-based, although their ties have weakened. These ties have buttressed the two-party system, making it very difficult for any third force to break into British politics. The Liberal Democrats have aimed at disaffected voters from the two major parties, and then tried (with varying degrees of success) to retain that support. The nationalist parties in Scotland and Wales have attempted to replace the class dynamic with a nationalistic (devolutionary or independence-aimed) focus but are again reliant upon winning over disaffected voters from the other parties.

5. Coalition of Interests

Once the two-party system became dominant, those aspiring to gain representation in Parliament realised even if their interests differed slightly from one of the two major parties, they stood a far greater chance of success working with and within one of the two major parties. Thus the labels used to describe modern political parties include: 'broad church', 'umbrella organisation', or 'coalition of interests'. As each label suggests, there are a number of factions within each political party. They work together in an attempt to achieve office. Once there, each faction attempts to get its supporters into key government positions. In the early 1980s, the various factions within the Labour were openly fighting each other. Between 1997 and 2006, there was a similar problem for the Conservatives. Success binds and unites a party; defeat causes bitterness and resentment, and potentially a civil war within the party.

Results of the Two Party System

It is a matter of contention as to the extent to which Britain has benefited from the two-party system. This polarisation may have prevented alternative avenues of policy being explored. For example, there was nationalisation versus privatisation, or state control versus the freedom of the markets. The two-party system encouraged this yes-no option. The issue of the European Union is the same – you are either for or against membership. No other alternatives are presented. The idea of compromise is considered to be a sign of weakness. This has definitely made Britain distinctive when contrasting it with the multi-party politics and coalition governments of other European states.

1. Centralised, Strong Executive

A striking feature of the British political system is its highly centralised nature, with a strong executive apparently controlling Parliament and Whitehall. Such a perception is a result of the Cabinet being able to rely on a single highly disciplined party to ensure legislation passes through the House of Commons. A premium is placed upon loyalty and discipline. MPs realise they owe their seats to the party label and in return they are expected to toe the party line. The party whips are there to make sure MPs do not forget this. The whips cajole and persuade any recalcitrant MPs, and occasionally have to resort to pressure and discipline. This occurs even within a coalition government.

Governments do, however, suffer backbench rebellions, and are defeated occasionally, even when they have large majorities in the Commons. Tony Blair suffered a large rebellion on the war in Iraq, although the vote was passed due to Conservative support. Similarly, David Cameron endured a rebellion of over 80 MPs on the issue of Europe (although he was not defeated). Defeats, when they occur, tend to be on minor pieces of legislation but they demonstrate governments can no longer take their backbenchers for granted all of the time.

2. Broad Coalition Concept Declining?

Throughout the 1980s, this trend was applicable to the Labour Party, as the party fragmented with the formation of the SDP. Under successive leaders –

Neil Kinnock, John Smith, and Tony Blair, the Labour Party developed into a broad coalition of interests, taking on board many of the economic reforms of the Thatcher years. In the post-1997 era, the Conservative Party appeared in decline. While there was no split similar to that of the SDP, there were defections to Labour, the Liberal Democrats and the UK Independence Party. The election of David Cameron as party leader saw the start of the reversal of these misfortunes. Yet even in power, the Conservatives are stilling seeing defections – suggesting there is not a happy coalition of interests within the party.

3. Consensus?

The charge of adversarial politics levelled at the British political system can to some extent be refuted when the 1950s and 1960s are considered. This is the period labelled the 'age of consensus' or 'Butskellism' (from R. A. Butler who was Chancellor of the Exchequer and Hugh Gaitskell who was leader of the Labour Party), when the two parties were in broad agreement on crucial areas like the welfare state and the mixed economy (partly state-ownership and partly privately owned).

The advent of Thatcherism broke the consensus. This ideological approach polarised issues and gave the electorate a stark choice between the ideology of a radical right (privatisation, reduce the role of the State, cut taxes, cut public spending) and the socialist left (nationalisation, increase the role of the state, increase public spending, promote a more egalitarian society). From the late 1980s, the Labour Party began to change its position on most of these issues. By the late 1990s, a new consensus appeared to have formed between the major parties. Again, they were in broad agreement on how the economy should be run, and the role of the State. This has continued through the global economic crisis of 2008, with the major parties in agreement there should be cuts to public spending, but disagreeing over the extent of the cuts.

During the consensus period of the 1950s and 1960s the Liberal Party was almost squeezed out of existence. When there was a stark choice in the 1980s, the minor parties flourished – particularly the Liberal-SDP Alliance. What is interesting about the new consensus is minor parties still flourish. The consensus shifted on to the old Thatcherite agenda leaving plenty of room to the left of centre for the nationalist parties and the Liberal Democrats.

Decline in the Two Party System

The predicted demise of the two-party system failed to materialise in the 1980s. The reasons for such predictions were the huge election victories in 1983 and 1987 for the Conservatives, the rise of the Alliance, and the decline of the Labour Party. After the 2001 election, with a second crushing defeat for the Conservatives, and the Liberal Democrats winning a larger number of seats at an election since 1929, questions were again being asked as to whether this was the end of the two-party system. The formation of a coalition government in 2010 makes such questions even more salient.

1. The decline in voting strength for the Conservatives and Labour
There has been a gradual decline in the number of votes being won by the two major parties. When voter turnout is taken into account, particularly in 2001, the decline is even more pronounced. The electoral system masks the extent of this decline. As in the 1980s, the overall number of votes received by a political party bears little relationship to the number of seats won. Yet, after the 2005 General Election, 92 MPs were elected who did not represent the two major parties sitting in Parliament. In 2010, this number fell to 85.

2. Parliamentary Practice
The Parliamentary procedures are based upon a two-party system – those who support and those who oppose the government. In fact, the layout of the House of Commons reflects this confrontational approach. Further, representation on select committees and other parliamentary bodies also reflects such a divide. It is also assumed voters divide just as neatly into opposing camps. A coalition government, in this respect, confuses matters a little – although the division between supporters and opponents of the government remains. Within Parliament, the increased non-Conservative/Labour representation means greater consideration needs to be taken in the participation in debates and questions.

3. Overlapping party systems
This was a phrase used by Dunleavy (2005) to highlight there is no longer a uniform party system across the UK. Similarly, Childs (2006) and Cowley (2011) have noted the continuing fragmentation of the British party system. In effect, there are different party systems covering the different geographical parts of the UK. On top of this, there are the different tiers of government – local, regional, national and EU.

Some commentators may persist in talking about Britain having a two party system. At best, this would apply only to the national government – and even that would be strongly contested. In Scotland, Wales and Northern Ireland, there are multi-party systems. Elections to the European Parliament see a different form of multi-party politics for each of the regions across the UK. At the local government level, it is even more complicated again, with different councils having different forms of party system. In the city of Leicester, for example, there was a Liberal Democrat-Conservative coalition after the 2003 elections. By 2011, each of these parties had one councillor, with all of the others coming from the Labour Party!

The Ideology and Structure of the Major Parties

It is easy enough to present the structure and origins of the three major parties, but this would be a futile exercise without including the ideological underpinnings of each. All three parties have undergone radical changes and in many respects bear little resemblance to their predecessors from the beginnings of the 20th century. The Liberal Democrats are included here, so as to distinguish them from the 'minor' parties that may not always gain representation in elections.

1. The Conservative Party

The British Conservative Party can be considered one of the most successful modern democratic parties. Such a claim can be measured by electoral success – in the period 1950-2000, the Conservatives held power for 34 years. During this time (if not during the entire 20th century) the Conservative Party has retained a solid core of support within the electorate. It has also developed a disciplined organisation, with a pragmatic approach to politics. By the end of the 20th century, the organisation and the support appeared to be crumbling. Yet, a decade later, the Conservatives were forming a coalition government.

Ideology – Principles

The underpinnings of the Conservative Party are very interesting. Traditional Conservatives would argue the party does not have any ideology as such – because 'ideologies' are both radical and extremist – but rather the Conservatives have a 'tendency'. The emphasis is very much upon pragmatism, but also authority, tradition and continuity. There is a disapproval of preconceived ideas being used to resolve problems. Traditional Conservatives prefer tried and tested solutions. If a solution has not been tried, it is unclear as to whether it will work.

Associated with pragmatic politics was the **One Nation Tory**. Society is traditionally hierarchical. Rather than having a divided nation between the rich and the poor, One Nation Tories argued the rich had an obligation to help the less well off. This 19th century approach was remodelled in the 20th century, with the State being given the powers to help the less well off, with the rich helping indirectly through the payment of taxes. Thus after the Second World War, the Conservative Party supported the broad principles of the Welfare State.

Under the leadership of Margaret Thatcher, the Conservative Party moved away from its One Nation approach. Thatcher belonged to the **New Right**. This approach to politics (sometimes labelled neo-liberal or liberal conservatism, and styled as Thatcherism in Britain) had a minimalist role for the State. It should intervene as little as possible in economic affairs. Thus nationalised industries were privatised, public spending and taxation were both cut, along with the powers of the trade unions. The New Right approach aims for the maximisation of freedom and choice. This can best be achieved with the 'free market', which operates far more effectively than State intervention. Thus individuals should help themselves because the State would no longer do so. The language used emphasised the changes. People should find work rather than scrounging off social security; they should have private pension schemes rather than being dependent upon the state pension; they should have private health care rather than being dependent upon the NHS. All of this was summarised as 'rolling back the frontiers of the State'.

Thatchers' approach, while wishing to reduce the role of the State, also envisaged a strong State. The emphasis here was upon law and order, as well as defence and patriotism. There was a need for more police on the street, with greater powers. There should be greater spending on defence to combat communism and the perceived threat from the USSR. Thus Thatcher cosied up to Ronald Reagan (the then-President of the USA), who had similar perceptions of the world and how it should be run. Europe was presented as a less acceptable and less viable alternative to the special relationship between Britain and the USA.

During the Major years, attempts were made to moderate the action and language of Thatcherism. Ideas about accountability for service delivery emerged, best exemplified in the Citizen's Charter. The Major Government carried on with the privatisation process (coal and railways). Under Major's successors (William Hague, Iain Duncan Smith and Michael Howard), the moderate language was reversed. Patriotism and English nationalism came to the forefront of Conservative language, with opposition to Europe and the Euro, asylum seekers, and anything else that might threaten Britain. The New Right ideology of the Thatcher years was reinforced.

Under David Cameron's leadership, the Conservative Party appeared to move away from the liberal conservatism of the Thatcher years and towards a more social conservatism – which is sometimes seen to be similar to One Nation Conservatism. Evans (2010, p. 326) has pointed out "it could be argued that Cameron has expressed a preference for a return to the sense of social priority that underpinned One Nation Conservatism, as opposed to a continuation of the economic obsessions of Thatcherism". This was best portrayed in Cameron's idea of 'the Big Society'. The problem Cameron had was an inability to bring the Conservative Party along with him. Consequently, some interpretations of 'the Big Society' have been portrayed as similar to Thatcher's 'rolling back the frontiers of the state' (see chapter 8) i.e liberal conservatism; the new right, reinforced.

The New Right is very much an ideological approach, and in this respect could be viewed as being outside the Conservative tradition. Traditional Conservative thinking argues life cannot be improved by theories which have not been tried and tested. The New Right approach was such a theory. Consequently, Thatcherism could be viewed as not being pure Conservatism.

Leadership

A Conservative leader enjoys a power unparalleled in a British political party and yet more Conservative leaders have been dismissed or have conveniently resigned than in any other political party. This paradox is easy to explain. Loyalty to the leadership is paramount but only as long as the leadership is successful (i.e. winning elections). Most party leaders have stepped down due to fears (or their realisation) of electoral defeat. Most notably, Harold Macmillan (1963) and Margaret Thatcher (1990) were persuaded to step down because they were perceived as electoral liabilities. Neither Thatcher nor Macmillan ever lost a general election. Alec Douglas Home, William Hague and Michael Howard never won an election; while Iain Duncan Smith never even had the opportunity to fight one.

The developments in the procedure for choosing the leader of the Conservative Party have been an interesting comment on how the party has evolved. Until 1965, the party leader 'emerged'. Discussions were held behind the scenes and a name was brought forth. The appointment of Douglas-Home as leader in 1963 caused such bitter acrimony the party moved to hold elections for the leadership. These were first held in 1965. Every Conservative MP could vote for the leader. The original method was a complicated procedure of a maximum of three 'wasting' ballots.

On the first ballot, the leading candidate needed an absolute majority and a lead of over 15% over their nearest rival. In the event of this not happening, anybody could stand for the second ballot, but the winner still needed an absolute majority. If there were still no winner, a third ballot would be held between the three leading candidates from the second ballot. This third ballot would use a preferential system of voting, which would eliminate the weakest candidate and eventually a winner would emerge with a majority of votes. One further innovation was made to this system in 1975. It was agreed the leader should be subject to annual re-election.

This process was reformed by William Hague in 1998. He proposed the party leader be elected by the party membership in a one member one vote system. MPs would vote in a series of elimination ballots to get a short list of two candidates to put to the membership. After each elimination ballot, the last placed candidate would be eliminated, and subsequent ballots held until two candidates remained. This is how both Iain Duncan Smith and David Cameron were elected (see Table 23.2 for the election process of David Cameron). Michael Howard was unopposed when he became party leader, thus removing the need for a ballot of the party membership.

Table 23.2 Results of the 2005 Conservative Party Leadership Election

Candidate	First Round (MPs)	Second Round (MPs)	Third Round (Party membership)
David Cameron	56	90	134 446
Kenneth Clarke	38	-	-
David Davis	62	57	64 398
Liam Fox	42	51	-

Despite the change to the election of the party leader in an attempt to democratise the party, the reverse may actually be the case. It is now going to be very difficult to depose a leader. It will take a motion of no confidence to be requested by 15% of Conservative MPs. If the parliamentary party passes this motion the leader must step down and take no further part in the process. An election will take place following the procedures detailed above. If the no confidence motion is defeated then there can be no further challenges to the party leader for twelve months.

The leader of the Conservative Party is still in a very powerful position, appointing the Party Chairperson and deputies, the Shadow Cabinet, and the Chief Whip and deputy whips. Finally, the party leader is still solely responsible for the party manifesto.

Conservative Board of Management

The formation of this body was part of Hague's reforms of the party, to have a single and unified party. The Board of Management is the supreme decision making body on any matters to do with the Conservative Party. It comprises the Conservative Central Office, the National Union of Conservative Associations, and the parliamentary party. Central Office, which had been formed in 1870, was seen as the civil service of the Conservative Party. It was under the direct control of the party leader but run by the party chairperson. Central Office was often perceived as a liaison point between activists and MPs. Hague's reforms have enabled Central Office to intervene in local constituency affairs.

The National Union, formed in 1867, had been the grassroots of the Conservative Party, representing the various constituency associations. Its key task had been to organise the annual party conference.

1922 Committee

This is a committee of all Conservative MPs. When in opposition, the party leader is excluded from this group, when in Office the entire front bench is excluded. The leader of the Conservative Party has little influence over this body. The 1922 Committee elects its own leader, from 2010 it has been Graham Brady. It advises the party leader of backbench concerns. It has no policy making role but is a channel of communication between the party leader and backbench MPs. This is the body to which Conservative MPs must write if they wish to hold a motion of no confidence in their leader. Any leader that loses the support of the 1922 Committee is likely to be removed.

Funding

Until 1968, no accounts for the Conservative Party were ever published. Thus it was difficult to find out exactly who was giving money to the Conservative Party. There were estimations that around two thirds of Conservative funds came from corporate donations in the 1960s, although this has since dropped. Instead, the Conservative Party seems to benefit from donations from wealthy individuals, including Michael Ashcroft (the former Deputy Chairman of the Conservative Party) and Paul Getty. In the past, such donations were normally kept secret. In 1998 the Committee on Standards in Public Life ruled there should be public disclosure of all donations over £5000 to any political party. Over half of the Conservative Party's finances come from donations and fundraising, as opposed to state funding, membership fees or any commercial activities (Clarke, 2011).

2) The Labour Party

The Labour Party's origins to some extent explain its ideology and structure. Unlike the Liberals and Tories who constructed their parties from within Parliament, Labour was formed in 1900 by a collection of a number of groups operating outside Parliament – including trade unions and socialist societies. Even when a single party was established in 1918 it continued to act as a coalition of interests rather than as a unified party.

Ideology

Labour's ideological underpinning went through a dramatic transformation during the 1980s and 1990s. It has changed its stance on a number of major issues – the most prominent being the change in Clause IV of the party constitution, which had committed the party to full scale nationalisation of the economy. Labour appeared to transform itself from a socialist party to a social democratic one. With Blair's commitment to the 'Third Way', even the label social democratic came under pressure. This has caused problems for subsequent leaders of the party, as to which ideological direction should be taken.

While the original Labour Party claimed to be socialist, an important proviso here is they were committed to achieving socialism via parliamentary means rather than through revolution. Socialism is a system based on the common ownership of the means of production and distribution. The drive is for an egalitarian (equal) system. Socialism was supposed to be a preparatory stage towards achieving the communist utopia. To be able to set up this socialist state, capitalism needed to be overthrown. This had to be achieved through violent and bloody revolution. Anything less would enable capitalism to survive, evolve and dominate. The writings of Karl Marx highlighted how history could only be understood in terms of class. A ruling class exploited the masses throughout time – feudal landowners dominated the peasants and serfs, the bourgeois factory owners dominated the working classes. Such a cycle could only be broken through revolution. The dictatorship of the bourgeoisie would be replaced by the dictatorship of the proletariat, rule by the people, democracy.

Some of the 19th century followers of Marx were Social Democrats. They believed socialism could be achieved through parliamentary means. The formation of the Labour Party could be viewed as the acknowledgement that Parliamentary means were probably the best option for a socialist future in Britain.

The Labour Representation Committee was formed in 1900. After the 1906 general election there were 29 Labour MPs. Keir Hardy was elected as chairman of the Parliamentary Labour Party (PLP). Support for the Labour Party continued to grow, even during World War One when the party was divided over whether or not to support the war cause – the war was perceived to be a consequence of capitalism.

In January 1924, Labour formed a minority administration under Ramsay MacDonald. It only lasted ten months but in that time the leadership demonstrated they could be trusted – even though they gave diplomatic recognition to the Soviet Union. A second minority administration ran from 1929 to 1931. After participating in the National Government of the 1930s and the wartime coalition, Labour won power with a landslide majority in 1945.

This Labour Government founded the Welfare State. The state could be used to create a fairer and more just society. Many industries were nationalised. A National Health Service was created. There was a strong emphasis upon social reforms and improving working conditions.

During the 1950s and 1960s, a revisionist debate arose within the Labour Party. Some in the Labour Party, such as Tony Crosland, argued many of the socialist goals had been achieved (e.g. freedom and equality). Therefore there was no need for further nationalisation. The emphasis should move to a mix of public and private sectors. This debate was to stay with the Labour Party into the 1980s.

After the defeat of the Labour Government in 1979, Michael Foot became party leader. Under his aegis the party moved to the left, adopting a more socialist stance. Policy proposals included greater nationalisation, withdrawal from the EEC, and a stronger emphasis upon the role of the state in providing services. Defeat in 1983 saw this move to the left halted and reversed. Under the leadership of Neil Kinnock, John Smith and Tony Blair, the party moved to the centre ground of British politics. The leadership of Tony Blair saw the public acceptance of many of the Thatcherite policies considered so abhorrent in the 1980s, including privatisation and deregulation. At the 1994 party conference,

Blair first used the label 'New Labour'. The underpinning of New Labour was the Third Way.

The approach of the Third Way was to 'borrow' the best bits of both left and right. There was to be a limited role for the state – it would not necessarily provide or deliver public services, it would make sure they were provided. The market was considered important, as was the concept of citizenship. Everyone has both rights and obligations, and these have to be met. The best way to achieve this is through co-operation and trust.

The clearest example of the extent to which Blair has moved the Labour Party away from its traditional ideological base was over Clause IV of the party constitution. Clause IV committed the party to nationalising all aspects of the economy. No Labour Government had ever implemented it. Even the 1945-51 Government was very selective in what it nationalised. Blair presented Clause IV as a symbol of the party's unwillingness to modernise itself, arguing if Labour wished to form a government ever again, it had to drop Clause IV. The 1918 version was replaced (see Table 2.1 for both versions).

During the Blair and Brown years, the Labour Party attempted to muffle any ideological debate within its ranks. To some extent even the Third Way was shelved. During Gordon Brown's tenure as party leader, Labour appeared to move back towards its ideological roots. This was seen as the best response to the global economic crisis if 2008. Interestingly enough, almost every country hit by this crisis adopted the Brown model to arrest the economic decline i.e. increased public spending, targeted as long term investment in the infrastructure of the country.

After the election defeat of 2010, there was much soul searching within the Labour Party. Many Blairites argued the best root forward was to follow the path laid out by Tony Blair – the Third Way, with its neo-liberal underpinnings. Other parts of the party have looked to the Brown model of targeted public spending, but have been castigated as being out of touch with economic reality. The concern for Labour is it may no longer have any ideological underpinning.

The Leader

Traditionally, a Labour Party leader appears to be at a decided disadvantage when compared with the position of the Conservative Party leader. The idea of a 'leader' can easily be associated with authoritarianism. In fact it was not until 1922 that Ramsay MacDonald was given the title.

The party leader and deputy were both elected by the party conference. This was done through an electoral college where the trade unions had a third of the votes, as did the Constituency Labour Party (CLP) and the Parliamentary Labour Party (PLP). Each third was **not** a block vote. Rather, a system of One Member One Vote (OMOV) existed within each part of the electoral college. In many respects this electoral college was a huge constraint upon the party leader, although it also made the leader rather difficult to remove should he/she wish to hang on to office. Traditionally the Labour leader has had to balance the attitudes of each third of the electoral college. OMOV has, to some extent, reduced this burden.

The election of Ed Miliband (see Table 23.3) highlighted the need for a Labour Party leader to garner support from all three thirds of the electoral college. His brother, David, had support from the PLP and the CLP – in fact, he was the clear favourite within both parts of the electoral college. The trade unions, on the other hand, saw David Miliband as another Tony Blair, and were less forthcoming in giving him their support. Ed Miliband subsequently changed the system to a 'one member, one vote' model, similar to that of the Conservatives, but with a different nomination system.

Table 23.3 Election result for the Labour Party leader (2010)*

Candidates	1st round	2nd round	3rd round	4th round
Dianne Abbott	0.88% PLP 2.45% CLP 4.09% Unions **Total 7.42%**			
Ed Balls	5.01% PLP 3.37% CLP 3.41% Unions **Total 11.79%**	5.17% PLP 4.22% CLP 3.83% Unions **Total 13.23%**	5.43% PLP 4.82% CLP 5.76% Unions **Total 16.02%**	
Andy Burnham	3.01% PLP 2.85% CLP 2.83% Unions **Total 8.68%**	3.03% PLP 3.30%CLP 4.08% Unions **Total 10.41%**		
David Miliband	13.91% PLP 14.69% CLP 9.18% Unions **Total 37.78%**	14.02% PLP 15.08% CLP 9.80% Unions **Total 38.89%**	15.78% PLP 16.08% CLP 10.86% Unions **Total 42.72%**	17.81% PLP 18.14% CLP 13.40% Unions **Total 49.35%**
Ed Miliband	10.53% PLP 9.98% CLP 13.82% Unions **Total 34.33%**	11.11% PLP 11.13% CLP 15.23% Unions **Total 37.47%**	12.12% PLP 12.42% CLP 16.71% Unions **Total 41.26%**	15.52% PLP 15.20% CLP 19.93% Unions **Total 50.65%**

* Figures do not always add up due to rounding

As party leader, both Neil Kinnock and Tony Blair took huge steps towards increasing their powers. Kinnock did so by removing dissenting elements within the Labour Party, most notably the Militant Tendency (a hard-left wing group with Trotskyist leanings which had successfully attempted to infiltrate the Labour Party). His groundwork in uniting the party made it easier for Blair to impose his will upon the party. Rather than being hamstrung by the annual conference - which still decides policy – Blair, with a huge electoral majority, was in a position to appeal directly to the membership and thus bypass conference. Being in office with a huge Parliamentary majority appeared to make Blair unassailable.

Annual Conference

The 1918 constitution made the Annual Conference the supreme policy making body of the Labour Party. This was enshrined in Clause V of the Labour Party constitution. As a consequence, the Annual Conference experienced many gladiatorial contests between the rank-and-file members and the leadership on issues such as Europe or unilateral nuclear disarmament.

For the most part, the Annual Conference has been dominated by the trade unions. Until the 1980s, the trade unions wielded between 80% and 90% of the conference vote. This influence has been reduced on two fronts. Firstly, the unions now wield around 50% of the conference vote. Secondly, but more importantly, is the role of the Annual Conference has changed.

The conference no longer initiates policy. It can still make policy decisions, but these tend to be voting on recommendations from other bodies. With the advent of New Labour there has been significant stage management of the Annual Conference. In many respects, the Annual Conference resembles its Conservative counterpart – a body that meets to cheer on the leadership.

The policy making powers of the Labour conference were surrendered in 1990. That year's conference approved the formation of the National Party Forum. This body, which comprises 175 members from all parts of the party, considers policy proposals before their presentation to conference.

National Executive Committee (NEC)

Like the Annual Conference, the NEC saw its role reduced under the Blair leadership, to the extent he was able to bypass it if the need arose. The role of the NEC was to make sure conference decisions were upheld. It is composed of 32 members from all parts of the party, all bar four of whom are elected by the conference, or at least sections of it. The exceptions are the party leader, deputy leader, party secretary and leader of the European Labour Party.

The NEC has a number of different roles to play. It oversees the party finances, as well as providing lists of suitable candidates to stand for election. The NEC also performs a disciplinary role within the party, and is involved in research and policy development, as well as publicity.

The party leader may be capable of bypassing the NEC, but this does not mean the leader can get their own supporters elected. Even Tony Blair was not always able to get his own supporters on to the NEC. Conference elected members in direct opposition to the preferred 'Blair' candidate (e.g. Liz Davies in 1998, Dennis Skinner in 1999). This appears to be one of the few ways in which the party conference can attempt to keep a check on the party leader.

Parliamentary Labour Party (PLP)
These are the MPs elected to Parliament. Within this group there is also the European Parliamentary Labour Party (EPLP). In theory, all members elected under the Labour Party label are bound to follow conference decisions. Traditionally, this was the case – at least when Labour was in opposition. When in government, the Labour Party leadership has always felt more comfortable in exerting their own authority, and the PLP have been no different.

Constituency Labour Party (CLP)
Although considered to be the weakest part of the Labour Party, the CLP does play an important role. Each constituency party selects its own candidate, using the OMOV system. The only restriction appears to be candidates are chosen from NEC lists of suitable candidates. In the mid-1990s, women-only shortlists were imposed on some constituencies (although this policy was later successfully contested). There have been occasions where the party leadership have either blocked a particular candidature (Liz Davies in Leeds North East in 1997) or imposed their own preferred candidate (Shaun Woodward in St. Helens South in 2001). For the most part, the various CLPs are able to select their own candidates.

Funding
This may appear to be the achilles heel of the Labour Party. They are dependent upon funding from the trade unions. Affiliation fees are the largest part of Labour's funding – comprising around a third of revenue. Donations and membership fees respectively comprise around a quarter and a sixth of Labour's funding. With the need to declare individual donations of over £500, most of the individual subscriptions and affiliation fees fail to reach such a threshold, thus Labour is under no obligation to reveal the sources of such funding. Accusations are thus made about the secret power that the trade unions wield over the Labour Party.

3. Liberal Democrats
The Liberal Democrats are the 'third' party in UK politics. They are the third largest party in UK politics, having formed coalition governments at Westminster, in both the Scottish Parliament and the Welsh Assembly, as well as running or forming coalitions in local councils throughout Britain.

The Liberal Democrats were formed in 1989 by the fusion of the majority of the Liberal Party and the majority of the Social Democratic Party (SDP). Their first leader was Paddy Ashdown. At that time, the Liberal Democrats belonged to what was described as the centre ground of British politics. This generally meant they positioned themselves between Labour and the Conservatives. Under Ashdown's leadership, the Liberal Democrats adopted a stance of being 'equi-distant' from each of the major parties. This proved to be impossible as Labour moved to the right, particularly under Smith and Blair. With the possibility of being squeezed out of existence with the movement of the Labour Party, the Liberal Democrats repositioned themselves a little to the left of New Labour. This did not mean the Liberal Democrats were a socialist party but rather they highlighted the need for some state involvement in areas such as running the economy, and providing public services (such as health and education). The Liberal Democrats advocated higher direct taxation to fund the state provision of these services.

Ideology
One of the problems when trying to identify the ideological underpinning of the Liberal Democrats is, as noted earlier, they are a fusion of two separate parties. The Social Democratic Party was a centre left party, created when Labour lurched to the left in the early 1980s. The merger with the Liberals appeared to be a good match as there was a degree of ideological overlap. A strand of social liberalism had dominated Liberal thinking since the late 1920s. This approach saw the need for state intervention in the economy, as well as to help create jobs. By the 1980s, there was a clear line of thinking about using the state to help individuals realise their potential. Within all of this, there was a clear overlap between social democracy and social liberalism.

Under the leadership of Nick Clegg, and this has been more noticeable since the formation of the coalition government in 2010, there has been a move away from social liberalism and back to classical liberalism. This is a very clear shift to the right within the Liberal Democratic Party. The emphasis moved to tax cutting (compared to the idea of putting a penny on income tax to fund education which the Liberal Democrats espoused between 1992 and 2003) and reducing the role of the state. This classical liberalism is a lot closer to many of the tenets of Thatcherism, which is probably one of the reasons why Nick Clegg feels more comfortable with the Conservatives than with Labour. It is also worth noting the top positions within the Liberal Democratic Party under Clegg were held by more classical liberals than social liberals.

The Leader
The leader of the Liberal Democratic Party is an extremely important person. As the 'third' party of British politics, they need a dynamic leader; one who can be recognized in the media and is able to get across the party's policies to voters. This was epitomised in Paddy Ashdown, the first leader. He set a benchmark none of his successors have reached.

All party members are involved in electing the leader. This is carried out in a postal ballot, using the Single Transferable Vote (STV) (see chapter 20).

Minor Parties

There are numerous minor parties in the UK. These are parties that fight elections, with little hope of winning overall control but which hope to gain representation.

i) UK Independence Party (UKIP)

This is the most prominent of the minor political parties in the UK, which is sometimes considered to be an offshoot from the Conservative Party. UKIP advocates withdrawal from the European Union, but surprisingly has had candidates elected to the European Parliament in every election since 1999.

ii) British National Party (BNP)

The BNP is often considered to be a fascist party. It advocates that non-Britons should be encouraged to return to their country of origin, but such a move should be voluntary. Under the leadership of Nick Griffin, the BNP has tried to present itself as a moderate party that puts British interests first. This has resulted in some electoral success at both the local and European level. Griffin and Andrew Brons were both elected to the European Parliament in 2009. Brons has since left the BNP to form his own party – the British Democratic Party.

iii) Green Party

The Greens were founded in 1973. As their name suggests, they are part of the environmental or ecological movement, which includes other organisations such as Friends of the Earth and Green Peace. The Green Party is not directly related to any of these other organisations.

The Green Party has had a chequered electoral history. This has been due, in no small part, to the major parties stealing their policies. After the 1989 elections to the European Parliament (where the Green Party won 15% of the vote but no seats), a brighter future was predicted. As ever, the major parties simply increased their emphasis upon environmental issues, and Green Party support faded.

Subsequently, the Green Party suffered a damaging internal conflict. Yet it has since emerged stronger and has gained representation at the local level, as well as in the Scottish Parliament, the Greater London Authority and the European Parliament. A significant breakthrough was made in the 2010 General Election when the then-party leader, Caroline Lucas, was elected as MP for Brighton Pavilion.

iv) Scottish Nationalist Party (SNP)

The SNP was formed in 1934 but did not really impinge upon British politics until the 1960s. In the 1970s, the SNP gained electoral success but after the defeat of the referendum on devolution in 1979 (see chapter 27), their success waned.

In the 1990s, the SNP experienced a major revival. While they have yet to achieve the votes and seats won in the 1974 elections, they established themselves as the opposition to Labour in Scotland, before becoming a minority government in Scotland and then a majority government in 2011.

The platform of the SNP is based upon an independent Scotland within Europe. The SNP treat the elections to the Scottish Parliament as being far more important than Westminster elections. A referendum on independence will be held in 2014, having received approval from Westminster.

v) Plaid Cymru

Whereas the SNP aim for Scottish independence, Plaid Cymru have set themselves far more modest aims. This is due, in no part, to their limited electoral success. Plaid Cymru aim to promote and defend the Welsh language and culture. Ideas of independence are no more than a pipe dream. Even demands for devolution have been limited. The devolution referendum was heavily defeated in 1979. The 1997 referendum saw a minuscule majority on a turnout of around 50% (see chapter 28). Thus there appears to be no great desire for an independent Wales at this stage.

Electorally, Plaid Cymru have not had the same success as the SNP. They do, however, consider themselves to be the opposition to Labour in Wales, and even formed a coalition with Labour (2007-2011). Prior to the 2011 elections, Plaid Cymru were the second largest party in the Welsh Assembly. Similarly, prior to the general election of 2010 they had more Welsh seats than the Conservatives or the Liberal Democrats at Westminster. The problem for the party was how to build upon this base. Plaid Cymru need to find a way of breaking out from their Welsh language heartlands in the Northwest of Wales. The problem has been in the last two sets of elections where they seem to have taken a step backwards.

vi) Northern Ireland Parties

Northern Irish politics should be viewed as completely different from the mainland political scene because of the issues of religious rivalries and the border between the North and the South of Ireland. Northern Ireland does, however, have an impact upon British politics – not least from the 18 MPs it sends to Westminster. Some of the Northern Ireland parties have been in the position of holding the balance of power during a hung Parliament (most recently during the latter stages of the Major Government).

There are several parties representing each side of the religious divide, as well as some non-sectarian parties. On the Protestant side the two main parties are the Ulster Unionist Party and the Democratic Unionist Party (who have links with the Orange Order). Of the two main parties, the Democratic Unionists are considered to be the more militant, but they are now the dominant unionist party.

On the Catholic side there is the Social Democratic and Labour Party (SDLP) and Sinn Fein. The SDLP has an open membership policy but is mainly supported by Catholics. Sinn Fein is the political arm of the IRA. Their Westminster MPs are unable to take their seats because they refuse to swear an oath of allegiance to the Monarch. The non-sectarian parties include the Alliance, who gained their first MP in 2010. All of the above parties have gained representation in the Northern Ireland Assembly (see chapter 29 for more information).

vii) Others
There are numerous other political parties operating in Britain. The most prominent of these is probably **Respect**. This party is led by George Galloway (who won the Bradford West by-election in 2012). It emerged out of the anti-Iraq war campaign, but has had little success beyond that of its leader.

Beyond this, there are many other small and fringe parties; some more serious than others. This includes a wide range of parties such as the Monster Raving Loony Party, the English Democrats and the Socialist Alliance.

Conclusion
Despite the decline of two party domination, the electoral system still favours two party politics with one party government. In the post-war era, there have been periods of minority government and, after the 2010 election, a coalition government. The previous period of coalition government was during World War Two, and before that, during the 1930s with the Government of National Unity.

The erosion of support for the two major parties suggests we are seeing the end of the two-party system, which has dominated British politics in the past. It must be noted, however, similar forecasts were made during the 1980s when the Labour Party stared into the abyss of electoral oblivion and the Liberal-SDP Alliance looked set to restructure British party politics. The results of 1983 and 1987 showed just how far out such predictions were.

At the same time, when looking at Scotland, Wales and Northern Ireland, the two-party system is broken. In both the Scottish Parliament and the Welsh Assembly there is four-party (or multi-party) politics and regular coalition governments. The Northern Ireland Assembly has coalition government and multi-party politics. Local government across the UK has also highlighted the growth in multi-party politics, where few electoral contests are a straight fight between Labour and the Conservatives. Thus what we are now seeing across the UK is not just the fragmentation or the fracturing of the party system. Rather, there are multiple party systems across different tiers of government in the UK.

Westminster is sometimes described as the only remaining example of two-party politics in Britain. Yet, after the 2010 election there were ten parties represented at Westminster. The 2012 by-election in Bradford West saw this number rise to eleven. Two-party politics is very much under pressure again.

Selected bibliography

Allern, Elin & Bale, Tim. (2012). "Political parties and interest groups: Disentangling complex relationships", *Party Politics* vol. 18-1, pp. 7-25.

Blyth, Mark & Katz, Richard. (2005). "From Catch-all Parties to Cartelisation: The Political Economy of the cartel Party", *West European Politics* vol. 28-1, pp. 33-60.

Buckler, Steve & Dolowitz, David. (2012). "Ideology Matters: Party Competition, Ideological Positioning and the Case of the Conservative Party under David Cameron", *British Journal of Politics and International Relations* vol. 14-4, pp. 576-594.

Clark, Alistair. (2012). *Political Parties in the UK*: Palgrave.

Gamble, Andrew. (2012). "Inside New Labour", *British Journal of Politics and International Relations* vol. 14-3, pp. 492-502.

Pedersen, Helene. (2012). "What do Parties Want? Policy versus Office", *West European Politics* vol. 35-4, pp. 896-910.

Websites

action.labour.org.uk/with-us
Homepage of the Labour Party

www.conservatives.com
Homepage of the Conservative Party

www.dup2win.com
Homepage of the Democratic Unionist Party

www.libdems.org.uk
Homepage of the Liberal Democratic Party

www.plaidcymru.org/
Plaid Cymru homepage

www.politicsresources.net/area/uk/man.htm
A list of election manifestos since 1945

www.sdlp.ie/index.php
Homepage of the Social Democratic and Labour Party

www.sinnfein.ie/
Sinn Fein homepage

www.snp.org.uk
Homepage of the SNP

www.uup.org
Homepage of the Ulster Unionist Party

Questions
1. To what extent do political parties impede Parliamentary democracy?
2. The two-party system that exists in Britain today is gradually being undermined. In what ways, if at all, may this be of benefit to British politics?
3. "Minor parties, when in coalition, wield power far beyond their numbers. This undermines democracy." Discuss.

CHAPTER 24 // MEDIA

Contents
- **Introduction**
- **The Political Role of the Media**
- **Ownership and the Media**
- **The Influence of the Press**
- **The Role of Television**
- **Coverage of By-elections and General Elections**
- **The 'New Media'**
- **Conclusion: The Trivialisation of Politics?**

Introduction

An examination of the political scene would be deficient without an analysis of the impact of the media. By this term, it is important to note it does not just include print and broadcast media, but also newer forms available via the internet, especially social media. The media comprises a range of methods of mass communication of such things as news, sport, and entertainment to a wide variety of audiences. This could be through a satellite television channel, a local newspaper or a blog.

A responsible mass media is of immense value to furthering democratic ideals. There is also an inevitable corollary that a blatantly biased and monopolistically controlled media is not just a distortion of the democratic process but can be anti-democratic. The trend in Britain towards the concentration of ownership not just in the written word (newspapers, journals, and publishing houses) but in satellite and cable television is regarded with ever-growing concern. It has been suggested media moguls such as Rupert Murdoch should not be seen as 'dangerous' yet, but the possibilities for oligopoly (domination by a few) obviously exist. Such a fear became more prominent after 2011, with the investigation into phone hacking at the *News of the World* and the subsequent Leveson Report of November 2012. As a result, around the world there were allegations about, and investigations into, such practices within the media.

There is the further confusion that in order to maximise sales and advertising revenue, the tabloid sector of the newspaper industry has reached new depths in trivialising issues, emphasising personalities often in an offensive manner and concocting scandals with little supporting evidence. This tendency has generally left readers with a superficial, distorted impression of the political process and social issues. To make matters worse, the broadsheet (or 'quality') papers also appear to be lowering some of their standards for exactly the same reasons.

With the growth in the number of television channels, there have been allegations of 'dumbing down' across all parts of the broadcast media. This has been made worse with the growth in the 'new' media. The sale of advertising on the internet is growing in proportion, compared to the more 'traditional' outlets of broadcast or print media. There is sometimes a suspicion of a race to the bottom within the media in an attempt to entice readers, viewers or listeners – as well as advertising revenue.

Other concerns have also been raised against the broadsheets. Apart from their biased manner on political issues, there is also a strong tendency to reflect middle class perspectives while claiming these positions to be both detached and analytical.

The importance of the print media has waned dramatically in recent years. Without disparaging the role of the press, television is the communication medium with the greatest political impact – even with the growth in the 'new media'. By law broadcast media is supposed to be impartial and evenhanded in its presentation. Yet there are constant complaints from both the 'left' and the 'right' of politics against a perceived bias in programmes. This shows just how difficult it is to achieve strict impartiality.

The implication of these complaints is that television is so significant a medium any detected bias is bound to be highly influential on the political preferences of viewers. Successive governments, whilst disclaiming any pressure on the BBC, ITV or Channels 4 and 5, have been anxious to utilise the channels for their own advancement. Satellite and cable television are also important players in the dissemination of information. Added to this is the suggestion that the influence of internet-based media as a means of obtaining information will outstrip – if it has not already done so – all other forms of media.

The Political Role of the Media

No real consensus has emerged among commentators on the influence print and broadcast media make on society as an entity and individuals as voters. It should always be borne in mind the vast majority of the population has only a passing interest in politics and hence, unlike activists, tend to obtain their information, and perhaps reinforcement of their prejudices, from the media. In Britain, despite there still being a bias in the majority of the press towards small 'c' conservatism, as well as the Conservative Party, there is considered to be sufficient variety of views and debates in the newspapers and on television for the media to have a significant impact on the democratic process.

There is, however, disagreement on how this impact is exercised. These can be separated under three broad headings: the objective or neutral approach; the liberal tradition; and, the radical interpretation.

i. The 'Neutral' Approach

This is often considered the aim which many in the media – both broadcast and print – would desire as being the ideal treatment of news and opinion. Within the print media, there is scant evidence of such an ideal ever being achieved.

There is even less balance on the internet. Blogs, for example, give opinions and possible interpretations of events without necessarily being accurate. As long as the press – be it magazines, journals, newspapers, or even books – is in private hands, the political partisanship of its proprietors is inevitable. The extent to which this may distort the presentation of information to the public is debatable. When there are allegations of stories being blocked, partisanship (or maybe personal or economic interests) may come to the fore. The refusal to publish Chris Patten's memoirs by Murdoch-owned publishers, HarperCollins, could be viewed as a case in point. Patten, the former Governor of Hong Kong, was somewhat scathing of the Chinese Government. Had these views been published, Murdoch's business ventures into the People's Republic of China may have been damaged. The publication of Patten's book was stopped on the grounds of his writings not being up to the required standard. This did not stop Pan from publishing Patten's memoirs instead.

Television does not escape censure either. Its critics constantly complain of bias. Phone-ins on radio and letters in the press accuse all channels of bias towards one or other of the parties. With the growth in 24-hour news coverage, there has been a similar growth in complaints of bias – but not just at the party-political level. The problem of 24-hour news is about the speed and accuracy of the reporting. This was best exemplified during the Iraq War in 2003, where the port of Umm Qasr was reported to have been captured nine times before it actually fell. The suggestions of bias (in the Iraq War) came as a result of correspondents reporting damage and civilian casualties from within Baghdad. The suggestion was such reporting would undermine support for the British troops.

Broadcast reporting, particularly at election time, is supposed to be impartial. Equal coverage should be given to the two major parties, but coverage should also be given of the Liberal Democrats and, in the case of Scotland and Wales, the nationalist parties as well. Thereafter, it becomes more problematic as to the levels of coverage each party should get – which may be dependent upon previous electoral success. If there is coverage of a particular constituency, all candidates must be mentioned – even if it means simply scrolling their names up the television screen. In general, at least at election time, the broadcast media does indeed act in a neutral way – although rigorous questioning of leading politicians by the likes of John Humphries on the Today Programme on Radio 4 suggested all candidates should be given as difficult a time as possible. This may not be considered neutral behaviour, as some interviewing techniques could be described as hostile, but it is generally evenhanded.

ii. The Liberal Tradition
This perspective tends to take a rather benign view of the role of government in its relationship with the media and in the plurality of views in society. It is acknowledged the government from time-to-time has the right to place curbs

on the divulging of information and comment e.g. during wartime and in combating terrorism. In emergency situations the public appear to accept the right of the government to clamp down on full media freedom. An example often cited here was in fighting the terrorist activities of the IRA. There was no public outcry against the ban on the right of Sinn Fein members being able to utter their views in their own voices on television in the 1980s. This may, however, have been because anyone voicing that perspective may have been included in the ban.

There has always existed disquiet in the media and amongst sections of the public of how excessive this kind of censorship can become. Successive British Governments have been accused of operating too frequently in a climate of secrecy unparalleled in most Western democracies. For instance, there is irritation at the imposition of 'D' notices. These are Defence Notices, which can be sent to newspapers or broadcasters requesting non-publication of specific material. While the system is voluntary, the media acquiesces to the 'D' notice requests because the alternative could be a more stringent form of censorship. The government can also apply pressure on the media not to release stories (e.g. the 'Death on the Rock' television documentary about the alleged murder by British security personnel of IRA suspects in Gibraltar).

Yet the media appear sometimes to be almost willing to work with the government over what should – or, more accurately, should not – be reported. There was self-censorship by both the BBC and ITN during the Iraq War (Stanyer, 2004). Dissent against the war was hardly covered, and, although there was acknowledgement of civilian casualties, the numbers were never reported. This self-censorship was again evident during the Libyan uprising against Gadhafi in 2011. NATO airstrikes were reported, but allegations of civilian deaths appeared to be questioned by reporters on a regular basis.

In the end, however, the liberal tradition stresses the more usual 'open government' approach which allows a free press to prosper and television channels are compelled by law to be objective and impartial. Through the lobby system and the so-called 'reliable sources' the media is able to convey government and parliamentary information and comment. Of course, this sometimes results in embarrassment for politicians, especially over the MPs expenses scandal prior to the 2010 General Election. Sadly, all MPs appeared to be tarred with the same brush, even when there was no evidence of wrong doing by individual MPs.

If it is contended that the price to be paid for this liberal free market tradition is a strongly biased press in favour of one political party, then the answer is there is nothing to stop rival newspapers being established favouring other political parties. In any case it is almost inevitable the Conservatives would benefit from the bias of the majority of the press, since in a free market it is natural the owners of private companies like the publishing corporations would favour the party that believes in free entreprise. This is one of the reasons why Tony Blair strongly courted Rupert Murdoch prior to the 1997 General Election. With only the *Mirror* and the *Guardian* giving open support to Labour in the mid-1990s, Labour needed to look elsewhere for backing. By adopting policies favourable to the Murdoch empire, and giving access to those papers, it enabled Blair to obtain personal support, if not support for his party. In 1997, 2001 and 2005, the *Sun* backed Blair specifically, rather than the Labour Party. Two years after Blair stepped down as party leader, the *Sun* reverted to the Conservatives.

iii. The Radical Concept

As with the liberal perspective, the radical interpretation acknowledges the media does have an influence on the politics of a nation. The emphasis is different, being placed upon the ability to mould public opinion through a positive consciousness to do so. It is not that the journalists, editors and owners do not simply reflect public attitudes but they actually help to shape public acceptance of traditional institutions like the law, Parliament, or the monarchy and what can be loosely dubbed as 'middle class' attitudes. Those who raise objections to such institutions and views can then be labelled as extremists, radicals or at least irresponsible. There are exceptional circumstances when individual papers challenge the orthodox perspective. An example of such a circumstance was in February 2001 when the *Guardian* newspaper challenged the Treason Felony Act of 1848, which makes it a criminal offence to advocate the abolition of the Monarchy. Although this court case was thrown out, it did enable the *Guardian* to publish a number of articles questioning the continued existence of the monarchy.

For the most part it is a myth to believe the media reflects a variety of competing opinions. In fact it generally confines itself to quite a limited band of conventional 'safe' culturally and societally stereotypical views. Attempts to establish and maintain a popular 'left wing' newspaper have proved singularly unrewarding. The demise of left wing or Labour supporting newspapers such as *The News on Sunday* in the 1980s and *Today* in 1995 is considered proof of this contention. The *Mirror*, while still the largest Labour-supporting newspaper, appears to have become far more 'conventional' in its outlook.

Even in television there is alarm at any attempt to depart from the safe, consensual view. In recent times, this was exemplified by the coverage of the public spending cuts. There appeared to be tacit acceptance of cuts across the board. Where there was debate was over the speed and depth of the cuts; any critics of the policy of spending cuts – those, for example, advocating no cuts whatsoever – tended to be marginalised.

This generally reinforces the radical view that it is virtually impossible for the media to be neutral or objective. Any news printed or broadcast is manufactured, in the sense it has been filtered through a highly subjective process of what is thought to be worth publishing. Thus many of the tabloids will focus on lurid headlines, dramatic events, and personalities rather than more analytical articles. For example in the treatment of industrial disputes much more attention appears to be paid to strikes especially if they are violent than to a description and discussion of negotiations leading up to strike action. The strikers will probably be interviewed on the picket line or outside the factory gates, with all the background noise and distractions, while the management representatives are more likely to be interviewed in the calm of an office, or in the studio, exuding an air of reasonableness and considered authority.

Another example is the way in which the tabloid press tends to concentrate on social security 'scroungers' rather than on tax evaders. Each appearance of a new social phenomenon receives screaming headlines in lurid terms such as 'lager louts', 'football hooligans', 'bogus asylum seekers' and 'chavs'. The use of such abusive phrases like 'loony lefties' or 'bully boys' soon becomes part of folklore embedded in readers' minds.

Ownership and the Media

The political bias within the press inevitably raises the question of its ownership. To hear the outcry of critics – mainly from the left – bemoaning the danger of a few proprietors pumping out their propaganda may make people think that this is a new phenomenon. Anybody studying the history of the popular press will see how exaggerated this view is. Rupert Murdoch is a household name, as was Robert Maxwell, but Northcliffe, Rothermere and Beaverbrook were equally prominent ones in the early part of the twentieth century. It was these newspaper owners pursuing such overt political aims who provoked the bitter comment, attributed to Prime Minister Baldwin in the 1930s, that they 'exercised power without responsibility'. The only thing that may have changed since then is the subtlety of newspaper owners with regard to the pursuit of their political aims.

Given the competitive, highly technical and expensive nature of press ownership it seems inevitable there would be a concentration of ownership once a mass readership was established. The concentration of ownership is one problem. There is also the issue of the other interests of the leading newspaper publishers, be it publishing, television, or other commercial interests. Currently eight publishers account for all daily national newspaper sales: Associated Newspapers, Guardian Media Group, Independent News and Media, News International, Northern and Shell Media, Pearson, Press Holdings, Trinity Mirror (OFT, 2008, p. 19). Table 24.1 details which national papers are owned by which groups, and the political parties to which they have given support in recent general elections. Table 24.2 gives a flavour of the extent to which regional and local newspapers have been bought up by the owners of the national dailies.

There are over a thousand weekly local or regional newspapers, and over a hundred local or regional dailies (OFT 2009), but they are owned, for the most part, by only five companies. What is also of note is the extent to which media magnates now have interests far beyond newspapers and broadcasting. News International, which is the British branch of Rupert Murdoch's News Corporation, is an extreme example of the breadth of ownership that now exists. It owns or has interests in newspapers (The Times, The Sunday Times, The Sun), publishing companies (HarperCollins, Fontana Books, Granada Books), broadcast media (BSkyB, LWT, cable television, Twentieth Century Fox, Metromedia), Reuters News Agency, property, oil, gas and transport.

Table 24.1 National Newspaper Ownership

PAPER	OWNER	PARTY PREFERENCE 2010 (2005, 1997)
The Dailies		
Daily Mail	Associated Newspapers	Con (Con, Con)
Telegraph	Press Holdings	Con (Con, Con)
Express	Northern & Shell	Con (Con, Con)
Mirror	Trinity Mirror	Lab (Lab, Lab)
Sun	News International	Con (Lab, Lab)
Guardian	Guardian Media Group	Lib Dem (Lab/Lib Dem,
Times	News International	Lab)
Independent	Independent News &	Con (Lab, Euro-sceptic)
Financial Times	Media	Lab/Lib Dem (Lib Dem,
Star	Pearson	Lab)
	Northern & Shell	Con (Lab, Lab)
The Sundays		Con (No preference, Lab)
Mail on Sunday		
Sunday Telegraph	Associated Newspapers	
Sunday Express	Press Holdings	Con (Con, Con)
Sunday Mirror	Northern & Shell	Con (Con, Con)
News of the World	Trinity Mirror	Con (Con, Con)
(now the Sun on	News International	Lab (Lab, Lab)
Sunday)		Con (Lab, Lab)
Observer	Guardian Media Group	
Sunday Times	News International	Lib Dem (Lab, Lab)
Independent on Sunday	Independent News &	Con (Lab, Con)
The People	Media	Lib Dem (Not Lab, Lab)
Daily Star Sunday	Trinity Mirror	Coalition (Lab, Lab)
	Northern & Shell	Con (No preference, did not exist)

Table 24.2 Regional Press Publishers (January 2014)

Group Name	Number of Titles	Total circulation
Trinity Mirror plc	130	8 533 436
Newsquest Media Group	185	5 434 471
Local World	107	4 697 195
Johnston Press plc	213	4 362 909
Associated Newspapers Ltd	1	3 871 525
Evening Standard Ltd	1	3 454 450
The Midland News Association Ltd	17	1 987 183
ARCHANT	66	1 463 939
D. C. Thomson & Co. Ltd	6	1 357 608
Tindle Newspapers Ltd	110	981 065
City AM	1	645 605
Independent News & Media	6	446 343
Romanes Media Group	28	398 941
NWN Media Ltd	14	398 187
Bullivant Media Ltd	9	305 303
CN Group Ltd	10	297 906
Irish News Ltd	1	245 502
KM Group	16	244 906
Guiton Group	5	189 144
Champion Newspapers	8	163 140
TOTAL (103 Publishers)	**1 111**	**40 607 310**

Source: www.newspapersoc.org.uk/sites/default/files/pdf/Top-20-
Publishers_January-2014.pdf

The Influence of the Press

There have been a number of deep analytical studies of the effects of the mass media in general and the press in particular on politics. Of particular note are works by Ralph Negrine, as well as James Curran and Jean Seaton.

For many years there was the comforting **reinforcement theory**, that is, the press simply reinforced readers' prejudices. Hence, newspapers did very little to change peoples' views. In fact surveys suggested, for example, during the 1980s the majority of *Sun* readers believed it actually supported the Labour Party despite its strident pro-Thatcher line. The accuracy of such claims have been questioned, as it appeared such readers either ignored the 'political' content of the paper or even if still Labour supporters had their views influenced by constant references to 'loony lefties' and stories directed against the Labour Party. The 1992 election campaign demonstrated this bias, with the *Sun* having a picture of Neil Kinnock with a blue light bulb behind him on the front page. Beneath this was a statement saying that if Kinnock became prime minister, would the last person to leave the country please turn out the light. The day after the campaign, the *Sun* headline read: "It was the Sun wot won it".

The reinforcement perspective has been supported by the agenda-setting theory. This states the media are not so foolish as to tell people what to think but hope to achieve their ends by more subtle means. They influence the public through establishing an all-pervasive set of factors encompassing what people think, as well as the perceived importance of certain political issues. Although the newspapers do not always achieve their aims by getting the public to accept their agendas, the constant interaction between the press and its audience sets the agenda which part of the readership are lulled into accepting.

An alternative school of thought, the **independent effect theory**, has a growing claim to attention. It asserts the press does indeed have a direct and independent effect on public attitudes and behaviour in certain circumstances even if these effects may be small. While there is insufficient evidence to provide conclusive findings, the general drift of this theory is not wholly incompatible with the previous theories.

The power of the media cannot be explained by the reinforcement of readers' and viewers' opinions. The press does have a short term impact, in the long run its influence can be crucial if only in the negative sense. For instance, if a political party is hardly ever mentioned in a particular newspaper, readers may well tend to ignore such a party. A former *Sun* editor recently admitted this was exactly the stance his paper had taken with the Liberal Democrats in the past.

The trouble with these theories is they suggest there is such a phenomenon as a grand media 'effect'. Pursuing this line of thought does not get us very far. It is more useful to think in terms of a number of intensities of effect. These could be conditioned by volatile factors like the changing economic, political and social scene.

Media effects theories tend also to play down the extent to which people's backgrounds and life experience shape their political outlook. These, until the saturation of the mass media, were always the most dominant in shaping political views.

It could be argued even if the media does not change people's minds, it is at least influential in deciding which issues people do think about. In particular, the news focus on a Royal event (wedding or funeral) at the expense of all other news coverage leaves very little for people to talk about. Even those complaining about such coverage are only able to do so as a result of the media coverage.

General elections, by-elections, social and economic issues all to some degree are shaped by press coverage. While in the 1987 general election the vast majority of the press gave Thatcher the most favoured of treatment, the 1997 election was simply the 'Get rid of the Tories' campaign. The 2001 campaign, in comparison, was tedious, and 2005 was little better. Labour was expected to win each time; the question was merely by how much? This was despite the influence of the Iraq War in the 2005 campaign. The 2010 election generated much greater interest. Much of this was a result of the three televised leaders' debates.

The Role of Television

With due respect to the press there can be no doubt it is the impact of television which has raised the most serious consideration of the connection between the media and politics. Between 1951 and 1964 the number of television sets rose from 1 million to 13 million (Curran and Seaton, 1999, p. 174). A BBC survey in 1962 found around 57% of adults named television as a major source of information for news, compared to around 33% naming newspapers. Ten years later, another study found the television figure had risen to almost 85%. With satellite, digital and cable television, plus television over the internet, virtually every household has access to television if they so wish.

With greater demand for information, television has increased its coverage of political activities. Televising the proceedings in the Houses of Parliament is one obvious example. There are also many news programmes (e.g. Panorama, Question Time), programmes with satirical comment (e.g. Have I Got News For You, The Mark Thomas Comedy Product, Bremner, Bird and Fortune), as well as numerous documentaries. Coverage of political issues such as the fuel protests of September 2000 has also increased. International political coverage, be it US Presidential Elections or the uprisings across the Arab World in 2011, is also much more prominent. Yet, while there is wider coverage of political issues (rather than simply politics), it is unclear as to the degree of influence television has. The reporting of political stories informs viewers, but whether that will then compel further activity is not clear. Many people have given financial aid to disaster relief charities as a result of television coverage e.g. the Indian Ocean tsunami on Boxing Day 2004, the floods in Pakistan in 2010, or to the famine in Somalia in 2011.

The Influence of Television

There is a whole range of ways in which it might be said television plays a part in influencing public opinion and shaping political response.

1. Television is primarily a visual medium. The vital ingredient is presentation. There have been numerous allegations that television prefers slick packaging to detailed verbal analysis, and there is some substance to them. This can be viewed as the tabloidisation of television, or even as dumbing down. Simply look to the recent makeovers to news broadcasts on the major terrestrial television channels – and the BBC in particular. Viewers have become accustomed to professional presentation and no longer simply want a 'talking heads' approach. While such programmes still exist (e.g. Newsnight and Question Time), and they give politicians the opportunity to explain and defend their views, these programmes are appearing in late evening slots rather than on prime time television. During the 2010 General Election, the leaders debates showed the extent to which presentation was more important than substance. David Cameron **was seen** to win the final debate, yet the content of his responses was often vacuous.

2. The selection of visual images can be vital in influencing viewers' perceptions. The way in which a demonstration is presented can prejudice the public against a cause. There have been charges of camera teams inciting demonstrators to extrovert behaviour in order to obtain newsworthy pictures.

3. To counter point 2), it is important to note public service broadcasting in Britain is bound to be impartial. The viewer is supposed to be able to obtain a balanced presentation of political news and comment. Politicians can be quizzed directly by interviewers and audiences, and quite possibly more effectively than in Parliament. An unsatisfactory answer can be queried on programmes such as Question Time in a way MPs cannot do in Parliament.

Unfortunately, there is a downside to this need for impartiality. In many news programmes the desire to pack in a number of items leads to a stopwatch mentality developing. This, in turn, frustrates full explanations and encourages blandness. Impartiality tends to operate within narrow confines, that is, between the Conservatives, Labour and the Liberal Democrats. Radical ideas, parties and personalities hardly ever get a look in, except if they are regarded as 'characters'. Even these are on the wane.

4. Rather than focusing on issues, the media as a whole tend to focus upon personalities. It was suggested, by the likes of Tony Benn, that this trivialises politics and distorts the issues. The problem is television thrives on visual presentation – a gladiatorial contest between party leaders, with a hostile audience – rather than on the intricate detail of particular policies. The political parties have recognised this, and consequently try to choose leaders who are telegenic (David Cameron has clearly modelled himself on Tony Blair). With general elections being more like presidential campaigns, the party leaders are the natural focus. The extent to which this is a desirable development appears immaterial.

5. This finally leads us to the endgame of media manipulation: spin. The political parties seem to believe elections are won and lost in the media - and particularly on television. Thus there is a need for media management. The spin doctors are not a new phenomenon. The likes of Tim Bell and Bernard Ingham helped model and present Margaret Thatcher, while Tony Blair had Alastair Campbell. The spin doctors work on the snappy angles and the soundbites. They present the opinions of their political bosses, and defend them. Not so much media managers as possible arch-propagandists.

Coverage of By-Elections and General Elections
Media coverage, and particularly that of television, is an essential part of election campaigns. With near blanket coverage it must be asked as to the effect such

coverage has on the outcome of a general election. By-elections do not always receive the same levels of coverage.

The first general election to be covered by television was in 1959, but it was in such a cursory, limited fashion as to be negligible in its effects on public opinion. Since then coverage has increased to the saturation levels of today. Political parties plan their campaigns to meet the demands of television, knowing full well success or failure can hinge on their performances. The visual impact was of great importance. In the 2001 campaign, the morning press conferences were covered live on television channels such as BBC News 24, where the daily agendas would be outlined very clearly. The soundbites were prepared and presented in a very slick manner by all the major parties. This has continued in subsequent elections, with occasional delays – almost as if to keep the press waiting. Press conferences that were supposed to start promptly at 8am, often started at quarter past the hour!

Despite the wealth of research it is still difficult, however, to pontificate on the influence of television in moulding public opinion during a general election campaign to the extent of changing the outcome of the result.

The 'New Media'

Recent general elections in the UK have seen numerous people heralding the importance of the 'new media'. These would be the internet elections, where people would surf the internet to found out their political information; and where blogs and web forums would lead discussions and debates on the latest political issues. Such proclamations have turned out to be far from accurate. The 'new media' does play a role, but it tends to be in conjunction with the so-called 'old' media.

A major misperception is that everyone in the UK has internet access at home. This is far from the truth. In 2011, around 82% of the UK population were using the internet – a figure that has increased by well over 230% in the last decade (www.internetworldstats.com/stats4.htm). There were eight European countries, in 2011, with higher rates of usage – Iceland topped the list at 97%. Across the EU, around two thirds of the population have internet access, while globally the number is barely over 30% (www.internetworldstats.com/stats9.htm).

There are numerous blogs, Facebook pages and Twitter accounts and many other forms of social media that provide political information. Guido Fawkes is one of the most prominent bloggers, while Alastair Campbell is a voracious tweeter. Yet information coming from sources such as these does not necessarily reach everyone. There is a need for the traditional forms of media (broadcast rather than print, in this case) to broaden the audience. Thus some news stories have their origins in statements on blogs or video footage from Youtube.

Added to this, viewers and readers are encouraged to send in their pictures or video footage for broadcast or publication as a supplement to ongoing news stories. Many pictures of the tsunami that hit Japan in 2011, for example, were taken on mobile phones. Stories emanating from Egypt, Yemen, Syria and Libya had "unsubstantiated footage" sent to broadcasters to supplement the news stories being reported. Traditional forms of media have realised the value of these new sources of information, and have shown a willingness to use them. The tools of the 'new media' are a vital supplement to the 'old' media. At this time, on its own, the 'new media' does not have the same capabilities as the 'old' media. This may, of course, change with time.

Conclusion: The Trivialisation of Politics?

What we can see in the media is a vast amount of information on political issues which needs to be condensed into digestible news articles. The problem is within this process much of the detail is lost. The broadcast media try to cover as many different items as possible, while attempting to remain impartial. This has led to accusations of 'dumbing down', and the tabloidisation of broadcast news.

The print media is little better. Sensationalism is to the forefront. Even the broadsheets have moved away from in-depth coverage of politics. Most broadsheets will have a couple of pages on politics, along with a leader or editorial comment. In their defence, the broadsheets do cover topical issues in greater detail, such as the uprisings in the Arab World and, of course, general elections, and try to offer analysis as well as basic reporting.

The tabloids look to the glitz, glamour, soaps, royals and sport for sensationalist headlines. The focus is more upon tittle tattle and trivia, sex and gossip rather than what could be described as 'real' news.

Much of this can be attributed to the 'ratings (or circulation) war'. Stories sell newspapers – even if the reports are light on 'facts'. As Seaton (2003, p. 181) notes: "as the supply of news increases, there is a more ruthless battle to catch the attention of the public above the cacophony of other news – and other sources of entertainment – clamouring for audiences". Stories are edited to make them more appealing and easier to absorb – and often at the expense of factual accuracy.

What can be seen is the trivialisation of politics. The subject is often characterised as boring, and many sections of the media do very little to stimulate any interest in the subject. When a topical issue does arise, for example the Euro, the tabloid media shed little light on the subject, but plenty of heat. If there is ever a referendum on the UK joining the Euro, or the UK remaining in the EU, the tabloid press in particular will probably present a jingoistic defence of the pound or of national interests, without necessarily bothering about the detail. This is not a useful style of reporting, and it does nothing for the standing of politics and politicians in Britain. If the strength of a country's democracy can be measured by the quality of its journalism, what does this say about the UK in the 21st century?

Selected bibliography

Barnett, Steven & Seaton, Jean. (2010). "Why the BBC Matters: Memo to the New Parliament about a Unique British Institution", *Political Quarterly* vol. 81-3, pp. 327-332.

Gibbons, Virginia. (2010). "Public Perceptions of the Media's Reporting of Politics Today", *Parliamentary Affairs* vol. 63-2, pp. 369-376.

Gunn, Sheila. (2011). *So You want to be a Political Journalist*: Biteback.

Seaton, Jean. (2003). "Public, Private and the Media", *Political Quarterly* vol. 74-2, pp. 174-183.

Stanyer, James. (2004). "Politics and the Media: A Crisis of Trust?", *Parliamentary Affairs* vol. 57-2, pp.420-434.

Temple, Mick. (2010). "In Praise of the Popular Press: The Need for Tabloid Racism", *Politics* vol. 30-3, pp. 191-201.

Wring, Dominic & Ward, Stephen. (2010). "The Media and the 2010 Campaign: the Television Election?", *Parliamentary Affairs* vol. 63-4, pp. 802-817.

Websites

www.aljazeera.com/
Al-jazeera news in English

www.bbc.co.uk/
BBC homepage

www.channel4.com/
Channel 4 homepage

www.independent.co.uk/
The Independent web pages

www.internetworldstats.com/stats4.htm
Internet users in Europe

www.internetworldstats.com/stats9.htm
Internet usage in the European Union

www.itn.co.uk/
ITN homepage

www.mediauk.com
Source of media ownership, with links to newspapers, magazines and broadcast outlets

www.newspapersoc.org.uk/a-to-z-of-local-newspaper-websites
The Newspaper Society lists a complete A to Z of local and regional newspapers in the UK

www.sky.com/
Sky homepage

www.telegraph.co.uk/
The Telegraph web pages

www.theguardian.com/uk
The Guardian web pages

www.thetimes.co.uk/tto/news/
The Times web pages

Questions

1. Evaluate the role of the media in general election campaigns. What are the strengths and weaknesses of their coverage?
2. To what extent does the ownership of the media affect the reporting of politics?
3. How far can viewers rely on broadcast coverage of UK politics? How does it differ from press coverage?

CHAPTER 25 // LOCAL GOVERNMENT

Contents

- **Introduction**
- **Development of Local Government**
- **Structure of Local Government**
- **Functions of Local Government**
- **Local Government Finance**
- **Centre-Local Relations**
- **Personnel**
- **The Localism Act (2011)**
- **Conclusion: what future for local government?**

Introduction

To many people, local government is not just considered to be a boring subject, but also one of a peripheral nature in British politics. Britain is a highly centralised, unitary country. Parliament is sovereign. Central government is viewed as being all-powerful, despite the introduction of devolution. Local government is invariably seen as being little more than a sideshow; a trifle that occasionally hits the headlines – and if that happens, then it is a result of the ineptitude of a specific local authority. Important policy decisions are supposedly taken by central government – policies to do with the economy, defence, or foreign affairs. Local government deals with what are often perceived as being the unimportant, or at least the less important, issues – street lighting, parks, or refuse collection. It does also deal with education and social services. Were such issues neglected, or such services not carried out, there would be a vociferous outcry. These often mundane areas play a significant part in most people's everyday lives. Wilson & Game (2011, p. 5) highlight the idea "local authorities 'look after you from the cradle to the grave' – or from sperm to worm – is both a cliché and an outdatedly paternalistic view of councils' wide-ranging responsibilities. But it is also literally true". The problem is this provision of services is frequently taken for granted.

The idea of local government was based upon a very simple concept; namely, that of providing a service for the local community. There was no specific plan for the creation and development of local government. It emerged, in part, as a pragmatic response to local demands with regard to issues such as sanitation. Enthusiasts can look back to medieval times with counties being administered by sheriffs, or to Elizabethan times with the Poor Relief Act of 1601 and the Poor Law Act of 1602 as examples of steps that gradually led to the formation of local government. The idea of a co-ordinated elected local government is, however, a much more recent development.

During the Thatcher years, questions were raised as to whether local government should be such a provider of services. In fact local government was arguably transformed in the 1980s from a service provider to a service enabler, and this process has continued. In 1988, Nicholas Ridley (then-Environment Secretary) envisaged a minimalist local government; it would no longer provide its traditional services like housing and education, but rather would regulate and monitor these and other services which would be provided by other bodies. This was seen as a rather extreme perspective at that time, with few people envisaging it would ever actually be realised. As will become apparent in this chapter, there is a mix of service provision by local government along with the enabling of service provision by other bodies, and an increasing use of partnerships between the public, private and voluntary sectors. In some cases, such as Peterborough City Council, Ridley's minimalist enabling authority has come into being.

Although perceived as being unimportant, local government plays a major role in Britain. It spends approximately one quarter of total government spending, around £175 billion in 2011/12. It employed about 1.9 million people in 2012, around 7% of the total workforce in Britain (and in many areas the local authority is still the largest employer). Local government remains very important. Unless there are major problems, local government does not get the media coverage it should. Even local government elections are seen as glorified opinion polls of a possible Westminster election. All of this undermines the idea of a locally elected body providing local services, or organising local service delivery. It is a case of government actually being closer to the people.

Development of Local Government

It was the Municipal Corporations Act of 1835, along with the Local Government Acts of 1888 and 1894 that established a system of local administration as we understand it today. This system consisted of 45 counties within which rural, urban and municipal or non-county borough districts operated. Within the counties, 79 'county boroughs' or towns were given self-governing status. This could mean the county had no jurisdiction over the larger, more important towns and cities. For example, Liverpool and Manchester were totally independent of Lancashire County Council.

This structure of local government remained largely unchanged throughout much of the 20th century, despite a range of growing pressures. During the 1960s, pressures came from the migration of population to the suburbs, increased car ownership, and higher expectations from citizens. Such pressures created a movement for local government reform. This culminated in the setting up of two Royal Commissions in 1966. One Commission was to consider the structure of local government in England (outside London) and was chaired by Lord Redcliffe-Maud. The other, chaired by Lord Wheatley, considered Scotland. Both reported in 1969.

These Commissions conducted the first real investigation into local government, although the reports were fairly predictable. A number of key points were highlighted: the system did not conform to the pattern of life and work in modern society; services were fragmented; there were too many councils, and some of these were too small; and, that highly professional staff were not being recruited in size and numbers.

The Redcliffe-Maud Commission advanced a number of recommendations to completely restructure local government in England. There were to be 58 unitary (or single tier) authorities, with three tiered authorities for Manchester, Liverpool and Birmingham. The reforms that were introduced in 1972 were significantly different. Conversely, the Wheatley reforms for Scotland were largely adopted. In both cases, there were underlying political considerations that affected the reform of local government at this time.

The 1972 Local Government Act saw the creation of tiered local authorities throughout England and Wales. These came into effect in 1974. Six Metropolitan County Councils were created, each of which centred on a major urban conurbation: Manchester, Merseyside (Liverpool), West Yorkshire (Leeds), South Yorkshire (Sheffield), West Midlands (Birmingham) and Tyne and Wear (Newcastle). There were also 39 Non-Metropolitan County Councils. Both types of county council had a tier of district councils beneath as shown in Figure 25.1.

The Local Government (Scotland) Act of 1973, which came into effect in 1975, proposed a mixture of tiered and unitary authorities. The 'island' councils of Orkney, Shetland and the Western Isles became 'most-purpose' authorities, while the remainder of Scotland became tiered.

Local government changed significantly in the 1980s. The 1985 Local Government Act abolished the six Metropolitan County Councils and the Greater London Council. While supposedly cogent reasons were advanced at the time as to why abolition was necessary, it is clear today political considerations were foremost. All seven councils were Labour controlled and were powerful opponents of the Thatcher Government. In 1988, the Inner London Education Authority (ILEA) was also abolished. Many of the functions carried out by the abolished bodies were taken over by the district councils and London boroughs. A large number of quangos and Joint Boards were also created. These quangos and Joint Boards co-ordinated the delivery of services across the areas where councils had been abolished.

During the 1980s there were numerous changes to local government in both structure and function. There were over 100 pieces of legislation that either directly or indirectly affected local government. At no other time has there been so much central government involvement in local government affairs. The role of local government arguably changed from service provider to service enabler (which is discussed later in the chapter). All subsequent governments have continued to interfere in local government affairs. The volume of central involvement may have been reduced but the impact remains.

Figure 25.1 The system of UK Local Government in the mid-1970s

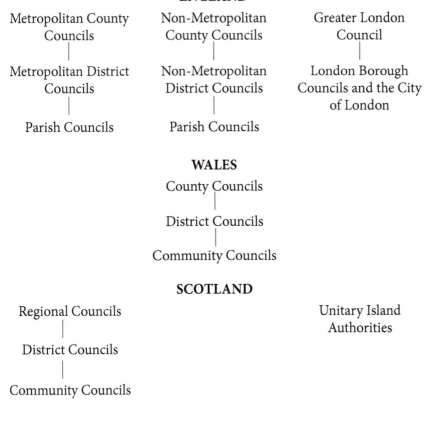

ENGLAND

Metropolitan County Councils	Non-Metropolitan County Councils	Greater London Council
|	|	|
Metropolitan District Councils	Non-Metropolitan District Councils	London Borough Councils and the City of London
|	|	
Parish Councils	Parish Councils	

WALES

County Councils
|
District Councils
|
Community Councils

SCOTLAND

Regional Councils   Unitary Island
| Authorities
District Councils
|
Community Councils

NORTHERN IRELAND

District Councils

Structure of Local Government

The structure of local government across England can be described as either "hybridity, or a dog's breakfast" (Wilson & Game, 2011, p. 67). There is not a single uniform structure. By contrast, in Scotland, Wales and Northern Ireland, there is a uniform structure in each country. In 2013, Scotland had 32 unitary authorities, all of which were responsible for delivering services such as education, leisure and recreation, planning and building standards, social services, housing, and refuse collection. At the same time, Wales had 22 unitary authorities, each with similar responsibilities. Northern Ireland has 26 unitary authorities, although this number is to be reduced to 11 in April 2015. The responsibilities of these new authorities has yet to be confirmed (in 2013). The 26 unitary authorities had relatively few responsibilities.

English local government is a mixture of unitary authorities and tiered authorities. The metropolitan areas of England have remained unchanged since 1986. London, by contrast, has seen the introduction of a directly elected mayor and the creation of the Greater London Authority (both directly elected since 2000). This is the re-establishment of tiered local government in London. The rest of England is a mixture of tiered and unitary authorities. Added to this, some local authorities have introduced directly elected mayors (which are discussed later in this chapter).

In 1992 the Local Government Commission was set up to investigate the structures of local government in non-metropolitan England. This body consulted with the public on proposals to reform local government structures. There was, however, suspicion of a hidden agenda when options for reform often excluded the status quo. A case in point here was Leicestershire, where a number of options were proposed, excluding that which already existed – a two-tier County with both Leicester City Council and Rutland District Council under the County's auspices. One option had a unitary Leicester City authority, with the County remaining tiered. A second had a unitary Rutland, a unitary City, and the remainder of the County tiered. This latter proposal was eventually adopted.

In 2013 there were 353 councils in England. These could be broken down into the following:

- 27 county councils, with 201 district or borough councils in a lower tier
- 33 London boroughs, including the City of London
- 36 metropolitan district or borough councils
- 55 unitary authorities
- Isles of Scilly council

A new authority was established in London in 2000 which covers the entire Greater London area. From 1986 to 2000 London was the only European capital city not to have its own umbrella council. Now, not only is there a Greater London Authority (GLA) but London also has an elected mayor. Rather than imposing this system upon the citizens of London, a referendum was held in 1998 to confirm popular support for such a move. Around 72% of voters expressed their desire to have this new system. Such an endorsement was marred however by the poor turnout of 35%.

The mayoral elections have been held under the Supplementary Vote system. This electoral system is explained in chapter 20 on Electoral Systems. The elections to the 25-member GLA were held under a form of Mixed Member-Proportional (MMP). The various London councils were compressed into 14 single member constituencies, with 11 top up members to be elected from across all of London. A full explanation of how MMP operates is also given in chapter 20.

The powers of the GLA and the London Mayor have been laid out very clearly. There is a clear separation of powers. The mayor speaks for the whole of London, in particular on issues such as transport, police, and the environment. The mayor also sets the budget for the GLA.

The GLA acts as a check on the mayor. It monitors the mayor's actions and performance, as well as the performance of various bodies including transport and policing. The GLA can amend the mayor's budget, but only with a two-thirds majority vote.

Functions of Local Government

The functions of local government have changed significantly over time. Traditionally, local government has been viewed as a provider of services for the local community. This role has now changed to that of enabler/partner. Local government no longer necessarily provides services, but rather makes sure the services are provided. In fact some councils no longer provide any services directly, but monitor and regulate the delivery of these services by other bodies.

To complicate matters, the formal functions of local authorities vary according to the type of authority. This is demonstrated in Table 25.1.

The complexities of the functions of local government are clearly demonstrated in Table 25.1. Councils are obliged to provide statutory services, which include many of those listed above. There is a legal obligation to provide such services. There are also discretionary services and mandatory services. Councils are likely to provide mandatory services, or provide them up to a certain standard of delivery, not because they have to but because there might be a legal challenge if they did not. This covers many social services. Discretionary services are those which the council chooses to provide e.g. community and leisure centres. These are also the services most likely to be cut during times of austerity.

As has already been noted, although councils are considered responsible for the delivery of services, they may not actually deliver these services. Local government provides some services but co-ordinates the delivery of others. Wilson and Game (2011) highlight this point in one of their chapters, entitled "Governance and Partnership". This highlights the extent to which local government has become one of the partners in the delivery of services. This shift from local government to local governance (which is not exclusive to local government, as can be seen in the final chapter of this book) has been happening since the late 1980s. As Wilson (2003, p. 319) notes: "local authorities have become but one of a number of bodies 'governing' at the local level".

Table 25.1 Distribution of Main Functions (2013)

	TWO TIER		UNITARY AUTHORITY
	COUNTY	DISTRICT	
Education	X		X
Highways	X	X	X
Transport	X		X
Social services	X		X
Housing		X	X
Fire & Rescue		X	X
Libraries	X		X
Strategic planning	X		X
Development control		X	X
Refuse collection	X	X	X
Refuse disposal			X
Recreation facilities		X	X
Licensing		X	X
Consumer protection	X		X
Council tax collection		X	X

Many local services are now provided by private or voluntary contractors. Refuse collection is an obvious example. Under the Compulsory Competitive Tendering (CCT) legislation, councils had to open a range of services to competition. Today, many councils no longer provide the weekly refuse collection service. Instead, private contractors provide this service, on behalf of the council.

Other services may also be provided on behalf of the council. In Peterborough, for example, most of the city's culture and leisure facilities are managed by a not-for-profit organisation, Vivacity.

The role of local government in service provision, however, remains essential. Not only did the Local Government Act (2000) reinforce local government's role as the primary co-ordinator of services at the local level, but the Localism Act

(2011) – which is covered later in this chapter – did the same. This is, however, a significant difference to the original idea of local government: as a provider of local services.

Local Government Finance

This is a very complex area of local government. One reason for this complexity is it is composed of both locally raised taxation, fees and charges, and central government grants. Another reason is the extent to which the financing of local government has changed over the years.

During the 1950s and 1960s local government expenditure grew rapidly. Much of this was in response to the development of the welfare state. In 1976, the Layfield Committee of Inquiry into Local Government Finance pointed out local government expenditure had grown eleven-fold since the early 1950s. Most of this had been funded through central government grants – in particular the Rate Support Grant which could be spent at the discretion of the local authority. The remainder was met through the rating system.

– Domestic Rates – a tax levied on each property in the area based on the notional rental value of that property.
– Business Rates – a tax levied on each commercial or industrial property in the area.

During the 1970s, the extent of local government expenditure came under increasing pressure from central government. In May 1975, the Secretary of State for the Environment, Tony Crosland, argued "the party's over" with regard to the levels of local government spending. Central government started to exercise greater control over the levels of local government spending.

It was the Conservative Government under Thatcher that sought control over local government spending. Measures such as 'capping' were introduced, where local government expenditure was capped at centrally prescribed limits. Any local authority which overspent was penalised through the Rate Support Grant – effectively losing grant income in proportion to the overspend.

The pinnacle of the Thatcher Government's involvement in local government finance was the introduction of the Community Charge or Poll Tax in April 1990 (for those living in Scotland it was April 1989). This was a tax levied against every individual aged over 18 years living in a property. It proved to be exceedingly unpopular and was a contributing factor in the downfall of Thatcher. The Poll Tax was replaced by the Council Tax in 1993.

At the same time as the introduction of the Poll Tax, there was also a reform of the Business Rates. These were replaced by the National Non-Domestic Rates (NNDR), sometimes known as the Uniform Business Rate. Whereas local government had set the old Business Rates, the NNDR was set nationally.

Although the NNDR remains a tax on local business (or, more accurately, on properties which are not used for domestic purposes), the proceeds are divided between areas according to a central government determined formula based on the population of the council area. Certain properties are exempt from NNDR, including farm lands and buildings, churches, and some properties used by the disabled.

The introduction of the Council Tax changed local taxation to a property-based system with an individual element. As can be seen in Table 25.2, there are seven bands. Each property is placed in a band according to its notional value in 1991, when this tax was first established. The Council Tax is set for Band D and the tax is then levied as a higher or lower proportion of the Council Tax. The valuations are different in Scotland and Wales. Welsh valuation bands were reviewed in 2003 and re-set in 2005.

Table 25.2 Council Tax Bands in England

BAND	VALUE OF PROPERTY	PROPORTION OF TAX AT BAND D LEVEL
A	Under £40 000	66.7%
B	£40 001 - £52 000	77.8%
C	£52 001 - £68 000	88.9%
D	£68 001 - £88 000	100%
E	£88 001 - £120 000	122.2%
F	£120 001 - £160 000	144.4%
G	£160 001 - £320 000	166.7%
H	Over £320 001	200%

There are some exemptions to the paying of the Council Tax. A single occupant of a property receives a 25% reduction in their bill. Students are currently exempt from paying council tax, while the least well off used to receive rebates. These rebates were stopped in April 2013.

The rebates, which could be up to 100% of the council tax bill, were means tested. They were replaced by a Council Tax Reduction Scheme. Whereas the rebates had been set nationally, the reduction scheme was co-ordinated at the local level. On top of this, central government cut their funding of such benefits by 15%. Consequently, many of the least well off people in society had to make a contribution to their council tax bills. Councils were left to set their own reductions. Leicester City Council set an upper limit of an 80% reduction, Brighton & Hove City Council at 91.5%, as did Newcastle City Council, and Rutland Unitary Authority set an upper limit of 75% for non-pensioners and 100% for pensioners.

Centre-Local Relations

As can be seen from both the structures and finance of local government, central government plays a very large, often domineering, role. The relationship is relatively straightforward in constitutional terms. Parliament is sovereign and can delegate powers to lesser tiers of government – either local government or to the devolved bodies. These powers can be re-centralised at any time. Parliament can also abolish local government, as was done in 1986, or restructure it – as seems to be done on a regular basis since the 1970s. Should a local authority take actions not stipulated by Parliament, then it is acting *ultra vires*. This term translates as 'beyond its powers' (see Table 17.2). Whenever you examine the relationship between central and local government, both Parliamentary sovereignty and the doctrine of *ultra vires* must be borne in mind.

One of the problems when looking at central-local relations is to treat both as single, cohesive blocs. Across the UK, there are some 433 councils. No two councils are alike. There may be similarities between the councils in Orkney and Shetland, but these island councils are significantly different to those for the Isle of Wight or the Scilly Islands. An inner city London borough council will be significantly different to that of rural England. Each will have its own priorities and concerns.

Similarly, it is a mistake to consider all of central government as a cohesive bloc. There are departmental rivalries. Individual departments will be protective of their 'empires' and their budgets. Different central government departments have their own idiosyncracies when dealing with local government.

This leaves a complicated relationship between central and local government. It is made worse by the fact the centre controls the purse strings. The centre can decide which, if any, funds should be ring-fenced. This can leave local government with little room for manoeuvre in the funding of some services, as has already been seen with the restructuring of council tax benefit.

Davis (2000) suggested central government has emasculated local government. Even where there appears to be an emphasis on local democracy – be it through local democratic renewal, the Big Society or the localism legislation – the reality is more central interference in local affairs and, ultimately, greater centralisation. At best, local government may be a *steward* of the centre, ultimately implementing the decisions made by the centre. A good steward, however, will ask questions, raise reservations or concerns about the decisions being made. This is no partnership, as the steward is may be little more than a manager or an administrator. The terms of such a relationship will be decided, ultimately, by the centre.

Personnel

In many respects, local government is a miniature version of central government. At Westminster there are MPs, while ministers are aided by civil servants. Local government is similar. There are elected councillors, and local government officers who perform a civil service type of role. There are also now a small number of directly-elected mayors in England. The creation of this post in a number of councils has had a significant impact on the role of both councillors and officers.

1. Councillors

Councillors are considered to be an important feature of democracy in Britain. They are directly elected by their community to represent them on the council. The fact some councillors are returned unopposed, or the turnout for local government elections averages less than 40%, is often considered immaterial. Councillors may be viewed as a symbol of democracy.

Although claiming to represent their communities, councillors are often unrepresentative of society as a whole. The vast majority of councillors represent the older sections of society. The average age of councillors in England in 2010 was 60 years – it had been only 55 years of age in 1997. On top of this, most councillors are male (68% in 2010) and white (96% in 2010). The representation of ethnic minorities on councils needs to be broken down. The aggregate figures distort representation. In cities such as Leicester, with a large ethnic minority community, their representation on the council is closer to their total population size. In 2011, ethnic minorities made up approximately 49.5% of Leicester's population and at the same time there were 22 councillors from ethnic minorities out of a total of 54.

The duties of a councillor are not clearly defined. In many respects, it may actually depend upon the interests and aspirations of the individual councillor. On top of this, where there are now directly-elected mayors, the role of a councillor may have changed. Although there is no set job description, Wilson & Game (2011, p. 273) have summarised the 'job' of a councillor as:

> to represent, be accountable to, and an advocate for all their electors...
> formulating policies and practices for the local authority...
> monitoring their effectiveness...
> and providing leadership for the community...
> while (of course) maintaining the highest standards of conduct and ethics.

The priorities in the role of a councillor may have changed, especially as a 'backbench' councillor, or one operating under a mayoral administration. The scrutiny role, in particular, has increased significantly. As Copus (2008, p. 591) notes, councillors are "central to ensuring that local political leaders were continually held to account". This role may have existed in the past, but it would have been more behind-the-scenes.

To complicate matters, councillors tend to be part-time in their post, with most holding down full-time jobs at the same time. Financial compensation is negligible, although it is left to local choice as to how much councillors are paid.

In many respects the job of a councillor is not too dissimilar to that of an MP. Councillors act as representatives for their wards or communities but are expected to pay a regard to the interests of the whole local authority area. Like MPs, councillors also deal with problems and issues raised by their constituents (e.g. schools, housing, or planning permission). As with MPs, councillors also have to work in the chamber – although a councillor's role may be more active and possibly even more influential. In many respects, like the job of an MP, the job of a councillor should really be a full-time post.

Although most councillors represent a political party, these ties are not normally perceived to be as strong as compared to those on an MP. Bottom & Copus (2011) found otherwise. For councillors who are elected under a party label, "the expectations and requirements of party unity and discipline in public is far greater than for MPs" (p. 284). In fact, all group decisions are taken under a three line whip, with party positions decided in pre-council meetings. It would seem that "councillors are, first and foremost, loyal to their political parties" (Copus & Erlingsson, 2013, p. 59).

It must be noted many councils in the UK are 'hung' i.e. there is no overall majority for a single party. In Scotland in 2013, of the 32 councils 23 were hung (although this may be attributable, at least in part, to the use of the Single Transferable Vote (STV) in these elections; see chapter 20), with a further three – Orkney, Shetland and the Western Isles – controlled by Independents. In Wales in 2013, ten of the 22 councils were hung, with a further two controlled by Independents; in England, 48 of the 355 councils were hung, with one other controlled by Independents. In each of these circumstances, local councillors were compelled to work with other parties.

Overall, party matters, even with the changing role of councillors. "A key role for the councillor now is to hold the policies and the initiatives of a mayoral administration up to critical review, without reference to party interest or advantage. So far, English councillors have been largely unwilling to do this in public" (Copus, 2008, p. 601).

For the most part, the job of the average councillor has remained the same. The scrutiny role has increased, especially with the potential over-concentration of power in the hands of a few.

2. Directly-elected Mayors

Until the Local Government Act, 2000, the management of councils had been organised around a system of committees. The full council would meet and delegate decision making powers to the various committees (these committees could include social services, planning, environment, and housing). The Local Government Act 2000 changed this. It compelled local authorities to consult with the public as to what form of political management they would like to adopt. There were four choices (although only three of them applied to most councils):

i. A directly elected mayor with a cabinet (appointed from the elected councillors)

ii. A cabinet with a leader (all appointed from the council)

iii. A directly elected mayor and a council manager (who would be an officer)

iv. A revised committee system (for authorities with a population under 85 000)

Most councils opted for the second choice, as it was the closest to what had existed prior to 2000. This entails the leadership of the council forming an executive or cabinet (with a maximum of ten members, regardless of the size of the council) while the remainder of the elected members performing a scrutiny role. Over a dozen have adopted the first choice, while one council, Stoke-on-Trent, opted for the third (although this has since been reversed in a referendum).

Berwick-upon-Tweed was the first council to hold a referendum for an elected mayor, but it was defeated. Watford was the first town outside of London to adopt a directly elected mayor in a local referendum. In the Local Government Act (2000), there was a requirement to hold a local referendum if the council wished to adopt an elected mayor. This pre-requisite was removed in 2006. One reason for this was only 12 local authorities had adopted elected mayors.

In February 2009, the Conservative Party indicated, should they win the 2010 General Election, an intention to hold referendums in the twelve largest cities in England (outside of London) for elected mayors. Of the twelve, both Leicester and Liverpool adopted mayoral systems without a referendum. Referendums were held in 2012 in the others, and only Bristol City Council voted for a mayoral system.

As of May 2013, there were 15 local authorities in England with directly elected mayors, plus the Mayor of London. The most recent one to be abolished was in Hartlepool.

The post of directly elected mayor may see a change in how local politics operates. Traditionally, party politics has dominated local government, and elected mayors disturb this pattern (Copus, 2011). The elected mayors have to provide a range of different forms of leadership. There is *civic leadership*, as leader of the community. There is also *political leadership*. This is not party-political leadership, as many mayors are Independents. Rather, it is about leadership of the political processes. As Copus (2011, p. 343) notes, "Independent mayors are faced with negotiation, deliberation, compromise and the need to construct a broad governing coalition of support". Arguably, this applies to all mayors, regardless of their political persuasion. Even in Leicester City, with a Labour mayor and all bar two of the councillors being Labour as of 2013, negotiations, deliberation and compromise are likely to prevail. Finally, but by no means the least important, is *corporate leadership*. This is, in effect, the leadership of the council bureaucracy. Such leadership may cause problems in the relationship with the Chief Executive of the local authority, who is the senior local government officer. Each elected mayor has to balance the three different forms of leadership.

There is a perception the directly elected mayors have usurped the role of councillors. In the past, concerned residents would go to their local councillor to remedy a problem. Where there are elected mayors, the concerned residents are now going directly to the mayor, by-passing the local councillor. Consequently, in some local authorities with elected mayors, moves are afoot to reduce the number of councillors.

3. Local Government Officers

Local authorities employ staff to assist in implementing policies, and to carry out various other duties. These are the local government officers. It could be suggested these officers play a civil service-type role, and this would not be an inaccurate assessment. One important difference is the local government officers tend to be professional experts in their field. Added to this, local government officers claim to work to a different set of values from those in other sectors of the economy. This is the **public sector ethos** – the idea of working for the public good.

There is a commonly held perception local government officers wield too much influence. They are the full-time, permanent professionals who are there to assist the part-time, transient elected members.

The senior officer for any council is usually called the *Chief Executive*. The relationship between the Chief Executive and the leader of the council is by far the most important. Yet as the political management changes, the role of the Chief Executive – if not all officers – may have to change as well. There has already been conflict between directly elected mayors and chief executives, as their roles overlap.

The Localism Act (2011)

This legislation, brought forward by the Coalition Government, was the backbone of David Cameron's 'Big Society'. One of the key features, as noted by Lowndes & Pratchett (2012) was the strengthening of local accountability. This was to be done through a range of methods.

> i. *more local referendums* – these could be initiated by citizens over, for example, council tax rises, especially if such rises were seen to be excessive. Local referendums are not a new device. It is just the Coalition Government envisage a greater use of them. As Lowndes & Pratchett (2012, p. 28) note, such referendums can "often promote short-term self-interest over broader community concerns and can militate against long term investments which are of wider community benefit".

ii. more directly elected mayors – as has already been noted, there were ten referendums for elected mayors in 2012, although nine were defeated. This leaves a question mark over how central government envisages local leadership being taken forward (based on the standard assumption the status quo is not an option)

iii. elections for Police and Crime Commissioners (PCCs) – these were introduced in November 2012. The elections were rushed through, with little consideration given to informing voters of the powers and roles of the PCCs. The knock-on effect of the lack of information was a phenomenally poor turnout – an average of 15% in England and Wales, and one polling station in Newport, Gwent, had a turnout of zero. The idea of electing the PCC was to make policing more accountable to the public. With such a poor turnout, questions were raised as to whether or not the PCCs had a popular mandate (see chapter 15).

iv. greater transparency of local bureaucracy – the idea here was to open up local government, and to make it more accountable to the public. This includes the publication of all local authority spending over £500, as well as the remuneration of senior local government officers, and the pay and expenses of councillors, mayors and Lord Mayors.

Questions have been raised about the extent to which the Localism Act (2011) is about local government. While the points above may be about local government, it must be questioned as to whether or not it is for the benefit of local government and the public. For example, imposing the PCC elections across England and Wales meant adding an extra tier of management on to a system that already appeared to be over-managed. Added to this, the idea that holding elections every four years as being the best way to hold policing to account is ludicrous. There were suggestions the installation of the PCCs undermined another function of local government. There are endless criticisms about excessive central interference in local government, and the Localism Act is no different. Yet there are now suggestions we are seeing the beginning of the end of local government.

Conclusion: what future for local government?

As has been the case for the last thirty years or more, the future of local government is unclear. While central government appears to want local government to ensure the provision of a greater number of services, and to ensure all services are of the highest quality, there are fewer resources to enable this to happen. Councils are being forced to compete against each other for extra resources. On top of this, council budgets are suffering severe cuts, as central government continues with its austerity measures. Consequently, the discretionary services provided by councils are being cut.

The response from the centre is quite simple – and part of this is in the localism/Big Society agenda. If people want the services to be provided, and the council is unable to do so – or any other service provider, for that matter – then the people should get together and provide the service themselves. This can be local schools, leisure centres, post offices, or any other services the people feel they need to have provided.

Yet what is really needed for local government to be able to function more effectively is greater powers and greater financial autonomy from the centre. Goss (2001, p. 119) noted over the last two decades of the twentieth century, local councils "lost power, money and status. The job has become more managerial, with less scope for making things happen". Leach (2009) has argued if there was to be a fundamental review of local government, both the structure and function of local government would need to be covered, along with the financing of local government, and its relationship with central government.

Local government in the UK is no longer 'local' government. Every time central government restructured local government, the local authorities became larger and larger. They are no longer 'local'. Cornwall, for example, is a unitary authority, but can a single tier of government of that size be considered 'local'? Councils have become too large to provide the services for the local community. Added to this, there are too few councillors per head of population for them to develop a meaningful relationship with the local community. The UK has the lowest ratio of councillors to population in Europe: 1 councillor for almost 3000 people (excluding parish councils). Within this figure there are a wide range of differences, with some urban councils seeing a ratio of 1:7000 but some rural councils at 1:1000. In Germany, by way of comparison, the ratio is one councillor per 350 people, and in France it is 1:118.

For there to be a meaningful future for local government, there is a need for smaller councils, with greater powers to deliver services at the local level. How this can be funded is an issue. With the huge disparities in wealth and income across the UK, there may need to be some central government 'interference' in the funding of local government. Finally, there is the whole relationship between central and local government. Even allowing for the formal constitutional relationship, there are times when local government should be allowed to get on with the job it is supposed to be doing, without too much central government involvement.

Selected bibliography

Buser, Michael. (2013). "Tracing the Democratic Narrative: Big Society, Localism and Civic Engagement", *Local Government Studies* vol. 39-1, pp. 3-21.
Chandler, Jim. (2010). "A Rationale for Local Government", *Local Government Studies* vol. 36-1, pp. 5-20.
Copus, Colin. (2010). "The Councillor: Governor, Governing, Governance and the Complexity of Citizen Engagement", *British Journal of Politics and International Relations* vol. 12-4, pp. 569-589.

Copus, Colin. (2011). "Elected mayors in English Local Government: Mayoral Leadership and Creating a new Political Dynamic", *Lex Localis – Journal of Local Self-Government* vol. 9-4, pp. 335-351.

Leach, Steve. (2009). "Reorganisation, Reorganisation, Reorganisation: A Critical Analysis of the Sequence of Local Government Reorganisation Initiatives, 1979-2008", *Local Government Studies* vol. 35-1, pp. 61-74.

Verheul, Wouter Jan & Schaap, Linze. (2010). "Strong Leaders? The Challenges and Pitfalls in Mayoral Leadership", *Public Administration* vol. 88-2, pp. 439-454.

Wilson, David & Game, Chris. (2011). *Local Government in the United Kingdom*: Palgrave, 5th edition.

Websites

www.leicester.gov.uk/homepage.aspx
Homepage of Leicester City Council. Many other councils have web pages. You can use the oultwood web pages to find them

www.lga.gov.uk
Homepage of the Local Government Association. This is a source of factual information on local government

www.gov.uk/government/organisations/department-for-communities-and-local-government
This is the home page for the Department for Communities and Local Government

www.london.gov.uk/
This is the homepage for the GLA and the Mayor of London

www.oultwood.com/localgov/countries/england.php
Links to all local government web sites throughout England. Instead of england, you can type in scotland, wales or northernireland to get access to local government in those regions

Questions

1. To what extent does central government control local government?
2. Does elected local government have a future?
3. "Elected mayors undermine the role of councillors and are having an adverse effect on local government." Discuss.

CHAPTER 26 // DEVOLUTION

Contents
- **Introduction**
- **What is devolution?**
- **Related concepts**
- **Asymmetric Devolution**
- **Funding Devolution in the UK**
- **Conclusion**

Introduction

The issue of devolution has been prominent in British politics for many years. It was to the forefront of politics in the 1970s and again in the 1990s. With the successful devolution referenda in 1997 in both Scotland and Wales, there appeared to be an assumption devolution no longer mattered. Such a perspective was reinforced when the attempt to have political devolution for the regions of England failed. Consequently, the issue has to some extent disappeared from the political agenda in England. Yet all of this is to condense a hugely important issue as something of little consequence for the English – and this is a grave mistake.

This chapter will introduce various forms of devolution – many of which are in existence in the UK today. A range of related concepts will be explained. This will be followed by a brief overview of the collective UK position on devolution. Subsequent chapters will examine, in far greater detail, devolution in Scotland, Wales, Northern Ireland and England.

What is devolution?

The concept of devolution is relatively straightforward to explain. It is the delegation of powers from a higher or superior tier of government to a lower one. Bogdanor has broadened out this definition much further. Devolution "consists of three elements: *the transfer to a subordinate elected body on a geographical basis, of functions at present exercised by ministers and Parliament*" (Bogdanor, 2001, p.2). Such functions could be:

- legislative – making laws
- executive – making decisions within an already established legal framework

Thus, the situations in Scotland, Wales and Northern Ireland fit this definition very well. Each devolved body has been granted specific powers, which had previously been exercised by Parliament or by government ministers. The geographic areas within which these powers are exercised are also clearly defined.

Yet this is a rather narrow understanding of devolution. For example, devolution has existed in some form or another in the UK since the 19th century, if not earlier. In 1885, the Scottish Office was created. This was a form of **administrative devolution**, as opposed to the **political devolution** that exists today in Scotland, Wales and Northern Ireland. The Welsh Office was created in 1964, and the Northern Ireland Office in 1972. Within England there has also been administrative devolution, and it still exists today. It can take the form of quangos, with bodies such as the East Midlands Regional Development Agency (although this agency, and all of the other regional development agencies, were abolished in 2012). The various utilities providers (water, gas, electricity) are all regionalised, and were so even when they were nationalised industries. What is lacking in England (arguably outside of London) is the political devolution that has been granted to the other component parts of the United Kingdom.

Thus, when talking about devolution, greater clarity is needed. Not only are there significant differences between political and administrative devolution, but also between these and other related concepts.

Before examining these related concepts, there is one very important point that must be borne in mind at all times when focusing on devolution in the UK: **the Westminster Parliament remains sovereign**. Parliament can devolve power, but it can also rescind such a decision. No Parliament can bind its successors. Parliamentary sovereignty is the underpinning of the British constitution. While political devolution may appear to change the political landscape, such a policy can be reversed. In Northern Ireland, for example, since 1998 the exercising of devolved powers has been suspended on four occasions, with the devolved powers being returned to Westminster. Although on each occasion it was an interim measure, such a move could be made permanent. And with administrative devolution, it is even easier to centralise power.

In sum, devolution is all about the centre handing power down to a lower tier of government. This power can be policy making, administrative, and perhaps even legislative. As noted before, this process can be reversed (although it is unlikely) because the Westminster Parliament remains sovereign.

There is, however, a caveat. Constitutionally (as noted in chapter 6), Britain is a unitary state. This means there is one political centre, and all areas across the country are treated in a similar manner. Devolution may have changed this.

> Westminster... is no longer a Parliament for the domestic and non-domestic affairs of the whole of the UK. It has been transformed into a Parliament for England, a federal parliament for Scotland and Northern Ireland, and a parliament for primary legislation for Wales. Westminster has become, it might be suggested, a quasi-federal parliament. (Bogdanor, 2010, p. 156)

Even this is now inaccurate for Wales, with the devolved Welsh Assembly having received some primary powers in 2011.

From a more centralised perspective, the UK may now be seen as a union state, rather than a unitary state. There may be one central position of power, but the country is no longer treated in a uniform manner. Westminster remains sovereign, but the perception of a quasi-federal parliament may not be inaccurate.

Related concepts

Two forms of administrative devolution are: **decentralisation** and **deconcentration**. Decentralisation is to do with policy making powers being handed out from central government (e.g. powers being given to local government, or, in the past, to the Scottish or Welsh Offices). These are not normally law making powers. Deconcentration is where central government posts are relocated around the country (e.g. the Inland Revenue headquarters being relocated to Nottingham).

Administrative devolution is more to do with service delivery. Bodies such as the Scottish, Welsh or Northern Ireland Offices were involved in service delivery, but were able to provide any particular peculiarities that were needed. For example, education in Scotland is a little different to that in the rest of the UK in that the Scots do not sit 'A'-levels. Instead, they sit 'Highers'. Prior to 1999, the Scottish Office co-ordinated all of this rather than the Department for Education (although it is quite likely both departments would have co-operated with each other).

A term that is often associated with devolution is **nationalism**. There is often an assumption when talking about devolution, that it is nationalists who wish to use devolution as a stepping stone towards independence.

The world is divided into nations. Each nation has its own unique character. This will have developed from history, culture, language and possibly even religion. These are a nation's *objective* characteristics. Added to this are the *subjective* characteristics – knowledge, awareness and feelings for your nationality. Nationalism promotes the idea of each nation being able to run its own affairs – national self-determination. In other words, each nation should be independent.

Yet devolution and nationalism are poles apart. Supporters of devolution may not necessarily view themselves as 'nationalists'. In fact they may even oppose the sentiments of nationalists. Quite simply, it is felt nationalism could lead to the break up of the United Kingdom. An old slogan of the Scottish Nationalist Party (SNP) sums up the position: "An Independent Scotland Within Europe". The SNP want Scotland to break away from the rest of the UK. Supporters of devolution may not want such an event to occur. They might prefer to see a more autonomous Scotland *within* the United Kingdom of Great Britain and Northern Ireland.

Devolution is also different to **federalism**. One key difference is the division of powers is permanent under a federal system. Devolved powers can be returned to the centre (Parliament cannot bind its successors). In a federal structure, the division of powers is enshrined in the constitution. This is very obvious in federal countries such as the United States, Australia, and Germany. The powers of both the central government and the individual state governments are clearly detailed. There is no overlap. Issues such as defence and foreign affairs are most likely to be conducted by the central government, while things such as speed limits or drinking laws are more likely to be decided at the state level. Each tier may not intercede in the affairs of another.

Yet, there is the suggestion of the UK becoming quasi-federal. While there is the appearance of the centre being able to intercede across the UK, the reality is significantly different. It is most unlikely the UK Parliament will ever intercede in Scottish or Welsh affairs. Northern Ireland, as a result of domestic circumstances, is not so clear cut.

A related concept to devolution, which is used by the European Union (EU), is **subsidiarity**. The principle of subsidiarity states decision making should be taken at the lowest and most appropriate tier of government. Within the context of the EU, this means decision making could be taken at the EU level, or central, regional, or even local government level. Subsidiarity may be viewed as a way of preventing the transfer of powers from individual EU member states up to Brussels. Devolution, on the other hand, focuses upon the transfer of power from the centre to a lower tier of government.

Asymmetric Devolution

Like Spain, the UK has introduced a form of asymmetric devolution. This means different devolved bodies have different powers and responsibilities. According to Colino (2008), the distribution of these powers and responsibilities in Spain is not clear cut. There are reserved powers (which are under the control of the centre), which include: criminal law, defence, external trade and immigration. The powers assigned to the devolved bodies (or Autonomous Communities, as they are called in Spain) include: agriculture, industry, culture, social services and tourism. Most policy areas have "concurrent or shared powers" (Colino, 2008, p. 576) between the two tiers of government. This suggests the central government and the Autonomous Communities work together, but it is not always the case. Central government could impose a framework for policies, and thus limit the extent of discretion for the Autonomous Communities.

The UK is similarly complicated with regard to devolution. In 1999, the devolved assembly in Wales was originally given a list of areas in which it had secondary law making powers. (The terms Primary Legislative Powers and Secondary Legislative Powers are explained in Table 26.1.) The Scots, on the other hand, were given a list of reserved powers – policy areas which remained under the control of Westminster. The rest was left up to them – for both primary and secondary legislation. In Northern Ireland, the devolved authorities were given the powers which had been wielded by the Northern Ireland Office.

Table 26.1 Primary and Secondary Legislation

Primary Legislation	This is the making of all laws. Parliament is the only body that may pass primary legislation, although this power has been granted to the Scottish Parliament, the Northern Ireland Assembly, and now also the Welsh Assembly (in specified areas).
Secondary Legislation	This is where laws are passed by Parliament, but then may be adjusted to suit local needs. The Welsh Assembly was originally granted such powers.

As has been noted earlier in this chapter, some commentators describe the post-devolution UK constitutional position as being "quasi-federal" (Kay, 2005, p. 552). The extent of some of the powers that have been devolved, in particular to Scotland, are such that they are far greater than those distributed within a federal structure. For example, how many federal regimes permit some states to adjust the levels of national taxation?

Added to this, the likelihood of the UK central government repealing the devolution legislation is very small indeed. The consequences of such an action may actually lead to the break up of the UK.

Funding devolution in the UK

Within the UK, finance is very much under the control of central government. Some expenditure is clearly 'national' e.g. defence. Other parts of expenditure are implemented regionally, or even locally.

The budgets of the devolved administrations in Scotland, Wales and Northern Ireland are determined in three ways:

– an unconditional block grant, which covers most activities
– specific allocations for services that must be implemented (through UK or EU policy)
– amounts raised by the devolved administrations, their local authorities and other public bodies
(Heald & McLeod, 2002, p. 149)

This system appears a little complicated, but it is the block grant which is, by far, the most important. The block grant is the major source of revenue. The system through which it is allocated has been utilised since 1978, with only minimal changes. It is known as the **Barnett formula** – named after Joel Barnett, who is credited with devising the formula while Chief Secretary to the Treasury. This formula is a population-based mechanism, not a needs-based mechanism (Heald & McLeod, 2002, p. 151). It is given in relation to the size of population in each devolved territory, and in relation to the amount of money being spent in England.

In effect, the Barnett formula gives a block grant to Scotland, Wales and Northern Ireland (although the latter was not originally included in the formula). The original formula was 85:10:5. This meant that for every £85 on comparable public expenditure on English services equivalent to those in Scotland or Wales, the Scottish block automatically received £10 (or 11.76% of English funding), and the Welsh £5 (or 5.88% of English funding). Northern Ireland received £2.75 for every £100 spent in England (Bogdanor, 2001, p. 243).

After the 1991 census, the funding allocations were reviewed. As of 2013, Scotland receives 10.66% of English funding (i.e. £10.66 for every £100 spent on comparable English expenditure), Wales 6.02%, and Northern Ireland 2.87%.

Thus, funding for the devolved bodies is passed as a block from central government. The devolved administrations, just like the secretaries of state who were in post prior to political devolution, distribute the funds as they see fit (Bell & Christie, 2005).

Conclusion
Within the UK, there are clear devolved structures. Scotland, Wales and Northern Ireland each have their own directly-elected assembly/parliament. Until 2012, England had a form of devolution as well, although (outside of London) it was unelected. This is clearly asymmetric devolution.

At the same time, however, the heavy hand of central government is still prominent. This is most notable through the centralised system of funding the devolved bodies. Yet, it is also prominent through the constitutional position: parliamentary sovereignty. In theory, any future government could repeal all of the devolution legislation. While this is seen as being highly unlikely to occur, it may not stop future governments from tampering with the devolution legislation. There remains the theoretical possibility of repealing the legislation.

Selected bibliography
Bell, David & Christie, Alex. (2005). "Finance: Paying the Piper, Calling the Tune?" in Trench, Alan (ed.); *The Dynamics of Devolution: The State of the Nations 2005,* imprinta academic, pp. 161-177.

Bogdanor, Vernon. (2001). *Devolution in the United Kingdom:* Oxford University Press.

Bogdanor, Vernon. (2010). "The West Lothian Question", *Parliamentary Affairs* vol. 63-1, pp. 156-172.

Heald, David & McLeod, Alasdair. (2002). "Beyond Barnett? Financing devolution" in Adams, John & Robinson, Peter (eds.); *Devolution in Practice: Public Policy Differences within the UK* IPPR, pp.147-175.

Mellett, R. (2009). "A Principles-based Approach to the Barnett Formula",

Political Quarterly vol. 80-1, pp. 76-83.

Trench, Alan. (2005c). "Whitehall and the Process of Legislation after Devolution" in Hazell, Robert & Rawlings, Richard (eds.); *Devolution, Law Making and the Constitution,* Imprint Academic, pp. 193-225.

Websites

news.bbc.co.uk/1/hi/uk_politics/election_2010/first_time_voter/8589835.stm
The BBC provides a beginners guide to devolution

www.ucl.ac.uk/constitution-unit/
The constitution Unit has some interesting material on devolution

Questions

1. "The UK should move from a system of devolution to one of federalism." Discuss.
2. Present the case for political devolution for the English regions.

CHAPTER 27 // SCOTLAND

Contents
- **Introduction**
- **History**
- **Referendum**
- **Elections**
- **Powers**
- **Personnel**
- **Conclusion**

Introduction

As noted in the previous chapter, the issue of devolution is separate to that of nationalism. Nationalists in Scotland may have been less than enthused about devolution, as it could be seen as another barrier to prevent Scottish independence. Conversely, supporters of devolution may have perceived it as a way of preventing the creation of an independent Scotland.

This highlights, to some extent, the issue of national identity. Moreno (2006) raises the idea of a dual identity – the extent to which people in Scotland see themselves as both Scottish and British. In many ways, devolution promotes this dual identity. Survey research supports this. From 1986, opinion polls in Scotland started to ask what has become known as the 'Moreno Question' (Moreno 2006). It focuses on perceptions of national identity. In effect, the question asks whether you feel yourself to be:

1. Scottish, not British
2. More Scottish than British
3. Equally Scottish and British
4. More British than Scottish
5. British, not Scottish

Very few respondents in Scotland perceive themselves to be British, not Scottish. The largest numbers perceive themselves as a mix of Scottish and British (although divided over the degree of mix – which covers three of the five options available to respondents). Thus it may be devolution fits the needs and perceptions of most Scots at this moment in time.

History

The Act of Union of 1707 is perceived as a pivotal point in Scottish politics. With this act, Scotland lost its own Parliament, although Scotland did retain its separate legal system. A separate banking system and a different education system were to emerge later. In 1885 the Scottish Office was formed, which was the beginning of administrative devolution for Scotland. Although, as Bogdanor (2001, p. 111) notes, the Scottish Office began "with hardly any functional responsibilities". Yet in some quarters this was perceived as being insufficient. The formation of the

SNP in 1934 focused attention upon the possibility of an independent Scotland. Electorally, the SNP was unsuccessful until the 1970s. Despite the occasional by-election success, the SNP was viewed as being on the fringes of mainstream politics. It was only as dissatisfaction grew with the three major parties that the SNP was able to develop a bedrock of support. Perceptions in Scotland suggested the English knew little and cared less about events in Scotland. This was the type of feeling upon which the SNP was able to capitalise. Such feelings existed despite the increasing role of the Scottish Office, which had seen "a continual accretion of functions until, by the 1960s, the Secretary of State was expected to take an interest in all matters affecting Scotland" (Bogdanor, 2001, p. 111).

In March 1979 a referendum was held on the issue of devolution for Scotland. The result caused some controversy as an absolute majority of people voted in favour. A special clause had been inserted requiring a minimum of 40% of those eligible to vote to support devolution before it could take effect. As can be seen in the table below, this threshold was not achieved.

Table 27.1 Support for Scottish Devolution at the 1979 Referendum

	% voters	% total electorate
YES	51.6	32.5
NO	48.4	30.4
DID NOT VOTE	-	37.1

Thereafter, support for the SNP declined, and apparently so did support for devolution. During the Thatcher years, the devolution debate re-emerged more strongly than ever. With events such as the imposition of the Community Charge (Poll Tax) a year prior to the rest of Britain, and ever-decreasing support for the Conservatives in Scotland, the Scottish people again looked towards running their own affairs. Consequently, support for the SNP started to rise.

Table 27.2 SNP support in General Elections since 1970

YEAR	SEATS	% SCOTTISH VOTE
1970	1	11.0
1974 (Feb.)	6	21.9
1974 (Oct.)	11	30.4
1979	2	17.3
1983	2	11.8
1987	3	14.1
1992	3	21.5
1997	6	22.1
2001	5	20.1
2005	6	17.7
2010	6	19.9

In both the 1992 and 1997 election campaigns, there were commitments from Labour and the Liberal Democrats for a referendum on devolution. With Labour winning the 1997 General Election, the commitment to a referendum was carried through.

Referendum

The 1997 referendum differed from that of 1979. A key point to note is the 1997 referendum was a **pre-legislative referendum** (i.e. people were asked to vote on the broad principle of devolution, with a Bill to follow). In 1979, the referendum was **post-legislative**. The legislation was already on the statute books, and therefore had to be repealed.

On 11 September 1997, a two-question referendum was held. The questions were:

- I agree that there should be a Scottish Parliament
- I agree that a Scottish Parliament should have tax-varying powers

Labour, the Liberal Democrats and the SNP all campaigned for a 'Yes-Yes' vote. The Conservatives campaigned for a 'No-No' vote. Unlike in the 1979 referendum, there were no thresholds to be achieved beyond a majority vote. The turnout in Scotland was surprisingly low at 60.4% (which was marginally lower than in 1979), with 73.4% voting for a Scottish Parliament, and 63.5% for tax-varying powers. Had there been a threshold as in 1979, the tax-varying powers would have been defeated.

The results were collated by council areas. Every council area had a majority for a Scottish Parliament. The support ranged from 84.7% (West Dunbartonshire) to 60.7% (Dumfries and Galloway). With regard to the vote on tax-varying powers, the support was not quite so strong. The City of Glasgow recorded 75% in favour of tax-varying powers. Two council areas, Orkney and Dumfries & Galloway, had majorities *against* tax-varying powers at 52.3% and 51.2% respectively. The turnout was varied across Scotland from 72.7% (East Dunbartonshire) to 51.5% in Shetland and 51.6% in the City of Glasgow.

With the success of the referendum, the Scotland Bill faced little opposition as it went through Parliament. It received Royal Assent in November 1998. The first elections to the Scottish Parliament were on 6 May 1999.

Table 27.3 Scottish Referendum (1997) results by Council Areas

Council area	Support for a Scottish Parliament (%)	Support for tax varying powers (%)	Turnout (%)
City of Aberdeen	71.8	60.3	53.7
Aberdeenshire	63.9	52.3	57.0
Angus	64.7	53.4	60.2
Argyll & Bute	67.3	57.0	65.0
East Ayrshire	81.1	70.5	64.8
North Ayrshire	76.3	65.7	63.4
South Ayrshire	66.9	56.2	66.7
Scottish Borders	62.8	50.7	64.8
Clackmannan	80.0	68.7	66.1
West Dunbartonshire	84.7	74.7	63.7
East Dunbartonshire	69.8	59.1	72.7
Dumfries & Galloway	60.7	48.8	63.4
City of Dundee	76.0	65.5	55.7
City of Edinburgh	71.9	62.0	60.1
Falkirk	80.0	69.2	63.7
Fife	76.1	64.7	60.7
City of Glasgow	83.6	75.0	51.6
Highland	72.6	62.1	60.3
Inverclyde	78.0	67.2	60.4
North Lanarkshire	82.6	72.2	60.8
South Lanarkshire	77.8	67.6	63.1
East Lothian	74.2	62.7	65.0
Midlothian	79.9	67.7	65.1
West Lothian	79.6	67.3	62.6
Moray	67.2	52.7	57.8
Orkney	57.3	47.7	53.5
Perth & Kinross	61.7	51.3	63.1
Renfrewshire	79.0	63.6	62.8
East Renfrewshire	61.7	51.6	68.2
Shetland	62.4	51.6	51.5
Stirling	68.5	58.9	65.5
Western Isles	79.4	68.4	55.8
ALL SCOTLAND	**74.3**	**63.5**	**60.4**

Elections

The elections to the Scottish Parliament are conducted under a form of the Mixed Member-Proportional (MMP) system (see Chapter 20). Each voter casts two votes. The first is for a constituency representative using Simple Plurality. The second is for a party list. This is to ensure a more proportional outcome. The lists were drawn on a regional basis, with Scotland being divided up into eight regions. There are 129 Members of the Scottish Parliament (MSPs). Of these, 73 are elected under Simple Plurality. The remaining 56 are the regional 'top ups'. The constituencies were the same as used for elections to Westminster in 1997, except for Orkney and Shetland. This Westminster constituency was separated into two constituencies for the Scottish elections. The regions are the Scottish constituencies to the European Parliament.

One of the reasons for selecting this particular electoral system was to reduce the possibility of an outright SNP victory. Labour, it appears, was willing to sacrifice the likelihood of having outright control of the Scottish Parliament (in its early years), to ensure the SNP would only ever gain power as a minority government, or as part of a coalition. In either case, legislation for an independent Scotland would never be passed. Yet, the 2011 elections to the Scottish Parliament returned a majority SNP government. Consequently, the issue of a referendum on independence returned to the political agenda.

In each of the elections to the Scottish Parliament, the focus has been upon the fight between the Labour Party and the SNP – and, more specifically, the extent to which the SNP would be likely to challenge Labour as the largest party at Holyrood. The Conservatives and the Liberal Democrats have been consigned to the background, while other smaller parties have been seen as even less consequential. It must be noted, however, in each election there appears to have been an assumption that Labour and the Liberal Democrats would be the most likely coalition partners. The results are detailed in Table 27.4 through to Table 27.6.

Table 27.4 Scottish Parliamentary Election results (total seats won)

Party	1999	2003	2007	2011
Conservative	18	18	17	15
Green	1	7	2	2
Labour	56	50	46	37
Liberal Democrat	17	17	16	5
Scottish Nationalist	35	27	47	69
Others	2	10	1	1

Table 27.5 Scottish Parliamentary election results (by constituency and list seats)

Party	1999		2003		2007		2011	
	Constit.	List	Constit.	List	Constit.	List	Constit.	List
Conservative	0	18	3	15	4	13	3	12
Green	0	1	0	7	0	2	0	2
Labour	53	3	46	4	37	9	15	22
Liberal Democrat	12	5	13	4	11	5	2	3
Scottish Nationalist	7	28	9	18	21	26	53	16
Others	1	1	2	8	0	1	0	1

Table 27.6 Scottish Parliamentary election results (% votes by constituency and list)

Party	1999		2003		2007		2011	
	Constit.	List	Constit.	List	Constit.	List	Constit.	List
Conservative	15.6	15.4	16.6	15.5	16.6	13.9	13.9	12.4
Green	0*	3.6	0*	6.9	0.1	4.0	0*	4.4
Labour	38.8	33.6	34.6	29.3	32.1	29.1	31.7	26.3
Liberal Democrat	14.2	12.4	15.4	11.8	16.2	11.3	7.9	5.2
Scottish Nationalist	28.7	27.3	23.8	20.9	32.9	31.0	45.4	44.0
Others	2.7	7.7	9.6	15.6	2.1	9.7	1.1	7.7

*The Green Party did not field any constituency candidates in this election

In the first two elections, Labour were the largest party in terms of seats won – and quite significantly so, although failing to gain an outright majority. In 1999, Labour fell seven seats short of an outright majority. Some pundits predicted this would be the closest any party would ever get to an outright majority in the Scottish Parliament. They were proven wrong in 2011.

In 2007, there was a stunning reversal. Not only did the SNP win more seats than Labour (by 1 seat), but they also outpolled Labour in terms of votes in both constituency votes and regional lists. Labour may have won the most constituency seats in 2007, but the SNP gained more constituency votes! This then proved to be a strong base for the SNP to be able to dominate the 2011 campaign: a minority government defending their record. In 2011, Westminster politics may have had some influence upon the collapse of Liberal Democrat support, but the SNP surged ahead, gaining 53 constituency seats (the same as Labour in 1999) but retaining regional list support to almost the same levels.

What is evident from the election results is the Conservatives and Liberal Democrats have a core of support, above which they seem unable to move – although much of this collapsed for the Liberal Democrats in 2011. If gains are made at the constituency level, as have been made by the Conservatives in 2003 and 2007, they result in a loss of 'top up' regional seats.

Overall, there appears to be a polarisation in Scottish politics, with the two major parties going toe-to-toe. Consequently, support for the minor parties diminishes, while support for the Conservatives and Liberal Democrats appears, at best, to be static.

Powers

The most notable power of the Scottish Parliament is that of varying the taxation levels. The Scottish Parliament can change the level of income tax by up to 3 pence. In fact during the first election campaign, the SNP proposed Scotland not receive a 1 pence reduction in income tax that had been proposed in the budget. They wished to invest that money (an estimated £690 million over three years) in public services such as health, housing and education. Labour, on the other hand, gave a commitment to leave this power unused during the first Parliament.

The key to the financing of public policy in Scotland is the Barnett Formula. Effectively, this is the Treasury grant to Scotland, which is the staple for financing the Scottish budget. The Scottish Executive has widespread discretion over the allocation of these funds within the total. The Barnett Formula was explained in Chapter 26.

The actual powers of the Scottish Parliament were detailed in the White Paper, *Scotland's Parliament* (Cm 3658), in July 1997. These were reiterated in the Scotland Act (1998). The key areas of responsibility included:

- health
- education
- transport
- housing
- training
- economic development
- agriculture
- the environment
- tourism
- law courts
- police
- fire service

Although the powers of the Act stipulated the responsibilities very clearly, the basic principle was 'what is not specifically reserved to Westminster is devolved'. This is the opposite to the situation in the 1970s where nothing was devolved unless specifically cited in the legislation.

Within each of the above areas, the Scottish Parliament had primary law making powers. For example, with regard to higher education, the Scottish Parliament abolished up-front tuition fees. Salary awards for school teachers in 2001 were significantly higher in Scotland (21.5% over three years) compared to the rest of the UK. Similar awards could be negotiated for the nursing profession in Scotland as well. Free personal care for the elderly has been provided by the state since April 2002, whereas in the rest of Britain it is means tested. In March 2006, a ban on smoking in public places was introduced in Scotland prior to anywhere else in the UK.

Many areas of policy making were reserved for Westminster. These included: constitutional matters; foreign and defence policy; most economic policy; social security; and, medical ethics. The Scottish Parliament cannot, for example, pass legislation proclaiming independence. Nor can it ban nuclear weapons from Scottish territory. Benefit levels cannot be adjusted either. Such decisions would have to be taken by central government. Should the Scottish Parliament attempt to legislate in these reserved areas, it would be acting *ultra vires* (or beyond the law). Within this, however, there are some areas of flexibility. For example, the electoral system cannot be changed for elections to the Scottish Parliament. The system used at local government level can, however, be changed. The Single Transferable Vote (STV) was introduced for local elections in Scotland in 2008.

There is one major issue over the power relationship between Holyrood and Westminster. Acts of the Scottish Parliament have the same force of law as those passed by Westminster. In the case of conflict between the two, the Scottish legislation prevails in Scotland (Page, 2005, p. 7). In the Scotland Act (1998), however, there was a clear caveat. "Once a bill has been passed there is a four week 'holding' period during which the United Kingdom or the Scottish Law Officers may refer the question of whether it is within the legislative competence of the Scottish Parliament to the Judicial Committee of the Privy Council" (Page, 2005, p. 31). Thus, any legislation passed by the Scottish Parliament is, in effect, vetted before it comes into law.

Added to this, the Westminster Parliament can intercede in Scottish affairs. This is straight forward if it is a reserved power e.g. defence. The **Sewel Convention** states Westminster will not normally legislate on devolved matters without the consent of the devolved legislature (Page, 2005; Winetrobe, 2005). In the first Scottish Parliament (1999-2003), 41 Sewel motions (now known as **Legislative Consent Motions**) were passed. A further 41 were passed in the 2003-2007 Parliament, and 31 were passed in the 2007-2011 Parliament (included in each of these sessions were Acts where Legislative Consent

Motions were not initiated). This means Westminster passed legislation on matters that were under the control of the Scottish Parliament (see Winetrobe, 2005). Yet the concern is not over who legislates on what issue. Some of the Sewel motions may have come from, for example, EU legislation. Others may be through the desire to have uniform UK-wide legislation, for example, the powers for the courts to confiscate assets of serious offenders.

> The central criticism of the Sewel Convention as a law making device, is that legislation subject to the Sewel process is not only *not* scrutinised by the Scottish Parliament in its usual ways... but also that it *is* scrutinised by the very place and by the very procedures whose perceived failings were a justification for both devolution and the devising of Holyrood's own legislative process. (Winetrobe, 2005, p. 42)

If the Scottish Parliament permits Westminster to legislate on a devolved matter, the Scottish Parliament does not even scrutinise the legislation. Such a situation is far worse (from a Scottish position) than existed pre-1999. At least then there were bodies representing Scottish interests who had input into, and scrutiny of, legislation. There appears now to be a perception in Westminster that if the Scottish Parliament gives consent to a Sewel motion, then it becomes a wholly Westminster issue.

A final point to note about the powers of the devolved bodies in Scotland is the name. While such a point may seem relatively unimportant, there was actually much at stake.

When political devolution came into effect in 1999, a Scottish Parliament was elected. From this was selected a Scottish Executive. When the SNP gained power in 2007, the name was changed from the Scottish Executive to the Scottish Government. There appeared to be few objections to this unilateral move. It does mean, however, the Scots can claim to be governing themselves rather than merely executing orders from elsewhere. And with the SNP winning outright in 2011, moves were afoot to increase the powers of the Scottish Government, if not outright independence.

The independence referendum campaign has seen David Cameron promise the Scots "Devo Max" if they vote against independence. In other words, he is willing to ask Parliament to devolve even more powers to the Scots in order to keep them in the Union. Some cynics have argued this is a 'win-win' situation for Alex Salmond. If the referendum returns a 'Yes' vote, Scotland gains independence. A 'No' vote will result in extra powers being devolved to Scotland.

Personnel

The members of the Scottish Government are becoming household names in Scotland. Throughout the rest of Britain, very few people actually know any of the post holders, beyond the First Minister. When Alex Salmond was First Minister of Scotland, he was able to generate an awareness of the Scottish Government across the UK. Apart from Donald Dewar – who was the first First Minister – no other Scottish politician has such a high UK-wide profile.

Table 27.7 The Scottish Executive, 2013

FIRST MINISTER	**ALEX SALMOND**
Deputy First Minister, and Infrastructure, Investment and Cities	**Nicola Sturgeon**
Finance, Employment and Sustainable Growth	**John Swinney**
Education and Life-Long Learning	**Michael Russell**
Justice	**Kenny MacAskill**
Rural Affairs and the Environment	**Bruce Lochhead**
Culture and External Affairs	**Fiona Hyslop**
Health and Wellbeing	**Alex Neil**

Mention must be made of the civil service (see Pyper (2001) for greater detail). The civil servants who worked for the Scottish Office (pre-1999) were transferred to the Scottish Executive (now Scottish Government). They remain part of the British or 'Home' civil service, with unchanged status, conditions of service, and so forth. The Scottish Government, however, has made it very clear as to where the Scottish civil servant's allegiances must lie. On the 'Frequently Asked Questions' section of the Scottish Government's website, it states that "civil servants working for the Scottish Government owe their loyalty to the devolved administration rather than the UK Government".

Some aspects of the civil service workload have changed, most notably the increased volume of work, and a change in the nature of the work. The Scottish Office was a relatively small government department. Today, these civil servants are serving a First Minister, a Cabinet, and sub-Cabinet ministers.

Conclusion

The election of the SNP minority government in 2007 had a profound impact upon Scotland. For the first time, there was an administration in Edinburgh that was not closely associated with the London Government. There had been a belief (rightly or wrongly) that every Labour First Minister was linked to either Tony Blair or Gordon Brown. With a coalition government in London, the relationship changed again. The Scottish Government under the SNP appeared more willing to assert their autonomy from the rest of the UK. There had been talk of a referendum on independence (after the election of the SNP minority government). Although such a referendum was not permitted under the devolution legislation, it did not stop a number of

Labour MSPs supporting the calling of such a referendum. The belief was the referendum would be defeated, and this would neuter the SNP – potentially permanently.

The relationship changed more significantly after the 2011 Scottish Parliamentary elections. Not only was there more talk of holding a referendum on Scottish independence, but Alex Salmond was also negotiating the devolving of further powers to Scotland. He was able to defend such demands by highlighting his mandate from the Scottish people. Salmond's position was enhanced further with the resignations of the leaders of the Scottish Conservative, Labour and Liberal Democrat party leaders! And on 18 September 2014 the Scots will vote on whether or not Scotland should be an independent country.

Selected bibliography

Cooke, Phil. (2005). "Devolution and Innovation: The Financing of Economic Development in the UK's Devolved Administrations", *Scottish Affairs* no. 50, pp. 39-51.

Crawford, Bruce. (2009). "Ten Years of Devolution", *Parliamentary Affairs* vol. 63-1, pp. 89-97.

Moreno, Luis. (2006). "Scotland, Catalonia, Europeanization and the 'Moreno Question'", *Scottish Affairs*, no. 54, pp. 1-21.

Page, Alan. (2005). "A Parliament that is Different? Law Making in the Scottish Parliament", in Hazell, Robert & Rawlings, Richard (eds.); *Devolution, Law Making and the Constitution,* imprint academic pp. 7-38.

Saunders, Ben. (2013). "Scottish Independence and the All-Affected Interests Principle", *Politics* vol. 33-1, pp. 47-55.

Websites

home.scotland.gov.uk/
The homepage of the Scottish Government

www.scotland.gov.uk/About/Sewel
The Scottish Government's explanation as to how the Sewel Convention operates. From here it is possible to go to adjoining pages that list all of the legislation passed through Sewel

www.scotreferendum.com/information/
This site provides information about the Scottish referendum on independence

www.scottish.parliament.gov.uk/
The homepage of the Scottish Parliament

Questions

1. Present the case for Scotland becoming an independent country.
2. "Scottish devolution makes the Union stronger." Discuss.

CHAPTER 28 // WALES

Contents
- **Introduction**
- **History**
- **Referendum on Devolution**
- **Elections**
- **Powers**
- **Personnel**
- **Conclusion**

Introduction

The history of Welsh nationalism, and more recently the demands for devolution, has had a significantly different emphasis compared to Scotland. In recent times, demands for Welsh independence have been few and far between. Added to this, demands for Welsh devolution appear to be met by apathy from many Welsh people. While there is a very strong vein of national feeling, this has not transformed into any great political demands.

Thus, whereas Scottish nationalism has focused upon independence, and many of the economic problems in Scotland, the fight in Wales has been largely over the protection of the Welsh language and culture. It could be argued such issues are just as easily defended and protected through administrative devolution as political devolution.

History

Wales was conquered by England in 1536. There was no formal Parliament or any other similar bodies, unlike in Scotland. The economic plunder of Wales followed this military conquest. There were also systematic attempts to eradicate the Welsh language and culture. From 1746, for governmental purposes, Wales was treated as part of England (Bogdanor, 2001). It was not until 1964 that the Welsh Office was created. This had been a manifesto pledge by the Labour Party in that year's general election.

Prior to the creation of the Welsh Office, there had been some administrative devolution. An example of this was in 1907, when the Welsh Department of the Board of Education was established (Bogdanor, 2001).

The party that has symbolised the Welsh struggle in recent years has been Plaid Cymru (the Party of Wales). Plaid was formed in 1925. It first won a Parliamentary seat in a by-election in Carmarthen in 1966. This was subsequently lost in the 1970 General Election. Compared to the SNP, Plaid has never had similar electoral success. Even in the 1970s, during the height of nationalist support, Plaid made a negligible impact on Welsh politics.

The referendum on devolution in 1979 symbolised the lack of support for both Plaid and for devolution. The 1979 referendum was soundly defeated.

Table 28.1 Support for Welsh Devolution at the 1979 Referendum

	% voters	% total electorate
YES	20.2	11.8
NO	79.8	46.5
DID NOT VOTE	-	41.7

Whereas in Scotland, apathy prevented the implementation of devolution, in Wales there was simply a lack of support. Much of this may have been due to the Labour Party in Wales being seriously split over the issue, with members such as Neil Kinnock being vehemently opposed to devolution at this time.

What was surprising was support for Plaid Cymru did not tail off in the way the SNP lost support after the defeat of the referendum. There was some drop off. Yet it was not until the 2001 election that Plaid was able to surpass the levels of support achieved in 1970. Again, there has since been a gradual tailing off of support back to the levels of 1970.

Table 28.2 Plaid Cymru support in General Elections since 1970

YEAR	SEATS	% WELSH VOTE
1970	0	11.5
1974 (Feb.)	2	10.7
1974 (Oct.)	3	10.8
1979	2	8.1
1983	2	7.8
1987	3	7.3
1992	4	8.8
1997	4	9.9
2001	4	14.3
2005	2	12.6
2010	3	11.3

After the 1997 General Election, Plaid was the second largest party in Wales, with regard to the number of seats held. This position was maintained after the 2001 election, although support for Plaid has eroded away in subsequent general elections. They have a bedrock of support in the Northwest and West of

Wales (although the constituency of Ynys Môn, which is the island of Anglesey, was lost in 2001). Yet support for devolution, even in the late 1980s and early 1990s was muted at best. Demand for devolution in Wales was very much on the shirt tails of Scottish demands. This was to have a profound impact upon the 1997 devolution campaign.

Referendum on Devolution

As with the 1997 Scottish referendum, the Welsh one was pre-legislative (and in 1979, as in Scotland, it had been post-legislative). The Welsh referendum was held one week after the Scottish referendum. With support for devolution decidedly lukewarm, the Blair Government hoped to create a bandwagon effect. On top of this, the proposed Welsh Assembly was to have very limited powers. The referendum was a single question.

- I agree that there should be a Welsh Assembly

Labour, the Liberal Democrats and Plaid Cymru all campaigned for a 'Yes' vote, while the Conservatives campaigned for a 'No' vote. As expected, the result was very close. A mere 50.3% voted 'Yes', but with a turnout of only 50.1%, there was no decisive move for devolution. The gap in support for the 'Yes' and 'No' campaigns was 6 721 votes. Apathy was the real winner as Wales stumbled into devolution.

There was a clear divide in Wales over support for devolution. West Wales supported devolution, East Wales (bordering England) did not. The only exception was Pembrokeshire, in the Southwest corner of Wales, which voted 'No'. As with Scotland, the result was reported by council area. The most notable result was from the capital city, Cardiff, as it voted against the formation of a National Assembly of Wales (NAW)

Of the twenty two councils, half voted in favour of a Welsh Assembly, and half against. Neath Port Talbot had the highest level of support (66.5%), while Monmouthshire had the most opposition (67.9% against a Welsh Assembly). The turnout, which was very poor across all of Wales, varied between council areas from a high in Gwynedd (59.8%) to a low in Flintshire (41%). There was no consistency between levels of turnout and support for the NAW between council areas.

Table 28.3 Welsh Referendum (1997) results by Council Areas

Council Area	Percentage support for a Welsh Assembly	Turnout %
Blaenau Gwent	56.4	49.3
Brigend	54.4	50.6
Caerphilly	54.7	49.3
Cardiff	44.4	46.9
Carmarthenshire	65.3	56.4
Ceredigion	59.2	56.8
Conwy	40.9	51.5
Denbighshire	40.8	49.8
Flintshire	38.2	41.0
Gwynedd	64.1	59.8
Merthyr Tydfil	58.2	49.5
Monmouthshire	32.1	50.5
Neath Port Talbot	66.5	51.9
Newport	37.4	46.1
Pembrokeshire	42.8	52.6
Powys	42.7	56.2
Rhondda Cynon Taff	58.5	49.9
City of Swansea	52.0	47.1
Torfaen	49.8	45.5
Vale of Glamorgan	36.7	54.3
Wrexham	45.3	42.4
Ynys Môn	50.9	56.9
ALL WALES	**50.3**	**50.1**

Elections

The elections to the NAW used the same electoral system as those for the Scottish Parliament. There were 40 constituency seats, and 20 top up seats, with five regions each returning four Assembly members. Labour was expected to be the largest party in the NAW. In fact, most forecasts predicted a working majority for the Labour Party. This was based largely upon the 1997 General Election result where Labour won 34 out of the 40 Welsh seats.

The Labour Party appeared to do everything they could to prevent such an outcome – most notably with the selection of the leader for the Labour Party in Wales, and probably First Minister designate. Unlike in Scotland, where Donald Dewar was clearly the top person for the job, there was a dispute in Wales. This was between Alun Michael, who was Tony Blair's choice for the post, and Rhodri Morgan, who was portrayed as 'Old Labour' but perceived as the people's choice. Alun Michael's selection appeared to be engineered and a backlash was delivered in the election.

Table 28.4 Welsh Assembly Election Results (seats)

Party	1999	2003	2007	2011
Conservative	9	11	12	14
Labour	28	30	26	30
Liberal Democrat	6	6	6	5
Plaid Cymru	17	12	15	11
Other	0	1	1	0

Table 28.5 Welsh Assembly Election Results (by constituency and list seats)

Party	1999		2003		2007		2011	
	Const	List	Const	List	Const	List	Const	List
Conservative	1	8	1	10	5	7	6	8
Labour	27	1	30	0	24	2	28	2
Liberal Democrat	3	3	3	3	3	3	1	4
Plaid Cymru	9	8	5	7	7	8	5	6
Other	0	0	1	0	1	0	0	0

Table 28.6 Welsh Assembly Election Results (% votes by constituency and list)

Party	1999		2003		2007		2011	
	Const	List	Const	List	Const	List	Const	List
Conservative	15.8	16.5	19.9	19.2	22.4	21.4	25.0	22.5
Labour	37.6	35.4	40.0	36.6	32.2	29.6	42.3	36.9
Liberal Democrat	13.5	12.5	14.1	12.7	14.8	11.7	10.6	8.0
Plaid Cymru	28.4	30.5	21.2	19.7	22.4	21.0	19.3	17.9
Other	4.7	5.1	4.7	11.9	8.2	16.3	2.9	14.6

Labour's failure to win control of the NAW in the first assembly elections was portrayed as an election defeat. Although Labour was comfortably ahead of second placed Plaid Cymru, the dilemma became whether or not to form a coalition government. Alun Michael decided not to go into coalition with the Liberal Democrats, but to lead a minority administration. Coalition with either the Conservatives or Plaid Cymru was not even considered. This administration came close to failure, before Rhodri Morgan took over as Labour leader in Wales, and First Minister, and formed a coalition with the Liberal Democrats.

Each of the subsequent elections has followed a similar pattern: will Labour be able to form a majority government? Labour's support has fluctuated. They have been involved in forming a government after every election to date, but they have never achieved an outright majority. This has resulted in coalition government with the Liberal Democrats, and with Plaid Cymru (2007-2011). Since the 2011 election, Labour has been in a minority administration.

Plaid Cymru's support seemed to peak in the first elections, and has gradually decreased in subsequent elections. It decreased more significantly after a term in coalition government with Labour. Conversely, the Conservatives have seen a gradual improvement in each election. The Liberal Democrats have appeared static, with a slight drop in 2011 (which could be attributed to Westminster politics rather than Welsh politics).

Powers
The Government of Wales Act, 1998 laid out very clearly the powers of the NAW. While the NAW has been viewed as little more than a 'talk shop', this is not strictly accurate. The legislation provided guidelines as to what the NAW could do. Originally, the perception was the NAW "would perform the functions both of Whitehall and Westminster" (Miers & Lambert, 2002, p. 663). In comparison, the Scottish Parliament was given more vague guidelines, and left to interpret its powers as it saw fit.

The Government of Wales Act (1998) devolved power to the NAW as a corporate body, combining (some) legislative, executive, scrutiny and administrative functions. Effectively, the powers of the Secretary of State for Wales were transferred. The problem was these powers were not clear cut. For example, if there was an education issue in Wales, which department would take the lead: the Department of Education or the Welsh Office? Therefore this needed "explicit recognition" (Miers & Lambert, 2002, p. 665) of the division of functions in all legislation. The NAW had the power to develop and implement policy in a number of fields. These are:

- agriculture, fisheries, forestry and rural development
- ancient monuments and historic buildings
- culture
- economic development
- education and training
- environment
- fire and rescue and promotion of fire safety
- food
- health and health services
- highways and transport
- housing
- local government
- National Assembly for Wales
- public administration
- social services

- sports and recreation
- tourism
- town and country planning
- water and flood defences
- the Welsh language

While this list seems far more extensive than that for the Scottish Parliament, it must be borne in mind this was a list of areas for policy implementation rather than policy formulation. The NAW was delegated secondary legislative powers, unlike the Scottish Parliament, which has primary legislative powers (see Table 26.1). This meant the NAW could only legislate to complete the details of Acts passed by Westminster. In other words, the NAW could make proposals as to how policy could be delivered rather than making the actual policy.

There was a suggestion this situation of 'completing the details' of the legislation meant far less input into the legislative process than had existed prior to devolution. The NAW was responsible for implementing legislation but it was "not party to the internal preparation of such legislation within Whitehall" (Patchett, 2005, p. 112). In pre-devolutionary times, the Welsh Office would have had some input into the preparation of any legislation that affected Wales. Thus, post-devolution, a concordat was drawn up between the NAW and the Welsh Office (Rawlings, 2001, p. 68). Both acknowledged the need to maintain a good working relationship. The Welsh Office made a commitment that the views of the NAW would be considered in legislation being drawn up in Whitehall that would have an impact on Wales (Rawlings, 2001, p. 68).

Where there was a significant change in the operation of politics in Welsh devolution was in consultation and openness. "The Government of Wales Act (1998) committed the National Assembly of Wales to a *legally binding* partnership with voluntary organisations" (Hodgson, 2004, p. 88). Thus there was a formalised relationship between the NAW and a range of voluntary organisations and pressure groups across the country. It enabled many groups to have the opportunity to liase with the NAW. Consequently, many groups employed dedicated staff to dealing with the NAW – although there was a criticism that many groups felt they were being swamped by the volume of information emanating from the Assembly.

Despite this partnership with voluntary organisations, there was a feeling devolution had failed to engage with many people in Wales. It was not necessarily due to a lack of support for devolution. One argument was with only secondary powers being devolved to the NAW, the elections were "classic 'second-order' elections" (Scully *et al*, 2004, p520). People did not engage or participate because it was perceived nothing could be changed.

The NAW established a rather complex committee structure. There are Legislation Committees, Scrutiny Committees and Other Committees. Members of the Welsh Executive are not permitted to sit on these committees.

The Legislation Committees, of which there are five permanent committees, consider and report on legislation proposed by Assembly Members, as well as Government legislation. They last a full term. The Scrutiny Committees are also established to last the lifetime of the NAW. They include the Communities and Culture Committee, and the Enterprise and Learning Committee. Their role is to monitor Welsh Government policies, action and spending in their respective fields. The Other Committees oversee the work of the NAW and the Executive, covering everything that is not covered by the Scrutiny Committees and Legislation Committees. They include the Business Committee, and the Scrutiny of First Minister Committee.

In June 2002, the Richard Commission was established to examine the powers and the electoral arrangements of the NAW. The Commission reported back in the spring of 2004. Its conclusions were greater powers ought to be devolved to Wales, including primary legislative powers by 2011. To get to this stage, a progressive transfer of secondary legislative powers was envisaged, with a possible referendum on the transfer of primary legislative powers.

The Government of Wales Act (2006) separated the executive from the NAW. This meant the Executive became a distinct body in its own right, rather than a committee of the NAW. Added to this, within each of the fields listed earlier in this chapter, the NAW was given greater legislative competence to pass Legislative Measures. These were, effectively, primary legislative powers.

On 4 March 2011, there was another referendum in Wales. This was about the NAW receiving full primary legislative powers in the 20 fields that had been devolved. There was no consideration of extending the powers of the NAW to match the Scottish Parliament. The question was not the most straightforward. It did not roll off the tongue:

Do you want the Assembly now to be able to make laws on all matters in the 20 subject areas it has powers for?

The fear was a 'No' vote could set back any consensus on devolution in Wales. The result, however, returned a 'Yes' vote. On a turnout of 35.4%, it was hardly a ringing endorsement for primary legislative powers in Wales.

Table 28.7 Referendum Results 2011 by Council area

Council Area	% voting Yes	Turnout (%)
Blaenau Gwent	68.9	32.0
Brigend	68.1	35.4
Caerphilly	64.3	34.5
Cardiff	61.4	34.9
Carmarthenshire	70.8	44.0
Ceredigion	66.2	43.8
Conwy	59.7	33.5
Denbighshire	61.8	34.1
Flintshire	62.1	29.2
Gwynedd	76.0	43.1
Merthyr Tydfil	68.9	30.2
Monmouthshire	49.4	35.4
Neath Port Talbot	73.0	37.6
Newport	54.8	27.8
Pembrokeshire	55.0	38.3
Powys	51.6	39.7
Rhondda Cynon Taf	70.7	34.4
Swansea	63.2	32.8
Torfaen	62.8	33.4
Vale of Glamorgan	52.5	39.7
Wrexham	64.1	26.8
Ynys Môn	64.8	43.5
ALL WALES	**63.5**	**35.4**

Unlike in the referendum on devolution in 1997, only one council area voted against the referendum – Monmouthshire, with 50.6% voting 'No'. In 1997, Monmouthshire had registered the most opposition to devolution. Gwynedd returned the highest level of support for primary legislative powers (76%), with three other counties also returning over 70% support. The top three supporters of devolution in 1997 (Gwynedd, Carmarthenshire and Neath Port Talbot) were the same in the 2011 referendum. The highest level of turnout was in Carmarthenshire (44%), while Wrexham had the lowest (26.8%). As with the referendum in 1997, there was no correlation between turnout and support for the referendum.

After the referendum, there were clear commitments by all of the major parties not to go wild with their newly acquired powers. With the poor level of turnout, it was not a ringing endorsement. As Scully *et al* (2004, p. 537) have noted with regard to the original establishment of the NAW: "creating new elected political institutions does not necessarily engage the interests of the public or revitalize the democratic process." If anything, this is even more the case after the 2011 referendum.

Personnel

As with Scotland, the members of the Welsh Executive are not household names throughout Britain. When he was First Minister of Wales, Rhodri Morgan was by far the most prominent member. As First Minister, he took steps to bring the NAW closer to the people of Wales (although there was a legal obligation to do so). Most notably, the minutes of Welsh Executive meetings are made public. These can be accessed on the internet three weeks after the meeting.

Table 28.8 The Welsh Executive, 2013

FIRST MINISTER OF WALES	CARWYN JONES
Economy, Science and Transport	Edwina Hart
Education and Skills	Huw Lewis
Finance	Jane Hutt
Health and Social Services	Mark Drakeford
Housing and Regeneration	Carl Sargeant
Communities and Tackling Poverty	Jeff Cuthbert
Natural Resources and Food	Alun Michael
Culture and Sport	John Griffiths
Local Government and Government Business	Lesley Griffiths

As with Scotland, the members of the Welsh Executive are more prominent in Wales. With the increased powers devolved to the NAW – most notably, primary legislative powers – the Welsh Executive is likely to become even more prominent in Wales. It may well be the case, as in Scotland, the devolved executive members are better known in Wales than their Westminster counterparts.

Conclusion

Welsh devolution is far from straight forward. The most notable thing about the referenda that have been held is the extent of apathy across much of the country on every occasion. Yet the move to increase the powers of the NAW may increase people's awareness of the role of the NAW and the Welsh Executive. Having been castigated as being little more than a 'talk shop', the NAW has the opportunity to reset the Welsh political agenda. Rhodri Morgan talked of the need to create 'clear red water' between Cardiff and Westminster. The Government of Wales Act 2006 and the referendum result in 2011 present a clear opportunity for such a move to go ahead.

Yet there needs also to be a word of caution. There was not a ringing endorsement of the increased powers. Current and future Welsh Governments need to continue engaging and collaborating with the Welsh people. Primary legislative powers in the devolved fields are a starting point to present a Welsh agenda. But the Welsh Government will need to take the people with them. Failure to do so could see the end of the devolution project in Wales.

Selected bibliography

Hodgson, Lesley. (2004). "The National Assembly for Wales, Civil Society and Consultation", *Politics* vol. 24-2, pp. 88-95.

Miers, David & Lambert, David. (2002). "Law making in Wales: Wales Legislation on-line", *Public Law* pp. 663-669.

Rawlings, Richard. (2005). "Law Making in a Virtual Parliament: the Welsh Experience" in Hazell, Robert & Rawlings, Richard (eds.); *Devolution, Law Making and the Constitution,* Imprint Academic pp. 71-111.

Report of the Richard Commission. (2004). *Commission on the Powers and Electoral Arrangements of the National Assembly for Wales.*

Scully, Roger; Wyn Jones, Richard & Trystan, Dafydd. (2004). "Turnout, Participation and Legitimacy in Post-Devolution Wales", *British Journal of Political Science* vol. 34-3, pp. 519-537.

Websites

wales.gov.uk/
The homepage of the Welsh Government

www.assemblywales.org/
The homepage of the Welsh Assembly

www.wales-legislation.org.uk
This site shows the powers of the NAW and the legislation that has been passed

Questions
1. Why was devolution introduced into Wales?
2. Present the case for the Welsh Assembly being given greater legislative powers in a similar manner to that of the Scottish Parliament.
3. "Welsh devolution should be reversed." Discuss.

CHAPTER 29 // NORTHERN IRELAND

Contents

- **Introduction**
- **History**
- **Elections to the Northern Ireland Assembly**
- **Powers of the Legislative Assembly**
- **The Executive**
- **Consociationalism**
- **Conclusion**

Introduction

When looking at the issue of devolution for Northern Ireland, a first impression presents a highly complicated scenario. This is not wrong. Through much of history, the relationship between the island of Ireland and mainland Britain has been extremely bloody. This violent relationship has spilled out of Ireland and Britain, and into parts of Europe and North America. Even today, with a peace process operating for over a decade, there is still a prospect for violence. What has become noticeable is some of the formerly violent protagonists are now condemning violent actions. Yet, at the same time, Northern Ireland is still highly polarised. Travelling on the tourist buses around Belfast, for example, you can see the so-called peace wall, which, in effect, divides the communities. There may be peace in Northern Ireland, but there is little integration of the two major communities.

History

There are several key dates to note in Irish history before focusing specifically upon Northern Ireland. The first is the Battle of the Boyne (12 July 1690), when William of Orange, a Protestant, defeated the deposed James II of England, a Catholic. After this battle, legislation was passed in the British Parliament preventing Catholics from becoming monarch. Parts of the Protestant community commemorate this battle every year – most obviously, the Orange Order – but such celebrations are sometimes marred by violence.

In 1801 there was the Act of Union. This incorporated all of Ireland into a union with mainland Britain – the United Kingdom of Great Britain and Ireland. Such a union was not welcomed by a majority of the Irish population. Continual agitation culminated in the Easter Rising of 1916, where there was an attempt to set up an independent Irish State. This rebellion was suppressed and the leaders shot.

In 1922 the Irish Free State was established. The six counties of Ulster (Fermanagh, Tyrone, Derry, Antrim, Down and Armagh) remained part of the United Kingdom. These counties were given the title Northern Ireland. The rest of Ireland took the name the Irish Free State. In 1949 this became Eire or the Republic of Ireland.

Devolution – Rule by Stormont (1920-1972)

In creating Northern Ireland the British Government granted it a concession that neither Scotland nor Wales enjoyed: its own Parliament, Stormont, based in Belfast. From its inception there was no attempt to accommodate the large Catholic minority. The Protestant majority, expressed through the Unionist Party, used the devolved power of Stormont to bolster its authority, to ensure Protestants occupied all the powerful positions. For example, in 1929, the electoral system for the Stormont elections was changed from the Single Transferable Vote (STV) to Simple Plurality, to reduce the chances of non-Unionist candidates getting elected. At the local level, blatant gerrymandering of the boundaries ensured Catholics were also excluded from important positions whilst discriminatory practices against Catholics were normal.

It might have been thought the British Government would have viewed such a position with concern and, while individual MPs did raise questions, Westminster appeared to be indifferent to events in Northern Ireland, mainly because there were few incidents that raised alarm. The extremists failed to stir the majority of Catholics to gross acts of violence and the Irish Republican Army (IRA) looked as if it was moribund.

All this began to change with the growth of the civil rights movement by Ulster Catholics in the late 1960s. Stormont responded haltingly despite urgent requests by the then-Labour Government to institute reforms giving Catholics a greater say and opportunities in political and economic life. Even the mild reforms introduced caused the Unionist Party to split. A new hard-line party was formed – the Democratic Unionist Party – headed by the Reverend Ian Paisley.

With the civil rights marches escalating into riots, it became apparent Stormont was losing control of the situation. This was to become known as **The Troubles** (explained below). The situation became so bad the British Government instituted **Direct Rule** from 30 March 1972. The Northern Ireland Office was established, with its Secretary of State given cabinet status.

The Troubles 1968-1995

The rioting that occurred forced the British Government to intervene using the military. The first troops were sent to the province in 1969 after the Battle of Bogside. The IRA came to prominence but so did a number of so-called 'Loyalist' paramilitaries, such as the Ulster Volunteer Force (UVF). In August 1971, internment (without trial) was introduced. Anyone suspected of terrorist activities could be arrested. On the first day alone, there were over 340 such arrests. Internment continued until December 1975, during which time almost 2000 people were interned – of which around 100 were Protestant.

Probably the most notable date of the Troubles was 30 January 1972 – **Bloody Sunday**. British troops fired upon a civil rights march in Londonderry. Thirteen civilians were shot and another thirteen injured, one of whom later died. The troops have always claimed to have been fired upon, and were simply returning fire. The Widgery Report (1972), which was the first investigation into the killings, backed the soldiers' claims. There have been a number of subsequent investigations in an attempt to verify such claims, and these culminated in the **Saville Report**, which was published in 2010. This report gave an unequivocal conclusion that the killings were unjustified, thus discrediting totally the Widgery Report. The Saville Report has also opened up the possibility of legal action against the troops who were involved in the killings.

On 1 March 1981, Bobby Sands started a hunger strike. He was the leader of the IRA members in the Maze Prison. Sands claimed all IRA members ought to be treated as prisoners of war rather than criminals. In April 1981, Sands won a Westminster Parliamentary by-election in the constituency of Fermanagh and South Tyrone. After 66 days of refusing food, Sands died. By the end of October 1981, ten other prisoners had also died from hunger strikes. Sands' death is commemorated every year. In some quarters, he is revered as a martyr.

As a consequence of these deaths, and the continued IRA activity both in Northern Ireland and on mainland Britain, the British Government started secret contacts with Sinn Féin (the political wing of the IRA), the Social Democratic and Labour Party (SDLP) of Northern Ireland (which at that time represented the majority of Catholics in the province), and the Irish Government. The objective was to remedy the situation. One result of these meetings was the **Anglo-Irish Agreement** of 1985, sometimes called the **Hillsborough Agreement**. In this agreement, the Irish Government recognised the province of Northern Ireland would continue as part of the United Kingdom. In return, the Irish Government would be given a say in the internal affairs of Northern Ireland. Mutual security arrangements were also reached, including the right of extradition of terrorists from Ireland to Britain.

The Peace Process
Bearing in mind such steps as the Hillsborough Agreement, it is not easy to pinpoint when the peace process began. If a date was needed, however, it is 15 December 1993 with the **Downing Street Declaration**. The respective Prime Ministers of Britain and of Ireland at that time, John Major and Albert Reynolds, endorsed the principles of Northern Ireland self-rule and of a permanent ceasefire. In effect, the decisions on the future of Northern Ireland were to be left to the people of the island of Ireland and the people of Northern Ireland. As for a permanent ceasefire, the IRA made such a declaration in August 1994 and Protestant paramilitaries soon followed suit.

The Hillsborough Agreement was followed, in January 1996, with the **Mitchell Report**. George Mitchell, a Democrat senator from the United States, proposed all-party talks if the principles of non-violence could be established. While the Unionist parties, in particular, disputed the extent to which the steps towards non-violence were being taken, the peace process did continue. The **Good Friday Agreement** (10 April 1998), also known as the **Belfast Agreement** (and hereafter known as the Agreement) detailed the powers of the new assembly along with the electoral system to be used. It was approved in referendums in both Northern Ireland and the Republic of Ireland. There were slightly different questions for each country. In Northern Ireland the question was:

Do you support the Agreement reached at the multi-party talks on Northern Ireland and set out in Command Paper 3883?

In the Republic of Ireland, the question was:

Do you approve of the proposal to amend the Constitution contained in the undermentioned Bill?
(Nineteenth Amendment of the Constitution Bill, 1998)

The referendum in the Republic approved a constitutional change that resulted in Dublin renouncing any 'claim' on Northern Ireland. The referendums paved the way for elections to the Northern Ireland Assembly, which took place in June 1998.

Table 29.1 Referendum Results on the Agreement

	Northern Ireland	Republic of Ireland
Yes	71.1%	94.4%
No	28.9%	5.6%
Turnout	81.1 %	55.6%

It is interesting to note the results of the referendum in Northern Ireland were not broken down by council ward (as is normally done in elections). Shirlow (2001, p. 745) claimed such a move "was undertaken due to fears that a breakdown of votes, by electoral ward, would indicate that a majority of Protestants voted against the Agreement". Many Protestants presented such arguments on numerous radio chat shows, including Late Night Currie on Radio 5 (in which one of the authors participated in the studio as an elections expert).

Despite the elections to the Northern Ireland Assembly, which are discussed below, the peace process has not continued smoothly. There were problems over the decommissioning of weapons. The IRA committed themselves to putting their weapons beyond use and, arguably, in a verifiable way. From the Unionist perspective, this was not considered decommissioning.

The annual Orange Order parades have also caused numerous problems. These parades commemorate the Battle of the Boyne of 1690. The Parades Commission has refused a number of the parades to go ahead, including the Drumcree march – which is the oldest of all Orange marches. This particular ban has led to widespread rioting and violence by Protestant paramilitaries, which brought into question as to whether or not there was still a ceasefire.

Finally, the Northern Ireland Assembly has been suspended on four separate occasions. While two of these suspensions lasted for 24 hours (10 August 2001 and 22 September 2001), the Assembly was also suspended for three months (between February and May 2000). This was only three months after the powers had been transferred to Stormont. The longest suspension was between 14 October 2002 and 8 May 2007. At that time, there were grave concerns as to whether or not the peace process could be restarted.

Elections to the Northern Ireland Assembly
The first elections to the Northern Ireland Assembly took place in June 1998, and have been held on a four-year cycle. Northern Ireland was divided up into eighteen multi-member constituencies, with six members to be elected from each. The electoral system used was the Single Transferable Vote (STV). This particular system was detailed in chapter 20.

Table 29.2 Northern Ireland Assembly Election Results (seats)

PARTY	1998	2003	2007	2011
SDLP	24	18	16	14
Ulster Unionists	28	27	18	16
Democratic Unionists	20	30	36	38
Sinn Féin	18	24	28	29
Alliance	6	6	7	8
UK Unionists	5	1	0	-
Progressive Unionists	2	1	1	0
Women's Coalition	2	0	-	-
Green	0	0	1	1
Traditional Unionist Voice	-	-	-	1
Others	3	1	1	1

(- means the party did not contest the elections.)

Table 29.3 Northern Ireland Assembly Election Results (votes)

PARTY	1998		2003	
	First preference	%	First preference	%
SDLP	177 963	22.0	117 547	17.0
Ulster Unionists	172 225	21.3	156 931	22.7
Democratic Unionists	145 917	18.0	177 944	25.7
Sinn Féin	142 858	17.7	162 758	23.5
Alliance	52 636	6.5	25 372	3.7
UK Unionists	36 541	4.5	5 700	0.8
Progressive Unionists	20 634	2.6	8 032	1.2
Women's Coalition	13 019	1.6	5 785	0.8
Others	47 470	5.9	31 959	4.5

PARTY	2007		2011	
	First preference	%	First preference	%
SDLP	105 164	15.2	94 286	14.2
Ulster Unionists	103 145	14.9	87 531	13.2
Democratic Unionists	207 721	30.1	198 436	30.0
Sinn Féin	180 573	26.2	178 224	26.9
Alliance	36 139	5.2	50 875	7.7
Traditional Unionist Voice	-	-	16 480	2.5
Green	11 985	1.7	6 031	0.9
UK Unionists	10 452	1.5	-	-
Progressive Unionists	3 822	0.6	1 493	0.2
Others	31 312	4.5	28 397	4.3

The first thing to note about these results is that in the 1998 elections to the Legislative Assembly, pro-Agreement parties won an overwhelming majority. Surprisingly, the SDLP won the most first preference votes but did not win the most seats. In the first elections, some cross-denominational groups won representation, including the Alliance and the Women's Coalition (who have subsequently disbanded). Most voting was on sectarian lines – and this voting pattern has continued. The vast majority of votes (normally over 80%) go to the four main parties – UUP, DUP, SDLP and Sinn Féin. They have also won at least 90 of the 108 Assembly seats in each election.

What is also of note, when examining these elections, is the way in which the Unionist parties have tended to fragment. This has been most obvious with the way in which the UUP appears to have imploded. If you look at other elections – such as those to Westminster – the UUP have disappeared. The DUP is also suffering a similar, if smaller problem. As the dominant Unionist body, there is a perception among some of their supporters they are giving too many concessions to the Nationalist parties. Consequently, some members (such as Jim Allister) have left the DUP and established a new party. In the case of Allister, it was the Traditional Unionist Voice. This party has taken support from both major unionist parties.

There has been far less fragmentation in support on the Nationalist side of Northern Ireland politics. The most obvious point to note is the SDLP has been replaced by Sinn Féin as the dominant party.

On both sides of the sectarian fence, the (perceived) moderate parties – UUP and SDLP – have seen their support erode away. More hard-line parties – DUP and Sinn Féin, have replaced them.

Powers of the Legislative Assembly

The actual powers of the Northern Ireland Assembly were outlined in the Agreement. In effect, it took over the powers of the Northern Ireland Department. The Assembly is the prime source of authority for all devolved responsibilities, and has full legislative and executive authority.

All Assembly members must be designated 'Unionist', 'Nationalist' or 'Other'. Thus, all decision-making is taken on a cross-community basis. This can take either of two forms:

i) Parallel consent – a majority of members present and a majority of Unionist and Nationalist designations present and voting
ii) Weighted majority – 60% of members present and voting and 40% of each designation present and voting

This is to make sure decision-making is not biased in favour or against any particular sectarian group. It also makes it very difficult to censure any member of the Assembly or Executive, as such action would require cross-community support. For example, no party can veto another party's membership of the Executive, although "the Assembly as a whole, through cross-community consent, could deem a party unfit for office" (McGarry & O'Leary, 2006b, p. 265).

On top of this, no party may change its designation between elections. In the past such actions have been permitted, as the Alliance Party redesignated themselves as Unionist in November 2001 to enable the election of David Trimble and Mark Durkan as First Minister and Deputy First Minister respectively. It has been suggested this move stopped the collapse of the Peace Process, but it also further polarised public opinion.

The Executive

The Executive has normally comprised members of the four largest parties in the Northern Ireland Assembly. Originally there were ten posts on the Executive (and this number was fixed), alongside the First Minister and Deputy First Minister. The addition of Policing and Justice has seen this number increase. Traditionally, the posts have been shared evenly between Unionists and Nationalists. This was not planned, although it was seen as an ideal outcome. The posts are allocated using the d'Hondt electoral system (see chapter 20). The largest party at Stormont (in terms of seats) gains the post of First Minister, the second largest gains the post of Deputy First Minister, and so forth. The only post not covered by this process was the Minister for Policing and Justice (which was allocated to the Alliance Party, after a cross-community Assembly vote).

Table 29.4 The Northern Ireland Executive, October 2012

FIRST MINISTER	**Peter Robinson (DUP)**
DEPUTY FIRST MINISTER	**Martin McGuinness (Sinn Féin)**
Justice	David Ford (Alliance)
Agriculture and Rural Development	Michelle O'Neill (Sinn Féin)
Culture, Arts and Leisure	Carál Ní Chuilín (Sinn Féin)
Education	John O'Dowd (Sinn Féin)
Entreprise, Trade and Investment	Arlene Foster (DUP)
Environment	Alex Attwood (SDLP)
Finance and Personnel	Sammy Wilson (DUP)
Health, Social Services and Public Safety	Edwin Poots (DUP)
Employment and Learning	Stephen Farry (Alliance)
Regional Development	Danny Kennedy (UUP)
Social Development	Nelson McCausland (DUP)

Although there is a First Minister and a Deputy First Minister, and the titles suggest a hierarchy, this is not the case. They are co-equal roles. In effect, there is a form of co-habitation. There is no 'marriage' between the leaders of the different sectarian groups. Instead, it is better to perceive the roles as being interdependent. Should one post holder resign, for example, the other would be obligated to do the same. Two junior ministers assist the two post holders.

Upon taking Office, Ministers take a Pledge of Office (rather than an Oath of Allegiance). Included in this pledge is a commitment to non-violence, as well as a commitment to the use of democratic means and processes. All ministers commit themselves to working for the collective good of all of the people of Northern Ireland.

The Executive works with a number of bodies that were either established in the Agreement, or are seen as partners in the Peace Process. Thus there is involvement with the UK Government and that of the Republic of Ireland. There are North-South bodies, which focus on the relationship between the two parts of the island. There are also East-West bodies, which draw in the relationship with the UK as well. The two most prominent bodies are the British & Irish Council and the North-South Ministerial Council.

Membership of the British & Irish Council comprises government representatives from the Republic of Ireland and the UK, as well as representatives from the Scottish Government, the Northern Ireland Executive, the Welsh Government, the Isle of Man Government, Jersey and Guernsey. Its overarching role is to aid the development of the Peace Process. It covers issues that are of importance to all participating parts of the British & Irish Council, including such things as the misuse of drugs, housing, and the environment.

The North South Ministerial Council was established as part of the Agreement to cover issues of mutual concern to both Northern Ireland and the Republic of Ireland. There are six areas of co-operation, but these are administered separately in each country:

- Agriculture
- Education
- Environment
- Health
- Tourism
- Transport

There is also a **Civic Forum**, which was established in the Agreement. This body represents interests that may not be included within the major parties. Thus the voices of those outside of conventional politics may also be heard (McGarry & O'Leary, 2006b).

Consociationalism

When examining the Northern Ireland Peace Process and, more generally, Northern Ireland politics, the extent of the polarisation becomes very clear. As McGarry & O'Leary (2006b, p. 255) have noted, there are two major communities with "distinct national identities, not merely ethnic heritages. Neither unionists nor nationalists want to be subsumed within the other's nation-state, even if they are guaranteed equal citizenship". What has been established to accommodate these rival aspirations is a form of power sharing. Some commentators have described the situation in Northern Ireland as a form of consociationalism – although there are others who would dispute the extent to which there is consociationalism in Northern Ireland.

Gormley-Heenan (2011, pp. 130-131; see also McGarry & O'Leary, 2006a) identifies four key characteristics of consociationalism:

- A grand coalition
- Decision-making through mutual agreement
- Representation on a proportional basis
- Segmented authority i.e. groups look after their own internal affairs.

The situation in Northern Ireland appears to fit these four characteristics. Yet this covers the political aspects of the governing of Northern Ireland. It could be argued the social dimension of consociationalism sees a fragmentation of society. As Pinkerton (2012, p. 142) has pointed out: "the years since the end of the armed conflict have not been accompanied by processes of inter-community healing. Rather, segregated social spaces remain, and have indeed increased in certain respects". Peace walls, for example, have proliferated, especially at points of sectarian tension. If anything, it could be argued the whole peace process and the Agreement were simply an agreement to disagree. It could even be argued the sectarian divides have become institutionalised.

The problem is there is no viable alternative to govern Northern Ireland. The country could not exist as an independent state. To go in the other direction, that of joint government by the UK and the Republic of Ireland, is just as unfeasible. Unifying the island of Ireland is not feasible any more than rule solely from Westminster. In this respect, the consociational approach is simply the least worst option.

Conclusion

Northern Ireland is still deeply divided. Yet, much progress has been made in just over a decade. From the Downing Street Declaration and the subsequent Good Friday Agreement/Belfast Agreement, the peace process moved very slowly. In July 2005, the IRA declared a formal end to its armed campaign, and, two months later, the head of the international decommissioning body, General Sir John de Chaistlain, declared the IRA's entire arsenal of weapons to have been destroyed. These are considered key points in the progress made in the peace process. The use of violence to achieve political ends was effectively over.

Almost five years later, the control of policing and justice powers was transferred from London to Belfast. The Royal Ulster Constabulary (RUC) was then replaced by the Police Service of Northern Ireland. This marked the completion of the devolution process (for those powers that could be devolved).

The question is really: where to from here? Currently, there is no answer. The next elections to the Northern Ireland Legislative Assembly are in 2016. It may well a crisis point could arise if the First Minister was to come from a Nationalist party rather than a Unionist party. The reaction to such an event, should it ever happen, will demonstrate just how far the peace process has come.

Selected bibliography

Birrell, Derek. (2012). "Intergovernmental Relations and Political Parties in Northern Ireland", *British Journal of Politics and International Relations* vol. 14-2, pp. 270-284.

Coakley, John. (2011). "The Challenge of Consociation in Northern Ireland", *Parliamentary Affairs* vol. 64-3, pp. 473-493.

Gormley-Heenan, Cathy & Devine, Paula. (2010). "The 'Us' in Trust: Who Trusts Northern Ireland's Political Institutions and Actors?", *Government and Opposition* vol. 45-2, pp. 143-165.

McGarry, John & O'Leary, Brendan. (2006a). "Consociational Theory, Northern Ireland's Conflict, and its Agreement. Part 1: What Consociationalists Can Learn from Northern Ireland", *Government and Opposition* vol. 41-1, pp. 43-63.

McGarry, John & O'Leary, Brendan. (2006b). "Consociational Theory, Northern Ireland's Conflict, and its Agreement. Part 2: What Critics of Consociation Can Learn from Northern Ireland", *Government and Opposition* vol. 41-2, pp. 249-277.

Perry, Robert. (2011). "The Devolution of Policing in Northern Ireland: Politics and Reform", *Politics* vol. 31-3, pp. 167-178.

Pinkerton, Patrick. (2012). "Resisting Memory: The Politics of Memorialisation in Post-conflict Northern Ireland", *British Journal of Politics and International Relations* vol. 14-1, pp. 131-252.

Websites

healingthroughremembering.info/day_of_reflection
A web page dedicated "to remember the events of the past in a non-confrontational, dignified and respectful manner"

www.cain.ulst.ac.uk
The website for the Conflict Archive on the Internet (CAIN). This is an excellent resource giving much information about the conflict in Northern Ireland

www.niassembly.gov.uk/
The home page of the Northern Ireland Assembly

www.northernireland.gov.uk/
The home page of the Northern Ireland Executive

Questions
1. Evaluate the alternatives to consociationalism in Northern Ireland.
2. To what extent has the peace process increased the polarisation of the different communities within Northern Ireland?
3. "The peace process is little more than a veneer over the ongoing conflict in Northern Ireland." Discuss.

CHAPTER 30 // ENGLAND

Contents
- **Introduction**
- **What are the different regions of England?**
- **Regional Development Agencies**
- **Regional Assemblies**
- **Regional Government Offices**
- **The Coalition Government and Regional Government in England**
- **The demand for an English Parliament**
- **Conclusion**

Introduction

When looking at devolution in England, there is often a misconception over whether or not such devolution exists. People look at the devolved structures in Scotland, Wales and Northern Ireland, and assume, because there is no such equivalent in England, there is no devolved government in England. Yet, there is devolved government in England. There is an argument over whether London is regional or local government. This will be examined later. Excluding that debate, there is still devolved government in England. It is merely unelected. Refer back to the different forms of devolution, as detailed in chapter 26. There are various forms of *administrative* devolution in place in England. There is also a question as to whether or not England should have a similar form of devolution as to what exists in Scotland. Since the creation of the elected devolved bodies in Scotland, Wales and Northern Ireland, support for an English equivalent has struggled to get above 20% in the opinion polls – although results could be dependent upon what is actually being asked!

What are the different regions of England?

One of the major problems when examining the idea of devolved regional structures for England is the drawing up of said regions. Regionalism in England is a rather artificial concept. People may talk of living in the North East of England, or the South West of England, but these tend to be rather vague labels. How far east or north do you travel, for example, before you are no longer in the "south west"?

England has been drawn up into nine different regions, as listed in Table 30.1. Yet, these appear rather artificial concepts. While England can be 'regionalised', there is simply no agreement as to what the regions are, or even if there is a specific regional identity. The East Midlands, for example, covers Leicestershire, Derbyshire, Nottinghamshire, Lincolnshire, Northamptonshire and Rutland. Yet, parts of Lincolnshire – those that border the Humber estuary – are considered part of Yorkshire and Humberside.

Table 30.1 The English Regions

- North East
- North West
- Yorkshire and Humberside
- East Midlands
- West Midlands
- East of England
- South East
- London
- South West

The South West is also fascinating, for similar reasons. When thinking of the counties in that region, Cornwall and Devon come to mind. Somerset, Dorset and the area around the city of Bristol may be included as well, and possibly Wiltshire. Yet, what of Gloucestershire? It could be argued Gloucestershire is part of the West Midlands, yet it is considered to be part of the South West. It is also interesting to note the European Parliamentary constituency for the South West of England includes Gibraltar.

Added to this, there are various other regional bodies in England – in health or the media, to name but two. These do not correspond to the English regions as utilised by the government. The BBC has twelve identifiable English regions, while ITV has ten. Some regions such as the West and the South West are uniform for these broadcasters, but for no other English regions. The "West" is not included in Table 30.1.

London is clearly identified as an English region. Yet, because there is an elected mayor for London, the city is considered to be part of local government. Its predecessor was the Greater London Council – clearly a local authority. Yet the Greater London Authority is so much more. There is the concept of the city-region, which has been created to describe some of the huge metropolises that exist around the world. London is of that ilk, along with around 300 other cities such as Mexico City, Shanghai, Cairo and Jakarta. Thus London was covered in chapter 25 under local government. Despite this, some references will be made to the region of London in this chapter.

Regional Development Agencies

The Regional Development Agencies (RDAs) were established in 1999. They were created to instil a sense of regional identity. To some politicians, most notably John Prescott, the RDAs had the potential to become devolved government bodies akin to those in Scotland, Wales and Northern Ireland. At the time of their establishment, they were simply quangos (see chapter 14), whose membership was appointed by the Secretary of State for the Environment, Transport and Regions.

As noted by Pearce & Ayres (2009, p. 541), the RDAs were given five statutory purposes:

– to further economic development and regeneration
– to promote business efficiency, investment and competition
– to promote employment
– to enhance development and application of skills relevant to employment
– to contribute to the achievement of sustainable development in the UK

As can be seen from the list, the powers of the RDAs were related solely to the economy. It was anticipated the RDAs would assist in strengthening regional economic performance, and, in doing so achieve balanced economic growth across the regions (Ayres & Pearce, 2005). To ensure this, the RDAs were given extra resources in 2002 and 2004. It is also interesting to note senior members of all of the RDAs across England had access to government ministers – in a way that was unprecedented for quangos.

The RDAs were considered a possible stepping-stone to the creation of regionally elected government in England. If there was local/regional demand, then there was the prospect of a referendum on such a move. Only one such referendum was held, in the North East of England, on 4 November 2004. The result of that referendum is presented in Table 30.2. Any further plans to hold other referenda across any of the other regions of England were shelved because of the result.

Table 30.2 Referendum result for an elected regional body in the North East of England

Yes	22.1%
No	77.9%
Turnout	47.7%

Not only was the plan given a resounding defeat, but every council area in the region returned a 'No' vote. Yet the result also masked a number of issues. Many people who voted 'No' were unaware there was already an unelected tier of regional government in the North East of England – and this did not just include the RDA. Such information only came to light after the referendum (Sandford & Hetherington, 2005). Further, there was a feeling the powers on offer to the proposed elected body were insufficient. The perception was any such elected body would wield fewer powers than the Welsh Assembly, which, at that time, had been described as little more than a glorified talking shop. The proposed elected body would be little more than a puffed up regional version of a local council – and many councils feared losing resources to such a body.

Regional Assemblies

The regional assemblies, or regional chambers as they were originally known, were established as a counter-balance to the RDAs. Although not directly elected, these bodies included local councillors from across each region. With the plans for the RDAs to become directly elected bodies, it was actually these assemblies that would then become the prominent bodies.

The only regional assembly that is directly elected is the London Assembly. It's role and function was examined in chapter 25.

The regional assemblies were one of the bodies that scrutinised the activities of the RDAs. Some assemblies were also involved in regional planning conferences (Tomaney, 2002). The Conservative Government established these conferences in the 1980s, to provide advice to the Secretary of State on regional planning matters. In effect, by having members on the assembly who were elected, there was a veneer of democratic accountability. The problem was the assemblies had no legislative or decision-making powers (Ayres & Pearce, 2004).

These regional assemblies were largely unknown and unnoticed across England. It is interesting to note awareness of the Regional Assembly for the North East of England increased after the referendum defeat on creating a directly elected assembly.

Regional Government Offices

The idea of regionalism did not belong solely to the Labour Governments of Blair and Brown. Previous Conservative Governments had also been aware of the regional dimension. It was the Major Government that established regional government offices in 1994, although government ministers were not formally allocated to these posts until 2007. Originally, there were ten such offices for the regions of England, overseeing the work of four government departments: Transport, Employment, Industry, and Environment (Mawson, 2007). Other departments were included at later dates – by 2010, there were thirteen government departments involved.

Originally, these regional government offices had a regulatory role, as opposed to collaborating with regional partners. In other words, these offices were involved in the co-ordination and delivery of policies rather than prompting policy proposals.

Prior to the General Election of 2010, these offices employed around 1700 staff. They were involved in delivering (or co-ordinating the delivery) of over £7 billion worth of services. Yet they had their critics. One of these was Alan Duncan (MP for Rutland and Melton) who spoke about these regional ministers in the House of Commons:

> These Ministers are fictitious Ministers, supposedly joining up the various tentacles of government and somehow making a Minister in

one Department tie his or her decisions in with those of a Minister in another Department. The people who should be held to account, if that is necessary, are the Ministers who take those decisions, not these supposed facilitators who have no executive responsibility whatever. They are faux Ministers — false Ministers — and they do not really exist as Ministers at all. (*Hansard*, 3 Mar 2009: Column 790)

The problem with the regional government offices was they were driven by Whitehall rather than by regional imperatives. The extent of the central domination was made clear with the establishment of a Regional Coordination Unit in Whitehall in 2001. This body oversaw the work of the regional offices. Such a body, based in Whitehall, highlighted the extent to which the centre was dominating the proceedings of supposedly regional governance.

The Coalition Government and Regional Government in England

After the 2010 General Election, the new coalition government announced plans to remove the entire tier of regional government in England. The RDAs were closed in March 2012, and abolished in July of that year. Prior to their abolition, the RDAs transferred a range of assets, liabilities, functions and activities - including ongoing project responsibilities - to other public sector bodies. For example, some land and property assets and liabilities were transferred to the Homes and Communities Agency.

The regional assemblies were closed down as well, while the regional government offices simply ceased to exist. In July 2010, the Secretary of State for Communities and Local Government, Eric Pickles, announced in principle, the abolition of the regional government offices, subject to a number of issues around the government spending review. These offices were perceived, by the coalition partners, to be the agents of Whitehall in the regions of England rather than regional voices speaking up in Whitehall.

Interestingly, the RDAs were replaced by **Local Economic Partnerships** (LEPs). There are 39 LEPs in England. The problem was the LEPs were not expected to be fully functioning until 2012, leaving a possible 18-month regional power vacuum. Added to this, their emphasis is clearly upon the local (or multiple local authorities) rather than the regional, which may give some cause for concern with regard to representation on the European Union's Committee of Regions, or accessing sources of revenue such as the European Regional Development Fund (ERDF). To counter this, the coalition proposed the management of the ERDF and ESF (European Social Fund) programmes continued in place until 2013 (when new six-year programmes started).

Whereas the RDAs had clear boundaries, related to local authorities, the same cannot be said of the LEPs. For example, the city of Chesterfield is in the Derby, Derbyshire, Nottingham and Nottinghamshire LEP, and in the Sheffield City

Region LEP. The councils of Bassetlaw, Bolsover and North East Derbyshire are included in both of these LEPs as well. North Hertfordshire is in the Hertfordshire LEP, and also in the Greater Cambridge and Greater Peterborough LEP. In fact, 37 local authorities are covered by two LEPs.

The LEPs highlight the extent to which the coalition government is moving away from the regionalism of the previous governments, towards a greater emphasis on localism. Regional government was perceived as an extra tier of bureaucracy, and, as most of it was not directly elected, it was not accountable to the people. The LEPs appear to have a greater degree of accountability because of the link to local authorities. The problem here is all LEPs cover multiple local authorities, and holding them to account may not be as easy as first imagined. Added to this, the coalition government expects half of the membership of the boards running the LEPs to come from the private sector. Other board members could include representatives from councils, local colleges, trade unions, faith groups, universities and other public sector bodies. Further, there is an expectation that due consideration be given to issues surrounding diversity i.e. sufficient women, ethnic minorities and the disabled having some adequate representation as well. This has the potential to leave very cumbersome boards, most of whose membership appear unaccountable. The reality may not be quite so bad, as can be seen in Table 30.3, although questions could be raised surrounding the issue of diversity.

Table 30.3 Membership of the New Anglia LEP (3 October 2012)

Board Member	Profession
Dr Andy Wood (Chairperson)	Chief Executive, Adnams Plc
Mark Jeffries	Senior Partner, Mills & Reeve
Erika Clegg	Managing Director, Spring
Mark Goodall	Area Manager, Aker Solutions
David Marsh	Various business and voluntary interests
Mark Pendlington	Group Director, Anglian Water
Davina Tanner	General Manager, Chapelfield Shopping Centre
Mark Bee	Leader Suffolk County Council
David Ellesmere	Leader, Ipswich Borough Council
John Fuller	Leader, South Norfolk Council
John Griffiths	Leader, St Edmundsbury Borough Council
Derrick Murphy	Leader, Norfolk County Council
Alan Waters	Deputy Leader, Norwich City Council
Professor Edward Acton	Vice Chancellor, University of East Anglia

Developed from www.newanglia.co.uk/Page.aspx?Id=156

The demand for an English Parliament

With devolved parliaments or assemblies in Scotland, Northern Ireland and Wales, the question has been raised as to why England does not have the same. Organisations such as the English Democrats are campaigning for the establishment of such a body. To date, they have received little support – although the former elected mayor of Doncaster was an English Democrat.

As Hazell (2006) has noted, there are a number of reasons as to why England should have an elected parliament. The primary idea is to give England a stronger political voice. This would, in effect, require a rebalancing of the union.

The argument is the English have 'lost out' when compared to the other devolved parts of the UK. There is no body representing English voices. The Parliament at Westminster passes legislation for all of the UK. Yet, there are legislative areas that do not impact upon, for example, Scotland (see chapter 27 for a list of the devolved powers). Thus Scottish MPs are able to vote on what are, in effect, seen as English matters, but the English are prevented from legislating on Scottish matters. This was known as the West Lothian Question, first raised by Tam Dalyell in the 1970s. Even today, with devolution in place, this question has not been resolved.

The most significant problem with an English Parliament is in the consequences of creating such a body. There would, in effect, be a federal state, with the different parts having the same powers (as in the United States, Germany, Australia, and any other federal country). England, through its size alone, would clearly dominate. Around 85% of the population of the UK, and a similar proportion of the UK's GDP, come from England. This has not stopped the English Democrats demanding an English Parliament.

The only way in which an English Parliament could work would be to sub-divide England, to stop the English Parliament from being dominant. In post-war Germany, as noted by Hazell (2006), Prussia was sub-divided to stop it from becoming dominant. The idea of sub-dividing England, as has already been noted in this chapter, is somewhat problematic. The regions that are currently in use are broadly similar in size, and all of them have larger populations than Scotland. This would stop any of them – with the possible exception of London – from becoming dominant. Yet there is little support for such an idea.

Conclusion

Outside of London, devolution in England is significantly different to the rest of the UK. There are no elections to any English Parliament, or to regional bodies within England. Yet there is no groundswell of opinion showing any demand to change the status quo in England. People get agitated when Scottish MPs are able to influence legislation affecting England but not Scotland; and there is a strong argument that Scottish MPs ought to exclude themselves from such a vote. One remedy to this situation has been to reduce the number of Scottish MPs sitting in the UK Parliament – but this does not resolve the problem.

To establish an English Parliament, similar to that which exists in Scotland, would require a complete overhaul of the UK political system. The problem is England would dominate the other parts through its size alone. A federal structure would not stop the English from dominating. Instead, England would need to be sub-divided – but there is no support for such a move.

The current coalition government is far less committed to regionalism than the government of Tony Blair. In fact, many of the parts of regional government established in England – as a possible stepping-stone to elected regional government in England – have been abolished. The current government places a far greater emphasis upon local government and local partnerships. Thus regionalism in England appears to be no more, and there is little chance of the creation of an English Parliament. This leaves the UK as, what Jeffery (2006) has described, a lopsided state.

Selected bibliography

Bryant, Christopher. (2008). "Devolution, equity and the English question", *Nations and Nationalism* vol. 14-4, pp. 664-683.

Chapain, Caroline & Comunian, Roberta. (2010). "Enabling and Inhibiting the Creative Economy: The Role of the Local and Regional Dimensions in England", *Regional Studies* vol. 44-6, pp. 717-734.

Jeffery, Charlie. (2006). "Devolution and the Lopsided State" in Dunleavy, Patrick; Heffernan, Richard; Cowley, Philip & Hay, Colin (eds.); *Developments in British Politics 8*: Palgrave, pp. 138-158.

Mawson, John. (2007). "Regional governance in England: past experience, future directions", *International Journal of Public Sector Management* vol. 20-6, pp. 548-566.

Pearce, Graham & Ayres, Sarah. (2009). "Governance in the English Regions: The Role of the Regional Development Agencies", *Urban Studies* vol. 46-3, pp. 537-557.

Pearce, Graham & Mawson, John. (2009). "Governance in the English regions: moving beyond muddling through?", *International Journal of Public Sector Management* vol. 22-7, pp. 623-642.

Tomaney, John. (2002). "The Evolution of Regionalism in England", *Regional Studies* vol. 36-7, pp. 721-731.

Websites

www.bis.gov.uk/policies/economic-development/leps
This is the Department for Business, Innovation and Skills web page for the Local Economic Partnerships (LEPs).

www.englishdemocrats.org.uk/
The homepage of the English Democrats, who campaign for, among other things, an English Parliament

www.thecep.org.uk/
This is the website for the Campaign for an English Parliament

Questions
1. Why might Britain be described as a lopsided state?
2. Should England have its own Parliament?

CHAPTER 31 // EUROPEAN UNION

Contents
- **Introduction**
- **The Constitutional Relationship**
- **The Political Relationship**
- **Institutions of the European Union**
- **The Europeanization of British Politics?**
- **Britain and the Euro**
- **Conclusion – Britain the 'reluctant European'?**

Introduction

Having been a member of the European Union (EU) and its predecessors since 1973, you might expect there to be a degree of enthusiasm for, or even interest in, the organisation within the UK, but it is far from the case. Britain's relationship with the EU is rather complicated, with Britain still being labelled a 'reluctant European'. This label is not unjustified. Historically, Britain refused to participate in the early years, with the formation of the European Coal and Steel Community (ECSC) in 1952 and the European Economic Community (EEC) in 1958. The reasons were Britain had recently nationalised both the coal and steel industries, it had an Empire to look after, and had a 'special relationship' with the United States. Europe was very low in British priorities in the early post-war years.

In the 1960s, however, with the success of the ECSC and the EEC, there was an apparent change of heart in Britain. An alternative organisation was established – the European Free Trade Association (EFTA). Although it had seven founding members (compared to the six of the EEC), EFTA was not a great success from a British perspective. The economies of the partner states were significantly smaller than that of Britain, and there was negligible benefit to the British economy. EFTA, it must be noted, continues today. Harold Macmillan applied to join the EEC in 1961, but the application was turned down in 1963. Similarly Harold Wilson applied unsuccessfully in 1967. It was not until the application by the Edward Heath Government that Britain was able to enter the EEC on 1 January 1973.

Even after joining, the relationship between Britain and the EEC was problematic. In 1974 the terms of entry were renegotiated by the Wilson-led Labour Government, and in 1975 these were put to a referendum. This was passed, with two thirds of voters deciding that Britain ought to remain a member.

When Margaret Thatcher became Prime Minister in 1979, the relationship between Britain and the EEC became even more fraught. Thatcher put British interests ahead of those of the EEC, and was often accused of 'handbagging' her European partners. If anything, Thatcher epitomised the 'reluctant European'. Narrow national interests always superseded transnational or supra-national interests, with Britain often appearing to be the odd-one out in Europe.

Her successors (John Major and Tony Blair) claimed to want to place Britain 'at the heart of Europe'. Such claims were treated with a degree of scepticism. Major negotiated opt-outs from the Treaty on European Union (TEU); and his government was unwilling to enforce some EU directives. An example of the latter is cited by Falkner *et al* (2004), where the Working Time and Young Workers Directives were opposed by the Major Government but were passed under Qualified Majority Voting (explained later in this chapter). The Major Government challenged the Working Time Directive in the European Court of Justice in March 1994, but lost the challenge in November 1996. Despite this, the Major Government "openly refused to accept the Court ruling" (Falkner *et al*, 2004, p. 457). No attempt was made to comply until just before the May 1997 General Election. Blair gave a verbal commitment to European leaders that Britain would join the Euro. He was, however, unable to deliver British membership of the Euro. Thus, even with more supposedly pro-European leadership, the UK appeared to remain a reluctant member.

All of this portrays the negative aspects of British membership of the EEC – and these are some of the reasons as to why Britain has earned the label 'reluctant European'. As will become apparent in this chapter, the relationship is not so clear-cut. Britain has a vital role to play in the EU – the problem is successive governments have failed to grasp the opportunity. Britain has led the way in a number of areas, including combating fraud, making the institutions more accountable to the public through the establishment of bodies such as the ombudsman, and in encouraging the EU to play a greater role in global politics. All of these positive roles played by the EU, and encouraged by the UK, appear to pass unnoticed.

The Constitutional Relationship

Britain's membership of the EU has been built into the constitution – and necessarily so. While Parliament remains sovereign, whenever there is conflict between EU law and national law, EU law takes precedence. This may appear to be a contradictory position. According to the British constitution, Parliament is supreme. With regard to local government or the devolved bodies, they are lesser institutions when compared to Parliament. It is Parliament that grants powers to these bodies, and Parliament can also rescind the powers as well. By signing the Treaty of Rome, however, and joining what was then called the EEC in 1973, Parliament granted powers to Europe which actually placed Europe in a dominant position. This has often been described as having "surrendered sovereignty" to Europe. In the late 1980s, Margaret Thatcher, in particular, complained that Britain had surrendered enough sovereignty.

Article 189 of the Treaty of Rome (1957) specifies the extent to which the EU can legislate for member states.

It can pass:

- *Regulations* – these are binding in every respect and have the direct force of law in every member state. They are directly applicable.
- *Directives* – these are binding on the member states to which they are addressed with respect to the results to be achieved. They need to be transposed into national law, but the means are left to the discretion of the national authority.
- *Decisions* – these may be addressed to a specific government, a private enterprise or an individual, and are binding in every respect on the parties involved.
- *Recommendations and Opinions* – these are purely advisory, with no binding authority.

The mere act of joining automatically involved an acceptance of this article and the judgements of the European Court of Justice based on it.

While on the surface it may appear Britain has indeed surrendered sovereignty to Europe, the constitutional position is actually far more complex. On the one hand, with the drive towards ever closer union, increased political and economic integration, and the introduction of the Euro, sovereignty is being lost. Yet the complaints about the loss of sovereignty appear to be peculiarly British. Part of this stems from Britain's history – Britain did not lose the Second World War; Britain has not been successfully invaded since 1066; all other member states have changed their constitutions (in particular after the Second World War) whereas the British constitution represents stability and continuity. This erosion of sovereignty started in 1973. To stop it, the option is quite simple: withdraw from the EU. In doing so, Parliamentary sovereignty can be reasserted properly. Britain can become truly independent again.

The problem is this option is no longer really valid, although Nigel Farage (leader of the UK Independence Party) would disagree. Britain has become integrated into Europe, economically as well as politically. The political option of withdrawal is not valid in economic terms – even if it is acceptable in political terms. Britain has been to the forefront in enabling the individual member states to reassert themselves within the EU context. The most notable success was during the TEU negotiations, with the introduction of the concept 'subsidiarity'. This concept means decision making, in particular circumstances, is removed from Brussels to national capitals, or even to lower tiers of government within each member state. Added to this, the British economy is well integrated into that of Europe – to the extent the EU is Britain's largest export market. Over half of all UK trade is conducted with the other 27 member states of the EU (and most of that is conducted with the Euro-zone states). Withdrawal would see trade barriers go up between Britain and the rest of the EU, with tariffs and duties to be paid on imports and exports. The US, China and the Commonwealth could never replace the lost markets of Europe. Added to this, if Britain was to withdraw but carry on trading with the EU, there would be a further complication. Any country that exports goods to the EU must ensure goods comply with all EU rules and regulations. British firms exporting to the EU would have to comply with these rules, but the British Government would have no input into their formulation. Even the most economically powerful countries in the world – the USA and China – must conform to these rules to be able to trade with the EU. It would be no different for Britain.

The Political Relationship

When examining the political relationship between Britain and the EU, there are two distinct sections. The first is the actual relationship between the two, and the second is to do with perceptions about the EU within British politics.

The perception of the EU within government has changed. An article in the *Observer* in December 1995 ("The Battle for Brussels is already lost") pointed out that dealing with Brussels was no longer considered to be foreign policy. This article went on to highlight the extent to which the EU has become an integral part of the government of Britain. At that time, approximately 70% of the Ministry of Agriculture, Fisheries and Food's work was Brussels-related. Issues such as terms of employment, or health and safety at work were dealt with in Brussels, along with health and hygiene standards. Such policies are developed by the member states (including Britain) as well as by the EU institutions. It is important to note there is British representation in each EU institution. What can be seen here, and is addressed later in this chapter, is the Europeanization of Britain.

The political relationship may be best exemplified by the attitudes of the MPs towards Europe. What is interesting here is the range of different attitudes that exist towards the EU. Most of this is not picked up in the media. The media representation of any debate on the EU is between Euro-philes and Euro-phobes, or pro- and anti-Europeans – those who like Europe against those who hate it. This is a gross oversimplification of the divisions in any debate on the EU. As Rosamond and Wincott (2006, p. 8) have noted, "[t]he notions of 'pro' and 'anti' European perhaps also conceal more than they reveal".

If the future of Europe is to become a superstate, with the individual members reduced in status to little more than a copy of the component states of the USA, then the vast majority of people would probably not support such a position. Does this make them all anti-Europeans? Similarly, if the future of Europe is to remain as it is now, with individual member states responsible for some areas of policy, and the EU responsible elsewhere, with possible enlargement but little further integration, there would probably be support for such a position. Does this make such supporters pro-Europeans?

During the debates on the TEU (also known as the Maastricht Treaty), Bill Cash (MP for Stone) highlighted the problem. He was opposed to the treaty but he believed Britain did have a role to play in Europe. As he was anti-Maastricht, however, he was portrayed in the media as being anti-European. Cash supported the idea of a European Community but was opposed to further integration. Such a position appears to have been considered too complex to convey to the public. Cash's position was reduced to the lowest possible denominator: that of being anti-European. As Cash (1992, p. 14) said:

> We are told that the choice is between accepting Maastricht or repudiating the European Community as a whole. To be anti-Maastricht is said to be anti-European. This is an insular argument, which assumes that the only question for the British is whether they should be in or out. But nobody wants to see Britain standing alone outside Europe. The questions it raises are much broader. Any argument based on this unreal alternative is untenable and anti-Community.

Within each of the two major parties there are a range of different attitudes to the EU. With regard to the various Conservative positions, what is most notable is the majority of MPs appear generally supportive of membership of the EU – if guardedly so. The problem really arises with the future development – both integration and enlargement. There appears to be a general belief that the individual member states are very important, and this identity should not be lost within a greater EU. There is clear opposition to ceding further powers to the EU. It would be very difficult, for example, to find any Tory MPs (or MEPs for that matter) who support the idea of a federal Europe. The Cameron position is somewhat vague. He appears to believe Britain should be in the EU but there does not appear to be any clear vision as to how the EU should develop, or what should be Britain's role within the organisation. Cameron has stated he wishes to renegotiate the terms of entry, and to put them to a straight 'In-Out' referendum in 2017. This sounds very similar to the actions of the Wilson Government in 1974 and 1975. What we see here is a 'soft' euro-sceptic position. There is a lack of happiness with the status quo, and a reluctance to go further down the integration route. But there is no appetite for withdrawal either.

Those opposed to membership with in the Conservative Party, and who argue for withdrawal (the "anti-marketeers"), are growing in number. These are the 'hard' euro-sceptics. The UK Independence Party (UKIP) has tapped into this anti-EU feeling and is garnering much support, especially but not exclusively from the Conservative Party. Issues such as immigration (especially after the enlargements of 2004 and 2007) have come to the forefront. The now-defunct EU constitution and the EU Reform Treaty have both been seen as further undermining national sovereignty, as have the economic problems of the so-called PIIGS economies (Portugal, Ireland, Italy, Greece and Spain). Financial bailouts for the smaller countries, and the potential need for such bailouts for Italy and Spain, saw an increasingly anti-Euro and anti-EU sentiment.

This, in turn, has led to an increase in anti-EU sentiment within much of the Conservative Party – especially at the grassroots level, but also at Westminster, where around 100 Conservative MPs attended a new anti-European group meeting in September 2011. Whether this will lead to the Conservative Party espousing a policy of withdrawal from the EU will remain to be seen. David Cameron, as already noted, is committed to renegotiating the terms of entry and putting them to a referendum – where he will campaign for a 'Yes' vote. Added to this, if there are any further treaties which involve handing power to the EU, these will also be put to a referendum.

Within the Labour Party, the situation is somewhat more complex than within the Conservative Party. There are anti-EU factions within the Labour Party – both to the left and to the right of the party. They are both, however, in a distinct minority. The likes of Tony Benn (who belonged to the anti-European Left and who espoused withdrawal) appeared almost irrelevant within the Labour Party of Tony Blair and Gordon Brown. It was even less likely a policy of withdrawal would re-surface under Ed Miliband.

Pro-Europeans are quite prevalent across the Labour Party. As with the Conservatives, there is a range of different perspectives. Tony Blair was clearly pro-European. He signed Britain up to the Social Charter almost immediately upon gaining Office in 1997. He was keen to join the single currency and develop the European Rapid Reaction Force.

Overall, Blair's enthusiasm for Europe appeared to filter down through much of the Labour Party. Yet questions always arose as to the strength of support for the Blair position, especially since his removal from office. Gordon Brown, on the other hand, while still keen to remain an active participant within the EU, was by no means as committed to the European project as his predecessor. There appeared to be considerable support for his position.

Under Ed Miliband's leadership, the position of the so-called "pragmatic centre" of the party appeared to dominate. There was an almost apathetic acceptance of EU membership, subject to guidance from the leadership of the party. Yet there appeared to be no leadership on this issue, thus leaving the apathy and a lack of desire to rock the boat from the backbenches.

The Institutions of the European Union

There are a number of important institutions in the EU. Some of these are detailed below. Britain's role within each will also be examined.

The Commission

This body is often perceived as being the civil service of the EU. Its role is actually far more extensive. While the Commission is the bureaucratic arm of the EU, it is also the 'Guardian of the Treaties'. In sum, the Commission drafts legislative proposals for consideration by other EU bodies but it also makes sure that the legislation is applied correctly. A key role of the Commission is to work towards ever closer union. It also monitors the free movement of goods, services, capital and people throughout the EU.

Within the UK, the Commission gets much bad press. Stories abound in parts of the media of the Commission wanting to ban bent cucumbers, ban the British sausage, or make donkeys wear nappies when working on beaches. All of these are scare stories, with barely a grain of truth to them. Yet the Commission is an easy target to blame. If it does decide to fight back, which of the euro-sceptic media outlets will publish the story?

Currently, there are twenty eight commissioners – one from each state. The President of the Commission, who is in post until May 2014, is José Manuel Barroso (a former Portuguese Prime Minister). Britain's commissioner until May 2014 is Catherine Ashton. Each commissioner has a portfolio (almost akin to a cabinet post). Ashton is the High Representative of the Union for Foreign Affairs and Security Policy. She is also one of the Vice-Presidents of the Commission.

While the Commissioners are allocated on a national basis, it is important to note that they do not actually 'represent' their home country (see Table 31.1). The Commissioners are independent, and actually swear such an oath, although their absolute neutrality can be questioned. They are nominated by their national governments, in consultation with the nominee for the President of the Commission. The nominations and their portfolios must be endorsed by the European Parliament, which can either accept or reject the entire Commission. The European Parliament may not object to an individual nomination, it can only reject (or accept) the whole package of nominations.

Table 31.1 The EU Commission (until May 2014)

Name	Country	Portfolio
José Manuel Barroso	**Portugal**	**President**
Catherine Ashton	UK	Vice President Foreign Affairs and Security Policy
Viviane Reding	Luxembourg	Vice President Justice, Fundamental Rights and Citizenship
Joaquín Almunia	Spain	Vice President Competition
Siim Kallas	Estonia	Vice President Transport
Neelie Kroes	Netherlands	Vice President Digital Agenda

Antonio Tajani	Italy	Vice President Industry and Entrepreneurship
Maroš Šefčovič	Slovakia	Vice President Inter-Institutional Relations and Administration
Olli Rehn	Finland	Vice President Economic and Monetary Affairs and the Euro
Janez Potočnik	Slovenia	Environment
Andris Piebalgs	Latvia	Development
Michel Barnier	France	Internal Market and Services
Androulla Vassiliou	Cyprus	Education, Culture, Multilingualism and Youth
Algirdas Šemeta	Lithuania	Taxation, Customs, Statistics, Audit and Anti-Fraud
Karel De Gucht	Belgium	Trade
Tonio Borg	Malta	Health
Máire Geoghegan-Quinn	Ireland	Research, Innovation and Science
Janusz Lewandowski	Poland	Financial Programming and Budget
Maria Damanaki	Greece	Maritime Affairs and Fisheries
Kristalina Georgieva	Bulgaria	International Cooperation, Humanitarian Aid and Crisis Response
Günter Oettinger	Germany	Energy
Johannes Hahn	Austria	Regional Policy
Connie Hedegaard	Denmark	Climate Action
Štefan Füle	Czech Republic	Enlargement and European Neighbourhood Policy
László Andor	Hungary	Employment, Social Affairs and Inclusion
Cecilia Malström	Sweden	Home Affairs
Dacian Cioloş	Romania	Agriculture and Rural Development
Nevin Mimica	Croatia	Consumer Policy

Developed from ec.europa.eu/commission_2010-2014/members/index_en.htm

There are a number of issues about the Commission the EU needs to address. The first of these is whether or not to restructure the entire Commission. In the EU Reform Treaty, the plan was to reduce the number of Commissioners by one third in 2014. Each member state would, therefore, have equal turns in not having a Commissioner (Palmer & Facey, 2008). This position was reversed after the Irish Referendum on the Reform Treaty, to one member-one commissioner. If there are any further enlargements, and a number of countries such as Iceland, Montenegro, Serbia and Turkey, are hoping to join in the near future, the Commission will become even more unwieldy than it is now. This will make the entire decision making process even slower than is currently the case. The profusion of portfolios also makes the Commission rather cumbersome, as there is significant overlap between what already exists. The proposed restructuring meant some countries would not get a commissioner. This did not prove to be very popular, leaving the Commission unable to reform itself properly.

There is also a pecking order of portfolios, not too dissimilar to that in a national government. Portfolios such as Competition, Trade, Justice or Economic and Monetary Affairs are much more important than the likes of Consumer Policy or Development. When a new Commission is nominated, there is always haggling over the allocation of portfolios and vice presidencies. With the last Barroso Commission, the French were upset not to have been allocated a vice presidency. They were, to some extent, appeased, by being allocated the Internal Market portfolio.

The Council of Ministers

This body is also known as the **Council of the European Union**, and is still the dominant body within the EU. The Council of Ministers is the legislative body of the EU, although it has been a co-decision maker since the implementation of the TEU. This means all legislative proposals must be approved by both the Council of Ministers and the European Parliament. Alongside its legislative role, the Council of Ministers also co-ordinates the general economic policies of the member states.

The composition of the Council of Ministers is one ministerial representative per Member State. If agriculture is being discussed then all member states agriculture ministers will attend; if transport is under discussion, then it will be the various transport ministers in attendance, and so on. When the Heads of Government meet, that particular council is called the European Council. Overall, in effect, you could argue there are a series of Councils of Ministers.

Until 2009, each member state had a turn at holding the Presidency of the Council of Ministers. The Presidency ran in a six monthly rotation. With there being 28 member states in the EU, each state would hold the Presidency for six months in every 14 years.

A new post, created in 2009, is the **President of the Council**. This has replaced the rotating presidency. The first post-holder was Herman Van Rompuy. He is the principal representative of the EU on the world stage. The **European Council** is the meeting of the Heads of Government of each member state. Arguably, this is the most important of all parts of the Council of Ministers. Van Rompuy, who chairs these meetings, took the decision to report back to the European Parliament after each meeting of the European Council, even though there was no obligation for him to do so.

Decision making in the Council of Ministers can be complicated. Some decisions are taken by simple majorities (e.g. anti-dumping legislation as part of the Common Competition Policy), and some through unanimity (e.g. enlargement). Most decisions are taken by **Qualified Majority Voting** (QMV). Various treaties have extended the number of policy areas which are decided under QMV.

Under QMV, each member state has a certain number of votes depending upon the size of the country. These are detailed in Table 31.2. To pass any legislation, 260 out of the 352 votes available must be cast in favour. In some cases, half, or even two thirds, of all member states must support the proposals. What this means is that the larger countries cannot impose their will on the smaller member states. Similarly, these countries cannot be held to ransom by the smaller countries, as it would only take four of the largest countries to defeat any proposed legislation.

Table 31.2 Weighting of Votes under Qualified Majority Voting (2013)

Votes	Countries
29	France, Germany, Italy, United Kingdom
27	Poland, Spain
14	Romania
13	Netherlands
12	Belgium, Czech Republic, Greece, Hungary, Portugal
10	Austria, Bulgaria, Sweden
7	Croatia, Denmark, Finland, Ireland, Lithuania, Slovakia
4	Cyprus, Estonia, Latvia, Luxembourg, Slovenia
3	Malta

The EU Reform Treaty changed QMV, but not significantly. From 2014, the new QMV rules state at least 50% plus one of the Member States (15/28 since Croatia joined), which must also represent at least 65% of the EU population, must vote in favour to pass any legislative proposals. Between 2014 and 2017, there will be a transition period, where the current rules may be applied if so requested by member states.

An alternative way of looking at QMV is what is needed to block legislative proposals. It requires 93 votes to block any proposals. The 'big four' could collectively block any proposals, or three of them along with any one country that has seven or more votes.

Once the laws have been passed, there is then the issue of their implementation. In this respect, the Commission devolves the enforcement of EU legislation to national governments. When examining the implementation of EU legislation, the UK is one of the better member states in implementing EU law. If a member state fails to implement EU legislation, a dialogue between the EU and the member state will ensue. If this fails to resolve the situation, the EU will issue a 'formal letter of notice' in which the member state has to explain the alleged breach. If this fails, a 'reasoned opinion' is then issued by the EU, which sets out the Commission's view on the breach. Failure to respond here will then see the breach referred to the Court of Justice. Between 1978 and 1999, there were 266 reasoned opinions issued against the UK. This compares with 983 against Italy over the same time period, 684 against France, 682 against Greece (who joined in 1981), 419 against Portugal and 317 against Spain (both of whom joined in 1986). Of the member states who joined prior to 1978, only Denmark and the Netherlands had fewer reasoned opinions issued against them than the UK (see Perkins and Neumayer (2007) for more information).

The European Parliament
The European Parliament has over the years become a powerful body within the EU. Until 1979, Members of the European Parliament (MEPs) were nominated from national parliaments. Since then, there have been direct elections on a fixed five-year term. The Treaty on European Union gave the European Parliament the power of co-decision maker. The majority of legislative proposals that come from the Commission and the Council of Ministers must also go through the European Parliament. Both institutions must agree to the legislative proposals for them to become law. Along with this legislative power, the European Parliament can hold the Commission to account for the EU budget, and can even reject the Commissions budgetary proposals. The European Parliament also scrutinises both the Council of Ministers and the Commission.

The 766 MEPs are elected at a national level. Britain, for example, has 73 MEPs, as does Italy. Germany, the largest country, has 99 MEPs while Malta, Luxembourg and Cyprus each have six. Although elected on a national basis, the MEPs do not sit in national groups. Rather, they sit in ideological trans-national groupings (or, in simple terms, with like-minded thinkers). This is shown in Table 31.3.

Table 31.3 Composition of the European Parliament, 2013

POLITICAL GROUPINGS	NUMBER OF MEPs	BRITISH MEPs
Group of the European People's Party	274	-
Group of the Progressive Alliance of Socialists and Democrats	195	13 Labour
Alliance of Liberals and Democrats for Europe	84	12 Liberal Democrats
Group of the Greens and the European Free Alliance	58	2 Greens 2 Scottish Nationalist 1 Plaid Cymru
European Conservatives and Reformist Group	57	25 Conservatives 1 Ulster Conservatives and Unionist 1 Unattached
European United Left and the Nordic Green Left	35	1 Sinn Féin
Europe of Freedom and Democracy	31	8 UK Independence
Non-attached	32	2 UK Independence 1 British National 1 British Democrat 1 Democratic Unionist 1 An Independence from Europe 1 We Demand a Referendum

The 2009 elections were most interesting in Britain, as UKIP came second in terms of votes won and seats gained. The more pro-European parties – the Liberal Democrats and Labour – fared far less well (as can be seen in Table 31.4). The Conservatives tapped into some of the anti-European sentiment, but also played upon domestic issues, most notably Blair stepping down as Prime Minister and Brown replacing him, but as an 'unelected' prime minister. As with all UK elections to the European Parliament, domestic issues were of far greater importance in the campaign than European issues. In fact, it was unlikely as to whether the voting public even knew of any major European issues apart from the single currency.

Table 31.4 European Parliamentary Election Result in Mainland Britain (June 2009)

Party	% vote in mainland Britain	Seats won in mainland Britain
Conservative	27.7	25
UK Independence	16.5	13
Labour	15.7	13
Liberal Democrat	13.7	11
Green	8.6	2
BNP	6.2	2
SNP	2.1	2
Plaid Cymru	0.8	1
Other	8.7	0

Although the SNP and Plaid Cymru percentage of votes look distinctly poor, it must be borne in mind each party only contested one constituency. The SNP won over 29% of the Scottish vote, while Plaid Cymru gained around 18.5% of the Welsh vote in 2009.

On top of this, there were also three seats contested in Northern Ireland, using STV with the entire province as a single constituency. The Democratic Unionists, Sinn Fein, and Ulster Unionists (although the MEP calls himself a Traditional Unionist, and the party is now known as the Ulster Conservatives and Unionists) each won one seat.

When looking at the results in 2009 and the party breakdown in 2013, there are some discrepancies. This has been to do with MEPs changing party groups. Edward McMillan-Scott left the Conservatives for the Liberal Democrats in March 2010, while David Campbell Bannerman left UKIP for Conservatives in June 2011. Other UKIP MEPs have left the party, setting up their own organisations, and sitting as Non-attached MEPs. Some UKIP members also sit with the Non-attached MEPs rather than in the Europe of Freedom and Democracy group. Similarly, the BNP has fragmented as well.

The Court of Justice

This body is based in Luxembourg. It currently comprises 28 Judges (one from each member state) and nine Advocates General, each appointed on renewable six year terms. In 2013, the 'British' judge was **Christopher Vajda** (who has been in post since October 2012). The appointment of the Advocates General is a little more complex. As of 2009, each of the six larger states has one, while the remainder are shared between the other member states in an alphabetical rotation. The British Advocate General is Eleanor Sharpston (who has been in post since 2006). All appointments to the Court of Justice are non-political (unlike in the United States) and are on merit.

The role of the Court of Justice is to ensure the laws are observed and there is consistency of interpretation across the EU. On top of this, the Court of Justice interprets the various treaties of the EU, and is also a court of appeal. An important point to note about the Court of Justice is it cannot intervene in any dispute by itself. Cases must be referred to it. Examples include: the Commission can bring cases if member states have failed to fulfil an obligation under Treaty requirements; EU members or bodies can have the legality of acts reviewed; and, national courts can refer to the Court of Justice for guidance on rulings.

As the judicial work has increased, a second court was established in 1988 – the Court of First Instance (renamed the **General Court** in 2009). Like the Court of Justice, the General Court has 28 judges – one from each member state – but no advocates general. In 2013, the British representative was Nicholas Forwood; his term of office runs until 2019. There is a clear divide between the two courts: the General Court focuses on the scrutiny of factual matters, while the Court of Justice focuses on matters of law.

The Committee of the Regions

This body was established through the TEU. It is a consultative committee comprising 353 members. The delegates are appointed on renewable five year terms, and they are generally from local and regional authorities. Each member state is designated a number of members on the Committee of the Regions, depending upon the size of the country.

Table 31.5 Membership of the Committee of the Regions (2013)

Number of Members	Member States
24	France, Germany, Italy, UK
21	Poland, Spain
15	Romania
12	Austria, Belgium, Bulgaria, Czech Republic, Greece, Hungary, Netherlands, Portugal, Sweden
9	Croatia, Denmark, Finland, Ireland, Lithuania, Slovakia
7	Estonia, Latvia, Slovenia
6	Cyprus, Luxembourg
5	Malta

Currently, of the 24 British members, most of them are councillors, although there are two representatives from the Scottish Parliament, and one from each of the Welsh, Northern Ireland and London Assemblies. The council representation stretches across all of the UK.

The creation of the Committee of the Regions was a key part of the subsidiarity within the TEU. As a result the Committee must be consulted on a number of matters pertaining to local or regional government. Since that time, the remit has been broadened still further. It now includes:

- education and youth
- employment
- environment
- climate change and energy
- economic and social cohesion
- public health
- transport
- the European Social Fund
- vocational training
- social affairs
- culture
- trans-European transport, energy and communication networks
- cross-border cooperation

The Committee of the Regions has the potential to become akin to a second chamber with the EU. It appeared to be, however, the European Parliament that prevented such a development. Having gained a number of powers via the TEU, the European Parliament seemed reluctant to share them. Until the Committee of the Regions is directly elected, it may suffer from an apparent lack of accountability.

The European Economic and Social Committee
This is an advisory body which was created in 1957 to ensure the representation of a range of different sections of society. The sections of society represented are employers, workers, and various other interests. These various other interests include farmers, small businesses, environmental organisations, consumer organisations and members of the scientific and academic communities. The committee is very much non-political. Like the Committee of Regions, it comprises 353 members, broken down in the same way for each member state. Thus Britain contributes 24 members. All members are proposed by their 'home' government for a renewable five year term. Of the British representatives, 8 represent the employers, 8 the workers, and 8 various interests. The European Economic and Social Committee (EESC) presents itself as being the forum where members of civil society can have their say.

The EESC has six sections:
- Agriculture, Rural Development and the Environment
- Economic and Monetary Union and Economic and Social Cohesion
- Employment, Social Affairs and Citizenship
- External Relations
- The Single Market, Production and Consumption
- Transport, Energy, Infrastructure and the Information Society

The EESC can only offer opinions in each of these areas, and, as stated before, these are purely advisory.

The Europeanization of British Politics?

One of the most interesting aspects of Britain's relations with the EU is the extent to which EU practices have filtered into the UK. This is sometimes presented as something to be resisted; that the British way of doing things may be polluted by these foreign influences. Yet the Europeanization of British politics is not solely about the EU telling Britain (and all the other member states) what to do. Such an approach over-simplifies a rather complex relationship. It is not just about central government either. Europeanization can also be linked to regional and local government (see Jones (2007) chapter 5 for the impact of the EU on sub-national government in the UK).

Europeanization is a contested term. For many Euro-sceptics in particular, Europeanization is about the process of creating a United States of Europe. This is probably the most extreme integrationist perception of Europeanization. There is a range of different approaches to the concept. Some ideas of Europeanization are the 'top down' enforcement, where the EU tells the member states what to do. Bulmer and Burch (1998, p. 602), for example, see Europeanization "as referring to the impact of EU-led changes upon at least two distinct aspects of member states' activities – policy and machinery". This can be seen in the legislative arena, where EU law overrides national law where the two conflict. Bulmer and Burch (1998) acknowledge there are both inter- and intra-state dimensions to Europeanization. The intra-state dimension focuses on the impact on member states (as noted above). The inter-state dimension looks at the impact of the actions of member states upon each other, and upon the EU. Although EU regulations and directives are binding on the states to which they are addressed, there will have been significant national influence in the legislative process (from more than one member state).

Yet Europeanization can also be about ideas, beliefs and attitudes. The EU can influence the way in which people think. This is not to say the EU transforms everyone into mindless pro-European automatons. Rather, it compels people to contemplate the impact of the EU on their everyday lives. Thus Europeanization may contribute to people developing an anti-EU perspective, or reinforcing anti-EU beliefs.

It must also be noted Europeanization is not a one-way street. Individual member states, tiers of sub-national government, and pressure groups can all influence the EU (as noted by Bulmer and Burch (1998) with the inter-state dimension of Europeanization). The good practice developed by these organisations may influence the operations of the EU, which, in turn, filters through to all member states. The UK national government has been to the forefront in fighting different forms of corruption within the EU. The good practices utilised by the UK have influenced how the EU fights corruption as well. This is sometimes seen as 'bottom up' Europeanization (Börzel & Panke, 2010).

As noted above, Europeanization is not just about national governments. It can influence specific policy areas, and have varying influences across different government departments. For an interesting evaluation of the impact on environmental policy and the Department of the Environment, see Jordan (2003). According to Börzel (2002), on environmental issues the UK used to be what she termed a 'foot dragger' (resistant to other states' domestic approaches being broadened out to apply to all EU members) or a 'fence sitter' (apathetic or indifferent to EU policies). At the turn of the century, Börzel saw the UK as a 'pace setter' on environmental policy – promoting specific British policies for adoption across the EU. All of this is part of the process of Europeanization.

When examining Europeanization, Radaelli (2000) asks some interesting questions:

1. Is Europeanization making the member states more similar?
2. Do different domestic policy structures 'refract' Europeanization in different directions?
3. If everything is Europeanized to a certain degree, what is **not** Europeanized?

Europeanization is a complex concept. It is often presented as the imposition of the EU and its ideas on to all of the EU. Yet it can produce divergence, as well as promoting integration. In the UK, there has been an emphasis on the negative impact of EU membership. This, too, can be part of the process of Europeanization. And it leaves Radaelli's last question unanswered: what is not Europeanized?

Britain and the Euro

One area where Britain has appeared resistant to the EU has been over the adoption of the Euro. During the TEU negotiations, then-Prime Minister John Major negotiated an opt-out of the final stage of European Monetary Union (EMU). Thus, while Britain participated in the first two stages of EMU, along with Denmark (and later, Sweden), the British Government declined the opportunity of joining the single currency.

As of 2013, of the 28 member states, 18 have joined up to the Euro. There is an obligation on all member states that joined in 2004 and 2007 to work towards joining the single currency. Only Denmark and the UK are permitted to opt out.

As Prime Minister, Tony Blair was initially quite keen for Britain to join the Euro. His Chancellor, Gordon Brown, was far less enthused. An agreement was reached between Blair and Brown that a referendum on British membership of the Euro would be held when Britain met the five economic tests devised by the Treasury (although there is speculation the tests were drawn up on the back of an envelope by Gordon Brown and Ed Balls). The tests are detailed in Table 31.6.

Table 31.6 Gordon Brown's Five Economic Tests for British membership of the Euro

• Would joining economic and monetary union create better conditions for firms making long-term decisions to invest in Britain?
• How would Britain's financial services be affected by adopting the single currency?
• Are business cycles and economic structures compatible with those of our European partners so that we can all live comfortably with a single interest rate?
• Is there sufficient flexibility to be able to deal with any problems?
• Will joining help promote growth, stability and a lasting increase in jobs?

The extent to which Britain has met these tests has been reported to Parliament on only one occasion – in October 1997, and at that time, only one test was considered to have been met. Since then, the issue of the UK joining the Euro has, at best, been on the back burner. There was a clear lack of public support for Britain joining the Euro. Added to this, other factors overtook the Euro as a salient political issue: the debate around the proposed European constitution; the global economic crash of 2008; and, the Euro-zone economic crisis and, in particular, the problems surrounding Greek membership of the Euro. The coalition government stated Britain will not join the Euro during the lifetime of the 2010-2015 Parliament.

Conclusion – Britain the 'reluctant European'?
Many people have described Britain as a 'reluctant European'. By this it is suggested Britain does not really want to be part of the EU unless it is in British interests. In the formative years, in the 1950s and 1960s, Britain was uninvolved. In the 1970s, Britain joined but participation was hesitant. In the 1980s, Thatcher placed British interests ahead of those of Europe. She looked across the 'pond' to the United States rather than across the 'ditch' to Europe. There is, though, a curious position with Thatcher. In 1986, she forced the

Single European Act through Parliament on a three-line whip, and guillotined the debate on the legislation in the House of Commons as well. Her perception was the Single European Act was 'economic' in nature, and did not mean greater political integration. In this evaluation, Thatcher has clearly been shown to be wrong.

In the 1990s, internal divisions within British politics meant that Europe has not remained high on the political agenda. John Major wanted to place Britain at the heart of Europe but many within his party were resistant. Tony Blair, while expressing similar sentiments, appeared rather timid on the issue of Europe, not wishing to upset the media – and the Rupert Murdoch-owned press in particular – which is for the most part Euro-sceptic or even Euro-phobic. That enthusiasm diminished under Brown, and has disappeared under Cameron.

Yet, when looking at Britain's track record in Europe, the label 'reluctant European' may not be totally deserved. Legislation such as the Single European Act, the Treaty on European Union and the EU Reform Treaty were passed by Parliament. Denmark, on the other hand, had to hold two referendums before passing the Treaty on European Union, and Ireland had to do the same for the Treaty of Nice. The EU Reform Treaty was also subject to a referendum in Ireland and, again, the Irish voted No. Sweden returned a 'No' vote on joining the Euro. France and the Netherlands blocked the proposed EU constitution by voting 'No' in national referendums.

Within the EU itself, Britain has been to the forefront in attempting to open up the EU to greater scrutiny (e.g. the creation of the Ombudsman) and in fighting fraud and corruption. Upon obtaining office, the Blair Government signed Britain up to the Social Charter. The Blair Government supported the development of the European Rapid Reaction Force, with a role that can complement NATO membership.

In sum, Britain's relationship with Europe has not been consistent. Much of the problem appears to lie with the popular perceptions of Europe, as portrayed in the media. Infamous headlines such as "Up Yours, Delors", or stories about the banning of British sausages, or donkeys having to wear nappies on beaches (both of which were fictitious) have added to a general hostility towards Europe. Sadly, there is a huge lack of awareness as to what the EU does for the UK. Instead, any mistakes made by the EU are highlighted, along with anything that appears even remotely detrimental to Britain. National flag-waving and anti-Europeanism seem to go hand-in-hand. It may well be this narrow nationalistic jingoism is what is making Britain appear as a 'reluctant European'.

Selected bibliography
Bache, Ian & Jordan, Andrew (eds.). (2008). *The Europeanization of British Politics:* Palgrave.
Cini, Michelle & Borragán, Nieves (eds.). (2010). *European Union Politics*: Oxford University Press, 3rd edition.

Gowland, David; Turner, Arthur & Wright, Alex. (2010). *Britain and European Integration Since 1945*: Routledge.

Jones, Alistair. (2007). *Britain and the European Union*: Edinburgh University Press.

McCormick, John. (2011). *Understanding the European Union: A Concise Introduction*: Palgrave, 5th edition.

Nugent, Neill. (2010). *The Government and Politics of the European Union*: Palgrave, 7th edition.

Steunenberg, Bernard. (2010). "Is big brother watching? Commission oversight of the national implementation of EU directives", *European Union Politics* vol. 11-3, pp. 359-380.

Websites

cor.europa.eu/Pages/welcome.html
This is the home page of the Committee of Regions

curia.europa.eu/
This website leads you to the Court of Justice and the General Court, formerly known as the Court of First Instance

ec.europa.eu/
This is the home page of the Commission

ue.eu.int
This is the home page of the Council of Ministers/Council of the European Union

www.eesc.europa.eu/
Home page of the Economic and Social Committee

www.europarl.europa.eu/
This is the home page of the European Parliament

Questions
1. Britain is not a "reluctant European". Most Britons do not want to be "European"; hence the desire to leave the EU. Comment.
2. A federal Europe is inevitable. Discuss
3. The EU is the most divisive of all issues in British Politics, yet we get few leads from our political leaders. Why is this the case? Justify your position.

CHAPTER 32 // POLITICS OF INEQUALITY: GENDER

Contents
- **Introduction**
- **Under-representation**
- **Reasons Advanced for Under-representation**
- **Feminine Conceptions of Politics**
- **Conclusion**

Introduction

The role of gender in politics – if not in society, business, and every other facet of peoples' lives – is receiving far greater attention. The problem in writing this chapter is the author is male. Consequently, there will be those who argue, and with justification, this chapter is biased. There is no way in which a man can know about the needs or experiences of women. In fact, a man writing this chapter will further entrench the male domination of society that has gone on for centuries. So, with a very guarded step forward, this man will attempt to scratch at the surface of a number of issues of great importance to women. The vast majority of references used in writing this chapter are female authors and academics. This may be a small, pitiful defence, but it is better than no defence at all.

In the UK, gender politics has been around for centuries. A prominent point in this timeline was in 1866, when a petition was presented to Parliament, requesting full rights for women. The petition was ignored, and the following year the National Society for Women's Suffrage was established. Their objective was to obtain full voting rights. New Zealand was the first state in the world to give voting rights to women (in 1893), although they were actually preceded by the U.S. state of Wyoming and by the Isle of Man. Eventually British women received the vote in 1918. The Representation of the People's Act gave all women, aged over thirty years, full voting rights. This was later extended to all women aged over 21 – bringing them in line with men – with the Equal Franchise Act (1928). It is sometimes questioned, however, as to what the extension of voting rights actually achieved. "The suffragettes, however mistakenly, perceived the vote not simply as a symbol of political emancipation but as a means to effective political participation" (Randall, 1987, p. 51). It is debatable as to the extent to which this has been achieved, as we approach the centenary of the emancipation of women in the UK.

Under-representation

Despite the fact women constitute over half of the UK adult population, they are woefully under-represented in Parliament, in the cabinet, in the legal professions and at the higher levels of public bodies. There are odd exceptions, such as the Welsh Assembly, which saw women constituting over half of all Assembly Members in 2003. This was the first body in the world to achieve parity of representation by gender, but this parity slipped back in subsequent elections.

Even in local government, where there is a perception of a more positive picture with regard to the representation of women, female representation lags far behind men. Table 32.1 presents details of female representation across a range of British institutions.

Table 32.1 Female Representation in British Politics

House of Commons (1992)	9.2%
House of Commons (1997)	18.2%
House of Commons (2010)	22.0%
UK Cabinet (2013)	18.2%
House of Lords (2013)	22.6%
High Court Judges (2013)	15.5%
Supreme Court (2013)	8.3%
Scottish Parliament (2003)	39.5%
Scottish Parliament (2011)	34.8%
Scottish Government (2013)	25%
Welsh Assembly (2003)	50%
Welsh Assembly (2011)	41.7%
Welsh Government (2013)	27.3%
Northern Ireland Assembly (2003)	16.7%
Northern Ireland Assembly (2011)	18.5%
Northern Ireland Executive (2013)	23.1%
Local Councils in England (2011)	31%
British Members of the European Parliament (2009)	34.7%

A major breakthrough in gender politics in Britain appeared to be with the election of Margaret Thatcher as Prime Minister in 1979. The counterbalance to this is the 1979 General Election saw the smallest number of women MPs (19) elected since 1951. There were gradual rises in the number of women elected in subsequent elections, and a great leap forward in 1997, when 120 women were elected. Of these, 101 were elected as Labour MPs, and were labelled in the press as "Blair's babes".

Compared to other countries, Britain lags behind in women's parliamentary representation. As of October 2013, Rwanda had the highest percentage of female representatives, with 64%. They are followed by Andorra (50%), Cuba (49%) and Sweden (45%). Britain was ranked 65th, with 22.5%. At the time of writing, there was a marginally higher percentage of female representation in the House of Lords than in the House of Commons. The fact ten other EU member states, and the USA, all have less female representation in their national parliaments than Britain should be of little consolation. The Federated States of Micronesia, Palau, Qatar and Vanuatu are the only countries in the world to have no female representation in their respective lower houses (although almost a quarter of representatives in Palau's upper house are women). For more information, see the Women in Parliaments website at www.ipu.org/wmn-e/classif.htm.

When Margaret Thatcher was Prime Minister, it almost appeared as if women were excluded from her cabinets – Baroness Young was the only one chosen. John Major caused a public outcry when his first cabinet contained no women – although he later promoted Gillian Shepherd and Virginia Bottomley. Tony Blair's first cabinet contained five women: Margaret Beckett, Mo Mowlam, Ann Taylor, Harriet Harman and Clare Short. In fact, during the Blair/Brown years, there were some notable firsts for women appointees to the cabinet: Ann Taylor was the first female Chief Whip, Jacqui Smith was the first female Home Secretary, and Margaret Beckett was the first female Foreign Secretary. The Coalition Government also had five female politicians appointed to the cabinet after the general election – most notably Theresa May as Home Secretary. The others were: Cheryl Gillan, Caroline Spelman, Justine Greening and Baroness Warsi.

Reasons Advanced for Under-representation
A number of reasons have been advanced as to why there is such a lack of women's representation. This does not just apply to politics and public life, but may also apply to a lack of representation of women in the upper echelons of the business world. This section should be read in conjunction with the section on Citizenship and Gender in Chapter 19.

1. Political Socialisation
Society in the UK is patriarchal; that is, it "systematically reproduces a gendered power imbalance and... systematically privileges men as a group in relation to women as a group" (Einspahr, 2010, p. 12). Einspahr continues: "patriarchy, or the male control of political, economic, social, and cultural institutions, backed up with force, constitutes the material and symbolic conditions of women's domination" (p. 12). Jones (1990, p. 782) highlights this situation even further:

> ...even if women achieve juridical/legal equality, gain more adequate political representation in law-making and administrative bodies, and possess the economic means and personal motivation to practice their rights; and even if women's duties to the state are broadened to include military service, women's membership in the political community will still be less full than men's.

Everything is represented through the perspective of men. The worlds of politics, business and economics are presented as "men's worlds", where women have to compete as if they were men. Until such a mindset is changed, gender imbalances and gender inequality will be self-perpetuating.

Thus, although there is increased female participation in the job market, and in a willingness to stand for election, barriers remain in place. For example, "the majority of the new employment opportunities taken up by women have been in part-time jobs, which bring limited employment related rights or benefits, and which tend to be offered at relatively low rates of pay" (Bondi & Christie, 2000, p. 331). This reinforces the stereotypical images of the male breadwinner and the female as a care giver. Worse still, in many cases women are being paid less than men for doing the same job – and this is despite legislation such as the Equal Pay Act (1970).

As far as political socialisation is concerned, an argument is advanced that boys and girls receive different nurturing. The family and schooling are probably the two most crucial sites of early socialisation. Through these, feelings and attitudes are developed on a range of subjects. One result appears to be a lack of interest in, and knowledge of, politics by girls.

Yet the evidence to support such a statement is, at best, thin. For example, a number of studies have cast doubt on such assertions, most notably as to what is meant by "politics". There is more than ample evidence to show women are indeed interested in "politics". This may not necessarily be through standing for election. Rather, it is in the wider sense of the word, as attested by their participation in a diverse range of fields, including community affairs, welfare campaigns, and green issues. Consider, for example, the anti-nuclear campaign – especially at Greenham Common – in the 1980s, where women were the high profile protestors. This is very much participation in 'low-politics'; that which concerns everyday life, rather than the 'high-politics' of the elected representative.

2. Barriers to selection as Parliamentary candidates

Before even looking at the selection of Parliamentary candidates, party membership must be acknowledged. The number of party members, at least for the major parties, has decreased significantly over the years – although there have been periodic drives to improve the levels of party membership. In the late 1970s and early 1980s, women comprised over half of the membership of the Conservative Party – although this has since dropped. Women comprised around 40% of the Labour Party membership in the same time period.

Political parties tend to advance the rather weak excuse for the disproportionate choice of males as Parliamentary candidates is not enough women put themselves forward. This may well be true, but it is a self-fulfilling defence. Many women who would certainly be eligible as candidates because of their occupational and educational experience are reluctant to apply owing to a range of formidable obstacles put in their way. While these obstacles may no longer be as overt as in the past, women are often asked questions about childcare – will your husband/ partner be resigning from their job to care for your children? After all, being an MP is seen as a full-time job (at least by the selection panels). The chances of a male prospective candidate being asked a similar question is, at best, minimal.

Table 32.2 Parliamentary candidates for the 2010 General Election

Party	Number of Candidates	Number of Women Candidates	% of women candidates
Conservative	631	153	24.2
Labour	631	191	30.3
Liberal Democrat	631	134	21.2
Plaid Cymru	40	7	17.5
Scottish Nationalist	59	17	28.8
Total	**4 152**	**874**	**21.1**

Compared to previous elections, the number of women standing as candidates has increased. A major issue, however, is the extent to which these seats are "winnable". Allegations have been made of tokenism – that female candidates have been selected in unwinnable seats, but a party can claim to have increased numbers of female candidates.

The Labour Party moved to the use of All-Women Shortlists, prior to the 2005 General Election, in the hope of bolstering the numbers of women elected to Parliament. The plan, at one stage, was for women to comprise around half of the candidates for the Labour Party. Such a move was challenged in the courts, and Labour backed down.

It is interesting to note Labour had thirty candidates who were selected for the 2005 election using All-Women Shortlists. Of these, 23 won their seats. Research into the seven who lost their seats has drawn some interesting conclusions. The seats were not necessarily lost because of a woman candidate, but because of the 'newness' of the candidate. Concerns are often expressed that new candidates do not understand the constituency for which they are standing, and voters may feel reluctant to support them – irrespective of the candidate's gender (see Cutts *et al*, 2008).

At the 2005 General Election, there was one seat where the imposition of an All-Women Shortlist caused a backlash within the Labour Party – Blaenau Gwent. A prospective male Labour candidate decided to stand as an Independent in retaliation against the use of an All-Women Shortlist. He won the election, with a 49% swing in votes. This one constituency – which was an exceptional case – has been presented by many party members (as well as others who are opposed to the use of such schemes to increase female representation in Parliament) as a justification for not having All-Women Shortlists (and ignoring the 23 victories for candidates selected using such shortlists). Despite these criticisms, Labour have persisted with the use of All-Women Shortlists.

While the Labour Party moved forward with the use of such lists, other parties have not been so progressive. Party leaders, such as David Cameron and Nick Clegg, have expressed the need for more women to stand as candidates, and to get them elected into Parliament. Yet few moves have been made in such a direction.

Research has been conducted into Conservative Party members' feelings about getting more women into Parliament, if not into public life more generally. While there is a willingness "to concede the principle of a more socially representative parliamentary party, ... they do not welcome all of the candidate-selection reforms that have been introduced in recent years" (Childs *et al*, 2009, p. 211). Instead, the emphasis is much more meritocratic – finding the best person for the candidacy.

3. Electoral Office

The 1997 General Election saw the largest ever number of women entering Parliament. The experiences of this intake were far from positive. They had to endure bad treatment from a number of misogynistic male MPs. Added to this, their portrayal in the media made their experiences even worse. The reporting of some of the female MPs actually undermined their role as an MP.

The way in which Parliament operates is very much like a gentlemen's club, where women are, at best, tolerated – although there were suggestions of many male MPs being far from tolerant of their female counterparts. Such an atmosphere is anything but conducive for carrying out the work of Parliament; any more than the 'yah-boo' politics within the House of Commons chamber.

The experiences of electoral office are not helped by the lack of facilities in Parliament. This does not just apply to female MPs, but to everyone who works at the Palace of Westminster. While there has been a rifle range for many years, crèche facilities were only introduced in 2010. The crèche facility has been derided as a £750 000 waste of money, as it cost so much to establish and is used by so few children. In fact, some MPs want it closed.

4. Public Bodies

Women are under-represented in Parliament, so it is hardly surprising there is under-representation across public bodies as a whole. While representation on quangos is on the increase, it has been a rather gradual process. Around a third of all 'quango-crats' are women. Across bodies such as school governors, there has been much greater female participation. The problem is such bodies are a long way down the food chain. The top decision makers are dominated by men. It is the ever-present glass ceiling. As an example, the Monetary Policy Committee of the Bank of England in 2013 had no women members. Other parts of the public sector with no female representation include the army (where the highest ranking woman officer is a colonel; although Brigadier Nicky Moffat resigned in 2012), the air force (the highest ranking woman officer is an air commodore) and the navy. It must be noted the numbers of senior officers is very small, but that is not much of a defence.

5. The Glass Ceiling
The concept of a glass ceiling has been in use for many years. It is an invisible barrier that limits the progress of women, as well as minority groups. Everyone can see and aspire to the top jobs, but the glass ceiling prevents many from ever progressing to the upper strata of decision making and power.

Table 32.1 gave a number of examples of where women have not reached the top echelons of power in politics. There are similar stories in business as well. One of the clearest examples of how a glass ceiling functions can be seen through the issue of pregnancy and childbirth. As Mandel (2009, p. 705) notes: "motherhood continues to be an obstacle to employment... even among educated women".

There has been some interesting research conducted by Marlow *et al* (2013) into the financing of small and medium-sized businesses. Women owners of such businesses may be disadvantaged by their femininity because it is seen to conflict with the entrepreneurialism desired by many stakeholders.

Within the larger companies, the position of women is actually worse than in politics. Looking at the FTSE100 companies, the percentage of directorships in these most prominent and most powerful UK businesses stands at 17.3%. As of March 2013, there were two women chief executives running FTSE100 companies. Suggestions have been made, by organisations such as the Fawcett Society, for the introduction of boardroom quotas (as has been done in Norway). Such quotas (of suitably qualified women) would help to achieve not only boardroom equality, but also might help in taking steps to address issues such as pay equality. An increased presence in the number of women at the boardroom level tends to equate with improved business performance!

Feminine Conceptions of Politics
Feminism is the word that tends to be associated with women and politics. Yet under this broad label, there are a number of distinct approaches towards politics. Consequently, there are a number of different interpretations as to what feminism is all about. A succinct definition, as a starting point, is provided by Scholz (2010, p. 1). "The most common and perhaps most general understanding of feminism is that feminism is about equal rights for women." Such a position,

focusing upon gender equality, is still problematic. As Bondi & Christie (2000, p. 340) ask: is it about extending to women opportunities that are available to others? If so, the implicit assumption is a man's opportunities are the norm. Thus, women pursuing the same rights as men actually reinforce gender roles and gender stereotypes!

There are, therefore, a number of different approaches to feminism. For example, there are various fields of feminism, which range from the political and the economic through to the environmental and the epistemological. Added to this are different approaches from national or ethnic perspectives (such as European, North American, Islamic, Black). There are also approaches to feminism by different individuals, such as Rosa Luxemburg. Consequently, there is no uniform position on feminism. There have been challenges from "groups of women whose identities and interests have been ignored, marginalized or subsumed under the figure of the equal or different women who was its subject" (Lister, 2005, p. 447). Whether such splintering strengthens or undermines the cause of feminism is open to debate.

Within this chapter, three separate approaches towards feminism are going to be examined briefly. Each of them will be explained in relation to politics:

1. *Radical*
2. *Marxist*
3. *Reformist*

While each approach highlights patriarchy as the problem, there are definitional problems with the concept of 'patriarchy' within each approach. Added to this, there are clear ideological divisions between all three (as well as between the many other approaches to feminism).

1. Radical

This perspective of feminism looks to a fundamental change not just in politics but in life. The fundamental division in society is seen as sex – divisions such as class and race are secondary. Such an approach is then developed with a focus on issues of physical or sexual aspects of male domination e.g. rape and abortion. The patriarchal society is "a system of control of women and women's bodies by men" (Scholz, 2010, p. 19). This male power/patriarchy is the source of the subordination of women.

Consequently, radical feminists believe in separatism. Men cannot be accepted as allies. To change the system of male domination requires revolution. Reform of the system will not work because men dominate the system: the politicians, the bureaucrats – those who would draw up and implement the legislation. Evidence can be cited of such legislation: the Equal Pay legislation of 1970. It was heralded as a great step forward in women's rights. Over forty years later, there are still disputes about the equality of pay. The legislation was flawed in its drawing up, and flawed in its execution. The radical perspective highlights politics not as an activity but as a power struggle – the ideas of conflict and control. Importantly, there is a rejection of mainstream politics and of the state by radical feminists. These are the symbols of patriarchy that must be torn down.

Finally, radical feminists argue you cannot distinguish between public and private (see Chapter 19 on feminist approaches to citizenship). There is a need for equality in political, economic, social and domestic life. Male domination exists in every sphere of life. For example, "[b]ecause women can bear children they have been relegated to the private sphere of the family or domestic life" (Scholz, 2010, p. 19). It is the patriarchal society which wants to separate the public from the private: a man's home is his castle, and a man can do whatever he wants there. The public (state) has no right to interfere! It is this type of idea radical feminists wish to tear down.

2. Marxist

Capitalist sources of oppression, along with the struggle between the classes, are at the forefront of this feminist approach. Consequently, it has been criticised for merely adding the oppression of women to a pre-existing Marxist framework. Regardless of this, the Marxist feminist perspective points out the struggle between the sexes will not disappear with the overthrow of capitalism.

Women's oppression is a direct result of capitalism. Gender inequality is part of the capitalist structure of society. "Capitalism relies on a class of people doing 'reproductive' labor [sic] that is unremunerated" (Scholz, 2010, p. 16). The male is the breadwinner and the property owner; the female is the housewife, or even the chattel.

As a result of this situation, women find it very difficult to organise themselves or to act collectively. The housewife who stays at home becomes very isolated. The capitalist structures also perceive women as a reserve pool of labour, ready to be called upon in times of labour shortages (such as during war, where the men go off to fight and the women pick up the jobs until the survivors return – at which point, the women will return home dutifully).

The Marxist feminist perspective also examines the economic aspects of women's oppression. Thus, there may be a push for equal pay and the advancement of women, but these are only transitional objectives. They may appear to improve the position of women but the struggle continues. A Marxist approach would not necessarily recognise equal pay as an achievement because the structures of class and patriarchy would remain untouched.

As with their radical counterparts, Marxist feminists have traditionally believed in revolutionary change. It is only with such a fundamental overhaul of society that true equality can be achieved. Any gradualist changes, such as through legislation, are little more than tinkering with the structures, without any actual change to the patriarchal class structures that endure.

3. Reformist

Reformist feminism is sometimes known as liberal feminism. This perspective emphasises reform rather than revolution (although the two are not necessarily incompatible). In the past, this label has been used as a catch-all for all feminists who did not fit under any other labels. This has, in fact, often confused things as some reformist feminists emphasise the economic aspects of their oppression (like the Marxists), while others emphasise the physical aspects (like the radicals). Thus the reformist label covers a wide range of approaches to feminism. An important feature of the reformist approach is they are willing to co-operate with non-feminist groups from across the political spectrum. In general, reformist feminists strive for economic and political equality within the existing capitalist structures.

One part of the reformist approach acknowledges the need for radical social change to 'liberate' women from patriarchy. The other end of the scale presents the plight of women as a minor and temporary handicap that can be redressed through legislation, such as equal rights. The underpinning demand from each side is that women be treated equally, or the same, as men. The emphasis is upon, for example, the equal rights of all citizens, and an end to all forms of discrimination. Thus, as Scholtz (2010, p. 15) notes, you can "identify the roots of the oppression of women in the lack of legal rights and equal opportunities afforded women".

One way in which this situation can be remedied is via the state (for example, through legislation). The reformist approach, however, presents the state as a neutral arbiter – in a manner not too dissimilar to that of pluralists. It suggests the state has no bias or value judgements that may influence the demands for change; state structures are little more than conduits through which policy ideas may be realised. Both radical and Marxist perspectives would refute this idea very strongly indeed. The idea the organs of the state do not have an agenda of their own, or civil servants can act totally impartially, is false.

Each of these approaches has made a huge contribution to the role of women in politics and society today – and will continue to do so. All of them have strengths and weaknesses. The reformist approach, for example, is rather naive in assuming the state to be neutral. It is very clearly male-dominated and is most unlikely to do anything that may rock the status quo. Yet, this is not to deride the reformist approach. It has had numerous successes, not all of which have received due acclaim. Table 32.3 lists some of the major legislative changes that have been introduced in the UK in the advancement of gender equality.

Table 32.3 Gender-related Legislation in the UK

Abortion Act (1967)
NHS (Family Planning) Act (1967)
Equal Pay Act (1970)
Sex Discrimination Act (1975)
Employment Protection Act (1975)
Domestic Violence and Matrimonial Proceedings Act (1976)
Equal Pay (Amendment) Act (1985)
Sexual Discrimination (Amendment) Act (1986)
Employment Act (2002)
Sex Discrimination (Election Candidates) Act 2002)
Equality Act (2006)
Work and Families Act (2006)
Single Equality Act (2010)

Of some concern is the suggestion of the demise of feminism among younger generations. Younger women are no longer portrayed as being 'feminist'. Yet feminism may simply have moved on: the fight for gender equality is merely being taken forward in different ways, as has always been the case. There are generational conflicts about feminism, in the same way as there have been many other conflicts about feminism.

Conclusion

There are more women in Parliament than ever before; there are more female candidates standing for election; in all aspects of life, women are coming to the fore; so, has gender equality been achieved? Despite all of the progress, and all of the legislation, the answer is still "No". To make matters worse, some regressive steps appear to be taking place, especially under the mask of 'austerity'.

The wheels of government can turn very slowly. In 1989, the "need for developing common knowledge and feminist debate around gender issues" (Hubert & Stratigaki, 2011, p. 171) was raised at the European level. Ten years later, the idea of a European Gender Institute was explicitly raised. In 2005, the **European Institute for Gender Equality** was established. This is fighting the cause for gender equality at the trans-national level.

Yet in the UK, the picture may not be quite so positive. There was some consternation when, in 2007, the Equal Opportunities Commission was wound up. It was, in effect, merged with the Commission for Racial Equality and the Disability Rights Commission to form a new Equality and Human Rights Commission. There were suggestions at that time this would undermine the campaign for gender equality. Things have got worse since then, as Waylen (2012) notes: "the current British coalition government has abolished the

Women's National Commission...; made big cuts to the single equality body, the Equality and Human Rights Commission; and ignored the gender equality duty introduced by the previous Labour government". All of these damage the cause of gender equality. There is even speculation the coalition government may consider abolishing the Equality Act.

Such moves highlight the precarious approach adopted by reformist feminists. What one government may give, another can take away. Radical feminists might, on the one hand, be thinking 'I told you so'; on the other hand, they will be considering ways in which to stop this patriarchal system of government, and the patriarchal society within which it operates, from doing untold damage to the cause of gender equality.

Selected bibliography

Annesley, Claire. (2012). "Campaigning against the Cuts: Gender Equality Movements in Tough Times", *Political Quarterly* vol. 83-1, pp. 19-23.

Campbell, Rosie & Childs, Sarah. (2010). "'Wags', 'Wives' and 'Mothers'... But what about women Politicians?", *Parliamentary Affairs* vol. 63-4, pp. 760-777.

Fox, Ruth. (2011). "'Boom and Bust' in Women's Representation: Lessons to be Learnt from a Decade of Devolution", *Parliamentary Affairs* vol. 64-1, pp. 193-203.

Hubert, Agnès & Stratigaki, Maria. (2011). "The European Institute for Gender Equality: A window of opportunity for gender equality policies?", *European Journal of Women's Studies* vol. 18-2, pp. 169-181.

Hunt, Karen. (2009). "Rethinking Activism: Lessons from the History of Women's Politics", *Parliamentary Affairs* vol. 62-3, pp. 211-226.

Public Policy & Administration vol. 24-2. (2009). Special Issue: Gender and Equality in Public Life.

Scholz, Sally J. (2010). *Feminism: A Beginners Guide*: Oneworld.

Waylen, Georgina. (2012). "Gender Matters in Politics", *Political Quarterly* vol. 83-1, pp. 24-32.

Websites

www.fawcettsociety.org.uk/
The Fawcett Society campaigns for women's equality and rights

www.feminist.com
An online community fostering awareness, education and activism for women around the world

www.thefword.org.uk/
An online magazine dedicated to contemporary feminism in the UK

www.parliament.uk/briefing-papers/RP13-65/women-in-parliament-making-a-difference-since-1918

A briefing paper from the House of Commons library on women in Parliament

Questions
1. In what ways can there be better representation of women and of women's issues?
2. "Gender equality can never be achieved." Discuss.
3. "Women-Only Shortlists undermine democracy." Discuss.

CHAPTER 33 // POLITICS OF EQUALITY: ETHNICITY

Contents
- **Introduction**
- **What is 'ethnicity'?**
- **Race Relations – Immigration**
- **Economic and Social Context**
- **Political Context**
- **Stephen Lawrence Case**
- **Conclusion**

As with the previous chapter, concern could be raised about the author writing this chapter. A white middle class male is not likely to be fully aware of the concerns of ethnic minorities, not having experienced their problems or fears. While acknowledging this point, the response is that it is far better to have a debate started on the issues of ethnicity and equality than to ignore it altogether.

Introduction

The significance of the 'black' and 'Asian' vote in general or local elections is increasing. There is already speculation with regard to the 2015 General Election about the impact of the potential ethnic minority vote. According to Operation Black Vote (OBV), this section of the voting population will have a significant impact in 168 marginal constituencies. In each of these constituencies, the ethnic minority vote is bigger than the majority of the sitting MP. Yet it appears as if politicians are oblivious to the concerns of these sections of society. They are, however, not alone. The killing of Mark Duggan in 2011 by police in Tottenham sparked off a series of riots that spread around the country. Questions were raised about the treatment of young, ethnic minority men by the police.

The question that must be posed at the outset is whether the British political and social system is capable of coming to grips with such a volatile situation. Yet rather than looking at the issue of British racism, the emphasis is shifted on to the ethnic minorities themselves. Even if the matter of racial prejudice based on colour is set aside, the incidents of high immigration, the concentration of ethnic minorities in the inner cities with the knock on effects for law and order, education, health, housing and employment are all perceived as a result of an ethnic influx. Some of this may be compounded by attempts to assimilate these ethnic groups into the British way of life. With increasing numbers of racially-motivated attacks and with implicit and explicit discrimination, the 'volatile situation' may actually be presented as a problem.

What is 'ethnicity'?

This is not an easy concept to explain. The New Zealand Federation of Ethnic Councils defined "ethnic" as: "pertaining to or relating to any segment of the population within New Zealand society sharing fundamental cultural values, customs, beliefs, languages, traditions and characteristics, that are different from those of the larger society" (Jones, 2000, p. 4). While this is a rather all-encompassing definition, it highlights the extent to which any of a range of factors could be covered to distinguish different ethnic groupings.

Modood (2005) highlights five dimensions of ethnic difference, with specific reference to the UK. Some of these overlap with those listed from the New Zealand Federation of Ethnic Councils. These are listed in Table 33.1. Modood acknowledges these dimensions are not wholly distinctive; there is a degree of overlap.

Table 33.1 Dimensions of Ethnic Difference

Cultural distinctiveness	Norms and practices of particular groupings of society. These could be in relation to gender roles, marriage, religion, etc.
Disproportionality	Identifying a particular group by a disproportional distribution of a specific characteristic. This could be high unemployment, athletic ability, etc.
Strategy	How a group responds to particular sets of circumstances. Such strategies can contribute to group consciousness. This could include responses to high unemployment or a reaction to a tragic event.
Creativity	Identifying a particular characteristic or innovation, even if such actions are taken on by mainstream society. This could include a particular style of fashion or dress.
Identity	Membership of a group can carry affective meanings; taking pride in that identity. This could include the Black Pride movement.

Developed from Modood (2005, p. 22)

With such differences, it is easy to identify particular nations or states, as opposed to ethnic groupings. Yet within most nations or states, specific ethnic groups still exist. Admittedly, some countries such as France do not record different ethnic groupings. Within the UK, on the other hand, there are multiple ethnic groupings, including both indigenous and immigrant ethnic groups.

Race Relations – Immigration

Britain has always boasted about its liberal attitudes towards immigration. Over the centuries Jewish, Irish and European nationalities have been allowed to enter the country. Some of this was economic migration, but a lot was due to the seeking of asylum or safe haven from persecution. In 1948, however, with the British Nationality Act the picture changed. All 'New' Commonwealth citizens were allowed to settle in Britain if they so wished - this meant virtually any citizen of the Commonwealth but was directly aimed at the 'Black' Commonwealth. With the need for cheap labour in public services like the NHS and transport, an influx from the 'New' Commonwealth began.

It should be pointed out at this stage the term 'Black' has become a general term to describe citizens from the 'New' Commonwealth (countries in Africa, the West Indies, and the Pacific, as well as India, Pakistan and Bangladesh). Such a term is actually misleading as it disguises the variety of cultures, customs, nations and religions within each of these regions or countries. The ethnic composition of Britain can be seen in table 33.2.

Table 33.2 Ethnic Composition of Britain (2011 census)

ETHNICITY	POPULATION
White	55 010 359 (87.1%)
Black*	1 904 684 (3.0%)
Indian	1 451 862 (2.3%)
Pakistani	1 173 892 (1.9%)
Bangladeshi	451 529 (0.7%)
Chinese	433 150 (0.7%)
Other – Asian	861 815 (1.4%)
British Mixed	1 250 229 (2.0%)
Other – Other	580 374 (0.9%)

* Black African and Black Caribbean are merged together because of different terminologies used in the Scottish census question.
Source: http://www.ons.gov.uk/ons/rel/census/2011-census/key-statistics-and-quick-statistics-for-local-authorities-in-the-united-kingdom---part-1/rft-ks201uk.xls

1) Immigration Measures
There were measures against immigration through legislation for the greater part of the twentieth century. In 1905, the Aliens Act was passed. While this reaffirmed Britain's commitment to giving political asylum, the legislation also enabled the British Government to refuse entry to anyone who could not support themselves or their dependants. It was clear in the early part of the twentieth century that while immigrants would be tolerated, they were not to place a burden upon the state.

With the onset of the First World War, this legislation was tightened up with the Aliens Restrictions Act (1914). This legislation was amended in 1919. The amendments repealed the 1905 Aliens Act. The 1919 legislation was renewed yearly until it was superseded by the Immigration Act 1971.

Yet there was also other legislation which affected immigration. There was the British Nationality Act (1948). This changed the manner in which British nationality could be acquired (Paul 1997). While various member states of the Empire could create their own nationality, this would merely provide access to becoming a British subject. The consequence of this was

[a]s subjects of the British Empire, colonial immigrants had the right of access to Britain and full rights of citizenship, including voting rights, the right to work in the civil service and the right to serve in the armed forces. (Layton-Henry, 1992, p. 9)

Thus there was a huge influx of immigrants from across the Empire throughout the 1950s. This was actively encouraged as there were labour shortages across the public sector.

The first signs of racial tension appeared in 1958 with riots in Nottingham and Notting Hill. The government's response to these disturbances was to look to limiting black immigration as a means to easing the tension. It is interesting to note after the 1958 riots, the issue of immigration became associated simply with non-white immigration (Layton-Henry, 1992, p. 73). The resulting attempt to curb immigration was the 1962 Commonwealth Immigrants Act, which was the first in a series of legislative measures to cut down the number of black immigrants. In 1968, a second Commonwealth Immigrants Act was passed which was aimed at tightening restrictions on immigration. It was followed, in 1971, by the Immigration Act, which imposed a quota system upon immigrants. The Nationality Act (1981) imposed even tighter restrictions upon immigration. It also made it more difficult to acquire British citizenship.

At the same time, the UK has been compelled to open up European immigration through the European Union. One of the main features of the EU is the free movement of people. Thus any residents in the EU may move freely around all 28 member states. There is a small caveat. Restrictions may be placed against free migration for new member states. Thus free movement was not permitted for Bulgarians and Romanians until 1 January 2014 – seven years after both countries joined the EU. The UK government placed restrictions against Croatians for two years after joining.

2) Race Relations Legislation

Successive governments' contentions have been that the attack on racial discrimination should be two-pronged. While there have been moves to limit the levels of immigration, there is also a need to protect the rights of those ethnic minorities who already live in Britain.

It could be argued that modern-day racism emerged as a consequence of the post-war immigration. Layton-Henry (1992, p.19) outlines the process:

> Even when recruited as a replacement labour force to do the work that the natives rejected and to occupy inner-city accommodation that the natives wished to leave, they could still be seen by those who remained as competitors for jobs, housing and other scarce resources. Immigration has thus provided a stimulus for xenophobia and for campaigns for racial control.

Such xenophobia could be directed against all immigrants. When directed against the non-European immigration, the attacks were described as 'racist'.

The first Race Relations Act was passed in 1965 and was followed by another in 1968. These stipulated there should be no discrimination in the public services (such as education, housing, and employment). The 1968 legislation also outlawed 'whites only' advertising. In 1976 another Race Relations Act came into effect. This strengthened the earlier legislation by outlawing both direct and indirect legislation. The 1976 Act also set up the **Commission for Racial Equality**. This body, which has since been merged into the **Equality and Human Rights Commission**, tackled discrimination and promoted ethnic equality.

Most recently, the Race Relations (Amendment) Act was passed in 2000. It came into force in April 2001. This Act updated the 1976 legislation, both strengthening and extending it. According to the 2000 Act it is now "unlawful to discriminate against anyone on grounds of race, colour, nationality (including citizenship), or ethnic or national origin" (www.cre.gov.uk/legaladv/rra.html). The types of harassment included range from verbal abuse to physical violence. This legislation should be read in conjunction with the Human Rights Act (1998) detailed in chapter seven.

3) Asylum Seekers

This is a topical area that seems to be separated from both immigration and race relations, with charges of bogus asylum seekers out to cheat the British welfare system. The reality is asylum seekers and refugees ought to be included as part of race relations. Their portrayal, especially in the media, suggests otherwise.

According to the United Nations Convention of the Status of Refugees of 1951 (amended in 1967), a refugee is:

> a person who is outside his or her country of nationality or habitual residence; has a well-founded fear of being persecuted because of his or her race, religion, nationality, membership of a particular social group or political opinion; and is unable or unwilling to avail him- or herself of the protection of that country, or to return there, for fear of persecution. (www.unhcr.org/4ec262df9.html)

While this appears to be a relatively straight forward definition, the actual interpretation of it is left to each signatory of the Convention. The UK Government has legislated on a number of occasions. In 1993 the Asylum and Immigration Appeals Act, outlined Britain's interpretation of refugee status. It was updated in 1996, making it more difficult to achieve refugee status. In 1999 the Immigration and Asylum Act introduced draconian measures which effectively blocked appeals against deportation. It also weakened any local government opposition to central government's control over how asylum seekers ought to be treated. Asylum seekers were pushed into designated accommodation by central government, potentially overriding any local government concerns. They were not eligible for any welfare support. Instead of receiving some form of state benefit, they received vouchers for food and other goods, and £10 cash per week. The vouchers could not be redeemed for cash, and had to be spent to their full value as change could not be given. Most shops, however, did not accept these vouchers, nor were they redeemable on public transport. These measures simply forced the asylum seekers to look for other means by which to live. Since then, the UK Borders Act (2007) and the Borders, Citizenship and Immigration Act (2009) have also been passed.

The UK Borders Act (2007) gave increased powers to the Borders and Immigration Agency (now known as the UK Borders Agency). It gave police-like powers to immigration officers, including entry, search and seizure powers. The idea was to tighten British frontiers to illegal immigration. The 2009 legislation was designed to simplify the immigration law, and to make it more difficult to gain naturalisation – from five up to eight years residency to gain naturalisation.

The body involved with both immigration and asylum seekers is the **UK Borders Agency**. It was previously known as the Immigration and Nationality Directorate (IND), and also the Borders and Immigration Agency. The UK Borders Agency comes under the auspices of the Home Office. As of April 2013, the UK Borders Agency was split in two separate operational units:

- UK Visas and Immigration: dealing with such things as visa applications, and applications for asylum
- Immigration Enforcement: is responsible for investigating immigration offences, and preventing abuse of the immigration system

The Home Office produces data on things such as visitor visa applications, applications for work visas or for study visas, as well as asylum applications. These are produced in quarterly reports – see www.gov.uk/government/collections/immigration-statistics-quarterly-release.

Economic and Social Context
Racial discrimination existed in British consciousness long before the advent of mass immigration from the New Commonwealth, and took the form of

personal insults and abuse which no amount of legislation was likely to eradicate. It was, however, far more significant to the welfare of immigrants to ensure discrimination was eliminated in the major areas of social and economic life. Here the state would play a significant role. Thus the legislation concentrated on employment, housing and education.

1) Employment

Contrasts have been drawn not only between levels of white and black unemployment, but also between types of employment. In December 2012, unemployment stood at 8% in mainland Britain. For the white ethnic population, the figure was 7%. For the black population it stood at 18%, and for those from an Asian ethnic background at 12%. When broken down by age, disparities were even worse: among 16-24 year olds the unemployment rate was 21%; for those from a Black ethnic origin the rate was 47%, compared to 20% for those from a white ethnic background, and 29% from an Asian ethnic background (House of Commons library, available at www.parliament.uk/briefing-papers/sn06385.pdf).

While there have been moves to improve the quality and the levels of employment among ethnic minorities, it is a slow process. This is exemplified in the civil service. In 1989, 1.4% of the senior civil service was made up of ethnic minority personnel. This rose to 1.7% in 1999, and 2.1% in 2000. By 2012, this had risen to almost 5%. Across the civil service as a whole, in 2012, 9.5% of the workforce came from ethnic minority backgrounds: specifically, 2.8% Black, 4.9% Asian, 0.2% Chinese, and the remainder were lumped together as 'other'.

2) Housing

It was almost inevitable the first waves of black immigrants, with little wealth and low qualifications, would gravitate towards the cheapest housing in the inner cities. Hence particular areas became known as black 'ghettos': Brixton in London, Sparkbrook in Birmingham, Toxteth in Liverpool and Moss Side in Manchester are examples. They became associated in the popular eye with overcrowding, squalor, drugs and crime.

There are signs that attempts are being made to break out of this pattern, particularly by the Asian population. In common with the general trend of movement to owner-occupier, an increasingly large number of black people are taking out mortgages, and gradually moving from the city centres into the suburbs.

3) Education

Closely linked to both housing and employment is education. This is not simply to do with educational attainment, but also opportunities in education. For example, the number of black children excluded from school is grossly out of proportion to the numbers on the school rolls. The reasons for this are normally attributed to behavioural problems. Yet this is to ignore where the schools are located (the inner cities) and the associated societal problems that can create educational difficulties.

When examining educational attainment on the grounds of ethnicity, a rather complex picture appears. Government data, focusing on state schools shows a mixed picture. When examining Key Stage 2 attainment in reading in 2013, 88% of all pupils made their expected progress (that is, progress of at least two levels). When broken down by ethnicity, 88% of both Black and White pupils made their expected progress. Asian pupils and Chinese pupils surpassed this progress. In both writing and mathematics, similar results were achieved. There is a small problem here. When looking at the percentage of pupils achieving Level 4 or above at Key Stage 2, fewer pupils from a Black ethnic background are achieving such progress. In fact, between one and three percent fewer Black pupils are making such progress when compared to the average in reading, writing and mathematics, or compared to other ethnic groups (developed from www.gov.uk/government/publications/national-curriculum-assessments-at-key-stage-2-2012-to-2013).

In that same year, leaping forward in educational levels, university entrance has seen some significant changes. In 2006, about 20% of pupils of Black ethnic origin applied to university. By 2013, this had increased to 34% (compared to 50% of Chinese and 29% of white pupils) (UCAS, 2013). This does, however, mask significantly different raw numbers – 500 000 students from a white ethnic background, compared to 2 000 from a Chinese ethnic background.

4) Law and Order

One of the most disturbing phenomena of recent years has been the disaffection of many members of the black community with prevailing white attitudes in general, but the police in particular. These attitudes appear more prevalent among the younger generation of blacks. The police are seen as being both discriminatory and threatening in their dealings with the black and Asian communities. Policies such as stop and search see black youths being stopped far more frequently than any other ethnic group; while Asian youths are far more likely to be stopped than white youths. Of course, the retaliatory actions as manifested in riots and civil disturbances have much deeper-seated causes than mere hatred of the police and their methods.

The list of significant racial disturbances is lengthy, including: Bristol (1980); Brixton (1981); Toxteth (1981); Handsworth (1985); Tottenham (1985); Bradford (1995, 2001); Oldham (2001); Tottenham (2011). These riots can be viewed as a result of severe social deprivation and alienation compounded by clumsy police tactics. Police attitudes are then regarded as an aggravating factor.

After the riots in Brixton, a report was commissioned into the causes of the disturbances. This report, written by Lord Scarman, acknowledged the problems of the social conditions – inner city deprivation, high levels of unemployment and discrimination – but argued they were not an excuse for a riot. Scarman instead highlighted the outburst of anger and resentment by young blacks against the police (Layton-Henry, 1992, p.131). This had been precipitated by a major police operation in Lambeth which had done little to endear the police to the local community. The riots in Handsworth and Tottenham in 1985 were both a result of police practices. No judicial inquiry, in the vein of Scarman, was commissioned into either if these disturbances.

In 2011, Mark Duggan was shot by a police marksman. This led to protests in Tottenham, which descended into rioting and was then followed by other copycat riots across the UK. At the inquest in 2013, Duggan's death was deemed to be a lawful killing by the police. There were immediate demands for a judicial review from Duggan's family. The family also requested that only peaceful protests be carried out; they did not want the death to be overshadowed by more rioting.

Political Context
No valid consideration of the position of ethnic minority people in British society could be complete without examining the political dimension of their aspirations and how the political parties propose to deal with them. In this context, it should be noted populism has not degenerated into any major support for extreme right wing movements. While there is no equivalent of the French National Party (led by Marine le Pen) or the neo-nazis in Germany, the rise in support for parties such as the BNP is a cause for concern.

1) Attitudes of the Major Political Parties
Until the 1970s Labour had such overwhelming support from the ethnic minority communities that the Conservatives made little attempt to capture that vote. This picture is gradually changing, although Labour is still the majority choice among ethnic minority voters. Comparing the 1997 and 2010 elections does not necessarily show any clear voting patterns beyond Labour domination.

Table 33.3 Ethnic Minority Voting Patterns in the 1997 General Election (%)

ETHNIC GROUP	Labour	Conservative	Liberal Democrat	Other
Black Caribbean	94	2	4	-
Black African	96	1	3	-
Black Other	88	2	4	6
Indian	72	18	1	4
Pakistani	55	39	1	4
Bangladeshi	83	13	1	3
Other	67	24	3	4

Source: www.obv.org.uk/2001aprjun/race_elect.html

Table 33.4 Ethnic Minority Voting Patterns in the 2010 General Election (%)

ETHNIC GROUP	Labour	Conservative	Liberal Democrat	Other
Black Caribbean	78	9	12	2
Black African	87	6	6	1
Indian	61	24	13	2
Pakistani	60	13	25	3
Bangladeshi	72	18	9	1

Source: www.runnymedetrust.org/uploads/EMBESbriefingFINALx.pdf

The 2010 General Election saw the largest ever number of ethnic minority candidates getting elected: 26. This compared with 15 in 2005. Of those 26 MPs, 11 are Conservative and 15 Labour. There are no ethnic minority MPs from any other party.

Ethnic minority representation in Parliament has been minimal. The first such MP to be elected was Dadabhai Naoroji in Finsbury in 1892. He was a Liberal MP who remained an MP until 1895. In 1895 Mancherjee Bhownaggree was elected in Bethnal Green North East. He was a Conservative MP until 1905, and was later knighted. Sharpurji Saklatvala was the first ethnic minority Labour MP to be elected (in Battersea in 1922-1923 and 1924-1929).

Between 1929 and 1987, there was no ethnic minority representation at Westminster. In 1987, Diane Abbott, Paul Boateng, Bernie Grant and Keith Vaz were all elected to Parliament as Labour MPs. Since then, ethnic minority representation at Westminster has increased to the current 26 MPs.

One reason for the poor number of elected black representatives is very few are selected by the parties. Those selected tend to be in unwinnable seats. As with the arguments surrounding the poor representation of women, the excuse appears to be that very few people from ethnic minorities put themselves forward as candidates. In the 2001 General Election there were 77 ethnic minority candidates – of these, 25 were Liberal Democrats, 16 Labour, 16 Conservative, 12 Socialist Labour, 6 Greens and 2 Socialists. In the 2010 General Election, this number had risen to 140. The spread between parties had changed: 50 Labour, 45 Conservative, 43 Liberal Democrat. It was also noteworthy that many ethnic minority candidates were selected in much more winnable seats.

2) Ethnic Minority Participation in Politics
There is a tendency to assume the aspirations of ethnic minorities must of necessity be different from white ones. Yet evidence supports the thesis that the political concerns of various ethnic groupings do not differ too greatly from those of whites, for example, in employment, housing and education.

Of course, it should be borne in mind the ethnic minority populace should never be regarded as a homogeneous group. Within a broad range of issues, there could be significant differences between, for example, Bangladeshis and Jamaicans.

On active participation in politics, it was only during the last quarter of the twentieth century that the ethnic minority communities and individuals began to show an interest. Bodies such as the 1990 Trust and Operation Black Vote (OBV) have been set up to encourage black participation. OBV was set up by the 1990 Trust and Charter88 in July 1996. It has a very clear mission statement:

> We believe that without a strong political voice for African, Asian, Caribbean, Chinese and other ethnic minorities, the ideal of equality of opportunity – regardless of race and colour – will remain an ideal... [O]vercoming stereotypical attitudes and institutional racism within the dominant cultural and political establishment will require willingness to communicate and co-operation from both Black and White to reach solutions. (www.obv.org.uk/about-us/mission)

In conjunction with the Commission for Racial Equality, OBV established two 'shadowing' schemes. The first, launched in July 1999, enabled 23 people from an ethnic minority background to each shadow an MP or a peer over a six month period. A second scheme was set up to shadow Magistrates, part of which has come as a response to the Stephen Lawrence case, which is detailed later in this chapter. In both 'shadowing' schemes, the people selected had little knowledge of the formal political processes. The hope is some of them may wish to get involved in the wider scope of government activities – as elected representatives or more involved in the communities in which they live and may, in the future, work.

3) Commission for Racial Equality
This body was established in 1976 under the Race Relations Act of that year. The Commission for Racial Equality (CRE) was a non-governmental body, or quango. This meant it operated at arms-length from the government (see chapter 14 on Quangos).

The main aim of the CRE was to tackle discrimination, both direct and indirect, and to promote racial equality. This was carried out through a variety of different means. Apart from enforcement work, the CRE was involved in many other roles: drafting codes of practice; monitoring legislation; helping individuals pursue cases of discrimination; funding and assisting local Community Relations Councils; and, advising public and private sector organisations. It also developed a code of practice to accompany the 1976 Race Relations Act. Thus, while the

CRE often received poor publicity in the media, particularly in the enforcement area, this did not cover the full range of activities being carried out.

In 2007, the CRE was merged into the **Equality and Human Rights Commission**. This was done through the Equality Act (2006). As a result of this merger with other bodies, a major concern was raised as to the extent to which race issues were being downplayed. Race is now one of a range of issues in which there may be discrimination.

Stephen Lawrence Case

The Stephen Lawrence case is a pivotal affair in race relations in Britain. Over twenty years later, this case is still a symbol of all that is wrong in race relations in the UK. The fallout from this race-motivated murder highlighted the inherent racism within sections of the British police force.

Stephen Lawrence was murdered on 22 April 1993. He was stabbed by a group of five white youths. The original investigation by the police was totally inadequate. Added to this, the family of Stephen Lawrence was very poorly treated by the investigating officers. A second investigation into the murder was carried out in a more sympathetic manner but by then it was too late. In 1996, the Lawrence family brought a private prosecution against three of the suspects. They were acquitted on the grounds of insufficient evidence. It was only through a change in the law in 2005 that allowed them to be tried again on the charge of murdering Stephen Lawrence. In 2012, two of the original suspects were tried and found guilty of murder.

An inquiry into the Stephen Lawrence case was carried out by Sir William Macpherson, commencing in 1997. This was published in February 1999. His conclusions were most scathing of those police officers who conducted the original investigation, accusing them not only of professional incompetence, but also of racism, and of the existence of institutional racism within the Metropolitan Police Force. Not only was there a lack of documentary evidence on the night of the murder, but witnesses and evidence were both dismissed, and the police refused to treat the case as being solely racially motivated. "Mere incompetence cannot of itself account for the whole catalogue of failures, mistakes, misjudgements, and lack of direction and control which bedevilled the Stephen Lawrence investigation" (Macpherson Report para. 6.44)

The Metropolitan Police Force was accused of both racism and institutional racism during the conduct of the first investigation into the Stephen Lawrence murder. According to the Macpherson Report, these terms are defined as:

Para. 6.4 "Racism" in general terms consists of conduct of words or practices which advantage or disadvantage people because of their colour, culture or ethnic origin. In its more subtle form it is as damaging as in its overt form.

Para. 6.34 "Institutional racism" consists of the collective failure of an organisation to provide an appropriate and professional service to people because of their colour, culture or ethnic origin. It can be seen or detected in processes, attitudes and behaviour which amount to discrimination through unwitting prejudice, ignorance, thoughtlessness, and racist stereotyping which disadvantage minority people.

The second investigation into the murder was praised by Macpherson, but by then the trail was cold. Following a cold case review in 2011, it was only in the light of new and substantial evidence, along with an earlier change in the law that enabled a prosecution to eventually go ahead.

The Macpherson Report made 70 recommendations as to how policing could be improved. These included a greater need for openness, better recording and reporting of racist incidents and crimes, and better police practices, training and education.

Questions still remain as to the extent to which the police and policing have changed, especially in dealings with ethnic minority communities. The allegations of racism and institutional racism have remained. Of particular note is the use of stop and search powers, where police appear to target young men from ethnic minority backgrounds. Added to this is the ethnic breakdown of police forces, which are still predominantly white. With regard to the charge of institutional racism, until the police acknowledge there has been (and, arguably, still is) a problem, then the charge will remain. The Metropolitan Police would respond that they have acknowledged the problem but the process of dealing with it is not about a quick fix.

Conclusion

Ethnic minority groups can no longer be dismissed as a 'problem', yet race issues remain. The riots in Oldham and other Northern England towns in 2001 had clear racist overtones – and these were further incited by the involvement of groups such as the BNP. It appears the major political parties have little idea as to how to deal with any race issues.

On the one hand, there is evidence of racism in British politics. On the other, there is evidence of increased participation by minority groups in mainstream politics. The racism being experienced by these minority groups, however, leaves a smouldering resentment against perceived discrimination and prejudice. There is a wish among many ethnic groups not to be assimilated into British culture, but rather to preserve their religion, language, customs and general culture. The difficulty for politicians and other interested groups is how to reconcile these tendencies – the need to involve all people, regardless of ethnicity, but at the same time to enable people to protect their heritage.

Selected bibliography

Huysmans, Jef & Buonfino, Alessandra. (2008). "Politics of Exception and Unease: Immigration, asylum and terrorism in parliamentary debates in the UK", *Political Studies* vol. 56-4, pp. 766-788.

Ministry of Justice. (2013). *Statistics on Race and the Criminal Justice System 2012: A Ministry of Justice publication under Section 95 of the Criminal Justice Act 1991.*

Modood, Tariq. (2005). *Multicultural Politics: Racism, Ethnicity and Muslims in Britain*: Edinburgh University Press.

Parliamentary Affairs vol. 66-2. (2013). Special Edition on Ethnic Representation in Britain.

Stolle, Dietland & Harell, Alison. (2013). "Social Capital and Ethno-racial Diversity: Learning to Trust in an Immigrant Society", *Political Studies* vol. 61-1, pp. 42-66.

The Stephen Lawrence Inquiry: Report of an Inquiry by Sir William Macpherson of Cluny, February 1999, Cm 4262-I The Stationery Office.

Uberoi, Varun & Modood, Tariq. (2010). "Who Doesn't Feel British? Divisions over Muslims", *Parliamentary Affairs* vol. 63-2, pp. 302-320.

Uberoi, Varun & Modood, Tariq. (2013). "Inclusive Britishness: A Multiculturalist Advance", *Political Studies* vol. 61-1, pp. 23-41.

Websites

www.blink.org.uk
Homepage to the Black Information Link, part of the 1990 Trust

www.equalityhumanrights.com
Home page of the Equality and Human Rights Commission

www.irr.org.uk
Institute of Race Relations homepage. This is a research body which focuses upon racial justice

www.ukba.homeoffice.gov.uk
UK Borders Agency home page

www.obv.org.uk
Homepage to Operation Black Vote. From here it is possible to get access to a range of information sources, presented from a black perspective

www.archive.official-documents.co.uk/document/cm42/4262/4262.htm
The official report of the Stephen Lawrence Inquiry, headed by Sir William Macpherson of Cluny. This is now an archived document

www.runnymedetrust.org
An independent think tank on ethnicity and cultural diversity

Questions
1. How have successive governments attempted to deal with the tensions arising from immigration?
2. What impact have ethnic minority groups made on the British political system?
3. "Groups which incite racial hatred should be outlawed. Their members should be prosecuted, and the organisation banned." Discuss.

CHAPTER 34 // ENVIRONMENTAL POLICY

Contents
- **Introduction**
- **Green Ideology**
- **Sustainable Development and Ecological Modernisation**
- **Government bodies dealing with the Environment**
- **What can the Government do to help the environment?**
- **Conclusion**

Introduction

In the 1970s, as the environment was coming on to the political agenda, Inglehart (1977) suggested the West was moving from a materialist world into a post-materialist one. He argued there was "a shift from overwhelming emphasis on material consumption and security toward greater concern with the quality of life" (Inglehart, 1977, p. 363). Rather than worrying about accruing material possessions, other factors were becoming more important in people's lives. One of these post-materialist issues was the environment.

While Inglehart's arguments on post-materialism can be questioned, the rise of the environment as an issue of concern is a little more obvious. Yet the concern may not be of a post-materialist nature (i.e. about the quality of life). Rather, it may be in response to natural or human-made disasters. The meltdown of the nuclear reactor at Chernobyl in 1986, which led to thousands of deaths and the abandonment of a city saw a rise in concern over environmental issues, especially linked to the dangers of nuclear energy and nuclear waste. In the UK, the BSE outbreak in the late 1980s and the foot-and-mouth outbreak in 2001 saw grave concerns being raised about the dangers of the industrialisation of agriculture and its impact on both people and the environment. The flooding across the UK in places such as Boscastle (2004), Workington (2009) and the Somerset levels (2013-2014), has raised concerns about the impact of climate change on our weather. These environmental issues are of a global nature, and may require global solutions.

Yet questions can be raised about what needs to be done, and what can be done, to protect the environment. Our current consumer culture, not to mention the amount of waste that follows, cannot be changed overnight. Most shoppers want the cheapest possible products, no matter, for example, out-of-season fruit and vegetables have to be shipped from all over the world to satiate demand. Even if people in the UK were to 'do their bit' to protect the environment, would it make any difference if the USA or China refused to follow suit? Added to this, the furore over the accuracy of scientific data goes on and on. The data demonstrating there is harmful human-made damage to the environment is questioned by climate change deniers. In turn, their evidence is refuted, but the circle goes round and round. Maybe, in the words of Private Frazer from the BBC television programme 'Dad's Army', "we're doomed, laddie, doomed!".

To complicate matters still further, the environment is sometimes seen as a 'wicked' or 'complex' problem. This means it is very difficult to resolve, or it cannot be resolved in a conventional manner. Take, for example, plans to improve traffic congestion. Traffic congestion causes increased amounts of pollution. One solution to resolve traffic congestion is to build more roads. Such road building schemes lead to a host of other environmental issues arising.

Green Ideology

One of the interesting aspects of green ideology is, as with all other ideologies, there is not a single cohesive body of thought. In very broad terms, as noted by Garner (2000, p. 7), it is about "promoting a society which places a good quality environment above one which worships material consumption". This is a very positive approach, presenting a constructive ideal. There are, however, numerous interpretations of "a good quality environment", starting with the most obvious question of to which environment are we referring?

Within green ideology, there are two broad positions. These have many different labels, as can be seen below:

- Dark Green versus Light Green
- Deep Ecology versus Shallow Ecology
- Ecocentric versus Anthropocentric
- Radical Environmentalists versus Reformist Environmentalists
- Ecologism versus Environmentalism

Within these pairings, there is a noticeable conflict. Those listed on the right tend to argue incremental changes may be enough to solve environmental issues, with a need for a degree of continuity. Those listed on the left argue for far more radical and fundamental changes, in fact, a paradigm shift – a change in basic assumptions about the role and importance of the environment. Approaches listed to the right may be associated with concepts such as **sustainable development** or **ecological modernisation** (both concepts are explained later in this chapter). How groups wish to pursue their environmental agenda will be influenced by the extent to which they follow a light or dark green approach. Weaker definitions, in environmental terms, of sustainable development may be presented as 'light green', but there are also 'dark green' approaches which are far more ecocentric. Thus some approaches to sustainable development may fit on the left hand side of the above list.

The more radical approaches tend to argue economic growth is incompatible with environmental objectives; that it is a zero-sum game. It is possible to strive for economic growth or to protect the environment; the two are incompatible. Hence a paradigm shift is needed with regard to the need to place environmental concerns above the pursuit of economic growth. The reformist approach would question such ideas, using sustainable development or ecological modernisation as examples of how there is a degree of compatibility.

In effect, the 'light' or 'environmental' approach "argues for a managerial approach to environmental problems, secure in the belief that they can be solved without fundamental changes in present values or patterns of production and consumption" (Dobson, 2007, p. 2). Here we have the continuity of policy, and the need to amend current policies. This is clearly an anthropocentric approach, putting human priorities ahead of those of nature. There is still an obvious desire to protect and maintain the environment.

The 'dark' or 'deep' or 'ecological' approach "holds that a sustainable and fulfilling existence presupposes radical changes in our relationship with the non-human natural world, and in our more of social and political life" (Dobson, 2007, p. 3). This is not necessarily being misanthropic (hating humankind), rather it is not prioritising humankind's needs. Humankind is but one part of the natural world. Merely protecting this natural world, or reducing the effects of humankind's exploitation of it, is not enough.

If a government was to adopt a more pro-environmental approach, it is likely to be a 'light' environmental approach. It is highly improbable any government will dismiss the current patterns of economic production and consumption. The question would merely be over the cost of being more pro-environment to the economy. Some political parties might question these patterns of production and consumption. The Green Party, for example, would argue it is more radical than any other and would question these patterns. They may be, for the most part, rather light green, but they are 'dark green around the edges'.

Sustainable Development and Ecological Modernisation
The concepts of sustainable development and ecological modernisation dominate the environmental agenda. They are two separate, but related, concepts which are sometimes used interchangeably. As will become apparent in this chapter, they are distinct concepts.

Sustainable development
Sustainable development came to the fore in the mid-1980s with the publication of a report by the World Commission on Environment and Development, better known as the **Brundtland Report** (after its chair, Gro

Harlem Brundtland), or, to give it the correct title: *Our Common Future*. This report was commissioned by the United Nations to investigate concerns over environmental issues as well as economic development. The definition of sustainable development adopted in the Brundtland Report has become the basis of all subsequent definitions.

> Humanity has the ability to make development sustainable – to ensure that **it meets the needs of the present without compromising the ability of future generations to meet their own needs**. The concept of sustainable development does imply limits – not absolute limits but limitations imposed by the present state of technology and social organization on environmental resources and by the ability of the biosphere to absorb the effects of human activities.
> (emphasis added; World Commission on Environment and Development, 1987, p. 8)

The Brundtland Report went further, listing a range of policy directions that needed consideration. These included:

- *population and human resources* – the growth in population numbers; the increased mobility of people; and the pressure this places on natural resources
- *food scarcity* – degradation of the resource base, i.e. the decline in the fertility of land; deforestation to create more arable land and the consequences of such action
- *species and eco-systems* – the disappearance of different species of plant and animal; loss of genetic variability;and how all of this impacts upon what remains
- *energy* – the dilemma over the use of fossil fuels; the use of nuclear energy; and the increasing demands for energy
- *industry* – the impact of industrial growth; the changing structures of world industry; and the decline in the natural resource base

Within these policy areas, there were some key questions. As highlighted in the definition (above), with the phrase "meet the needs", what are the needs today? What are likely to be the future needs? What are the limits? It may also be worth considering 'what' is to be sustained? This could be present levels of economic growth, or even current consumption practices. But at present rates of consumption, what will be left for future generations?

It could, therefore, be argued the Brundtland Report raised more questions than answers with regard to the concept of sustainable development. Regardless, the concept has been taken on board by governments and businesses around the world.

What is most obvious within the concept of sustainable development is its anthropocentrism (the inherent focus on meeting the needs of humankind). There is a sustainable development triangle: people, planet, profit – although the latter is often replaced by prosperity (see Seghezzo, 2009; Thiele, 2013). Within this triangle, different groups will have different priorities. They all matter in this *triple bottom line* upon which sustainability rests (see Table 34.1).

Table 34.1 The Triple Bottom Line

The bottom line for any business is profit. If there is no profit, the business will fail. The Triple Bottom Line, first used in 1994, presents the case for three different bottom lines: profit, people and planet. The concern about profit is no different to before. Yet consideration needs also to be taken about the people – the social responsibility of the business. Planet is about the environmental responsibilities of the business. Thus the triple bottom line is about the financial, social and environmental performance of a business.

There are many approaches to sustainable development. Voisey & O'Riordan (1997), for example, highlighted a number of definitions, including an economic definition, and a language of development definition. Thus, from an economic perspective, sustainable development "seeks to use interventions in market prices and in regulatory mechanisms to correct the imperfections of under-valuation of polluting discharges, over-depletion of non-renewable resources, and pollution damage to sites or species of aesthetic or biological significance" (Voisey & O'Riordan, 1997, p. 25). When the actions of the UK Government are examined later in this chapter, this economic approach dominates.

Yet, when examining sustainable development through the language of development, a significantly different emphasis emerges. It is about "helping developing economies to grow in accordance with environmental protection objectives, so that economic growth is not hindered by environmental degradation" (Voisey & O'Riordan, 1997, p. 26). Economic priorities are still prevalent in this definition, highlighting a clear anthropocentric underpinning, but it is about achieving that economic growth without doing insurmountable harm – if indeed any harm – to the environment.

There is also a 'local' approach to sustainable development which is highlighted by Voisey & O'Riordan (1997, p. 26) which "focuses on public participation, local involvement, and sees the concept as a social transition as much as an environmental one". This can be seen in such slogans as "Think global; act local".

A blueprint for implementing sustainable development was hammered out at the Rio Earth Summit in 1992, which resulted in among other ideas, Agenda 21 – a global agenda on sustainable development into the twenty first century (see below).

Ecological modernisation

From an environmental perspective, Baker (2007) points out sustainable development is all about how the environment will be managed. Ecological modernisation has a wholly different emphasis, asking who will manage the environment, and in whose interests? Within the approach of sustainable development, there is an acknowledgement of a link between economic growth and environmental degradation. Ecological modernisation tries to break that link. Gouldson & Murphy (1996, p. 11) note the "theory of ecological modernization suggests that policies for economic development and environmental protection can be combined with synergistic effect". Economic development should not be associated with environmental degradation, and environmental protection should not limit economic development.

Within the broad approach of sustainable development, the extent of the anthropocentrism can be questioned. There are 'light green' approaches to sustainable development which are more anthropocentric, but there are also 'dark green' approaches which are much more ecocentric. Not so with ecological modernisation. It is very clearly anthropocentric. This is most obvious in the four key themes of ecological modernisation (Gouldson & Murphy, 1996; Baker, 2007):

1. there is a synergy between economic development and environmental protection
2. environmental policy goals need to be integrated into all aspects of government policy and activity
3. alternative and innovative policy measures, or new environmental policy instruments (see Jordan *et al*, 2003), need to be developed
4. there is sector-specific activity, looking at invention, innovation and diffusion of new, cleaner technologies

Within the ecological modernisation approach is a simple mantra: "what is good for the environment is also good for business" (Richardson, 2009, p. 608). The government takes the lead in strategic planning, with industry and business as the centre of attention. By integrating economic and environmental policies, there is a potential win-win situation for the government: economic growth and environmental protection. Arguably, this requires a more pro-active environmental policy agenda from the government, which is something that has not been prevalent among most governments around the world. Obvious exceptions are Denmark and Germany, both of which place a very strong emphasis upon such environmental issues; while Japan was once considered to be the forerunner of the Ecological Modernisation movement.

Yet, as Baker (2007, p. 313) notes, ecological modernisation "does not address the underlying contradictions in capitalism: a logic of ever-increasing consumption in a world characterised by material resource limitations". Ecological modernisation presents an opportunity to push for economic growth which can lead to environmental protection. With ever-increasing levels of consumption, neither sustainable development nor ecological modernisation, at this time, have a plan to prevent ecological disaster. This may well be why the dark green ecologists have so little time for such timid approaches.

Government bodies dealing with the Environment

Successive British Governments have expressed the desire to protect the environment. This could be seen with the establishment of a Department for the Environment in 1970, with the minister given full cabinet status. In 1997, it was merged with the Department of Transport to form the Department of the Environment, Transport and the Regions. After the foot and mouth outbreak in 2001, it became the Department of the Environment, Food and Rural Affairs (DEFRA).

One of the main roles of DEFRA is environmental protection. Yet this has to be balanced with the other priorities such as the rural economy, and food and farming. Arguably, some of these priorities might be complementary, while others may be contradictory. In 2013, DEFRA placed greater emphasis upon sustainable development across all of central government. Each department must have a business plan which includes actions contributing towards sustainable development.

DEFRA is assisted by a number of government agencies, the more prominent of which are examined below. As with government-agency relations, DEFRA set the parameters by which the different agencies may operate.

Environment Agency
The Environment Agency is a quango (see chapter 14) which was established in 1996. In theory, it is the most important government body with regard to environmental issues. Its remit is to protect and improve the environment, as well as promoting sustainable development.

The Environment Agency works with a range of partners, including businesses, central and local government, and communities. Consequently, it has numerous functions. These include protecting people from flooding, looking after wildlife and helping to protect endangered species, working with farmers and with industry, and fining those who fail to take their environmental responsibilities seriously (www.environment-agency.gov.uk/aboutus/work/35696.aspx).

In a study of the roles and functions of the Environment Agency, Bell & Gray (2002) were critical of the organisation. They argued the Environment Agency lacked a coherent vision because it was doing too much. For example, it was formed through the amalgamation of 86 predecessor bodies. Added to this, it was seen as being too close to the government – especially as the

Environment Agency appeared to avoid conflict with the government. Bell & Gray noted also the perceptions of the Environment Agency as held by industry and by environmental organisations. There were claims from industry that the Environment Agency was inefficient, inconsistent, slow, expensive and confrontational. On the other hand, environmental organisations made the opposite claims: the Environment Agency was too close to business (Bell & Gray, 2002, p. 87). With so many stakeholders in the Environment Agency, with such diverse demands, it was almost impossible to please many of them. Carter (2007) has also noted the Environmental Agency as being a rather weak organisation. Much of this was attributed to the breadth of its operations.

Sustainable Development Commission (SDC)

The SDC was established in 2000, but ceased to exist in 2011. It was closed down as part of the Coalition Governments cull of quangos. The major function of the SDC was as a watchdog, scrutinising government on the implementation of sustainable development. Their focus was on government, not the private sector. If anything the SDC tried to raise awareness in government circles about the relevance and importance of sustainable development.

In the closing press release, the following statement was made: "The establishment of the Sustainable Development Commission (SDC) in 2000 was, in part, a recognition that government is not yet structured to be able to rise above the limitations of short term political and budgetary cycles and narrow departmental remits to make the kinds of long-term decisions and connected responses that these major challenges demand" (www.sd-commission.org.uk/presslist.php/119/what-next-for-sustainable-development).

Committee on Climate Change

The Committee on Climate Change (CCC) was established under the Climate Change Act (2008). It is a quango, with its role being to advise the UK Government and the devolved administrations in Scotland, Wales and Northern Ireland on emissions targets. The CCC also reports to Parliament on progress made in reducing greenhouse gas emissions and preparing for climate change.

A number of policy sectors come under the remit of the CCC. These include energy and power, transport, agriculture, and buildings. In each of these areas, the CCC gives advice and recommendations related to carbon emissions, for example, a report published in 2011, "The Renewable Energy Review", covered a range of scenarios on how renewable energy could be deployed in the UK, in conjunction with more mainstream alternatives.

Having greater autonomy than the Environment Agency has enabled the CCC to be much more frank and open with the government with regard to advice and recommendations. While there is no obligation to follow any advice from the

CCC, their status has become such that they are seen as one of the most eminent environmental bodies in the UK.

While the Coalition Government, like its predecessors, claims to be committed to sustainable development, and to combating climate change, concerns have been expressed about the degree of commitment. Many environmental bodies or projects have been abolished. The Sustainable Development Commission was one of the most prominent, but there have been many others. The list includes: the Royal Commission on Environmental Pollution, the Health Protection Agency (which became part of Public Health England in 2013), Sustainable Schools (which was taken over by Sustainable and Environmental Education when the government withdrew support), the Commission for Architecture and the Built Environment (which was merged into the Design Council), the Advisory Committee on Carbon Abatement Technologies, and the Expert Panel on Air Quality Standards. The need to cut public spending as part of the Coalition Government's austerity measures was part of the justification for closing down these bodies. Their functions were taken over by other bodies in most circumstances.

What can the Government do to help the environment?

Having examined some of the bodies involved in monitoring and protecting the environment, it is now useful to look at what they have or have not achieved. One example is the idea of sustainable development, which has been most prominent in government literature. Yet there is no "sustainable development policy" reaching across all of government. In fact, when looking at the environmental policies of different governments, the word "piecemeal" comes to mind. There has been no coherent platform to develop policies to protect and nurture the environment. Instead, policies are developed in fits and starts. This can be seen in a sample of policies on the environment detailed below.

Agenda 21

Agenda 21 had its origins in the Rio Earth Summit of 1992. It was a voluntary agreement to encourage aspects of sustainable development – although the voluntary nature meant that no government was obliged to implement the proposals.

The document was broken down into four sections. The first of these highlighted the social and economic dimensions of sustainable development. This included the need to combat poverty, with an emphasis on developing countries, and the need to promote good health. The second section focused on the conservation and management of resources. Issues such as deforestation, atmospheric protection, control of pollution, protecting fragile eco-systems, and conserving biodiversity were all covered. The third section covered the roles of the different actors in the sustainable development debate. This included the roles of local authorities, non-governmental organisations, pressure groups, women, children and young people. Finally, section four examined the means of implementation i.e. how to implement sustainable development. This covered the use of technology, education, financial mechanisms, and the role of international institutions.

Implementation of Agenda 21 at the level of local government was called Local Agenda 21. The idea was if everyone acted in their own day to day life to do their bit to help protect the environment, then there would be a global benefit. Consequently, local authorities, in conjunction with local communities, examined the sustainability of a number of local authority practices, and how sustainability could be integrated into all policies and practices. The major problem in trying to implement this was central government dedicated no extra resources to help local authorities. As a result, implementation of sustainable development has been far from uniform across the UK.

The Stern Report
This report was commissioned by the Treasury to examine the effects of climate change on the world economy. It was published in 2006. Sources of greenhouse gas emissions were identified, with power generation accounting for almost a quarter of such emissions. Transport, industry and agriculture each contributed around 14% of total global greenhouse gas emissions (McLean, 2008).

According to the Stern Report, at least 5% of global GDP was being lost as a result of climate change – and this was likely to rise to 20% if nothing was done. Global GDP is the value of all the goods and services produced in a year from around the world. In 2012, this was estimated at over $US 83 trillion. Thus 5% of this – or just over $US 4.2 trillion – is being lost, and this will rise to over $US16 trillion. To put this into context, the UK GDP in 2012 was about $US 2.4 trillion.

The Stern Report estimated from 2006, 1% of global GDP needed to be invested to counteract the effects of climate change – 1% for every year thereafter. The longer it takes to commit the resources to address climate change, the greater the cost.

The key elements to address climate change were listed in the Stern Report. These included emissions trading (examined later in this chapter), technology co-operation, and reduction of deforestation. With regard to reducing deforestation, in 2007 the President of Guyana came up with a plan. He pledged to protect all of the rainforest in his country – over 70 million acres – in return for sustainable development funds. In effect, he was asking to be paid not to chop down the rainforest in his country. This proposal was backed by the British Government at that time. Britain had also backed much smaller schemes in Brazil and Indonesia. In 2009, Guyana received $US 250 million to protect and preserve its rainforests.

British Governments have been broadly supportive of the Stern Report, however it caused consternation at a global level. Particular policies, such as emissions trading, have been adopted enthusiastically.

Emissions Trading

There are two broad approaches to emissions trading. These are "cap and trade" and "baseline and credit". With the "cap and trade" approach, there are a fixed number of permits created, each of which allow a fixed amount of pollution. Businesses work out how much pollution they will create. If they produce less pollution than permitted, they can trade the excess permits with businesses that are going to over-pollute. It must be noted, however, in each subsequent year the amount of pollution permitted will be reduced. Thus even the least-polluting of businesses will have to consider ways in which to reduce their pollution.

The "baseline and credit" approach sets each a business a target to achieve in the amount of pollution that may be produced: a baseline. Credit is generated by beating the baseline i.e. producing less pollution than the baseline. These credits can be traded with those businesses that are likely to fail to meet their baseline. The baseline targets will be adjusted on a regular basis, making them more difficult to achieve.

Baldwin (2008, p. 197) raises an interesting concern. Quite simply, he asks what are the objectives in emission trading? With both of the approaches cited above, there is no benefit to the environment. Greenhouse gas emissions will not be reduced. Businesses which pollute below their targets will sell their excess permits or credits to those businesses which are likely to over-pollute. In the short term at least, there will be little incentive for most businesses to look at ways of reducing their greenhouse gas emissions. The under-polluters will sell; the over-polluters will buy – at least until it is no longer cost-effective to continue polluting. How far in the future will this be? How much damage will continue to be done to the environment?

Despite these criticisms, emissions trading schemes have resulted in a reduction in greenhouse gas emissions. There have been issues over how much pollution has been permitted, and how challenging the year-on-year reductions in permitted pollution have been. Such novel schemes had to start somewhere. The important point is getting all businesses and governments on board.

Britain started a voluntary Emissions Trading Scheme in 2002, utilising a "cap and trade" approach. It now runs parallel with the EU Emissions Trading Scheme. Questions were raised about how demanding the UK scheme has been. There have been suggestions the targets set for the businesses involved in the original UK scheme were not demanding enough. It had also been noted while some businesses had reduced their emissions significantly, not all of those reductions could be attributed to the trading scheme.

The current EU Emissions Trading Scheme runs from 2013 to 2020. The first phase ran from 2005 to 2007, and the second from 2008 to 2012. The "cap" on emissions reduces by almost 2% every year. By 2020, the cap will have been reduced by 21% from what was first set in 2005.

Energy Policy

One of the major sources of greenhouse gases is the energy sector. In the past, the UK had many coal-fired power stations, which were heavy-polluting. Their closure, at least in environmental terms, has seen a huge benefit The 2008 Climate Change Act (see below) set targets in the reduction of greenhouse gases for the UK. One target was to reduce emissions to 35% below 1990 levels by 2020. The closures of these stations see a strong likelihood of the 2020 targets being met.

The problem, acknowledged at the Rio Earth Summit and in the Stern Report, is there is a huge energy demand globally. China, for example, is forecast to see its energy demand increase by around 50% between 2010 and 2030.

The Royal Commission on Environmental Pollution published a report in 2000 entitled *Energy – The Changing Climate* (Cm 4749). It examined the predicted UK energy consumption to 2050, and considered how that demand might be met. The potential damage to the environment was also considered within the report. The report noted:

A sustainable energy policy for the UK should protect the interests of the generations to come, but it must also seek to achieve social justice, a higher quality of life and industrial competitiveness today. Achieving the right balance is formidably difficult; current policies do not strike it. (p. 1)

Thus energy production and environmental protection clash. In general, renewable energies such as wind, wave and solar power are promoted by the environmentalists. Gas and coal-fired power stations are promoted by those who wish to promote economic growth. A concern is Britain is becoming dependent on energy imports – for example, gas from Norway. Consequently, alternatives are being explored, such as fracking for shale gas. The problem here is the environmental consequences of such techniques are unknown.

The issue of nuclear power is divisive. Supporters of nuclear power note it is the cleanest and greenest way in which to generate power; it is carbon-free power. Opponents to nuclear power ask about the nuclear waste or the risks of nuclear disaster such as Three Mile Island or Chernobyl. With regard to waste, the half life of plutonium 239, for example, is 24 000 years (plutonium 239 is used in the production of nuclear weapons and is one of the fuels used in nuclear reactors). By that time, only half of its radio activity will have decayed. To make matters worse, the hazardous life of nuclear waste is around ten times the half life. To highlight the toxicity of this substance, one milligram of plutonium 239 would most likely cause cancer for one person. It is hardly surprising organisations such as Greenpeace ask if it is possible to "manage" nuclear waste for 240 000 years.

Climate Change Act (2008)

Arguably, the most significant piece of environmental legislation in recent times has been the Climate Change Act (2008). This legislation had cross-party support through Parliament. It set out the targets for the UK with regard to greenhouse gas emissions: at least 35% below 1990 levels by 2020, and 80% below 1990 levels by 2050. Added to this was the introduction of a carbon budgeting scheme, which set out caps on carbon emissions over 5-year periods. This plans a trajectory to enable the UK to meet the 2050 target for emissions. As noted earlier in this chapter, a Committee on Climate Change was also established.

Within this legislation, a number of measures were introduced or reinforced to reduce greenhouse gas emissions. The Emissions Trading Scheme was broadened out; the use of bio-fuels was promoted; and there were incentives to encourage greater recycling of household waste.

There has, however, been a degree of scepticism as to whether or not the targets set are achievable. Factors such as increasing population size do not appear to be taken into consideration. Further, while challenging targets have been set, there does not appear to be a plan as to how they can be achieved.

In sum, there has been a range of different policies implemented, and investigations into the extent of environmental problems. Other environmental concerns, such as foot and mouth, flooding, and disaster planning, have also had government policies to cover them – on top of what has already been done. The problem is this not a coherent package. Lowe & Ward summarise British environmental policy making in a succinct manner. Although written in 1998, their observations are still pertinent today. "The traditional style of British environmental policy would be characterised as: low politics; pragmatic; piecemeal and incremental; reliant on scientific and expert consensus; and involving close (and closed) consultation with affected interests; devolved implementation; and a preference for informal regulation" (1998, p. 29).

Conclusion

Current strategies to protect the environment, to reduce greenhouse gas emissions, or to combat climate change are still anthropocentric in nature. Any government that adopts an ecocentric approach is likely to be castigated for downplaying the importance of the economy. Yet ecological modernisation approaches and some under sustainable development appear to assume by merely tinkering with economic policies, the environment can be protected.

The Stern Report suggested otherwise, highlighting the **economic** cost of climate change. As a result, there was a short-lived surge in concern about the environment – in relation to protecting economic growth. Economic priorities seem to trump the environment every time. The fear in the Stern Report was by the time people were aware of the damage to the environment, the economic costs would be too high, and it may then be too late to reverse the damage. The words of Private Frazer may resonate even more strongly.

Selected bibliography

Carter, Neil. (2007). *The Politics of the Environment: Ideas, Activism, Policy*: Cambridge University Press, 2nd edition.

Carter, Neil. (2008). "Combating Climate Change in the UK: Challenges and Obstacles", *Political Quarterly* vol. 79-2, pp. 194-205.

Compston, Hugh. (2010). "The Politics of Climate Change Policy: Strategic Options for National Governments", *Political Quarterly* vol. 81-1, pp. 107-115.

Dobson, Andrew. (2007). *Green Political Thought*: Routledge, 4th edition.

Gavin, Neil. (2009). "Addressing climate change: a media perspective", *Environmental Politics* vol. 18-5, pp. 765-780.

Lovell, Heather; Bulkeley, Harriet & Owens, Susan. (2009). "Converging agendas? Energy and climate change policies in the UK", *Environment and Planning C: Government and Policy* vol. 27-1, pp. 90-109.

Luke, Timothy. (2005). "Neither Sustainable or Development: Reconsidering Sustainability in Development", *Sustainable Development* vol. 13-4, pp. 228-238.

Seghezzo, Lucas. (2009). "The five dimensions of sustainability", *Environmental Politics* vol. 18-4, pp. 539-556.

The World Commission on Environment and Development. (1987). *Our Common Future*: Oxford University Press.

Thiele, Leslie Paul. (2013). *Sustainability*: Polity Press.

Websites

archive.excellencegateway.org.uk/141443
This is the Stern Report on the Economics of Climate Change (2006)

www.environment-agency.gov.uk/
The home page of the Environment Agency

www.sd-commission.org.uk
This was the website for the Sustainable Development Commission. This body ceased operating in March 2011. Much of the material linked to this website has been archived and is accessible

www.theccc.org.uk/
The committee on Climate Change home page

www.un.org/esa/sustdev/agenda21.htm
The United Nations' web page on Agenda 21

Questions
Evaluate the strengths and weaknesses of sustainable development and ecological modernisation. How effective are they in addressing climate change?
Consider how an ecocentric government might operate. What differences would be seen to the current form of government?
Why should the Stern Report be taken so seriously?

CHAPTER 35 // GOVERNANCE IN BRITAIN

Contents
- **Introduction**
- **What is Governance?**
- **Governance in the UK**
- **Conclusion**

Introduction

This has been a wide-ranging text book, covering a range of features of the British political system, as well as much more. The challenge in this chapter is to pull these often disparate strands together. As was noted in the introduction, there is clear overlap between different chapters: the Cabinet and the Prime Minister; electoral systems and voting behaviour; the different parts of government beyond the centre; and so forth.

Government, it was often believed, was relatively straightforward. Politicians were voted in, at whatever tier of government (central or local), and they introduced policies, and made decisions which impacted on the lives of the population. These decisions were then judged at the subsequent election. The cycle would then repeat.

That description is a huge oversimplification. The politicians no longer make all of the decisions, assuming they ever did. There is a complex, multi-level structure of government that could start at the international level, with the United Nations and the World Trade Organisation. There is also the European Union – a supra-national and intergovernmental body. Then there is central, regional and local government across the UK.

Yet even this description is incomplete. There are so many other actors involved in the formulation and the implementation of policies. The chapters on regulation, the state, and local government have highlighted the range of actors who may be involved in running the country – be it making policies, advising on policies or delivering services. It is not solely the government which does this any more. Instead, there is a complex, multi-tiered system of governance.

What is Governance?

Such a question is worthy of a book in its own right. There are a multitude of ways in which the concept of governance can be defined. Gray (2000, p. 285), for example, examines how the state has moved from being a provider of services to an enabler and a regulator of the provision of these services. He goes further, arguing the central state has "lost control of the management and administration of goods and services" (p.288). This is all part of a move from government to governance. The managing and administration of these services is done by those who provide them – and that tends not to be the government. Instead, there are bodies who provide these goods and services on behalf of government.

Rhodes (1997; 2007) has argued for many years the state has become 'hollowed out'. "The state has been hollowed out from above (for example, by international interdependence); from below (by marketisation and networks); and sideways (by agencies and the several species of parastatal bodies)" (Rhodes, 2007, p. 1248). Bache & Flinders (2004, p. 97) similarly describe governance as "the increased role of non-governmental actors in public policy making and delivery". In other words, quangos and other public bodies, as well as private companies, pressure and lobby groups, and voluntary organisations may all have a role to play in the formulation and delivery of public services at every tier of government.

Rather than the state delivering all of the services the public needs, the state instead finds other organisations to deliver these same services – but to do so more cost-effectively. This suggests the state actively, or at sub-national levels is actively encouraged or even forced, to find partners to deliver services. Offe (2009, p. 553) presents two rather blunt explanations of governance:

Private actors... substituting for deficient state capacities.

Private actors... take advantage of their power position in order to usurp genuinely public tasks.

There is a whole debate here about the extent to which non-state bodies are delivering state-funded services, and the extent to which they should be doing this. Such a debate is not just about the provision of services originating from central government; it applies to every tier of government. Should private organisations be permitted to deliver state services, and to do so while generating a profit out of such service delivery? Under the PF2 scheme (Private Finance 2, which is the successor to the Private Finance Initiative or PFI) as proposed by George Osborne, the public sector must have an involvement in these schemes. If there is any profit generated, the public sector will get their share: a twenty per cent stake in the service delivery will see twenty per cent of the profits. Is it right such profits should be made? Could the service not be delivered even more cost-effectively so there is no profit, but no loss either?

All of these debates do not just apply to one tier or level of government. Rather it is across the board. There is a whole debate about multi-level or multi-tier governance or a plethora of interchangeable titles, depending upon the source of the literature.

Hooghe & Marks (2003) identify different types of multi-level governance. Regardless of the type of multi-level or multi-tier governance, it is seen "as an *alternative* to hierarchical government" (Hooghe & Marks, 2003, p. 234, their emphasis). According to Hooghe & Marks, there are two major types of multi-level governance. Type I sees "dispersions of authority to general purpose, non-intersecting, and durable jurisdictions" (Hooghe & Marks, 2003, p. 233). This can be seen within a federal structure, where power is shared between different tiers of government. There are clear boundaries in which the actors perform, and these boundaries, and the actors as well, are difficult to transform. Using the USA as an example, it would be very difficult indeed to create or abolish different tiers of government.

Type II governance sees "task specific, intersecting and flexible jurisdictions" (Hooghe & Marks, 2003, p. 233). Such an approach is seen as much more helpful to citizens, giving them a range of choice of service providers. The focus is upon the different services which need to be provided rather than who is providing these services. Different service providers may offer their services to different regions and locales, rather than being stuck within, for example, a single geographically-based unit such as a local council.

The reality with these two types of governance is they can and do co-exist. It is possible to see both types existing within the service delivery structures of a state. Both of them are clearly present within what has become the governance of the UK.

Governance in the UK

Throughout this book it should have become apparent the different tiers of government in the UK, while still very important, are declining in much of what they do. Local government has moved from being a provider of services to an enabler of services; quangos, at local, regional and national levels, are picking up greater responsibilities. More and more, the role of the government has become that of a regulator rather than as a deliverer of services. Within the UK there is now a complex, multi-tiered system of governance.

Offe, commenting more generally on governance, raises an important concern:

> the co-option of non-state actors... might either increase the efficiency and effectiveness of the policy in question through the coordination of responsibilities, or it might lead to the systematic creation of dependency of public authorities on private actors ("state capture") and outright corrupt practices. (Offe, 2009, p. 553)

The positive side of the above quote presents the reasons as to why the private sector or the voluntary sector may be better at delivering services than the public sector. Rather than the Type I governance of a rigid system of state provision within a geographically-confined area, the Type II approach, which focuses on the service being delivered rather than the deliverer of that service, might be seen as a better format. Such arguments would resonate most strongly with all those who want to gain government contracts or enter into public-private partnerships.

The second part of Offe's quote is one which tends not to be addressed – at least, not by those who want such structures to be put in place. If things go wrong, as they did with the privatisation of the British railway infrastructure, the building of the Channel Tunnel, the partnership established for the National Air Traffic Services (NATS), and the failure by a number of private businesses to run state schools properly, then the service delivery stops. Alternatively, the problem is transferred back to the state to pick up the pieces and to continue the service delivery. As was noted in the chapter on regulation, some services are too important to fail. Governments, at all levels, may become captivated by the enticing promises of better service delivery, and the promise of the transfer of risk. Yet, if penalty clauses were to be put in place for the delivery of public services, it is suggested very few private contractors would be interested. This could mean the state dependency on private suppliers is already here.

One of the concerns around governance in the UK is the issue of accountability. Arguably, politicians are held to account for the way in which government is run – be it national, regional or local government. Whether holding such an election every three to five years is actually holding politicians to account can be debated. Arguably, that is still far more accountable than when a private company delivers a service on behalf of a public sector body. When such contracts last for ten of even twenty years, how does the average person in the street hold the supplier to account? It is suggested the private company is held to account, contractually, by the public sector partner e.g. the local council. Yet, if there is dissatisfaction with the delivery of the service, but it is within the contractual obligations, it would appear nothing can be done. Voting out the council may not help. The incoming ruling party may wish to break the contract, but there is likely to be a huge financial penalty for doing so. Such expense may be difficult to justify. As Kjær (2004) notes, for governance the focus is on efficiency. Democratic accountability is sometimes sidelined. The people want the most cost-effective service delivery possible, regardless as to who provides that service.

Conclusion

The complex system of multi-level governance in the UK is here to stay. While it may be possible to tinker with this system through, for example, the negotiation of better contracts, any fundamental change is not likely to happen. Any politician who stands up to question the role of the private sector in the delivery of public services is likely to be portrayed as coming from 'cloud cuckoo land'; as being out of touch with reality. The austerity package forced on the public sector has made it even less likely this idea of governance can be challenged.

Those who do wish for change, and look back on some mythical golden era, when there was fantastic public service delivery by public sector bodies as being the model that ought to be in place, are looking at history through rose-tinted spectacles. There were many things wrong with the system of government in the post-war era, much of it can be linked to the electoral cycle. With a general election every five years, there was a need for the economy to look healthy in every fifth year – although snap elections were often called at opportune moments, when the economy was looking healthier than expected. Quality of service delivery was not measured, although measuring such quality does not guarantee a quality service. Those who wish to turn the clock back to some pre-Thatcherite era need to consider just how much things have changed over the last few decades.

In generations to come, when people look back at the second half of the twentieth century and into the early part of the twenty-first, they may talk of a rather odd experiment where the state tried to provide as many services as possible, to keep as many people in work as possible, to provide generous benefits to those who needed them, to provide generous state pensions to everyone, and to be actively involved in running the economy. The bill for taxpayers might have been huge, but the state ran up large debts to help as many people as possible. Attempts were made to tinker with the system, but these proved to be unsuccessful. It was only through the great financial crisis of the early twenty-first century, when governments and the people finally realised the system was unaffordable, that such an experiment was finally ended.

Selected bibliography

Bache, Ian & Flinders, Matthew (eds.). (2004). *Multi-level Governance:* Oxford University Press.

Gray, Clive. (2000). "A 'Hollow State'?" in Pyper, Robert & Robins, Lynton (eds.), *United Kingdom Governance*: Macmillan, pp. 283-300.

Hooghe, Liesbet & Marks, Gary. (2003). "Unraveling the Central State, but How? Types of Multi-level Governance", *American Political Science Review* vol. 97-2, pp. 233-243.

Kjær, Anne Mette. (2004). *Governance*: Polity Press.

Offe, Claus. (2009). "Governance: An "Empty Signifier"?", *Constellations* vol. 16-4, pp. 550-562.

Rhodes, R. A. W. (2007). "Understanding Governance: ten years on", *Organization Studies* vol. 28-8, pp. 1243-1264.

Rutter, Jill. (2011). "The State of UK Governance", *Public Policy and Administration* vol. 27-1, pp. 89-95.

Websites

www.civilsociety.co.uk
Presents some interesting perspectives on governance from the perspective of charities and the voluntary sector

www.good-governance.org.uk/
The Good Governance Institute is an advisory organisation which focuses on aspects of good governance, especially in relation to the provision of health and healthcare

www.gov.uk/government/organisations/hm-revenue-customs/about/our-governance
The perspective of governance from a quango

Questions
1. "We should no longer talk about the government of the UK but rather the governance of the UK." Discuss
2. "The whole concept of the welfare state, with the state also playing an active role in the running of the economy was little more than an experiment – and one which failed." Comment.

APPENDIX // HOW DO THE DIFFERENT ELECTORAL FORMULAS WORK?

Below is a brief overview of the different electoral formulas presented in the Multi-Dimensional Approach to Electoral Systems presented in Table 20.5.

Simple Plurality
The candidate with the most votes is the winner.

Block Vote
In a two-member constituency, the top two candidates (with the most votes) are declared the winners. In a three-member constituency, it will be the top three candidates, and so forth.

Second Ballot
If a candidate wins an absolute majority of votes, then that candidate is declared the winner. If no candidate is successful, there is a second ballot. There may be pre-conditions as to who may qualify for the second round. For example, in the French Presidential elections, only the top two candidates (in terms of votes received) go on to the second round. In the French Assembly elections, all candidates who gain over 12.5% of the vote proceed to the second round. The winner of the second round is decided by Simple Plurality.

Condorcet
The winning candidate is the one that is preferred by more voters in relation to every other candidate. This can be done by conducting a series of pair-wise comparisons.

Borda
Points are given for to each candidate on a voter's ballot paper: 0 for last, 1 for second last, all the way up to the most preferred candidate. The candidate with the most points is the winner.

Alternative Vote
A candidate needs an absolute majority of votes to gain election. If no candidate gains an absolute majority, the last placed candidate is eliminated, and their votes are redistributed according to the next listed preference. Votes are then counted to see if an absolute majority has been achieved. If not, the process is repeated until there is a winner.

Supplementary Vote

Voters rank two preferences. All of the first preferences are counted. If a candidate gains an absolute majority of first preference votes, then that candidate is declared the winner. If there is no winner, the two candidates with the most votes progress to the second round. The second preference votes for all of the other candidates are then redistributed (or declared void if not for one of the top two candidates who have progressed to the second round). The candidate with the most votes then wins.

Approval Voting

Each voter may vote for (or 'approve') of as many candidates as he or she wishes. The candidate with the most votes wins. (This could be considered a Plurality system rather than a Majoritarian system).

Exhaustive Voting

Each voter casts a single (or multiple) preference. If the leading candidate gains an absolute majority, that candidate is declared the winner. If there is no winner, the last placed candidate is eliminated (sometimes thresholds of votes are used e.g. 5% in the first round, 10% in the second and so forth) and another ballot is held. This process continues until a candidate gains an absolute majority of votes.

Single Non-Transferable Vote

In a three member constituency, the three candidates with the most votes gain election. In a four member constituency, it will be the top four candidates, and so forth.

Cumulative Vote

Under this system, it is possible for a voter to cast multiple ballots for a single candidate. For example, in a constituency where three candidates are to be elected, it is possible for a voter to cast all three of their preferences for one candidate. The candidates with the most votes gain election. In a three-member constituency, it will be the three candidates with the most votes. As a formula, this could be considered a Plurality system.

Limited Vote

In a three member constituency, voters are likely to have two votes (it will always be fewer votes than there are candidates to be elected). These are categoric choices. The candidates with the most votes gain election. In a three-member constituency, it will be the three candidates with the most votes. As a formula, this could be considered a Plurality system.

Single Transferable Vote

To gain election a target number of votes needs to be achieved. For STV, this is done via the Droop Quota:

$$\frac{\text{Total votes cast in the constituency}}{\text{Number of candidates to be elected} + 1} + 1$$

For example:

$$\frac{10\ 000\ \text{votes}}{4\ \text{candidates to be elected} + 1} + 1 = 2001\ \text{votes}$$

Thereafter, STV follows the same rules as the Alternative Vote, with last placed candidates being eliminated and votes redistributed until the target number of candidates are elected.

d'Hondt

This is a highest average method of allocating seats in a party list system. A grid may be presented of each party's votes. If 5 seats are to be allocated, each party's vote may be divided by 1 through to 5. The five largest numbers are then allocated the seats (see hypothetical example below, with emboldened figures denoting election).

Party	Votes / 1	Votes /2	Votes /3	Votes /4	Votes /5	Seats won
A	**7 000**	**3 500**	2 333.333	1 750	1 400	2
B	2 000	1 000	666.666	500	400	0
C	**4 500**	2 250	1 500	1 125	900	1
D	900	450	300	225	180	0
E	**5 000**	**2 500**	1 666.666	1 250	1 000	2

Imperiali

This is a highest average method of allocating seats in a party list system. It follows the d'Hondt system (above) except that the first seats are allocated in the /2 column. As with the above example, the five largest numbers are allocated the seats (see hypothetical example below, with emboldened figures denoting election).

Party	Votes / 1	Votes /2	Votes /3	Votes /4	Votes /5	Seats won
A	7 000	**3 500**	**2 333.333**	**1 750**	1 400	3
B	2 000	1 000	666.666	500	400	0
C	4 500	**2 250**	1 500	1 125	900	1
D	900	450	300	225	180	0
E	5 000	**2 500**	1 666.666	1 250	1 000	1

Saint Laguë

This is a highest average method of allocating seats in a party list system. It follows the d'Hondt system (above) except that the votes are divided by odd numbers, as shown in the hypothetical table below. As with the above examples, the five largest numbers are allocated the seats (with emboldened figures denoting election).

Party	Votes / 1	Votes /3	Votes /5	Votes /7	Votes /9	Seats won
A	**7 000**	**2 333.333**	1 400	1 000	777.777	2
B	2 000	666.666	400	285.714	222.222	0
C	**4 500**	1 500	900	642.857	500	1
D	900	300	180	128.571	100	0
E	**5 000**	**1 666.666**	1 000	714.286	555.555	2

Hare

This is a largest remainder method of allocating seats in a party list system. It uses a simple formula of Total votes cast divided by the total number of seats to be allocated. This gives a divisor by which to divide each party's votes, with the largest remainders gaining any remaining seats (see following table)

Party	A	B	C	D	E	Total
Votes	7 000	2 000	4 500	900	5 000	19 400
Seats						5
Hare Quota						3 880
Votes / quota	1.8	0.5	1.2	0.2	1.3	
Automatic seats	1	0	1	0	1	3
Remainder	0.8	0.5	0.2	0.2	0.3	
Highest remainder seats	1	1	0	0	0	2
Total seats	2	1	1	0	1	5

Niemeyer

This is a largest remainder method of allocating seats in a party list system. It follows the Hare system. Hence this system is sometimes called **Hare-Niemeyer**.

Hagenbach-Bischoff

This is a largest remainder method of allocating seats in a party list system. It follows the Hare method but uses the formula of total votes divided by seats (plus one).

Party	A	B	C	D	E	Total
Votes	7 000	2 000	4 500	900	5 000	19 400
Seats + 1						6
H-B Quota						3 233.333
Votes / quota	2.2	0.6	1.4	0.3	1.5	
Automatic seats	2	0	1	0	1	4
Remainder	0.2	0.6	0.4	0.3	0.5	
Highest remainder seats	0	1	0	0	0	1
Total seats	2	1	1	0	1	5

Additional Member System

Under this system, as proposed by the Hansard Society in 1976, most MPs are elected under Simple Plurality. A number of MPs (around 100) would be selected from a list of losing candidates (sub-divided across four or five regions of the UK). Thus the best losing candidates in each region would also gain election. The hope is this will lead to a more proportional result.

AV Plus

The AV part of this electoral system follows the Alternative Vote (a candidate needs an absolute majority of votes to gain election, with the last placed candidates being eliminated and their votes redistributed until one candidate has an absolute majority of votes). Around 15-20% of MPs would be elected by a regional top up vote (utilising a regional party list formula (probably d'Hondt), to increase the proportionality of the result.

Mixed Member-Proportional

Around half of the MPs are elected under Simple Plurality. The remainder are elected under a party list system in an attempt to ensure a more proportional result. Under some systems of MMP (as used in Scotland, Wales, Germany and New Zealand), the percentage of votes cast for the party lists should equate (approximately) with the total percentage of seats won by each party. In Russia, the results of the two parts of the vote are kept apart.

Bibliography

Abraham, Ann (2008); "The Ombudsman and Individual Rights" *Parliamentary Affairs* vol. 61-2, pp. 370-379

Abraham, Ann (2009); "Good Administration: Why We Need It More Than Ever" *Political Quarterly* vol. 80-1, pp. 25- 32

Alkire, Sabina (2002); "Global Citizenship and Common Values" in Dower, Nigel & Williams, John (eds.); *Global Citizenship: A Critical Reader* Edinburgh University Press, pp. 169-180

Allan, Graham & Crow, Graham (2001); *Families, Households and Society* Palgrave

Allen, Nicholas (2011); "Dishonourable members? Exploring patterns of misconduct in the contemporary House of Commons" *British Politics* vol. 6-2, pp. 210-240

Allen, Nicholas & Dean, Jonathan (2008); "No (Parliamentary) Gender Gap Please, We're British" *Political Quarterly* vol. 79-2, pp. 212-220

Allen, Nicholas & Ward, Hugh (2009); "'Moves on a Chess Board': A Spatial Model of British Prime Ministers' Powers over Cabinet Formation" *British Journal of Politics and International Relations* vol. 11-2, pp. 238-258

Allern, Elin & Bale, Tim (2012); "Political parties and interest groups: Disentangling complex relationships" *Party Politics* vol. 18-1, pp. 7-25

Allington, Nigel & Peele, Gillian (2010); "Moats, Duck Houses and Bath Plugs: Members of Parliament, the Expenses Scandal and the Use of Web Sites" *Parliamentary Affairs* vol. 63-3, pp. 385-406

Almond, Gabriel & Verba, Sydney (1963); *The Civic Culture* Princeton University Press

Amundsen, Helene; Berglund, Frode & Westkog, Hege (2010); "Overcoming barriers to climate change adaptation – a question of multi-level governance?" *Environment and Planning C: Government and Policy* vol. 28-2, pp. 276-289

Anckar, Carsten (2000); "Size and Party System Fragmentation" *Party Politics* vol. 6-3, pp. 305-328

Andrews, Rhys & Martin, Steve (2007); "Has Devolution Improved Public Services?" *Public Money and Management* vol. 27-2, pp. 149-156

Annesely, Claire (2010); "Gender, Politics and Policy Change: The Case of Welfare Reform Under New Labour" *Government and Opposition* vol. 45-1, pp. 50-72

Annesley, Claire (2012); "Campaigning against the Cuts: Gender Equality Movements in Tough Times" *Political Quarterly* vol. 83-1, pp. 19-23

Annesley, Claire & Gains, Francesca (2013); "Investigating the Economic Determinants of the UK Gender Policy Agenda" *British Journal of Politics and International Relations* vol. 15-1, pp. 125-146

Anthony, Gordon & Morison, John (2005); "Here, There, and (Maybe) Here Again: The Story of Law Making for Post-1998 Northern Ireland" in Hazell, Robert & Rawlings, Richard (eds.); *Devolution, Law Making and the Constitution* Imprint Academic, pp. 155-192

Armstrong, Kenneth (2006); "The 'Europeanisation' of Social Exclusion: British Adaptation to EU Co-ordination" *British Journal of Politics and International Relations* vol. 8-1, pp. 79-100

Asad, Talal (1990); "Multiculturalism and British Identity in the Wake of the Rushdie Affair" *Politics & Society* vol. 18-4, pp. 455-480

Asenova, Darinka & Hood, John (2006); "PFI and the Implications of Introducing New Long-Term Actors into Public Service Delivery" *Public Policy and Administration* vol. 21-4, pp. 23-41

Asquith, Andy (2008); "A bullock, a monkey and Robocop: an assessment of the directly elected mayor in English local government" *Policy and Politics* vol. 36-1, pp. 39-53

Audit of Political Engagement 7: The 2010 Report with a focus on MPs and Parliament" (Hansard Society, 2010)

Aughey, Arthur (2001); *Nationalism, Devolution and the Challenge to the United Kingdom* Pluto Press

Ayres, Ian & Braithwaite, John (1992); *Responsive Regulation: Transcending the Deregulation Debate* Oxford University Press

Ayres, Sarah & Pearce, Graham (2004); "Devolution to the English regions: Assessing its implications for transport" *Town Planning Review* vol. 75-2, pp. 231-255

Ayres, Sarah & Pearce, Graham (2005); "Building regional governance in England: the view from Whitehall" *Policy & Politics* vol. 33-4, pp. 581-600

Ayres, Sarah & Stafford, Ian (2009); "Deal-making in Whitehall: Competing and complementary motives behind the *Review of Sub-national Economic Development and Regeneration*" *International Journal of Public Sector Management* vol. 22-7, pp. 605-622

Bache, Ian & Flinders, Matthew (2004); "Multi-level Governance and British Politics" in Bache, Ian & Flinders, Matthew (eds.); *Multi-level Governance* Oxford University Press, pp. 93-106

Bache, Ian & Jordan, Andrew (2008a); "Britain in Europe and Europe in Britain" in Bache, Ian & Jordan, Andrew (eds.); *The Europeanization of British Politics* Palgrave pp. 3-16

Bache, Ian & Jordan, Andrew (2008b); "Europeanization and Domestic Change" in Bache, Ian & Jordan, Andrew (eds.); *The Europeanization of British Politics* Palgrave pp. 17-33

Bache, Ian & Jordan, Andrew (2008c); "The Europeanization of British Politics" in Bache, Ian & Jordan, Andrew (eds.); *The Europeanization of British Politics* Palgrave pp. 265-279

Baggott, Rob (1995); *Pressure Groups Today* Manchester University Press

Baggott, Rob (2000); *Pressure Groups and the Policy Process* Sheffield Hallam University Press

Bailey, Alan (2003); "The Governance of the Public Sector" *Political Quarterly* vol. 74-2, pp. 158-163

Baker, Susan (2007); "Sustainable Development as Symbolic Commitment: Declaratory Politics and the Seductive Appeal of Ecological Modernisation in the European Union" *Environmental Politics* vol. 16-2, pp. 297-317

Baldi, Gregory (2006); "Europeanising Antitrust: British Competition Policy Reform and Member State Convergence" *British Journal of Politics and International Relations* vol. 8-4, pp. 503-518

Baldwin, Robert (2008); "Regulation lite: The rise of emissions trading" *Regulation & Governance* vol. 2-1, pp. 193-215

Baldwin, Robert & Black, Julia (2008); "Really Responsive Regulation" *The Modern Law Review* vol. 71-1, pp. 59-94

Baldwin, Robert; Scott, Colin & Hood, Christopher (eds.) (1998); *A Reader on Regulation* Oxford University Press

Bale, Tim (2009); "'Cometh the Hour, Cometh the Dave': How far is the Conservative party's Revival All Down to David Cameron?" *Political Quarterly* vol. 80-2, pp. 222-232

Ball, Rob; Heafey, Maryanne & King, David (2002); "The Private Finance Initiative and public sector finance" *Environment and Planning C: Government and Policy* vol. 20-1, pp. 57-74

Bandelow, Nils (2008); "Government Learning in German and British European Policies" *Journal of Common Market Studies* vol. 46-4, pp. 743-764

Baraitser, Lisa (2009); "Mothers who make things public" *Feminist Review* no. 93, pp. 8-26

Barberis, Peter (2000); "Prime Minister and Cabinet" in Pyper, Robert & Robins, Lynton (eds.); *United Kingdom Governance* Macmillan, pp. 14-38

Barder, Brian (2001); "Britain: Still Looking for that Role?" *Political Quarterly* vol. 72-3, pp. 366-374

Barker, Rodney (2011); "Big Societies, Little Platoons and the Problems with Pluralism" *Political Quarterly* vol. 82-1, pp. 50-55

Barnett, Steven (2013); "Leveson Past, Present and Future: The Politics of Press Regulation" *Political Quarterly* vol. 84-3, pp. 353-361

Barnett, Steven & Seaton, Jean (2010); "Why the BBC Matters: Memo to the New Parliament about a Unique British Institution" *Political Quarterly* vol. 81-3, pp. 327-332

Barrett, Maxwell (2001); *The Law Lords: An Account of the Workings of Britain's Highest Judicial Body and the Men who Preside over It* Macmillan

Barry, Frank & Begg, Iain (2003); "EMU and Cohesion: Introduction" *Journal of Common Market Studies* vol. 41-5, pp. 781-796

Bartle, Ian & Vass, Peter (2007); "Self-Regulation within the Regulatory State: Towards a New Regulatory Paradigm?" *Public Administration* vol. 85-4, pp. 885-905

Bartle, John & Laycock, Samantha (2006); "Elections and Voting" in Dunleavy, Patrick; Heffernan, Richard; Cowley, Philip & Hay, Colin (eds.); *Developments in British Politics 8* Palgrave, pp. 77-97

Beaujouan, Éva & Ní Bhrolcháin, Maíre (2011); "Cohabitation and marriage in Britain since the 1970s" *Population Trends* number 145

Beetham, David (2003); "Political Participation, Mass Protest and Representative Democracy" *Parliamentary Affairs* vol. 56-4, pp. 597-609

Bell, David & Christie, Alex (2005); "Finance: Paying the Piper, Calling the Tune? in Trench, Alan (ed.); *The Dynamics of Devolution: The State of the Nations 2005* Imprint Academic, pp. 161-177

Bell, Derek & Gray, Tim (2002); "The Ambiguous Role of the Environment Agency in England and Wales" *Environmental Politics* vol. 11-3, pp. 76-98

Bellamy, Richard (2008); "The democratic constitution: why Europeans should avoid American style constitutional judicial review" *European Political Science* vol. 7-1, pp. 9-20

Benenson, Harold (1991); "The "Family Wage" and Working Women's Consciousness in Britain, 1880-1914" *Politics & Society* vol. 19-1, pp. 71-108

Bennear, Lori (2008); "What do we really know? The effect of reporting thresholds on inferences using environmental right-to-know data" *Regulation & Governance* vol. 2-1, pp. 293-315

Berlinski, Samuel; Dewan, Torun & Dowding, Keith (2007); "The Length of Ministerial Tenure in the United Kingdom, 1945-1997" *British Journal of Political Science* vol. 37-2, pp. 245-262

Bernhagen, Patrick & Trani, Brett (2012); "Interest group mobilization and lobbying patterns in Britain: A newspaper analysis" *Interest Groups & Advocacy* vol. 1-1, pp. 48-66

Bernstein, Steven (2002); "Liberal Environmentalism and Global Environmental Governance" *Global Environmental Politics* vol. 2-3, pp. 1-16

Bertelli, Anthony (2008); "Credible Governance? Transparency, Political Control, the Personal Vote and British Quangos" *Political Studies* vol. 56-4, pp. 807-829

Bevir, Mark (2008); "The Westminster Model, Governance and Judicial Reform" *Parliamentary Affairs* vol. 61-4, pp. 559-577

Bevir, Mark & Rhodes, R. A. W. (2006); "Prime Ministers, Presidentialism and Westminster Smokescreens" *Political Studies* vol. 54-4, pp. 671-690

Birch, Kean & Cumbers, Andrew (2007); "Public Sector Spending and the Scottish Economy: Crowding Out or Adding Value?" *Scottish Affairs* no. 58, pp. 36-56

Birrell, Derek (2012); "Intergovernmental Relations and Political Parties in Northern Ireland" *British Journal of Politics and International Relations* vol. 14-2, pp. 270-284

Biscop, Sven; Howorth, Jolyon & Giegerich, Bastian (2009); *Europe: A Time For Strategy* (Egmont Paper 27, Academia Press, Ghent)

Bishop, Jeff (2010); "From Parish Plans to Localism in England: Straight Track or Long and Winding Road?" *Planning Practice & Research* vol. 25-5, pp. 611-624

Black, Julia (2001); "Decentring Regulation: Understanding the Role of Regulation and Self-Regulation in a 'Post-Regulatory' World" *Current Legal Problems* vol. 54, pp. 103-147

Black, Julia (2007); "Tensions in the Regulatory State" *Public Law* vol. 51-1, pp. 58-73

Black, Julia (2008); "Constructing and contesting legitimacy and accountability in polycentric regulatory regimes" *Regulation and Governance* vol. 2-2, pp. 137-164

Blau, Adrian (2004); "Fairness and Electoral Reform" *British Journal of Politics and International Relations* vol. 6-2, pp. 165-181

Bleich, Erik (2011); "Social Research and 'Race' Policy Framing in Britain and France" *British Journal of Politics and International Relations* vol. 13-1, pp. 59-74

Blondel, Jean (1974); *Voters, Parties and Leaders: The Social Fabric of British Politics* Penguin

Blühdorn, Ingolfur & Welsh, Ian (2007); "Eco-politics beyond the Paradigm of Sustainability: A Conceptual Framework and Research Agenda" *Environmental Politics* vol. 16-2, pp. 185-205

Blyth, Mark & Katz, Richard (2005); "From Catch-all Parties to Cartelisation: The Political Economy of the cartel Party" *West European Politics* vol. 28-1, pp. 33-60

Bogdanor, Vernon (2001a); *Devolution in the United Kingdom* Oxford University Press

Bogdanor, Vernon (2001b); "Civil Service Reform: A Critique" *Political Quarterly* vol. 72-3, pp. 291-299

Bogdanor, Vernon (2010); "The West Lothian Question" *Parliamentary Affairs* vol. 63-1, pp. 156-172

Bogdanor, Vernon (2011); *The Coalition and the Constitution* Hart Publishing

Bogdanor, Vernon; Khaitan, Tarunabh & Vogenauer, Stefan (2007); "Should Britain Have a Written Constitution?" *Political Quarterly* vol. 78-4, pp. 499-517

Bondi, Liz (1990); "Feminism, Postmodernism, and Geography: Space for Women?" *Antipode* vol. 22-2, pp. 156-167

Bondi, Liz; & Christie, Hazel (2000); "The best of times for some and the worst of times for others? Gender and class divisions in urban Britain today" *Geoforum* vol. 31-3, pp. 329-343

Boney, Norman (2012); "Some constitutional issues concerning the installation of the monarch" *British Politics* vol. 7-2, pp. 163-182

Borer, Robert & Krutz, Glen (2005); "The Devolved Party Systems of the United Kingdom: Sub-national Variations from the National Model" *Party Politics* vol. 11-6, pp. 654-673

Börzel, Tanja (2002); "Pace-Setting, Foot-Dragging, and Fence-Sitting: Member State Responses to Europeanization" *Journal of Common Market Studies* vol. 40-2, pp. 193-214

Börzel, Tanja & Panke, Diana (2010); "Europeanization" in Cini, Michelle & Borragán, Nieves (eds.); *European Union Politics* Oxford University Press, 3rd edition, pp. 405-417

Börzel, Tanja & Risse, Thomas (2000); "When Europe Hits Home: Europeanization and Domestic Change" *European Integration online Papers* vol. 4, no. 15, available at eiop.or.at/eiop/texte/2000-015a.htm

Boston, Jonathan (1998); *Governing Under Proportional Representation: Lessons from Europe* Institute of Policy Studies, New Zealand

Bottom, Karin & Copus, Colin (2011); "Independent Politics: Why Seek to Serve and Survive as an Independent Councillor?" *Public Policy & Administration* vol. 26-3, pp. 279-305

Bovaird, Tony & Russell, Ken (2007); "Civil Service Reform in the UK, 1999-2005: Revolutionary Failure or Evolutionary Success?" *Public Administration* vol. 85-2, pp. 301-328

Bowler, Shaun & Farrell, David (2006); "We Know Which One We Prefer but We Don't Really Know Why: The Curious Case of Mixed Member Electoral Systems" *British Journal of Politics and International Relations* vol. 8-3, pp. 445-460

Boyne, George; James, Oliver; John, Peter & Petrovsky, Nicolai (2008); "Executive Succession in English Local Government" *Public Money and Management* vol. 28-5, pp. 267-274

Boyne, George; James, Oliver; John, Peter & Petrovsky, Nicolai (2009); "Does Political Change Affect Senior Management Turnover? An Empirical Analysis of Top-Tier Local Authorities in England" *Public Administration* vol. 88-1, pp. 136-153

Bradbury, Jonathan (2006); "*Territory and Power* Revisited: Theorising Territorial Politics in the United Kingdom after Devolution" *Political Studies* vol. 54-3, pp. 559-582

Bradbury, Jonathan & Mitchell, James (2001); "Devolution: New Politics for Old?" *Parliamentary Affairs* vol. 54-2, pp. 257-275

Brandsma, Gijs & Blom-Hansen, Jens (2010); "The EU Comitology System: What role for the Commission?" *Public Administration* vol. 88-2, pp. 496-512

Brazier, Alex & Fox, Ruth (2011); "Reviewing Select Committee Tasks and Modes of Operation" *Parliamentary Affairs* vol. 64-2, pp. 354-369

Brewer, Brian (2007); "Citizen or customer? Complaints handling in the public sector" *International Review of Administrative Sciences* vol. 73-4, pp. 549-556

British and Irish Ombudsman Association (2009); *Guide to principles of good governance*

Broad, Matthew & Daddow, Oliver (2010); "Half-Remembered Quotations from Mostly Forgotten Speeches: The Limits of Labour's European Policy Discourse" *British Journal of Politics and International Relations* vol. 12-2, pp. 205-222

Broadbent, Jane & Gray, Andrew with Jackson, Peter (2003); "Public-Private Partnerships" *Public Money and Management* vol. 23-3, pp. 135-136

Broadbent, Jane & Laughlin, Richard (1997); "Evaluating the 'New Public Management' Reforms in the UK: A Constitutional Possibility?" *Public Administration* vol. 75-3, pp. 487-507

Broscheid, Andreas & Coen, David (2003); "Insider and Outsider Lobbying of the European Commission: An Informational Model of Forum Politics" *European Union Politics* vol. 4-2, pp. 165-189

Bruce, Steve & Glendinning, Tony (2010); "When was secularisation? Dating the decline of the British churches and locating its cause" *The British Journal of Sociology* vol. 61-1, pp. 107-126

Bryant, Christopher (2008); "Devolution, equity and the English question" *Nations and Nationalism* vol. 14-4, pp. 664-683

Bryson, Alex & Forth, John (2010); "The evolution of the modern worker: attitudes to work" in Park, Alison; Curtice, John; Clery, Elizabeth & Bryson, Caroline (eds.); *British Social Attitudes: Exploring Labour's Legacy. The 27th Report* National Centre for Social Research pp. 103-130

Buckler, Steve & Dolowitz, David (2012); "Ideology Matters: Party Competition, Ideological Positioning and the Case of the Conservative Party under David Cameron" *British Journal of Politics and International Relations* vol. 14-4, pp. 576-594

Bull, Martin (2009); "Introduction: religion and politics – American and European experiences and contrasts" *European Political Science* vol. 8-3, pp. 270-272

Buller, Jim & Flinders, Matthew (2005); "The Domestic Origins of Depoliticisation in the Area of British Economic Policy" *British Journal of Politics and International Relations* vol. 7-4, pp. 526-543

Bulmer, Simon & Burch, Martin (1998); "Organizing for Europe: Whitehall, the British State and European Union" *Public Administration* vol. 76-4, pp. 601-628

Bulmer, Simon & Burch, Martin (2005); "The Europeanization of UK Government: From Quiet Revolution to Explicit Step-Change?" *Public Administration* vol. 83-4, pp. 861-890

Burchell, Jon & Cook, Joanne (2011); "Banging on open doors? Stakeholder dialogue and the challenge of business engagement for UK NGOs" *Environmental Politics* vol. 20-6, pp. 918-937

Burnett, Jon (2007); "Britain's 'civilising project': community cohesion and core values" *Policy & Politics* vol. 35-2, pp. 353-357

Burns, Charlotte (2006); "Co-decision and Inter-Committee Conflict in the European Parliament Post-Amsterdam" *Government and Opposition* vol. 41-2, pp. 230-248

Buser, Michael (2013); "Tracing the Democratic Narrative: Big Society, Localism and Civic Engagement" *Local Government Studies* vol. 39-1, pp. 3-21

Butler, Clare; Finniear, Jocelyn & Hill, Steve (2011); "How do we do public service? The socio-psychological status of public servants" *Public Money & Management* vol. 31-6, pp. 395-402

Butler, David & Stokes, Donald (1974); *Political Change in Britain: The Evolution of Electoral Choice* 2nd edition, Macmillan

Butnett, Jon (2007); "Britain's 'civilising project': community cohesion and core values" *Policy & Politics* vol. 35-2, pp. 353-357

Buttel, F. H. (2000); "Ecological modernization as social theory" *Geoforum* vol. 31-1, pp. 57-65

Byrne, Iain & Weir, Stuart (2004); "Democratic Audit: Executive Democracy in War and Peace" *Parliamentary Affairs* vol. 57-2, pp. 453-468

Cairney, Paul (2007); "The Professionalisation of MPs: Refining the 'Politics-Facilitating' Explanation" *Parliamentary Affairs* vol. 60-2, pp. 212-233

Campbell, Colm; Ni Aoláin, Fionnuala & Harvey, Colin (2003); "The Frontiers of Legal Analysis: Reframing the Transition in Northern Ireland" *The Modern Law Review* vol. 66-3, pp. 317-345

Campbell, Rosie & Childs, Sarah (2010); "'Wags', 'Wives', and 'Mothers'... But what about Women Politicians?" *Parliamentary Affairs* vol. 63-4, pp. 760-777

Campbell, Rosie; Childs, Sarah & Lovenduski, Joni (2009); "Do Women Need Women Representatives?" *British Journal of Political Science* vol. 40-1, pp. 171-194

Carey, Sean & Burton, Jonathan (2004); "Research Note: The Influence of the Press in Shaping Public Opinion towards the European Union in Britain" *Political Studies* vol. 52-3, pp. 623-640

Carter, Neil (2001); *The Politics of the Environment* Cambridge University Press

Carter, Neil (2006); "Party Politicization of the Environment in Britain" *Party Politics* vol. 12-6, pp. 747-767

Carter, Neil (2007a); *The Politics of the Environment: Ideas, Activism, Policy* Cambridge University Press 2nd edition

Carter, Neil (2007b); "Transforming Environmental Policy: Does Europe Lead the Way?" Review Essay *Political Quarterly* vol. 16-3, pp. 523-528

Carter, Neil (2008); "Combating Climate Change in the UK: Challenges and Obstacles" *Political Quarterly* vol. 79-2, pp. 194-205

Carter, Neil (2009); "Vote Blue, Go Green? Cameron's Conservatives and the Environment" *Political Quarterly* vol. 80-2, pp. 233-242

Carter, Neil (2013); "Greening the mainstream: party politics and the environment" *Environmental Politics* vol. 22-1, pp. 73-94

Cash, William (1992); *Europe: The Crunch* Duckworth

Catt, Helena (1996); *Voting Behaviour: A Radical Critique* Leicester University Press

Chadwick, Andrew & Stanyer, James (2011); "The Changing News Media Environment" in Heffernan, Richard; Cowley, Philip & Hay, Colin (eds.); *Developments in British Politics 9* Palgrave, pp. 215-237

Chandler, J. A. (2001); *Local government today* Manchester University Press, 3rd edition

Chandler, James (2008); "Liberal Justifications for Local Government in Britain: The Triumph of Expediency over Ethics" *Political Studies* vol. 56-2, pp. 355-373

Chandler, Jim (2010); "A Rationale for Local Government" *Local Government Studies* vol. 36-1, pp. 5-20

Chapain, Caroline & Comunian, Roberta (2010); "Enabling and Inhibiting the Creative Economy: The Role of the Local and Regional Dimensions in England" *Regional Studies* vol. 44-6, pp. 717-734

Chapman, Richard & O'Toole, Barry (2010); "Leadership in the British Civil Service" *Public Policy and Administration* vol. 25-2, pp. 123-136

Childs, David (1995); *Britain Since 1939: Progress and Decline* Macmillan

Childs, Sarah (2006); "Political Parties and Party Systems" in Dunleavy, Patrick; Heffernan, Richard; Cowley, Philip & Hay, Colin (eds.); *Developments in British Politics 8* Palgrave, pp. 56-76

Childs, Sarah & Krook, Mona Lena (2008); "Critical Mass Theory and Women's Representation" *Political Studies* vol. 56-3, pp. 725-736

Childs, Sarah; Webb, Paul & Marthaler, Sally (2009); "The Feminisation of the Conservative Parliamentary Party: Party Members' Attitudes" *Political Quarterly* vol. 80-2, pp. 204-213

Chisholm, Michael & Leach, Steve (2011); "Dishonest Government: Local Government Reorganisation, England 2006-2010" *Local Government Studies* vol. 37-1, pp. 19-41

Christensen, Jørgen (2010); "EU Legislation and National Regulation: Uncertain Steps Towards a European Public Policy" *Public Administration* vol. 88-1, pp. 3-17

Clark, Alistair (2012); *Political Parties in the UK* Palgrave

Clarke, Alistair & Wilford, Rick (2012); "Political Institutions, Engagement and Outreach: The Case of the Northern Ireland Assembly" *Parliamentary Affairs* vol. 65-2, pp. 380-403

Clarke, Harold; Sanders, David; Stewart, Marianne & Whiteley, Paul (2009); "The American voter's British cousin" *Electoral Studies* vol. 28-4, pp. 632-641

Clarke, John (2005); "New Labour's citizens: activated, empowered, responsibilized, abandoned?" *Critical Social Policy* vol. 25-4, pp. 447-463

Clarke, John (2010); "Scrutiny, inspection and audit in the public sector" Bovaird, Tony & Löffler, Elke (eds.); *Public Management and Governance* Routledge, 2nd edition, pp. 199-211

Clarke, Michael (2000); *Regulation: The Social Control of Business between Law and Politics* Macmillan

Clough, Emily (2007); "Strategic Voting Under Conditions of Uncertainty: A Re-Evaluation of Duverger's Law" *British Journal of Political Science* vol. 37-2, pp. 313-332

Coakley, John (2011); "The Challenge of Consociation in Northern Ireland" *Parliamentary Affairs* vol. 64-3, pp. 473-493

Cockburn, Cynthia (2002); "Resisting Equal Opportunities: The issue of maternity" in Jackson, Stevi & Scott, Sue (eds.); *Gender: A Sociological Reader* Routledge, pp. 180-191

Cocker, Phil & Jones, Alistair (2005); *Essential Topics in Modern British Politics and Government* Liverpool Academic Press

Coker, Christopher (1992); "Britain and the New World Order: the special relationship in the 1990s" *international Affairs* vol. 68-3, pp. 407-421

Colino, César (2008); "The Spanish model of devolution and regional governance: evolution, motivations and effects on policy making" *Policy & Politics* vol. 36-4, pp. 573-586

Colomer, Josep (2005); "It's Parties That Choose Electoral Systems (or, Duverger's Laws Upside Down)" *Political Studies* vol. 53-1, pp. 1-21

Colomer, Josep & Negretto, Gabriel (2005); "Can Presidentialism Work Like Parliamentarism?" *Government and Opposition* vol. 40-1, pp. 60-89

Compston, Hugh (2010); "The Politics of Climate Change Policy: Strategic Options for National Governments" *Political Quarterly* vol. 81-1, pp. 107-115

Cooke, Phil (2005); "Devolution and innovation: The Financing of Economic Development in the UK's Devolved Administrations" *Scottish Affairs* no. 50, pp. 39-51

Copus, Colin (2004); "Directly Elected Mayors: A Tonic for Local Governance or Old Wine in New Bottles?" *Local Government Studies* vol. 30-4, pp. 576-588

Copus, Colin (2008); "English Councillors and Mayoral Governance: Developing a New Dynamic for Political Accountability" *Political Quarterly* vol. 79-4, pp. 590-604

Copus, Colin (2009); "English national parties in post-devolution UK" *British Politics* vol. 4-3, pp. 363-385

Copus, Colin (2010); "The Councillor: Governor, Governing, Governance and the Complexity of Citizen Engagement" *British Journal of Politics and International Relations* vol. 12-4, pp. 569-589

Copus, Colin (2011); "Elected mayors in English Local Government: Mayoral Leadership and Creating a new Political Dynamic" *Lex Localis – Journal of Local Self-Government* vol. 9-4, pp. 335-351

Copus, Colin & Erlingsson, Gissur (2013); "Formal institutions versus informal decision-making. On parties, delegation and accountability in local government" *Scandinavian Journal of Public Administration* vol. 17-1, pp. 51-69

Copus, Colin; Sweeting, David & Wingfield, Melvin (2013); "Repoliticising and redemocratising local democracy and the public realm: why we need councillors and councils" *Policy & Politics* vol. 43-3, pp. 389-408

Cottle, Simon (2006); "Mediatized rituals: beyond manufacturing consent" *Media, Culture and Society* vol. 28-3, pp. 411-432

Cottle, Simon (2008); "Reporting demonstrations: the changing media politics of dissent" *Media, Culture and Society* vol. 30-6, pp. 853-872

Cowley, Philip (2009); "The Parliamentary Party" *Political Quarterly* vol. 80-2, pp. 214-221

Cowley, Philip (2011); "Political Parties and the British Party System" in Heffernan, Richard; Cowley, Philip & Hay, Colin (eds.); *Developments in British Politics 9* Palgrave, pp. 91-112

Cowley, Philip & Stuart, Mark (2004); "Parliament: More Bleak House than Great Expectations" *Parliamentary Affairs* vol. 57-2, pp. 301-314

Coxall, Bill & Robins, Lynton (1998); *British Politics since the War* Macmillan

Craig, John (2010); "Introduction: e-learning in politics" *European Political Science* vol. 9-1, pp. 1-9

Crawford, Bruce (2010); "Ten Years of Devolution" *Parliamentary Affairs* vol. 63-1, pp. 89-97

Crick, Bernard (2001); "Introduction" in Crick, Bernard (ed.); *Citizens: Towards a Citizenship Culture* Blackwell, pp. 1-9

Crouch, Colin (2001); "The Divine Comedy of Contemporary Citizenship" in Crick, Bernard (ed.); *Citizens: Towards a Citizenship Culture* Blackwell, pp.149-154

Curtice, John (2008); "Where stands the Union now? Lessons from the 2007 Scottish Parliament election" Institute for Public Policy Research

Curtice, John; Seyd, Ben; Park, Alison & Thomson, Katarina (2000); "Wise After the Event? Attitudes to Voting Reform Following the 1999 Scottish and Welsh Elections" Paper for the *Political Studies Association – UK*, 10-13 April 2000

Curtis, Mark (2004); "Britain's Real Foreign Policy and the Failure of British Academia" *International Relations* vol. 18-3, pp. 275-287

Cutts, David; Childs, Sarah & Fieldhouse, Edward (2008); "'This is what happens when you don't listen'. All-women Shortlists at the 2005 General Election" *Party Politics* vol. 14-5, pp. 575-595

Czaika, Mathias (2009); "Asylum Cooperation among Asymmetric Countries: The Case of the European Union" *European Union Politics* vol. 10-1, pp. 89-113

Dahlstedt, Magnus (2008); "Now you see it, now you don't: reconsidering the problem of representation" *Policy Studies* vol. 29-2, pp. 233-248

Davies, Jonathan (2000); "The hollowing out of local democracy and the 'fatal conceit' of governing without government" *British Journal of Politics and International Relations* vol. 2-3, pp. 414-428

Davies, Jonathan (2012); "Active citizenship: navigating the Conservative heartlands of the New Labour project" *Policy & Politics* vol. 40-1, pp. 3-19

Davies, Jonathan & Pill, Madeleine (2012); "Empowerment or abandonment? Prospects for neighbourhood revitalization under the big society" *Public Money & Management* vol. 32-3, pp. 193-200

Davies, Steve (2011); "Outsourcing, public sector reform and the changed character of the UK state-voluntary sector relationship" *International Journal of Public Sector Management* vol. 24-7, pp. 641-649

Davis, Evan (2011); *Made in Britain: How the Nation Earns its Living* Little, Brown

Davis, Fergal (2010); "The Human Rights Act and Juridification: Saving Democracy from Law" *Politics* vol. 30-2, pp. 91-97

Deakins, Eric; Dillon, Stuart; Al Namani, Hamed & Zhang, Chao (Kevin) (2010); "Local e-government impact in China, New Zealand, Oman and the United Kingdom" *International Journal of Public Sector Management* vol. 23-6, pp. 520-534

Dean, Jonathan (2012); "On the march or on the margins? Affirmations and erasures of feminist activism in the UK" *European Journal of Women's Studies* vol. 19-3, pp. 315-329

Delphy, Christine & Leonard, Diana (2002); "The Variety of Work Done by Wives" in Jackson, Stevi & Scott, Sue (eds.); *Gender: A Sociological Reader* Routledge, pp. 170-179

Denton, Matthew (2006); "The Impact of the Committee on Standards in Public Life on Delegated Governance: The Commissioner for Public Appointments" *Parliamentary Affairs* vol. 59-3, pp. 491-508

Denver, David (1989); *Elections and Voting Behaviour in Britain* Philip Allan

Denver, David (2007); *Elections and Voters in Britain* 2nd edition, Palgrave

Denver, David (2010); "The Results: How Britain Voted" *Parliamentary Affairs* vol. 63-4, pp. 588-606

Denver, David & Garnett, Mark (2012); "The Popularity of British Prime Ministers" *British Journal of Politics and International Relations* vol. 14-1, pp. 57-73

Department for Communities and Local Government (2010); "Draft Structural Reform Plan" Department for Communities and Local Government, July 2010

Dermody, Janine; Hanmer-Lloyd, Stuart & Scullion, Richard (2010); "Young people and voting behaviour: alienated youth and (or) an interested and critical citizenry?" *European Journal of Marketing* vol. 44-3/4, pp. 421-435

Diamond, Patrick & Kenny, Mike (2011); "Reviewing New Labour in Government: Progressive Dilemmas?" in Diamond, Patrick & Kenny, Michael (eds.); *Reassessing New Labour: Market, State and Society under Blair and Brown* Wiley Blackwell, pp. S4-S15

Dickens, Linda (2007); "The Road is Long: Thirty Years of Equality Legislation in Britain" *British Journal of Industrial Relations* vol. 45-3, pp. 463-494
Diefenbach, Thomas (2009); "New Public Management in Public Sector Organizations: The Dark Sides of Managerialistic 'Enlightenment'" *Public Administration* vol. 87-4, pp. 892-909
Dietl, Ralph (2008); "Suez 1956: A European Intervention?" *Journal of Contemporary History* vol. 43-2, pp. 259-278
Dixon, Timothy; Pottinger, Gaye and Jordan, Alan (2005); "Lessons from the private finance initiative in the UK: Benefits, problems and critical success factors" *Journal of Property Investment and Finance* vol. 23-5, pp. 412-423
Dobson, Andrew (2000); "Sustainable Development and the Defence of the Natural World" in Lee, Keekok; Holland, Alan & McNeill, Desmond (eds.); *Global Sustainable Development in the 21st Century* Edinburgh University Press, pp. 49-60
Dobson, Andrew (2003); *Citizenship and the Environment* Oxford University Press
Dobson, Andrew (2005); "Globalisation, Cosmopolitanism and the Environment" *International Relations* vol. 19-3, pp. 259-273
Dobson, Andrew (2007); *Green Political Thought* Routledge 4th edition
Dodds, Anneliese (2006); "The Core Executive's Approach to Regulation: From 'Better Regulation' to 'Risk-Tolerant Deregulation'" *Social Policy and Administration* vol. 40-5, pp. 526-542
Doherty, Brian; Paterson, Matthew; Plows, Alexandra & Wall, Derek (2003); "Explaining the fuel protests" *British Journal of Politics and International Relations* vol. 5-1, pp. 1-23
Doherty, Brian; Plows, Alexandra & Wall, Derek (2003); "'The Preferred Way of Doing Things': The British Direct Action Movement" *Parliamentary Affairs* vol. 56-4, pp. 669-686
Doig, Alan (2006a); "Ten Years After Nolan: Introduction" *Parliamentary Affairs* vol. 59-3, pp. 454-457
Doig, Alan (2006b); "Regional Variations: Organisational and Procedural Dimensions of Public Ethics Delivery Ten Years After Nolan" *Parliamentary Affairs* vol. 59-3, pp. 458-473
Dorey, Peter (1995); *British Politics since 1945* Blackwell
Dorey, Peter (2006); "1949, 1969, 1999: The Labour Party and House of Lords Reform" *Parliamentary Affairs* vol. 59-4, pp. 599-620
Dorey, Peter (2009); "'Sharing the Proceeds of Growth': Conservative Economic Policy under David Cameron" *Political Quarterly* vol. 80-2, pp.259-269
Dorey, Peter & Garnett, Mark (2012); "No such thing as the 'Big Society'? The Conservative party's unnecessary search for 'narrative' in the 2010 general election" *British Politics* vol. 7-4, pp. 389-417

Dover, Robert (2005); "The Prime Minister and the Core Executive: A Liberal Intergovernmentalist Reading of UK Defence Policy Formulation 1997-2000" *British Journal of Politics and International Relations* vol. 7-4, pp. 508-525

Dowding, Keith (2013); "The Prime Ministerialisation of the British Prime Minister" *Parliamentary Affairs* vol. 66-3, pp. 617-635

Dower, Nigel (2002); "Global Citizenship: Yes or No?" in Dower, Nigel & Williams, John (eds.); *Global Citizenship: A Critical Reader* Edinburgh University Press, pp. 30-40

Dower, Nigel (2003); *An Introduction to Global Citizenship* Edinburgh University Press

Downs, Anthony (1957); *An Economic Theory of Democracy* Harper

Drewry, Gavin; Blom-Cooper, Louis & Blake, Charles (2007); *The Court of Appeal* Hart Publishing

Dryzek, John & Dunleavy, Patrick (2009); *Theories of the Democratic State* Palgrave

Duckenfield, Mark & Aspinwall, Mark (2010); "Private interests and exchange rate policies: The case of British business" *European Union Politics* vol. 11-3, pp. 381-404

Duggett, Michael (2009); "The State of UK Governance: Whitehall – Structures and Functions under Brown" *Public Policy and Administration* vol. 24-1, pp. 103-111

Dumbrell, John (2009); "The US-UK Special Relationship: Taking the 21st-Century Temperature" *British Journal of Politics and International Relations* vol. 11-1, pp. 64-78

Dummett Michael (1997); *Principles of Electoral Reform* Oxford University Press

Dunbar, Katrina (2000); *Citizenship and You* Heinemann

Dunleavy, Patrick (2005); "Facing Up to Multi-Party Politics: How Partisan Dealignment and PR Voting Have Fundamentally Changed Britain's Party System" *Parliamentary Affairs* vol. 58-3, pp. 503-532

Dunleavy, Patrick & Husbands, Christopher (1985); *British Democracy at the Crossroads: Voting and Party Competition in the 1980s* George Allen and Unwin

Dunleavy, Patrick & Jones, G. W. (with Burnham, June; Elgie, Robert & Peter Fysh) (1995); "Leaders, Politics and Institutional Change: The Decline of Prime Ministerial Accountability to the House of Commons, 1868-1990" in Rhodes, R. A. W. & Dunleavy, Patrick (eds.), *Prime Minister, Cabinet and Core Executive* Macmillan, pp. 275-297

Dunleavy, Patrick & Margetts, Helen (2005); "The Impact of UK Electoral Systems" *Parliamentary Affairs* vol. 58-4, pp. 854-870

Dunleavy, Patrick & O'Leary, Brendan (1987); *Theories of the State: The Politics of Liberal Democracy* Macmillan

Dunleavy, Patrick & Rhodes, R. A. W. (1990); "Core Executive Studies in Britain" *Public Administration* vol. 68-1, pp. 3-28

Dunne, Tim (2004); "'When the shooting starts': Atlanticism in British security strategy" *International Affairs* vol. 80-5, pp. 893-909

Durham, Martin (1997); "'God Wants us to be in Different Parties': Religion and Politics in Britain Today" *Parliamentary Affairs* vol. 50-2, pp. 212-222

Durose, Catherine; Greasley, Stephen & Richardson, Liz (2009); "Changing local governance, changing citizens: introduction" in Durose, Catherine; Greasley, Stephen & Richardson, Liz (eds.); *Changing local governance, changing citizens* Policy Press, pp. 1-12

Dyson, Stephen (2009); "Cognitive Style and Foreign Policy: Margaret Thatcher's Black-and-White Thinking" *International Political Science Review* vol. 30-1, pp. 33-48

Eason, Christina (2009); "Women Peers and Political Appointment: Has the House of Lords Been Feminised Since 1999?" *Parliamentary Affairs* vol. 62-3, pp. 399-417

Edwards, Aaron (2007); "Social Democracy and Partition: The British Labour Party and Northern Ireland, 1951-64" *Journal of Contemporary History* vol. 42-4, pp. 595-612

Edwards, Gwyn (2001); "A very British subject: questions of identity" in Lambert, David & Machon, Paul (eds.); *Citizenship through Secondary Geography* Routledge/Falmer, pp. 109-121

Edwards, Rebecca; Smith, Graham & Büchs, Milena (2013); "Environmental management systems and the third sector: exploring weak adoption in the UK" *Environment and Planning C: Government and Policy* vol. 31-1, pp. 119-133

Einspahr, Jennifer (2010); "Structural domination and structural freedom: a feminist perspective" *Feminist Review* no. 94 pp. 1-19

Eising, Rainer (2008); "Interest groups in EU policy-making" *Living Reviews in European Governance* vol. 3-4, [on-line article accessed 28 June 2011 at www.livingreviews.org/lreg-2008-4]

Elcock, Howard (2008); "Elected mayors: Lesson Drawing from Four Countries" *Public Administration* vol. 86-3, pp. 795-811

Elliott, Mark (2006); "United Kingdom: Detention without trial and the 'war on terror'" *International Journal of Constitutional Law* vol. 4-3, pp. 553-566

Erdos, David (2010); "Smoke but No Fire? The Politics of a 'British' Bill of Rights" *Political Quarterly* vol. 81-2, pp. 188-198

Erikson, Robert & Goldthorpe, John (2010); "Has social mobility in Britain decreased? Reconciling divergent findings on income and class mobility" *The British Journal of Sociology* vol. 61-2, pp. 211-230

Eschle, Catherine & Maiguashca, Bice (2009); "Feminist Scholarship, Bridge-Building and Political Affinity" *International Relations* vol. 23-1, pp. 127-134

Esmark, Anders (2009); "The Functional Differentiation of Governance: Public Governance Beyond Hierarchy, Market and Networks" *Public Administration* vol. 87-2, pp. 351-370

Evans, Geoffrey (2000); "The Continued Significance of Class Voting" *Annual Review of Political Science* vol. 3, pp. 401-417

Evans, Stephen (2008); "Consigning its past to History? David Cameron and the Conservative Party" *Parliamentary Affairs* vol. 61-2, pp. 291-314

Evans, Stephen (2010); "'Mother's Boy': David Cameron and Margaret Thatcher" *British Journal of Politics and International Relations* vol. 12-3, pp. 325-343

Everitt, Anthony (2001); "Culture and Citizenship" in Crick, Bernard (ed.); *Citizens: Towards a Citizenship Culture* Blackwell, pp. 64-73

Ewing, K. (2004); "The Futility of the Human Rights Act" *Public Law* pp. 829-852

Fabre, Cécile (2000); "A Philosophical Argument for a Bill of Rights" British Journal of Political Science vol. 30-1, pp. 77-98

Falk, Richard (2002); "An Emergent Matrix of Citizenship: Complex, Uneven, and Fluid" in Dower, Nigel & Williams, John (eds.); *Global Citizenship: A Critical Reader* Edinburgh University Press, pp. 15-29

Falkner, Gerda; Hartlapp, Miriam; Leiber, Simone & Treib, Oliver (2004); "Non-Compliance with EU Directives in the Member States: Opposition through the Backdoor?" *West European Politics* vol. 27-3, pp. 452-473

Farrell, David (2011); *Electoral Systems: A Comparative Introduction* Palgrave 2nd edition

Farrell, David & Gallagher, Michael (1999); "British voters and their criteria for evaluating electoral systems" *British Journal of Politics and International Relations* vol. 1-3, pp. 293-316

Farthing, Rys (2010); "The politics of youthful antipolitics: representing the 'issue' of youth participation in politics" *Journal of Youth Studies* vol. 13-2, pp. 181-195

Faulkner, David (2008); "Government and Public Services in Modern Britain: What Happens Next?" *Political Quarterly* vol. 79-2, pp. 232-240

Fenwick, John; Elcock, Howard & McMillan, Janice (2007); "'Flagship Councils that will lead the Way'? Issues and Tensions in the Reorganisation of the English Counties" Public Administration Committee Annual Conference, University of Ulster

Fenwick, John; McMillan, Janice & Elcock, Howard (2009); "Local Government and the Problem of English Governance" *Local Government Studies* vol. 35-1, pp. 5-20

Fieldhouse, Edward & Sobolewska, Maria (2013); "Introduction: Are British Ethnic Minorities Politically Under-represented?" *Parliamentary Affairs* vol. 66-2, pp. 235-245

Fielding, Stephen (2009); "Introduction: Cameron's Conservatives" *Political Quarterly* vol. 80-2, pp. 168-171

Fingland, Lisa & Bailey, Stephen (2008); "The EU's Stability and Growth Pact: Its Credibility and Sustainability" *Public Money and Management* vol. 28-4, pp.223-230

Fisher, Stephen; Lessard-Phillips, Laurence; Hobolt, Sara & Curtice, John (2008); "Disengaging voters: Do plurality systems discourage the less knowledgeable from voting?" *Electoral Studies* vol. 27-1, pp. 89-104

Fitzgerald, Rory; Harrison, Eric & Steinmaier, Frank (2010); "Age identity and conflict: myths and realities" in Park, Alison; Curtice, John; Clery, Elizabeth & Bryson, Caroline (eds.); *British Social Attitudes: Exploring Labour's Legacy. The 27th Report* National Centre for Social Research pp. 179-202

Flinders, Matthew (1999a); "Setting the Scene: Quangos in Context" in Flinders, Matthew & Smith, Martin (eds.); *Quangos, Accountability and Reform: The Politics of Quasi-Government* Macmillan, pp. 3-16

Flinders, Matthew (1999b); "Quangos: Why Do Governments Love Them?" in Flinders, Matthew & Smith, Martin (eds.); *Quangos, Accountability and Reform: The Politics of Quasi-Government* Macmillan, pp. 26-39

Flinders, Matthew (2002); "Shifting the Balance? Parliament, the Executive and the British Constitution" *Political Studies* vol. 50-1, pp. 23-42

Flinders, Matthew (2005a); "Majoritarian Democracy in Britain: New Labour and the Constitution" *West European Politics* vol. 28-1, pp. 61-93

Flinders, Matthew (2005b); "The Politics of Public Private Partnerships" *British Journal of Politics and International Relations* vol. 7-2, pp. 215-239

Flinders, Matthew (2006); "Public/Private: The Boundaries of the State" in Hay, Colin; Lister, Michael & Marsh, David (eds.); *The State: Theories and Issues* Palgrave pp. 223-247

Flinders, Matthew (2007); "Analysing Reform: The House of Commons, 2001-5" *Political Studies* vol. 55-1, pp. 174-200

Flinders, Matthew (2009); "Constitutional Anomie: Patterns of Democracy and 'The Governance of Britain'" *Government and Opposition* vol. 44-4, pp. 385-411

Flinders, Matthew (2010); "Explaining Majoritarian Modification: The Politics of Electoral Reform in the United Kingdom and British Columbia" *International Political Science Review* vol. 31-1, pp. 41-58

Flinders, Matthew & Curry, Dion (2008); "Deliberative democracy, elite politics and electoral reform" *Policy Studies* vol. 29-4, pp. 371-392

Flinders, Matthew & Kelso, Alexandra (2011); "Mind the Gap: Political Analysis, Public Expectations and the Parliamentary Decline Thesis" *British Journal of Politics and International Relations* vol. 13-2, pp. 249-268

Flinders, Matthew & McConnel, Hugh (1999); "Diversity and Complexity: The Quango Continuum" in Flinders, Matthew & Smith, Martin (eds.); *Quangos, Accountability and Reform: The Politics of Quasi-Government* Macmillan, pp. 17-25

Flinders, Matthew & Skelcher, Chris (2012); "Shrinking the quango state: five challenges in reforming quangos" *Public Money & Management* vol. 32-5, pp. 327-334

Flinders, Matthew; Matthews, Felicity & Eason, Christina (2011); "Are Public Bodies Still 'Male, Pale and Stale'? Examining Diversity in UK Public Appointments 1997-2010" *Politics* vol. 31-3, pp. 129-139

Flynn, N. (2007); *Public Sector Management* Sage 5th edition

Foley, Michael (2004); "Presidential Attribution as an Agency of Prime Ministerial Critique in a Parliamentary Democracy: The Case of Tony Blair" *British Journal of Politics and International Relations* vol. 6-2, pp. 292-311

Foley, Paul & Alfonso, Ximena (2009); "eGovernment and the Transformational Agenda" *Public Administration* vol. 87-2, pp. 371-396

Follesdal, Andreas (2002); "Citizenship: European and Global" in Dower, Nigel & Williams, John (eds.); *Global Citizenship: A Critical Reader* Edinburgh University Press, pp. 71-83

Foster, Emma; Kerr, Peter; Hopkins, Anthony; Byrne, Christopher & Ahall, Linda (2013); "The Personal is Not Political: At Least in the UK's Top Politics and IR Departments" *British Journal of Politics and International Relations* vol. 15-4, pp. 566-585

Foster, Steven (2006); *The Judiciary, Civil Liberties and Human Rights* Edinburgh University Press

Fowler, Carwyn & Jones, Rhys (2005); "Environmentalism and Nationalism in the UK" *Environmental Politics* vol. 14-4, pp. 541-545

Fox, Ruth (2011); "'Boom and Bust' in Women's Representation: Lessons to be Learnt from a Decade of Devolution" *Parliamentary Affairs* vol. 64-1, pp. 193-203

Franklin, Mark N. (1985); *The Decline of Class Voting in Britain: Changes in the Basis of Electoral Choice 1964-1983* Clarendon Press

Furlong, Andy & Cartmel, Fred (2012); "Social Change and Political Engagement Among Young People: Generation and the 2009/2010 British Election Survey" *Parliamentary Affairs* vol. 65-1, pp. 13-28

Gains, Francesca & Stoker, Gerry (2009); "Delivering 'Public Value': Implications for Accountability and Legitimacy" *Parliamentary Affairs* vol. 62-3, pp. 438-455

Gallop, Geoff (2011); "New development: Public leadership, public value and the public interest" *Public Money & Management* vol. 31-5, pp. 371-376

Gamble, Andrew (1990); "Theories of British Politics" *Political Studies* vol. 38-3, pp. 404-420

Gamble, Andrew (2003); *Between Europe and America: The Future of British Politics* Palgrave

Gamble, Andrew (2012a); "Better Off Out? Britain and Europe" *Political Quarterly* vol. 83-3, pp. 468-477

Gamble, Andrew (2012b); "Inside New Labour" *British Journal of Politics and International Relations* vol. 14-3, pp. 492-502

Game, Chris (2009); "Twenty-nine per cent Women Councillors after a Mere 100 Years" *Public Policy & Administration* vol. 24-2, pp. 153-174

Garner, Robert (2000); *Environmental Politics: Britain, Europe and the Global Environment* Palgrave, 2nd edition

Garry, John (2009); "Consociationalism and its critics: Evidence from the historic Northern Ireland Assembly election 2007" *Electoral Studies* vol. 28-3, pp. 458-466

Gash, Tom & Rutter, Jill (2011); "Reports and Surveys: The Quango Conundrum" *Political Quarterly* vol. 82-1, pp. 95-101

Gavin, Neil (2009); "Addressing climate change: a media perspective" *Environmental Politics* vol. 18-5, pp. 765-780

Gavin, Neil (2010); "Pressure Group Direct Action on Climate Change: The Role of the Media and the Web in Britain – A Case Study" *British Journal of Politics and International Relations* vol. 12-3, pp. 459-475

Gearty, Conor (2007); "Terrorism and Human Rights" *Government and Opposition* vol. 42-3, pp. 340-362

Gibbons, Virginia (2010); "Public Perceptions of the Media's Reporting of Politics Today" *Parliamentary Affairs* vol. 63-2, pp. 369-376

Gibbs, David (2000); "Ecological modernisation, regional economic development and regional development agencies" *Geoforum* vol. 31-1, pp. 9-19

Gibson, Alex & Asthana, Sheena (2012); "A Tangled Web: Complexity and Inequality in the English Local Government Finance Settlement" *Local Government Studies* vol. 38-3, pp. 301-319

Giddens, Anthony (1998); *The Third Way: The Renewal of Social Democracy* Polity Press

Gilad, Sharon (2008); "Exchange without Capture: The UK Financial Ombudsman Service's Struggle for Accepted Domain" *Public Administration* vol. 86-4, pp. 907-924

Gillespie, Andy & Benneworth, Paul (2002); "Industrial and regional policy in a devolved United Kingdom" in Adams, John & Robinson, Peter (eds.); *Devolution in Practice: Public Policy Differences within the UK* IPPR, pp. 69-85

Glover, Julian (2008); "Climate more urgent than economy" *The Guardian* (July 2, 2008)

Goodall, Kay (2004); "Ideas of 'Representation' in UK Court Structures" in Le Sueur, Andrew (ed.); *Building the UK's New Supreme Court: National and Comparative Perspectives* Oxford University Press, pp. 67-94

Gormley-Heenan, Cathy (2011); "Power Sharing in Northern Ireland" in Heffernan, Richard; Cowley, Philip & Hay, Colin (eds.); *Developments in British Politics 9* Palgrave, pp. 130-151

Gormley-Heenan, Cathy & Devine, Paula (2010); "The 'Us' in Trust: Who Trusts Northern Ireland's Political Institutions and Actors?" *Government and Opposition* vol. 45-2, pp. 143-165

Goss, Sue (2001); *Making Local Governance Work: Networks, Relationships and the Management of Change* Palgrave

Gouldson, Andrew & Murphy, Joseph (1996); "Ecological Modernization and the European Union" *Geoforum* vol. 27-1, pp. 11-21

Gowland, David; Turner, Arthur & Wright, Alex (2010); *Britain and European Integration Since 1945* Routledge

Grant, Wyn (1989); *Pressure Group Politics and Democracy in Britain* Philip Allen

Grant, Wyn (2001); "Pressure Politics: From 'Insider' Politics to Direct Action?" *Parliamentary Affairs* vol. 54-2, pp. 337-348

Grant, Wyn (2002a); *Economic Policy in Britain* Palgrave

Grant, Wyn (2002b); *Pressure Groups and British Politics* Macmillan

Grant, Wyn (2004); "Pressure Politics: The Changing World of Pressure Groups" *Parliamentary Affairs* vol. 57-2, pp. 408-419

Grant, Wyn (2005); "Pressure Politics: A Politics of Collective Consumption?" *Parliamentary Affairs* vol. 58-2, pp. 366-379

Grant, Wyn (2012); "Forty years studying British politics: The decline of Anglo-America" *British Politics* vol. 7-1, pp. 30-42

Gray, Clive (2000); "A 'Hollow State'?" in Pyper, Robert & Robins, Lynton (eds.); *United Kingdom Governance* Macmillan, pp. 283-300

Gray, Clive (2009); "Managing Cultural Policy: Pitfalls and Prospects" *Public Administration* vol. 87-3, pp. 574-585

Gray, Clive (2011); "Museums, Galleries, Politics and Management" *Public Policy and Administration* vol. 26-1, pp. 45-61

Greaves, Justin (2009); "Biopesticides, Regulatory Innovation and the Regulatory State" *Public Policy and Administration* vol. 24-3, pp. 245-264

Green-Pedersen, Christoffer & Stubager, Rune (2010); "The Political Conditionality of Mass Media Influence: When Do Parties Follow Mass Media Attention?" *British Journal of Political Science* vol. 40-3, pp. 663-677

Greenslade, Roy (2003); *Press Gang: How newspapers make profits from propaganda* Macmillan

Greenwood, John (2000); "Should the Civil Service become fully politicised?" in Robins, Lynton & Jones Bill (eds.), *Debates in British Politics Today* Manchester University Press, pp.63-77

Greenwood, John; Pyper, Robert & Wilson, David (2002); *New Public Administration in Britain* Routledge, 3rd edition

Greenwood, Justin & Dreger, Joanna (2013); "The Transparency Register: A European vanguard of strong lobby regulation?" *Interest Groups & Advocacy* vol. 2-2, pp. 139-162

Greer, Scott & Jarman, Holly (2010); "What Whitehall? Definitions, Demographics and the Changing Home Civil Service" *Public Policy and Administration* vol. 25-3, pp. 251-270

Greer, Steven (2010); "Anti-Terrorist Laws and the United Kingdom's 'Suspect Muslim Community': A Reply to Pantazis and Pemberton" *British Journal of Criminology* vol. 50-6, pp. 1171-1190

Gualmini, Elisabetta (2008); "Restructuring Weberian Bureaucracy: Competing Managerial Reforms in Europe and the United States" *Public Administration* vol. 86-1, pp. 75-94

Gunn, Sheila (2011); *So You want to be a Political Journalist* Biteback

Gunningham, Neil (2009); "Shaping Corporate Environmental Performance: A Review" *Environmental Policy and Governance* vol. 19-4, pp. 215-231

Gunther, Richard & Diamond, Larry (2003); "Species of Political Parties: A New Typology" *Party Politics* vol. 9-2, pp. 167-199

Gutiérrez Romero, Roxana; Haubrich, Dirk & McLean, Iain (2010); "To what extent does deprivation affect the performance of English local authorities?" *International Review of Administrative Sciences* vol. 76-1, pp. 137-170

Hakhverdian, Armen (2010); "Political Representation and its Mechanism: A Dynamic Left-Right Approach for the United Kingdom, 1976-2006" *British Journal of Political Science* vol. 40-4, pp. 835-856

Haldenby, Andrew; Parsons, Lucy; Rosen, Greg & Truss, Elizabeth (2009); "Fit for purpose" Reform Research Trust

Hamlin, Alan (2010); "Fixed-Term Parliaments: Electing the Opposition" *Politics* vol. 30-1, pp. 18-25

Hampton, Philip (2005); *Reducing administrative burdens: effective inspection and enforcement* (HM Treasury)

Hankivsky, Olena & Christoffersen, Ashlee (2011); "Gender mainstreaming in the United Kingdom: Current issues and future challenges" *British Politics* vol. 6-1, pp. 30-51

Hargrove, Erwin (2001); "The presidency and the prime ministership as institutions: an American perspective" *British Journal of Politics and International Relations* vol. 3-1, pp. 49-70

Harling, Philip (2001); *The Modern British State: An Historical Introduction* Polity

Harlow, Carol (2000); "Disposing of Dicey: from Legal Autonomy to Constitutional Discourse?" *Political Studies* vol. 48-2, pp. 356-369

Harries, Bethan & Richardson, Liz (2009); "Citizen aspirations: women, ethnicity and housing" in Durose, Catherine; Greasley, Stephen & Richardson, Liz (eds.); *Changing local governance, changing citizens* Policy Press, pp. 71-89

Harris, Margaret; Cairns, Ben & Hutchinson, Romayne (2004); ""So Many Tiers, So Many Agendas, So Many Pots of Money": The Challenge of English Regionalization for Voluntary and Community Organizations" *Social Policy & Administration* vol. 38-5, pp. 525-540

Harvey, David (1976); "The Marxian Theory of the State" *Antipode* vol. 8-2, pp. 80-89

Haverland, Markus (2000); "National Adaptation to European Integration: The Importance of Institutional Veto Points" *Journal of Public Policy* vol. 20-1, pp. 83-103

Hay, Colin (2006); "(What's Marxist about) Marxist State Theory?" in Hay, Colin; Lister, Michael & Marsh, David (eds.); *The State: Theories and Issues* Palgrave pp.59-78

Hay, Colin (2007); *Why We Hate Politics* Polity Press

Hay, Colin (2009); "Disenchanted with democracy, pissed off with politics" *British Politics* vol. 4-1, pp. 92-99

Hay, Colin (2010); "Chronicles of a Death Foretold: the Winter of Discontent and Construction of the Crisis of British Keynesianism" *Parliamentary Affairs* vol. 63-3, pp. 446-470

Hay, Colin & Lister, Michael (2006); "Introduction: Theories of the State" in Hay, Colin; Lister, Michael & Marsh, David (eds.); *The State: Theories and Issues* Palgrave pp. 1-20

Hazell, Robert (2005); "Westminster as a 'Three-In-One' Legislature for the UK and its Devolved Territories" in Hazell, Robert & Rawlings, Richard (eds.); *Devolution, Law Making and the Constitution* Imprint Academic, pp. 226-251

Hazell, Robert (2006); "The English Question" The Constitution Unit (first published in *Publius* vol. 36-1, January 2006)

Hazell, Robert (2007); "The Continuing Dynamism of Constitutional Reform" *Parliamentary Affairs* vol. 60-1, pp. 3-25

Heald, David & McLeod, Alasdair (2002); "Beyond Barnett? Financing devolution" in Adams, John & Robinson, Peter (eds.); *Devolution in Practice: Public Policy Differences within the UK* IPPR, pp.147-175

Hearl, Derek (1995); "Britain and Europe since 1945" in Ridley, F. F. & Michael Rush (eds.); *British Government and Politics since 1945* Oxford University Press, pp. 17-31

Heater, Derek (2002); "The History of Citizenship Education: A Comparative Outline" *Parliamentary Affairs* vol. 55-3, pp. 457-474

Heater, Derek (2004); *A Brief History of Citizenship* Edinburgh University Press

Heath, Anthony; de Graaf, Nan Dirk & Li, Yaojun (2010); "How fair is the route to the top? Perceptions of social mobility" in Park, Alison; Curtice, John; Clery, Elizabeth & Bryson, Caroline (eds.); *British Social Attitudes: Exploring Labour's Legacy. The 27th Report* National Centre for Social Research pp. 29-50

Heath, Anthony; Jowell, Roger & Curtice, John (1985); *How Britain Votes* Pergamon Press

Heffernan, Richard (2003a); "Prime ministerial predominance? Core executive politics in the UK" *British Journal of Politics and International Relations* vol. 5-3, pp. 347-372

Heffernan, Richard (2003b); "Political Parties and the Party System" in Dunleavy, Patrick; Gamble, Andrew; Heffernan, Richard & Peele, Gillian (eds.); *Developments in British Politics 7* Palgrave, pp. 119-139

Heffernan, Richard (2005a); "Why the Prime Minister cannot be a President: Comparing Institutional Imperatives in Britain and America" *Parliamentary Affairs* vol. 58-1, pp. 53-70

Heffernan, Richard (2005b); "Exploring (and Explaining) the British Prime Minister" *British Journal of Politics and International Relations* vol.7-3, pp. 605-620

Heffernan, Richard (2006); "The Blair Style of Central Government" in Dunleavy, Patrick; Heffernan, Richard; Cowley, Philip & Hay, Colin (eds.); *Developments in British Politics 8* Palgrave, pp. 17-35

Heffernan, Richard (2013); "There's No Need for the '-isation': The Prime Minister Is Merely Prime Ministerial" *Parliamentary Affairs* vol. 66-3, pp. 636-645

Helbling, Marc & Tresch, Anke (2011); "Measuring party positions and issue salience from media coverage: Discussing and cross-validating new indicators" *Electoral Studies* vol. 30-1, pp. 174-183

Hellowell, Mark & Pollock, Allyson (2007); "New Development: The PFI: Scotland's Plan for Expansion and its Implications" *Public Money and Management* vol. 27-5, pp. 351-354

Helms, Ludger (2008); "Governing in the Media Age: The Impact of the Mass Media on Executive Leadership in Contemporary Democracies" *Government and Opposition* vol. 43-1, pp. 26-54

Henn, Matt & Foard, Nick (2012); "Young People, Political Participation and Trust in Britain" *Parliamentary Affairs* vol. 65-1, pp. 47-67

Henn, Matt; Weinstein, Mark & Forrest, Sarah (2005); "Uninterested Youth? Young People's attitudes towards Party Politics in Britain" *Political Studies* vol. 53-3, pp. 556-578

Henn, Matt; Weinstein, Mark & Wring, Dominic (2002); "A generation apart? Youth and political participation in Britain" *British Journal of Politics and International Relations* vol. 4-2, pp. 167-192

Hennessy, Peter (2000a); "The Blair Style and the Requirements of Twenty-first Century Premiership" *Political Quarterly* vol. 71-4, pp. 386-395

Hennessy, Peter (2000b); *The Prime Minister: The Office and its Holders since 1945* Allen Lane

Hennessy, Peter (2005); "Rulers and Servants of the State: The Blair Style of Government 1997-2004" *Parliamentary Affairs* vol. 58-1, pp. 6-16

Herrschel, Tassilo & Newman, Peter (2000); "New Regions in England and Germany: An Examination of the Interaction of Constitutional Structures, Formal Regions and Informal Institutions" *Urban Studies* vol. 37-7, pp. 1185-1202

Heywood, A. (2007); *Politics* Palgrave 3rd edition

Hiebert, Janet (2005); "Interpreting a Bill of Rights: The Importance of Legislative Rights Review" *British Journal of Political Science* vol. 35-2, pp. 235-255

Hiebert, Janet (2006); "Parliament and the Human Rights Act: Can the JCHR help facilitate a culture of rights?" *International Journal of Constitutional Law* vol. 4-1, pp. 1-38

Hill, Christopher (1979); "Britain's elusive role in world politics" *British Journal of International Studies* vol. 5-3, pp. 248-259

Hindmoor, Andrew (2006); "Public Choice" in Hay, Colin; Lister, Michael & Marsh, David (eds.); *The State: Theories and Issues* Palgrave pp. 79-97

HM Government (2008) *Code of Practice on Consultation* Crown Copyright

Hodgson, Lesley (2004); "The National Assembly for Wales, Civil Society and Consultation" *Politics* vol. 24-2, pp. 88-95

Holliday, Ian (2000); "Is the British State Hollowing Out?" *Political Quarterly* vol. 71-2, pp. 167-176

Hood, Christopher & Dixon, Ruth (2012); "A Model of Cost-cutting in Government? The Great Management Revolution in UK Central Government Reconsidered" *Public Administration* vol. 91-1, pp. 114-134

Hooghe, Liesbet & Marks, Gary (2003); "Unraveling the Central State, but How? Types of Multi-level Governance" *American Political Science Review* vol. 97-2, pp. 233-243

Hopkin, Jonathan (2011); "Elections and Electoral Systems" in Jones, Erik; Heywood, Paul M.; Rhodes, Martin & Sedelmeier, Ulrich (eds.); *Developments in European Politics* Palgrave, pp. 81-99

Hopkin, Jonathan & Wincott, Daniel (2006); "New Labour, Economic Reform and the European Social Model" *British Journal of Politics and International Relations* vol.8-1, pp. 50-68

Hopkins, John (2002); *Devolution in Context: Regional, Federal and Devolved Government in the European Union* Cavendish Publishing

House of Commons (2001a); *Measuring the Performance of Government Departments* Report by the Comptroller and Auditor General. HC301 session 2000-2001: 22 March 2001 (The Stationery Office, London)

House of Commons (2001b); *Better Regulation: Making Good Use of Regulatory Impact Assessments* Report by the Comptroller and Auditor General. HC329 session 2001-2002: 15 November 2001 (The Stationery Office, London)

House of Commons Library (2006); "Judicial Review: A short guide to claims in the Administrative Court" *Research Paper 06/44*, 28 September 2006

Howard, Alistair (2006); "UK Corporate Governance: To What End a New Regulatory State?" *West European Politics* vol. 29-3, pp. 410-432

Hubert, Agnès & Stratigaki, Maria (2011); "The European Institute for Gender Equality: A window of opportunity for gender equality policies?" *European Journal of Women's Studies* vol. 18-2, pp. 169-181

Humphreys, Peter & Simpson, Seamus (2008); "Globalization, the 'Competition' State and the Rise of the 'Regulatory' State in European Telecommunications" *Journal of Common Market Studies* vol. 46-4, pp. 849-874

Hunt, Karen (2009); "Rethinking Activism: Lessons from the History of Women's Politics" *Parliamentary Affairs* vol. 62-3, pp. 211-226

Hutchings, Kimberly (2002); "Feminism and Global Citizenship" in Dower, Nigel & Williams, John (eds.); *Global Citizenship: A Critical Reader* Edinburgh University Press, pp. 53-62

Hutchins, Brett & Lester, Libby (2006); "Environmental protest and tap-dancing with the media in the information age" *Media, Culture & Society* vol. 28-3, pp. 433-451

Hutton, Will (1995); *The State We're In* Jonathan Cape, London

Huysmans, Jef & Buonfino, Alessandra (2008); "Politics of Exception and Unease: Immigration, asylum and terrorism in parliamentary debates in the UK" *Political Studies* vol. 56-4, pp. 766-788

Imray, Linda & Middleton, Audrey (2002); "Public and Private: Marking the Boundaries" in Jackson, Stevi & Scott, Sue (eds.); *Gender: A Sociological Reader* Routledge, pp. 155-158

Inglehart, Ronald (1977); *The Silent Revolution: Changing Values and Political Styles Among Western Publics* Princeton University Press

Inglehart, Ronald (1990); *Culture Shift in Advanced Industrial Society* Princeton University Press

Internet World Stats at www.internetworldstats.com/stats4.htm (accessed 31 August 2010)

Internet World Stats at www.internetworldstats.com/stats9.htm (accessed 31 August 2010)

Iversen, Torben & Soskice, David (2006); "Electoral Institutions and the Politics of Coalitions: Why Some Democracies Redistribute More Than Others" *American Political Science Review* vol. 100-2, pp. 165-181

Iyengar, Shanto (1990); "The Accessibility Bias in Politics: Television News and Public Opinion" *International Journal of Public Opinion Research* vol. 2-1, pp. 1-15

Jackson, Peter (2009); "The size and scope of the public sector" in Bovaird, Tony & Löffler, Elke (eds.); *Public Management and Governance* Routledge, 2nd edition, pp. 27-40

Jalalzai, Farida & Krook, Mona Lena (2010); "Beyond Hillary and Benazir: Women's Political Leadership Worldwide" *International Political Science Review* vol. 31-1, pp. 5-21

James, Simon (1992); *British Cabinet Government* Routledge

Jay, Lord of Ewelme (2008); "Who makes British foreign policy?" *Policy & Politics* vol. 36-3, pp. 449-456

Jeffery, Charlie (2006); "Devolution and the Lopsided State" in Dunleavy, Patrick; Heffernan, Richard; Cowley, Philip & Hay, Colin (eds.); *Developments in British Politics 8* Palgrave, pp. 138-158

Jenkins, Kate (2008); "Politicians and Civil Servants: Unfinished Business – The Next Steps Report, Fulton and the Future" *Political Quarterly* vol. 79-3, pp. 418-425

Jensen, Carsten (2010); "Neo-functionalism" in Cini, Michelle & Borragán, Nieves (eds.); *European Union Politics* Oxford University Press, 3rd edition, pp. 71-85

Jensen, Christian; Slapin, Jonathan & König, Thomas (2007); "Who Calls for a Common EU Foreign Policy? Partisan Constraints on CFSP Reform" *European Union Politics* vol. 8-3, pp. 387-410

John, Peter (2004); "Strengthening Political Leadership? More Than Mayors" in Stoker, Gerry & Wilson, David (eds.); *British Local Government into the 21st Century* Palgrave, pp. 43-59

John, Peter (2009); "Citizen governance: where it came from, where it's going" in Durose, Catherine; Greasley, Stephen & Richardson, Liz (eds.); *Changing local governance, changing citizens* Policy Press, pp. 13-29

John, Peter; Fieldhouse, Edward & Liu, Hanhua (2011); "How Civic is the Civic Culture? Explaining Community Participation Using the 2005 English Citizenship Survey" *Political Studies* vol. 59-2, pp. 230-252

Johnston Miller, Karen & McTavish, Duncan (2009); " Editorial: Special Issue: Gender and Equality in Public Life" *Public Policy & Administration* vol. 24-2, pp. 115-118

Jones, Alistair (1998); "New Labour Government: What About Electoral Reform?" *Talking Politics* vol. 10-2, pp. 143-145

Jones, Alistair (2007a); *Britain and the European Union* Edinburgh University Press

Jones, Alistair (2007b); "Teaching Citizenship?" *Teaching Public Administration* vol. 9-2, pp. 1-17

Jones, Alistair (2008); *A Glossary of the European Union* Edinburgh University Press

Jones, Derek (2000); *A Ten Year History of the New Zealand Federation of Ethnic Councils Inc. 1989-1999* NZ Federation of Ethnic Councils

Jones, Kathleen (1990); "Citizenship in a Woman-friendly Polity" *Signs: Journal of Women in Culture and Society* vol. 15-4, pp. 781-812

Jordan, Andrew (2003); "The Europeanization of National Government and Policy: A Departmental Perspective" *British Journal of Political Science* vol. 33-2, pp. 261-282

Jordan, Andrew & Lorenzoni, Irene (2007); "Is There Now a Political Climate for Policy Change? Policy and Politics after the Stern Review" *Political Quarterly* vol. 78-2, pp. 310-319

Jordan, Andrew; Wurzel, Rüdiger; Zito, Anthony & Brückner, Lars (2003); "Policy Innovation or 'Muddling Through'? 'New' Environmental Policy Instruments in the United Kingdom" *Environmental Politics* vol. 12-1, pp. 179-198

Judge, David (2004); "Whatever Happened to Parliamentary Democracy in the United Kingdom?" *Parliamentary Affairs* vol. 57-3, pp. 682-701

Juss, Satvinder Singh (2006); "Constitutionalising Rights Without a Constitution: The British Experience under Article 6 of the Human Rights Act 1998" *Statute Law Review* vol. 27-1, pp. 29-60

Karagiannis, Yannis (2010); "Collegiality and the Politics of European Competition Policy" *European Union Politics* vol. 11-1, pp. 143-164

Karp, Jeffrey & Banducci, Susan (2008); "Political Efficacy and Participation in Twenty-Seven Democracies: How Electoral Systems Shape political Behaviour" *British Journal of Political Science* vol. 38-2, pp. 311-334

Kavanagh, Aileen (2006); "The Role of Parliamentary Intention in Adjudication under the Human Rights Act 1998" *Oxford Journal of Legal Studies* vol. 26-1, pp. 179-206

Kavanagh, Aileen (2011); "From Appellate Committee to United Kingdom Supreme Court: Independence, Activism and Transparency" in Lee, James (ed.); *From House of Lords to Supreme Court: Judges, Jurists and the Process of Judging* Hart Publishing, pp. 35-55

Kay, Adrian (2005); "Territorial Justice and Devolution" *British Journal of Politics and International Relations* vol. 7-4, pp. 544-560

Keating, Michael (2002); "Devolution and public policy in the United Kingdom: divergence or convergence?" in Adams, John & Robinson, Peter (eds.); *Devolution in Practice: Public Policy Differences within the UK* IPPR, pp. 3-21

Kelly, Richard (2008); "It's Only Made Things Worse: A Critique of Electoral Reform in Britain" *Political Quarterly* vol. 79-2, pp. 260-268

Kelly, Richard; Gay, Oonagh & White, Isobel (2005); "The Constitution: Into the Sidings" *Parliamentary Affairs* vol. 58-2, pp. 215-229

Kelso, Alexandra (2006); "Reforming the House of Lords: Navigating Representation, Democracy and Legitimacy at Westminster" *Parliamentary Affairs* vol. 59-4, pp. 563-581

Kelso, Alexandra (2007a); "The House of Commons Modernisation Committee: Who Needs It?" *British Journal of Politics and International Relations* vol. 9-1, pp. 138-157

Kelso, Alexandra (2007b); "Parliament and Political Disengagement: Neither Waving nor Drowning" *Political Quarterly* vol. 78-3, pp. 364-373

Kenny, Michael (2012); "The Political Theory of Recognition: The Case of the 'White Working Class'" *British Journal of Politics and International Relations* vol. 14-1, pp. 19-38

Kerr, Peter & Kettell, Simon (2006); "In Defence of British Politics: The Past, Present and Future of the Discipline" *British Politics* vol. 1-1, pp. 3-25

Kilby, Ian (2010); "The Interpretation of Article 260 TFEU (ex 228 EC)" *European Law Review* vol. 35-3, pp. 370-386

King, Anthony & Allen, Nicholas (2010); "'Off With Their Heads': British Prime Ministers and the Power to Dismiss" *British Journal of Political Science* vol. 40-2, pp. 249-278

King, Desmond & Waldron, Jeremy (1988); "Citizenship, Social Citizenship and the Defence of Welfare Provision" *British Journal of Political Science* vol. 18-4, pp. 415-443

King, Roger & Kendall, Gavin 2004); *The State, Democracy and Globalization* Palgrave

Kirby, Jill (2009); "From Broken Families to the Broken Society" *Political Quarterly* vol. 80-2, pp. 243-247

Kirby, Michael (2011); "A Darwinian Reflection on Judicial Values and Appointments to Final National Courts" in Lee, James (ed.); *From House of Lords to Supreme Court: Judges, Jurists and the Process of Judging* Hart Publishing, pp. 9-34

Kirkham, Richard; Thompson, Brian & Buck, Trevor (2009); "Putting the Ombudsman into Constitutional Context" *Parliamentary Affairs* vol. 62-4, pp. 600-617

Kisby, Ben (2007); "New Labour and Citizenship Education" *Parliamentary Affairs* vol. 60-1, pp. 84-101

Kisby, Ben (2010); "The Big Society: Power to the People?" *Political Quarterly* vol. 81-4, pp. 484-491

Kjær, Anne Mette (2004); *Governance* Polity Press

Klausen, Jytte (2009); "Why religion has become more salient in Europe: four working hypotheses about secularization and religiosity in contemporary politics" *European Political Science* vol. 8-3, pp. 289-300

Klug, Francesca & Starner, Kier (2005); "Standing Back from the Human Rights Act: how effective is it five years on?" *Public Law* pp. 716-728

Klüver, Heike & Saurugger, Sabine (2013); "Opening the black box: The professionalization of interest groups in the European Union" *Interest Groups & Advocacy* vol. 2-2, pp. 185-205

Knill, Christoph; Tosun, Jale & Bauer, Michael (2009); "Neglected Faces of Europeanization: The Differential Impact of the EU on the Dismantling and Expansion of Domestic Policies" *Public Administration* vol. 87-3, pp. 519-537

Knox, Colin (2011); "Cohesion, sharing, and integration in Northern Ireland" *Environment and Planning C: Government and Policy* vol. 29-3, pp. 548-566

Koppell, Jonathan (2003); *The Politics of Quasi-Government: Hybrid Organizations and the Dynamics of Bureaucratic Control* Cambridge University Press

Korris, Matt (2011); "Standing up for Scrutiny: How and Why Parliament Should Make Better Law" *Parliamentary Affairs* vol. 64-3, pp. 564-574

Kostakopoulou, Dora (2008); "The evolution of european union citizenship" *European Political Science* vol. 7-3, pp. 285-295

Kotler-Berkowitz, Laurence (2001); "Religion and Voting Behaviour in Great Britain: A Reassessment" *British Journal of Political Science* vol. 31-3, pp. 523-554

Krieger, Kristian & Rogers, M. Brooke (2010);"Green partnerships in Britain's energy sector – classifying non-governmental organisations and exploring their varying potential to co-operate with energy companies" *Environmental Politics* vol. 19-6, pp. 910-929

Krook, Mona Lena (2010); "Why Are Fewer Women than Men Elected? Gender and the Dynamics of Candidate Selection" *Political Studies Review* vol. 8-2, pp. 155-168

Krook, Mona Lena; Lovenduski, Joni & Squires, Judith (2009); "Gender Quotas and Models of Political Citizenship" *British Journal of Political Science* vol. 39-4, pp. 781-803

Kumarasingham, Harshan (2006); "'For the Good of the Party': An Analysis of the Fall of British Conservative Party Leaders from Chamberlain to Thatcher" *Political Science* vol. 58-2, pp. 43-63

Laffin, Martin (2007); "Coalition-formation and Centre-Periphery Relations in a National Political Party: The Liberal Democrats in a Devolved Britain" *Party Politics* vol. 13-6, pp. 651-668

Laffin, Martin (2008); "Local Government Modernisation in England: A Critical Review of the LGMA Evaluation Studies" *Local Government Studies* vol. 34-1, pp. 109-125

Laffin, Martin; Shaw, Eric & Taylor, Gerald (2007); "The New Sub-national Politics of the British Labour Party" *Party Politics* vol. 13-1, pp. 88-108

Lambert, David & Machon, Paul (2001); "Introduction: setting the scene for geography and citizenship education" in Lambert, David & Machon, Paul (eds.); *Citizenship through Secondary Geography* Routledge/Falmer, pp. 1-8

Landman, Todd (2005); "Review Article: The Political Science of Human Rights" *British Journal of Political Science* vol. 35-3, pp. 549-572

Lankina, Tomila & Phillips, Michael (2009); "The House of Lords: The Working of the Electoral Process in the 1999 Act of Parliament" *Political Quarterly* vol. 80-1, pp. 42-48

Lasswell, Harold (1936); *Politics: Who Gets What, When, How* McGraw Hill

Law Commission; (2008); "Administrative Redress: Public Bodies and the Citizen. A Consultation Paper" Law Commission Consultation paper No. 187

Layton-Henry, Zig (1992); *The Politics of Immigration: Immigration, 'Race' and 'Race' Relations in Post-war Britain* Blackwell

Le Sueur, Andrew (2004); "The Conception of the UK's New Supreme Court" in Le Sueur, Andrew (ed.); *Building the UK's New Supreme Court: National and Comparative Perspectives* Oxford University Press, pp. 3-20

Leach, Steve (2009); "Reorganisation, Reorganisation, Reorganisation: A Critical Analysis of the Sequence of Local Government Reorganisation Initiatives, 1979-2008" *Local Government Studies* vol. 35-1, pp. 61-74

Leach, Steve (2010); "The Labour Government's Local Government Agenda 1997-2009: The Impact on Member-Officer Relationships" *Local Government Studies* vol. 36-3, pp. 323-339

Leach, Steve & Wilson, David (2008); "Diluting the Role of Party Groups? Implications of the 2006 Local Government White Paper" *Local Government Studies* vol. 30-3, pp. 303-321

Lee, Bill (2012); "New public management, accounting, regulators and moral panics" *International Journal of Public Sector Management* vol. 25-3, pp. 192-202

Lee, James (2011); "Introduction" in Lee, James (ed.); *From House of Lords to Supreme Court: Judges, Jurists and the Process of Judging* Hart Publishing, pp. 1-7

Lees-Marshment, Jennifer (2008); *Political marketing and British political parties* Manchester University Press, 2nd edition

Leonard, Dick (1996); *Elections in Britain Today* Macmillan, Third Edition

Lester, Anthony (2008); "Citizenship and the Constitution" *Political Quarterly* vol. 79-3, pp. 388-403

Lester, Libby (2006); "Lost in the wilderness? Celebrity, protest and the news" *Journalism Studies* vol. 7-6, pp. 907-921

Levy, Jessica (2010); "Public Bill Committees: An Assessment Scrutiny Sought; Scrutiny Gained" *Parliamentary Affairs* vol. 63-3, pp. 534-544

Lewis-Beck, Michael & Nadeau, Richard (2011); "Economic voting theory: Testing new dimensions" *Electoral Studies* vol. 30-2, pp. 288-294

Lijphart, Arend (1985); "The Field of Electoral Systems Research: A Critical Survey" *Electoral Studies* vol. 4-1, pp. 3-14

Lister, Michael (2005); "'Marshall-ing' Social and Political Citizenship: Towards a Unified Conception of Citizenship" *Government and Opposition* vol. 40-4, pp. 471-491

Lister, Ruth (2003); *Citizenship: Feminist Perspectives* Palgrave 2nd edition

Lister, Ruth (2005); "Being Feminist" *Government and Opposition* vol. 40-3, pp. 442-463

Little, Richard (2008); "In response to Lord Jay: 'Who makes British foreign policy?'" *Policy & Politics* vol. 36-3, pp. 457-458

Local Government Ombudsman (2010); "The Local Government Ombudsman's Annual Review: Leicester City Council for the year ending 31 March 2010"

Loveland, Ian (2003); *Constitutional Law, Administrative Law and Human Rights: A Critical Introduction* (Butterworths) 3rd edition

Lovell, Heather; Bulkeley, Harriet & Owens, Susan (2009); "Converging agendas? Energy and climate change policies in the UK" *Environment and Planning C: Government and Policy* vol. 27-1, pp. 90-109

Lovenduski, Joni (2008); "State Feminism and Women's Movements" *West European Politics* vol. 31-1/2, pp. 169-194

Lowndes, Vivien (2000); "Women and Social Capital: A Comment on Hall's 'Social Capital in Britain'" *British Journal of Political Science* vol. 30, pp. 533-540

Lowndes, Vivien (2004); "Reformers or Recidivists? Has Local Government Really Changed?" in Stoker, Gerry & Wilson, David (eds.); *British Local Government into the 21st Century* Palgrave, pp. 230-246

Lowndes, Vivien & Pratchett, Lawrence (2012); "Local Governance under the Coalition Government: Austerity, Localism and the 'Big Society'" *Local Government Studies* vol. 38-1, pp. 21-40

Luke, Timothy (2005); "Neither Sustainable or Development: Reconsidering Sustainability in Development" *Sustainable Development* vol. 13-4, pp. 228-238

Lundberg, Thomas Carl (2007); "Electoral System Reviews in New Zealand, Britain and Canada: A Critical Comparison" *Government and Opposition* vol. 42-4, pp. 471-490

Lusk, Sean (2008); "Why does government find it so hard to be strategic? An analysis of what stands in the way of strategic work in the public sector, and of ways to overcome the obstacles." Public Administration Committee Annual Conference, University of York

Lynch, Peter (2006); "Governing Devolution: Understanding the Office of First Ministers in Scotland and Wales" *Parliamentary Affairs* vol. 59-3, pp. 420-436

Macalister, Terry (2008); "Clean tech: Green energy is the modern gold rush" *The Guardian* (July 2, 2008)

Macaulay, Michael & Lawton, Alan (2006); "Changing the Standards? Assessing the Impact of the Committee for Standards in Public Life on Local Government in England" *Parliamentary Affairs* vol. 59-3, pp. 474-490

Mackay, R. Ross & Davies, Rhys (2012); "Collective Learning, Effective Demand, Loss of Work and Loss of Direction: The Growing Regional Divide within the UK" *Regional Studies* vol. 46-7, pp. 859-871

Maddock, Su (2009); "Gender Still Matters and Impacts on Public Value and Innovation and the Public Reform Process" *Public Policy & Administration* vol. 24-2, pp. 141-152

Madeley, John (2009); "Unequally yoked: the antinomies of church-state separation in Europe and the USA" *European Political Science* vol. 8-3, pp. 273-288

Maer, Lucinda; Hazell, Robert; King, Simon; Russell, Meg; Trench, Alan & Sanford, Mark (2004); "The Constitution: Dragging the Constitution out of the Shadows?" *Parliamentary Affairs* vol. 57-2, pp.253-268

Maier, Jürgen & Rittberger, Berthold (2008); "Shifting Europe's Boundaries: Mass Media, Public Opinion and the Enlargement of the EU" *European Union Politics* vol. 9-2, pp. 243-267

Mair, Peter (2007); "Political Opposition and the European Union" *Government and Opposition* vol. 42-1, pp. 1-17

Majone, Giandomenico (1997); "From the Positive to the Regulatory State: Causes and Consequences of Changes in the Mode of Governance" *Journal of Public Policy* vol. 17-2, pp. 139-167

Majone, Giandomenico (1998); "Rise of the Regulatory State in Europe" in Baldwin, Robert; Scott, Colin & Hood, Christopher (eds.); *A Reader on Regulation* Oxford University Press, pp. 192-215

Majone, Giandomenico (1999); "The Regulatory State and its Legitimacy Problems" *West European Politics* vol. 22-1, pp. 1-24

Mallesson, Kate (2009); "Diversity in the Judiciary: The Case For Positive Action" *Journal of Law and Society* vol. 36-3, pp. 376-402

Mandel, Hadas (2009); "Configurations of gender inequality: the consequences of ideology and public policy" *British Journal of Sociology* vol. 60-4, pp. 693-719

Maor, Moshe & Stevens, Handley (1997); "Measuring the Impact of New Public Management and European Integration on Recruitment and Training in the UK Civil Service" *Public Administration* vol. 75-3, pp. 531-551

Marks, Gary & Hooghe, Liesbet (2004); "Contrasting Visions of Multi-level Governance" in Bache, Ian & Flinders, Matthew (eds.); *Multi-level Governance* Oxford University Press, pp. 15-30

Marlow, Sue; Vershinina, Natalia & Rodionova, Yulia (2013); "SME financing and credibility: does entrepreneur's gender matter?" Institute for Small Business & Entrepreneurship Conference, Cardiff, 12-13 November

Marriage, Divorce and Adoption Statistics, England and Wales (Series FM2), No. 35, (2007) available at www.ons.gov.uk/ons/publications/re-reference-tables.html?edition=tcm%3A77-39669

Marsden, Bill (2001); "Citizenship education: permeation or pervasion? Some historical pointers" in Lambert, David & Machon, Paul (eds.); *Citizenship through Secondary Geography* Routledge/Falmer, pp. 11-30

Marsh, David (2009); "The future of politics?" *British Politics* vol. 4-1, pp. 117-126

Marsh, David; Smith, M. J. & Richards, D. (2000); "Bureaucrats, Politicians and Reform in Whitehall: Analysing the Bureau-Shaping Model" *British Journal of Political Science* vol. 30-3, pp. 461-482

Marshall, T. H. (1963); "Citizenship and Social Class" in Marshall, T. H.; *Sociology at the Crossroads and other essays* Heinemann

Massey, Andrew & Pyper, Robert (2005); *Public Management and Modernisation in Britain* Palgrave

Masterman, Roger (2009); "Labour's 'Juridification' of the Constitution" *Parliamentary Affairs* vol. 62-3, pp. 476-492

Matthews, Felicity (2008); "Redefining the Scope of Public Service Delivery – The UK Government and the Challenge of Climate Change" Paper presented at the Public Administration Committee (PAC) Annual Conference, University of York

Matthews, Felicity (2011); "The capacity to co-ordinate – Whitehall governance and the challenge of climate change" *Public Policy and Administration* vol. 26-2, pp. 169-189

Mawson, John (2007); "Regional governance in England: past experience, future directions" *International Journal of Public Sector Management* vol. 20-6, pp. 548-566

Mawson, John (2009); "Local Economic Development and the Sub-National Review: Old Wine in New Bottles?" *Local Government Studies* vol. 35-1, pp. 39-59

May, Peter (2007); "Regulatory Regimes and Accountability" *Regulation & Governance* vol. 1-1, pp. 8-26

McAuley, James (2003); *An Introduction to Politics, State and Society* Sage

McAuley, James & Tonge, Jonathan (2010); "Britishness (and Irishness) in Northern Ireland since the Good Friday Agreement" *Parliamentary Affairs* vol. 63-2, pp. 266-285

McCormick, John (2011); *Understanding the European Union: A Concise Introduction* Palgrave 5th edition

McCormick, John (2012); *Contemporary Britain* Palgrave 3rd edition

McCourt, David (2009); "What was Britain's "East of Suez Role"? Reassessing the Withdrawal, 1964-1968" *Diplomacy & Statecraft* vol. 20-3, pp. 453-472

McCourt, David (2011); "Rethinking Britain's *Role in the World* for a New Decade: The Limits of Discursive Therapy and the Promise of Field Theory" *British Journal of Politics and International Relations* vol. 13-2, pp. 145-164

McElroy, Gail & Benoit, Kenneth (2007); "Party Groups and Policy Positions in the European Parliament" *Party Politics* vol. 13-1, pp. 5-28

McGarry, John & O'Leary, Brendan (2006a); "Consociational Theory, Northern Ireland's Conflict, and its Agreement. Part 1: What Consociationalists Can Learn from Northern Ireland" *Government and Opposition* vol. 41-1, pp. 43-63

McGarry, John & O'Leary, Brendan (2006b); "Consociational Theory, Northern Ireland's Conflict, and its Agreement. Part 2: What Critics of Consociation Can Learn from Northern Ireland" *Government and Opposition* vol. 41-2, pp. 249-277

McGlynn, Catherine & Mycock, Andrew (2010); "Parliamentary Affairs: A Special Edition of Britishness" *Parliamentary Affairs* vol. 63-2, pp. 223-228

McGrattan, Cillian (2010); "Learning from the past or laundering history? Consociational narratives and state intervention in Northern Ireland" *British Politics* vol. 5-1, pp. 92-113

McLaren, Laura (2012); "Immigration and Trust in Politics in Britain" *British Journal of Political Science* vol. 42-1, pp. 163-185

McLean, Iain (2008a); "Review Article: In Riker's Footsteps" *British Journal of Political Science* vol. 39-1, pp. 195-210

McLean, Iain (2008b); "Climate Change and UK Politics: From Brynle Williams to Sir Nicholas Stern" *Political Quarterly* vol. 79-2, pp. 184-193

McLeod, Douglas & Detenber, Benjamin (1999); "Framing Effects of Television News Coverage of Social Protest" *Journal of Communication* vol. 49-3, pp. 3-23

McNeill, Desmond (2000); "The Concept of Sustainable Development" in Lee, Keekok; Holland, Alan & McNeill, Desmond (eds.); *Global Sustainable Development in the 21st Century* Edinburgh University Press, pp. 10-29

McRobbie, Angela (2002); "Clubs to Companies: Notes on the Decline of Political Culture in Speeded Up Creative Worlds" *Cultural Studies* vol. 16-4, pp. 516-531

Meadowcroft, John (2001); "Community Politics, Representation and the Limits of Deliberative Democracy" *Local Government Studies* vol. 27-3, pp. 25-42

Mellett, Russell (2009); "A Principles-based Approach to the Barnett Formula" *Political Quarterly* vol. 80-1, pp. 76-83

Messer, Anne; Berkhout, Joost & Lowery, David (2010); "The Density of the EU Interest System: A Test of the ESA Model" *British Journal of Political Science* vol. 41-1, pp. 161-190

Micklem, Ros (2009); "Gender Equality and the Equality and Human Rights Commission" *Public Policy & Administration* vol. 24-2, pp. 213-217

Miers, David & Lambert, David (2002); "Law making in Wales: Wales Legislation on-line" *Public Law* pp. 663-669

Mike, Károly (2007); "An Unhappy Consensus: EU Membership and Party Collusion in Hungary" *World Political Science Review* vol. 3-4, pp. 1-32

Milburn, Richard (2012); "Mainstreaming the environment into postwar recovery: the case for 'ecological development'" *International Affairs* vol. 88-5, pp. 1083-1100

Miller, Laura (2008); "e-Petitions at Westminster: the Way Forward for Democracy?" *Parliamentary Affairs* vol. 62-1, pp. 162-177

Miller, Raymond (1999); "From Pre-selection to Coalition Government: Scotland and New Zealand Compared" Paper to the *Political Studies Association, UK*, 23-25 March 1999

Miller, Raymond (2000); "Adapting to Proportional Representation: The Public and Political Response to Coalition Failure in New Zealand" Paper to the *Political Studies Association, UK*, 10-13 April 2000

Ministry of Justice (2013); *Statistics on Race and the Criminal Justice System 2012: A Ministry of Justice publication under Section 95 of the Criminal Justice Act 1991*

Mitchell, James (2005); "Scotland: Devolution Is Not Just for Christmas" in Trench, Alan (ed.); *The Dynamics of Devolution: The State of the Nations 2005* imprint academic pp. 23-41

Modood, Tariq (2005); *Multicultural Politics: Racism, Ethnicity and Muslims in Britain* Edinburgh University Press

Mol, Arthur (2000); "The environmental movement in an era of ecological modernisation" *Geoforum* vol. 31-1, pp. 45-56

Moran, Michael (2002); "Review Article: Understanding the Regulatory State" *British Journal of Political Science* vol. 32-2, pp. 391-413

Moran, Michael (2003); *The British Regulatory State: High Modernism and Hyper-Innovation* Oxford University Press

Moreno, Luis (2006); "Scotland, Catalonia, Europeanization and the 'Moreno Question' " *Scottish Affairs*, no. 54, pp. 1-21

Morgenstern, Scott & Potthoff, Richard (2003); "The Components of Elections: District-Time Effects, District Heterogenity, and Volatility" Working Paper 213, Institute of Political and Social Sciences, Barcelona

Morison, John (2001); "Democracy, Governance and Governmentality: Civic Public Space and Constitutional Renewal in Northern Ireland" *Oxford Journal of Legal Studies* vol. 21-1, pp. 287-310

Morrell, Kevin (2009); "Governance and the Public Good" *Public Administration* vol. 87-3, pp. 538-556

Morris, Justin (2011); "How Great is Britain? Power, Responsibility and Britain's Future Global Role" *British Journal of Politics and International Relations* vol. 13-3, pp. 326-347

Mosher, James & Trubek, David (2003); "Alternative Approaches to Governance in the EU: EU Social Policy and the European Employment Strategy" *Journal of Common Market Studies* vol. 41-1, pp. 63-88

Mulgan, Richard (2000); "'Accountability': An Ever-Expanding Concept?" *Public Administration* vol. 78-3, pp. 555-573

Mullard, Maurice (1995); "Introduction" in Mullard, Maurice (ed.); *Policy-Making in Britain* Routledge

Müller, Wolfgang; Bovens, Mark; Chrsitensen, Jørgen; Jenny, Marcelo & Yesilkagit, Kutsal (2010); "Legal Europeanization: Comparative Perspectives" *Public Administration* vol. 88-1, pp. 75-87

Murphy, Joseph (2000); "Ecological modernisation" *Geoforum* vol. 31-1, pp. 1-8

Murphy, Joseph & Gouldson, Andrew (2000); "Environmental policy and industrial innovation: integrating environment and economy through ecological modernisation" *Geoforum* vol. 31-1, pp. 33-44

Murphy, Kristina; Tyler, Tom & Curtis, Amy (2009); "Nurturing regulatory compliance: Is procedural justice effective when people question the legitimacy of the law?" *Regulation and Governance* vol. 3-1, pp. 1-26

Mycock, Andrew (2010); "British Citizenship and the Legacy of Empires" *Parliamentary Affairs* vol. 63-2, pp. 339-355

National Audit Office (2008); *Regulatory quality: How regulators are implementing the Hampton vision* National Audit Office, London

Nedergaard, Peter (2008); "The Reform of the 2003 Common Agricultural Policy: an advocacy coalition explained" *Policy Studies* vol. 29-2, pp. 179-195

Needham, Catherine (2006); "Customer Care and the Public Service Ethos" *Public Administration* vol. 84-4, pp. 845-860

Negrine, Ralph (1994); *Politics and the Mass Media in Britain* Routledge 2nd edition

Niblett, Robin (2007); "Choosing between America and Europe: a new context for British foreign policy" *International Affairs* vol. 83-4, pp. 627-641

Nickels, Henri; Thomas, Lyn; Hickman, Mary & Silvestri, Sara (2012); "Constructing 'suspect' communities and Britishness: Mapping British press coverage of Irish and Muslim communities, 1974-2007" *European Journal of Communication* vol. 27-2, pp. 135-151

Nielsen, Vibeke & Parker, Christine (2009); "Testing Responsive regulation in regulatory enforcement" *Regulation and Governance* vol. 3-4, pp. 376-399

Nisar, Tahir (2007); "Value for money drivers in public private partnership schemes" *International Journal of Public Sector Management* vol. 20-2, pp. 147-156

Norris, Pippa (1995); "Introduction: The Politics of Electoral Reform" *International Political Science Review* vol. 16-1, pp. 3-8

Norris, Pippa (2003); "Young People & Political Activism: From the Politics of Loyalties to the Politics of Choice" Report for the Council of Europe Symposium: "Young people and democratic institutions: from disillusionment to participation" Strasbourg, 27-28 November, 2003. Available at www.hks. harvard.edu/fs/pnorris/Acrobat/COE%20Young%20People%20and%20 Political%20Activism.pdf

Nugent Neill (2010); *The Government and Politics of the European Union* Palgrave, 7th edition

O'Donnell, Aidan (1994); "Legal and Quasi-legal Accountability" Pyper, Robert (ed.); *Aspects of Accountability in the British System of Government,* Tudor pp. 82-118

O'Brien, Nick (2008); "Equality and Human Rights: Foundations of a Common Culture?" *Political Quarterly* vol. 79-1, pp. 27-35

O'Brien, Nick (2012); "Administrative Justice: A Libertarian Cinderella in Search of an Egalitarian Prince" *Political Quarterly* vol.83-3, pp. 494-501

O'Donnell, Clara Marina & Whitman, Richard (2007); "European policy under Gordon Brown: perspectives on a future prime minister" *International Affairs* vol. 83-1, pp. 253-272

O'Donnell, Sir Gus (2007); "The Civil Service – The Way Forward" *Public Money and Management* vol. 27-2, pp.89-91

O'Hara, Glen (2009); "'This is What Growth Does': British Views of the European Economies in the Prosperous 'Golden Age' of 1951-73" *Journal of Contemporary History* vol. 44-4, pp. 697-718

O'Malley, Eoin (2006); "Investigating the Effects of Directly Electing the Prime Minister" *Government and Opposition* vol. 41-2, pp. 137-162

O'Malley, Eoin (2007); "The Power of Prime Ministers: Results of an Expert Survey" *International Political Science Review* vol. 28-1, pp. 7-27

Offe, Claus (2009); "Governance: An "Empty Signifier"?" *Constellations* vol. 16-4, pp. 550-562

Office for the Commissioner for Public Appointments (1996); "The Commissioner for Public Appointments' Guidance on Appointments to Executive Non-Departmental Public Bodies and NHS Bodies"

Office of Fair Trading (2008); "Newspaper and magazine distribution in the United Kingdom: Introductory overview paper on the newspaper and magazine supply chain" OFT1028

Office of Fair Trading (2009); "Review of the local and regional media merger regime: Final report" OFT1091

Ogus, Anthony (1995); "Rethinking Self-Regulation" *Oxford Journal of Legal Studies* vol. 15-1, pp. 97-108

Oliver, Dawn (2004); "Constitutionalism and the Abolition of the Office of Lord Chancellor" *Parliamentary Affairs* vol. 57-4, pp. 754-766

Olsen, Johan (2002); "The Many Faces of Europeanization" *Journal of Common Market Studies* vol. 40-5, pp. 921-952

Orr, Kevin & Vince, Russ (2009); "Traditions of Local Government" *Public Administration* vol. 87-3, pp. 655-677

Orsato, Renato & Clegg, Stewart (2005); "Radical Reformism: Towards *Critical* Ecological Modernization" *Sustainable Development* vol. 13-4, pp. 253-267

Orwell, George (1951); *Animal Farm* Penguin

Osborne, Stephen & Brown, Louise (2011); "Innovation, Public Policy and Public Services Delivery in the UK: the word that would be king?" *Public Administration* vol. 89-4, pp. 1335-1350

Osbourne, R. D. (2008); "Emerging Equality Policy in Britain in Comparative Context: A Missed Opportunity?" *Public Money & Management* vol. 28-5, pp. 305-312

Osmond, John (2005); "Wales: Towards 2007" in Trench, Alan (ed.); *The Dynamics of Devolution: The State of the Nations 2005* Imprint Academic, pp. 43-62

Page, Alan (2005); "A Parliament that is Different? Law Making in the Scottish Parliament" in Hazell, Robert & Rawlings, Richard (eds.); *Devolution, Law Making and the Constitution* Imprint Academic pp. 7-38

Page, Edward (2010); "Has the Whitehall Model survived?" *International Journal of Public Sector Management* vol. 76-3, pp. 407-423

Palmer, John & Facey, Peter (2008); "The European Union Reform Treaty: How will it affect the UK?" Unlock Democracy, London

Panitch, Leo (1977); "Profits and Politics: Labour and the Crisis of British Capitalism" *Politics & Society* vol. 7-4, pp. 477-507

Pantazis, Christina & Pemberton, Simon (2009); "From the 'Old' to the 'New' Suspect Community: Examining the Impacts of Recent UK Counter-Terrorist Legislation" *British Journal of Criminology* vol. 49-5, pp. 646-666

Pappalardo, Adriano (2007); "Electoral Systems, Party Systems: Lijphart and Beyond" *Party Politics* vol. 13-6, pp. 721-740

Parkinson, John (2007); "The House of Lords: A Deliberative Democratic Defence" *Political Quarterly* vol. 78-3, pp. 374-381

Parliamentary Affairs vol. 51-3 special edition on "Protest Politics: Cause Groups and Campaigns" edited with Grant Jordan

Parliamentary and Health Service Ombudsman (2009a); *Principles for Remedy*

Parliamentary and Health Service Ombudsman (2009b); *Principles of Good Administration*

Parliamentary and Health Service Ombudsman (2009c); *Principles of Good Complaint Handling*

Parpworth, Neil (2013); "The Succession to the Crown Act 2013: Modernising the Monarchy" *Modern Law Review* vol. 76-6, pp. 1070-1093

Patchett, Keith (2005); "Principal or Pragmatism? Legislating for Wales by Westminster and Whitehall" in Hazell, Robert & Rawlings, Richard (eds.); *Devolution, Law Making and the Constitution* Imprint Academic pp. 112-154

Paterson, Matthew; Doran, Peter & Barry, John (2006); "Green Theory" in Hay, Colin; Lister, Michael & Marsh, David (eds.); *The State: Theories and Issues* Palgrave pp. 135-154

Patterson QC, Frances (General Editor) (2011); *Judicial Review: Law and Practice* Jordans

Patterson, Alan & Gray, Tim (2012); "Unprincipled? The British government's pragmatic approach to the precautionary principle" *Environmental Politics* vol. 21-3, pp. 432-450

Pattie, Charles & Johnston, Ron (2009); "The Conservatives' Grassroots 'Revival'" *Political Quarterly* vol. 80-2, pp. 193-203

Pattie, Charles & Johnston, Ron (2011); "How Big is the Big Society?" *Parliamentary Affairs* vol. 64-3, pp. 403-424

Pattie, Charles; Seyd, Patrick & Whiteley, Paul (2004); *Citizenship in Britain: Values, Participation and Democracy* Cambridge University Press

Paul, Kathleen (1997); *Whitewashing Britain: Race and Citizenship in the Postwar Era* Cornell University Press

Pearce, Graham & Ayres, Sarah (2007); "Emerging Patterns of Governance in the English Regions: The Role of Regional Assemblies" *Regional Studies* vol. 41-5, pp. 699-712

Pearce, Graham & Ayres, Sarah (2009); "Governance in the English Regions: The Role of the Regional Development Agencies" *Urban Studies* vol. 46-3, pp. 537-557

Pearce, Graham & Mawson, John (2009); "Governance in the English regions: moving beyond muddling through?" *International Journal of Public Sector Management* vol. 22-7, pp. 623-642

Pearce, Graham; Mawson, John & Ayres, Sarah (2008); "Regional Governance in England: A Changing Role for the Government's Regional Offices?" *Public Administration* vol. 86-2, pp. 443-463

Pedersen, Helene (2012); "What do Parties Want? Policy versus Office" *West European Politics* vol. 35-4, pp. 896-910

Perkins, Richard & Neumayer, Eric (2007); "Do Membership Benefits Buy Regulatory Compliance? An Empirical Analysis of EU Directives 1978-99" *European Union Politics* vol. 8-2, pp. 180-206

Perry, Robert (2011); "The Devolution of Policing in Northern Ireland: Politics and Reform" *Politics* vol. 31-3, pp. 167-178

Peters, B. Guy (2010); *The Politics of Bureaucracy: An Introduction to Comparative Public Administration* Routledge, 6th edition

Peters, B. Guy & Pierre, Jon (2006); "Governance, Government and the State" in Hay, Colin; Lister, Michael & Marsh, David (eds.); *The State: Theories and Issues* Palgrave pp. 209-222

Peterson, John and Steffensen, Rebecca (2009); "Transatlantic Institutions: Can Partnership be Engineered?" *British Journal of Politics and International Relations* vol. 11-1, pp. 25-45

Phelps, Nicholas (2009); "From branch plant economies to knowledge economies? Manufacturing industry, government policy, and economic development in Britain's old industrial regions" *Environment and Planning C: Government and Policy* vol. 27-4, pp. 574-592

Phillips of Worth Matravers, Lord (2012); "The Birth and First Steps of the UK Supreme Court" *Cambridge Journal of International and Comparative Law* vol. 1-2, pp. 9-12

Pilkington, Colin (2002); *Devolution in Britain Today* Manchester University Press

Pinkerton, Patrick (2012); "Resisting Memory: The Politics of Memorialisation in Post-conflict Northern Ireland" *British Journal of Politics and International Relations* vol. 14-1, pp. 131-252

Pitt, Michael; Collins, Norman and Walls, Andrew (2006); "The private finance initiative and value for money" *Journal of Property Investment and Finance* vol. 22-4, pp. 363-373

Plümper, Thomas & Troeger, Vera (2006); "Monetary Policy Autonomy in European Non-Euro Countries, 1980-2005" *European Union Politics* vol. 7-2, pp. 213-234

Pollitt, Christopher (2009); "Bureaucracies Remember, Post-Bureaucratic Organizations Forget?" *Public Administration* vol. 87-2, pp. 198-218

Pratchett, Lawrence (1999); "New Fashions in Public Participation: Towards Greater Democracy?" *Parliamentary Affairs* vol. 52-4, pp. 616-633

Pratchett, Lawrence & Leach, Steve (2004); "Local Government: Choice within Constraint" *Parliamentary Affairs* vol. 57-2, pp. 366-379

Preuß, Ulrich (1996); "Two Challenges to European Citizenship" *Political Studies* vol. 44-3, pp. 534-552

Price, Vicky & Simpson, Graeme (2007); *Transforming Society? Social Work and Sociology* Policy Press

Prince, Sue (2004); "The Law and Politics: Upsetting the Judicial Apple-Cart" *Parliamentary Affairs* vol. 57-2, pp. 288-300

Prince, Sue (2005); "Law and Politics: Rumours of the Demise of the Lord Chancellor have been Exaggerated..." *Parliamentary Affairs* vol. 58-2, pp. 248-257

Prosser, Tony (1997); *Law and the Regulators* Oxford University Press

Prosser, Tony (2000); "Regulation, Markets and Legitimacy" in Jowell, Jeffrey & Oliver, Dawn (eds.); *The Changing Constitution* Oxford University Press, 4th edition, pp. 229-257

Pulzer, Peter (1967); *Political Representation and Elections in Britain* George Allen & Unwin

Pyper, Robert (1994); "Introduction The Parameters of Accountability" Pyper, Robert (ed.); *Aspects of Accountability in the British System of Government* Tudor, pp. 1-12

Pyper, Robert & Burnham, June (2011); "The British Civil Service: Perspectives on 'Decline' and 'Modernisation'" *British Journal of Politics and International Relations* vol. 13-2, pp. 189-205

Quinn, Thomas (2012); "Spin doctors and political news management: A rational-choice'exchange' analysis" *British Politics* vol. 7-3, pp. 272-300

Quinn, Thomas (2013); "From Two-Partism to Alternating Predominance: The Changing UK Party System, 1950-2010" *Political Studies* vol. 61-2, pp. 378-400

Radaelli, Claudio (2000); "Whither Europeanization? Concept stretching and substantive change" *European Integration online Papers* vol. 4 No. 8, available at eiop.or.at/eiop/texte/2000-008a.htm

Radaelli, Claudio (2010); "Regulating Rule-Making via Impact Assessment" Governance vol. 23-1, pp. 89-108

Radaelli, Claudio & Meuwese, Anne (2009); "Better Regulation in Europe: Between Public Management and Regulatory Reform" *Public Administration* vol. 87-3, pp. 639-654

Rallings, Colin & Thrasher, Michael (2000); "Electoral Change for Local Government: Out of the frying pan and into the fire?" Paper to the Political Studies Association, UK, 10-13 April 2000

Randall, Vicky (1998); "Gender and Power: Women engage the State" in Randall, Vicky & Waylen, Georgina (eds.); *Gender, Politics and the State* Routledge, pp. 185-205

Rawlings, Richard (2001); "Quasi-Legislative Devolution: Powers and Principles" *Northern Ireland Legal Quarterly* vol. 52-1, pp. 54-81

Rawlings, Richard (2005); "Law Making in a Virtual Parliament: the Welsh Experience" in Hazell, Robert & Rawlings, Richard (eds.); *Devolution, Law Making and the Constitution* Imprint Academic, pp. 71-111

Redclift, Michael (2000); "Global Equity: The Environment and Development" in Lee, Keekok; Holland, Alan & McNeill, Desmond (eds.); *Global Sustainable Development in the 21st Century* Edinburgh University Press, pp. 98-113

Redclift, Michael (2005); "Sustainable Development (1987-2005): An Oxymoron Comes of Age" *Sustainable Development* vol. 13-4, pp. 212-227

Reilly, Niamh (2011); "Rethinking the interplay of feminism and secularism in a neo-secular age" *Feminist Review* no. 97, pp. 5-31

Renn, Ortwin & Schweizer, Pia-Johanna (2009); "Inclusive Risk Governance: Concepts and Application to Environmental Policy Making" *Environmental Policy and Governance* vol. 19-3, pp. 174-185

Report of the Richard Commission (2004); *Commission on the Powers and Electoral Arrangements of the National Assembly for Wales*

Report on Non-Departmental Bodies Cmnd. 7797 (1980) HMSO

Rhodes, R. A. W. (1997); *Understanding Governance* Open University Press

Rhodes, R. A. W. (2001); "United Kingdom: 'everybody but us'" in Rhodes, R.A.W. & Weller, Patrick (eds.); *The Changing World of Top Officials* Open University Press, pp. 111-151

Rhodes, R. A. W. (2007); "Understanding Governance: ten years on" *Organization Studies* vol. 28-8, pp. 1243-1264

Rhodes, R. A. W. (2013); "Political anthropology and civil service reform: prospects and limits" *Policy & Politics* vol. 41-4, pp. 481-496

Rhodes, R. A. W. & Wanna, John (2009); "Bringing the Politics Back In: Public Value in Westminster Parliamentary Government" *Public Administration* vol. 87-2, pp. 161-183

Richards, David (2011); "Changing Patterns of Executive Governance" in Heffernan, Richard; Cowley, Philip & Hay, Colin (eds.); *Developments in British Politics 9* Palgrave, pp. 29-50

Richards, David; Blunkett, David & Mathers, Helen (2008); "Old and New Labour Narratives of Whitehall: Radicals, Reactionaries and Defenders of the Westminster Model" *Political Quarterly* vol. 79-4, pp. 488- 498

Richardson, Benjamin (2009); "Climate Finance and its Governance: Moving to a low carbon economy through socially responsible financing?" *International and Comparative Law Quarterly* vol. 58-3, pp. 597-626

Richardson, Liz & John, Peter (2012); "Who Listens to the Grass Roots? A Field Experiment on Informational Lobbying in the UK" *British Journal of Politics and International Relations* vol. 14-4, pp. 595-612

Rimington, John (2009); "Public Management and Administration: a Need for Evolution" *Political Quarterly* vol. 80-4, pp. 562-568

Roberts, Geoffrey (2007); "Modes of Environmental Activism" Review Essay *Environmental Politics* vol. 16-4, pp. 677-682

Robins, Lynton (1992); "Britain and the European Community: twenty years of not knowing" in Jones, Bill & Lynton Robins (eds.); *Two Decades in British Politics* Manchester University Press, pp. 243-255

Robinson, Nick (2002); "The Politics of the Fuel Protests: Towards a Multi-Dimensional Explanation" *Political Quarterly* vol. 73-1, pp. 58-66

Rolandsen Agustín, Lise (2012); "(Re)defining women's interests? Political struggles over women's collective representation in the context of the European Parliament" *European Journal of Women's Studies* vol. 19-1, pp. 23-40

Rootes, Christopher (2013); "From local conflict to national issue: when and how environmental campaigns succeed in transcending the local" *Environmental Politics* vol. 22-1, pp. 95-114

Rootes, Christopher & Carter, Neil (2010); "Take blue, add yellow, get green? The environment in the UK general election of 6 May 2010" *Environmental Politics* vol. 19-6, pp. 992-999

Rosamond, Ben & Wincott, Daniel (2006); "Constitutionalism, European Integration and British Political Economy" *British Journal of Politics and International Relations* vol. 8-1, pp. 1-14

Rosamund, Ben (2003); "The Europeanization of British Politics" in Dunleavy, Patrick; Gamble, Andrew; Heffernan, Richard & Peele, Gillian (eds.); *Developments in British Politics 7* Palgrave, pp. 39-59

Rowlingson, Karen; Orton, Michael & Taylor, Eleanor (2010); "Do we still care about inequality?" in Park, Alison; Curtice, John; Clery, Elizabeth & Bryson, Caroline (eds.); *British Social Attitudes: Exploring Labour's Legacy. The 27th Report* National Centre for Social Research pp. 1-28

Rubin, James (2008); "Building a New Atlantic Alliance" *Foreign Affairs* vol. 87-4, pp. 99-110

Russel, Duncan & Turnpenny, John (2009); "The politics of sustainable development in UK government: what role for integrated policy appraisal?" *Environment and Planning C: Government and Policy* vol. 27-2, pp. 340-354

Russell, Meg (2001); "What are Second Chambers for?" *Parliamentary Affairs* vol. 54-3, pp. 442-458

Russell, Meg (2009); "House of Lords Reform: Are We Nearly There Yet?" *Political Quarterly* vol. 80-1, pp. 119-125

Russell, Meg (2011); "'Never Allow a Crisis Go To Waste': The Wright Committee Reforms to Strengthen the House of Commons" *Parliamentary Affairs* vol. 64-4, pp. 612-633

Rutter, Jill (2011); "The State of UK Governance" *Public Policy and Administration* vol. 27-1, pp. 89-95

Saalfeld, Thomas & Bischof, Daniel (2013); "Minority-Ethnic MPs and the Substantive Representation of Minority Interests in the House of Commons" *Parliamentary Affairs* vol. 66-2, pp. 305-328

Sanders, David (1990); *Losing an Empire, Finding a Role: British Foreign Policy since 1945* Macmillan

Sanders, David (1997); "Britain and the world" in Robins, Lynton and Bill Jones (eds.); *Half a century of British Politics* Manchester University Press, pp. 7-28

Sanders, David; Clarke, Harold; Stewart, Marianne & Whiteley, Paul (2011); "Downs, Stokes and the Dynamics of Electoral Choice" *British Journal of Political Science* vol. 41-2, pp. 287-314

Sandford, Mark & Hetherington, Peter (2005); "The Regions at the Crossroads: The Future for Sub-National Government in England" in Trench, Alan (ed.); *The Dynamics of Devolution: The State of the Nations 2005* Imprint Academic, pp. 91-113

Sartori, Giovanni (1994); *Comparative Constitutional Engineering: An Inquiry into Structures, Incentives and Outcomes* Macmillan

Sartori, Giovanni (2005); "Party Types, Organisations and Functions" *West European Politics* vol. 28-1, pp. 5-32

Saunders, Ben (2013); "Scottish Independence and the All-Affected Interests Principle" *Politics* vol. 33-1, pp. 47-55

Saunders, Clare (2012); "Reformism and radicalism in the Climate Camp in Britain: benign coexistence, tensions and prospects for bridging" *Environmental Politics* vol. 21-5, pp. 829-846

Schaffer, Gavin (2010); "*Till Death Us Do Part* and the BBC: Racial Politics and the British Working Classes 1965-75" *Journal of Contemporary History* vol. 45-2, pp. 454-477

Schlembach, Raphael; Lear, Ben & Bowman, Andrew (2012); "Science and ethics in the post-political era: strategies within the Camp for Climate Action" *Environmental Politics* vol. 21-5, pp. 811-828

Schmidt, Vivien (2006); "Adapting to Europe: Is it Harder for Britain?" *British Journal of Politics and International Relations* vol. 8-1, pp. 15-33

Scholz, Sally J. (2010); *Feminism: A Beginners Guide* Oneworld

Scott, Colin (2000); "Accountability in the Regulatory State" *Journal of Law and Society* vol. 27-1, pp. 38-60

Scott, Jonathan M. & Irwin, David (2009); "Discouraged advisees? The influence of gender, ethnicity, and education in the use of advice and finance by UK SMEs" *Environment and Planning C: Government and Policy* vol. 27-2, pp. 230-245

Scully, Roger; Wyn Jones, Richard & Trystan, Dafydd (2004); "Turnout, Participation and Legitimacy in Post-Devolution Wales" *British Journal of Political Science* vol. 34-3, pp. 519-537

Seaton, Jean (2003); "Public, Private and the Media" *Political Quarterly* vol. 74-2, pp. 174-83

Sedelmeier, Ulrich (2011); "The Differential Impact of the European Union on European Politics" in Jones, Erik; Heywood, Paul; Rhodes, Martin & Sedelmeier, Ulrich (eds.); *Developments in European Politics 2* Palgrave, pp. 28-44

Sedley, The Rt. Hon. Lord Justice (1999); *Freedom, Law and Justice* Sweet & Maxwell

Seghezzo, Lucas (2009); "The five dimensions of sustainability" *Environmental Politics* vol. 18-4, pp. 539-556

Seneviratne, Mary & Cracknell, Sarah (1988); "Consumer Complaints in Public Sector Services" *Public Administration* vol. 66-2, pp. 181-193

Seyd, Patrick; Whiteley, Paul & Pattie, Charles (2001); "Citizenship in Britain: Attitudes and Behaviour" in Crick, Bernard (ed.); *Citizens: Towards a Citizenship Culture* Blackwell, pp. 141-148

Seymoure-Ure, Colin (1991); *The British Press and Broadcasting since 1945* Blackwell

Shaw, Eric (2012); "New Labour's Faustian Pact" *British Politics* vol. 7-3, pp. 224-249

Shaw, Jo (1998); "The Interpretation of European Union Citizenship" *The Modern Law Review* vol. 61-3, pp. 293-317

Sheail, John (2007); "Torrey Canyon: The Political Dilemma" *Journal of Contemporary History* vol. 42-3, pp. 485-504

Shell, Donald (1992); *The House of Lords* Harvester Wheatsheaf, 2nd edition

Shell, Donald (2004); "The Future of the Second Chamber" *Parliamentary Affairs* vol. 57-4, pp. 852-866

Sherrington, Philippa (2006); "Confronting Europe: UK Political Parties and the EU 2000-2005" *British Journal of Politics and International Relations* vol. 8-1, pp. 69-78

Shirlow, Peter (2001); "Devolution in Northern Ireland/Ulster/the North/Six Counties: Delete as Appropriate" *Regional Studies* vol. 35-8, pp. 743-752

Shlaim, Avi (1975); "Britain's Quest for a World Role" *International Relations* vol. 5-1, pp. 838-856

Simpson, Kirk (2013); "Political strategies of engagement: Unionists and dealing with the past in Northern Ireland" *British Politics* vol. 8-1, pp. 2-27

Sjoberg, Laura (2009); "Feminist Interrogations of Terrorism/Terrorism Studies" *International Relations* vol. 23-1, pp. 69-74

Skelcher, Chris (1998); *The Appointed State: Quasi-governmental Organizations and Democracy* Open University Press

Skelcher, Chris & Torfing, Jacob (2010); "Improving democratic governance through institutional design: Civic participation and democratic ownership in Europe" *Regulation & Governance* vol. 4-1, pp. 71-91

Skelcher, Chris; Weir, Stuart & Wilson, Lynne (2000); *Advance of the Quango State: A Report for the LGIU* Local Government Information Unit

Skjærseth, Jon Birger & Wettestad, Jørgen (2009); "The Origin, Evolution and Consequences of the EU Emissions Trading System" *Global Environmental Politics* vol. 9-2, pp. 101-122

Sloam, James (2007); "Rebooting Democracy: Youth Participation in Politics in the UK" *Parliamentary Affairs* vol. 60-4, pp. 548-567

Sloam, James (2012); "'Rejuvenating Democracy?' Young People and the 'Big Society' Project" *Parliamentary Affairs* vol. 65-1, pp. 90-114

Smith, Graham & Wales, Corinne (2000); "Citizens' Juries and Deliberative Democracy" *Political Studies* vol. 48-1, pp. 51-65

Smith, Karen (2008); *European Union Foreign Policy in a Changing World* Polity 2nd edition

Smith, Martin (1995); "Interpreting the Rise and Fall of Margaret Thatcher: Power Dependence and the Core Executive" in Rhodes, R. A. W. & Dunleavy, Patrick (eds.), *Prime Minister, Cabinet and Core Executive* Macmillan, pp. 108-124

Smith, Martin A. (2011); "British nuclear weapons and NATO in the Cold War and beyond" *International Affairs* vol. 87-6, pp. 1385-1399

Smith, Mitchell (2008); "All Access Points are Not Created Equal: Explaining the Fate of Diffuse Interests in the EU" *British Journal of Politics and International Relations* vol. 10-1, pp. 64-83

Smith, Neil (2007); *UK Parties and Pressure Groups* Philip Allen

Sobolewska, Maria; Fieldhouse, Edward & Cutts, David (2013); "Taking Minorities for Granted? Ethnic Densitu, Party Campaigning and Targeting Minority Voters in 2010 British General Elections" *Parliamentary Affairs* vol. 66-2, pp. 329-344

Sørensen, Georg (2004); *The Transformation of the State: Beyond the Myth of Retreat* Palgrave

Sørensen, Georg (2006); "The Transformation of the State" in Hay, Colin; Lister, Michael & Marsh, David (eds.); *The State: Theories and Issues* Palgrave pp. 190-208

Soroos, Marvin (2001); "Global Climate Change and the Futility of the Kyoto Process" *Global Environmental Politics* vol. 1-2, pp. 1-9

Stanyer, James (2004); "Politics and the Media: A Crisis of Trust?" *Parliamentary Affairs* vol. 57-2, pp. 420-434

Stegmaier, Mary; Lewis-Beck, Michael S. & Smets, Kaat (2013); "Standing for Parliament: Do Black, Asian and Minority Ethnic Candidates Pay Extra?" *Parliamentary Affairs* vol. 66-2, pp.268-285

Steunenberg, Bernard (2010); "Is big brother watching? Commission oversight of the national implementation of EU directives" *European Union Politics* vol. 11-3, pp. 359-380

Stevens, Andrew (2006); *The Politico's guide to Local Government* Politico's 2nd edition

Stockemer, Daniel (2008); "Women's Representation: A Comparison between Europe and America" *Politics* vol. 28-2, pp. 65-73

Stockemer, David & Byrne, Maeve (2012); "Women's Representation around the World: The Importance of Women's Participation in the Workforce" *Parliamentary Affairs* vol. 65- pp. 802-821

Stoker, Gerry (2006); *Why Politics Matters* Macmillan

Stoker, Gerry (2009); "What's wrong with our political culture and what, if anything, can we do to improve it? Reflections on Colin Hay's 'Why We Hate Politics'" *British Politics* vol. 4-1, pp. 83-91

Stolle, Dietland & Harell, Alison (2013); "Social Capital and Ethno-racial Diversity: Learning to Trust in an Immigrant Society" *Political Studies* vol. 61-1, pp. 42-66

Street, John (2004); "Celebrity Politicians: Popular Culture and Political Representation" *British Journal of Politics and International Relations* vol. 6-3, pp. 435-452

Street, John; Inthorn, Sanna & Scott, Martin (2012); "Playing at Politics? Popular Culture as Political Engagement" *Parliamentary Affairs* vol. 65-2, pp. 338-358

Sweeting, David & Copus, Colin (2012); "Whatever happened to local democracy?" *Policy & Politics* vol. 40-1, pp. 20-37

Szreter, Simon (2003); "Health, Class, Place and Politics: Social Capital and Collective Provision in Britain" in Berridge, Virginia & Blume, Stuart (eds.); *Poor Health: Social Inequality before and after the Black Report* Frank Cass, pp. 27-57

Tam, Henry (2001); "The Community Roots of Citizenship" in Crick, Bernard (ed.); *Citizens: Towards a Citizenship Culture* Blackwell, pp. 123-131

Taylor, Andrew (2007); "The Strategic Impact of the Electoral System and the Definition of 'Good' Governance" *British Politics* vol. 2-1, pp. 20-44

Temple, Mick (2010); "In Praise of the Popular Press: The Need for Tabloid Racism" *Politics* vol. 30-3, pp. 191-201

"The House of Lords (Again)" Commentary. *Political Quarterly* vol. 80-1, pp. 165-167

The LSE GV314 Group (2012); "New Life at the Top: Special Advisers in British Government" *Parliamentary Affairs* vol. 65-4, pp. 715-732

The Royal Commission on Environmental Pollution (2000); *Energy – The Changing Climate* The Stationary Office (Cm 4749)

The Stephen Lawrence Inquiry: Report of an Inquiry by Sir William Macpherson of Cluny, February 1999, Cm 4262-I The Stationery Office

The Stern Review (2006); *The Economics of Climate Change* available at archive. excellencegateway.org.uk/141443

The World Commission on Environment and Development (1987); *Our Common Future* Oxford University Press

Theakston, Kevin (2000); "Ministers and Civil Servants" in Pyper, Robert & Robins, Lynton (eds.); *United Kingdom Governance* Macmillan, pp. 39-60

Theakston, Kevin (2005); "Prime Ministers and the Constitution: Attlee to Blair" *Parliamentary Affairs* vol. 58-1, pp. 17-37

Theakston, Kevin & Gill, Mark (2006); "Rating 20th-Century British Prime Ministers" *British Journal of Politics and International Relations* vol.8-2, pp. 193-213

Thiele, Leslie Paul (2013); *Sustainability* Polity Press

Thomas, Graham (2000); "Has Prime Minister Major been replaced by President Blair?" in Robins, Lynton & Jones, Bill (eds.); *Debates in British politics today* Manchester University Press, pp. 13-26

Thompson, Grahame (1990); *The Political Economy of the New Right* Pinter

Thomson, Robert; Torenvlied, René & Arregui, Javier (2007); "The Paradox of Compliance: Infringements and Delays in Transposing European Union Directives" *British Journal of Political Science* vol. 37-4, pp. 685-709

Thorlakson, Lori (2011); "Britain's Place in the European Union" in Heffernan, Richard; Cowley, Philip & Hay, Colin (eds.); *Developments in British Politics 9* Palgrave, pp. 257-279

Tilley, James; Evans, Geoffrey & Mitchell, Claire (2008); "Consociationalism and the Evolution of Political Cleavages in Northern Ireland, 1989-2004" *British Journal of Political Science* vol. 38-4, pp. 699-717

Toke, David (2010); "Foxhunting and the Conservatives" *Political Quarterly* vol. 81-2, pp. 205-212

Toke, David & Marsh, David (2003); "Policy Networks and the GM Crops Issue: Assessing the Utility of a Dialectical Model of Policy Networks" *Public Administration* vol. 81-2, pp. 229-251

Tomaney, John (1999a); "In Search of English Regionalism" *Scottish Affairs* no. 28

Tomaney, John (1999b); "New Labour and the English Question" *Political Quarterly* vol. 70-1, pp. 75- 82

Tomaney, John (2002); "The Evolution of Regionalism in England" *Regional Studies* vol. 36-7, pp. 721-731

Tonra, Ben (2003); "Constructing the Common Foreign and Security Policy: The Utility of a Cognitive Approach" *Journal of Common Market Studies* vol. 41-4, pp. 731-756

Towns, Ann (2009); "The Status of Women as a Standard of 'Civilization'" *European Journal of International Relations* vol. 15-4, pp. 681-706

Tremblay, Manon (2005); "Women's Political Representation: Does the Electoral System Matter?" *Political Science* vol. 57-1, pp. 59-75

Trench, Alan (2005a); "Introduction: The Dynamics of Devolution" in Trench, Alan (ed.); *The Dynamics of Devolution: The State of the Nations 2005* Imprint Academic, pp. 1-19

Trench, Alan (2005b); "Intergovernmental Relations Within the UK: The Pressures Yet To Come" in Trench, Alan (ed.); *The Dynamics of Devolution: The State of the Nations 2005* Imprint Academic, pp. 137-159

Trench, Alan (2005c); "Whitehall and the Process of Legislation after Devolution" in Hazell, Robert & Rawlings, Richard (eds.); *Devolution, Law Making and the Constitution* Imprint Academic, pp. 193-225

Treverton, Gregory (1990); "Britain's role in the 1990s: an American view" *International Affairs* vol. 66-4, pp. 703-710

Trouille, Jean-Marc (2007); "Re-Inventing Industrial Policy in the EU: A Franco-German Approach" *West European Politics* vol. 30-3, pp. 502-523

Tsolakis, Andreas (2010); "Opening Up Open Marxist Theories of the State: A Historical Materialist Critique" *British Journal of Politics and International Relations* vol. 12-3, pp. 387-407

Turner, Bryan (2001); "The erosion of citizenship" *British Journal of Sociology* vol. 52-2, pp. 189-209

Uberoi, Varun & Modood, Tariq (2010); "Who Doesn't Feel British? Divisions over Muslims" *Parliamentary Affairs* vol. 63-2, pp. 302-320

Uberoi, Varun & Modood, Tariq (2013); "Inclusive Britishness: A Multiculturalist Advance" *Political Studies* vol. 61-1, pp. 23-41

UCAS Analysis and Research (2013); *Demand for full-time undergraduate higher education (2013 cycle, March deadline)*

Unalan, Dilek & Cowell, Richard (2009); "Europeanization, Strategic Environmental Assessment and the Impacts on Environmental Governance" *Environmental Policy and Governance* vol. 19-1, pp. 32-43

Ungericht, Bernhard & Hirt, Christian (2010); "CSR as a Political Arena: The Struggle for a European Framework" *Business and Politics* vol. 12, issue 4, article 1. Available at www.bepress.com/bap/vol12/iss4/art1

Van der Waal, Jeroen; Achterberg, Peter & Houtman, Dick (2007); "Class Is Not Dead – It Has Been Buried Alive: Class Voting and Cultural Voting in Postwar Western Societies (1956-1990)" *World Political Science Review* vol. 3, issue 4, article 3. Available at www.bepress.com/wpsr/vol3/iss4/art3

Van Dorpe, Karolien & Horton, Sylvia (2011); "The Public Service Bargain in the United Kingdom: The Whitehall Model in Decline?" *Public Policy and Administration* vol. 26-2, pp. 233-252

Van Schendelen, Rinus (2002); "The GMO food arena in the EU (1998-2001)" *Journal of Public Affairs* vol. 3-3, pp. 225-231

Van Thiel, Sandra (2001); *Quangos: Trends, Causes and Consequences* Ashgate

Vannoni, Matia (2013); "The determinants of direct corporate lobbying in the EU: A multi-dimensional proxy of corporate lobbying" *Interest Groups & Advocacy* vol. 2-1, pp. 71-90

Verdun, Amy (2008); "Policy-Making and Integration in the European Union: Do Economic Interest Groups Matter?" *British Journal of Politics and International Relations* vol. 10-1, pp. 129-137

Verheul, Wouter Jan & Schaap, Linze (2010); "Strong Leaders? The Challenges and Pitfalls in Mayoral Leadership" *Public Administration* vol. 88-2, pp. 439-454

Voisey, Heather & O'Riordan, Tim (1997); "Governing Institutions for Sustainable Development: The United Kingdom's National Level Approach" *Environmental Policy* vol. 6-1, pp. 24-53

Vucetic, Srdjan (2010); "Bound to follow? The Anglosphere and US-led coalitions of the willing, 1950-2001" *European Journal of International Relations* vol. 17-1, pp. 27-49

Wallace, William (2005); "The collapse of British foreign policy" *International Affairs* vol. 82-1, pp. 53-68

Watts, Duncan (2000); *British Electoral Systems: Achieving a Sense of Proportion* Sheffield Hallam University Press

Watts, Duncan (2006); *British Government and Politics: A Comparative Guide* Edinburgh University Press

Waylen, Georgina (2012); "Gender Matters in Politics" *Political Quarterly* vol. 83-1, pp. 24-32

Weakliem, David & Adams, Julia (2011); "What Do We Mean by "Class Politics"?" *Politics & Society* vol. 39-4, pp. 475-495

Webb, Paul & Childs, Sarah (2010); "Wets and Dries Resurgent? Intra-Party Alignments Among Contemporary Conservative Party Members" *Parliamentary Affairs* vol. 64-3, pp. 383-402

Webb, Paul & Poguntke, Thomas (2013); "The Presidentialisation of Politics Thesis Defended" *Parliamentary Affairs* vol. 66-3, pp. 646-654

Weihe, Guðrið (2008); "Public-Private Partnerships and Public-Private Trade-Offs" *Public Money and Management* vol. 28-3, pp.153-158

Weir, Stuart & Hall, Wendy (eds.) (1994); *EGO TRIP: Extra-governmental organizations in the United Kingdom and their accountability* Charter 88 Trust

West, Anne & Currie, Peter (2008); "The role of the private sector in publicly funded schooling in England: finance, delivery and decision making" *Policy & Politics* vol. 36-2, pp. 191-207

Whitaker, Richard (2006a); "Ascendant Assemblies in Britain? Rebellions, Reforms and Inter-Cameral Conflict" *Parliamentary Affairs* vol. 59-1, pp. 173-180

Whitaker, Richard (2006b); "Backbench Influence on Government Legislation? A Flexing of Parliamentary Muscles at Westminster" *Parliamentary Affairs* vol. 59-2, pp. 350-359

Whiteley, Paul (2003); "The State of Participation in Britain" *Parliamentary Affairs* vol. 56-4, pp. 610-615

Wiener, Antje (1997); "Assessing the Constructive Potential of Union Citizenship – A Socio-Historical Perspective" *European Integration online Papers* vol. 1 No. 17. Available at eiop.or.at/eiop/texte/1997-017a.htm

Wilford, Rick (2010); "Northern Ireland: The Politics of Constraint" *Parliamentary Affairs* vol. 63-1, pp. 134-155

Wilford, Rick & Wilson, Robin (2005); "Northern Ireland: While You Take The high Road" in Trench, Alan (ed.); *The Dynamics of Devolution: The State of the Nations 2005* Imprint Academic, pp. 63-89

Williams, Steve & Scott, Peter (2011); "The Nature of Conservative Party Modernisation Under David Cameron: The Trajectory of Employment Relations Policy" *Parliamentary Affairs* vol. 64-3, pp. 513-529

Wilson, David (2003); "Unravelling control freakery: redefining central-local relations" *British Journal of Politics and International Relations* vol. 5-3, pp. 317-346

Wilson, David (2004); "New Patterns of Central-Local Government Relations" in Stoker, Gerry & Wilson, David (eds.); *British Local Government into the 21st Century* Palgrave, pp. 9-24

Wilson, David & Game, Chris (2011); *Local Government in the United Kingdom* Palgrave 5th edition

Wimbush, Erica (2011); "Implementing an outcomes approach to public management and accountability in the UK – are we learning the lessons?" *Public Money & Management* vol. 31-3, pp. 211-218

Winetrobe, Barry (2005); "A Partnership of Parliaments? Scottish Law Making under the Sewell Convention at Westminster and Holyrood" in Hazell, Robert & Rawlings, Richard (eds.); *Devolution, Law Making and the Constitution* Imprint Academic pp. 39-70

Woll, Cornelia & Alvaro Artigas (2007); "When trade liberalization turns into regulatory reform: The impact on business-government relations in international trade politics" *Regulation & Governance* vol. 1-1, pp. 121-138

Woodhouse, Diana (1997); *In Pursuit of Good Administration: Ministers, Civil Servants and Judges* Clarendon Press

Woodhouse, Diana (2001); "The Law and Politics: More Power to the Judges – and to the People?" *Parliamentary Affairs* vol. 54-2, pp. 223-237

Worthy, Benjamin (2008); "The Future of Freedom of Information in the United Kingdom" *Political Quarterly* vol. 79-1, pp. 100-108

Wright, Erik Olin (1984); "A General Framework for the Analysis of Class Structure" *Politics & Society* vol. 13-4, pp. 383-423

Wright, Scott (2006); "Government-run Online Discussion Fora: Moderation, Censorship and the Shadow of Control" *British Journal of Politics and International Relations* vol.8-4, pp. 550-568

Wright, Tony (2010); "What are MPs for?" *Political Quarterly* vol. 81-3, pp. 298-308

Wring, Dominic & Ward, Stephen (2010); "The Media and the 2010 Campaign: the Television Election?" *Parliamentary Affairs* vol. 63-4, pp. 802-817

Young, Alasdair (2009); "Confounding Conventional Wisdom: Political not Principled Differences in the Transatlantic Regulatory Relationship" *British Journal of Politics and International Relations* vol. 11-4, pp. 666-689

INDEX